McGRAW-HILL SERIES IN MARKETING

Consulting Editor
Charles Schewe
University of Massachusetts

ADVERTISI

ADVERTISING

Fourth Edition

JOHN S. WRIGHT

School of Business
Georgia State University

DANIEL S. WARNER

Professor Emeritus
School of Communications
University of Washington

WILLIS L. WINTER, JR.

School of Journalism
University of Oregon

SHERILYN K. ZEIGLER

College of Communications
University of Tennessee

McGRAW-HILL BOOK COMPANY

New York   St. Louis   San Francisco   Auckland   Bogotá   Düsseldorf
Johannesburg   London   Madrid   Mexico   Montreal   New Delhi
Panama   Paris   São Paulo   Singapore   Sydney   Tokyo   Toronto

This book was set in Memphis Light by Black Dot, Inc.
The editors were William J. Kane, Marjorie Singer, and Laura D. Warner;
the designer was Joan E. O'Connor;
the production supervisor was Thomas J. LoPinto.
New drawings were done by J & R Services, Inc.
The cartoonist was Fred Haynes.
R. R. Donnelley & Sons Company was printer and binder.

ADVERTISING

34567890DODO7832109

Library of Congress Cataloging in Publication Data

Wright, John Sherman, date
   Advertising.

   (McGraw-Hill series in marketing)
   Includes index.
   1. Advertising. I. Title.
HF5823.W7 1977   659.1   76-43997
ISBN 0-07-072067-3

CONTENTS

PART ONE   INTRODUCTION

Chapter 1   What Is Advertising?   4

Advertising Defined   A Brief History of Advertising   The Development
of Modern Advertising   Advertising in a Microcosm   Why Study
Advertising?

Summary

Chapter 2   Advertising and Society   40

Advertising and Economics   The Soviet Experience   Social Effects of
Advertising   Advertising and Freedom of the Press   The Case
for Advertising

Summary

PART TWO   ADVERTISING'S ROLE IN THE
              MARKETING PROCESS

Chapter 3   Marketing: The Product and Advertising   76

What Is Marketing?   The Marketing Concept   Advertising and the
Marketing Mix   Primacy of the Product   The Package   The Brand

PART FOUR   ADVERTISING MESSAGES

PART FIVE   PLANNING AND MANAGING THE ADVERTISING CAMPAIGN

PART SIX THE FUTURE OF ADVERTISING

PREFACE

When ADVERTISING first appeared in 1962, we set out to interest students, regardless of their academic areas, in how advertising functions, and to inform them of its importance in society. At the same time, we aimed to stimulate further study and to lay the groundwork for those considering advertising as a career. This book differed significantly from others in the field because all three points of view from which advertising is usually discussed were taken into account: the management-marketing viewpoint, the communications-creative viewpoint, and the viewpoint of the consumer-citizen who uses, and is affected by, advertising every day.

The underlying philosophy of ADVERTISING has stood the test of time and is as valid today as it was in the early 1960s. Thus, the book remains fundamentally unchanged; yet, because advertising itself is so dynamic, each edition has been revised to reflect changing conditions, and this fourth edition is no exception. Indeed, this edition boasts a rather substantial facelift, since recent years have seen increased advertising-related activity in several sectors of our economy.

Those not familiar with previous editions of the book will find that it differs from most advertising texts in approach, organization, and treatment of topics. The characteristics of media are analyzed before discussion of the creation of advertising messages; students have demonstrated a keener understanding of the problems of copy, art, and production when bolstered by knowledge of the media vehicles used to distribute ads and commercials. Furthermore, while the importance of information input is stressed at the beginning of the section dealing with creation of advertising, formal research is not presented as a topic until Part Five, Planning and Managing the Advertising Campaign. Clearly, however, the structure of this book is flexible enough for instructors to rearrange its parts to suit the needs of their individual teaching styles.

Although theory and practice are two sides of the same coin, this text focuses primarily on general principles and broad viewpoints rather than emphasizing specific techniques. Important details that beginning students often find difficult to understand—and even more difficult to retain—are included, but simplified. An introductory text cannot make students expert in the production of either printed advertisements or broadcast commercials, but it can help them learn to communicate with, and use the basic skills of, specialists in both fields. Nor can any book teach students how to write copy, but even an introductory text can give them an understanding of the problems and challenges the copywriter must face and solve in creating an effective message.

This edition should appear as an old friend to those familiar with earlier editions. Like an old friend, it has changed in some respects, but we hope the book has improved with age. The chapter dealing with consumer behavior has been moved from the opening portion of the book to the beginning of Part Four, Advertising Messages. It is believed that this location is more useful and relevant to students as they set about learning how advertising is created. In addition, recognizing the fast-changing regulatory climate that advertising faces these days, we have taken the old appendix on advertising legislation and developed it into the new Chapter 20, The Legal Framework of Advertising. It incorporates such topics as advertising substantiation, comparative advertising, corrective advertising, and industry self-regulation.

Part Three, Advertising Media, now starts off with an overview (Chapter 6), which lays the groundwork for detailed discussions of the major advertising media. Broadcast advertising has received more extensive treatment (in Part Four) than was the case in earlier editions, and is discussed *with* print advertising instead of after it as a "special problem." Budget and media selection decisions, formerly discussed in a single chapter, now appear separately (Chapters 17 and 18). Finally, many chapters—notably Chapter 2, Advertising and Society; Chapter 11, Consumer Behavior and Advertising; and Chapter 16, Research for Advertising Planning—have been completely rewritten to include up-to-date concepts and fresh insights.

We hope you will find the study of ADVERTISING as fascinating as the activity itself is in the world of business.

John S. Wright
Daniel S. Warner
Willis L. Winter, Jr.
Sherilyn K. Zeigler

ACKNOWLEDGMENTS

Writers of any textbook are indebted to many, many people, and we want to call attention to some whose contributions proved invaluable.

First, our own students contributed immeasurably to the content of ADVERTISING by providing the "test market" for many of the ideas incorporated in this book.

Second, since the first edition appeared in 1962, a number of professors have been kind enough to send along ideas for improvement of the "product." At the request of the publisher, the following advertising instructors reviewed the third edition and provided many useful ideas for change and improvement in this new edition:

Professor Kenward L. Atkin
California State University
at Fullerton

Professor Laurence Jacobs
University of Hawaii

Professor John Mertes
University of Arkansas
at Little Rock

Professor Leon Quera
San Francisco State College

Professor Billy Ross
Texas Tech University

Professor Jack Z. Sissors
Northwestern University

Professor Harry M. Tobin
Skagit Valley Community College

Professor Louis J. Wolter
Drake University

Another group of teaching colleagues reviewed all or part of the manuscript for this edition and also made many helpful suggestions:

Professor Edward L. Grubb
Portland State University

Professor William G. Nickels
University of Maryland,
College Park

Professor Nathan Weinstock
Orange County Community College

Professor Timothy Wright
Lakeland Community College

In-depth assistance was given on specific chapters by the following persons:

Professor James Ferguson
University of Rochester

Mr. Kenneth A. Hollander
Kenneth Hollander Associates, Inc.

Professor Marshall C. Howard
University of Massachusetts

Professor H. Keith Hunt
Brigham Young University

Professor Richard Joel
University of Tennessee

Professor Rom Markin
Washington State University

Professor Frank B. Thornburg, Jr.
University of Tennessee

The usual caveat is offered: the authors, and not those just mentioned, are responsible for any errors of omission or commission.

Third, the advertising industry has been extremely gracious in providing illustrative materials for the book. In most cases, the advertiser is clearly recognized by the mere presence of the firm's advertisement; the advertising agency behind the ad, unfortunately, remains anonymous in some instances.

Similarly, publishers of books and periodicals have given permission to quote from their materials.

Fourth, each of us received cheerful and dependable service from departmental secretarial support groups and from student assistants. Without such aid the job would never have been completed.

Finally, to Daniel S. Warner goes special appreciation. Now retired from teaching, though still active in the practice of advertising, he was not directly involved in the preparation of the fourth edition of ADVERTISING. Nevertheless, his influence on its content and orientation remains.

To all these people, and to those unmentioned, our heartfelt thanks.

ADVERTISING

ONE

INTRODUCTION

Advertising is an exciting, dynamic, and truly challenging enterprise—often misunderstood, but essential to business and industry as we know them today.

What the activity called "advertising" is all about is explained in Chapter 1. After the term is defined, a short historical perspective is presented. Five actual examples of the real-life use of advertising are then given, followed by reasons for studying the subject.

In Chapter 2 the role of advertising in our society is discussed. First, we examine the economic role played by advertising in the United States. This discussion is followed by an evaluation of advertising's social effects.

CHAPTER 1

WHAT IS ADVERTISING?

Ubiquitous ... brash ... pervasive ... materialistic ... intrusive ... dynamic ... alluring ... annoying ... pesky ... indispensible ... fascinating. These adjectives are among the many used to describe advertising. The average consumer in the United States is exposed to hundreds of advertisements daily. A carefully designed study revealed that 21 typical Milwaukee residents saw anywhere from 117 to 484 ads per day in four major forms of advertising media.[1] Advertisements are but one part of the advertising process—the tangible part which is alternately praised and criticized. Certainly, anyone living in an economically developed nation knows from personal experience what advertising is. Yet that understanding is often imprecise, and it is characterized by myths and half-truths. This chapter (and for that matter, the entire book) is an explanation of what the advertising process really is and how it functions in the world of business.

(Advertising is a powerful communication force and a vital marketing tool—helping to sell goods, services, images, and ideas (or ideals) through channels of information and persuasion.) Notice the word "helping" in the last sentence. By itself, advertising almost never "sells" products. Though it is often credited with making cash registers ring or blamed for failing to do so, advertising is, after all, but one part of the marketing and communication processes. The "greatest ad" in all the world cannot sell a product which is not in the store because the distribution system has broken down. Nor will it convince people to buy products which they feel cost too much, are poorly packaged, or in some other way do not live up to their expectations. Even if advertising does help sell such a product once, repeat sales are virtually impossible to obtain; and few advertisers today can survive on one-time sales.

It is crucial to our understanding of advertising, therefore, that we appreciate from the start the dual nature of this process, which draws from both marketing and behavioral science disciplines. It interacts with numerous other marketing concerns, including personal selling, product development and servicing, branding of merchandise, and research. Advertising is also forever intertwined with the social-psychological needs, wants, and backgrounds of consumers.

ADVERTISING DEFINED

Every occupation, trade, and profession has its own language, nomenclature, and jargon. The practitioner of each field must know and understand the terms used by his or her colleagues. Advertising

[1]Steuart Henderson Britt, Stephen C. Adams, and Allan S. Miller, "How Many Advertising Exposures Per Day?" *Journal of Advertising Research*, December 1972, p. 9.

people must learn its specialized terminology. The obvious starting point is with the hardest term of all to describe adequately, *advertising* itself. The function of advertising can be viewed in two basic ways: as a *tool of marketing* and as a *means of communication.*

The Marketing Point of View

The American Marketing Association (AMA) recommends this definition:

> Advertising is any paid form of nonpersonal presentation and promotion of ideas, goods, and services by an identified sponsor.[2]

Although purists might well point out that the AMA definition actually describes an advertisement, rather than advertising, these words deserve careful scrutiny. Four phrases warrant clarification.

"Paid Form" When products or services are mentioned favorably in the media—newspapers, magazines, radio, or television—the item appears because it is presumed to provide information or entertainment for the audience. This is publicity, and no payment is made by the benefited organization. Advertising, on the other hand, is published or broadcast because the advertiser has purchased time or space to tell his story.

"Nonpersonal Presentation" Personal selling takes place when a personal face-to-face presentation is made. Although advertising complements, or may substitute for, personal selling, it is done in a nonpersonal manner through intermediaries—or media.

"Ideas, Goods, and Services" From this phrase we can see that advertising is concerned with much more than the promotion of tangible goods. In recent years the United States has been characterized as a "service economy," and banks, insurance companies, airlines, resorts, restaurants, and dry cleaners advertise as aggressively as do the makers of automobiles, detergents, or beer.

Although most advertising is designed to help sell goods and services, it is being used increasingly to further public interest goals.

"An Identified Sponsor" This phrase distinguishes advertising from propaganda. Propaganda attempts to present opinions and ideas in order to influence attitudes and actions. So does advertising. Often the propagandist remains anonymous and the source of the idea is

[2]Ralph S. Alexander and the Committee on Definitions, *Marketing Definitions*, American Marketing Association, Chicago, 1963, p. 9.

unknown, which makes evaluation difficult. Advertising, on the other hand, discloses or identifies the source of the opinions and ideas it presents. To do otherwise would be a wasteful expenditure of funds.

The Communications Point of View

The "paid form" phrase in the AMA definition is too restricted for many advertising professionals. The phrase was designed to distinguish between advertising, which is delivered through space or time for which the advertiser has paid, and publicity, which is delivered without charge as part of the news or entertainment content of the medium. In 1975 the Advertising Council arranged for $529 million worth of broadcast time and print media space to be devoted to advertisements for national distribution to promote public service projects such as continuing education, safe driving, and litter control. None of this advertising was paid for in the usual sense; various media and advertisers gave the necessary advertising space and time. Furthermore, the creative skill used in writing, illustrating, and producing the advertisements was not paid for either. An even larger dollar volume of public service messages was produced and delivered without cost for local community projects, such as the United Fund and support of the symphonies and the art galleries. To the media that deliver these messages and to the men and women who create and produce them, they are advertisements just as much as are messages designed to increase the sale of soap.

Information and Persuasion

The words "presentation" and "promotion" in the AMA definition fail to do justice to advertising's role. The words describe an exhibition and an advancement of the featured item. In doing so, the advertiser is engaging in a highly important function of advertising, namely that of *informing* prospective buyers and users of the availability of his product. Advertising, which provides the communication link between someone with something to sell and someone who needs something, is often just that simple: the advertiser is providing information to persons who are seeking it. Surely advertising is the most efficient means of reaching people with product information. For example, Coca-Cola reaches one person with an ad for Coke at a cost of $.002, but the cost of an average personal sales call today exceeds $60.

The terms, however, hardly suggest an active attempt to influence people to action or belief by an overt appeal to reason or emotion; that is *persuasion*, which is a major objective of modern advertising.

Clyde R. Miller points out that "all successes in business, in

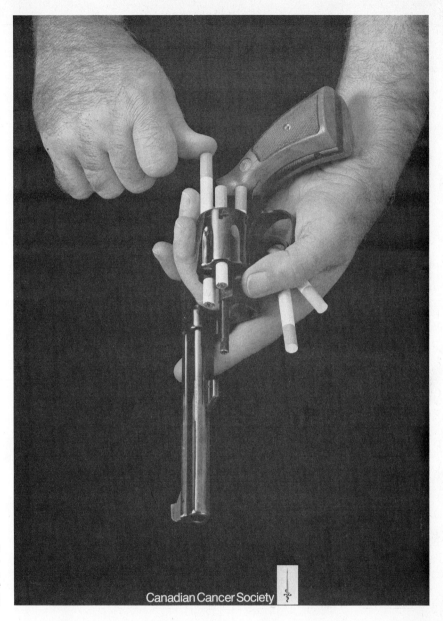

FIGURE 1.1
A telling point is made in this public service poster. [*Canadian Cancer Society.*]

industrial production, in invention, in religious conversion, in education, and in politics depend upon the process of persuasion."[3] Persuasion is the essence of a democratic society. Its opposite is coercion. And in the words of Sir Arthur Quiller-Couch, "Persuasion is the only true intellectual process."[4]

[3]Clyde R. Miller, *The Process of Persuasion*, Crown Publishers, Inc., New York, 1946, p. 16.
[4]Arthur Quiller-Couch, *On the Art of Writing*, G. P. Putnam's Sons, New York, 1916, p. 161.

In modern markets, the producer who is content with advertising that merely identifies or informs may soon find himself in a vulnerable competitive position. Moreover, the creator of advertising—unlike the reporter, editor, or commentator—needs to remember that his or her creative effort must do more than merely inform or entertain. It must change or reinforce an attitude or behavior. And the consumer—the "man in the street"—should always be aware of the advertiser's persuasive intent, no matter how restrained and informative the message may be.

To avoid restricting the scope of advertising to completely commercial functions, and at the same time to convey adequately its purpose and the creative communications processes required to achieve that purpose, this definition of advertising is recommended:

> *Advertising is controlled, identifiable information and persuasion by means of mass communications media.*

We have already discussed the importance of the words "information" and "persuasion" in this definition of advertising. Let us consider the meaning and purpose of three other key terms.

"Controlled"   To the creator of advertising or the advertiser who pays for it, the word "controlled" provides an important distinction between advertising and either personal selling or publicity. The content, time, and direction of an advertising message are controlled by the advertiser. The advertiser says what he wants to say—no more and no less. And by careful selection of the medium that delivers the message, it is directed to the people whom he wants to receive it. The same cannot be said of personal selling, as almost any sales manager or retail proprietor can verify. The salesperson may tell only part of the story, and may not tell that part clearly or effectively. The message may be wasted on the wrong people or not be delivered at the most advantageous time.

The word "controlled" also distinguishes advertising from publicity. The advertiser cannot control the content, time, or direction of publicity. The story may not be presented as desired, at the time chosen, or to the people selected to be reached. In fact, much publicity material is never presented at all. When the advertiser contracts for advertising space or time, on the other hand, definite results can be expected. The message will be published in the way it was prepared—in the same words and the same pictures—and it will be delivered to the specific audience or group served by the medium, it will be of a certain size or length, and it will appear at a certain time.

"Identifiable"   This word is used in preference to such terms as "by an identified sponsor" to indicate that the receiver of the advertising message is able to identify both source and purpose. The source is responsible for the message, and recognizes—or should recognize—that its purpose is to persuade the receiver to accept the ideas or opinions it presents. Publicity or propaganda may not offer these aids to evaluating the message.

"Mass Communications Media" This qualification is designed to separate personal selling and advertising and also to convey the concept of multiple messages delivered to groups of people simultaneously. Basically there are only two mechanisms of mass communications, and they were developed 500 years apart.

The first of these is the printing press, or more accurately the *process of printing from movable type.* With this innovation in the fifteenth century it was possible for the first time to produce with speed and economy many copies of the same message. Today, by way of the printing press in its modern variations, newspapers, magazines, outdoor posters, direct-mail material, and store displays deliver messages to thousands or millions of people at the same time.

The second basic mechanism of mass communications is the *electronic transmitter*—the radio or television station—which, as we know, did not appear until the first part of the twentieth century, and it made available a means of broadcasting messages simultaneously to many people, even to those who could not read. Radio, of course, makes its impression only through sound; television combines sight with sound.

Many other less conspicuous methods of delivering advertising messages exist to service specialized needs of advertisers. These will be discussed later, but most modern advertising is delivered through newspapers, magazines, radio, direct mail, and television.

A BRIEF HISTORY OF ADVERTISING

Institutions appear when a need for them is recognized. No mysterious process of self-generation spews forth an institution unless a variety of external forces are present to nourish its development. Similarly, institutions are not assured of immortality. To survive, an institution must be dynamic and adapt to changing conditions. In this section we explore how advertising came to be an institution in our society. We present this information in the belief that the past helps explain the present and provides guides to the future.

Early Advertising

Advertising in ancient and medieval times was crude when measured by present-day standards. Nevertheless, the basic reason for employing the technique was the same then as now: to communicate information and ideas to groups of people in order to change or reinforce an attitude.

Our knowledge of advertising in ancient times naturally is fragmentary. The diggings of archaeologists in the countries rimming the Mediterranean Sea have turned up evidence that the Romans and some of their predecessors had learned that "it pays to advertise." Three forms of advertising were used prior to the time the printing press began to open the door to the development of modern mass communication media.

Trademarks Pride in workmanship led early craftsmen to place their own individual marks on goods such as pottery. As the reputation of one particular artisan spread by word of mouth, buyers came to look for his distinctive mark just as we look for trademarks and brand names on merchandise today.

The guild system, with its trade monopolies, gave legal protection to those persons permitted to make a certain type of product. Goods could not be sold unless they carried a guild mark, and severe penalties were imposed for placing counterfeit marks on the output of nonguild members. Thus, the trademark has a long history in the world of commerce and still performs its prime functions of protecting (1) the consumer by ensuring that he receives the goods he wants and (2) the manufacturer by preventing inferior goods from being palmed off as his product.

Signs Some traders, like the Phoenicians, painted commercial messages on prominent rocks along trade lanes, much in the fashion of some present-day religious sects. These messages extolled the wares that were for sale and were forerunners of modern outdoor advertising. Excavations at Pompeii reveal that each little shop had an inscription on the wall next to the entrance to tell the passerby whether the shop was a place to buy bread, wine, pottery, or other merchandise.

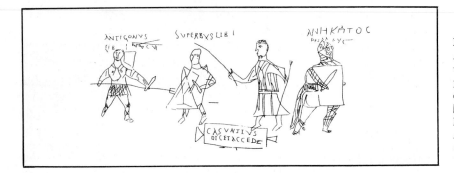

FIGURE 1.2
Advertisings on a wall in Pompeii, promoting a gladiatorial contest. [*Dick Sutphen*, The Mad Old Ads, *McGraw-Hill Book Company, New York, 1966.*]

Town Criers In Greece, during its Golden Age, public criers were a civic institution. Men were paid to circulate through the streets of the city, advising the citizens of important news and announcing public events. Later, during the Middle Ages, the only available means of advertising except signs was the spoken word.

Early Printed Advertising

The first known printed advertisement in the English language appeared in 1473. At that time, William Caxton, an English adapter of Gutenberg's idea of movable type, printed and distributed a handbill which called the attention of potential buyers to a book of ecclesiastical rules he had just published. By the middle of the seventeenth century, weekly newspapers, called "mercuries," started to appear in

FIGURE 1.3
Fifteenth-century printer's marks. The mark in the center was used by William Caxton, who printed the first known advertisement in the English language.

England. The printing press was then being used in a fashion which led to the gradual growth and development of advertising, by providing a practical, readily available medium to deliver advertising messages to the literate portion of the public. Most early newspaper advertisements were in the form of announcements. Prominent among early advertisers were importers of products new to England. For instance, the first offering of coffee was made in a newspaper ad in 1652, followed by an offering of chocolate in 1657, and of tea in 1658.

Evidence of "competitive" advertising, as contrasted with "pioneering" advertising that aims at building acceptance for a previously unknown product, can be found as early as 1710 when razor strop and patent medicine advertisements attempted to convince magazine readers of the advertised product's superiority over similar products. Many of the claims certainly were excessive and, to the more sophisticated reader of today, transparently unbelievable. Printed advertising was in general use by the mid-eighteenth century.

THE DEVELOPMENT OF MODERN ADVERTISING

Although American advertising has its roots in the English background, if any institution other than democracy itself can be said to be synonymous with America, that institution is advertising. For a variety of reasons, however, English and American advertising did not follow parallel paths of development. Of the number of different forces contributing to the difference in advertising's rate of growth in the two countries, a particularly significant obstacle to its expansion in England was the tax imposed by the Crown on both newspapers and their advertisements. The imposition of excise taxes was one of the grievances of American colonists, and when the United States successfully waged its War of Independence, no such taxes were enacted by the government of the new republic.

When the *Boston News-Letter* published its first issue on April 24, 1704, it contained advertisements much like those of contemporaneous English newspapers. But in addition to the absence of taxes already referred to, a number of social and economic advances were necessary before American advertising could approach its present stature. The turning point came at approximately the middle of the nineteenth century. While we shall consider each of these socioeconomic advances individually, we should bear in mind that they are closely interrelated.

The Industrial Revolution in the United States

The Industrial Revolution, following Watt's discovery of the principle of steam power, led to expanded manufacturing in England and later on

GREAT ENCOURAGEMENT

AMERICAN REVOLUTION

What a Brilliant Prospect does this Event hold out to every Lad of Spirit, who is inclined to try his Fortune in that highly renowned Corps

The Continental Marines

When every Thing that swims the Seas must be a

PRIZE!

Thousands are at this moment endeavoring to get on Board Privateers, where they serve without Pay or Reward of any kind whatsoever; so certain does their Chance appear of enriching themselves by PRIZE MONEY! What an enviable Station then must the *CONTINENTAL MARINE* hold,—who with far superior Advantages to thefe, has the additional benefit of liberal Pay, and plenty of the best Provisions, with a good and well appointed Ship under him, the Pride and Glory of the Continental Navy; furely every Man of Spirit muft blufh to remain at Home in Inactivity and Indolence, when his Country needs his Assistance.

Where then can he have fuch a fair opportunity of reaping Glory and Riches, as in the Continental Marines, a Corps daily acquiring new Honors, and here, when once embarked in American Fleet, he finds himself in the midft of Honor and Glory, furounded by a fet of fine Fellow, Strangers to Fear, and who ftrike Terror through the Hearts of their Enemies wherever they go?

He has likewise the infpiring idea to know, that while he fcour the Ocean to protect the Liberty of these states, that the Hearts and good Wifhes of the whole American peoples attend him; pray for his fuccefs, and participate in his Glory!! Lofe no Time then, my Fine Fellows, in embracing the glorious Opportunity that awaits you; YOU WILL RECEIVE

Seventeen Dollars Bounty,

And on your Arrival at Head Quarters, be comfortably and genteely CLOTHED,—And fpirited young BOYS of a promifing Appearance, who are Five Feet Six Inches high, WILL RECEIVE TEN DOLLARS, and equal Advantages of PROVISIONS and CLOTHING with the Men. And thofe who wish only to enlist for a limited Service, fhall receive a Bounty of SEVEN DOLLARS, and Boys FIVE. In Fact, the Advantages which the *MARINE* poffefses, are too numerous to mention here, but among the many, it may not be amifs to state.—That if he has a *WIFE* or aged *PARENT*, he can make them an Allotment of half his *PAY*; which will be regularly paid without any Trouble to them, or to whomsoever he may directs that being well Clothed and Fed on Board Ship, the Remainder of his *PAY* and PRIZE MONEY will be clear in Reserve for the Relief of his Family or his own private Purpofes. The Single Young Man on his Return to Port, finds himself enabled to cut a Dafh on Shore with his GIRL and his GLASS, that might be envied by a Nobleman.—Take Courage then, seize the Fortune that awaits you, repair to the *MARINE RENDEZVOUS*, where in a FLOWING BOWL of PUNCH, an Three Times Three, you shall drink

Long Live The United States, and Success to the Marines.

The Daily Allowance of a Marine when embarked, is—One Pound of BEEF or PORK.—One Pound of BREAD,—Flour, Raisins, Butter, Cheese, Oatmeal, Molasses, Tea, Sugar, &c. &c. And a Pint of the beft WINE, or Half a Pint of the best RUM or BRANDY; together with a Pint of LEMONADE. They have liberty in warm Countries, a plentiful Allowance of the choicest FRUIT. And what can be more handsome than the Marines' Proportion of PRIZE MONEY, when a Sergeant shares equal with the First Class of Petty Officers, such as Midshipmen, Assistant Surgeons, &c. which is Five Shares each; a Corporal with the Second Class, which is Three Shares each; and the Private with the Able Seamen, one Share and a Half each.

Desiring greater Particulars, and a more full Account of the many Advantages of this invaluable Corps, apply to CAPTAIN MULLAN, at TUN TAVERN, where the Bringer of a Recruit will receive THREE DOLLARS.

* * * * * * * *

January, 1776

FIGURE 1.4

Marine recruits were sought by this persuasive ad during the Revolutionary War. The crude production of the advertisement reflected the primitive state of printing at that time. [*U.S. Marine Corps.*]

in the United States. The Civil War accelerated the trend, and an expanded domestic market provided an outlet for factory-made products. As the Industrial Revolution altered the relationship between the maker and the user of goods, a need for advertising developed.

The Need for Communication

Mechanization turned out goods faster than they could be absorbed in the region of manufacture. A need arose to extend markets geographi-

FIGURE 1.5
Marine recruits are still needed, and contemporary advertising approaches are employed. Note the shift of emphasis to a dominant illustration and little copy. [*U.S. Marine Corps.*]

cally, and the manufacturer had to find a way of communicating the value of his products to people who knew nothing of his reputation, as was the case when goods were made to order by local craftworkers. Advertising provided the needed communication vehicle. Later on, it helped raise consumption so that the full use of the machinery was possible, thus bringing about lower per-unit costs of manufacture.

The Need for Transportation

Granted that a high degree of industrialization must precede an advertising system of any magnitude, there are several other important elements to such a development. A comprehensive transportation system must come first. A network of waterways, highways, railroads, and airlines is needed to carry the goods to scattered markets. This same system is needed to carry printed advertising media to prospective buyers living far from the producer.

In the United States the railroads provided this network, and by 1890 all of our country was served by the "iron horse." In 1896 the federal government inaugurated rural free delivery (RFD). This system of package delivery to farm homes led to the expansion of markets by the mail-order houses, such as Montgomery Ward and Sears Roebuck. Slowly, the country became a more homogenized market instead of a series of a local and regional markets.

The Need for Education

Before the Industrial Revolution and the existence of a transportation system were to have any effect on the need for advertising, people had to be able to read. Until the advent of radio in the 1920s, people could be reached only through the printed word. Our nation was an early believer in the doctrine of compulsory public education, and a high rate of literacy resulted.

The Growth of Newspapers and Magazines

These trends in transportation and education were reflected in the growth of printed media in the United States. The *Boston News-Letter* was the first newspaper of any continuous life in our country. By 1830 there were 1,200 papers in the nation, growing to 3,000 in 1860 and to a high point of 15,000 in 1914. Today over 11,400 newspapers serve the reading public of our nation.

In 1741, two magazines were published in Philadelphia. Both failed, and the following century saw many attempts to establish magazine ventures. By 1850 there were some 700 struggling magazines in the United States. The number increased to 1,200 in 1870 and doubled again to 2,400 by 1880. The improvement in levels of education of the population, the expansion of transportation facilities, the benefits of low-cost mailing privileges granted by Congress in 1879, and the development of the rural free delivery system—all of these combined with an increased trend by manufacturers toward national marketing—to the doubling of the number of magazines in the two decades between 1880 and 1900. Publishers, recognizing that advertising revenues could replace subscription income, lowered prices on their magazines and aggressively promoted advertising sales to fill the revenue gap. Circulations skyrocketed, and today there are more than 9,600 magazines in the United States.

The Development of the Modern Advertising Agency

For advertising to become an institution, a need for it had to be recognized; its availability had to be communicated to potential users. This was accomplished by the advertising agent, from which the modern advertising agency evolved. Volney Palmer, the first American advertising agent, began business in the early 1840s. The first agents originally were only brokers of space in newspapers and magazines who contracted with publishers for advertising space at bulk rates and resold the space to advertisers at a higher rate. They provided none of the creative or planning services that are the primary functions of advertising agencies today. However, in the days when the knowledge of available advertising media was meager at best, and even the basic function of advertising in accelerating distribution was understood by few producers, the limited services of these space-broker agents justified their existence. About 1890, as advertisers became more sophisticated, markets increased in size, advertising budgets grew bigger, and agencies began to add such services as the writing of advertising messages, the creation of illustrations, the choice of typography, and sometimes even market analysis, rudimentary though it was by present standards of marketing research. By the beginning of the twentieth century, agencies had come to assume the role they perform today—the planning, creation, and execution of complete advertising campaigns—in return for commissions paid by media or fees received from advertisers.

The Advent of Radio and Television

Two twentieth-century events gave added impetus to the growth of advertising, namely, the appearance of radio and of television on the American scene. The invention of the electronic transmission of messages, with its subsequent commercial applications, is second only to the invention of printing in the development of advertising media.

For the first time, except for the minor use of town criers, it became possible to advertise goods and services to illiterates. Of course, by the time of the invention and commercial application of radio, nearly everyone in America could read. Still, some advertising messages can be delivered more easily and more quickly through the ear than through the eye. Furthermore, in countries less well developed—in Latin America, Africa, and the Near East, for example—radio has played a more important role in marketing and mass communication than have newspapers or magazines.

The first wireless message was transmitted by Marconi in 1895. The first broadcasting station established for commercial application of the radio broadcasting principle was by KDKA of East Pittsburgh, Pennsylvania, which carried presidential election returns in 1920. The Federal Communications Commission (FCC) had licensed 30 radio stations by January 1, 1922. Today there are over 6,800. The founding of the National Broadcasting Company (NBC) in 1926 made it possible for all Americans to hear the same program at the same time.

Television, of course, changed the role of radio as TV became the major source of in-home entertainment in the 1950s. Television sets were the fastest-selling appliances in the 1950s, and advertisers switched dollars from radio and print media to take advantage of even larger audiences. For the first time, a medium of mass communication combined the impact of sound with that of sight and motion.

By 1976 there were 963 television stations licensed in the United States alone, of which 252 were educational; the medium was second only to newspapers as a repository of advertising dollars. The addition of color transmissions in the 1960s furthered the growth of television as an advertising medium.

It is difficult to predict what the next major breakthrough will be in the history of advertising. One can safely predict, however, that whatever it is, it will be exciting.

ADVERTISING IN A MICROCOSM

Now that we have defined advertising and told something of its history, it may be useful to examine several true-life examples of how advertising does, in fact, work. To accomplish this goal, and to help disclose the fascination inherent in the advertising process, we present five short examples of how advertising operates in the day-to-day world. These cases are not the product of Madison Avenue advertising agencies; instead, each originated in 1974 in Atlanta, Georgia, an average American city and the home of one of the authors of this book. Similar examples could be found in any metropolitan center—Kansas City, Boston, Denver, New Orleans, Dallas, Seattle, and so on. These advertising campaigns are not particularly glamorous in planning or execution; rather, each was selected as being representative of advertising in general. Each campaign was successful in achieving the objectives of its sponsor. Some of the terms and phrases will be new to the beginner in advertising. It is hoped that all will be clearer by the end of the course. For the present time read the cases in a broad, open fashion, concentrating on what is taking place rather than on minute details. The objectives of the five campaigns were as follows:

1 Introduce a new consumer product nationwide (Grease Relief by Texize)
2 "Demarket" a product in an age of shortage (Georgia Power Company)
3 Promote a special event (Bob Dylan Concert Tour)
4 Raise funds for a charity (Georgia Heart Fund)
5 Promote retail-store traffic and increase sales (House of Denmark)

Grease Relief

Consumer products designed for use in the home are synonymous in our minds with such sophisticated marketing firms as Procter & Gamble. Nevertheless, many of the new products in the category are developed by small, entrepreneurial firms located most anywhere in the nation. Such is the case of Grease Relief.®

Grease Relief was developed in 1973 as a growth vehicle for Intex, a new company in Greenville, South Carolina. The product as developed was suitable for use in both the kitchen and the laundry and

FIGURE 1.6
Two versions of the Grease Relief package are shown. The one at the right has a spray dispenser; the other contains the product to be used to refill the dispenser.

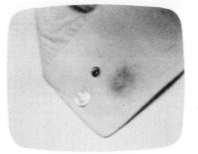

(Silent)

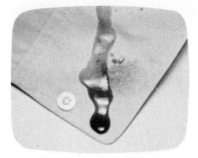

ANNCR: There's got to be another way.

SINGERS: Get relief . . . Grease relief

ANNCR: Made just to degrease

SINGERS: Easy!

ANNCR: Or the new pull-top

FIGURE 1.7
This photoboard shows the television commercial used to introduce Grease Relief.

ANNCR: Grease relief degreaser for the laundry . . . kitchen, too.

Now easier . . .

Grease spots. Grimy collars and cuffs.

There's got to be an easier way.

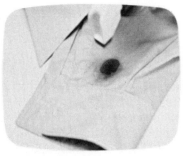

only easier now with the

new Trigger Control Top

economy squeeze

SINGERS: Easy!

more economical

from Texize.
SINGERS: Get Grease relief.

competed against such giants as Lever Brothers' Wisk for laundry usage; various liquid detergents for dishes, pots and pans; and all-purpose cleaners for range tops and other surfaces. After extensive consumer research, including focus groups, simulated test markets, and personal interviews by such well-known organizations as Yankelovich, Skelly, and White, Inc., the product was positioned in the marketplace as a "degreaser" for kitchen and laundry. Ninety percent of the surveyed housewives thought grease was their single most difficult cleaning problem, indicating a need for a product of this type.

The price was set at 79 cents for a 22-ounce bottle. Intex retained Weltin Advertising, a new Atlanta-based agency, and it was decided to begin the product rollout in several adjoining states located in the Southeast with the intent to go national as soon as practical. Color page advertisements were run in regional editions of *Family Circle*, *Good Housekeeping*, *Southern Living*, *Woman's Day*, and Sunday newspaper supplements. The bulk of the advertising, however, was placed in television, using a combination of daytime, late-night, and prime-time network spot announcements. The product met with good consumer acceptance during this regional marketing. However, Intex was not set up for expeditious national distribution of a single product line, and the product was sold to Texize. Now Grease Relief was ready for its exciting thrust into the national market. To that end, the national marketing plan was drawn up and the following marketing objectives were set down:

1 To introduce and expand the brand nationally through grocery stores
2 To obtain and maintain a minimum of 80% all commodity volume (ACV) distribution nationally with a maximum of 5 percent out of stocks
3 To generate national awareness and trial comparable to that achieved in test markets
4 To identify potential heavy users of Grease Relief and apply extra effort to attract these consumers

In developing the creative strategy behind the advertising, an attempt was made to integrate all elements—name, package size and design, and advertising—in order to communicate quickly the product's major benefit, relief from grease. Figure 1.7 is a television commercial used in the 1974 campaign.

The media strategy was to aim Grease Relief advertising at homemakers of all ages but to slant it toward the upper income brackets, to reach this market frequently enough to create brand awareness and generate trial usage, and to use a combination of media for these specific reasons:

1 *Television.* To serve as the primary mass medium because the advertiser

believes TV to be the most effective means of communicating with the consumer. TV embodies sight, sound, and action in living color.

2 *Magazines.* To "heavy-up" (reach more frequently) against better prospects.

3 *Sunday magazines.* To generate added impact upon consumers while providing the means of distributing a coupon.

Grease Relief budgeted $4,605,604 for media advertising in 1974, divided in this manner:

Television: $4,186,400

Women's service magazines: $100,330

Sunday magazines: $318,874

Consumer promotion strategy used cents-off coupons to stimulate trial purchases; trade promotion strategy provided off-invoice allowances and guarantees to retailers.

Thanks to a carefully researched, planned, and executed introductory campaign, today's homemakers are using some 15 million bottles of Grease Relief annually to solve an annoying problem.

Georgia Power Company

In the first half of the twentieth century, public utilities, including electric utilities, were urged to produce and distribute their commodities at the lowest price possible so that more people might enjoy their benefits. Increased use of electricity and efficiency in production led to lower prices until electricity became not a luxury but a labor-saving convenience. In such times, public utilities, through advertising, were urging consumers to take advantage of these bargain rates. Figure 1.8 shows a Georgia Power advertisement promoting outdoor lighting service, which, in addition to giving consumers a desired service, added to the company sales volume.

With the onset of national inflation and environmental concern in the late 1960s, however, utilities became hard pressed to maintain low rates. Governmental approval was sought to raise rates to cover higher costs. At this time it also became prudent to assess the value of product promotion. Thus, instead of stimulating power usage, the objective of electric utility advertising shifted to communicating information about the company to its public: image advertising, if you will.

In the 1970s, inflation continued and a new dimension was added to the picture in the form of fuel shortages and unprecedented costs for the energy industries. Although consumers remained free to impose demands on electric utilities at any time, the utilities began to try to tailor those demands to fit the resources available. The firms began to

BRILLIANT SECURITY

For as little as $4 a month, our dusk-to-dawn lighting service helps safeguard your property.

At nightfall—automatically—your home, farm, business or industry is bathed in brightness with an electric dusk-to-dawn security light.

It gives you safety, convenience and protection. All at a low cost.

Security lights are especially bright because they contain powerful mercury-vapor lamps. And each has a photoelectric cell which automatically turns the lamp on at dusk and off at dawn. A carefree feature you will appreciate.

There are two lights to choose from: a 7,000-lumen fixture for $4 a month and a 20,000-lumen fixture for $6.75 a month. Cost includes installation on an existing pole, maintenance, lamp replacement and electricity used.

For details on Georgia Power's dusk-to-dawn lighting service, call or come by our nearest office. Or, if you prefer, mail the coupon below.

Georgia Power Company
Box 4545, Atlanta, Ga. 30302   Advertising Dept.

I want to know more about the dusk-to-dawn security lighting service. Please send me a free descriptive folder without obligation.

Name

Address

Town_____Phone_____

GEORGIA POWER COMPANY

FIGURE 1.8
A public utility promotes additional uses for its product in the days before America recognized that a shortage of energy existed. The ad appeared in newspapers in the fall of 1968.

take a new marketing approach, called *demarketing*, which is defined as "a state in which demand exceeds the level at which the marketer feels able or motivated to supply it."[5]

Georgia Power is a summer-peak company; heavy use of air

[5]Philip Kotler, *Marketing Management*, 3d ed., Prentice-Hall, Inc., Englewood Cliffs, N.J., 1976, p. 11.

conditioning during the summer months places the greatest demands of the entire year on the system, as contrasted with the winter-load problem in Northern states. If power isn't there when needed, a brownout or a blackout is sure to occur.

To ward off such occurrences and to inform customers of increased prices in summer, Georgia Power began an advertising program designed to encourage the wise use of electricity, especially during the air conditioning season. A series of newspaper ads was run suggesting numerous ideas for preventing power waste, including turning thermostats higher during summer months, adding insulation and weatherstripping, and keeping doors and windows closed. Figure 1.9

How does 73° differ from 78°?

It takes 25 percent more electricity.

Imagine what that does to your electric bill. Air conditioning can use more power than all your other electric appliances put together. When you set the thermostat lower than necessary for comfort, the extra power is needless expense.

Rates went up last year and will be reflected in cooling costs this summer. But

there are ways to use electricity more efficiently and cut down on your bill.

Set the thermostat on 78°. And adjust it 5° higher while you're away from home. Keep filters clean. Clogged filters will overwork the system.

Keep windows and doors shut, and close

draperies in sunny rooms. Shade trees help, too. Good insulation and weather stripping can lower operating costs. Air conditioning is even affected by heat from a light bulb. So turn off unnecessary lights.

Starting to save electricity may take a conscious effort. But it can become a money-saving habit.

Georgia Power Company
A citizen wherever we serve®

FIGURE 1.9
By spring 1972 the same company was showing consumers how to use less of its product. A demarketing strategy was being followed.

shows one of the ads in the campaign. A bill stuffer was mailed to the company's residential customers—almost 1 million of them. Later, two television spots and a statewide radio campaign were used. Although Georgia Power's chief fuel is coal and there appears to be no immediate shortage of electricity from this fuel, the company continues its program of conservation information, emphasizing that electricity is "too good to waste."

Bob Dylan Concert Tour

Early in 1974 Bob Dylan, the reigning balladeer and poet-conscience of the young and the not-so-young, set out on a 21-city tour of the United States. His first public appearance in over eight years, the series of concerts was advertised solely through the placement of one newspaper advertisement in each city where he was scheduled to sing. Figure 1.10 shows how this ad appeared in the *Atlanta Journal* and *Constitution.*

Response was almost unbelievable. Within hours after mail-order tickets were put on sale, more than 5 million letters, each requesting an average of three tickets, descended upon post offices along the tour route. By the tour's end, it was estimated that approximately 7.5 percent of the nation's population had requested $90 million worth of tickets.

The Atlanta newspaper ad, 7 by 10 inches, cost $991.90 and succeeded in filling the 15,000-plus seat Omni International Auditorium; concert promoters achieved a 11,250 percent gross return on their investment. Thus, a small, simple informational ad had communicated its message successfully and benefited both seller and buyer.

The Heart Fund

Advertising is becoming increasingly important to the success of charitable, nonprofit organizations, as is illustrated by the Georgia Heart Fund campaign.

The American Heart Association is interested in raising money to support research into the causes of heart disease and to mount educational campaigns aimed at reducing the losses brought about by America's number one health problem. Each year the national headquarters prepares a series of specialized kits which are developed for use by the Heart Association of each state. Each kit includes promotional materials such as 20-, 30-, and 60-second commercials for television; magazine advertisements and logos; newspaper ads; and prepared speeches. The Heart Association of each state has the responsibility for distributing these kits to proper media and for seeing that the materials are used. Each association enlists local support, coordinates volunteers, and stimulates promotional efforts throughout the state.

Although the Heart Association is a nonprofit organization, it

BOB DYLAN/THE BAND

APPEARING AT

THE OMNI

Monday & Tuesday, January 21 & 22, 8:00 P.M.
Ticket Prices $8.50, $7.50, $6.50 plus $.25 service charge per ticket
(Limit 4 per person)
TICKETS BY MAIL ORDER ONLY TO:
BOB DYLAN BOX OFFICE (Ticket Price/Date)
100 Techwood Drive N.W., Atlanta, Georgia 30303

Indicate on your envelope the price/date tickets you are requesting. Enclose self-addressed
stamped envelope with your payment, payable to BOB DYLAN. (Do not send cash or personal
checks). Note: No mail orders will be accepted postmarked earlier than December 2, 1973.
IMPORTANT: Indicate if you will take the best available if all tickets at the price/date indicated are sold out.

FIGURE 1.10
This simple an-
nouncement ad
led to a sellout for
the Bob Dylan
concert.

approaches fund raising with the idea that there is a "product" to sell,
namely, each local heart fund and the importance of supporting it; and
the product is promoted through advertising. For example, the kits for

each state association contain mats (copy that can be duplicated) for advertisements similar to the one in Figure 1.11. The owners of newspapers and magazines are persuaded to contribute free space to reproduce these messages, which contain health suggestions for avoiding heart disease and ask for support for local heart funds.

FIGURE 1.11
This print advertisement was reproduced from a mat developed and distributed by the Heart Fund. It was run gratis by publishers of newspapers and magazines.

In 1974, the efforts of the Georgia Heart Association centered on increasing public knowledge of the dangers of high blood pressure, which accounts for more deaths among people between the ages of forty-five and sixty-four than any other cause. The promotion of information on high blood pressure serves two purposes: one, to encourage people to have their blood pressure checked and obtain medical treatment if necessary; two, to raise funds for additional research into the causes and treatment of this disease, which takes more than 6,000 lives a year in Georgia alone. An example of an advertisement communicating the desired information is shown in Figure 1.12. It appeared on a full newspaper page as a public relations gesture by one of Atlanta's leading department stores.

The goal set for the Georgia Heart Fund campaign for 1974 was $1 million. Through the use of the promotional strategies discussed, the goal was met with a small overage of $8,000. Although there is no way of knowing the number of people who were persuaded to have their blood pressure checked, it is believed that the campaign was instrumental in alerting the general public to the problem.

House of Denmark

The House of Denmark is a small retail furniture company. It specializes in imported Scandinavian furniture and accessories and operates one store in an Atlanta suburb and a warehouse several miles away. Its merchandise is priced in the medium and upper ranges; the store appearance and mood is one of lightness and young sophistication. The House of Denmark sales staff also is young, sophisticated, and college-educated; sales personnel often have an art-design background. Customers are drawn primarily from young, professional married couples who are furnishing their first house or apartment.

On one Sunday in 1974, the store ran a one-column, 21-inch newspaper advertisement in the *Atlanta Journal* and *Constitution* (Figure 1.13). The ad was simple and straightforward, was entirely informative, and showed no furniture, which usually is an integral part of House of Denmark advertising. The newspaper charged $185 for the space. Along with the newspaper ad, the store sent out 1,750 announcement cards, printed with the same selling message, to its mailing list of regular customers. This element of the promotion cost $28.75 for printing the cards and $140 for postage. From a total advertising expenditure of $353.75, the House of Denmark drew large numbers of people to its warehouse. In a five-hour period, 535 items were sold; sales totaled more than $60,000.

These five examples should help the reader appreciate the various ways that advertising can be employed to help solve business and nonbusiness problems. How advertising strategies and tactics are planned and the great variety of advertising techniques are used to

With the startling news that an estimated 800,000 Georgians have High Blood Pressure, and that more than half this number don't even know they have it, The Georgia Heart Association has launched a campaign of HBP Control. Naturally, the first step is detection, and perhaps the most interesting facet of this is a project in Carrollton where fifth, sixth and seventh graders are being taught to read blood pressures, and thus are able to screen members of their families and report to a team of medical volunteers for evaluation. This project is so successful that the teaching unit will be employed in many elementary schools in Georgia in the near future. If kids can take blood pressures easily, then having yours taken should be even easier. How about it,

FIGURE 1.12
A large retailer ran this newspaper ad, which highlights the dangers of high blood pressure (HBP), as a public service.

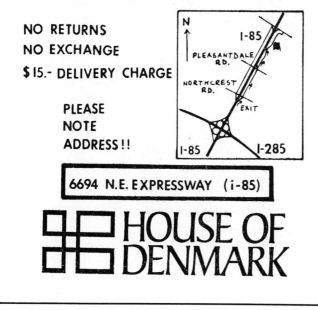

achieve advertising objectives is discussed throughout the rest of this book. We trust that some of advertising's excitement has already rubbed off onto the reader. Additional reasons for studying advertising are now provided.

WHY STUDY ADVERTISING?

There are many good reasons for having an understanding of advertising. It has social importance and international significance, it can add to our effectiveness as consumers, and it possesses career applications.

Social Importance

Most college students recognize that a study of advertising helps prepare them for careers in business, journalism, commercial art, or media management. Most informed citizens also realize, to a degree, that advertising is an important institution in our society—a force that helps shape the lives of all of us. The following remarks by historian David M. Potter emphasize the social significance of advertising:

> For millions of people throughout the world, during the last three centuries, America has symbolized plenty. This profusion of wealth, this abundance of goods, has borne a significance that far transcends the field of economics. American democracy, in the broad sense, was made possible to begin with by a condition of economic surplus, and the constant incidence of this abundance has differentiated American democracy from the democracy of other, less richly endowed countries.

> Abundance, then, must be reckoned a major force in our history. But one may question whether any force can be regarded as possessing major historic importance unless it has developed its own characteristic institution. Democracy, for instance, produces the institution of popular government—the whole complex of parties, elections, representative bodies, constitutions and the like. Religion manifests itself in the church, with a canon law, a clergy, and a whole ecclesiastical system. Science and learning find institutional embodiment in universities with all their libraries, laboratories, faculties, and other apparatus of scholarship. If abundance can be regarded as a great historical force, what institution is especially identified with it? Does any such institution exist?

> . . . If we seek an institution that was brought into being by abundance without previous existence in any form, and, moreover, an institution which is peculiarly identified with American abundance rather than with abundance throughout Western civilization, we will find it, I believe, in modern American advertising. . . .

Father John O'Leary.

If he's not in church, he's probably in jail.

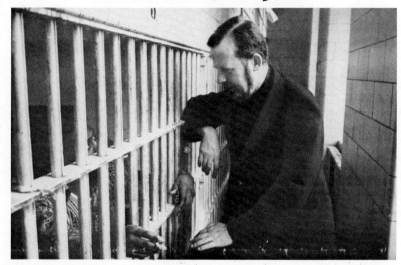

He was put in for good behavior.

His work as a counselor to high school youths brought him to the attention of Catholic authorities when they needed a new chaplain for the Manhattan House of Detention. (You may have heard it referred to as "The Tombs.")

So several months ago, John O'Leary's world changed from classrooms to cell blocks.

His 'flock' is an ever-changing group of 1400 men who are waiting for trial or sentencing. They're packed in, two men to a cell barely big enough for one, and from where they sit God can seem to be very far away.

But what can one priest do?

A prisoner put it pretty well: "He brings you your freedom." It's that simple and that complicated. It's exactly what Christ brought to a world of prisoners 2000 years ago.

At first glance, the dedicated social workers and psychologists at The Tombs might seem to be doing the same work. But what makes John O'Leary special in the eyes of many of the men is his priesthood.

It's both the outward sign of commitment and the inward source of strength he uses to do a difficult job.

The kind of job you do for love, not for money.

But there's so much more work to do in the New York Archdiocese—and too few priests. Could you do what John O'Leary does? Have you ever thought about it? There's a phone number where you can reach him. Just dial P-R-I-E-S-T-S (774-3787). Or write: PRIESTS, 555 West End Avenue, New York, N.Y. 10024.

He'll be happy to talk to you about his vocation. And yours too.

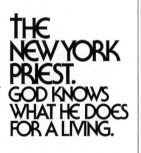

THE NEW YORK PRIEST.
GOD KNOWS WHAT HE DOES FOR A LIVING.

FIGURE 1.14
Advertising is used to interest young men in becoming priests.

But advertising as an institution has suffered almost total neglect. One might read fairly widely in the literature which treats of public opinion, popular culture, and the mass media in the U.S. without ever learning that advertising now compares with such longstanding institutions as the school and the church in the magnitude of its social influence. It dominates the media, has vast power in the shaping of popular standards, and it is really one of the very limited group of institutions which exercise social control. Yet analysts of society have largely ignored it. Historians seldom do more than glance at it in their studies of social history, and, when they do, they usually focus attention upon some picturesque or titillating aspect, such as the way advertising has reflected or encouraged a new frankness about such previously tabooed subject as ladies' underwear. Histories of American periodicals and even of the mass media deal with advertising as if it were a side issue. Students of the radio and of the mass-circulation magazines frequently condemn advertising for its conspicuous role, as if it were a mere interloper in a separate pre-existing, self-contained aesthetic world of actors, musicians, authors, and script-writers; they hardly recognize that advertising created modern American radio and television, transformed the modern newspaper, evoked the modern slick periodical, and remains the vital essence of each of them at the present time. Marconi may have invented the wireless and Henry Luce may have invented the newsmagazine, but it is advertising that has made both wireless and newsmagazines what they are in America today.[6]

International Significance

Although *modern* advertising developed more rapidly in this country, its essential techniques came from Britain and Europe with the first printing press transported to our shores. The roots of advertising application are to be found in the Industrial Revolution, which also was imported to our land. We recognize that the application of modern advertising methods is not limited to the American society of abundance. As the world changed from colonialism and exploitation to self-determination and economic development, thinking about international trade also changed, and many cartels and prohibitive tariffs have given way to competitive enterprise and customs unions. These changes in the world environment have permitted modern advertising to spread beyond the United States to such unlikely nations as the Soviet Union and Kenya. Figure 1.15 shows how a soap powder is advertised in the heart of Africa.

Most of the largest advertising agencies are American in origin. Their overseas offices, however, outnumber their branches in our country. Furthermore, Dentsu, a Japanese agency, does more advertising for clients than any other agency in the world, although most of its

[6]David M. Potter, *People of Plenty*, The University of Chicago Press, Chicago, 1954, pp. 166–168.

Je unajua?

Gharama ya kufua na Extra Active OMO ni ndogo sana ukilinganisha na sabuni ya kawaida...

...watumia OMO chache tu kwa kung'arisha hata nguo chafu zaidi!

K-OMO-4/SW-O&M/1105

Je, umeshajiunga na wanaong'aa? Hao ndio watu wanaosisitiza kutumia Extra Active Omo kila wanapofua nguo zao. Wanajua kwamba hakuna sabuni nyingine ya unga au ya mti iliyo na 'active brightener' maalum kama Omo - na sasa Omo imeongezwa active brightener nyingi zaidi.

Hii ndiyo sababu Omo haigharimu kuliko sabuni ya kawaida.

Watumia Omo chache tu, kwa kusafisha vingi - kwa maji ya moto au baridi. Tumia Extra Active Omo kila mara unapofua kung'arisha nguo zako.

Extra Active OMO hung'arisha hata zaidi_na huonyesha wazi

FIGURE 1.15
American advertising techniques are employed in the promotion of a soap product in an African country. The copy is written in the Swahili language.

business is done within its native country. Courses in advertising are taught in such European universities as Louvain, Göttingen, Berlin, Bergen, Helsinki, and Geneva, as well as several business schools including INSEAD (Fontainebleau), London, and IMEDE (Lausanne).

American advertising executives lecture on the topic throughout the world.

Advertising is indeed an important American institution, but one major development of the twentieth century has been the tremendous expansion of international marketing, and consequently advertising has become an important force in many other nations as people seek to improve their lots in world society. Regardless of our career intentions, an understanding of advertising should be a part of the broad background for citizenship—a better understanding of the world in which we live and the world of the future.

FIGURE 1.16
A familiar advertising theme, "Let your fingers do the walking," is featured in a French-language billboard ad. The campaign has stimulated increased usage of the yellow pages directory in Belgium where it appeared. [*ITT.*]

Practical Value

Despite the economic importance of advertising in our country and throughout the world, the general public has a poor understanding of this form of mass communication. Loose comments about advertising by intellectuals in our society compound the problem. Since advertising is, or can be, powerfully persuasive, it sometimes is misused and therefore subject to adverse reaction—just as nuclear physics is downgraded for providing bombs. Knowledge of advertising, therefore, should help you to evaluate both the criticisms of and the claims for advertising in order to form your own opinion.

If we understand what advertising is and what it isn't—its possibilities and limitations—we shall be able to apply the forces of advertising to further social and community projects and to use it in our own pursuit of happiness, for our own welfare and that of others.

An understanding of advertising will help us allocate our own limited funds among unlimited choices available in the marketplace. We can become better-informed consumers and our purchases more satisfying.

Career Applications

Many readers of this textbook may have set advertising as their career goal. Most students, however, do not plan on entering the field upon graduation. This is a healthy situation because the pool of jobs in advertising is more limited than, say, accounting, selling, or management. Advertising can be an exciting and rewarding career, but knowledge of its functioning also is valuable to those opting for other careers.

Commercial art students, for instance, should study advertising since most of their creative output will be used in one form of advertising or another. Industrial design students have a similar interest, for the product they design usually must serve also as an advertisement for the product.

Students who plan to work in media—whether print or broadcast—should understand the main source of revenue for these media. Nearly all income of radio and television stations comes from advertising, and approximately 65 percent of the total income of newspapers and magazines stems from that source.

Executives in nearly every form of business need to know the fundamentals of advertising. In businesses where advertising is a highly significant factor in company success—cosmetics, for example—decisions on advertising are made at the highest level in the corporation. Every chief executive officer of Procter & Gamble over the past 50 years has come from early duty in the advertising department.

A business executive's need for knowledge about advertising will vary with his or her area of responsibility. Marketing people obviously require the most thorough comprehension of advertising. Often business leaders whose interests lie in production tend to accept advertising as a necessary complexity; such individuals must strive, however, to make goods that can be profitably advertised and sold. Financial officers, too, frequently view advertising with a jaundiced eye; their perception of advertising is that of an unnecessary deduction from earnings rather than an investment essential to maintaining present sales volume and developing future business. If a smooth interplay of the parts of the business machinery is to be achieved, each part must know how it intermeshes with others. Thus a basic course in advertising helps to provide future executives, no matter what their area of specialization, with additional perspective needed for success in a market economy.

SUMMARY

Advertising is a pervasive force in the American society and is becoming increasingly important in other nations throughout the world. Primarily a tool of business—big and small, local and national—in the never-ending search for customers, advertising also can make significant contributions to nonbusiness ventures.

Advertising can, and should, be viewed from both a marketing and a communications perspective. It is undergirded by two forms of mass communications mechanisms—the printing press (printing and movable type) and radio and television stations (electronic transmission). The first was introduced in the fifteenth century, but advertising did not really start in the modern sense until the 1700s, with true growth coming late in the nineteenth century. Commercial broadcasting came in the early 1920s with the introduction of radio. Its universal success was replicated in the 1950s with the advent of television. Now advertising relies on a blend of printed and broadcast media.

Advertising is a well-established institution today, but before it could reach such status a number of events had to preexist. A primary requisite is the industrialization of the economy, bringing a need for manufacturers to seek markets. This necessitates a means of communicating with prospects who know nothing of the maker's reputation. Advertising helps to fill that void. Mass transportation facilities and well-developed mass media also are essential. Before the development of broadcast media, a high rate of literacy was needed if advertising messages were to be understood.

Understanding of advertising and its role in modern society is one facet of being an informed person in today's world. Advertising provides information for better buyer behavior. Furthermore, knowledge of advertising's functions and techniques is vital to career success in such fields as journalism, public relations, television, commercial art, industrial design, marketing, and business management.

QUESTIONS FOR DISCUSSION

1 For the city where you attend college (or a nearby city), isolate current advertising similar to that used for (a) the Bob Dylan concert tour, (b) the Georgia Heart Fund, and (c) the House of Denmark campaigns. Bring examples to class, along with your evaluation of the ability of each campaign to communicate with consumers.

2 Find an advertisement which seems to be "demarketing" a product in a fashion similar to the Georgia Power campaign. Bring it to class.

3 Which view of advertising—marketing or communications—is most useful

to you? Why? Why do we need to recognize the existence of both viewpoints? Discuss.

4 Do you agree with the idea that advertising is often classified as "persuasion"? Is such a classification undesirable to the advertiser's way of looking at the matter? To the public's?

5 Distinguish, in a precise fashion, how advertising differs from (*a*) publicity, (*b*) propaganda, (*c*) personal selling.

6 Do you believe that David Potter is correct when he gives advertising status as an "American institution"? Explain your argument, giving specific examples.

7 Why should a newspaper editor or the producer of a television program understand the functions of advertising?

8 Is it likely that the Third World nations of Africa will adopt advertising as part of the nations' way of doing business? What conditions will have to be present for this to take place?

9 One premise is that advertising came on the American scene because there was a need for it; a corollary is that advertising will leave if such need no longer exists. Do you foresee such a contingency? Explain.

10 At least three forms of advertising preceded the development of the movable-type principle. What were these advertising forms? Give examples of their use in modern America.

FOR FURTHER REFERENCE

Burke, John D.: *Advertising in the Marketplace*, McGraw-Hill Book Company, New York, 1973.

Emery, Edwin, Phillip H. Ault, and Warren K. Agee: *Introduction to Mass Communications*, Dodd, Mead & Company, Inc., New York, 1973.

Kleppner, Otto, and Irving Settle: *Exploring Advertising*, Prentice-Hall, Inc., Englewood Cliffs, N.J., 1970.

Peterson, Theodore: *Magazines in the Twentieth Century*, The University of Illinois Press, Urbana, 1964.

Sargent, Hugh W: *Frontiers of Advertising Theory and Research*, Pacific Books, Palo Alto, Calif., 1972.

Sutphen, Dick: *The Mad Old Ads*, Dick Sutphen Studio, Inc., Minneapolis, 1966.

Wright, John S., and John E. Mertes: *Advertising's Role in Society*, West Publishing Company, St. Paul, Minn., 1974.

CHAPTER 2

ADVERTISING AND SOCIETY

Few topics are more confusing, or controversial, than advertising's role in society. In this chapter we shall look at advertising from a broad viewpoint. In the United States today, advertising is a powerful socioeconomic force. Sophisticated management of media has made advertising visible everywhere, and nearly everyone is exposed to it. The preparation of an advertising campaign or marketing program is not carried out in a vacuum. If a particular audience is hostile, then the most carefully planned campaign will fail. It is important then to know how advertising, as a social and an economic force, works in society as a whole.

We stated in Chapter 1 that advertising is informational and persuasive, and business people have found these properties to be an advantage in reaching potential customers. Because of its visibility and influence, however, advertising has come under criticism, particularly in the last decade and notably by economists. The problems of the 1970s—such as inflation, shortages of resources (particularly oil), high unemployment, changes in life-styles, and shifting value systems—have added to the criticisms of advertising. In this chapter we shall analyze some of the well-known arguments against advertising and give counterarguments showing the benefits of advertising.

The economic criticisms of advertising—three in number—are examined first. They lay the ground for and pose some overlap into the social issues in advertising.

ADVERTISING AND ECONOMICS

Simply put, economics is the study of the allocation of scarce resources. Although there are many possible definitions, this is the definition most generally accepted by economists. In the allocation of resources, the normal functioning of a free enterprise economy is based on the idea that the consumer makes this allocation in that he or she is free to make choices: a person can choose one type of job or profession over another and is free to choose this product instead of that one. Just as our wants differ, so do our abilities to satisfy our wants. Channeling or directing wants so that they will be socially beneficial is accomplished not by coercion, but by persuasion.

Advertising Is Wasteful

The traditional economic view that advertising is wasteful is based on the assumption that consumers already possess perfect information and can make their choices (allocate resources) without advertising. That assumption does not hold up. That people do not have complete

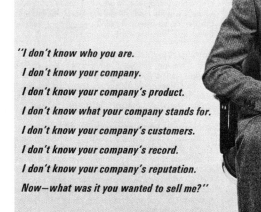

"*I don't know who you are.*

I don't know your company.

I don't know your company's product.

I don't know what your company stands for.

I don't know your company's customers.

I don't know your company's record.

I don't know your company's reputation.

Now—what was it you wanted to sell me?"

MORAL: Sales start **before** your salesman calls—with business publication advertising.

McGRAW-HILL MAGAZINES
BUSINESS•PROFESSIONAL•TECHNICAL

FIGURE 2.1
Advertising helps the business buyer know about persons attempting to make a sale. This ad, promoting the placement of advertising in business publications, dramatically makes this important point.

information and that they seek information is attested to by subscribers to consumer magazines. Information is an economic good and is subject to the laws of supply and demand as are other economic goods. Advertising has proved to be a more efficient (less costly) source of information than other sources. If this were not true, then advertised brands would cost more relative to quality, and consumers would choose unadvertised brands. Thus consumers, in buying advertised brands, are allocating resources to advertising; they consider that for obtaining information, advertising is the most efficient use of resources.

It may not seem necessary that we be offered a choice of dozens of competing detergents or brands of after-shave lotions. But when we view this selection as a manifestation of the whole philosophy of freedom of choice, which builds from trivial decision to matters of ultimate concern such as choosing our elective leaders, it takes on new significance. Advertising is sometimes referred to as the "voice of free choice," and certainly manufacturers seeking to serve diverse wants under a system of free choice should have the opportunity to communicate the news about the availability of their products to potential buyers.

Advertising Is Persuasive—Not Informative

Economists who take this position believe that advertising is not interested so much in fulfilling the desires of consumers as in changing desires to fit that which has been produced. In other words, people's tastes are changed so that they will buy what has been manufactured. This criticism in reality is a negation of the concept of consumer sovereignty, which claims that "the free market generates the flow of production along the lines that satisfy consumer tastes; their tastes determine what shall be produced."[1] Producer sovereignty governs the consumer, according to this argument. And argue we could over whether the consumer is king or not. In Chapter 1 we stated flatly that advertising is persuasion and that persuasion can be exercised for good ends. Rather than engage in a long harangue over consumer versus producer sovereignty in the marketplace, we prefer to turn our attention to the question of whether advertising is informative. If, in fact, it is informative, is it less informative because it also is persuasive?

Advertising as Information[2] At one time economists distinguished between "informative" advertising and "competitive" advertising. The latter was designed primarily to shift demand from one brand to another and therefore was called undesirable, uneconomic, and wasteful. Informative advertising, on the other hand, was in favor; examples of informative advertising under this system of classification were classified advertising in newspapers, price-oriented advertisements sponsored by retailers, and so on. In a pure sense, only price and terms of sale were classified as information. However, it came to be realized that every ad, if it is to be effective, must contain some elements of information; and identifying advertising as competitive is difficult, if not wholly unrealistic.

Some economists have been devoting considerable thought to this problem and have concluded that all advertising is informative,

[1] Israel M. Kirzner, "Advertising," *The Freeman*, September 1972, p. 516.
[2] This section is based in part on Phillip Nelson, "The Economic Value of Advertising," in Yale Brozen (ed.), *Advertising and Society*, New York University Press, New York, 1974, pp. 43–65.

FIGURE 2.2
Highly educational information about trees is provided by this advertisement. The sponsor is a leading producer of lumber.

although different kinds of advertising convey different kinds of information. Nelson postulates: "There are two possible ways by which advertising can increase sales: either advertising changes tastes, or advertising provides information." He rejects the taste-changing role because there is no theory of taste or taste change and therefore no possible empirical test for it. He goes on to develop "a theory of advertising as information."

Nelson's theory starts out with the belief that consumers have far less than perfect information about products, and he goes on to state that it costs resources to distribute product information and, more importantly, it costs resources, largely time, to acquire product information. Consumers, furthermore, are acting rationally when they limit expenditures on information acquisition, and they will respond to advertising only if it provides information to them at a *lower* cost than do alternative sources of information. Consumers are not at the complete mercy of sellers; they do have some other sources of information about goods.

Information about product quality can be obtained to some extent through physical inspection; sofas can be viewed in furniture showrooms, and suits can be tried on in clothing stores. Items which can be obtained less expensively in this fashion are labeled as *search goods* by Nelson.

Probably more concern over the consumer's relative bargaining strength in the marketplace exists over products whose quality is not so easily ascertained. Such items as toothpaste or canned dog food do not convey much information about their quality through mere physical inspection of their packages, or even the contents thereof. Information about their worth is obtained by experimentation among several brands. Such products are designated as *experience goods* by Nelson. Through repeat purchases of such products consumers exercise control over the market for experience goods. Because such experimentation for even relatively inexpensive items is costly, consumers often seek information prior to purchase. Polling friends and relatives or reading articles in newspapers or magazines may well give the needed information. However, these information sources often are not available or are inadequate, and advertising fills the informational gap.

The pertinent question is over the authenticity of the information provided by the advertiser. Nelson states that in the case of search goods the problem is simple: if the characteristics featured in the advertising are at variance with the product when inspected, no purchase will result. Although the advertisement might attract the prospective customer to the store, it is a waste of money (for the advertisement) and time (of the salesperson) if advertising claims and product qualities aren't equal.

As mentioned earlier, the purchaser of experience goods exercises

TITLE: "SON OF HOT DOG STAND"
COMMERCIAL No.: MGAM 3606

LENGTH: 60 SECOND TV
PRODUCT: WIENERS

WOMAN (ON CAMERA): I'd like to show you a very special recipe.

The recipe for Oscar Mayer Wieners. We start with 14 ounces of meat.

pork shoulder and side. All U. S. Government inspected.

There are no fillers or cereals because meat is one of the best sources of complete protein.

FIGURE 2.3
In a 60-second television commercial, a food processor gives information to the consumer about the product's ingredients and quality.

Then we cook and smoke delicately for the best tasting pound of Wieners you can buy.

That's right. That's the recipe for one pound of Oscar Mayer Wieners.

Beef cuts from the brisket, chuck,

flank and round . . .

Now for some seasonings: nutmeg, allspice, and ground mustard.

Finally a little water for mixing, some sugar, salt, cure and vitamin C.

It's nice to know there's a food with good meat protein that kids love.

Oscar Mayer Wieners are number one in America, and now you know why.

PRODUCED BY J. WALTER THOMPSON CO.

FIGURE 2.4
One airline's newspaper ad is primarily information about departure and arrival times. Only the few lines above the photograph can be described as persuasive in nature.

control through repeat purchases, and to a lesser extent through recommending or not recommending the product to friends. Because repeat purchase is the goal, the seller wishes the buyer to use his product in such a way that satisfaction will be maximized. Thus, the information in his advertisements should be geared to the consumer's needs. As Nelson expresses it, "... advertisements almost always correctly relate brand to function." This is direct information, but most experience goods advertising messages convey only indirect information to the consumer: namely, that the brand is advertised—that the product has been successful enough to sustain the cost of the advertising program for the brand. Only brands of high quality and high repeat purchase potential can sustain heavy advertising over a period of time. Consumers are aware of this.

We're American Airlines. Doing what we do best.

Leading the way in air travel is one of the things we do best.

1926
The first scheduled flight for what was eventually to become American Airlines took off—flying mail from St. Louis to Chicago and piloted by a young man named Charles Lindbergh.

1930
American inaugurated the country's first all-air transcontinental service.

1936
American introduced the DC-3. Built to American's specifications, the DC-3 became the most reliable, popular, and long-lived aircraft ever made.

As a business traveler, you want comfort and convenience. That's why American has always set the standards the industry lives and flies by. Take a look at some of our firsts.

1959
American pioneered transcontinental jet service, flying the first Boeing 707 in just 5 hours 25 min. between New York and Los Angeles.

1970's
American became the first to introduce the DC-10, and the exciting DC-10 Video System. Plus the DC-10 Cockpit Camera. And we haven't stopped yet. We're still constantly looking for new ways to improve our service both on the ground and in the air. Finding new ways to make air travel more convenient is another one of the things we do best.

American

FIGURE 2.5
A different airline uses a more persuasive approach in a magazine advertisement. However, a great deal of information is present. The goal, of course, is to enhance the reputation of the firm.

From the mere presence of advertising of brands of experience goods, consumers learn of winning products, for those are the ones most heavily advertised. Often market success permits lower prices than competitive brands, and the consumer benefits from that development. Above all, the indirect information carried in advertisements may aid consumers in making up their mind when confronted with perplexing product choices in the marketplace; it saves their most scarce resource—time. In many instances, consumers want quick, cheap information, and advertising is its purveyor. Otherwise the consumer may resort to random selection.

Advertising Fosters Monopoly

The claim has been made by some economists that advertising creates product differentiation, which leads to more inelastic demand curves; this means that the demand for the product does not change in proportions relative to changes in price. As a result, prices of advertised products will be less sensitive to price competition. Advertising has this effect because it has set the product apart as being different from—superior to—other brands. It is argued that "advertising *increases* barriers to entry and reduces competition as measured by increases in concentration and increases in monopoly profits.[3]

The argument that advertising reduces competition is based on the assertion that the cost of advertising a new product is prohibitive for any but the "entrenched giants" of industry. In other words, advertising superiority enables large existing producers to block new competition from entering a market and results in the establishment of monopolies with high prices and profits. This situation, the argument continues, leads to more advertising power, and the vicious cycle continues. In an interesting variation on this theme, Procter & Gamble was ordered by the Federal Trade Commission (FTC) to divest itself of ownership of its Clorox division because P&G obtained a competitive advantage for the Clorox brand in the form of quantity discounts when buying advertising.[4]

One economist states that persons who believe that advertising decreases competition make two basic assumptions: (1) "that advertising by established firms changes consumers' tastes and creates durable brand loyalties" and (2) "that there are increasing returns to advertising."[5] We have dealt with the first assumption in the previous section on advertising as information insofar as the taste-changing capability of advertising is concerned. The following quotation sheds light on the brand loyalty issue:

[3] James M. Ferguson, *Advertising and Competition: Theory, Measurement, Fact*, Ballinger Publishing Company, Cambridge, Mass., 1974, p. 15.

[4] 386 U.S. 568 (1967).

[5] Ferguson, op. cit., pp. 4–5.

No proof has yet been offered that it is easier for the first advertiser to win a consumer's patronage than it is for a second advertiser to shift it to him. The fact that the soap companies are constantly bringing out new brands suggests a taste for novelty on the part of the consumer that does not square with the theory of the first advertiser's advantage.[6]

Under the second assumption, it is claimed that monopoly power is increased because increasing returns to advertising bring about the concentration of industry and furthermore erect barriers to entry into the industry. After a thorough examination of the studies conducted by the proponents of this point of view, Ferguson found no direct evidence that increasing returns to advertising do in fact exist.[7] Nevertheless, the concentration and barrier to entry criticisms are so prevalent in the literature of economics that a brief commentary on the subject is in order.

A University of Chicago economist, Lester G. Telser, has studied the concentration of industry–advertising relationship closely. His findings are summarized in these words:

> One measure of competition in an industry, widely accepted by economists, is the concentration of sales among the four leading firms in the industry. The larger the share of the total going to the four leading firms, the less the competition. If advertising reduces competition, then there ought to be high levels of advertising in those industries where the leading firms have small shares. This seems to be true in some industries, for instance, soaps, cigarettes, and breakfast cereals, but it is false in other industries, drugs, and cosmetics. The best way to test the proposition is to examine the data for all consumer-product industries. Such an examination shows a negligible positive association between advertising intensity and concentration. In other words, the exceptions to the hypothesis nearly outweigh the conforming cases. Changes in concentration and advertising intensity ought to move in the same direction according to the hypothesis that advertising lessens competition. The data for the period 1947–57 show, if anything, the opposite relation—an inverse association between changes in advertising intensity and changes in concentration. The weakness of the hypothesis claiming a positive association between advertising and monopoly is shown by another fact. Industries that produce industrial goods hardly advertise and yet may be highly concentrated. Thus if all manufacturing industries were examined to determine the relations between advertising intensity and the concentration of sales among the leading firms, no systematic pattern would emerge.[8]

---

[6] Richard Posner, quoted in U.S. Congress Subcommittee on Monopoly of the Senate Select Committee on Small Business, *Role of the Giant Corporations*, part I-A, July 1969, p. 923.

[7] Ferguson, op. cit., p. 5.

[8] L. G. Telser, "Some Aspects of the Economics of Advertising," *Journal of Business*, April 1968, as reproduced in John S. Wright and John E. Mertes (eds.), *Advertising's Role in Society*, West Publishing Company, St. Paul, Minn., 1974, pp. 38–39.

A casual glance at the recent inroads into the markets of such giants as General Motors, Bulova, and RCA by Volkswagen, Datsun, and Toyota, and by Timex and Sony finds ample evidence of newcomers successfully competing with entrenched leaders. The communication channels offered by modern mass advertising media are open to all entrepreneurs, and all innovations have a better chance of acceptance than in days when communication processes were slower.

Financial strength, according to Backman, is not an insurmountable barrier to entering a product field. Entry is easier when advertising can be used. Small companies operating in regional areas have an opportunity for saturation in their marketing and advertising activities that even the largest companies have difficulty combating. The phenomenal success Coor's beer has experienced in the Western part of the United States is an illustration of this point. The regional brewer has secured first position in several states in competition with the large national brewers. Furthermore, there is evidence that over a period of years the leaders in specific product categories have been replaced or rearranged on the sales-volume scale by newcomers. Backman sums up the relationship between advertising and monopoly with these words:

> Companies with relatively high advertising-sales ratios tend to have somewhat higher profit rates than less intensive advertisers. These higher profits appear to reflect the larger volume resulting from successful advertising rather than the exercise of market power to charge high monopolistic prices. . . . The relationship between advertising intensity and high economic concentration is nonexistent. There appears to be no link between advertising intensity and price increases. . . . The record shows clearly that advertising is highly competitive, not anti-competitive.[9]

The statement "Companies with relatively high advertising-sales ratios tend to have somewhat higher profit" may result from accounting procedures, that is, failure to capitalize the advertising investment.

The three principal criticisms of advertising on the grounds of economic theory are not borne out by empirical evidence. The data support the view that advertising (1) is economically productive, (2) is informative, and (3) does not shut out competition.

Advertising's Economic Utility[10]

Robert L. Steiner, formerly president of a major American toy manufacturing firm, relates how advertising brought down the price of toys

[9] Jules Backman, *Advertising and Competition*, New York University Press, New York, 1967, p. 157.
[10] Based on Robert L. Steiner, "Does Advertising Lower Consumer Prices?" *Journal of Marketing*, October 1973, pp. 19–26; as reproduced in John S. Wright and John E. Mertes (eds.), *Advertising's Role in Society*, West Publishing Company, St. Paul, Minn., 1974, pp. 212–225.

MUSIC & SINGERS:
Hey, look a there . . .

. . . is that the Chattanooga
Choo Choo?

Tyco's new train . . .

. . . has got a real famous
name.

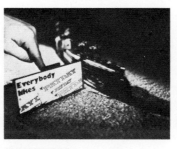

ANNOUNCER:
Tyco's new Chattanooga Choo
Choo smokes and whistles
SFX: TRAIN WHISTLE

MUSIC & SINGERS:
You'll see the smoke a puffin'
rough a puffin' out of the
stack.

Watch it as it chugs and chugs
along on the track.

Whistle for a warning,
every night and morning.
Woo-woo Chattanooga by Tyco.

Woo-woo Chattanooga by Tyco.

FIGURE 2.6
A 30-second televi-
sion commercial is
used to promote
an electric train.
Such commercials
were aired by the
manufacturer in
the pre-Christmas
season.

to consumers. Historically, toys were advertised in print media and
through radio commercials. These media did not reach the primary
audience for the toys, which is three- to seven-year-old children.
Considerable promotional effort was placed on department-store dem-

FIGURE 2.7
The same product is featured by a large retail chain in its newspaper advertising (upper right-hand corner). Note the emphasis on price, which was absent in the television commercial shown in Figure 2.6.

onstrations at that time. However, only major outlets were feasible locations for these "live" demonstrations of toys.

In the 1950s the growth of television as a mass medium and the development of child-oriented TV programming enabled toy manufacturers to reach their desired target audience with impact and efficiency, and the level of toy advertising increased greatly. In addition to the manufacturer-sponsored television commercials aimed at children, major toy dealers ran ads in local newspapers aimed at the secondary toy market—parents. Discount retailers soon learned that ads featuring TV-advertised toys at cut prices were capable of generating major sales results. This new combination of media—TV to reach children and newspapers to reach parents—brought about a large increase of sales output from a dollar of advertising input. The consequent higher levels of demand for toys permitted substantial economies of large-scale production in toy manufacturing. Increased spending for advertising made the factory salesperson's job easier, thus reducing that form of selling cost.

Two other events of the era—the growth of discount stores and the decline of fair trade laws in the United States—coincided with the growth of television advertising of toys. Discount-store operators learned that the new TV-promoted toy was an ideal vehicle for promotion. The approach brought about heavy floor traffic to the store, as well as more toy sales. Retailer margins obviously dropped significantly as a result of this price cutting. By 1970, strongly advertised toy merchandise enjoyed a distribution margin (markup) nearly 25 percent less than nonadvertised goods, while the overall toy distribution margin as a percentage of retail price fell by one-third, from 49 percent in 1958 to 33 percent in 1970.

The savings resulting from increased manufacturing productivity that was brought on by increased consumer demand stimulated by advertising were passed on to the retail trade. More effective advertising, along with mass retailing efficiencies, made distribution more productive, and distribution margins and retail prices were reduced. Consumer demand for toys is elastic. From 1958 to 1970 toy sales increased nearly 80 percent (in constant dollars), and toy makers experienced factory cost savings of 10 percent. Part of the growth in demand was in response to the relative fall in the price of toys which was provided because of television, a more efficient advertising medium.

Interestingly, the toy industry of the United Kingdom was not able to duplicate the American success story because retail-price maintenance practices prevented the discounting of toy prices. In France, on the other hand, commercial television advertising of toys was not permitted. So although discounting of toy prices was prevalent in France, demand remained lower than in the United Kingdom. The strong product identity which TV advertising produces was lacking in the French market. Thus, in sum, the United States consumer has benefited from materially lower toy prices because of their being advertised on TV.

THE SOVIET EXPERIENCE

The Soviet Union provides a dramatic example of advertising in a controlled economy—an economy founded on the Marxian philosophy that any marketing operation other than simple retailing is parasitic and of no value to society. The traditional communist view of advertising has been that it is a total social waste which forces unwanted goods on consumers. But the Soviet view of advertising is changing, and the present growth of advertising in the Soviet Union, and particularly in the Eastern European countries, supports our view that advertising is a productive force in economic life.

For centuries Russia was in the primary stage of economic development; its population was largely agricultural, the standard of living was very low, and a seller's market for consumer goods prevailed. In the late 1950s, the U.S.S.R. entered into a secondary stage of economic development. Supplies of certain consumer goods exceeded demand, and an increasing number of citizens possessed some discretionary income for the purchase of more than the bare necessities of life. In this secondary stage, the social ideal of a planned balance between production and consumption still appeared far away. The managers of the Soviet economy, therefore, started to adopt methods of distribution which resemble those employed in capitalistic economies. In 1958, the Ministry of Trade was reorganized, and a state-controlled advertising agency, *Torgreklama*, was established with branches in most Soviet cities. Advertising is playing an increasingly important role in both export and domestic marketing. The state advertising agency prepares advertising, for a commission, to be placed in a full array of media, which includes newspapers, magazines, outdoor posters, radio, and television, all of which are state-owned.

In our present era of closer trade ties between the United States and Russia, it seems strange that a precedent-shattering event occurred as recently as 1967, when Amtorg Trading Corporation placed a large advertisement in the *New York Times*.[11] Amtorg is a Soviet organization which serves as an agent for the foreign trade of Russia in its business transactions in the United States. The advertisement described 35 Soviet organizations that wanted to sell in our country. The concept and the flavor of the copy in this celebrated message are encapsulated in the following excerpt:

Despite ideological differences, firms from many countries are engaged in

[11] Drawn from Thomas V. Greer, *Marketing in the Soviet Union*, Frederick A. Praeger, Inc., New York, 1973, p. 94. Also see Marshall I. Goldman, "Product Differentiation and Advertising: Some Lessons from Soviet Experience," *Journal of Political Economy*, August 1960.

successful business transactions with Soviet foreign trade organizations who are ready to strike up relations with you.[12]

The Russian government publishes and distributes an English-language magazine, *Soviet Life*, in the United States. This quality publication compares favorably with other class magazines and shows the competent employment of Western techniques in Russia's efforts to communicate with the American public and business community.

More significantly, however, is the increased use of advertising domestically—within Russia itself for the purpose of communicating with the citizenry of the country. Several uses for advertising include the sale of unacceptably large inventories and of obsolescent goods and seasonally produced goods which are perishable in nature. There is some advertising to support new brands of services and design changes in old brands. Noteworthy is the advertising aimed at building store patronage for specific retail outlets. Classified advertising for services and secondhand goods flourishes, and there is a great deal of public service advertising.[13] Anastas I. Mikoyan, an important U.S.S.R. political leader, articulated the governmental view as:

> The task of Soviet advertising is to give people exact information about the goods that are on sale, to help to create new demands, to cultivate new tastes and requirements, to promote the sale of new kinds of goods and to explain their uses to the consumer.[14]

One additional quotation, this from a Soviet advertising executive, should be sufficient to show that advertising is being recognized in the U.S.S.R. as an important institution:

> It is incorrect to think of advertising as solely a directional, local tactic to provide information on goods and services. Every year it is becoming more and more an effective way to promote our life style and achievements. To a certain extent, therefore, it performs a social function. . . .
>
> Good advertising not only creates favorable conditions for a product or service, but also molds rational needs on the part of the consumer.[15]

SOCIAL EFFECTS OF ADVERTISING

Advertising touches our lives in four significant ways: (1) through its persuasive abilities, (2) because of its truthfulness or untruthfulness, (3)

---

[12] Greer, loc. cit.

[13] Ibid., pp. 96–97.

[14] Quoted in David Ogilvy, *Confessions of an Advertising Man*, Atheneum Publishers, New York, 1963, p. 150, as found in Greer, op. cit., p. 98.

[15] Ye. Kanevsky, "The Effect of Advertising," *Pravda*, Apr. 1 1972, p. 3. *CDSP*, 24 (Apr. 26, 1972), p. 32, as found in Greer, op. cit., p. 100.

through its tastefulness or tastelessness, and (4) by its cultural impact on our values and life-styles.[16] Advertising's economic roles—its persuasive and informative powers—have been discussed in the first half of this chapter. The question of truth in advertising is examined in Chapter 20, which deals with legal constraints on the practice of advertising. Thus, we now consider its social effects—taste in advertising and cultural impact. The discussion is framed in the reference of criticisms in order to parallel the previous material on the economic effects of advertising.

Advertising Lacks Taste

What constitutes good taste as contrasted with bad taste is a matter of individual perception. Each individual ends up exercising a personal opinion; sometimes an effort is made to project that opinion over the behavior of other individuals. In a sense, this is similar to the criticisms that "advertising makes people want things they shouldn't have." There is no law or universal guideline regarding good and bad taste.

In determining which advertising is in good taste and which fails to meet the test, the primary concern is the *manner* in which the advertising is done rather than its content *matter*.[17] Involved are those ethical, moral, and aesthetic considerations regarding the manner in which advertising is handled. Advertising can be classified as of questionable taste on four principal scores:

1 Moral concern over the product itself: products such as liquor, cigarettes, contraceptives, and feminine hygiene sprays.
2 Inappropriate time or context for the message exposure: laxative advertising at the dinner hour; lingerie ads on early-evening TV.
3 Use of objectionable appeals, such as fear or sex.
4 Use of objectionable techniques: excessive repetition of messages, loud volume, silliness of presentation.[18]

Concern over Product   If a person objects to a product itself, it is natural that its advertising will be deemed objectionable and will suffer as a consequence. Advertising is just the most visible part of the total product entity. Rationally, objection to the product should be distinguished from objection to its advertisement. The banning of cigarette advertising from the broadcast media illustrates this dilemma. The product has legal sanction; it is subject to special taxation.

---

[16] Stephen A. Greyser, "Advertising: Attacks and Counters," *Harvard Business Review*, March–April 1972, p. 22.
[17] Ibid., p. 32.
[18] Based on Michael Pearce, Scott M. Cunningham, and Avon Miller, *Appraising the Economic and Social Effects of Advertising.* Marketing Science Institute, Cambridge, Mass. 1971, p. 4.31, and Greyser, op. cit., p. 28.

Logically its processors should have the right to promote it on television and radio. If cigarettes are believed to be truly harmful to people, they should be banned from sale in interstate commerce. Certainly it is inconsistent to permit their advertising in forms of media other than broadcast. Moral judgments over the use of specific products need to be universally held before the advertising of them should be outlawed, and the sounder approach is to ban the sale of such products.

Message Timing and Context   Certainly the poor *timing* of advertising for an otherwise acceptable product may show a lack of taste on the part of the advertiser, as in the case of the laxative advertisement at dinnertime. Of course, one might counter that dining and watching television simultaneously is also in bad taste. The clutter of advertising messages on television can be irritating to the viewer. Heavy concentration of advertisements in other media, such as pre-Christmas issues of magazines and newspapers, is tolerated much more readily by the typical consumer. True, one can flip by ads in newspapers and magazines easier than one can avoid advertising on television. However, in the welter of messages, some may be relevant to part of the audience, and communication value is received by these persons. What messages, if any, should be allowed at times when children listen heavily to television, such as Saturday mornings, is a highly debated question and still is in the process of being resolved.

Objectionable Appeals   Opinions on matters of sex are subjective to the utmost degree. Although no advertiser knowingly will use sex appeal in a manner which will offend the majority of the target audience, there is no doubt that such appeals do create interest in advertising messages. "It is not always so much what is in the ad as what the viewer brings to it."[19] What is deemed to be sexy by one person may be bland to another, and we all recognize that the standards of what is socially acceptable are subject to rapid change in our society.

Insofar as the appeal to fear is concerned, this approach has been used to sell products which are of little interest to consumers when so-called rational appeals are employed. Even in cases where the product fulfills a generally recognized need, such as in the case of life insurance, fear appeals are needed to sell policies. However, appeals to fear, such as in the case of the cancer hazard in cigarette smoking, are often rejected by receivers of such messages. A more questionable use of the fear appeal is over body odors and the possible effect such odors may have on one's social acceptance. The end result is a fresher-smelling society, but is the advertising in bad taste? Once again, the answer is a subjective one.

[19] Pearce et al., op. cit., p. 4.36.

FIGURE 2.8
Information is persuasively presented in this public service ad designed for use on transportation car cards. [*Advertising Council.*]

VD is for everybody.

If you need help, see a doctor.

A Public Service of
Transit Advertising &
The Advertising Council **Ad Council**   American
Social Health
Association

Some people object to the appeals being made in advertisements on the grounds that they are too simple-minded, that "they insult a person's intelligence." Part of this criticism is based on the fact that many messages are meant for the mass market and thus are run in the mass media, which, in turn, do include persons in the audience not in the target market for the advertised product. To these people, the messages may seem inane. This is one of the difficult problems that advertisers face.

Objectionable Techniques   Techniques of advertising such as repetition of message, use of high volume, or the employment of unpleasant people, voices, or music are all part of the intrusive nature of advertising, especially the television medium. These techniques are used to attract the attention of the audience under circumstances in which such attention may be difficult to obtain. In other words, it is claimed by some advertising people that these tactics are unavoidable if advertising is to carry out its function of communicating with target audiences. On the other hand, others firmly believe that their use is a reflection of the bankruptcy of creativity on the part of the advertising community and would not be needed if more time and thought were devoted to advertising message development. However, advertisers spend money and time on testing alternative advertising techniques and would abandon any that resulted in decreased brand sales. And for experience goods, the very fact of advertising is the important point, not the content of the advertising message. There is no doubt that some advertising irritates some people, but clearly not most people, or the technique would be found unproductive and would be discontinued. Furthermore, extreme use of such techniques can be counterproductive; for example, the use of excessive repetition can lead to a backlash, a sort of protest, even to the point of consumer rejection of the product featured so frequently.

Conclusion A basic problem is that different people have different standards. At least three problems are present when determining the line between good taste and bad taste in advertising:

1 Ethics, morals, and aesthetics—or general standards of behavior, specific standards of behavior, and artistic standards—are problems involving mores and philosophy that may often differ widely in America's heterogeneous population.
2 Whatever the standards of taste (or tastefulness) are, they change over time.
3 There are semantic problems with the variable called taste.[20]

Furthermore, one can argue that the presence of garish, loud advertising is a cost of affluence. Consumers have a scarcity of time, and they seek fast, cheap information about products. In providing that need, advertisers on occasion may overstep the boundaries of good taste, at least in the view of the more sensitive members of the population.

Advertising Has an Adverse Effect on Values and Life-Styles

As Greyser so well puts it, "Of all the social issues involving advertising, the broadest has to do with its impact on life styles."[21] Five areas invoking the greatest concern when the impact of advertising on values and life-styles is under examination have been isolated: (1) materialism, instant gratification, and level of consumption; (2) moral, ethical, and aesthetic standards; (3) conformity and diversity; (4) interpersonal and group relationships; and (5) children.[22]

---

[20] Ibid., pp. 4.31–4.32.
[21] Greyser, op. cit., p. 140.
[22] Pearce et al., op. cit., p. 4.44.

Materialism   The desire to possess tangible goods is called material-ism, and the prevalence of this trait among Americans is judged to be undesirable by many intellectuals. People should be interested, their argument runs, in the "finer things of life"—music, poetry, paint-ing—rather than in owning suburban homes, automobiles, snowmo-biles, recreation vehicles, motor boats, and the many other symbols of the materialistic life. In characterizing our society as materialistic, a comparison is often made between the amounts of money spent for material goods and for the arts.

Because advertising is used to promote products which satisfy the materialistic requirements of consumers, it is accused of promoting materialism among our population. It is also true, however, that advertising is used to promote "back to nature" items such as natural foods and Earth Shoes and also denim—all representing a rejection of the "materialism" of the establishment.

This criticism of materialism has been broadened to include the idea that advertising brought about the "revolution of rising expecta-tions" among our people with the concomitant demand for "instant gratification" of material desires. The ghetto resident, watching the life-styles presented on the living room screen, therefore wants the goods that will allow him or her to emulate the manner of living represented on that screen. Many of the most enticing items people see on their TV screens are not in the commercials, of course, but are part of the stage settings used for dramas and are given away as prizes on game shows. Advertising, nevertheless, is often blamed.

The problem with this line of thinking is that advertising, to be effective, reflects the attitudes of its intended audience. It is true that advertising:

> . . . is the chief means of communicating (and reinforcing) to people the range of reasons for which they might want to acquire material objects. It is probable that as long as these reasons are ones which the culture recognizes, e.g., that a given object can indeed be viewed as a symbol of status, it is unlikely that advertising can or will be prevented from appealing to such reasons. If we regard as undesirable these materialistic values in our society, we must look beyond advertising for change.[23]

The conflict existing between the intellectual's view of advertis-ing's role in developing materialistic attitudes is clarified in the following quotation, which states that it depends on how one views others in the society:

Most of the things we want are not material but mental. We want states of

[23] Raymond A. Bauer and Stephen A. Greyser, *Advertising in America: The Consumer View*, Division of Research, Harvard Business School, Boston, 1968, p. 368.

mind. The advertiser, beginning with a material object which is to be sold, suggests the states of mind which may be achieved by the purchaser. . . . You can either rejoice that human beings have wants, and that other human beings try to satisfy them and be paid for their trouble; or you can deplore the nature of humanity.[24]

Moral, Ethical, and Aesthetic Standards   One accusation leveled against advertising is that it is a force for perverting or debasing our aesthetic or cultural standards. Although much advertising certainly is not an artistic triumph (bargain advertising by retail establishments, for instance, does not kindle a spark of aesthetic appreciation even in the most uncultured breast), other advertisements with a different purpose may display artwork of the finest illustrators and designers, bringing their creations before the eyes of millions. Artistic satisfaction from drawings, paintings, photographs, music, and drama are as subjective as are other wants. It is unrealistic to assume that advertising has a responsibility to raise or even to maintain cultural standards. Advertising's function is to transmit information from the advertiser to groups of people—to persuade. In attempting to persuade some, it is almost sure to offend others.

Mass communication media, supported by advertising, are also accused of satiating the public with the most superficial information and entertainment. In doing this, it is said, they have encouraged what is popular rather than what is good, and they have fostered material rather than spiritual and cultural values. Television is the medium most frequently cited, and it would be difficult indeed to make a case for the cultural contributions of many TV situation comedies and programs crammed with violence. But can advertising in a free enterprise society be held responsible for the complacency, the erosion of morality, and the cultural lag which may exist in our society? George J. Stigler, professor of economics at the University of Chicago, believes such a position is analogous to "blaming the waiters in restaurants for obesity."[25] He goes on to state that "advertising itself is a completely neutral instrument, and lends itself to the dissemination of highly contradictory desires."[26] Furthermore, he feels that "the intellectuals would gain in candor and in grace if they preached directly to the public instead of using advertising as a whipping boy."[27] It is a historical fact that only a small minority in any society have ever exhibited "good taste," or have been equipped with the capacity and the temperament to prefer the serious over the frivolous. There is no

[24] Walter Taplin, *Advertising: A New Approach*, Hutchinson & Co., Publishers, Ltd., London, 1960.
[25] George J. Stigler, *The Intellectual and the Market Place*, The Free Press, New York, 1963.
[26] Ibid.
[27] Ibid.

FIGURE 2.9
This shoe adver-
tisement appeared
in Hungarian
magazines. The
graphics employed
parallel those
found in Western
nations. [*Black-
Russel-Morris.*]

real evidence, moreover, that our cultural standards are lower than
they were before modern advertising became an important institution
in our society. Enumeration of the amounts spent for symphony concert
tickets, lecture series, works of art, books, and other forms of cultural
expression belies the claim that our society is completely lacking in
what are generally considered to be cultural standards. In fact,
advertising is used to promote cultural events.

Conformity and Diversity Another criticism revolves around the idea that advertising persuades as many people as possible to buy the featured product, with the end result being conformity in behavior, a homogenous populace. When advertising programs are highly successful and the item is purchased by most of the population, conformity actually results. We know, however, that obtaining universal acceptance of any product is extremely rare. On the other hand, advertising facilitates the introduction of new products and permits the news of their availability to spread rapidly and economically. When this takes place, *diversity*—not conformity—occurs in the society.

Interpersonal and Group Relationships In an urbanized society such as ours, individuals tend to lose their identity, and depersonalization takes place. Relationships between individuals tend to become strained. It is contended that the relationships between people of different races, religions, sexes, income, and age can become tense through the influence of advertising.

The protestations of the feminists provide an excellent illustration of this point of view. They feel that the portrayal of women in sterotyped roles, such as homemakers or secretaries, and not in career-oriented roles, leads to the acceptance of these roles as the norm by the population as a whole, and by the young in particular. Thus, women who hope to pursue other careers or life-styles resent the showing of a sterotyped homemaker ecstatically admiring the floor which she has just waxed. They resent the implication that this is all they are capable of. A highly successful campaign sponsored by National Airlines which bore the headline "I'm Cheryl. Fly Me!" was protested by NOW (National Organization for Women) on the grounds that it cast women in the role of sex objects.

Similarly, ethnic groups dislike the portrayal of nationalities in a demeaning light, such as in the Frito-Bandito commercials; Mexican-Americans do not like to be shown as lazy robbers. One active issue has been over the use of black models in advertisements. Once thought to be a concept unacceptable to significant portions of the American public, integrated advertising is now commonplace.

Resolution of this question hinges on whether advertisements should picture society as it really exists, or in some sort of idealistic view of what it should be. Minorities, who are also consumers, certainly have rights that should not be infringed upon, and, of course, pragmatic advertisers, in their own self-interest, avoid confrontation over any portrayal which might be offensive to the public, or to a part of it.

Children Because children constitute such a large minority and are viewed as being especially vulnerable to influences, their case warrants special consideration. How advertising, primarily over the television medium, operates in the socialization of children has received

"Hire him. He's got great legs."

If women thought this way about men they would be awfully silly.

When men think this way about women they're silly, too.

Women should be judged for a job by whether or not they can do it.

In a world where women are doctors, lawyers, judges, brokers, economists, scientists, political candidates, professors and company presidents, any other viewpoint is ridiculous.

Think of it this way. When we need all the help we can get, why waste half the brains around?

Womanpower. It's much too good to waste.

For information: NOW Legal Defense and Education Fund Inc., 127 East 59th Street, Dept. K, New York, New York 10022

FIGURE 2.10
The National Organization for Women (NOW) makes its point about discrimination against women in this humorous advertisement. [Reprinted with permission of the NOW Legal Defense and Education Fund.]

considerable attention in recent years. The typical child spends more of his or her time in the company of the television set than reading or being entertained by any traditional medium.

Determining whether television advertising does, in fact, lead to the corruption of children by instilling values which are not acceptable in our society is a difficult assignment. Normal research methodology, complicated enough when ascertaining adult behavior, is inadequate in the case of children. Bias is a problem, and the subjects are not capable of the same degree of cooperation with the researcher. For these reasons, the question of the effect of television advertising, as constrasted with television viewing, has only recently been examined scientifically. Tentative findings are that children are not helpless victims of television advertising; they do tune out the messages under certain circumstances. Some learning, nevertheless, does take place from viewing this form of marketing communication. Thus, the likelihood is great that we shall see greater control, by government, the media, and advertisers, of television advertisements aimed at children and the time when they may be aired.

FIGURE 2.11
Parents are given suggestions on how to answer difficult questions often posed by their children.

ADVERTISING AND FREEDOM OF THE PRESS

It has been said that "advertising controls the press." The implication of this criticism is that mass media are at the mercy of their advertisers, who dictate editorial policy and force publishers to kill stories or articles of which the advertiser disapproves. The importance of a free press to a democratic society is so obvious that any attempt to restrict this freedom, whether it comes from advertisers, churches, governments, or any other special interest groups, demands both attention and action.

At the same time, we should keep in mind that freedom is a relative rather than an absolute, and that inherent in any organizational system, whether commercial, religious, or political, is a person's tendency to respond to power and to anticipate the effect of one's acts on those in the organizational hierarchy. The influence of advertisers on editorial policy and content will naturally vary from medium to medium, and generally in indirect ratio to the effectiveness of the medium as a vehicle for advertising messages. The medium which can be "bought" declines in prosperity, in vitality, and in influence. Most media owners value the respect of their audiences too highly to risk destroying it, and most advertisers realize the importance of the medium's influence on the buyers whom they hope to sell.

The exceptions seem to be found most frequently in broadcast media, and especially in television network programming. In television, unlike newspapers and magazines, the advertiser not only pays for the time his commercials are on the air, but also may pay the cost of the entertainment between his commercials. In a sense he is at the same time both advertiser and publisher, or producer. There is no doubt that, in the past, advertisers have exerted considerable influence on the content of programs they have sponsored and paid for. However, as television costs have mounted, more and more advertisers have turned to the use of spot announcements or joint participation with other advertisers in programs produced and controlled by networks or stations. Advertisers have little or no influence in this situation.

Historically, mass communications media have been notably unsuccessful in attempting to survive on income received solely from readers, listeners, or viewers. The essential financial support has come from political parties, from government, or from advertisers. Unlike governments or political parties, advertisers are rarely interested in the editorial or entertainment policies of media except as they may affect the type or size of audience to whom the advertiser wishes to deliver his sales message. Moreover, the attitude or action sought by one advertiser is frequently the reverse of that sought by another, and the number of different advertisers is legion. Advertising support seems to promise

greater freedom of the press than is possible through subsidy by
government or political parties.

THE CASE FOR ADVERTISING

Neither scholars nor advertising and marketing professionals suggest
that advertising is an institution above criticism. However, those who
maintain that, on balance, advertising's socioeconomic influence is
more beneficial than harmful often list contributions such as these to
support such an evaluation:

1 Advertising is a buyer's guide for both consumers and industrial purchasers, providing the former with news of new merchandise and special prices
   and the latter with information about new materials, equipment, and
   technology.
2 Advertising reduces distribution costs by simplifying the task of personal
   selling or by replacing it entirely.
3 Advertising encourages competition and also fosters product quality
   through clear brand identification and producer or distributor accounta-
   bility.
4 Advertising adds value to products by adding to time, place, and possession utility.
5 Advertising publicizes the material and cultural incentives of a democratic,
   free enterprise society, and so helps motivate increased productive effort by
   both management and labor.
6 Advertising enables both printed and broadcast communications to maintain independence from government, political parties, or other special
   interest groups.
7 Advertising stimulates thought and action on national and local social
   problems.

SUMMARY

Advertising decisions by the business firm are made in a societal setting;
advertisements are aimed at members of society. Society is affected by
advertising in economic and in social ways. This chapter analyzes the overall
effects of advertising on society, as a background for advertising's more
specific roles.

Advertising has been criticized on three major points: (1) it is wasteful of
resources; (2) it is persuasive, not informative; and (3) it fosters monopoly.
Economists are concerned with the allocation of resources, and some charge
that advertising wastes resources. First of all, they claim that advertising just

adds costs to the price of the product. Although advertising is a cost of doing business and must be included in the selling price, it may also bring about substantial reduction in production and distribution costs and result in lower prices paid by consumers. Although much advertising does aim at shifting demand from one brand to another, the process leads to better products for consumers and is not really an inefficient allocation of resources. If advertising made people worse off, they would not respond to it. The idea that advertising makes people want things they don't need and therefore leads to an inefficient use of resources denies the whole concept of freedom of choice underlying our economic order.

Effective advertising is persuasive. It influences people to buy its sponsor's product. But advertising also informs consumers, and thereby justifies its economic existence. The critics' model assumes consumers have perfect knowledge (information), but that assumption is not valid in real life. Through advertising consumers learn of the existence of products, and furthermore, they learn which products are successful from the mere fact that they do advertise. Producers try to determine what people want, make the item, and then advertise its availability. The opposite sequence of trying, through advertising, to get people to want what is being made does not work out. Consumer sovereignty exercises its veto power readily and frequently.

Careful empirical studies have uncovered little evidence that the presence of advertising leads to the concentration of industry or that it erects barriers to entry into industry. In the American toy industry, the availability of television advertising has led to increased sales of the product at lower prices to consumers. Furthermore, communist economies are starting to employ advertising as part of their marketing mixes, further evidence of the economic worth of advertising.

On the social side, we see that advertising touches members of our society in four ways: (1) through its persuasive abilities, (2) because of its truthfulness or untruthfulness, (3) through its tastefulness or tastelessness, and (4) by its cultural impact on values and life-styles. Advertising is persuasive in nature, but there are adequate laws in existence to handle untruthful advertising, which, of course, is not desirable.

Critics say that advertising is often in bad taste. This charge may come about because the product itself is deemed to be undesirable; in such cases, advertising is not at the heart of the problem. Others believe that some advertising messages appear at the wrong time, or that objectionable appeals are made, or that the techniques of advertising employed are not acceptable. Each of these three areas is fraught with the hazards of personal subjectivity; what one person thinks is objectionable will not disturb another. Furthermore, standards of taste change over time and the very definition of "taste" poses problems. Errors in judgment may on occasion lead to tasteless advertising, but a generalization to the whole institution of advertising is unwarranted.

Whether advertising has an adverse effect on values and life-styles is doubtful. It is claimed that advertising breeds materialism, but it is probably more correct to say that advertising reflects the values of people. Thus, advertising appeals to the material wants of people rather than creating them.

Similarly, advertising does not debase the moral, ethical, or aesthetic standards of our society. Insofar as values are concerned, advertising is a neutral instrument.

QUESTIONS FOR DISCUSSION

1 What is the gist of the criticism that advertising constitutes economic waste? How can this criticism be answered?
2 Do you believe that advertising is persuasive? Give an example. Do you believe advertising is also informative? Give an example.
3 Goods can be categorized into two main types: search goods and experience goods. Explain how the role of advertising differs in the case of each type. Cite an illustration for each.
4 Does advertising foster monopoly? Or is it conducive to the establishment of a more competitive market? Develop your answer in some detail.
5 What is the interrelationship between the concept of freedom of choice prevalent in our economy and advertising? Why do controlled economies such as Russia use advertising? Explain.
6 Cite an instance from current advertising in which you believe bad taste has been evidenced. Which of the fourfold classification of ways advertising can be in questionable taste does your case exemplify? How could the advertiser's approach be changed to bring the ad into an acceptable condition?
7 Has advertising affected your own personal life-style in any fashion? Explain. Has this been undesirable? Worthwhile?
8 "Advertising affects the freedom of the press." Give both sides of this debatable statement.
9 What are some products, other than toys, where the consumer has benefited in relatively lower prices because of their being advertised in efficient mass media?
10 Write a short paragraph giving your opinion on the role of advertising in the establishment of stereotypes in our society.

FOR FURTHER REFERENCE

Backman, Jules: *Advertising and Competition*, New York University Press, New York, 1967.

Brozen, Yale (ed.): *Advertising and Society*, New York University Press, New York, 1974.

Buzzi, Giancarlo: *Advertising: Its Cultural and Political Effects*, University of Minnesota Press, Minneapolis, 1968.

Comanor, William S., and Thomas N. Wilson: *Advertising and Market Power*, Harvard University Press, Cambridge, Mass., 1974.

Corkindale, David, Sherril Kennedy, Harry Henry, and Gordon Wills: *Advertising Resource Allocation*, Cranfield School of Management, Cranfield, England, 1975.

Divita, S. F.: *Advertising and the Public Interest*, American Marketing Association, Chicago, 1975.

Ferguson, James M.: *Advertising and Competition: Theory, Measurement, Fact*, Ballinger Publishing Company, Cambridge, Mass., 1975.

Firestone, O. J.: *The Economic Implications of Advertising*, Methuen & Co., Ltd., Toronto, 1967.

Greer, Thomas V.: *Marketing in the Soviet Union*, Frederick A. Praeger, Inc., New York, 1973.

Howard, John A., and James Hulbert: *Advertising and the Public Interest*, Crain Communications, Inc., Chicago, 1973.

Moskin, J. Robert (ed.): *The Case for Advertising*, American Association of Advertising Agencies, Inc., New York, 1973.

Myers, John G.: *Social Issues in Advertising*, American Association of Advertising Agencies, Inc., New York, 1971.

Nicosia, Frandesco M.: *Advertising, Management, and Society*, McGraw-Hill Book Company, New York, 1974.

Pearce, Michael, Scott M. Cunningham, and Avon Miller: *Appraising the Economic and Social Effects of Advertising*, Marketing Science Institute, Cambridge, Mass., 1971.

Schmalensee, R.: *The Economics of Advertising*, North-Holland Publishing Company, Amsterdam, 1972.

Wright, John S., and John E. Mertes: *Advertising's Role in Society*, West Publishing Company, St. Paul, Minn., 1974.

TWO

TWO

**ADVERTISING'S ROLE IN THE
MARKETING PROCESS**

With some historical, social, and economic perspectives in mind, we now examine the usefulness of advertising to the business firm, particularly in its marketing programs. Advertising enables the selling firm to communicate with prospective buyers in order to inform them of its product and to persuade them to buy and use it.

To understand the role of advertising, we must recognize its importance in the marketing process. Therefore, Chapter 3 starts by defining marketing and then shows how the qualities of the product are used in advertising it. Included are such components of the total product as its package, label, brand name, trademark, and trade characteristics.

How advertising lubricates the channels of distribution and facilitates the movement of products from producers to consumers is explained in Chapter 4. The objectives of advertising are outlined, and various forms of advertising described. A discussion of the consumer's role in the marketing and advertising process concludes the chapter.

Many specialized business enterprises exist to help carry out the advertising process; three major types are described in Chapter 5. First of all, there are the *advertisers* who sponsor advertising. Second, *advertising agencies* create and place advertisements for advertisers. Third, *special-service groups*, such as photographers, engravers, artists, and production studios, help by providing their specialized assistance. The fourth type of business found in advertising—the *media* where ads appear—is handled in detail in Part Three.

CHAPTER 3

MARKETING: THE PRODUCT
AND ADVERTISING

Today's breakfast table illustrates the complexity of the task assigned to marketing in our industrial society. Coffee comes from Brazil, sugar from Colorado or Louisiana, orange juice from Florida, bacon from Iowa, toast from flour ground out of North Dakota spring wheat, and dairy products from nearby farms. All are brought to our tables as a result of the marketing process.

WHAT IS MARKETING?

The traditional definition of marketing reads: "The performance of business activities that direct the flow of goods and services from producer to consumer or user."[1] Marketing, however, is more than the mere physical movement of goods from the place of production to where they are consumed. For in addition to transportation and storage, key marketing functions include buying, selling (including advertising), financing, standardizing and grading, risk bearing, and the gathering of market information. These activities, blended together, constitute marketing as it is practiced in developed economies. However, another, more recent definition of the term probably better reflects marketing's broad-ranging scope:

> Marketing is a total system of interacting business activities designed to plan, price, promote, and distribute want-satisfying products and services to present and potential customers.[2]

Business, of course, is more than marketing. It is usually thought of as involving three principal activities: production, finance, and marketing. Production creates the goods and services which are offered to the public. Finance is concerned with regulating the flow of money to production, to marketing, and to the owners of the business. But the goods produced by production and fiscally managed by finance must be sold, for unsold goods and services are as pointless as unreceived messages in the communication process. They also are a waste of time and money and are a detriment to the economic health of the firm. Products made by the firm must reach the homes, offices, and plants where they are consumed; they must be marketed.

[1]Ralph S. Alexander and the Committee on Definitions, *Marketing Definitions*, American Marketing Association, Chicago, 1963, p. 15.
[2]William J. Stanton, *Fundamentals of Marketing*, 4th ed., McGraw-Hill Book Company, New York, 1975, p. 5.

THE MARKETING CONCEPT

Previous concern of business executives over the functions of production and finance has shifted to a considerable degree to problems of marketing because of its implications for the other two functions. This focus of attention is called by its advocates the *marketing concept.* Weeks and Marks describe the idea very nicely:

> The marketing concept of management is a unifying approach marshalling and directing the total resources of a business firm toward the determination and satisfaction of customer and consumer wants and needs in a way planned to enhance the firm's over-all profit position.[3]

Under the marketing concept, the marketing department becomes the dominant force in the business enterprise. It sets the tempo for all departments, including production and finance. This philosophy is expounded by Peter Drucker, the famous management professor, consultant, and writer, as follows:

> Fifty years ago the typical attitude of American businessmen toward marketing was still: "The sales department will sell whatever the plant produces." Today it is increasingly: "It is our job to produce what the market needs."

> Marketing is so basic that it cannot be considered a separate function (i.e., a separate skill or work) within the business, on a par with others such as manufacturing or personnel. Marketing requires separate work and a distinct group of activities. But it is, first, a central dimension of the entire business. It is the whole business seen from the point of view of its final result, that is, from the customer's point of view. Concern and responsibility for marketing must, therefore, permeate all areas of the enterprise .[4]

The central idea in Drucker's last paragraph above is usually referred to in marketing circles as *customer orientation,* a theme which permeates this textbook. It is also an integral part of sound marketing programs. Successful marketing means the satisfying of consumers' needs and wants. The skillful employment of the marketing concept lessens the imbalance between the supply of a good or service and the demand for the good or service. The sudden shifts in these relationships which occurred in 1974 and 1975 are evidence that the balance between supply and demand is indeed precarious; they also highlight the need for flexibility in marketing practice.

[3]Richard R. Weeks and William J. Marks, "The Marketing Concept in Historical Perspective," *Business and Society*, Spring 1969, p. 25.
[4]Peter Drucker, *Management: Tasks, Responsibilities, Practices*, Harper & Row, Publishers, Inc., New York, 1973, pp. 61–63.

ADVERTISING AND THE MARKETING MIX

Another concept useful in explaining where advertising fits in the marketing process is known as the *marketing mix*.[5] An analogy can be drawn between the procedure followed by the marketing manager and that used by the baker who wishes to make a cake. The baker's first decision is what *kind* of cake to produce—chocolate, angel food, or spice. The necessary ingredients are then assembled and blended into a "mix" to be placed in the oven. If the correct portions of sugar, flour, shortening, and other items are used, the cake will be a success; otherwise, it will fail. Another day the baker's objective may be a different kind of cake, and different ingredients will be used.

In a similar vein, the marketing manager has a set of ingredients to blend to accomplish the firm's business objective. The marketing "recipe" is a "mix" of five basic elements, as essential as sugar, flour, and shortening are to baking cake. The elements of the marketing mix are (1) product, (2) price, (3) distribution channels, (4) personal selling, and (5) advertising. Sometimes the arrangement is described as the *four P's* of marketing, wherein personal selling and advertising are combined into "promotion" and distribution channels are called "place." The four P's then are product, price, place, and promotion.[6]

Marketing programs vary widely in the mixture of these five ingredients. Some firms omit personal selling and use direct-mail advertising as the sole promotional ingredient; others may omit advertising completely. For instance, Hershey's chocolate was long cited as an eminently successful product that did no consumer advertising, standing on product quality and excellent distribution for sales. However, the company's products lost leadership to other candy manufacturers and, finally, in 1969 commenced advertising to consumers in the United States. By 1971 Hershey's was among the top-100 television advertisers, ranking ninety-sixth on the list, with expenditures of $7.3 million. Total advertising expenditures were $14,416,000 in 1972. After a severe cutback in 1974 due to ingredient shortages, a strong comeback in advertising was launched in 1975 and more than $10 million was spent for advertising in 1976. The company learned that without advertising it lost ground to its competitors.

Marketing executives decide which marketing mix elements to use and the portions to blend into their marketing programs. There is no cookbook to consult for marketing program recipes. Other marketing programs can be consulted for ideas, but, as in baking a cake, any variation in the ingredients will likely produce different results. Right

[5]Neil Borden, "The Concept of the Marketing Mix," *Journal of Advertising Research*, June 1964, pp. 2–7.
[6]See E. Jerome McCarthy, *Basic Marketing*, 5th ed., Richard D. Irwin, Inc., Homewood, Ill., 1975, pp. 75–80.

choices determine the executive's success and make for the marketer's reputation.

Most consumer-goods manufacturers, and many makers of industrial products, include advertising in their marketing mixes. Its specific function is *preselling* to present and potential customers. Weir explains this process:

> With an awareness that some kind of communication occurs in every phase of marketing, and that, in the end, the product itself performs the principal and decisive act of communication, management may come to realize that the actual aim of advertising (excluding mail order) is not to "sell" but to induce people to try the product or service offered and to prepare them for satisfaction in its use by "pre-sampling" it verbally.[7]

Products reaching consumers through self-service outlets such as supermarkets are "sold" largely through display and shelf positions. However, if the consumer knows the brand name and the benefits to be derived from using a product, it is obviously easier to sell that product. The selling process is accelerated when the item has been *positioned* favorably in the consumer mind. *Product positioning* is a marketing strategy which takes into consideration how consumers perceive a product relative to competitive offerings. Thus, mass retailers prefer that a product have consumer advertising support before agreeing to stock the item on their shelves.

It is clear that advertising is an important function in the marketing programs of most mass-produced, mass-marketed consumer goods. In the marketing of many industrial products, advertising is used to uncover unknown prospects and to help the salesperson obtain a hearing. As the costs of maintaining salespeople in the field continue to rise, this benefit takes on increasing importance. In 1975 the cost of an industrial sales call averaged over $70.

In the past decade it has been realized that marketing thinking, approaches, and techniques could be well applied to noncommercial situations. This philosophy was spelled out in an article titled "Broadening the Concept of Marketing."[8] The idea caught on, and one of the article's authors has followed up with a major book on the topic.[9] All of this adds up to many new challenges for marketing people, providing new jobs and opportunities to serve.

Advertising, of course, has long lent support to noncommercial ventures. Political candidates used banners, pins, outdoor signs, and newspaper advertising in the early days of American politics. Candi-

[7]Walter Weir, *On the Writing of Advertising*, McGraw-Hill Book Company, New York, 1960, p. 156.
[8]Philip Kotler and Sidney J. Levy, *Journal of Marketing*, January 1969, pp. 10–15.
[9]Philip Kotler, *Marketing for Nonprofit Organizations*, Prentice-Hall, Inc., Englewood Cliffs, N.J., 1975.

dates adapted readily to radio and television advertising media when these media appeared on the scene. In addition to being employed in securing political office, advertising is used to help convert people to a particular religious belief, to encourage learning, to secure financial support for charitable causes, and to achieve many other noncommercial objectives.

Although this book deals primarily with the advertising of products and services, bear in mind that the word "idea" usually can be substituted for the word "product." Advertising strategy for selling ideas, such as the conservation of energy, the reduction of drunk driving or litter, and the prevention of forest fires, closely parallels that used for tangible products.

PRIMACY OF THE PRODUCT

The product is the starting point—the very heart—of any advertising program. An old marketing axiom states that "without a good product, you have nothing." This truism is illustrated by a bit of advice from Howard J. Morgens, former chairman of Procter & Gamble Company, the nation's largest advertiser:

> The only way you can succeed in business is with a good product. You can't do it with advertising. It all gets down to the fact that if you've got a good product, you can be successful with a reasonable marketing expenditure, but if you haven't got the product, the surest way to go broke is to pour your money behind it.

No amount of marketing effort can sell a bad product over an extended period of time. Promotional effort may help make initial sales, but long-run success depends on customer satisfaction with the product, which provides the foundation to sound advertising. Product knowledge, therefore, is essential to the practitioner of advertising.

Product Defined

Stanton describes a product:

> ... in a very narrow sense as simply a set of tangible physical and chemical attributes assembled in an identifiable form. Each different product category carries a commonly understood descriptive name, such as apples, steel, shoes, or baseball bats.[10]

Our use of the term "product" is broader in scope. Services, as well

[10]Stanton, op, cit., p. 171.

as physical goods, are considered products. In fact, more of our dollars go toward the purchase of services, including those furnished by banks, hotels, restaurants, and airlines, and they, too, are advertised extensively in our affluent society. Much more than tangible products are encompassed in our analysis of the concept of product. Included are items such as the package, brand name, trademark, trade character, and package label—all influencing the salability of products. The advertising implications of these product components are examined in this chapter, followed by an analysis of the role played by the product itself in the advertising process.

Product Classification

When products are classified, the most elementary breakdown is between consumer and industrial goods. Those products which satisfy our personal wants and desires, such as food, clothing, and household items, are examples of the *consumer-goods* category. *Industrial goods* are used for a multitude of business purposes, ranging from blast furnaces, pig iron, and forklift trucks to sweeping compounds and typing ribbons.

The distinction is based on the use to which the product is put. Oil used to heat a home is classified as a consumer product: the same item is an industrial good when used to fuel a diesel truck. Thus producers often can sell their products in both the consumer and industrial markets. For that reason, a company such as Morton Salt has separate advertising directors for its table salt product line and for the hundreds of varieties of salt processed for industrial uses. This reflects different marketing characteristics of consumer and industrial goods and the need for different marketing strategies. The two types of goods do not reach the same market, and they do not require the same advertising. Therefore, every advertiser must know where the primary market lies—in the consumer or the industrial area.

Consumer Goods   There are three types: convenience, shopping, and specialty. *Convenience goods* are those items that are frequently purchased, are low in cost, and are bought at the most accessible retail outlet shortly after a need for the product is felt. The most desirable marketing strategy is to place the product in every possible retail outlet where a consumer might reasonably look for it. The advertising campaigns of soft-drink, candy-bar, food, and household products provide examples of convenience-goods advertising. The advertising for convenience goods seeks to familiarize the consuming public with the product name and its want-satisfying qualities. The consumer, it is hoped, will recognize the advertised brand and purchase it. At the same time, the manufacturer seeks to persuade retailers, through personal selling and trade advertising, to stock the product.

FIGURE 3.1
Services as well as products may be advertised. Here (*opposite page*) a large stock brokerage firm presents the case for making investments through its offices.

No way. Not when there are Gillette Twinjector® Blades around. Because, face it, a smoother, closer, safer injector shave is hard to find. Twinjector blades even have rinse slots. Specially-designed openings to help reduce clogging.

**The Gillette Twinjector® Shave.
Beautiful, baby.**

© The Gillette Co., Boston, Mass.

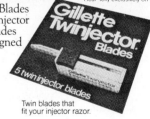

Twin blades that
fit your injector razor.

FIGURE 3.2
Convenience goods are promoted through consumer advertising. [*Reprinted with the permission of the Gillette Company, Safety Razor Division, Boston, Mass.*]

Products purchased after a careful consideration of quality, price, and suitability are classified as *shopping goods*. Style may be an additional factor in the decision. In this case, the product is infrequently purchased and has a high unit price. It is considered to be a major purchase. Family discussions may be held to decide where available

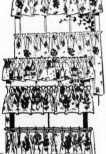
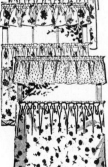

FIGURE 3.3
Furniture is an example of a shopping good which is frequently advertised in newspapers.

discretionary spending power is to be expended. Once a decision to buy is made, the consumer "shops" a number of retail outlets.

The marketing strategy of the shopping-goods manufacturer calls for placing products in comparatively few outlets. Retail outlets in main shopping centers are preferred so that comparison shopping by consumers may be facilitated. The decisive factor in the final purchase decision often lies in the store name, because it represents the quality, price, or style sought by the buyers. Thus, much of the advertising responsibility is placed upon the retailer. Dress shops and furniture outlets provide good examples of shopping-goods advertising.

The characteristics of high unit price and infrequent purchase are also present for *specialty goods*. The buying process, however, is quite different. As a guide in purchasing, the buyer relies on brand name and unique product characteristics, instead of shopping. A specialty good is a branded item which the consumer has become convinced is superior to all competitive brands. The retail outlet handling the brand is sought out by the consumer, and substitutes will not be accepted if the preferred brand is not in stock.

Many forces help the consumer develop a favorable attitude toward one brand: recommendations of friends and previous experience with the brand combine to create brand insistence. Advertising, of course, is often important in the picture. The manufacturer of a specialty product stresses the superiority of the firm's brand over competitive offerings. Advertisements for photographic equipment, sporting goods, and quality men's shoes show how specialty-goods manufacturers go about convincing consumers of brand superiority. Moreover, the manufacturer makes certain that consumers who are convinced by the claims made for the product can find retail outlets handling the brand without too much difficulty: yellow page advertising in the telephone directory is often used; the stores selling the brand may be listed in magazine ads for the brand; or a toll-free phone number from which the prospect can obtain the name and location of the nearest outlet may be provided.

Industrial Goods A fivefold classification is generally used for industrial goods: raw materials, fabricating materials and parts, operating supplies, installations, and accessory equipment. Our approach in Part Two is largely consumer-oriented. The special creative problems of industrial advertising are considered later in the book.

Product Positioning[11]

By the 1970s a new expression of marketing strategy had become popular, namely, *product positioning*. The underlying premise is that

[11]This section is based on the work of Jack Trout and Al Ries. See *Advertising Age*, April 24, May 1, and May 8, 1972. Copyrighted by Crain Communications, Inc., and used by special permission.

Why everybody's pretending they're us.

These are not Earth shoes. Just because they look like Earth shoes doesn't mean they are Earth brand shoes.

There was a time when the EARTH° negative heel shoe was the only shoe in the world with the heel lower than the toe.

In those days the other people who made shoes just laughed at us.

But things have changed. And now that you love our Earth brand shoes so much the shoe companies have stopped laughing and started copying.

The Earth brand shoe comes in styles for men and women, from open sandals to high boots. From $23.50 to $42.50. Prices slightly higher in the west.

The shoes that look like, seem like, but don't work like the Earth shoe.

Today, a lot of people are trying to imitate our shoe. Some even use names that sound like ours, and have ads that look like ours!

It seems like everybody's trying to be us.

But what they don't understand is this. Merely lowering the heel of a shoe isn't enough. And imitating the outside of our shoe isn't enough. Just because a shoe looks like the Earth shoe doesn't mean it works like the Earth shoe.

It took many years to perfect the Earth brand shoe. And those years are crucial. They make our shoe different from all its imitators.

How the Earth® Shoe was invented.

It started years ago when Anne Kalsø had the original idea for the negative heel shoe.

She saw footprints in the sand, and realized that with every footprint the body was designing a shoe. A natural shoe. A shoe with the heel lower than the toe. A shoe that would work in harmony with your entire body. But that was just the beginning. Then came the years

of research and hard work to get every detail just right. To perfect the arch. To make the toes wide, comfortable and functional. To balance the shoe. To mold the sole in a special way so that it would allow you to walk in a natural rolling motion. Gently and easily even on the hard jarring cement of our cities.

To get an idea of how the Earth shoe works, stand barefoot with your toes up on a book. Feel what begins to happen.

Patent '3305947. Why the Earth® shoe is unique.

The Earth shoe is patented. That means it can't be copied without being changed.

And if it's changed it just isn't the Earth shoe.

So to be sure you're getting the real thing, look on the sole for our patent number and our trademark. Earth. If they're not

Anne Kalsø.
Inventor of the EARTH negative heel shoe.

there it's not the Earth brand shoe.

Sold only at Earth® shoe stores.

And there's one more thing that makes our shoes so special.

Earth shoes are sold only at Earth shoe stores. Stores that sell no other shoe but ours, and are devoted entirely to the Earth shoe concept.

How our shoes fit you is very important to us. There's a special technique to fitting them. Our people are trained to fit you properly and we wouldn't trust anyone else to do it.

Find out for yourself.

To really appreciate Earth shoes you must try them.

When you do you'll see, perhaps for the first time in your life, what it's like to walk more gracefully, naturally and comfortably.

Earth Kalsø shoe

° EARTH is the registered trademark of Kalsø Systemet, Inc. for its negative heel shoes and other products.
©1975. Kalsø Systemet, Inc.

Our shoes are sold at stores that sell only the EARTH°shoe.

FIGURE 3.4
Specialty goods, such as this brand of shoe, are featured in ads which stress that the product is sold only in selected stores. When this ad appeared in some magazines, a list of retail stores selling the product appeared on the opposite page.

our society suffers from overcommunication; thus, to be successful an advertiser must create a niche in the prospect's mind. This niche—or "position"—involves not only the strengths and weaknesses of the product but also the manner in which the product differs from those of

A glorious, full-color picture of the Goodrich Blimp.

FIGURE 3.5
In this unusual advertisement a tire manufacturer uses a humorous approach to "position" itself against the industry leader by highlighting the company name.

What? No blimp?
Look again.
Not at the picture, the name.
Goodrich.
Not Goodyear.
Goodrich doesn't have a blimp,
Goodyear does.
　　　We haven't advertised as much
as Goodyear, either. So it's not too
surprising a lot of people forget our
name and remember theirs.
　　　And if you're confused about our
blimps, when we don't even have one,
just imagine how confused you can get about our tires.
　　　Who knows, you might even go to Goodyear to get them. And that's too bad.
　　　You see, in 1965, Goodrich introduced the first American-made radial tire.
　　　For five years, nationally, we've advertised nothing else.
　　　Not because everybody wanted radials.
　　　But because the radial tire was, and is, the most important innovation in tires
in nearly a quarter century.
　　　No conventional tire we've ever made, none, stops as fast, corners as well, and
lasts as long as our Goodrich Lifesaver Steel Radial.
　　　It's the result of our company's commitment, for ten years, to make the most
advanced radial tire on the road.
　　　Now you watch. You'll probably see Goodyear featuring a steel radial, too.
　　　Along with all their other tires.
　　　It'll be good. But it won't be Goodrich.
　　　And if you still get our names confused, just look up in the sky.
　　　If you see an enormous blimp with somebody's name on it, we're
the other guys.

B.F.Goodrich
America's Premier Radial Tire Maker

Lifesaver® Steel Radials.
If you want Goodrich, you'll just have to remember Goodrich.

major competitors. Sheer volume of advertising is not sufficient, because there is a limit to the amount of information that the consumer's mind can take in and handle. The mind is selective and filters out information which does not parallel its previous experience. Thus, if RCA advertises "RCA computers are best," most minds will respond by rejecting this statement since they believe that IBM, not RCA, holds the number one position. Most minds would probably associate RCA with other products, such as radio equipment. For a computer manufacturer to secure a favorable position, IBM must be dislodged (probably an impossibility), or a relationship of his product to IBM must be established.

One example of the implementation of the positioning concept is that of Seven-Up's "un-cola" campaign. The product was usually thought of as a mixer—something to be blended with hard liquor. Although sales were good and steady, the potential was nothing like that available to such soft-drink brands as Coca-Cola and Pepsi-Cola. A great deal more than half of the soft-drink-product category is the cola drinks. In its "un-cola" advertising, Seven-Up says to potential consumers that its product is a viable alternative to Coke and Pepsi. Seven-Up sales increased 10 percent in the first year after the new positioning approach, and the product has continued to maintain a healthy brand share.

Johnson & Johnson's baby shampoo, which for years had been positioned as a product for use on children's hair and was promoted to young mothers, found its sales potential drying up with the declining birthrate. Therefore, in the early 1970s the company sought to shift from that position to one as a general shampoo, serving the needs of every member of the family. Advertising messages were designed which showed virile men and even grandmothers using Johnson & Johnson's baby shampoo. The advertising pointed up the shampoo's performance characteristics as a mild, basic shampoo for use by anyone, changing what had been an appeal to a segmented market to one of universal acceptance and use. The brand replaced Procter & Gamble's brand, Head and Shoulders, as the leading shampoo, despite the retention of a name which previously had provided its own limited positioning as a children's product.

Advertising and New Products

If products are the heart of the marketing process, then new products are its lifeblood. New-product development provides a good example of the axiom "Marketing is dynamic," for changes come fast and often on this front. About 25 years ago, American manufacturers started to emphasize the strategy of *market segmentation*. This means that producers attempt to modify their product offerings in a manner that fits the special needs they have perceived to exist among a group (segment) of potential buyers.[12] Various strategies, including advertising, are then employed to inform members of the market segment of the product's availability and to convince them of its acceptability. In contrast, the *product differentiation* strategy hopes to get consumers to adjust their demands to the manufacturer's product as it exists, or to a changed existing product, or to a completely new product. Advertising is used in the product differentiation context to persuade consumers that they should purchase the item.

Although the term "new product" conjures up mental pictures of technological breakthroughs and revolutionary ways of doing things, its use in marketing is much broader, including modifications of existing products, imitations of competitive products, and product-line acquisitions. If the product is new to the firm, it is classified as a "new product." Although each new-product development carries stimulating challenges, it presents knotty problems for the marketing executive. But the success of many firms may be traced directly to the ability of their management to ferret out latent consumer desires and to develop new products to meet these demands. The demise of other firms came about because their executives became wedded to older, more stable, and once successful products, failing to stay in tune with changing demand trends.

One success story illustrating this point is that of Procter & Gamble. Contrary to the popular impression that consumer package-goods companies pour out an almost unending stream of new products, P&G introduced only two to the national market during the period 1970–1974—Sure deodorant and Pringles potato chips. Sure was just another entry into the growing antiperspirant market, providing a minor modification in the generic product. Pringles, however, was a totally new kind of potato chip. The giant potato-chip industry—almost $1 billion a year—always had been beset by the twin problems of spoilage and breakage. Aware of these problems because the company sold edible oils to potato-chip manufacturers, P&G set out to solve them. Instead of slicing and frying fresh potatoes, P&G dehydrated them and then reconstituted them as a mash that could be pressed and fried in a precise shape that would allow them to be stacked in a cylindrical container. Exhaustive testing (research and development work on Pringles began in the mid-1950s) resulted in a new chip that would stay fresh in the package for a year, six times the two-months' shelflife of the ordinary potato chip. And because of its stacking and protective container, Pringles could be shipped anywhere in the country without breakage. The result was that Pringles sold at an annual rate of approximately $200 million in 1975. This figure represented one-fifth of the market and was achieved only two years following national introduction of the product.

[12]See Wendell R. Smith, "Product Differentiation and Market Segmentation as Alternative Marketing Strategies," *Journal of Marketing*, July 1956, pp. 3–8.

Whether a product differentiation or a market segmentation strategy is followed, advertising usually bears a large portion of the responsibility for letting the public know about the attributes of the product. Advertising can introduce new products, call attention to changes in old products, and weld together a family of products made by the same manufacturer. Without the assistance of advertising, a great deal of the incentive for product development would be missing, for the returns from the acceptance of the new product would be much slower in materializing. Communication through advertising speeds the process of informing the marketplace of product innovations, thus benefiting consumers as well as producers.

A halt in the emphasis on new-product development came with the environmental movement and energy crisis during the first half of the 1970s. As was discussed in Chapter 1, many of the nation's leading utilities implemented "demarketing" programs. What advertising's role should be in an era of shortages was debated, and it became clear that "marketers must integrate the changes in the business environment into effective new product, pricing, distribution, and promotion strategies."[13] There was some evidence that "de-proliferation—the removal from product lines and models any options which do not affect profits or basic market penetration one way or the other (elimination of the frill factor)"[14]—might become common. At the same time, interest in new-product development did not die, as illustrated by this headline in an advertising trade publication: "Gillette to launch new product blitz. . . ."[15] But, today, another important factor must be considered when developing new products—the impact of the product on the total environment where it is produced, marketed, and ultimately consumed.

THE PACKAGE

A product's package is an important part of consumer acceptance. Daniel Boorstin correctly points out that packaging, as we know it and distinguish it from packing, came upon the American scene as a phenomenon of the early twentieth century, as the following quotation reveals:

> In the Old World, even after the industrial age had arrived, only expensive items were housed in their own box or elegantly wrapped. A watch or jewel would be presented in a carefully crafted container, but the notion

[13]David Cullwick, "Positioning Demarketing Strategy," *Journal of Marketing*, April 1975, p. 51.
[14]Ernest A. Jones, in a talk before the Detroit chapter of the American Marketing Association as reported in *Advertising Age*, Mar. 31, 1975, p. 87.
[15]*Advertising Age*, Apr. 21, 1975, p. 3.

that a pound of sugar or a dozen crackers should be encased and offered for purchase in specially designed, attractive material seemed outlandish. Essential to the American Standard of Living were new techniques for clothing objects to make them appealing advertisements for themselves. Industries spent fortunes improving the sales garb of inexpensive objects of daily consumption—a pack of cigarettes or a can of soup.[16]

That packaging, which is a concept considerably advanced from product packing, is vital to the marketing success of most consumer products is almost axiomatic in its simplicity. The mental image of the product which comes to the consumer's mind is of its package. In a real sense, the package is the product; as the old adage states, "Clothes make the man." Products are often judged by their packages, and an attractive package starts the product on its way to purchase. Perfume is an obvious example of this phenomenon.

There exists a close interrelationship between the advertising and packaging components of the marketing equation. Many advertisements boldly feature the product in its package. For this reason, there is a need for close coordination between package design and advertising programs. For product categories which possess little physical differentiation (for example, cigarettes and soap powders), the package may serve as an effective device for establishing consumer preferences. In such cases, advertisements obviously will key in on the package.

One way of establishing packaging's importance in modern-day marketing is on the basis of money spent for it. The bill for packages in the United States was $32 billion in 1975.[17] More is spent for packaging each year than for advertising. The packaging industry is characterized by continuous changes, some brought about through competition and others resulting from concerns over the environmental impact of packages. In the latter category are such issues as litter, solid-waste disposal, and deterioration of the atmosphere.

Purposes of Packaging

Products were originally packed as a means of *protection* during transportation and storage. The goal was to prevent damage to products in transit and their deterioration while they were being stored. Goods were received by merchants in bulk, that is, in barrels and boxes, and then sold in small quantities to consumers. The famous old cracker barrel of the country stores is an example.

Products still need this kind of protection. The responsibility for this

[16]Daniel J. Boorstin, *The Americans: The Democratic Experience*, Vintage Books, Random House, Inc., New York, 1974, p. 434.
[17]*U.S. Industrial Outlook, 1976*, Bureau of Domestic Commerce, Washington, January 1976, p. 177.

facet of packaging rests with the manufacturer's production department. Advertising people get involved only when the protective packaging is featured as a campaign theme. Moreover, the marketing department wants assurance that the product is presented in its best light to the consumer and protected as well or better than competitive products.

Our interest is primarily in the package as a *marketing* tool, rather than as a protective device. The package serves as a vehicle for *identification* by carrying the manufacturer's name, trademark, and the brand name. It also provides information about ingredients and instructions for product use. These services are important to sound marketing. There are, however, three other aspects of packaging that must be taken into consideration.

Consumer Desire for Convenience Because consumers look for increased convenience in products they use, manufacturers soon discovered that the package might provide this benefit. In other words, product differentiation was gained through the package. Soda crackers were first wrapped in family-size containers by the National Biscuit Company in 1899. Now most food is sold in family-size containers; recently Campbell's Soup introduced a single-portion can size for use by single-person households.

Package superiority in such areas of convenience as ease in opening is also used to differentiate one brand over competitors. Ease in pouring and storability are additional examples of the use of packaging as sales generators.

Packaging designed for convenience in use, such as boil-in-bag vegetables, is probably the most important category. The aerosol package, which made fighting insects and adding whipping cream to a strawberry pie easier tasks, illustrates the point; however, recently it has been claimed that the gaseous material used may have harmful impact on the atmosphere, and the aerosol device may be removed from the market. Even if this does come to pass, unless nonpollutant substitute propellant gases can be found, it can be predicted that another ingenious package will be developed to fill the desire for convenience in doing otherwise messy jobs. Consumer packaging is a parade of innovations which has included pull-tab cans, unbreakable shampoo bottles, and vacuum-seal plastic lids. Home "displayability" has become a characteristic of containers of such household products as facial tissue.

Packages may also be designed to have a reuse value, such as placing cream cheese in a juice glass, and are sometimes designed as gift items. Alcoholic beverages are sold at holiday seasons in elegantly designed decanters, for example, and other products are gift wrapped at the factory.

FIGURE 3.6
This container for
lemon juice was
designed for later
use as a cruet.

Competition for Shelf Space Another marketing dimension of packaging is to be found in the intense competition for space on the
retailer's shelf. Inasmuch as the revolution in packaging has coincided
with the conversion of much of America's retailing to the self-service
principle, it is clear that a product will not sell easily if it is not visible in
the supermarket shelf. Thus, the package should be designed so that

the important first sale to the retailer is facilitated; the retailer must be encouraged to place the product into stock. The large number of new products makes this task more difficult each year; some retail chains now say, in effect, "When you bring in a new one, tell us which one is to be thrown out." If the product is designed to give the retailer an advantage in stocking the item—in addition to the usual promotional support—the retailer is more inclined to make a decision favorable to the manufacturer. Thus, the two-bulb and the four-bulb packages solved the loose light bulb stocking problem and provided a good reason (at that time) for taking on the Sylvania brand. In sum, the package should be designed to fit into its retail environment.

Packaging as Advertising at the Point of Sale Retailers are highly interested in stock turnover; therefore, packaging which stimulates the rate of sale is desirable. In addition to brand familiarity and shelf position of the product, the attractiveness of the package itself may influence purchase in the self-service store. Packages with eye appeal stand out on the shelf; some consumers will reach out for the product in the attractive package. Packages must do the work of the fast-

FIGURE 3.7
The importance of the package in self-service merchandising is spoofed in this cartoon. [*Reprinted by special permission from* Advertising Age.]

"The new package looks so good on the shelves the customers are leaving it on the shelves."

1906 **1930** **1942**

1967 **1970** **1973**

FIGURE 3.8
Packages need modernizing to coincide with public ideas of acceptable art styles. A leading food manufacturer has made many such changes over the past three-quarters century.

vanishing salesperson. For this reason, considerable research and experimentation go on in the area of package design. Such dimensions as color, shape, and size of the package are examined for impact on consumers. The ability of the product to convey status to its possessor may be enhanced by the package design. Recognizing the marketing importance of the package, many firms make periodic reviews with packaging updating in mind. Specialized consulting firms and the major packaging manufacturers are involved in the activity. The changes made by one company over a period of years is shown in Figure 3.8. The Kellogg Company has updated its package for corn flakes many times to keep pace with changing standards of consumer acceptance.

Multiple-unit packaging also can increase sales, as the six-pack for soft drinks and beer illustrates. Many items are consumed on impulse—and at a faster rate if the item is already on the pantry shelf. Multiple-unit packaging helps build up the shelf inventory. A higher rate of consumption must be preceded by actual purchase. Lately, there has been a trend to larger containers for many products such as dog food or detergents. Affinity packaging is another approach to getting larger sales of a manufacturer's product line. Two or more products—different in composition but used jointly—are combined in one package to be sold as one unit.

Significance of Packaging

All of this discussion adds up to the observation that packaging is the biggest advertising medium of all. It has been estimated that a typical grocery product may get more than 15 billion potential exposures to the public in a year. This would cost nearly $50 million if conventional media were used.[18] The package has evolved from a protective device into an extremely important sales tool. In some product categories, package innovation is as crucial as product development itself. Although our discussion has revolved around consumer goods, packaging is also becoming increasingly important to the marketing success of industrial-goods manufacturers.

THE BRAND NAME

Once a good product is developed and appropriately packaged, an appealing name is needed. An analogy can be drawn to the birth and naming of a child for identification and communication purposes. We are assuming, at this point, that the manufacturer has already decided to sell the product under his or her name rather than to make it available to others for private labeling or branding.

The Reason for Brands

Cattle ranchers brand livestock in order to distinguish their herds from those of neighbors. Manufacturers want consumers to be able to pick their product over that made by competitors, hoping to build brand loyalty for their output over a period of time.

A *brand name* is the title given to a product by its manufacturer. Brand names should be distinguished from *trade names*, which are the names of business firms. General Mills, for example, is the trade name of a grocery-products manufacturer which originated as a flour-milling company. Its best flour bears the brand name of *Gold Medal*.

Names facilitate communication. Social relationships would be difficult indeed if people did not have names. Similarly, manufacturers

---

[18]Dik Warren Twedt, "How Much Value Can Be Added through Packaging," *Journal of Marketing*, January 1968, p. 61.

use names to expedite the communication of ideas about their products. Advertising would be pointless unless attention to the product could be called by a name which is capable of being remembered. The consumer, after seeing the ad and being stimulated to buy the product, may seek out the retailer selling Earth Shoes, or he or she may ask the supermarket manager, "Where do you stock Wonder bread?" Matters are simplified, for the consumer knows what he or she wants and the retailer knows what the consumer is talking about; everyone is satisfied. There has been communication.

This situation is intensified when the product is sold through self-service. All communication may be done impersonally. The brand name acts as a handy purchasing aid for the consumer and as a promotional vehicle for the manufacturer. Furthermore, the brand name makes the manufacturer accountable for the quality of the product. National advertising would be nigh impossible in the absence of brand names.

Choosing a Brand Name

Choosing a brand name is a complex and frustrating activity. When Esso Chemical Company found it necessary to change its company name, the computer was fed various vowel and consonant combinations and 44,990 four-letter and 500,000 five-letter combinations came out. EXXON was finally chosen because of its distinctiveness and graphic design possibilities. Other firms have created name banks to help in the naming of future products.

In a study of old company and brand names, Leonard Carlton isolated five benchmarks which seem to have dominated the name-choosing process in the past:[19]

1 *The founder.* Procter & Gamble, Borden, and Campbell Soup Company were named after the founders of each firm.

2 *Identification with great events.* The Great Atlantic and Pacific Tea Company (A&P) was named in honor of the opening of the coast-to-coast railroad.

3 *Identification with experience.* Carnation Milk was named in honor of President McKinley's ever-present boutonniere.

4 *Coinage.* The classic example is Kodak, which George Eastman named in 1888 because he liked the letter "K" and wanted a name incapable of misspelling.[20]

[19]Leonard Carlton, "The Oldtime Name Game," *Advertising Age*, Nov. 29, 1971, pp. 37–39.
[20]For a fascinating story, see "The Name Game" in *Forbes*, Nov. 15, 1973, pp. 70, 72. The thrust of the article is that businesspeople are superstitious, or "Why else would they need high priests to tell them how to change their companies' names?" This refers to firms such as Lippincott & Margulies which specialize in the design of corporate symbols. The writer goes on to emphasize the apparent appeal of the letter "X" as used in EXXON and in Xerox.

100

ADVERTISING'S
ROLE
IN THE
MARKETING
PROCESS

5   *Remembering the old hometown.* Beatrice Food's namesake is a town in Nebraska, and Oneida Community Plate honors an upstate New York town.

These choices from the pages of the past do not provide much in the nature of guidance when choosing a brand name today. As a general statement, it can be said that these approaches are the wrong way to go about the job. The overwhelmingly important consideration is *appropriateness.* The manufacturer must first determine what kind of image he wishes to create for his brand in the consumer's mind. Along with product quality, recommendations of friends, resellers' opinions, and advertising of the brand name help mold attitudes toward various products. We like some words; others rub us the wrong way. Individual attitudes are colored by past experiences. Once a particular Nancy snubbed us; now we subconsciously reject others bearing that same name. Many words are almost universally liked, and others generally disliked. The person picking a brand name must take such factors into consideration.

The marketing implications of such decisions can be found in scores of case examples. One is the share-of-market victory of Taster's Choice brand of freeze-dried coffee over the Maxim brand.[21] The battle was between two highly successful packaged-goods manufacturers, General Foods and Nestlé. General Foods was first in the field with its Maxim brand and took an early lead in sales. Nevertheless Nestle's Taster's Choice garnered a higher brand share in spite of spending appreciably less for promotion. The reasons for this apparent inconsistency are to be found in the areas of name choice and package design. The name "Maxim" was a spin-off of General Foods' highly successful Maxwell House Coffee brand. But inasmuch as freeze-dried coffee was essentially a new-product category, the tactic backfired as consumers perceived the brand as a by-product of the established line. Much of Maxim's sales came from the cannibalization of the Maxwell House brand. Nestlé, on the other hand, divorced its new product from its instant coffee, Instant Nescafe. An unusual name—Taster's Choice—was selected to enhance the product's uniqueness and its properties of quality and robust flavor. We are not concerned at this point in the differences in the product packaging of the two products; suffice it to say, the Taster's Choice package was less traditional than that used by Maxim.

The soap manufacturer who desires an image of "gentleness" for his product would not choose "Grit" as a brand name; "Dove" would be more appropriate. Words and their connotations are much more subtle, of course, than this example. Generally speaking, negative words are seldom desirable in brand names. While the name may

[21]This whole paragraph was excerpted from Walter P. Marguilies, "How Nestle Beat General Foods in Freeze-Dried Coffee Battle," *Advertising Age*, June 21, 1971, pp. 51–52.

merely identify the product, preferably it should hold some attraction for the customer. A name, such as A-1 Sauce or Perfection, conveys the idea of quality, or is pleasant (Sunshine), or suggests product composition (Pennzoil), or femininity (White Shoulders), or even the benefit resulting from its use (Easy-Off Oven Cleaner).

The brand name should have *graphic possibilities.* How the brand name will look on the package and how it can give something around which a promotional campaign can be built should be weighed. Some brand names lend themselves to use in singing jingles.

Many technical rules surround the choice of a brand name. One is to avoid foreign words, which, although they may connote fashion or prestige, may require the advertiser to spend scarce dollars attempting to teach the elements of, for example, French pronunciation. Other ideas are that brand names be short, unique, accurate, not too imitative, and not capable of unfavorable backward reading or initial-letter reading. How words affect people is the essential knowledge needed when struggling with the creative task of producing a successful brand name.

If a firm wishes to ensure its right to exclusive use of a brand name, it must take affirmative steps to prevent the use of the name by other manufacturers. DuPont lost its right to exclusive use of the name "cellophane" because the public came to think of any and all viscose solidified in thin, transparent waterproof sheets as "cellophane." Other registered trademarks which have passed into the public domain include aspirin, zipper, and linoleum—now all considered to be generic names for the products. A *generic name* is one used to describe a product category, and thus cannot be used exclusively by one manufacturer. More recently, the American Thermos Products Company lost the exclusive right to the name "thermos." One can think of other products that may be in danger of slipping into the generic name pit, such as Kleenex for facial tissue and Baggies for cellophane containers for food products.

TRADEMARKS AND TRADE CHARACTERS

Brand names and trademarks are similar in function; both are designed to identify the product of a specific maker. The word "brand" includes both terms within its scope and is defined as "a name, term, sign, symbol, or design, or a combination of them which is intended to identify the goods or services of one seller or group of sellers and to differentiate them from those of competition."[22] The brand name is

---

[22]Alexander, *Marketing Definitions*, p. 9.

described as that part of a brand which can be vocalized—the utterable.[23]

One useful definition of a trademark is found in a standard dictionary: "A name, symbol, or other device identifying a product, officially registered and legally restricted to the use of the owner or manufacturer."[24] Although there are a few isolated exceptions (such as service marks for businesses which provide services like dry cleaning and termite control), it is helpful to think of the trademark as a device attached to a product for the purpose of identifying its maker. The trademark may be a distinctive symbol, or it may consist of a special way of writing the brand name. Most manufacturers use both brand names and trademarks.

A highly technical body of law has developed governing the protection of trademarks. The Lanham Act, passed by Congress in 1946, is the basic law covering the trademark area and is discussed in Chapter 20. The small symbol ® indicates that a trademark has been registered; its use in product promotion helps protect the manufacturer's right to exclusive use of the trademark and his investment in the brand name.

The magnitude of the registration process is highlighted by the fact

[23]Ibid., p. 10.
[24]*The American Heritage Dictionary of the English Language*, Houghton Mifflin Company, Boston, 1969, p. 1360.

that on December 17, 1974, the U.S. Patent Office issued its one-millionth trademark registration certificate for a change in design for the Sweet 'N Low mark. Approximately 25,000 trademarks were registered in 1974, and approximately 500,000 were on the federal register as of early 1975.[25]

Trademarks and Advertising

The trademark should appear in every advertisement for the product. The advertiser wants consumers to recall the ad and its featured product when shopping. Thus there is a strong incentive to develop a distinctive and easy-to-remember trademark. Because the trademark is an important factor in the product's brand image, the style or graphic approach in which it is promoted probably should be revised from time to time to keep it contemporary. The Bell System has done this over the last century. Such changes, however, may be expensive. The costs mount for changes in letterheads and everywhere else the trademark appears. The Bell System had to repaint 128,000 vehicles when its trademark was last modernized. The physical representation of the trademark in an ad is usually called the *logo*.

Trade Characters

Many sellers use symbols in the form of animals, people, birds, and other animate objects in association with their products. The goal is to enhance the memorability of the products in the consumers' minds. The Jolly Green Giant is an example of the trade character, which is basically a device around which to build promotional programs. Recently the Green Giant has been joined by a sidekick named the "Little Green Sprout," who served as a spokesman for the company, whereas the Giant's vocabulary has been limited to "Ho, Ho, Ho." The Orange Bird is used similarly to promote the idea of drinking Florida orange juice, and for years the Pillsbury Dough Boy character has touted the company's convenience items and their location in the store—the dairy case. The great value of trade characters is to provide continuity to advertising programs, for the public seems able to remember trade characters better than it does brand names, trademarks, or slogans. Nearly everyone in America knows Betty Crocker. And a recent survey determined that Ronald McDonald is better known, among children, than Santa Claus. While not strictly an extension of the product, but rather of the promotional program, trade characters have a general similarity to trademarks and when entertainingly presented enhance brand awareness.

[25]Sidney A. Diamond, "Trademark No. 1,000,000 Goes to 'Sweet 'N Low'—Diamond Looks Back to No. 1," *Advertising Age*, Feb. 3, 1975, p. 39.

104
ADVERTISING'S
ROLE
IN THE
MARKETING
PROCESS

Save gasoline. Walk to Corn-on-the-Curb Days.

Anybody who has ever seen the Jolly Green Giant breeze through a corn patch will tell you: the big guy never runs out of energy.

Speaking of which, he hopes you'll have enough gas for a trip to the valley for Corn-on-the-Curb Days. If not, it's worth the walk.

It's a yearly event in Le Sueur, Minnesota (the Giant's hometown), to celebrate the corn harvest by gathering along the streets of town and eating fresh ears of Niblets corn. There's a traditional corn-eating contest, plus plenty to do for the little sprouts.

So do try to come. The date is August 4th. But either way, drop a line to the Green Giant, Box 50-452, Le Sueur, Minnesota 56058. He'll send you an official Corn-on-the-Curb Days Map and directions to Le Sueur.

(Turn left at Minneapolis)
You can't miss Le Sueur. It's a small town, but it has a big Giant.

Green Giant
Good things from the garden

FIGURE 3.10
The Jolly Green Giant is a well-established trade character. He and his sidekick, Little Green Sprout, create a personable image of the company.

GREEN GIANT, JOLLY GREEN GIANT, the Giant Figure, LITTLE GREEN SPROUT, and the Little Green Sprout Figure are trademarks of Green Giant Company. © GGCo.

THE LABEL

Another important extension of the product is the label. It is attached physically either to the product or to its package. A label that informs the buyer of the product's brand name and its manufacturer is called a *brand label*. Other kinds of information can appear on the label, for instance, the grade of the product. Some countries, notably Canada, have compulsory grade labeling for some product categories.

Certain information may be required by legislation to accompany the product. In the United States, the Federal Food, Drug, and Cosmetic Act requires that the labels on certain products include the product name, the manufacturer and his address, the quantity and nature of the contents, and any artificial flavorings or preservatives. In 1973, the Food and Drug Administration (FDA) released standards for nutritional labeling for all food products. Warnings of possible harmful effects are mandated for products such as over-the-counter drugs. Cigarette packages must carry a health warning, and the alcoholic content of beer, wines, and liquor must be on their containers. The Wool Products Labeling Act and the Synthetic Fibers Act prescribe that certain information concerning fabric content and washing instructions be conveyed on the label.

The label also can be used as a selling tool when instructions about the proper use and care of the product are placed on it. The consumerism movement is motivated to a degree by the desire for more product information. Thus imaginative use of the label can forestall aggressive action against the manufacturer on this score. Almost every question about the product which an average consumer might pose can be answered by a skillfully written label. Once again, this information-providing strategy is especially desirable when the product is sold via self-service. Informational labeling possesses a much neglected opportunity for the stimulation of product sales. Since product dissatisfaction often springs from user inefficiency, it is doubly important to make sure that instructions are clear, thus ensuring that the buyer is fully satisfied with his or her purchase and will add word-of-mouth advertising support to the seller's promotional mix. Labels may also serve to reinforce buyers' confidence concerning the wisdom of a purchase.

As with the other elements found in the product already discussed in this chapter, the label design should be done in good taste. It is an integral part of that intangible force which creates a brand image for the product. There is a need for modernizing labels from time to time unless an image of old-fashioned quality is being sought. A change in label, however, must be publicized, or regular buyers may become confused and even lost to the brand.

A recent development in labeling is the Universal Product Code (UPC). Described as the greatest collective change in labeling information in the history of the American food industry, UPC is a voluntary system wherein manufacturers place on all package labels a series of linear bars and a 10-digit number which describes the particular product. Once supermarkets obtain the necessary optical scanning equipment, a system of computerized checkout will be possible. This will speed up the checkout process and will enable store operators to have an almost instant check on inventory levels. What brands are selling, in what sizes, and similar information will be at their fingertips.

Is that really Alex Karras hugging a great big banana?

You bet, it's NFL All-pro defensive lineman Alex Karras. And he's hugging that big banana because he loves it.

You'll love it, too. In fact, you may be hugging that great big banana all the way to the bank. Because it's really gonna' sell bananas!

That great big banana is the Dole Banana Buddy. It's 4½ feet tall, inflatable and has a funny face kit. Dole is offering it for $2.95 plus two Dole banana labels. And kids across the country are going to find out about the Dole Banana Buddy on prime time television this spring, (parents, too). They'll also read about the Buddy in the Sunday Comics. So naturally, they're going to want one.

And since you'll have the Dole Banana Buddy display in your produce department, they'll be buying bananas from you!

Let's put that all together—the Dole Banana Buddy, prime time television, comic ads, Banana Buddy display, Dole bananas and your produce department—it all adds up doesn't it?

No one is doing more to help you sell bananas than Dole.

The implications for advertising are at least threefold: (1) test-market experiments on new products or size/packaging modifications can be monitored on a day-to-day basis; (2) the success of special promotions, displays, and point-of-purchase advertising can more accurately be assessed; (3) misinterpretation of these data caused by time lag and human error will to a great extent be eliminated.

THE IMAGE OF THE PRODUCT AND THE BRAND

The use of the concepts of behaviorial science in the creation of advertisements which will stimulate favorable consumer responses is discussed fully in a later chapter. Without going into a detailed analysis here, we wish to point out that every phase of marketing can utilize such behaviorial concepts, because what today's consumer buys is not merely the end product of certain raw materials processed to certain specifications. What is wanted, sought, and bought are the benefits, physical and psychological, that the product can deliver to the buyer. One aspect of these benefits is the *image* of a product, which includes all the ideas the consumer possesses about it—the sort of people who make or use it, the kind of stores that sell it, the drama of the ingredients that go into it, the character of the advertising promoting it, the "personality" of the manufacturer. The image of the product is the sum of all the stimuli received by the buyer related to the product.

This bundle of psychological attributes is called the *product image*. Most advertisers, however, are more concerned with the *brand image*. The goal is not usually to sell more of the generic product, such as cars or toothpaste, but to sell a particular brand of automobile or dentifrice against competitive brands of the product. When considering the relative inherent interest in two different products, such as sports cars and life insurance, the concept of product image is, of

FIGURE 3.12
This label from a soup can contains the UPC markings which will help to automate supermarket checkouts.

Campbell's CONDENSED Cream of **Mushroom**

RECIPE REG. U.S PAT OFF

SOUPER GRAVY
When preparing gravy for roasted or fried meats, remove meat from pan; spoon off excess fat, saving drippings. On top of range, in roasting pan, add 1 can Campbell's Cream of Mushroom Soup, 2 to 4 tbsp. drippings. Heat, stirring to loosen browned bits. Thin to desired consistency with water. Serve with beef, chicken, turkey, pork, or potatoes. Makes about 1½ cups.

Campbell's

Now Improved... CREAMIER!

Cream of **Mushroom**

NET WT. 10¾ OZ. (305 GRAMS)

INGREDIENTS: WATER, MUSHROOMS, ENRICHED WHEAT FLOUR, CREAM, VEGETABLE OIL, SALT, NONFAT DRY MILK, MODIFIED FOOD STARCH, MONO-SODIUM GLUTAMATE, NATURAL FLA-VORING, YEAST EXTRACT AND DE-HYDRATED GARLIC.

CAMPBELL SOUP COMPANY
CAMDEN, N.J., U.S.A. 08101

DIRECTIONS: Stir soup in pan. Gradually stir 1 can of water into soup. Heat to boiling, stirring occasionally. For extra richness, prepare as above using ½ milk and ½ water. Makes about 2½ cups.

CREAM SAUCE: Stir contents well. Stir in ¼ to ½ cup of milk. Heat to boil; simmer 2 minutes, stirring. Makes 1½ cups. Serve on hamburgers, other meats, vegetables.

SOUP NET WT. 10¾ OZ.

108

ADVERTISING'S
ROLE
IN THE
MARKETING
PROCESS

course, useful. Some product categories do intrigue consumers more than others; obviously, it is easier to advertise products successfully if they are inherently interesting and appealing to potential buyers.

The concept of brand image helps to explain why two products that are technically identical are purchased by different people for different reasons. Thus, toilet soap A is preferred by young college women, while soap B, which has the same essential ingredients, is preferred by women over forty. When there are many similar products and a large number of brands, as in the case of beer, development of a distinct brand image is vital to market success. Advertising often contributes a great deal to such brand-image development.

A classic instance of this is the case of Marlboro cigarettes. As Draper Daniels relates in his book, *Giants, Pigmies, and Other Advertising People*, the Marlboro cigarette had a feminine image until the time when the Leo Burnett agency was awarded the account.[26] Furthermore, attitudinal research showed that all filter cigarettes were thought to be slightly more feminine than masculine. The Burnett and Marlboro people set about trying to revise the image of a filter-tip smoker. The package was redesigned, and the ad campaign featured rugged-appearing male models with the famous tattoo on one hand. A headline reading, "New from Philip Morris . . . the filter that delivers the goods on flavor," was devised to help convey the masculinity of the product. The rest is advertising history; the brand became a runaway best seller, and the Marlboro campaign is still running, projecting essentially the same image, although a cowboy and Marlboro Country have replaced the tattoo as the central visual element in the ads.

GOVERNMENT AND THE PRODUCT

For the past decade or more, American manufacturers have been under considerable pressure from activist groups in our society. The beginning of the modern consumerist movement is usually traced to the publication of Ralph Nader's book, *Unsafe at Any Speed*, in 1965. This exposé dealt with the lack of safety features in certain automobiles, and led to the demise of at least one model and the passage of several laws dealing with the physical makeup of various products, culminating in the establishment of the National Commission on Safety in 1969.

These laws deal with product characteristics per se, and are, of course, of great importance to manufacturers of affected product categories. The legislation dealing most directly with advertising is the Fair Packaging and Labeling Act, which became effective in 1961. Known as the "Truth-in-Packaging Act," the law seeks to make it easier for consumers to ascertain the quantity of contents in packages in order to permit value comparisons. Unfair and deceptive packaging

[26]Draper Daniels, *Giants, Pigmies, and Other Advertising People*, Crain Books, Chicago, 1974, pp. 238–242.

Catherine Deneuve for Chanel

N° 5
CHANEL
PERFUME

CHANEL

Perfume in the classic bottle from 9.50 to 400. Eau de Toilette from 7.00 to 20.00. Eau de Cologne from 4.50 to 20.00. Spray Perfume 7.00, and Spray Cologne 6.50.

110

ADVERTISING'S
ROLE
IN THE
MARKETING
PROCESS

and labeling were the target of the legislation, which prescribed rather technical rules. Package proliferation was diminished as a result of the law, and it is believed that passage of the act encouraged regulatory bodies to become more aggressive in other areas. As a consequence, a movement for governmental evaluation of products and the publication of the results in a fashion similar to *Consumer Reports* has developed. Two writers describe the situation in these words: "The consumer's rights to safety and product choice have been broadened to include the right to be informed. . . . It is possible that in the future the seller will have to justify all product and information innovations on the basis of consumer research."[27] The public policy issues involved are truly complex and must be monitored closely by marketing people.

SUMMARY

In this chapter we have continued to show how advertising serves business firms and their customers by examining how it is used in marketing. We then looked at the product itself and its position as the basis, the core of the advertising program. Advertising performs its role within the framework of marketing. Marketing is the function concerned with ensuring that products are ready when and where needed by users and that they are what is desired and will be purchased by those users. This is known as the marketing concept. It is a departure from early thinking which involved making products and then seeking to get users to buy what had already been made.

At the heart of the marketing process is the product itself. The term "product" encompasses more than tangible goods; it includes services and even ideas. The needs of both consumers and industrial users are served by products. The emphasis in this book, however, is on consumer products, which can be classified into three groups: convenience, shopping, and specialty goods. Each group has a different buying pattern, which calls for varying advertising strategies. Product positioning is a strategy which became popular in the early 1970s and involves considering not only the product's own physical characteristics and its image, but the way it is perceived by consumers in relationship to competitive brands. New products serve to keep individual firms dynamic and competitive and provide challenging opportunities for advertising.

The product, as the prime component of the marketing mix, involves more than its tangible entity. In its broader dimension are included the package, the brand name, trademarks and trade characters, and the label. These components must be given serious coordination when a comprehensive marketing program is being developed for the product. All facets are melded together to enhance the product and brand image. Furthermore, guidelines established by laws and governmental agencies must be followed. Added together, decisions over product policy are complex and affect—and are affected by—advertising strategies and tactics.

[27]Warren A. French and Leila O. Schroeder, "Package Information Legislation Trends and Viewpoints," *MSU Business Topics*, Summer 1972, p. 43.

QUESTIONS FOR DISCUSSION

1 What is the role of advertising in the marketing process? In the marketing mix? Discuss.
2 How does advertising operate in a firm that has adopted and practices the marketing concept? Bring to class three ads that demonstrate this process in action.
3 From current advertising, describe a promotional campaign that illustrates the broadening of the concept of marketing. If feasible, bring tear sheets from the campaign.
4 Explain how the advertising strategy employed is varied when the product involved is a convenience good; a shopping good; a specialty good.
5 Describe product positioning, and explain how it is implemented through advertising planning and execution.
6 What are the principal means by which a product's package can help the consumer who purchases an item?
7 Explain the interrelationship between the brand name, trademark, and trade character of a given product. Is one more important than the others? Explain.
8 What is the purpose of the label found on a product or its package?
9 What impact will the Universal Product Code (UPC) have on the advertising of products?
10 Distinguish between the concepts of product image and brand image. Give an example of a product possessing a positive brand image? Why?

FOR FURTHER REFERENCE

Barach, Arnold B.: *Famous American Trademarks*, Public Affairs Press, Washington, 1971.

Corkindale, David, Sherril Kennedy, Harry Henry, and Gordon Wills: *Advertising Resource Allocation*, Cranfield School of Marketing, Cranfield, England, 1975.

Dichter, Ernest: *The New World of Packaging*, Cahners Books, Boston, 1975

Dreyfuss, Henry: *Symbol Sourcebook*, McGraw-Hill Book Company, New York, 1972.

Kotler, Philip: *Marketing Management: Analysis, Planning and Control*, 3rd ed., Prentice-Hall, Inc., Englewood Cliffs, N.J., 1976.

Neubauer, Robert G.: *Packaging: The Contemporary Media*, Van Nostrand Reinhold Company, New York, 1973.

Schwartz, David J.: *Marketing Today*, Harcourt, Brace, Jovanovich, New York, 1973.

Stanton, William J.: *Fundamentals of Marketing*, 4th ed., McGraw-Hill Book Company, New York, 1975.

Wasson, Chester R.: *Product Management*, Challenge Books, St. Charles, Ill., 1971.

CHAPTER 4
ADVERTISING AND DISTRIBUTION

In a society that relies on mass production to satisfy its demand for goods, most products reach the consumer after passing through many steps from raw materials to finished goods, from producer to sales outlet, from retail stores to the ultimate user—the consumer. In a craft society, an artisan makes an entire product from start to finish and may even be responsible for finding the component raw materials. When the product is complete, the artisan must meet with the potential customer on a face-to-face basis. In our economy, or the economy of any developed nation such as Japan or the countries of Western Europe, the labor needed to produce most products has been subdivided. The channels of distribution—the paths that products take in moving from producers to ultimate consumers—have also changed. A group of specialists is responsible for facilitating this flow of goods. In this chapter we shall examine the channels of distribution and show how advertising aids marketing people, the specialists in distribution, in informing the buying public about their products.

CHANNELS OF DISTRIBUTION

Marketing people think of a channel of distribution as a sequence of marketing institutions, consisting principally of wholesalers and retailers. Wholesalers buy from producers and sell to retailers or to firms purchasing goods for business purposes. Retailers buy for resale to consumers for personal use. The function of marketing is to facilitate the closing of the gap which separates producers from consumers. Four marketing activities are involved: transportation, inventory, promotion, and transaction.[1] Our concern, of course, is with the promotional part of the gap-filling process.

Two parallel systems operate within the channels of the distribution framework. The obvious one is the *physical distribution* of goods and involves the transportation and inventory activities. The other equally important part of the channel system is *communication*, and here the promotion and transaction functions dominate. Promotion, as we are using the term, deals with all activities that provide information, including persuasion. Four basic marketing activities are available for use in a promotional mix. They are personal selling, advertising, sales promotion, and public relations. The goal in using these promotional methods is, of course, to close the perceptual—or knowledge—gap existing between producer and consumer. How advertising functions

[1] This discussion is based in part on William P. Dommermuth and R. Clifton Anderson, "Distribution Systems—Firms, Functions, and Efficiencies," *MSU Business Topics*, Spring 1969, p. 52.

114

ADVERTISING'S
ROLE
IN THE
MARKETING
PROCESS

in closing this gap is more easily understood against a background of channel structure and strategy.

Channel Strategy and Promotional Activity

The choice of the correct channel of distribution is a critical decision for manufacturers, complicated by the large array of alternatives available to them. Some combinations of intermediaries are much more efficient in tapping potential markets than are others, and the marketplace is ever-changing, thus causing new intermediaries to appear and established ones to disappear. This decision dilemma is complicated further by the tendency for markets to become segmented with different groups seeking preferred products at different retail outlets. To reach different market segments successfully may require the use of several different trade channels by one manufacturer. The proper identification of these market segments requires a knowledge of consumer behavior patterns.

Three useful devices are available to manufacturers to help them move their products through the channels of distribution: (1) price, (2) personal selling, and (3) advertising. These three devices can be characterized as the lubricants for the machinery of marketing, and to a considerable degree success in marketing depends upon the ability to decide which of these three tools to use and in what combination.

At first blush, price would seem to be the easiest lubricant to use. A low-price approach usually is the quickest way to move goods. But using price as the primary appeal in selling a product has many drawbacks. It is easy for competitors to meet the low price, thus eroding the initial advantage to the price-cutter; a price war may ensue and eventually force one out of business. Equally serious is the possibility that a product's image of quality will be lost through a drastic reduction in price. When an attempt is made to return to the former higher price, consumer resistance and resentment can be encountered. Product quality may also deteriorate when manufacturers are caught in price wars. Obviously, profits can be reduced below healthy levels if prices are lowered to extremes. Thus, sellers have several good, sound business reasons for trying to minimize price as a key element in their marketing strategies.

Manufacturers and intermediaries therefore may emphasize personal selling or advertising, or both, when avoiding a strategy based on price cutting. These promotional activities are designed to substitute persuasion for price as the reason for buying products. Reasons for buying—other than price—are provided to prospective customers, showing the benefits to be derived from the purchase of the product.

Personal selling receives high priority in marketing programs for products needing personal contact and face-to-face presentations to get consumers to make the purchase decision. This is true also when demonstration and detailed explanation of the product are important, when the item being sold is an intangible such as life insurance, or when the purchase is a major one for the consumer as in the case of cars and homes. Personal selling remains an important mover of goods in the United States, although its relative role has been lessened by the trend toward self-service retailing. Personal selling and advertising often work together in a complementary way, with advertising paving the way for the salesperson's approach, making the sales presentation easier and shorter as the prospect already has some information about the product from advertising.

How advertising lubricates the distributive process constitutes the main thrust of this chapter. One approach to explaining the process is to classify advertising according to the nature of the selling task to be done. From this point of view, there are at least three broad categories of advertising: (1) national, (2) retail, and (3) business. These categories, often called the *functional forms of advertising*, are determined by the potential extent or type of audience coverage. Before describing them, however, the subject of advertising objectives is explored.

GENERAL OBJECTIVES OF ADVERTISING

Advertising is only one facet of business enterprise, really a subactivity of marketing which, along with production and finance, is one of the major functions of business management. To discharge their managerial responsibilities fully, managers should be capable of evaluating all aspects of their business operations. From a societal and philosophical viewpoint, the primary objective of any business endeavor is to fulfill the needs of its customers. Failure to accomplish this basic goal can lead to business failure and economic waste.

We are interested here, however, in the practical, business point of view. Put bluntly, the primary objective of business is *to make sales which yield a profit in the long run*. The influence of advertising on sales and profits thus becomes the important consideration. Every business manager needs to know how advertising helps in the achievement of the broader objectives of business.

Effect of Advertising on Demand

Advertising can maximize the demand for goods and services. Inactive demand is often latent within the consumer, waiting to be brought into each person's consciousness through advertising or other forms of stimulation. Although, technically speaking, advertising does not create demand for products, most advertising is designed to stimulate demand.

One way of obtaining more total revenue is for the firm to charge a

116

ADVERTISING'S
ROLE
IN THE
MARKETING
PROCESS

higher price for each unit of its output. By pointing out the advantages of a product or enhancing its image in a way that is of value to some consumers, advertising is a means of convincing prospects that the product is worth the price charged. A more usual alternative is to use advertising to increase the number of units sold. The total sales revenue for the producer is increased in either case.

Some products are more sensitive to increased advertising than are others; that is, the demand for some products can be stimulated more than for other products. This situation involves the concept of *expansibility of demand*, which exists when the use of advertising and/or personal selling will bring about an increase in the total demand for a product.

Advertising can stimulate the demand for any product in three basic ways. First, present users may be persuaded to increase present rates of product consumption. No better example can be found than the "take more pictures" strategy followed by Kodak for many decades. Thus, we see in Figure 4.1 that Kodak urges camera owners "to feed your camera this weekend." A second way is to tell present users about new uses for the product. This approach is beautifully illustrated by the Arm & Hammer Baking Soda case. The brand, while synonymous in consumers' minds with its product category, was in a sales slump as home baking declined. When the company hit upon the idea of selling its product as a "freshener" for the home refrigerator, a single television commercial explaining this product-use concept put the familiar A&H box into 40 million refrigerators.[2] The company further has advocated the use of baking soda in cat litter boxes, for brushing teeth, as a fire extinguisher, in a variety of camping situations, and in swimming pools to reduce eye burn from chlorine. Company sales have increased sharply, and a commodity product suddenly has marketing glamour. Drawing new users into the market for the product is the third alternative for the firm seeking to increase demand. The airlines have been engaged in a longtime quest for "nonfliers." When one realizes that 45 percent of American adults have never flown in a regular passenger airplane, the latent potential for the airlines of America can be readily grasped. However, no airline has been able to develop ads which are able to get large numbers of nonfliers to buy tickets.

Effect of Advertising on Profits

Increased sales are worthless unless they lead to increased profits. Although profits may be overlooked in the short run in order to obtain certain other worthwhile objectives, future profits, of necessity, are paramount in the manager's thinking and planning. Advertising may

---

[2] *Advertising Age*, Sept. 2, 1974, p. 10.

Pick up several rolls of your favorite kind of Kodak film
at your supermarket. And have a memorable weekend.

Kodak makes your pictures count.

FIGURE 4.1
A film manufactur-
er encourages
product users to
stock up. The idea
behind this ad is
that if there is film
in the camera, the
item is more likely
to be used.

affect the profit performance of a business firm in two important ways.

If advertising does increase sales, the increase may favorably affect *product costs*. If plant capacity is fully utilized and other cost reductions are employed (such as specialization of labor and quantity discounts on raw materials), the per-unit cost of the product will often be lowered. As manufacturing costs are lowered, profits are increased. Advertising similarly may affect *marketing costs*. Less personal selling may be required because of the advertising program. Other marketing costs, such as transportation and storage expenses per unit, may be reduced because of increased sales.

SPECIFIC OBJECTIVES OF ADVERTISING

Having seen how advertising fits into the overall business and marketing framework of the firm, we now deal with the specific objectives of advertising. The importance of the topic is expressed in the following quotation:

> In its search for new sources of productivity gains, management can find no more fertile field than advertising. A shockingly large share of the 12 billion spent annually for advertising is wasted for one fundamental reason: lack of well-defined objectives.

> In search of profit and growth, corporate management has focused its attention on the technological aspects of business. In the past, here was where the big productivity gains could be made; and here was where top management felt most competent and comfortable. But improved technology is no longer the whole answer. A drug company president tells me: "Advertising has become the second largest item in our corporate budget.

GIRD THYSELF, PADRE!
The menu said Roquefort. You said Roquefort.
Wilt abide "something else"—and PAY for Roquefort?

Roquefort means <u>Roquefort</u> Cheese. Made of sheep's milk. Ripened in the Roquefort Caverns. Not "something like it." Definitely not blue cheese. Better restaurants welcome the chance to show you they serve the real thing. Ask to see <u>Roquefort</u> on the label of the portion or the loaf. Just like the label on a vintage wine.

Roquefort Association, Inc., 41 E. 42 St., N.Y., N.Y. 10017

FIGURE 4.3
The specific objective of this ad is to prevent product substitution.

120

ADVERTISING'S
ROLE
IN THE
MARKETING
PROCESS

The chips are getting so blue that top management can no longer afford to be uninformed—naive, if you will—about advertising."[3]

More than 15 years have passed since Colley made this challenging statement, and total advertising expenditures are in excess of $30 billion; nevertheless, his observation is still true, and the need for better productivity in business has increased.

Each ad and every advertising campaign should have a basic keynote idea if it is to be successful; the theme must be designed to attain *specific* objectives, which are manifestations of the current strategy being employed by the advertiser to secure the general objectives of increased sales volume and profit improvement. The advantages of an "advertising by objectives" program are:

a The advertising effort is integrated with other marketing mix elements, leading to a consistent, logical marketing plan.

b The advertising agency can prepare and evaluate relevant plans and also recommend appropriate media.

c Advertising budgets can be determined more accurately.

d Top management can appraise advertising plans and can maintain control over advertising activities.

e It permits meaningful measurement of advertising performance.[4]

The number of specific objectives for advertising can be infinite. Thus, we shall not attempt to enumerate them comprehensively. Instead, we shall discuss briefly a few common instances to illustrate the point.

Advertising can be used to produce sales directly, as is done in mail-order selling, or as it is now sometimes called, "direct-response marketing." Such advertising asks consumers to send money in payment for the product being featured. Increasing floor traffic in the store is the aim of most retail advertising. Advertising also may be employed to produce leads to prospective customers as in the case where the consumer sends for a booklet which is delivered by a salesperson in search of a sale.

The objectives we have been describing are the *marketing objectives* of advertising. Most national consumer advertisements, however, are less direct in their objectives. For some time now a controversy has raged among advertising executives over whether a statement of advertising objectives can be couched in marketing terms at all. One view is that advertising goals should be stated in communication terms

[3] Russell H. Colley, "Squeezing the Waste Out of Advertising," *Harvard Business Review* September–October 1962, p. 76.
[4] David Corkindale, Sherril Kennedy, Harry Henry, and Gordon Wills, *Advertising Resource Allocation*, 1974, Cranfield School of Management, Cranfield, England, summarizing from S. Majaro, "Advertising Objectives," *Management Today*, January 1970.

only, if meaningful measurement of results is to follow.[5] The rationale is that marketing goals are dependent on the total marketing effort, which includes advertising, but advertising cannot take full credit when marketing goals are reached.

An advertising goal is defined by Colley as a "specific communication task, to be accomplished among a defined audience to a given degree in a given period of time."[6] Consumer awareness of a product or an idea, for example, can be surveyed before and after the advertising campaign is run. Upon comparison of before-and-after results of the two surveys, it is easy to determine if the communication goal has been achieved. Colley's thinking is that the statement of advertising goals should be made specific as to (1) audience, (2) degree, and (3) terms. He also urges that the statement of goals be put in writing.

Some advertisements may feature special merchandise offers; others aim to introduce a new product, model, or innovation. The objective may be to weld a family of products together so that the public will associate all the items in the advertiser's product line in its thinking, or the advertiser might wish to dispel a wrong impression about the product, remove prejudices about the product, create a favorable brand image, or reach influential people. Probably the most commonly stated objective is in terms of awareness. Thus, Rexham Corporation once set as its advertising objective "to raise the level of awareness of Rexham from 0% to 20% in 12 months."[7] The company had changed its name and wanted customers, present and prospective, to know. A series of four-color ads were run in business magazines, and the level of awareness increased from 0 percent to 38 percent in 12 months.[8]

The objective of advertising in consumer media may be to increase employees' pride in the company, or it may be to convince intermediaries of the desirability of stocking a certain brand. Another objective might be to convince financial leaders of the firm's importance in the national economy. If you take a current magazine and attempt to classify each full-page advertisement according to its apparent specific objective, you will recognize the great variety of possible advertising objectives. Although an advertisement may fail to achieve its immediate specific objective, it could still contribute to the creation of a favorable attitude toward the product, which in the long run might result in the achievement of the general objective of sales and profit.

[5] Discussion based on Russel H. Colley, *Defining Advertising Goals for Measured Results*, Association of National Advertisers, Inc., New York, 1961.
[6] Ibid., p. 14.
[7] *Objectives & Results* No. 2, American Business Press, Inc., New York, 1972, p. 6.
[8] Ibid.

122

ADVERTISING'S
ROLE
IN THE
MARKETING
PROCESS

Just because you love avocado doesn't mean it has to be fattening.

Because of our smooth, creamy texture and satisfying flavor some people think avocado might be too high in calories. Yet in half of an 8¼ ounce avocado there are 145 calories. And avocado gives you vitamins A, C, B6 and folic acid. So count avocado *in*, when you're counting calories. So you shouldn't feel deprived.

FIGURE 4.4
Dispelling a mis-
conception is the
objective of the
advertisement.

THE ROLE OF ADVERTISING IN
THE MARKETING CHANNEL

Advertising can be classified according to its function, and each functional classification possesses its own distinctive characteristics. Collectively these various forms of advertising close the perceptual gap which exists between producers and consumers of goods and services.

National Advertising

A manufacturer who decides to sell under his own brand name is faced with the need to stimulate consumer demand for the product. Engaging in national advertising is one way to approach this task. *National advertising* is any advertising done by a manufacturer of a consumer product for the purpose of convincing consumers that they will benefit from the purchase and use of the product. It is advertising done by the manufacturer or producer in contrast to that done by a retailer.

The word "national" conveys a picture of mass markets extending from coast to coast and calls to mind such names as Procter & Gamble, General Motors, and Exxon. Such large firms do, of course, employ national advertising in large quantities, but the term also applies to the promotional efforts of companies with limited market coverage. National advertising exists when a trademarked product that has the *potentiality* of being sold throughout the nation is, in fact, advertised.

When a new manufacturing firm appears on the business scene, it usually does not seek immediate national distribution; funds are limited, production capacity is low, personnel are few, and distribution know-how is limited. Management sells its output in the local community, and as conditions warrant, extends market coverage in concentric circles fanning out from the home plant. Well-established companies often introduce new-product items on a limited regional basis, too, through a plan of test markets.

In such situations, embarking upon an advertising campaign in nationally circulated media would be foolish. Potential customers would have little chance of seeing the message. Therefore, the manufacturer uses media serving the geographic area to be tapped. Local newspapers, local radio and television stations, and local outdoor plants provide appropriate media vehicles. This advertiser, nevertheless, is classified as a national advertiser, because his purpose is to get customers to purchase his product at any retail outlet which may stock the item.

Retail Advertising

In national advertising the message says, in effect, "Buy *our* brand." The manufacturer cares very little where the product is purchased. The

124

ADVERTISING'S
ROLE
IN THE
MARKETING
PROCESS

retail advertiser, on the other hand, has a different goal. His advertising message says, "Buy X brand at *our* store." Where the consumer makes the purchase is more important to the retailer than is the brand purchased.

Not all retail advertisements feature nationally advertised brands. Retailers may place selling messages for unbranded merchandise, as is common in the case of shopping goods, in their advertisements. Large-scale retailers stock private label goods which are promoted in a fashion similar to nationally advertised brands; that is, messages for these products may appear in the mass media. Recently Sears Roebuck & Co. has become the third largest advertiser in the United States with total national advertising expenditures of $220 million in 1974.[9] Over 90 percent of the company's sales volume is from its own brands, or put another way, less than 10 percent comes from nationally advertised brands. Retail-store advertising by the chain amounted to more than $275 million in the same year.[10] Giant retailers, thus, employ both national and retail advertising in their promotional mixes, and their private brands become, in effect, national brands which are sold exclusively in their own retail stores.

Retail and national advertising differ in at least five ways: (1) territory covered, (2) customer relationship, (3) target-audience interest, (4) expected response, and (5) use of price. Generally speaking, the retailer works in a more restricted geographic market than does the national advertiser. This proximity to the market means that the retailer's message can be closer to the likes, preferences, prejudices, and buying habits of the intended audience, which is usually more receptive than the national advertising audience. The prospective retail customer, in many instances, seeks out the advertisements of his or her favorite stores. The retail advertiser strives for an immediate response to most of his advertising, while the national advertiser usually is more interested in establishing long-range favorable attitudes. The retailer frequently stresses price in retail copy; the national advertiser may play down or ignore this inducement, as prices may vary from region to region. The difference between retail and national advertising can be seen in Figures 4.5 and 4.6. Here the Goodyear Tire & Rubber Company wears two advertising hats simultaneously. In its national advertising Goodyear is interested in showing the superiority of the Goodyear brand of tire, in its retail ads the goal is to pull bargain hunters into Goodyear outlets.

The Local Advertising Concept

We use the term "retail advertising" in a precise and narrow framework, namely, to describe the advertising done by actual retail

---

[9] *Advertising Age*, Aug. 18, 1975, p. 184.
[10] Ibid.

establishments for reasons described above. As a cursory examination of the local media in any community will reveal, there is an appreciable amount of advertising sponsored by local business firms which falls outside this narrow definition, for example, the advertising done by service institutions such as banks, dry cleaners, beauty parlors, and karate schools. The advertiser's aim is to convey the consumer benefits to be derived by the local buying public from the use of the advertised services; brand loyalty, so to speak, must be created for these services. The advertising done by these service establishments is carried in local media. This advertising possesses some of the characteristics of retail advertising and some of national advertising. It should not be classified as retail advertising just because it is run by a local establishment; therefore, we recommend that the special label of "local advertising" be used.

The other important part of the distribution channel—the wholesaler—usually plays an insignificant role as an advertiser. Wholesalers may be involved in the administration of cooperative advertising, which we shall now discuss. In general, however, these intermediaries perform other important marketing functions but do little advertising.

Cooperative Advertising

Some manufacturers have a special interest in the advertising efforts of their dealers, particularly in the case of specialty goods. When the producer mounts an extensive program of national advertising of a product, he or she doesn't want prospective purchasers to have trouble finding retail outlets that handle the product. Affirmative action should be taken to make such store identification easy for the consumer. Street signs and window displays can make a contribution, but the most fruitful means of identifying the retail outlet selling the manufacturer's product is to advertise over the dealer's name. To facilitate this goal, a procedure known as *cooperative advertising*—a technique which is an important part of the promotional programs of many manufacturers—has developed.

Cooperative ads appear to the general public to be regular retail advertisements of a local store. The featured product is a nationally advertised brand of merchandise, and the signature is that of the local retail store. The brand manufacturer often provides the retailer with the material or guidelines from which the ad is actually produced, thus assuring that the message says what the manufacturer wants it to say. The media costs are often shared. The managerial details of the cooperative advertising arrangement are discussed thoroughly in a later chapter.

Business Advertising

Our discussion of the functional forms of advertising up to this point has revolved around consumer products and the interrelationship

126
ADVERTISING'S
ROLE
IN THE
MARKETING
PROCESS

IT KEEPS ITS FEET EVEN IN THE RAIN

FIGURE 4.5
A tire manufacturer advertises his brand through national media. The ad appeared as a black-and-white spread in *Sports Illustrated*. Note the emphasis on product features.

between their distribution and advertising. From the discussion in Chapter 3 we know that there is another broad category of products known as industrial goods, which are sold for business use rather than for personal consumption. Manufacturers of industrial products face many problems that are similar to those challenging national advertis-

THE SECRET OF BIGFOOT CAPTURED ON FILM

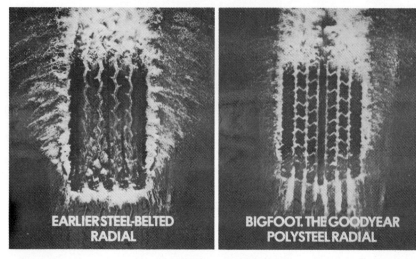

ers of consumer products. Prospective users must be told of the product's existence, and persuasion often is required before the item is purchased. Advertising is an integral part of the marketing mix of firms producing industrial goods. Advertising designed to communicate with buyers acting in a role of "producer" rather than "consumer" has been given many names, including "trade advertising," "industrial

128
ADVERTISING'S
ROLE
IN THE
MARKETING
PROCESS
.

MAY...1975

BIGFOOT
GOODYEAR POLYSTEEL RADIAL
25% OFF
save $60 to $92 per set of four tires

40,000 MILE "CUSTOM POLYSTEEL" RADIALS

These Goodyear steel belted radials (1) save money, (2) use less fuel, (3) provide longer mileage, and (4) help conserve America's resources. Now is the time to buy these Custom Polysteel Radial tires that are original equipment on many 1975 new cars. Sale prices remain in effect through Tuesday night May 27.

RAIN CHECK — If we sell out of your size we will issue you a rain check, assuring future delivery at the advertised price.

WHITEWALL SIZE	FITS MODELS OF	REGULAR PRICE	25% OFF
AR78-13	Vega, Pinto, Gremlin, Colt, Falcon, Toyota & others	$60.85	$45.63
BR78-13	Vega, Colt, Dart, Pinto, Falcon, Mustang & others	$65.20	$48.90
DR78-14	Gremlin, Hornet, Javelin, Valiant, Duster, Barracuda, Maverick & others	$67.85	$50.88
ER78-14	Matador, Ambassador, Nova, Chevelle, Camaro, Dart, Mustang, Cougar & others	$69.00	$51.75
FR78-14	Torino, Ambassador, Camaro, Cutlass, Chevelle, Challenger, Roadrunner, Charger & others	$74.55	$55.91
HR78-14	Matador Wagon, Sportwagon, Vista Cruiser, LeMans Wagon, Charger Wagon & others	$83.75	$62.81
JR78-14	Chevrolet Wagon, Olds 98, Pontiac Wagon, Chrysler Town and Country Wagon	$87.80	$65.85
GR78-15	Chevrolet, Polara, Galaxie, Monterey, Fury, Catalina & others	$79.80	$59.85
HR78-15	Buick, Chrysler, Dodge, Ford, Olds, Pontiac	$85.75	$64.31
LR78-15	Buick, Cadillac, Chevrolet Wagon, Plymouth, Pontiac & Lincoln Continental	$92.85	$69.63

Plus $2.02 to $3.46 F.E.T. per tire and old tire.

Lube and Oil Change
$4.88
Up to 5 qts. of major brand multi-grade oil
• Complete chassis lubrication & oil change • Helps ensure longer wearing parts & smooth, quiet performance • Please phone for appointment • Includes light trucks

Engine Tune-Up
$32.95
Add $4 for 8 cyl., $2 for air cond.
• With electronic equipment our professionals fine-tune your engine, installing new points, plugs & condenser • Helps maintain a smooth running engine for maximum gas mileage • Includes Datsun, Toyota, VW & light trucks

SEE THE INDY RACE ON TV
ABC network, 8:30-10:30 (E.D.S.T.) Sunday, May 25

Sale Ends Tuesday Night May 27

GOODYEAR

7 Ways to Buy
• Cash • Our Own Customer Credit Plan • Master Charge • BankAmericard • American Express Money Card • Carte Blanche • Diners Club

See Your Independent Dealer For His Price. Prices As Shown At Goodyear Service Stores.

Ad No. 550-111"(B&W) 6 Col. x 18.5"

FIGURE 4.6
The same product is displayed locally in newspapers as retail advertising. Note the emphasis on price. Usually store locations are added to this material as created by the manufacturer's advertising department.

advertising," "vocational advertising," and "business advertising." We prefer to use the last-mentioned term and include four specific categories within the broad classification: (1) trade advertising, (2) industrial advertising, (3) farm advertising, and (4) professional advertising.

Trade Advertising Manufacturers use trade advertising to persuade retailers to stock their products, to feature them in their stores, and to "tie in" with national advertising campaigns in their retail ads. Retailers stock those items that customers will buy, are generally limited in shelf space, and are short of funds for inventory; therefore, retailers must be convinced that stocking the products of individual manufacturers is to their advantage. Personal selling, by the manufacturer's sales force or by wholesalers, often carries the major responsibility for this job, but trade advertising makes the personal selling task easier.

Direct mail and specialized business publications are the principal media employed in trade advertising. Nearly every retail-business category has one or more specialized magazines or newspapers which circulate among retailers in each kind of specific endeavor. Grocery-store operators, for example, may read *Progressive Grocer, Chain Store Age, Supermarketing*, or any number of regional publications aimed specifically at them.

Trade advertising also may be directed to the operators of service establishments and to wholesalers. Some advertising placed in mass consumer media may be directed to retailers or other special groups in order to get the attention of the retailer, industrial user, or professional person when in a relaxed mood. *Vogue*, as an example, carries advertisements by synthetic materials manufacturers, such as Du Pont, aimed not only at consumers but at garment manufacturers and retailers as well. The thrust of the advertisement meant for retailers would be classified as trade advertising; that meant for other manufacturers would be industrial advertising.

Industrial Advertising A vast array of items, including machinery, equipment, raw materials, semiprocessed materials, parts, and operating supplies, are used by manufacturers and other producers to facilitate the performance of their basic productive function. The manufacturers of industrial goods wish to see that their products are bought by other producers, and they are not concerned with securing retail distribution. Personal selling is significantly more important in the distribution of industrial goods than in the case of consumer products. Prospective buyers are fewer; they tend to be in concentrated geographic locations, and their average purchase is considerably larger. Advertising is used to speed the sales of industrial products, to reduce the costs of personal sales efforts, and to improve sales effectiveness. For example, in one study involving the marketing of

130

ADVERTISING'S
ROLE
IN THE
MARKETING
PROCESS

The case for

- Full line of consistent high quality products.
- Efficient service from 41 strategically located distribution centers.
- Number one selling brand of Wieners, Cold Cuts and Bacon.
- Responsive to consumer needs and preferences.
- Exclusive packaging innovations for product protection and consumer convenience.
- Advertising reach and frequency that presells your customers.
- Peg displays and other merchandising aids to increase product turnover.

FIGURE 4.7
Several reasons
why retailers
should stock the
manufacturer's
brand are given in
this trade ad.

heavy electrical equipment to the public utility industry, it was shown that when a client had been called upon by a salesperson and also had been exposed to advertising for the product, preference for the brand increased 21 percent over instances in which sales calls alone were present.[11]

The list of industrial magazines is long and varied. The advertising

[11] *How Advertising Works in Today's Marketplace*, McGraw-Hill Publications, New York, 1971, p. 5.

KELLY , NASON
INCORPORATED
Advertising

Client: CHURCH & DWIGHT
Product: ARM & HAMMER BAKING SODA
Title: "REFRIGERATOR/SINK"

Comm'l. No.: ZCTB 2063
Length: 30 SECONDS

(WOMAN OPENING REFRIGERATOR)
I've got a secret in my refrigerator . . .

it's there way in back. See?

An open box of Arm & Hammer Baking Soda. It actually absorbs food odors . . .

whether you have cheese, onions, broccoli, even fish . . .

it will keep your refrigerator sweeter, cleaner and fresher smelling . . .

At the end of two months, put in a new box . . .

and pour the old box down a drain . . .

to help make it clean-smelling.

Arm & Hammer Baking Soda. A nice little secret for your refrigerator.

FIGURE 4.2
This photoboard shows a now classic television commercial used by a baking soda manufacturer to expand demand for the product by showing new uses for it.

The reduction in manufacturing or marketing costs which can result from advertising must be weighed against the costs of that advertising before we can say the advertising has helped to improve the profits of the firm. These possibilities—the reduction of production and marketing costs through the use of advertising—are tied directly to the role of advertising in increasing sales volume for the product.

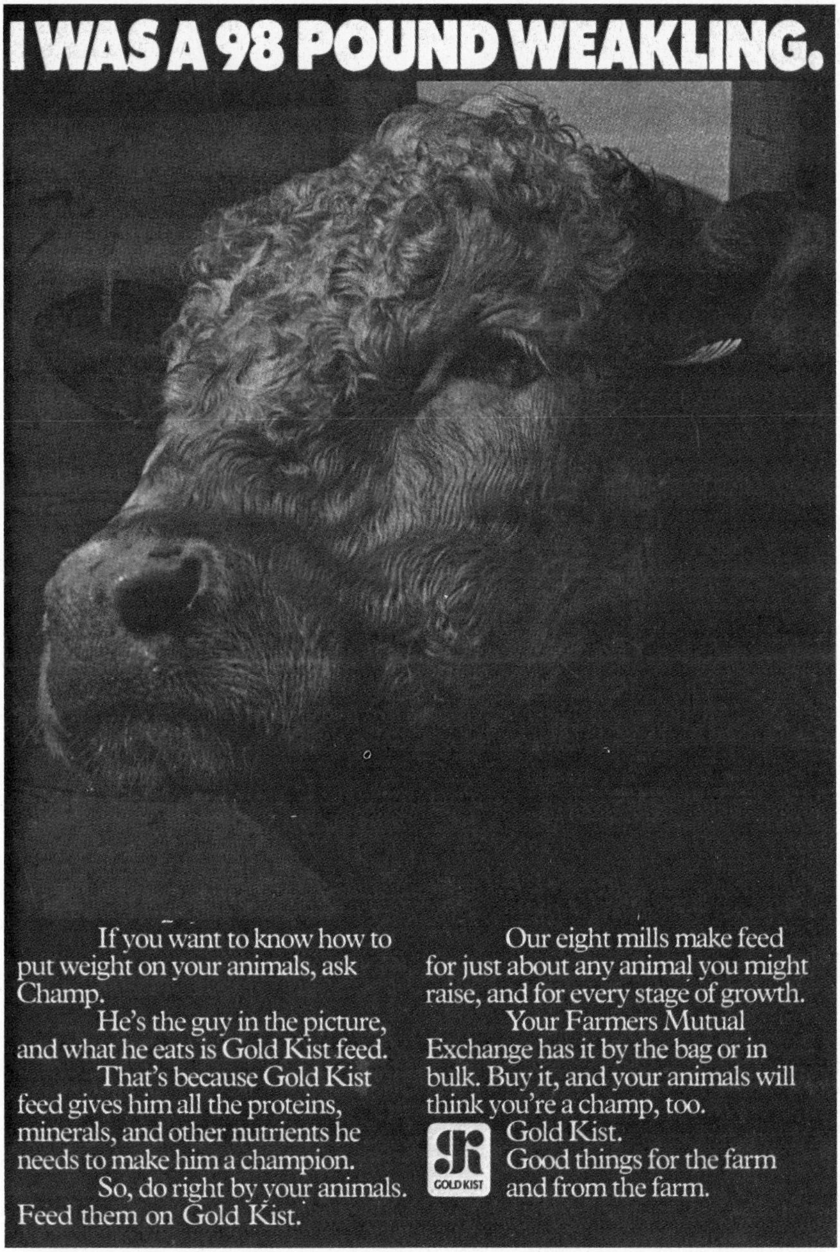

I WAS A 98 POUND WEAKLING.

If you want to know how to put weight on your animals, ask Champ.

He's the guy in the picture, and what he eats is Gold Kist feed.

That's because Gold Kist feed gives him all the proteins, minerals, and other nutrients he needs to make him a champion.

So, do right by your animals. Feed them on Gold Kist.

Our eight mills make feed for just about any animal you might raise, and for every stage of growth.

Your Farmers Mutual Exchange has it by the bag or in bulk. Buy it, and your animals will think you're a champ, too.

 Gold Kist.
Good things for the farm and from the farm.

FIGURE 4.9
Farm products resemble industrial products. Promotional strategies are very similar as shown in this farm ad.

contain a mixture of editorial material and advertising. On the one hand, the contents are really industrial in nature, aimed at the farmer as a producer. Feed and fertilizer manufacturers present testimonials indicating how other farmers profited from giving their cattle "brand X" feed or how soybean crop yields were improved after spreading

134

ADVERTISING'S
ROLE
IN THE
MARKETING
PROCESS

"brand Y" fertilizer on their land. The profit motive is the basic appeal in this part of farm advertising, as it is in most forms of business advertising. The industrial nature of farming has recently been recognized by the introduction of farm publications appealing only to the business side of farm life. Thus, *Big Farmer* is received by farmers who earn $25,000 or more a year from farming. Yet farm magazines are now listed in the consumer magazine edition of *Standard Rate And Data Service* (SRDS). The duality still exists and confuses the classification of farm advertising, which in the overall array of advertising is very small, accounting for about 0.3 of 1 percent of all advertising dollars in the United States.

Professional Advertising   Historically, professional people, such as doctors, dentists, lawyers, and architects, have been restricted by ethical standards from advertising their desire to secure clients. This restriction by professional associations seems about to be relaxed, and we may soon see ads by such individuals going beyond announcements of a new office location or the acquisition of a new partner. Our concern here, however, is for advertising aimed *at* the professional person, not *by* him or her. This kind of advertising is known as *professional advertising.*

Professional advertising in many ways is similar to trade advertising, except that the professional does not buy goods for the purpose of reselling them to clients; his or her role is to prescribe or recommend to the client the purchase of certain products. The physician designates specific drugs through the pharmacist, and the dentist says, "Use Crest toothpaste." The architect specifies a brand of insulation material to be used in the house being built under his guidance.

Personal selling also is very important in reaching professional people. Manufacturer's sales representatives, called "detail men," go out into the field and talk about company products to doctors, dentists, and architects. Ads in professional journals, such as *Medical Economics* or *Architectural Forum*, tell how the client of the reader can benefit from the use of the product. Direct mail and product samples also are important in the promotional mix of such manufacturers. Because the professional's career success depends upon the satisfaction of his clients and does not result from the sale of specific goods, it is to his benefit to keep abreast of the newest developments in his field. Professional journals and their advertising are must reading.

OTHER WAYS TO CLASSIFY ADVERTISING

We have classified advertising by the kind of selling task facing the advertiser, and we have studied the essentials of national, retail, and business advertising. These explanations have revolved around *who*

Certainly not...

Clearly, no one in his senses would use chewing gum at a time and place such as this.

However there are times and places where the use of chewing gum can be most beneficial; in fact its discreet use is a mark of tact and consideration for others as it is a definite aid to oral hygiene.

Doublemint chewing gum is especially made for such people. Its ingredients are carefully selected throughout, even its flavour has been double distilled; in fact, as its name implies, Doublemint is double good and gives you double benefits in many ways.

Try some at the right time and in the right place and see for yourself.

FIGURE 4.10
An unusual primary-demand stimulation advertisement, which led to an 83 percent increase in use of the advertiser's brand in three years, is shown. [*Wrigley Company Ltd.*]

136

ADVERTISING'S
ROLE
IN THE
MARKETING
PROCESS

sponsors the advertising. Other classification systems emphasize the *strategy behind the advertising*, regardless of sponsorship. Several alternative approaches to advertising, many of which are used in combination by a typical advertiser, are now discussed.

Primary and Selective Demands

The goal of primary-demand advertising is to stimulate a demand for a class or category of product, while selective-demand advertising

DANCER - FITZGERALD - SAMPLE, Inc.

Client: COFFEE COMMITTEE
Product: COFFEE
As Filmed/Recorded: COLOR

1. (MUSIC THROUGH-OUT) CHORUS: Coffee beans and human beings

2. were meant to be the best of friends.

5. with the wake-up aroma of roasted beans.

6. WOMAN: It warms the chill of a winter's day.

9. Its divine taste is super-natural.

10. CHORUS: Coffee beans and human beings

FIGURE 4.11
This 30-second tel-evision commer-cial is designed to stimulate primary demand for coffee, regardless of brand. [*United States Coffee Council.*]

attempts to create a demand for a particular brand in the product category. The distinction can be explained by the example of coffee. This product category has experienced a decline in per capita consumption over a long period of years. Americans drank 38.8 gallons of coffee per person in 1964 and only 34.4 gallons by 1973. Thus, the United States Coffee Association, representing many coffee producers, was understandably concerned about the situation and started to advertise in 1975 to see if Americans wouldn't consider coffee as one of their beverage alternatives. Figure 4.11 is an example of this *primary-*

Title: "NOV.-DEC. #4"
Commercial No.: CPCT5316
Date: 11/26/75   **Length:** 30 SECONDS

3. MAN: (VO) Good morning.

4. Coffee helps you start the day's routines

7. MAN: (VO) The price is never much to pay. Get it?

8. Relax with a cup, be more rational.

11. were meant to be the best of friends.

Got a special machine?
Get a special coffee:
New Maxwell House®A.D.C.™

A.D.C. means 'automatic drip coffee'.
A special blend, a special grind just for automatic drip coffee makers.

At last, perfect coffee. That's what new Maxwell House A.D.C. makes in any home automatic drip coffee maker.

Perfect, because A.D.C. is blended and ground just for the new machines. For smooth, full-flavored, utterly satisfying coffee. *Perfect coffee.*

That's why we say A.D.C. *means* 'automatic drip coffee'.

So if you've got a special machine, get a special coffee. New A.D.C.—only from Maxwell House.

new

MAXWELL HOUSE COFFEE

NET WT.

A.D.C.
Automatic Drip Coffee, New from Maxwell House

FIGURE 4.12
In this print ad, a coffee manufacturer seeks consumer purchase of his brand of coffee. The product featured is a line extension for the brand and is designed for users of coffee makers.

demand stimulation campaign. The goal here is increased coffee consumption regardless of brand choice, and major roasters of brand coffees contributed financial support to the campaign.

At the same time, various brands of coffee—Maxwell House, Folgers, Hills Brothers, and so forth—continue to seek larger shares of coffee sales. This goal is accomplished by *selective-demand advertising*, which stresses the superiority of a particular brand. Figure 4.12 is an example of the selective-demand strategy used by one company to promote its brand of coffee.

Primary-demand strategy may be used when a new type of product is introduced. There is no direct competition, and the consuming public needs to be educated about the product's benefits. Mazda's advertising of its Wankel engine in the early 1970s is an example. To get a car with a rotary engine meant buying a Mazda, and so the ads simply stressed the revolutionary engine.

In those rare cases in which the brand is heavily dominant in its share of the whole market for the product category, primary-demand appeals may also be featured. Campbell's Soup, with more than 90 percent of all condensed soup sales, stresses the idea of "soup for lunch" in its advertising, fully realizing that if primary demand for soup is thereby stimulated, the Campbell brand will benefit most by the increased sales. Generally speaking, however, the primary-demand stimulation strategy is inappropriate for most manufacturers, as the money spent helps competitors as well as the advertiser who pays the bill.

Product Reputation and Corporate Advertising

Our discussion so far, and for that matter throughout the entire book, is focused on advertising designed to influence the attitudes of prospective buyers and users toward specific advertised goods and services. Such advertising, which is aimed at promoting the sale of brand-name products, is called *product reputation advertising*, and it accounts for the bulk of advertising expenditures in the United States.

One class of advertising which has a different goal is variously called "institutional," "public relations," or "corporate" advertising. Although fine distinctions are sometimes drawn between these three categories, we consider them as one class and use the "corporate advertising" label. The overall objective of corporate advertising is to create a favorable attitude—or image—toward the business doing the advertising.

One reason for employing this strategy is to enhance the corporate image as part of a public relations program. When *Saturday Review* was making its annual advertising awards for 1974, it chose the campaign by Exxon, as shown in Figure 4.13, as the best in this

140
ADVERTISING'S
ROLE
IN THE
MARKETING
PROCESS

The new

Exxon is developing energy technology for this century and beyond.

Across our country Americans are coming to terms with the energy shortage. Faced with lines at service stations and limited supplies of heating oil, we have all become aware of the need for conservation.

Yet, even with conservation, by the year 2000 our country will probably require three times as much energy as it does today. Fossil fuels will continue to supply an important part of that energy. But a good deal of America's future supply in this century and beyond will have to come from new technology.

Exxon is already working on this technology to develop several new sources of energy.

Energy right from the sun.

One of those sources is the ultimate source of almost all of our energy—the sun itself.

The sun's energy is enormous

This five-cell solar module absorbs sun rays, producing 1½ watts of electricity.

and widely available. It can be collected and converted to electricity by *solar cells,* like those that produced electrical power for Skylab.

Solar energy in use today.

Today, as Exxon examines ways to improve its solar-cell technology, solar-cell units are already in use. In parts of Africa solar cells power instructional television. On boats, they maintain the charge in batteries. On marker buoys they supply electricity for warning lights and foghorns.

One of Exxon's research aims is to cut the present high cost of solar-cell electricty.

Super-batteries to store energy.

To efficiently use the energy generated by solar cells and other devices, we'll need super-batteries with much greater storage capacity. Batteries to store the sun's energy for use as electricity at night. Batteries to store energy that power plants produce in low-demand periods for later use when the demand for electricity is high.

Better batteries would also speed the development of electric vehicles. Exxon's target is a battery that would be light enough, reasonable enough in cost and charging demands, and powerful enough to drive a car 100 miles on a single charge from a wall outlet. This kind of battery, which still requires inten-

sive research, could make possible a practical electric passenger car.

Electricity from chemicals.

We're also developing a *fuel cell.* Different from the solar cell, which uses the sun, a fuel cell generates electricity when certain simple gases, like hydrogen and oxygen, or a simple liquid fuel like methanol, are fed continuously into the cell.

Potentially, fuel cells are efficient sources of electricity. They could provide silent energy for mobile homes or remote vacation homes. They also might be designed as total energy systems for shopping centers or as a way for public utilities to supply additional power during high-demand periods.

Solar cells, fuel cells and improved batteries should come into greater use during the 1980's. Meanwhile, Exxon is looking for energy sources for the next century. Nuclear fusion is one possibility.

Improved lead-acid batteries make electric-powered vans practical for urban delivery. The next step—practical battery-powered cars.

FIGURE 4.13
Exxon won a *Saturday Review* award as the best corporate advertising for 1974 with this print ad.

category.[12] The oil crises and shortages of the era had caused a serious public relations problem for the firm, which exceeded all other firms in the country in sales for the year. The Exxon campaign consisted of six

[12] *Saturday Review,* July 12, 1975, p. 41.

energy.

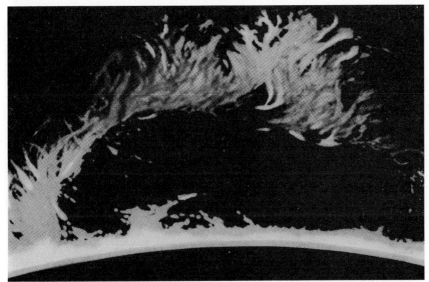

Developing ways to convert the sun's light and heat into usable, storable energy may make solar power a practical supplement to oil, natural gas and coal in this century.

Fusion reactors-a new kind of nuclear power.

Today's nuclear power plants operate on the familiar principle of nuclear fission, a process of splitting atoms apart. Nuclear *fusion* is just the opposite. Atoms are fused together to release a remarkable amount of energy.

Fusion is the main process feeding the fires of the sun and stars. Today, at the University of Rochester, Exxon and others are participating in a laser fusion feasibility project. It seeks to use the energy of high-powered lasers to heat frozen hydrogen pellets to sunlike temperatures of hundreds of millions of degrees in less than a hundred-billionth of a second—and thereby produce a fusion reaction.

At the University of Rochester, Exxon is participating in a nuclear fusion project. We are attempting to simulate the action of the sun by focusing powerful laser beams on a tiny piece of matter inside this metal chamber.

Harnessing fusion energy is one of the greatest challenges scientists have ever undertaken. However, even if our efforts or those of others are successful, commercial use of fusion reactions to produce energy is many decades away.

We can't begin too soon.

These new energy technologies may seem far away. But if our present energy situation holds any lesson, it is that we can't begin too soon to find energy supplements to oil, natural gas and coal. That's why Exxon is already at work on the new energy technology America will need in the next century.

double-page spreads and three single-page ads in selected print media and explained the difficulty of obtaining oil as well as the reasons behind record profits.

The winner in the other major category—public interest advertising—was the Distilled Spirits Council of the United States, a trade

142

ADVERTISING'S
ROLE
IN THE
MARKETING
PROCESS

association, which ran a series of advertisements on alcoholism and the problems it causes. A campaign sponsored by General Electric won special mention; the ad dealing with how to check for breast cancer, as shown in Figure 4.14, is representative of the GE campaign.

Thus, we see that corporate advertising may be employed to help a firm when it faces a public relations problem, or it may help to enhance the company's image by promoting good causes. The ultimate goal may be to increase sales, but such diverse objectives as favorable legislative treatment, stockholder and financial community interest in the company, better labor relations, and simple goodwill of the general public may motivate the corporate advertising campaign.

A comprehensive survey conducted recently by the Association of National Advertisers provides a good summary of the objectives of corporate advertising as it is viewed by the sponsors. Such advertising is designed to:

1 Enhance or maintain the company's reputation or goodwill among specific public or business audiences
2 Establish or maintain a level of awareness of the company's name and nature of business
3 Provide a unified and supportive marketing approach (umbrella) for a combination of present and future products and services
4 Educate the audience on subjects of importance to the company's future (for example, profits, free enterprise, economics)
5 Establish the company's concern for environmental or social issues
6 Bring about a change in specific attitudes of the audience toward the company or its products[13]

Retail establishments may stress the institutional character of the stores, trying to build their store image. Most users of corporate advertising also engage in product reputation advertising.

Push and Pull Strategies

Push strategy is aimed at intermediaries with the goal of getting retailers to aggressively promote the manufacturer's brand to consumers. It can be used when consumers rely heavily on dealers for advice on product use. Thus, specialty stores often emphasize the push strategy with a lesser emphasis on advertising. The consumer picks a specific sporting-goods store, camera shop, or jeweler because of faith in its reputation and then buys what is stocked.

Pull strategy, in its extreme form, uses advertising to stimulate

[13] Harry L. Darling, *Current Company Objectives and Practices in the Use of Corporate Advertising*, Association of National Advertisers, Inc., New York, 1975, pp. 6–7.

Until now, the first warning sign of breast cancer has been to suddenly feel a lump.

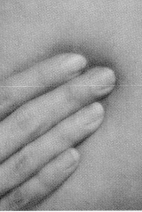

The sooner breast cancer is detected, the greater the chance of successful treatment.

That's why it's so important that a woman examine her breasts monthly. This is how 95% of all breast cancer is first discovered. The GE Spectrotherm A new weapon in the battle against breast cancer But, unfortunately, it's not a foolproof measure.

In many cases, by the time a tumor is big enough to be felt, the cancer has already spread to other parts of the body. This is particularly true if the tumor has started deep within the breast.

Now General Electric has a way to help doctors detect breast cancer at its earliest stages. The GE Spectrotherm.

Complete examination in a few minutes.

The Spectrotherm is an infrared scanning unit. It can detect the heat from a tumor (or another source) deep inside the breast. A tumor nearly always gives off more heat than the tissue surrounding it.

It's a simple procedure which can identify an area for further study.

There's no radiation. And nothing touches the patient.

The American Cancer Society and National Cancer Institute are setting up a program of 27 breast cancer detection centers. Most of them will be using the Spectrotherm along with physical examinations and x-rays.

Their goal is to screen hundreds of thousands of women. They hope to detect breast cancer early enough to give women a better than 85% chance of survival.

Someday infrared scanning devices like the Spectrotherm may be as common as chest x-ray equipment. And may do for breast cancer what the x-ray has done for tuberculosis. Sharp, clear pictures for easy diagnosis

The GE Spectrotherm. It can give women the weapon they need to win the battle against breast cancer. Time.

Progress for People.

GENERAL ⚡ ELECTRIC

FIGURE 4.14
General Electric won a special award from *Saturday Review* for this public interest advertisement dealing with breast cancer detection.

consumer demand to a sufficient degree that retailers are forced to stock the brand in order to please their customers. The promotional campaigns of most manufacturers, of course, are a blend of the two approaches. Deciding where to place the emphasis, however, is not always easy; the choice of approach depends on the nature of the product and the buying habits of consumers.

A knowledge of the essential differences between the various kinds of advertising is important. The terminology and the concepts are major communication tools throughout the advertising world.

144

ADVERTISING'S
ROLE
IN THE
MARKETING
PROCESS

THE CONSUMER'S ROLE IN THE DISTRIBUTION SYSTEM

The ultimate test of the impact of the promotional program for any product is actual purchase, and the buyer of products should not be viewed as a passive automaton in the distribution of goods and services. Serving the consumer efficiently is what the whole distribution process is all about. Similarly, the consumer, who is the receiver of advertising messages, should not be treated as a blob of inert protoplasm upon which the desires of the seller are inflicted without resistance or complaint. Not only is such an attitude undesirable from a social point of view, as discussed in Chapter 2, but it is poor business, for it results in ineffective advertising.

Advertising is often an important factor in building satisfaction in the consumer mind. It helps to interpret the want-satisfying characteristics of products in the framework of consumer thinking and action. Consumer orientation is important in all aspects of marketing, including, advertising. This subject is examined rather thoroughly in Chapter 11 as a backdrop to the discussion dealing with the creation of advertising. However, we wish to point out, in general terms, how consumers think about ads and advertised products. Such attitudes are influential in the whole marketing communications process. The consumer's role in the distribution process to a large degree depends on how he or she perceives and uses advertising.

Consumer View of Advertising

Some people feel that the consumer is a captive for advertising messages—exposed to them because there is no defense available from the onslaught. As the consumer employs the various kinds of media in search of entertainment or knowledge, the accompanying advertisements are absorbed through an osmosislike process and the advertising message penetrates the consciousness of the consumer, who then does the bidding of the manufacturer by purchasing the advertised product. Research, however, has shown that this view is not borne out in fact; consumers tend to be inattentive to most advertising and exercise a high degree of *selective perception*. This term describes a psychological pattern which indicates that of the vast amount of advertising being generated daily, the consumer pays attention to only that which fits into his personal concerns. The remaining advertising messages are unreceived.

On the other hand, the consumer often seeks out advertising in a positive, searching manner. Obvious examples might include newspaper classified advertising, yellow page advertising, fashion ads in women's magazines, and retail grocery advertising. When the consumer is acting as the family buying agent, for example, the market is searched for products that are needed to replenish or extend the household's assortment or inventory of goods. The real role of advertising in the consumer's life thus emerges as summarized in the following quotation:

> Advertising tells the consumer what's available; offers a parade of suggestions on how she may spend her money; and gives the freedom to accept or reject these options as she wishes.[14]

The consumer thus uses advertising as a *source of information*.

Advertising also can serve as a *time-saver* for the consumer. Once a person knows what he or she wants to buy, where to obtain the item is the next step in the buying process. Retail advertising tells the local source of the product. National advertising itself can save the consumer's time by assisting in the preselection process; instead of shopping every furniture store in the city, the consumer can analyze ads of furniture manufacturers and narrow the choice to two or three brands, which then may be examined in retail-store showrooms before an ultimate purchase is made. The increasing number of families consisting of two working adults, with the consequent shortening of time available for in-store shopping, should lead to more use of advertising as a time-saver.

If a manufacturer invests large sums of money advertising the quality of his product, it is only logical for the consumer to feel that the product must be of good quality. The surest way for a product to fail quickly is to successfully advertise an inferior product; after one trial followed by no repeat purchases, a product will soon be yanked from retailer shelves. When the consumer's choice is between a brand well known because of familiarity through continuous advertising and an unknown product, picking the known product is the natural reaction. Thus, advertising serves the consumer as an *assurance of quality*, which can be an important service when the multiplicity of products and brands is contemplated.

Lastly, ads are a *source of entertainment*. In one survey, approximately 20 percent of the population listed entertainment value as a consumer benefit derived from advertising.[15] One frequent comment is that television commercials are better than the programming. Of course, on a cost basis the money spent on a 30-second commercial is usually much greater than for that length time segment of program material. Although some specific advertising may irritate some consumers, much advertising relies on an entertaining approach to attract consumer attention and interest to the message.

---

[14] *What Does Advertising Do for the Consumer?* U.S. Department of Commerce, National Business Council for Consumer Affairs, 1972, p. 8.
[15] Rena Bartos, "The Consumer View of Advertising—1974," talk before the 1975 Annual Meeting of the American Association of Advertising Agencies, March 1975, p. 43.

146

ADVERTISING'S
ROLE
IN THE
MARKETING
PROCESS

Consumer Attitude toward Products

The consumer's mental attitude toward a product passes through several stages as he or she takes in advertising messages. These possible mental attitudes can be thought of as a hierarchy of effects. The least desirable attitude—other than outright dislike—that a consumer can have toward the manufacturer's brand is one of *ignorance* or unawareness. Awareness of the product is the first rung on the ladder of product success, and a great deal of advertising is aimed at achieving a state of product awareness in the minds of consumers. *Acceptance* is a step higher; now consumers will buy the brand as readily as any other brand offered for sale. *Preference* exists when the brand is desired over other offerings. *Insistence* indicates that the advertised brand is well along in the product attitude scale; no substitute brand will be considered.

The advertiser may aim at any one of these mental attitudes. If the product is new, he may wish to achieve a degree of awareness among the buying public. If his product is quite similar to competitive products, he may seek brand acceptance only. In order to move into the preference and insistence stages, the advertiser aims at product differentiation. Most advertising does not seek direct action; therefore, actual purchase rarely can be attributed to advertising alone. A knowledge of why consumers refer to advertisements and of an understanding of the mental processes going on in the consumer's mind cannot be stressed too strongly. The consumer is at the end of the distribution channel, and *good advertising must be customer-oriented.*

SUMMARY

Producers of consumer goods usually are geographically separated from their customers. Wholesalers and retailers operate the channels of distribution and facilitate the flow of goods between makers and users of goods. In addition to the physical movement of goods in the distribution channel, there exists a parallel channel of communication which gets information about products disseminated in the marketplace.

National advertising is the name given to efforts sponsored by the manufacturers of brand products. Its purpose is to familiarize consumers of the product so that it will be sought, or at least recognized, in the retail store. Retail advertising, on the other hand, is aimed at getting consumers to patronize a specific retail store; the emphasis shifts from the brand to the retail outlet. Many service institutions in a community advertise in a fashion similar to the strategy employed by the national advertiser; this advertising is called local advertising. Sometimes a plan of sharing promotional responsibilities, called cooperative advertising, is employed by a manufacturer and the retail stores selling his products.

Business advertising embraces four major subgroups: (1) trade advertising, which attempts to persuade retailers to stock the advertiser's merchandise; (2) industrial advertising, which is aimed at getting other businesses to use the advertiser's products in carrying out their business functions; (3) farm advertising, which communicates with farmers in their roles as producers and consumers; and (4) professional advertising, which seeks to have the advertiser's products recommended by professional people to their clients.

Advertising can be employed to stimulate primary demand. Most advertising seeks to enhance the reputation of the product, although corporate advertising is used instead when company reputation is given precedence over the product in the firm's advertising strategy. Promotional programs may stress a push approach or a pull approach.

All advertising programs need objectives if they are to be fully effective. Setting such objectives leads to more efficient advertising messages and provides a vehicle for measuring the effectiveness of advertising programs.

There are at least four ways in which the consumer uses advertising: (1) as a source of information, (2) as a time-saver, (3) as an assurance of quality, and (4) as a source of entertainment. The advertiser should keep the consumer uppermost in mind when planning advertising.

QUESTIONS FOR DISCUSSION

1 How does advertising serve to close the gap which separates the producer and the consumer of goods?
2 Why do many manufacturers prefer promotional strategies over price concessions as devices to lubricate the channels of distribution?
3 What are the general objectives of advertising? How do they differ from specific objectives of advertising?
4 Bring three magazine advertisements from current issues to class, each illustrating one of the three different ways that demand for goods and services can be expanded.
5 What is the fundamental difference between (a) national and retail advertising, (b) product reputation and corporate advertising, (c) primary-demand stimulation and selective-demand stimulation, (d) push and pull strategies?
6 When does a manufacturer use each of the following forms of business advertising: (a) trade advertising, (b) industrial advertising, (c) professional advertising?
7 Keep a log for three days, noting your personal use of advertising in your own purchase behavior. Categorize each example according to the four uses discussed in the chapter.
8 What is cooperative advertising? At whose initiative is a program of this nature started? Why?
9 What is local advertising? Bring a tear sheet showing a good example of its use in your city.

148

ADVERTISING'S
ROLE
IN THE
MARKETING
PROCESS

10 Cite examples of several current advertising campaigns that appear to be designed to communicate with consumers at different levels in the hierarchy of effects.

FOR FURTHER REFERENCE

Boone, Louis E., and James C. Johnson: *Marketing Channels*, General Learning Press, Morristown, N.J., 1973.

Colley, Russell H.: *Defining Advertising Goals for Measured Advertising Results*, Association of National Advertisers, Inc., New York, 1961.

Corkindale, David, Sherril Kennedy, Harry Henry, and Gordon Wells: *Advertising Resource Allocation*, Cranfield School of Management, Cranfield, England, 1974.

Darling, Harry L.: *Current Company Objectives and Practices in the Use of Corporate Advertising*, Association of National Advertisers, Inc., New York, 1975.

Engel, James F., Hugh G. Wales, and Martin R. Warshaw: *Promotional Strategy*, 3d Ed., Richard D. Irwin, Inc., Homewood, Ill., 1975.

Jacobs, Laurence W.: *Advertising and Promotion for Retailing: Text and Cases*, Scott, Foresman and Company, Glenview, Ill., 1972.

Kotler, Philip: *Marketing Management: Analysis, Planning and Control*, 3d ed., Prentice-Hall, Inc., Englewood Cliffs, N.J., 1976.

Robinson, Patrick J., and David J. Luck: *Promotional Decision Making: Practice and Theory*, McGraw-Hill Book Company, New York, 1964.

Sands, Saul S.: *Setting Advertising Objectives*, National Industrial Conference Board, Inc., New York, 1966.

Schwartz, David J.: *Marketing Today*, 2d ed., Harcourt, Brace, Jovanovich, New York, 1977.

Stanton, William J.: *Fundamentals of Marketing*, 4th ed., McGraw-Hill Book Company, New York, 1975.

Webster, Frederick E., Jr.: *Marketing Communication*, The Ronald Press Company, New York, 1971.

CHAPTER 5

CHAPTER 5

THE BUSINESS OF ADVERTISING

Once a firm has decided to pursue a program of advertising to increase sales or to increase the public awareness of its products, it requires some system to achieve this goal. First, the management of the company establishes a budget for the program, and it falls to the jurisdiction of the *advertising department* and its manager to follow through on this program. We shall explain the function of this department in the first part of the chapter. The firm's advertising department usually will rely on outside experts, often the *advertising agency*, which prepares the advertising messages and places them in appropriate media so that they are seen by a large section of the public, preferably potential buyers of the firm's products. Other businesses, called *special-service groups*, assist in the production of the advertisements themselves: printers, film makers, billboard painters, etc. Finally, the *media* participate in the presentation of ads. TV stations program commercials and show them at the proper time, and newspapers and magazines place advertising copy and artwork on the plates from which the papers are printed. This aspect of advertising preparation and presentation is so complex that we have devoted all of Part Three of the book to an analysis of each important advertising medium.

Thus, as John Crichton, president of the American Association of Advertising Agencies, stated: "Advertising is a business." We now take a closer look at each of the first three subareas, which will put the "business of advertising" in proper perspective.

THE FIRM: ORGANIZING FOR ADVERTISING DECISION MAKING

Earlier we learned that American businesses spend more than $30 billion annually to advertise their products and services. This amount is a significant cost of doing business because it is essential to the maintenance, or increase, of sales levels to firms that rely on it. Because it is such a huge expense for many companies, advertising budgets must be carefully managed. However, mismanagement of an advertising program can produce more than a wasted expense for a company—it can affect the company's sales level and threaten its chances for economic survival. The return from the investment in advertising must be maximized.

Firms have always searched for an organizational structure designed to facilitate the accomplishment of this goal of maximization and effectiveness. American business relies on specialization of labor to perform tasks most efficiently. It is only natural that division of labor be employed in the creation of advertising so that skilled individuals devote their best talents to an advertising program. Executive duties,

152
ADVERTISING'S
ROLE
IN THE
MARKETING
PROCESS

therefore, are broken into small units, and specialists are hired to perform the work of those units. The *advertising department* found in the organizational structure of many national firms exists solely to handle the advertising of the firm. Figure 5.1 shows where the department is positioned on the organization chart of the firm.

The Advertising Department

Departmental Functions   The advertising manager and the advertising staff have two main functions: (1) planning of the advertising program and (2) liaison with the advertising agency. The advertising manager, assisted by the advertising agency, develops the company's advertising program. The flexibility of the program is limited by the budget. The advertising manager will advise the corporate management about policy decisions, since they will affect the corporate image and sales potential. Involvement of top management in advertising policy is especially important for those firms where advertising is necessary for total company success. The late president of Revlon, Charles Revson, for example, was closely involved in the advertising of that cosmetic firm.

The advertising manager is responsible for the *overall* planning of the advertising program, which includes such issues as the product to be advertised, the market to be reached, and whether an outside agency will be employed. This responsibility also includes maintaining conformity with the financial and public relations guidelines set down

FIGURE 5.1

The position of the advertising department in a typical firm is shown in this organization chart. [*Victor P. Buell*, Changing Practices in Advertising Decision-Making and Control, *Association of National Advertisers, Inc., New York, 1973, p. 21.*]

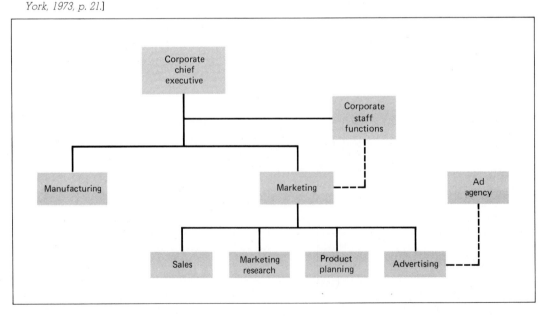

by corporate management. Most corporate firms employ an advertising agency, which, with a skilled staff, plans and provides the more *detailed* aspects of the advertising plan. The advertising manager's role then includes that of the liaison person, operating between the advertiser firm and the advertising agency. Although the agency is responsible for the execution of the program, the advertising manager assists by seeing that company policy and philosophy are understood and implemented by agency executives and by furnishing relevant product and market information to the agency. The advertising manager is consulted constantly as advertising messages are being developed and media choices are being made. The manager is responsible to his or her management for the progress made in carrying out the firm's advertising program. When necessary, the advertising manager may recommend that a change in agency be made.

Some creative work, such as supplementary or "collateral" advertising, may be done in the advertising department. Historically, the work done in the firm's advertising department is of the type which does not carry commissions from advertising media (discussed later). Recently, under an in-house arrangement, some advertisers have elected to create more of their own advertising—work normally performed by the advertising agency. This subject is discussed after we have explained the operation of the advertising agency.

Internal Structure   The work performed by the company's advertising department is divided into manageable units so that the advantages of specialization of labor are attained. One plan commonly used is to divide the work according to the *subfunctions* of advertising, with separate departments responsible for ad creation, media selection, and advertising production. A similar division can be made by *media*, with specialists handling print, broadcast, and out-of-home media. These plans are used when considerable volume of advertising is actually created within the department.

An alternative organization for a company's internal advertising structure is based on *end users*. One major manufacturer of medical supplies, for example, divides its advertising department into two major groups: (1) surgical dressings, tapping medical doctors and hospital users, and (2) baby products, reaching consumer markets. This alignment may appear to be a breakdown based on product class, but it is more truly a division by product end user. Major petroleum marketers provide another example of organization of advertising by end user. Separate executives, at both headquarters staff and regional- and divisional-line marketing levels, supervise motor fuels and lubricants sales through retail service stations and to fleet owners, to the commercial aviation market, and to the marine field. Their advertising programs are similarly organized.

154
ADVERTISING'S
ROLE
IN THE
MARKETING
PROCESS

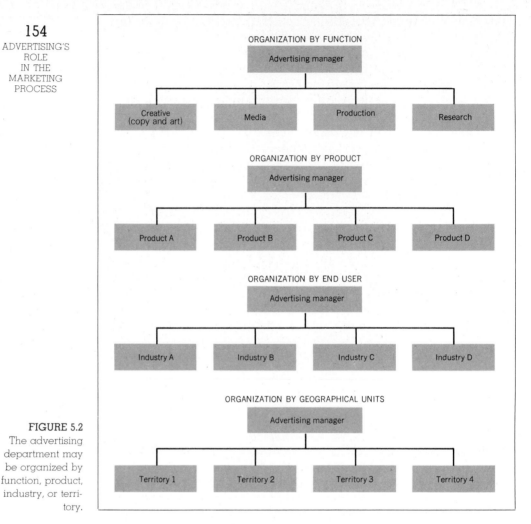

FIGURE 5.2
The advertising department may be organized by function, product, industry, or territory.

Another way of dividing the advertising task is on the basis of *geographical units*. A major brewery divides the advertising task among seven divisional advertising managers. Each manager has the advertising responsibility for one of the firm's seven major sales territories. These organizational patterns are illustrated in Figure 5.2.

Product Managers

The advertising manager system just described is still widely used in many businesses. In some instances it recently has been supplanted, however, by the *product manager system*. The product manager has particular knowledge of the product, and under the product manager

FIGURE 5.3
A product manager is reviewing an advertising layout with an agency account supervisor and a copywriter assigned to her coffee account. [*General Foods Corp.*]

advertising system he or she is the executive responsible for its advertising. A survey conducted by the Association of National Advertisers in 1973 revealed that 85 percent of responding firms that were engaged in the manufacture of packaged goods used product managers as their chief executives in charge of advertising; the percentage rose to 93 percent for those firms spending more than $10 million annually for advertising. For those firms manufacturing other consumer goods, the figure stood at 34 percent; for producers of industrial goods, 55 percent charged product managers with the responsibility for their advertising.[1]

The product management system came into general use in the 1950s as a "response to the organizational problem of providing sufficient management attention to individual products and brands when there are too many for any one executive to coordinate effectively all of the aspects of the marketing mix."[2] If the product line is limited, however, the functional plan of organization is indicated. The product management system, which was nurtured by Procter & Gamble, came to be highly popular with packaged-goods producers. The organiza-

[1] *Current Advertising Practices: Opinions as to Future Trends,* Association of National Advertisers, Inc., New York, 1974, p. 4.
[2] Victor P. Buell, "The Changing Role of the Product Manager in Consumer Goods Companies," *Journal of Marketing,* vol. 39, July 1975, p. 5.

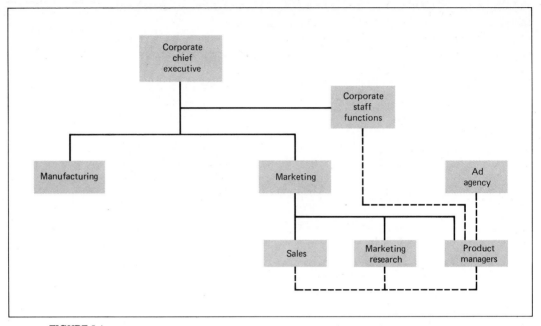

FIGURE 5.4

This organization
chart shows how
the arrangement
shown in Figure
5.1 changes when
the firm adopts the
product manager
system. [*Victor P.
Buell*, Changing
Practices in Adver-
tising Decision-
Making and Con-
trol, *Association of
National Advertis-
ers, Inc., New York,
1973, p. 23.*]

tional pattern found in a typical product management system is shown
in Figure 5.4.

Under the product management system the advertising manager
and the advertising department were replaced by the product manager, who "ran the brand" insofar as all marketing activities, including
advertising, were concerned. Companies with extensive product lines
would have several product or brand managers. Under this arrangement the company tends to take over more of the planning function
from the advertising agency, leaving the creation and placement
(media) functions as the agency's principal areas of responsibility.

Who Makes Advertising Decisions?

When the product manager position was first used, the managers
frequently performed as "little presidents" and acted as if the brand
under his or her management was in effect a little company whose
responsibility for profitability was held solely by the manager. It was
soon learned that the typical product manager was too limited in
experience and/or background to make key decisions concerning the
creation of advertisements. One commentator has stated that "at P&G
the brand manager's job was to make recommendations for his brand.
He did not make final decisions."[3] He goes on to state the product

[3] Henry Achachte, "Should the Agency Man Jump Ship for the Client in Today's Job
Market?" *Advertising Age*, July 28, 1975, p. 25.

management system developed by P&G was misused by imitators and led to consequent dissatisfaction with the system.

Buell made an important distinction between what he calls "operating decisions" and "policy decisions."[4] Operating decisions are those concerned with such categories as (1) strategies on how advertising is to achieve the objectives set down in the advertising plan, (2) creative and media decisions about how strategies are to be implemented, and (3) budgets. On the other hand, policy decisions involve those that "affect how the public feels about a company, its divisions, and brands."[5] Regardless of this distinction, top management may be involved in "operating" as well as "policy" decisions. For example, David Foster, president of Colgate-Palmolive, stated in an interview in 1975 that he personally approved all company advertising and added:

> I want it to be in good taste and believable. I am a strong believer in having products live up to their advertising. You must let the consumer know that you really care about the choice that he or she makes. In other words, don't give lip service to your products and let it go at that.[6]

Generally, however, product managers are free to make operating decisions; in fact, they are expected to do so. Policy decisions are reserved for higher levels of management. The significance of this arrangement has been heightened by rising consumer criticism of advertising and more governmental intervention in the advertising process. Who then should make advertising decisions? It depends on the type and relative importance of the decision. Product managers are charged with day-to-day operating matters; top management sets the overall policy. These generalizations also apply, obviously, to the advertising management system of organization. Under the product management situation, however, the lines of decision-making authority become more clouded.

The Retail Advertising Department

Both the function and the structure of retail advertising departments differ materially from those of the typical manufacturer's advertising department. Most retail firms do not employ the services of an advertising agency. There are many reasons why they do not, but an important one is the economic factor. Since some advertising media do not allow commissions on retail or local advertising, the retail store that wishes to use an agency must pay the agency a fee approximating 20 percent of its advertising expenditure in order to compensate the

[4] Victor P. Buell, "Where Advertising Decisions Should Be Made," *Journal of Advertising Research*, vol. 15, no. 3, June 1975, p. 8.
[5] Ibid.
[6] "The Marriage of Marketing and Technology to Improve Company Performance: How David Foster Runs Colgate-Palmolive," *Nation's Business*, August 1975, p. 44.

158

ADVERTISING'S
ROLE
IN THE
MARKETING
PROCESS

agency for handling its work. Therefore, many retail firms maintain their own advertising departments, whose functions are considerably broader than those of their counterparts in a manufacturing firm.

The time factor in retailing is also important. Often there is a need for last-minute changes in retail copy. Weather conditions may cause the cancellation of an overcoat sale or call for prompt promotion of swimwear or air conditioners. Special purchases or a delay in the arrival of merchandise may bring about an urgent need for promptness in altering media schedules or advertising content. Processing advertising through a third party such as an advertising agency would reduce the flexibility which the retailer who has his own advertising department enjoys. Moreover, the great variety of products which many retail stores wish to advertise would place a heavy burden on the personnel of an advertising agency working on the retailer's account. Someone might well have to stay right on the spot if the needs of the retail advertiser were to be fully served.

Thus, most large retail outlets feel they can do the job more economically—and possibly better—through the use of their own personnel. Retail advertising departments are more heavily involved in the creative function of advertising than similar departments maintained by national advertisers. Copywriting, artwork, production, and research are all done internally. The planning function remains, but there is no external liaison function to perform. On the other hand, the retail advertising department must maintain close contact with the various selling departments of the store. Good advertising requires a feel for the merchandise being featured, and this comes only from familiarity with the products and the people who sell them.

In a sense, the retail advertising department is a miniature advertising agency serving only one client. The variety of media employed is often more limited, with newspapers holding the dominant position. Small retail stores obviously cannot maintain separate advertising departments. Occasionally, the owner or one of the major executives will handle the advertising job. More often, the creative function is turned over to sales representatives from newspapers and television and radio stations.

THE ADVERTISING AGENCY

The folklore of glamour and excitement surrounding the advertising agency is more myth than fact and should not cause us to underestimate the agency's very real and important role in modern advertising. A full-service agency has many similarities to a large medical clinic. Each has a variety of specialists operating as a group under business management for profit objectives. In place of internists, orthopedists, radiologists, and the many other skills found in a clinic, the advertising agency has writers, artists, media experts, researchers, television producers, account executives, etc. Agency specialists work together to analyze the advertiser firm's condition in the marketplace and prescribe a course of action designed to keep the business healthy. Advertising specialists, unlike medical doctors, compound their own prescriptions by developing appropriate advertising plans and strategies and by creating advertisements and media plans to carry out those strategies.

Evolution of the Advertising Agency[7]

Space Broker Stage   Around 1840 various men began to act as sales representatives for out-of-town newspapers in such metropolitan centers as New York and Philadelphia. At first these men acted as simple agents selling space for their client newspapers on a commission basis. Later on, some would buy a set number of pages from a given newspaper and then resell portions at whatever price could be obtained from advertisers. This has been called the *space broker stage* in the evolution of the modern advertising agency. The arrangement led to price cutting as advertisers sought the lowest possible price. There was little emphasis on planning of advertising by the agent, or on the development of the best possible media schedule for advertisers. Inefficiency characterized the advertising field at this time.

Standard Services Stage   In 1876 the N. W. Ayer & Son agency devised a plan which was eventually to minimize the dubious practice of brokering advertising space. Ayer entered into agreements with advertisers whereby they promised to place all their advertising through the agency. In return the agency bought space for its clients only at established rates as published by newspapers and magazines. Thus, the agent became a buyer of space for the advertiser instead of a seller of space to the advertiser.

As this arrangement became adopted generally, agencies, in the competitive struggle for clients, started to take on duties now considered normal—copywriting, artwork, layout, media selection, and research. Before 1900 the Ayer agency had established departments for both copywriting and artwork, and the *standard services stage* in the evolution of the advertising agency had commenced. Over the next several decades advertising agencies improved the quality of their services to clients and added additional offerings. Agency personnel were trusted with solving more of their clients' problems.

[7] This section has drawn, in part, from Gordon E. Miracle and Bernard M. Bullard, "Evolution of Advertising Agencies," in Leonard W. Lanfranco (ed.), *Making Advertising Relevant: Proceedings of the 1975 American Academy of Advertising*, Columbia, S.C., 1976, pp. 125–127.

160

ADVERTISING'S
ROLE
IN THE
MARKETING
PROCESS

COASTING

is the term given by bicycle riders to their practice of taking the feet from the pedals and allowing the machine to run with the momentum acquired from previous effort.

This is the season when many business men are tempted to try "coasting" with their Newspaper Advertising.

The newspapers themselves however do not "coast." They are regularly issued, and regularly read, and the advertisers who have learned that

Keeping
Everlastingly At It
Brings Success

are **regularly represented** therein. They would no more "coast" with their advertising than with their employees, or any other every-day business necessity.

Coasting is a down-grade exercise. Success is an up-hill station. We have been there ourselves. We have gone there with many successful Newspaper Advertisers. We will be glad to start with you.

Correspondence solicited.

N. W. AYER & SON,
Newspaper Advertising Agents,
Philadelphia.

FIGURE 5.5

This 1893 ad by a well-known advertising agency was designed to encourage the buying of media.

Agency Recognition Policy One additional change had to take place, however, before the climate for agency development was fortuitous. Some agencies were rebating part of their commissions to clients, and in 1901 the Curtis Publishing Company promulgated its *agency recognition policy* to combat the rebate practice. Curtis stated that its magazines would no longer accept advertisements coming from agencies known to be rebating commissions to their clients. All agencies had to charge advertisers the rates prescribed by the publications. The result of this policy was that an advertiser would divert his efforts from trying to get a rebate to finding the agency which would provide the most and best services. The cost would be the same. Curtis further stated that commissions would be granted only to recognized agencies. Direct placement of advertising by the advertiser would not be permitted, or at least the advertiser would not be able to collect a commission from the medium. The only sensible course of action for a national advertiser thereafter was to use an advertising agency. The question "*Should* we use an agency?" became "*Which* agency should we use?"

Marketing Services Stage   Once these favorable changes had become permanently entrenched, growth of advertising agencies was rapid. Of course, industrial expansion in the United States was an important factor in this growth. By 1950 agencies were offering more varied and highly skilled services to the client, taking consumer psychology into account when creating ads, as well as furthering the role of advertising in the marketing mix by coordinating it with other marketing procedures. Advertising agencies thus entered into the *marketing services stage*, from which evolved the so-called full-service agency, which is representative of most large advertising agencies in the United States today.

Functions of the Full-Service Agency

The overriding function of the advertising agency is to see that its client's advertising leads to greater profits in the long run than could be achieved without the agency. The agency thus plans, prepares, and places advertising to this end. The customer is the key, and the agency supplies an "outside point of view" to the advertiser in his efforts to communicate with prospective purchasers of his product. The distinguishing characteristics between various advertising agencies lie in the creative skills of the personnel of each organization and in the philosophies of advertising held by each agency. The agency size could be a significant factor in its effectiveness, as, generally speaking, the larger agency is in a position to offer more services. Smaller agencies argue, however, that they can give more personalized service to their clients.

Advertising Planning   In planning the advertising program for a firm, the agency must have a thorough knowledge of the firm's product, the firm's past advertising, its present market, and its present distribution methods, and should provide research on potential new markets.

162

ADVERTISING'S
ROLE
IN THE
MARKETING
PROCESS

Knowledge about the client's product is keyed to its consumer benefits—and shortcomings—in relation to competitive products. A successful advertising program is built on a good product, and the advertising theme adopted is built around the product's strong points.

In order to gain the information needed, the agency engages in extensive research into the market for the client's product. Products come and go in the dynamic marketplace of our economy. To market a product successfully, market studies need to be conducted to ascertain the extent of the market for the product—who buys it, when, where, how, and why. Correct direction and timing of advertising campaigns are aided by such marketing information, and the advertising message is influenced by the nature of the market. What competitors are doing is also important.

In planning the advertising for a particular product, the agency analyzes marketing methods and distribution channels used in the past for the product in order to obtain specific information about the business environment in which the advertising message is to operate. The advertising must be relevant to the present (that is, fit conditions as they are) and of such a nature that it is aesthetically acceptable to the consumer and to the trade.

The agency knows the character and the influence of each advertising medium, in addition to audience figures and comparative costs. The advertising message must be adapted to the medium in which it is to appear. For example, the product advertisement to be heard on the radio probably will be different from the advertising message with visual impact, that is, on television. The printed medium would probably offer opportunity for longer messages. Different advertising media do have varying impacts on different segments of the market for specific products. The agency knows the physical requirements of each medium and creates ads that fit the space or time requirements of the medium.

From this background of product, market, distribution, and media knowledge, the agency can recommend plans for presenting the product to prospective buyers. These ideas, written up into an advertising plan, are submitted to the client for approval. Upon approval of the plan, the agency is ready to carry it out—to create the ads and place them. In addition, a full-service agency can provide many other marketing services to its clients: for example, postadvertising market studies are conducted to evaluate the effectiveness of the advertising.

Creation and Execution   Media choices are made before the ads are created. Contracts are made with the media selected; then advertising messages are prepared in correct mechanical form for running in those media. Specific advertisements are created. Copy is written; layouts are done; illustrations are drawn or photographed; and commercials are produced. Once the messages have been published or aired, the agency verifies the fact, pays the media, and bills the client.

Coordination   Agency responsibility does not end when the advertisement appears and the media have been paid. The agency often assists the client by working with his sales force and distribution network to ensure the long-run success of the advertising program. Maximum sales from the combined efforts of salespersons, distributors, and retailers—all assisted by advertising—are the goal.

Thus, the functions of the agency are (1) planning, (2) creation and execution, and (3) coordination. When additional services not normally done for the client in return for the media commission are undertaken, additional charges are made. In such cases the agency is in competition with special-service groups for the advertiser's business.

Although the agency relieves the client of many details involved in advertising, the client still makes the major decisions, as pointed out earlier. One fundamental decision is whether to advertise or not. Once the decision to advertise is made, the client chooses an agency to represent him. Large advertisers may engage a number of different agencies to handle various brands in their product line. Thereafter, decisions are concerned with the strategy to be used in the advertising program. The ideas of the agency are approved, modified, or disapproved. The following section describes the personnel in typical advertising agencies. By looking at agency personnel and their work, we get a more complete idea of what an advertising agency does.

Agency People and Their Work

In large agencies advertising specialists are assigned to specific tasks in the preparation of ads or the performance of other services. These tasks are now discussed.

Account Management   Keeping the client satisfied with the services rendered is of paramount importance to the business success of the advertising agency. This is the primary duty of the account executive, who acts as a liaison between agency and advertising department (advertiser) personnel. The account executive represents the client by explaining the advertiser's point of view to all agency personnel working on the account; he also represents the agency point of view to the client. The job, therefore, calls for diplomacy and tact. Merely representing the two sides of the agency-client relationship and keeping the channels of communication open in the relationship is not all there is to account management. The account executive is extremely important in the planning phases of the advertising program and in many ways is in charge of its administration.

The brunt of all misunderstandings arising between agency and

164

ADVERTISING'S
ROLE
IN THE
MARKETING
PROCESS

client is borne by the account executive. If the job is mishandled, the account may be lost. Occasionally an account executive may leave the employment of one agency and take a major account with him. For example, in 1975 J. Walter Thompson filed a lawsuit against one of its former executives for such alleged behavior. One of the qualities which an agency seeks in hiring an account executive, therefore, is loyalty.

Creative Department Once advertising plans are firm, advertisements are designed by creative personnel to carry out the plan. An agency retains a varied group of creative people, including writers, artists, designers, television producers, and graphic arts specialists. The creative function may be under one department, or it may be divided into several separate departments, such as copy, art, broadcast, and production.

Creativity is not a mechanical technique. It involves a novel or infrequent expression, response, or concept. And creativity in advertising is more than introversive expression, for it must be oriented to and correlated with the marketing situation and serve as a communication problem solver. Advertising creativity has been described as presenting a product in a way that people want to buy it. This creativity often goes beyond the creation of physical properties called advertisements; an agency may recommend new products, different distribution methods, or a distinctive selling idea. The outside point of view shines through in these recommendations. The ideal agency has personnel who can generate new marketing and communication ideas.

Media Selection Another highly specialized agency function is media selection. The goal of media people in the agency is to choose the advertising medium—or combination of media—which will do the most effective job of reaching the client's prospects. Securing the right audience is the most important factor in media choices, but decisions, of course, are affected by costs. From a maze of statistical data concerning rates, circulations, populations, audiences, incomes, and other relevant information the most productive assortment of advertising media is chosen.

Research A major service performed by advertising agency people is research to support the decisions made in the creative and media areas. The gathering of factual information is often a specialized agency function.

Internal Control and Other Services Every business must manage its finances, personnel, and office staff. Every advertising agency contains an *administrative* arm which conducts routine, behind-the-scenes business operations because it is a business enterprise. In addition, it is essential that individual jobs be coordinated and done on time since deadlines must be met. This function is performed by a specialized traffic department. Furthermore, larger agencies often have a legal department to pass on the legality of advertisements created by the agency; smaller agencies rely on law firms for such advice. Some agencies maintain merchandising departments; others provide public relations services for clients.

Agency Administration

Organizational Structure Multifunctional businesses often adopt formal organization structures to bring about better delegation of authority and to permit control of activities. Figure 5.6 shows in a general way how large advertising agencies organize their personnel. Smaller agencies do not have such elaborate organizational structures, but the essential functions are usually provided, although they may be consolidated into fewer departments, or even delegated to special-service groups independent of the agency itself.

The structure of the advertising agency can be arranged in one of two basic ways: on a departmentalized basis or on a group basis. Under the departmentalized form (typical of smaller agencies), all major departments, including copy, art, media, production, and research, are available to each account executive to facilitate service to the client. In the group approach (used by most large agencies), specific individuals are assigned to a team which does the planning, creative work, media buying, and similar activities for clients assigned to the group. Other groups, or teams, handle different accounts. In effect, several small agencies are created within the framework of the large agency.

Many agencies maintain plans boards, or review boards, in order to reassure clients that they are receiving the benefit of the best minds in the agencies. A plans board consists of departmental heads, or senior specialists, representing the major departments of the agency. The plans board meets with the account executive to review, criticize, and make suggestions on both the overall strategy and the specific tactics to be used in a client's advertising.

Administrative personnel give direction to departmental operations. Thus, there is a creative (copy) director, art director, research director, media director, office manager, and so forth. The typical agency has a president charged with the responsibility of seeing that the agency operates in a businesslike fashion. A large agency is likely to have a chairman and board of directors, and possibly, an executive committee, to set policy. One peculiarity of the advertising agencies is the prevalence of vice-presidents; one of the largest, J. Walter Thompson Company, had as many as 295 vice-presidents in 1974. Vice-presidents are usually department or group heads, or are responsible

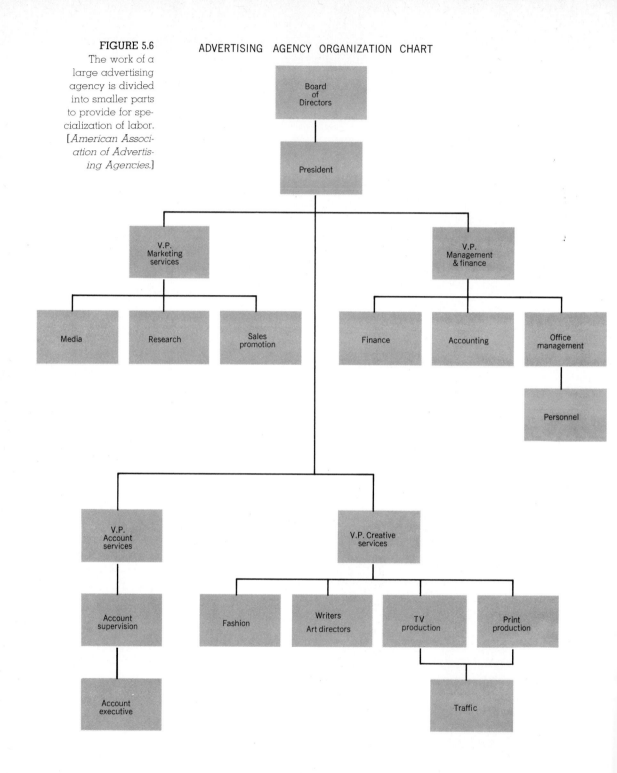

FIGURE 5.6
The work of a large advertising agency is divided into smaller parts to provide for specialization of labor. [*American Association of Advertising Agencies.*]

ADVERTISING AGENCY ORGANIZATION CHART

Board of Directors

President

V.P. Marketing services

V.P. Management & finance

Media

Research

Sales promotion

Finance

Accounting

Office management

Personnel

V.P. Account services

V.P. Creative services

Account supervision

Fashion

Writers Art directors

TV production

Print production

Account executive

Traffic

CUT OUT AND
WE'LL SEND YOU O

For an unlimited time only, you can send us one of these coupons, and we'll send you one of these men: Pete Little, John Feight or Hugh Lovewell.

Why should you spend 10¢ on somebody who's obviously going to try to sell you something? You shouldn't. Unless you've got something to sell yourself. In which case you should spend 73¢ and return the coupon Air Mail Special Delivery.

Because Pete, John and Hugh are Account Supervisors at Lawler Ballard Little Advertising. And we don't look at advertising like most of the agencies you've ever worked with.

Advertising, in fact, is the last thing we do. The first is marketing homework. That's why our clients get a lot more out of their budgets than awards from the local ad club. They get results. They get it from our marketing expertise. They get it from our advertising. They get it from our two subsidiary firms: Corporate Designs and Public Relations Institute.

Which are some of the reasons our agency is where it is today: Among the top ten in the Southeast in billings. With offices in Atlanta, Norfolk and Richmond. Plus our share of awards, too. And not just from the local ad club. But from practically every major advertising competition around.

So look at our coupon as a special introductory offer. And send it in.

Because what you get introduced to isn't just Pete, John or Hugh.

What you get introduced to is a whole new way of advertising.

Pete Little
The "Little" in Lawl
Vice President an
Atlanta office. P
land and industri
advertising mana
tern Railway for w
"Industrial Advertis
Industrial Marketing
president of the Atlanta
Marketing Association
Marketing Associatio
the Association o

Name

Company_____ Phone

City_____ State_

Lawler Ballard Little Adve
1800 Peachtree Road, N.W., Atla

John Feight
Director of Agency S
office. His backgrou
utive experience at
York where he wor
Efferdent, Chemwa
accounts. Since co
the senior account
account at Marschal
Account Supervisor
Kelley, where he wor
Cascade and other ac
elect of the Atlanta C
Marketing Associat

Name

Company_____ Phone

City_____ State_

Lawler Ballard Little Adve
1800 Peachtree Road, N.W., Atla

Hugh Lovewell
Director of New Busi
Supervisor in our Atla
extensive experience
counts and new prod
BBDO Minneapolis a
Atlanta. Some of the a
include Blue Plate Fo
Hormel, Pepsi Cola (F
Thermo-King Corpora

Name

Company_____ Phone

City_____ State_

Lawler Ballard Little Adve
1800 Peachtree Road, N.W., Atla

reputations of past performances as the principal mear
new clients. In any event, the function of getting busi
handled well if an agency is to grow and prosper
executives in the agency, therefore, nearly always are
facet of agency operations. Often the top executive of t
chosen for the post because of his or her strength in a
business.

We interrupt this ho-ho-hoing to say, "Happy Anniversary, Leo Burnett Company."

As you know, years to the Jolly Green Giant are just the times in between one harvest and the next. He rarely stops to count them.

So when someone reminded him it was forty years ago that he and the Leo Burnett Company first got together, the Giant was surprised. And delighted.

"Has it been that long already?" he asked. And went right back to work.

The Giant was just a green kid back in 1935 when you set out your first bowl of apples and opened your agency. You took him in and showed him a thing or two about advertising. Even taught him to "Ho-ho-ho."

Now here it is 1975. Forty years later. The Giant's bigger and so are you. But things haven't changed all that much in all that time.

Principles like "Reach for the stars" still apply.

So we say a special "Ho-ho-ho and happy anniversary." But if the Giant doesn't hang up his hoe and reminisce long into the night you'll understand why.

You always said it was impossible to work looking back over your shoulder.

FIGURE 5.7
Long-lasting relationships may exist between an advertising agency and its client. This unusual ad, paid for by the client, ran when the agency celebrated its fortieth anniversary.

168
ADVERTISING'S
ROLE
IN THE
MARKETING
PROCESS

for important accounts. The
executives or sold to the g

New Business Our discu
dwelled, as it should, on cl
another vital duty—to get
(1) by growing with presen
The first method involves
on increased business fr
involves acquisition of ne
agement acts as the sales

The importance of ad
emphasized when the tu
agencies is recognized. Fc
million in 1974 alone. Clier
agency may do a better jc
become the scapegoat wh
of whether advertising is
accounts where there is a
and the agency. Furthermc
agency not to represent
competition, and such age
tion. On the other hand, m
agencies for generations.

Executives charged
must know the politics of ac
ing changes in agency-cl
tions building up betweer
leads for approaching pro
ly solicit new business; oth
Agencies themselves eng
shown in Figure 5.8.

The actual selling p
which is a description of
accounts, and successes. T
singly or in competition w
require that a "speculative
tions the agency executive
it should be given to this
amount to tens of thousan
stration materials. Some
merely use the device t
personnel. The practice is
other business practices,
agency will win the acco

170
ADVERTISING'S
ROLE
IN THE
MARKETING
PROCESS

Alternatives to the Full-Service Agency[8]

As the full-service advertising agency matured, innovators saw new opportunities. New types of agencies developed. One, of course, was the multinational agency which came on the scene in the late 1950s when American advertising agencies followed their multinational clients to overseas locations, a development discussed in Chapter 21. Three other types are worth knowing about.

Boutique Agency The 1960s was a period when creativity was the byword of the advertising world. Clients wanted to be assured that the people working on their advertising were the most creative available, and star copywriters and art directors were motivated to leave full-service agencies and set up their own shops, which came to be known as creative "boutiques." The boutique agency performs only the creative function. This is done for a negotiated fee or for a percentage of the media expenditure. By the mid-1970s the interest in the approach had waned somewhat, and the future of this agency form is uncertain. Clients tend to want the usual agency services, and creative "geniuses" often do not have the talents needed to run a business. Moreover, many successful boutiques have grown into full-service agencies as the need for additional services has become apparent.

A la Carte Agency Under this type, each service of the agency is sold to clients on an optional basis. A separate fee is charged for each service desired by the client. This form may be referred to as the "department-store" or "smorgasbord" agency.

In-House Agency This variation probably has had the greatest impact on the full-service agency. The in-house agency, as its name implies, is owned outright by the advertiser and operates under his direct supervision. The in-house agency performs all of the creative and media services provided by the traditional full-service agency. A major goal in adopting this approach is to reduce the total cost of advertising, for the in-house agency receives the media commissions. If all the necessary work can be done for less money than the commissions total, the remainder goes directly to the profits of the company. Critics of the in-house agency claim that the outside point of view is lost as the creative personnel are working on only one account or product line and tend to become stale over time. Furthermore, a certain independence of thought is lost in the consequent hierarchical relationship of which the in-house agency is a part. Nevertheless, the form appears to be gaining popularity especially among heavy users of

[8] Based in part on "Now There Are Six Kinds of Ad Agencies," *Media Decisions*, December 1970, p. 78.

television advertising. Thus, such companies as J. B. Williams, Norton Simon, and General Electric are sponsors of in-house agencies.

Agency Compensation

The advertising agency receives its operating revenue from two basic sources: (1) commissions received from advertising media and (2) services fees charged to clients. In general, about two-thirds of an agency's revenue comes from commissions.

Commission System   The usual rate of commission granted by media to agencies is 15 percent of the rate charged for media space or time. Outdoor firms allow commissions of $16^2/_3$ percent, and some trade publications allow 20 percent. Although 15 percent is almost universal in the United States, commissions vary widely throughout the world.

A hypothetical example is given to demonstrate how the commission system works. An agency places a full-page advertisement in a magazine as part of the client's advertising program. A full-page ad in the magazine sells for $20,000. After the advertisement has run, the magazine bills the agency for $17,000 ($20,000 less 15 percent, or $3,000). The agency then bills the client for the regular media rate charge of $20,000, leaving $3,000 in the agency's operating funds. For this $3,000 the agency must pay the costs of planning, creating, and placing the advertisement, as well as make a contribution to overhead expenses and to profits. A cash discount of 2 percent is given by most media if payment is made within 10 days of the billing date. This discount usually is passed along to the prompt-paying client.

The commission system has the sanction of long usage. The system simplifies the task of the media greatly, as the agency often is solely responsible for payment of media charges. It also has stimulated a high level of productivity from agencies; competition for accounts is keen under the commission system.

A potential disadvantage of the system to the advertiser lies in its built-in temptation for the agency to recommend an advertising program which calls for extensive use of expensive media or of media which require little in the way of agency services. This argument has minimal validity over a period of time, for loading a client with unneeded advertising or inappropriate media not only would be unethical but would cause client dissatisfaction. The client must be satisfied with the results of his advertising or he will change agencies.

Agencies are often evaluated on the basis of their billings. Instead of saying that the agency achieved a certain sales volume for the year or had operating revenues equaling so many dollars, the amount of advertising placed by the agency is quoted. If an agency placed $10 million with various media during the year, it "billed" $10 million.

172

ADVERTISING'S
ROLE
IN THE
MARKETING
PROCESS

Income from this phase of the agency's activities, of course, totaled only $1.5 million.

Fee System Some agency executives argue that 15 percent is insufficient return in light of the many services rendered to the client. Advertisers, on the other hand, feel that the rate is too high. Heavy users of the television medium are often in this camp, for once a television commercial is created, it may be used for long periods of time and at millions of dollars of media billings. This controversy has led to the movement toward in-house agencies by some advertisers and to the development of the fee system.

The first big breakaway from the commission system came in 1960 when the Shell Oil Company entered into an agreement with its advertising agnecy, Ogilvy & Mather, Inc., whereby agency compensation would consist exclusively of service fees. The arrangement was made on the basis of cost plus 25 percent. Within a five-year period the agency had more than one-half of its billings on a fee basis. A rapid change to the fee system was predicted; however, a survey of member practices by the Association of National Advertisers in 1973 revealed that 78 percent of the 209 responding firms still were using media commissions as the basic method of agency compensation.[9] Fee arrangements were found primarily among industrial companies spending under $1 million. Such fee arrangements usually came about at the request of the agency.[10] The future pattern for the fee system is difficult to predict.

Other Income Advertising agencies do not rely on commissions and fees as their sole sources of revenue. The client pays for costs incurred in preparing materials for reproduction of advertisements. The client, in other words, pays for artwork, typography, photoengravings, commercial production, and the many other special services to be discussed in the next section. In addition to the actual cost of these services, the advertiser also pays a service charge of 17.65 percent more for the work than the agency pays. This service charge added to the cost of work is equivalent to the standard 15 percent commission discounted from billings by commissionable media.

Service fees also are charged for certain work on which commissions are not available. Retail advertising, for instance, is not granted a commission by some advertising media. Catalogs, point-of-purchase materials, sales materials, and direct-mail pieces usually do not involve commissions. Extra charges may be made when the media budget is so low that commissions do not pay for the work done on the

[9] *Current Advertising Management Practices: Opinions as to Future Trends*, Association of National Advertisers, Inc., New York, 1974, p. 39.
[10] Ibid.

advertising, such as the industrial advertising situation mentioned above. Finally, developmental work on a client's new products or any other unusual projects are often done on a special fee basis.

Usually a letter of agreement between the agency and the client spells out clearly the areas of responsibility assumed by the agency in return for the 15 percent commission received on advertising placed for the client. Those services for which the client is expected to pay extra and the rates of pay are also included in the agreement. A contract of employment, however, usually does not exist between the agency and the client, for their relationship is similar to that between the physician and patient or lawyer and client. Once mutual trust is lacking, the agency no longer can serve the advertiser, and the relationship is broken off.

SPECIAL-SERVICE GROUPS

Any keen observer of the business world cannot help but be impressed by the presence of alert entrepreneurs who are constantly seeking opportunities to provide services to consumers and to other business enterprises. There is a great multiplicity of such firms on the American scene whose objective is to provide advertisers, advertising agencies,

FIGURE 5.9
Printers are an important special-service group. This press serves the need generated through advertising (Hantscho web offset press).

174
ADVERTISING'S
ROLE
IN THE
MARKETING
PROCESS

FIGURE 5.10
Two special-
service groups,
model agency and
photographer, pool
efforts on an ad-
vertising project.
[*Courtesy of
Peachtree Center
Models.
Photographer:
Dwight Howard;
model: Vera Alex-
ander.*]

and the advertising media with a host of specialized services. These firms collectively are called *special-service groups*, and they are by far the least-known component of the advertising industry. Knowledge of their availability and function is vital if the structure of the advertising business is to be fully understood.

Use of the printed media involves printers, lithographers, photoengravers, and typographers. Other supplier groups are needed when additional forms of advertising are included in the advertising mix. Broadcast advertising may involve commercial production studios, musicians, actors, recordings, tapes, transcriptions, and packaged television shows from outside organizations.

Free-lance artists, photographers, and copywriters sell their creative output for use in advertisements. Models, package designers,

FIGURE 5.11
This interesting ad is seeking business for a special-service group specializing in the area of broadcasting.

public relations counselors, and independent market research firms, are additional examples of the extensive list of special-service activities that are available to serve the needs of advertisers.

Who should bear the responsibility for handling the many highly

176

ADVERTISING'S
ROLE
IN THE
MARKETING
PROCESS

specialized creative processes and mechanical details which precede the appearance of an advertisement? This is a perplexing managerial question. One of three organizations must take this responsibility. The advertiser can perform the specific task internally. Larger retailers adopt this approach, but the typical manufacturer's advertising department is less concerned with the creative aspects of the advertising program than with the planning and coordinating phases.

The advertiser may turn these duties over to the advertising agency. More and more of these jobs are being performed by agency personnel. Many large advertising agencies, for instance, have become recognized as specialists in the production of television commercials. Not only may agency personnel originate the script, but they may also direct and shoot the film for the commercial, or they may purchase the service from a production company.

Lastly, the advertising media can perform the creative and production phases of advertising. Many radio and TV commercials are taped or filmed by stations for their advertisers. Newspaper personnel write copy and do artwork for smaller advertisers in the paper.

Some facet of the job, regardless of who assumes overall responsibility for production of the ad, is likely to be turned over to a special-service group. If the particular need is occasional, the advertiser, the agency, or the media involved will tap the services of specialists. However, when the need is continuous, the decision should be based on where the best job can be done at the lowest cost.

Advertising media, the remaining part of the business of advertising to be discussed, is the topic for Part Three of this book.

SUMMARY

Advertising is a business, and it encompasses four major kinds of enterprises: (1) advertisers, (2) advertising agencies, (3) special-service groups, and (4) advertising media. We have analyzed the function of the first three.

Most medium-to-large businesses relying on advertising in their marketing mix maintain a special department to handle the advertising function. The person in charge, often called the advertising manager or advertising director, has two principal duties: (1) to plan the advertising program within budget limitations and (2) to coordinate its implementation. The work of the advertising department may be broken down along functional, media, geographic, or end-user bases.

Larger firms with multiproduct lines often adopt the product management system instead of using the advertising manager arrangement. In the former, an individual is placed in charge of all marketing activities for a specific product—an assignment which includes responsibility for the advertising of the product.

Regardless of the system employed, key advertising policy decisions are still reserved for the firm's top management. The advertising—or product—manager makes only operational decisions. The depth of top-management involvement in advertising decision making is dependent primarily on how important advertising is in the ultimate success of the firm.

The advertising agency is a highly specialized service organization. It has evolved over the past 140 years from simple media space selling to its present status as the supplier of a complete set of services for its advertiser clients. The agency's major functions today include: (1) advertising program planning, (2) the creation and execution of the program, and (3) the coordination of program activities.

To accomplish these objectives a collection of specialists, including account executives, creative people, media experts, and research personnel, is assembled. These people are organized within the agency structure on either a departmentalized or a group basis. Superimposed on the organization is a hierarchy of managerial people, including top management who has the generation of new business as a highly important responsibility. Recently, such alternatives to the full-service agency as the creative boutique and the in-house agency have appeared.

Agencies are paid either by media commissions or by client fees. The commission system originated from the space selling background of the advertising agency and usually is figured at 15 percent of the advertising billings placed in the traditional advertising media. Clients may agree to pay specified fees for work done by the agency instead of using the commission system, but the latter still accounts for more than three-fourths of all agency compensation.

Special-service groups are specialized businesses which furnish a variety of necessary products and services to the advertising industry. An important decision in advertising is who should do specific tasks—the advertiser, the agency, or the media. All three tap special-service groups when carrying out an assignment.

QUESTIONS FOR DISCUSSION

1 Explain the various types of business that participate in the business of advertising.
2 Who has the prime responsibility for advertising in the typical manufacturing firm's organizational structure? What are the person's principal duties?
3 List some advantages to a product manager system. Contrast the use of product manager with other types of market organizations.
4 Name the two major kinds of advertising decisions. Who is responsible for making each kind and why?
5 Why are advertising agencies paid commissions by advertising media? What are the shortcomings of this system of compensation? What alternative is available? When is it used?

178

ADVERTISING'S
ROLE
IN THE
MARKETING
PROCESS

6　Describe the operation of the full-service advertising agency. What alternatives to it have emerged recently? Why?

7　How is the work of the full-service advertising agency organized? What services may it provide to clients?

8　Why is new-business generation so important to the advertising agency? Who has the major responsibility for this activity?

9　Explain what we mean by special-service groups. How do they fit into the business of advertising? Is their importance growing or waning?

10　Interview one executive engaged in any one of the forms of advertising business described in this chapter, and write a description of the person's specific job.

FOR FURTHER REFERENCE

Aaker, David A., and John G. Myers: *Advertising Management*, Prentice-Hall, Inc., Englewood Cliffs, N.J., 1975.

Barton, Roger (ed.): *Handbook of Advertising Management*, McGraw-Hill Book Company, New York, 1970.

Buell, Victor P.: *Changing Practices in Advertising Decision-Making and Control*, Association of National Advertisers, Inc., New York, 1973.

Current Advertising Management Practices, Association of National Advertisers, Inc., New York, 1974.

Jones, Bob: *The Business of Advertising*, Longman Group Limited, London, 1974.

Ogilvy, David: *Confessions of an Advertising Man*, Antheneum Publishers, New York, 1963.

Reeves, Rosser: *Reality in Advertising*, Alfred A. Knopf, Inc., New York, 1961.

Simon, Julian L.: *The Management of Advertising*, Prentice-Hall, Inc., Englewood Cliffs, N.J., 1971.

Stansfield, Richard H.: *Advertising Manager's Handbook*, The Dartnell Corporation, Chicago, 1969.

THREE

THREE

ADVERTISING MEDIA

Media, the means by which advertisers reach their prospective customers with advertising messages, were introduced in Chapter 5 as the fourth category of businesses that constitute the advertising industry.

Except for advertisers themselves, more people in the advertising industry work in media than in any other division. Furthermore, of all the dollars spent in the planning and execution of advertising programs and campaigns, approximately two-thirds go to the media.

Whether one is involved in planning marketing, devising advertising strategy, or creating and producing advertising itself, a knowledge of the basics of each medium is indispensable.

In this section, we shall first present a broad overview of media and then, in subsequent chapters, investigate television and radio, publication media, direct mail, out-of-home media, and the other collateral media so important in many advertising campaigns.

CHAPTER 6
THE WORLD OF MEDIA: AN OVERVIEW

We have spent a significant portion of our lives being entertained and informed by the mass media—television, radio, newspapers, magazines, direct mail, and billboards, to name a few. From the advertisers' point of view, however, the media serve a different, but equally important, function. *Media* are the vehicles by which advertisers convey their messages to large groups of prospects and thereby aid in closing the gap between producer and consumer as described in Chapter 4. But beyond the viewpoint of audiences and advertisers, there is still another perspective from which media can be viewed—from the position of the medium itself.

Media owners and managers see their companies as manufacturing or service organizations bent on fulfilling a need among consumers for entertainment and information. Thus, television and radio stations program their broadcast fare in a manner designed to attract large segments of the public. In the same manner, newspapers and magazines attempt to build their circulations among readers who are drawn to the type of material they publish, be it local news, national news, or some specialized category of interest such as information published to appeal to persons interested in psychology, home decorating, or cross-country skiing.

Once a medium has established itself and built a significant audience, it is in a position to attract advertisers who are willing to pay for the privilege of reaching that audience with their advertising messages.

But not all media attract their audiences through programming or editorial offerings. Some, such as outdoor signs, direct mail, or the posters we see in retail stores, offer the consumer only the information contained in the advertising itself; but they offer advertisers a channel through which they can reach potential buyers at the right place and time. Regardless of the basis on which media secure their audiences, they constitute, collectively, one of the four categories of businesses (along with advertisers, agencies, and special service groups) that make up the advertising industry.

In this chapter we present an overview of the world of media: how they came to be conveyors of advertising; the range of media competing for the advertisers' dollar; the theory behind media charges; the institutions that exist behind the media we see; and the characteristics that make media attractive or unattractive to advertisers in meeting advertising objectives. In ensuing chapters we shall probe more deeply into the selection and use of a variety of the more important media.

THE EVOLUTION OF MEDIA INTO ADVERTISING VEHICLES

In the nineteenth century, publishers of newspapers and magazines discovered that both the circulations and the profits of their publications were drastically limited when they attempted to cover their writing and production costs through subscription and newsstand revenues alone. Some were threatened with business failure until they discovered that the secret to success lay not in raising their prices, but in lowering them. This action resulted in huge increases in circulation and enhanced the media's desirability as channels through which advertisers might reach prospective buyers. Everyone seemed to benefit from this arrangement. Publishers increased their audiences, profits, and spheres of influence; at the same time, the advertising not only subsidized their production costs, but even provided, in many cases, a handsome profit. Manufacturers and retailers welcomed the opportunity to present messages concerning goods and services in media whose reach far transcended the potential of the word-of-mouth or street-sign advertising they had been confined to. The general public, in turn, benefited through lower-priced magazines and newspapers and from the many advantages inherent in exposure to advertising, as discussed in Chapter 2.

In more recent years, as media choices have expanded, advertising has been the primary source of revenue for the newcomers—radio, television, elaborate outdoor posters and bulletins, and the many others we see about us each day. Thus, it is not surprising to find that today almost every medium in the country includes in its organization a department, or number of departments, dedicated to selling advertising. In many cases, we also find departments devoted to planning and creating advertising for potential customers. Furthermore, like most astute business organizations, these media maintain departments charged with promoting the medium to advertisers and their agency media buyers through advertising and other activities. This division, commonly called the *promotion department*, also works to build audiences or circulation and may be responsible for helping to enhance the image of a medium through public service and other public relations activities. The *Chicago Tribune* has done this by sponsoring the annual All-Star football game, with proceeds from ticket sales going to charity.

TYPES OF MEDIA

To a media buyer there is a seemingly endless variety of salespeople selling a wondrous spectrum of advertising media ranging from barnstorming fliers who sell the merits of skywriting or of dragging a streamer over a crowded stadium to the sophisticated and high-priced television networks or huge magazine publishing companies. Some of these salespeople, such as those who extol the virtues of specialty advertising, may offer in their catalogs more than a thousand different items to enable an advertiser to meet his media needs. While we shall restrict our analysis of media to the major forms, it is important for the reader to note that many others are available and will be encountered in the advertising world. The fundamental media competing for advertisers' dollars are as follows:

I   Broadcast media
   A   Radio
   B   Television
II   Printed media
   A   Publication media
      1   Newspapers
      2   Magazines
   B   Direct advertising
      1   Direct mail
      2   Specialties
III   Point-of-purchase advertising
IV   Out-of-home media
   A   Outdoor advertising
   B   Nonstandardized signs
   C   Transit advertising
V   Other media
   A   Advertising on film
   B   Directory advertising

The media listed above may appear endless when one considers the fact that each category represents hundreds or even thousands of competing businesses. But the money any advertiser appropriates for the purchase of media space or time is limited, and media sellers work to convince advertisers and other media buyers that the media they represent would best meet advertiser needs. Most media buyers ultimately build their campaigns around a few media that they believe reach their markets best and meet predetermined advertising objectives most effectively.

MEDIA EXPENDITURES

One way to ascertain the popularity of the various media as advertising vehicles is to examine how advertising dollars are being distributed among them. Table 6.1 provides an interesting breakdown of advertising expenditures during 1974–1975. As you can see, newspa-

FIGURE 6.1
Two radio stations
take diametrically
opposite ap-
proaches to build-
ing audiences.
One is all talk, the
other all jazz.

If you were running a newspaper...

9.8ˊLB

Would you sell 72 cents worth of newsprint for 60 cents?

The December 1, 1974, issue of the Sunday New York Times contained 770 pages, weighed 6 pounds, 2 ounces and the raw newsprint alone cost The Times 72 cents. To figure its total cost you'd have to add ink, printing, distribution and a share of the salaries of some 5,000 Times employes.

Yet you could buy a copy for only 60 cents all over town. It sounds like a short cut to the poorhouse, doesn't it?

Fortunately, The Times is in the *news-paper*, not the bulk paper business. And

it takes a big newspaper to cover the rich and varied interests of its over four-million highly educated readers. For instance, on this particular day there were three sections of main news and a section each on Arts & Leisure, Business/Finance, The Week in Review, Sports, Real Estate, Travel & Resorts and Classified. Plus a 128-page Magazine and a 112-page Book Review.

It also takes a big newspaper to carry the messages all kinds of buyers and sellers want Times readers to *see*. Whether it's apartments, houses, jobs, cars, boats, bonds or any number of other products

or services, The Times is *the* market-place in print for both the nation and for its Number 1 market. Advertisers spend more dollars to reach high-income, highly placed Times readers than they do to reach readers of any national magazine.

Because of this, that issue of the Sunday Times cost you only 9.8 cents a pound. Can you think of anything else at that price that's nearly as nourishing you can buy for yourself or your family these days?

The New York Times
Makes things happen where affluence and influence meet

FIGURE 6.2
The *New York Times* may lose money on its newspaper sales, but it makes it up on advertising revenue. [New York Times.]

pers have garnered the largest share of advertising dollars. This has been true in the past and will continue to be true in the years to come because newspapers have natural advantages stemming from the fact that most are monopolies in the cities of their origin. This makes them powerful competitors for local and retail advertising dollars. Another important source of dollars, classified advertising, flows to newspapers

TABLE 6.1

ADVERTISING VOLUME IN THE UNITED STATES IN 1974 AND 1975

MEDIUM	1974		1975	
	MILLIONS OF DOLLARS	PERCENTAGE OF TOTAL	MILLIONS OF DOLLARS	PERCENTAGE OF TOTAL
Newspapers				
Total	8,001	29.9	8,450	29.8
National	1,194	4.5	1,200	4.2
Local	6,807	25.4	7,250	25.6
Magazines				
Total	1,504	5.6	1,475	5.2
Weeklies	630	2.3	605	2.1
Women's	372	1.4	375	1.3
Monthlies	502	1.9	495	1.8
Farm publications	72	0.3	75	0.3
Television				
Total	4,851	18.1	5,325	18.8
National	2,145	8.0	2,325	8.2
Spot	1,495	5.6	1,645	5.8
Local	1,211	4.5	1,355	4.8
Radio				
Total	1,837	6.9	2,020	7.1
National	69	0.3	80	0.3
Spot	405	1.5	440	1.5
Local	1,363	5.1	1,500	5.3
Direct mail	3,986	14.9	4,125	14.6
Business papers	900	3.4	920	3.3
Outdoor				
Total	345	1.3	340	1.2
National	225	0.8	220	0.8
Local	120	0.5	120	0.4
Miscellaneous				
Total	5,284	19.7	5,590	19.7
National	2,760	10.3	2,875	10.1
Local	2,524	9.4	2,715	9.6
Total				
National	14,755	55.1	15,380	54.3
Local	12,025	44.9	12,940	45.7
Grand total	26,780	100.0	28,320	100.0

SOURCE: *Advertising Age*, Dec. 29, 1975.

because advertisers have no significant alternative when seeking to sell a used car, find a baby sitter, or hire an experienced machinist.

Although television is the newest of the major media, having arrived on the scene only 30 years ago, it has grown in importance, now capturing over $5 billion, or almost 19 percent, of total advertising dollars annually. It is a surprise to some that direct mail places a strong third, ahead of both radio and magazines in competing for advertising dollars. Part of direct mail's strength stems from its universal application. It is a rare company, large or small, that cannot find some advantage in communicating with its potential customers through some form of advertising delivered through the mails. The large miscellaneous figure in Table 6.1 represents an estimate of all the expenditures in collateral media such as in-store posters and signs, weekly newspapers, advertising specialties such as matchbooks or calendars, and other media too numerous to mention. This explains why the miscellaneous column total is such a huge figure—$5.5 billion.

MEDIA AS ADVERTISING CENTERS

Tens of thousands of advertising men and women are employed in the production and sale of advertising media. Some of the businesses for which they work are easily discerned by the layperson. Others that play a role in the appearance of the advertising we are so familiar with are less obvious. For example, publishing companies that produce newspapers and magazines are familiar examples of firms that sell and produce advertising. Direct-mail advertising, on the other hand, is commonly produced by specialized direct-mail firms that may contract with advertisers or agencies to handle particular assignments for them. Or a client or advertising agency may do all the planning and preparing of a direct-mail campaign and then turn the project over to a printing company for final production. Working in conjunction with direct-mail houses and printers is a subindustry of firms that specialize in compiling mailing lists to aid advertisers in reaching the most desirable groups of prospects.

FIGURE 6.3
Media advertising staff members provide the bulk of the income for all media. Here a salesperson helps a client plan advertising for the coming year. [Eugene Register-Guard.]

Out-of-Home Media

Everyone is familiar with out-of-home signs and posters, but few people have ever been inside a sign painting company, or the basic institution of the outdoor advertising business—an outdoor *plant*. These businesses vary in size from small local organizations to large national companies such as Foster & Kleiser or General Outdoor that sell outdoor advertising in a multitude of cities. Men and women who work in local outdoor offices engage in selling advertising to prospective clients and in the production of local signs or posters. When posters or signs are displayed in great numbers, independent printing companies are often brought in to prepare them.

Radio and Television

Most national and some local advertising that we see or hear on radio or television is prepared by advertising agencies for their clients. However, much of the local broadcast advertising we are exposed to is planned and prepared by advertising people who work in conjunction with the stations' sales personnel in expediting the placement of advertising on the station for which they work. The salespeople themselves are the heart of the broadcast business in the sense that their success or failure in selling time on the stations they represent is fundamental to the stations' ability to survive.

The Media Representative Firm

Most radio and television stations, as well as most magazines and newspapers, need some sort of sales organization to sell the advantages of their media to clients and agencies in the large business centers such as New York, Chicago, Detroit, and Los Angeles. Out of this need has grown another advertising sales arm of the media business—the *media representative firm*. The typical representative office employs a number of salespeople, commonly called *reps*, who represent a number of noncompetitive media located throughout the United States, for example, a group of newspapers or radio stations located in different cities. In return for their services, they receive a commission from the media amounting to about 10 percent of the advertising purchased in the media they represent. Some representative firms may include only a few large publications or stations among their list of principals; others may handle hundreds. Although the primary role of the rep is to sell national advertising for publishers or stations, like all good salespeople he or she accomplishes this end by providing service to their buyers. Thus, good representatives stand ready to provide advertisers or agency media buyers with current information concerning their media and markets. In this fashion, they are vital resource persons for media buyers in the large advertising centers.

Television Station Representatives

ABC TELEVISION SPOT SALES, INC.
Tv B
Media Code 6 000 0050 9.00
New York 10019—1330 Avenue of the Americas
Richard N. Savage, Pres.
Kent Fredericks, Gen'l Sales Mgr.
Stephen P. Mathis, Eastern Sales Manager
Darrell Anderson, Eastern Reg. Sales Manager
Phone 212-581-7777.
Chicago 60602—360 N. Michigan Ave.
Richard Taylor, Midwestern Sales Manager
Stuart Mackle, Midwestern Reg. Sales Mgr.
Phone 312-263-0800
Los Angeles 90026—4151 Prospect St.
Philip L. Gore, Sales Manager
Phone 213-663-3311
San Francisco 94111—1 Jackson Place, 633 Battery St.
James Sherbert, Sales Mgr.
Phone 415-863-0077
Detroit 48075—24175 North Western Hwy, Southfield, Mich.
Michael Berman—Sales Mgr.
Phone 313-444-1111

ACTION ADS, INC.
Media Code 6 000 0062 4.00
Newark, N. J. 07102—1180 Raymond Blvd.
Phones 201-622-7780, 212-267-6360 (N. Y. Tie-Line)

ADVERTISING REPS, INC.
Media Code 6 000 0075 6.00
Miami, Florida 33101—Box 3191
J. Van Dolen, Pres.
Phone 305-361-2122

ALASKA RADIO-TV SALES
Media Code 6 000 0200 0.00
Seattle 98101—715 Securities Bldg., 3rd & Stewart
Phone 206-624-6333
For all other cities—See Adam Young Inc.

ALEXANDER, PEARSON & DAWSON
Media Code 6 000 0207 5.00
Toronto, Ontario M5B 1K5—14 Carlton St., 8th Floor. Phone 416-361-1291.
Montreal, Quebec H3B 2V6—1115 Metcalf St., Suite 2101.
Phone 514-871-8490.

ALL-CANADA RADIO AND TELEVISION LIMITED
Media Code 6 000 0215 8.00
New York 10020—1271 Avenue of the Americas, Suite 550
Bill Mitchell, Alex Findlay
Phone 212-246-1425
Telex 126433
Chicago 60611—Wrigley Bldg., 400 N. Michigan Ave.
Rick Kapnick
Phone 312-263-0491
Hollywood 90028—6922 Hollywood Blvd.
Hugh Wallace
Phone 213-462-8641
Detroit 48076 — 26011 Evergreen Rd., Suite 218. Southfield, Mich.
Dallas 75205—5327 N. Central Expressway
Ed Outland, Sales Mgr.
Phone 214-521-8150
TWX 910-861-4319

AVERY-KNODEL, INC.
NAB SRA Tv B
Media Code 6 000 0250 5.00
New York 10022—437 Madison Ave.
J. W. Knodel, Chairman
Robert J. Kizer, Pres.
Richard A. O'Donnell, Vice-Pres., Dir. TV Sales
Stuart M. Krane, New York Sales Mgr.
Phone 212-421-5600.
TWX 710-581-2785.
Chicago 60601—2206 Prudential Plaza
F. Robert Kalthoff—Exec. Vice-Pres. & Midwest TV Sales Mgr.
M. W. Harms, Jr., Vice-Pres. & Ass't Midwest TV Sales Mgr.
Phone 312-467-6111
TWX 910-221-0333.
St. Louis 63102—10 Broadway, Suite 1170.
Fred W. Johnson
Phone 314-241-5051
TWX 910-761-1188
Detroit-Troy, Mich. 48084—1017 Naughton
David Brangan
Phone 313-524 9424
TWX 810-232-1642
Los Angeles 90005—633 S. Shatto Place
Douglas MacLatchie, Sr. Vice-Pres.
Phone 213-385-6394
TWX 910-321-3894.
San Francisco 94104—155 Montgomery St.
William E. Moore, Vice-Pres.; David B. Meblin
Phone 415-986-8082
TWX 910-372-7478
Dallas 75219—3626 N. Hall St., Oakwood Tower, Suite 600.
Wallis S. Ivy, Jr., Vice-Pres.
Phone 214-528-1741, 1742
TWX 910-861-4061
Atlanta 30309—1252 W. Peachtree St. N. W.
John DelGreco, Vice-Pres.
Phone 404-872-3871
TWX 810-751-3204
Philadelphia—Enterprise 6242
Minneapolis—Zenith 2870

AYERS INC. OF CHARLOTTE (formerly James S. Ayres Co., Inc.)
Media Code 6 000 0300 8.00
Charlotte 28202—230 S. Tryon St. Suite 580
Guy Vaughan, Jr., Mrs. Winton Coughenour
Phone 704-375-6146
Market Division:
Harry B. Smart—Pres.
Oliver T. Trittler—Vice-Pres. & Gen'l S.s. Mgr.
Arthur C. Stringer — Vice-Pres. & N. Y. Sls. Mgr
John T. Bray—Sales Mgr., American
James R. Bloom—Sales Mgr., National.
Special Sales:
Harold M. Pingree, Jr.—Vice-Pres. & Dir. Special Proj.
Service:
Richard W. Gideon—Vice-Pres., Sales Strategy Div.
Josef B. Rosenberg, Vice-Pres., Communications
Alfred B. Cannarella—Research Mgr./ABC.
John J. Scott—Research Mgr./CBS.
Andy Coscia—Research Manager/NBC.
Joseph N. R. Poulin—Research Mgr./Market Division.
Lawrence J. Lynch—Program Director.
Spot Development Div:
James R. Kelly—Vice-Pres. & Mgr.
Chicago 60611—645 N. Michigan Ave.
Phone 312-787-2300
TWX 910-221-1187
Brian P. Hogan—Vice-Pres. & General Sales Mgr.
Gust J. Theodore—Chicago Sales Mgr./ABC.
Leon Serruys—Chicago Sales Mgr./NBC.
James McGillen—Chicago Sales Mgr./CBS.
Atlanta 30308—600 W. Peachtree St., N. W. Suite 1145.
H. W. Maier—Vice-Pres.
Phone 404-881-1145
TWX 810-751-8492
Boston 02116—535 Boylston St.
Floyd Gelini—Manager
Phone 617-536-6230
TWX 710-321-1085
Dallas 75219—Two Turtle Creek Village, Suite 720
Steven F. Beard—Vice-Pres. & Mgr.
Phone 214-522-4100
TWX 910-861-4561
Detroit 48202—1129 Fisher Bldg.
Gabriel P. Dype—Vice-Pres. & Mgr.
Phone 313-871-3060
TWX 810-221-6293
Jacksonville 32207—Gulf Life Tower, Suite 2204
John M. Farris, Mgr.
Phone 904-399-1900
TWX 801-827-5761
Los Angeles 90036—5670 Wilshire Blvd.
Robert S. Billingsley—Vice-Pres. & Mgr.
Phone 213-937-5020
TWX 910-321-4137
Philadelphia 19102—Three Girard Plaza
Jack Satterfield—Vice-Pres.
Phone 215-568-0290
TWX 710-670-0479
San Francisco 94108—650 California St.
W. Ralph Abell—Vice-Pres. & Mgr.
Phone 415-434-2393
TWX 910-372-7436
St. Louis 63102—10 Broadway, Suite 660

FIGURE 6.4
Radio and TV station representatives tend to cluster in major advertising centers, as this listing shows. [*Standard Rate & Data Service, Inc.*]

Networks

Networks such as ABC, NBC, or CBS are important elements in the broadcasting business, providing programming for their own stations and for affiliated stations across the country. An important arm of each network is the sales division, dedicated to selling time for commercials to be run in conjunction with network programs as well as advertising that is originated directly from their local affiliates. In the latter role,

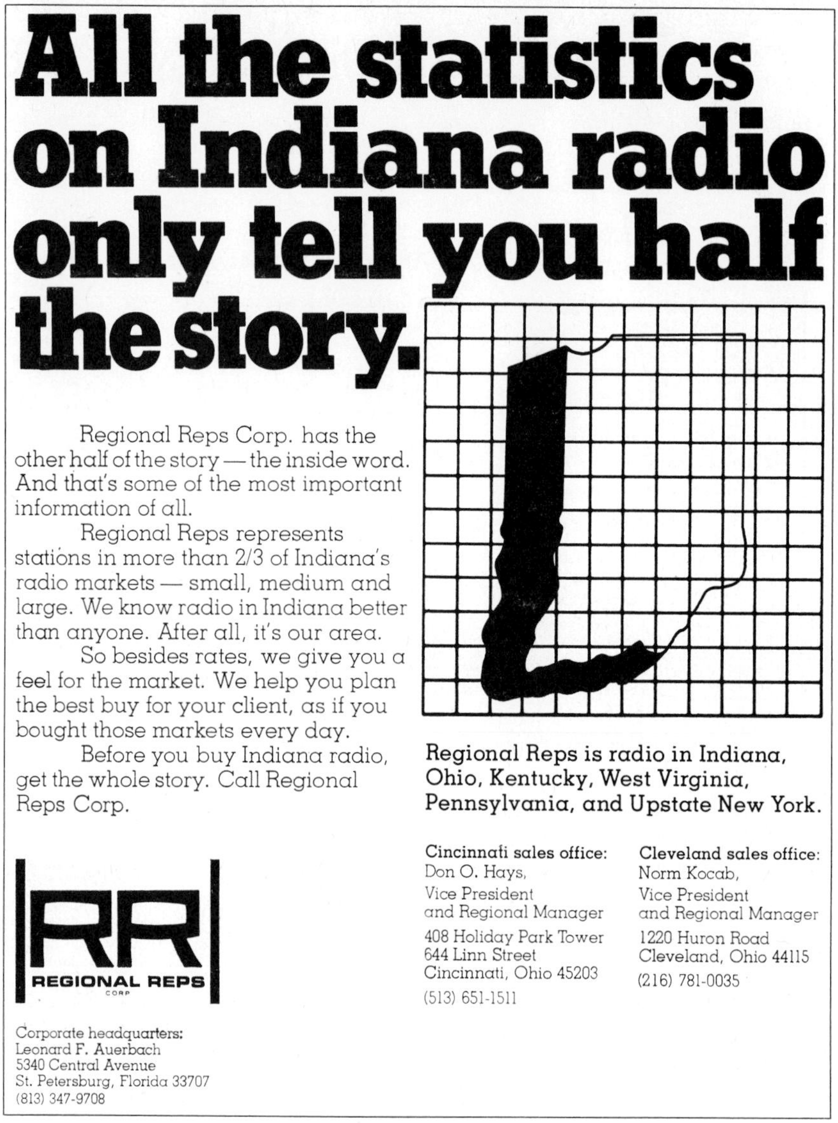

All the statistics on Indiana radio only tell you half the story.

Regional Reps Corp. has the other half of the story — the inside word. And that's some of the most important information of all.

Regional Reps represents stations in more than 2/3 of Indiana's radio markets — small, medium and large. We know radio in Indiana better than anyone. After all, it's our area.

So besides rates, we give you a feel for the market. We help you plan the best buy for your client, as if you bought those markets every day.

Before you buy Indiana radio, get the whole story. Call Regional Reps Corp.

Regional Reps is radio in Indiana, Ohio, Kentucky, West Virginia, Pennsylvania, and Upstate New York.

RR
REGIONAL REPS CORP

Corporate headquarters:
Leonard F. Auerbach
5340 Central Avenue
St. Petersburg, Florida 33707
(813) 347-9708

Cincinnati sales office:
Don O. Hays,
Vice President
and Regional Manager
408 Holiday Park Tower
644 Linn Street
Cincinnati, Ohio 45203
(513) 651-1511

Cleveland sales office:
Norm Kocab,
Vice President
and Regional Manager
1220 Huron Road
Cleveland, Ohio 44115
(216) 781-0035

FIGURE 6.5
This advertisement for a representative firm demonstrates how media reps serve the advertising business with information about media and markets.

they operate in a manner similar to the representatives mentioned above.

Advertising Specialties

When retail or national advertisers present you with a pen, key chain, thermometer, or more elaborate gift marked with a company or brand name, you are the target of *specialty* advertising, sometimes called *remembrance* advertising. Nearly every medium-to-large city has one or more firms called *specialty distributors* that engage in this business. Behind the distributors are manufacturers who provide the specialties. Giant manufacturers such as Brown and Bigelow of St. Paul, Minnesota, may have their own sales representatives located throughout the country. These people take pride in their ability to help plan successful specialty campaigns in terms of appropriate and creative tie-ins with their clients' advertising objectives.

It is obvious from the foregoing examples that the variety of institutions and job opportunities—sales, creative planning, production, and promotion—is extensive within the media division of the advertising business.

MEDIA CHARACTERISTICS

With the wide variety of media available to advertising people charged with selecting the best combination of media for a given campaign, one might wonder how a seller tries to convince a buyer that a medium is right for a given campaign. The answer begins with an understanding of basic *media characteristics.* These characteristics describe the dimensions by which media may be compared. Once you understand these qualities, it is easy to apply them to any medium under consideration. Here are some of the more important possibilities.

Selectivity

This quality can be viewed in two ways—(1) the ability of a medium to hit a specific geographical area such as a city or a region and (2) the ability of a medium to reach specific kinds of people who possess certain common traits. *Geographical selectivity* is obvious. One would not buy advertising in a national magazine to reach the inhabitants of Boulder, Colorado, when a local newspaper could accomplish the job with little waste circulation; that is, few copies of the publication would not be delivered directly to the market (prospects) we are trying to reach.

The concept of *class selectivity*, defined as the ability of a medium to reach particular classes of persons with common traits, is, in a sense, the opposite of reaching mass markets where your only objective is to expose great numbers of people to your advertising message. In considering media on the basis of class selectivity, people are classified in a hundred or more different ways, and advertising salespeople soon learn to interpret their media in terms of the needs of specific types of clients. One medium may do a better job of reaching women than men—*Ms.* magazine, *Glamour*, and *Good Housekeeping* are obvious examples. Another medium, the *Wall Street Journal*, may

FIGURE 6.6
The geographical
selectivity of Ohio
newspapers and
radio and TV sta-
tions is indicated
on this media
map. [*Standard
Rate & Data Ser-
vice, Inc.*]

reach an older, more affluent audience than *Time* magazine or
Esquire. A rock radio station attracts a younger audience than one
featuring classical music, but each may play an important role
depending on the objectives of the campaign and the market that
media buyers are trying to reach.

So far, we've considered class selectivity as it applied to *demographic breakdowns* of media audience; that is, we have viewed these audiences in terms of sex, age, religion, education, income, or other factors. More subtle and fascinating breakdowns may occur when TV viewers, radio listeners, and publication subscribers are viewed in the light of such dimensions as life-style, innovativeness, or other psychological variations that might have a bearing on their willingness to buy particular products. Considerations such as these are often referred to as *psychographics*—as opposed to demographics—and might include a tendency to be a *heavy user* of a particular type of product. The importance of the concept of the heavy user is easily illustrated in the beer industry, where 20 percent of the beer drinkers are said to consume 80 percent of the beer sold in the United States. Media salespeople are anxious to have psychographic findings available to prove the appropriateness of their media for certain types of product advertising.

Coverage

This expression, also called *penetration*, is sometimes used simply to refer to the size of an audience a medium can generate. In that context a medium's coverage might be expressed as 10 million people or homes. More properly, however, the word *coverage* means the ability of a medium to reach a certain percentage of homes in a given area, or persons within a particular market segment. Thus a local newspaper might claim 82 percent coverage of homes in a given city, or a regional chess magazine might claim to reach 36 percent of the chess players in the Middle Atlantic states. A television network might claim that one of its programs reaches 20 percent of all the TV homes in the United States.

Flexibility

Another basis for comparing advertising media is their *flexibility*, that is, the ease and amount of time required to place an ad in a medium. Newspapers and radio stations afford advertisers relatively short deadlines in placing advertising. Under certain circumstances this quality can be extremely important to media buyers—when they are trying to meet a competitive situation, make an unexpected announcement, or react to a timely news event. Conversely, flexibility is important when, for some reason, an advertiser is forced to kill an ad shortly before it is scheduled to appear.

Politicians know the importance of reserving outdoor advertising space as long as a year before an election; otherwise it may not be available. Retailers advertising in local magazines or the rotogravure sections of Sunday newspapers must plan well in advance in order to

It would take eighteen 30-second TV commercials to tell you what's on this page... and other reasons why I like print.

By Al Hampel

Executive Vice President and Director of
Creative Services,
Benton & Bowles, Inc.

When I was a kid, I sold magazines door to door. I didn't do it for the money because they paid you in prizes. I did it because it was the only way I could get to read the magazines.

Of all of them I liked Liberty the best. Before there was Evelyn Wood, there was Liberty magazine. Liberty gave you the reading time for every article. *You have now read about 65 words of this ad or about 30 seconds of TV copy—and, see, we have only just begun.*

I will not deny that writing TV commercials can be exciting and producing them can be glamorous, sometimes even fun. But for me there's still no kick to compare with filling a page with copy—even though I find it more difficult to do than TV.

Without the benefit of motion and bedazzling optical effects, without the impact of music and sound, I know copywriters who become paralyzed with fear at the thought of writing a print ad. Can you blame them? They are part of the generation of TV baby copywriters whose experience with print is limited to an occasional trade ad or a cents-off promotion. The shortage of good print writers is acute and so is the shortage of good print ads.

Print—the amazing new medium.

I sometimes wonder what would have happened if print had followed TV as an advertising medium. Think of print as a *brand-new* medium and the possibilities become astounding. Imagine a new form of advertising that lets you stretch out and sell your product in ways that no 30- or 60-second time span could possibly handle. For example, if you sell toothpaste for cavity prevention on TV, in print you can reveal ten ways you can get children to brush with your toothpaste—a story too long to be squeezed into a TV commercial.

Even in less than single-page units you can often say more than you can in a TV commercial. Grab your prospect with a provocative headline and an interesting visual, write bright informative copy, make it easy to read, and smaller space becomes no obstacle to good print advertising.

Great recipe for selling.

It may look like just another ad to you, but to the woman of the house it's tonight's dessert—or Saturday night's dinner. Any food or beverage advertiser who doesn't consider print for recipes or serving suggestions does so at his own risk.

And in print the recipes aren't limited to food or drink. Learn how to select a mattress or a fine vintage wine. Get a crash course in make-up or how to insulate a house. Cut along the dotted line and file an airline schedule in your wallet. Find a new color for a rug and take it to the store when you shop. No TV set can convey color as accurately as four-color print. There are as many variations of hues on TV as there are sets in use.

And only in print: The information in an ad is yours to keep and refer to as long as the paper lasts.

Coupons–the choicest cut of all.

If you've been at a supermarket check-out counter lately, you'll know the family scissors have been working overtime. The person who invented the cents-off coupon must have loved manufacturers, retailers, and consumers alike. There is scarcely a more useful promotion tool in all of marketing.

A recent issue of a popular magazine contained coupons worth $52.39.

Overnight response.

If you have a son or daughter who wants to be a copywriter, encourage him or her to get a job in a department store. It's the best training they could get. When you write retail print copy, you can expect response to your ad at the point of sale the day after it runs. The buyer of ladies' ready-to-wear will tell you within days how good a copywriter you are. You won't need research to tell you.

Print vs. the subliminal address.

In print, when you invite someone to write for something, your address is available forever. Like this:

Free! Handsome button containing
the immortal words:
IT'S NOT CREATIVE UNLESS IT SELLS.
Send to: Free Button Offer
P.O. Box 5035, F.D.R. Post Office Station
New York, N.Y. 10022

Name_____
Address_____
City_____State_____Zip_____

Could you have remembered that address or copied it from a TV screen in three seconds?

Aubrey Joel, President of Southam Business Publications in Canada, says: "One of print's primary advantages is its ability to free time. A page in a magazine can hold a reader five, ten, fifteen minutes, long enough to fill out a coupon, write a check, make a phone call, or take some other action. And isn't action the ultimate purpose of advertising?"

MAIN IDEA and secondary ideas.

In print you can highlight a main selling idea in your headline. Your secondary selling idea can go in a sub-headline. Other key points can be emphasized with crossheads. And, of course, you can get down to details in the body copy.

This is not as easily done in TV where every word carries as much weight as every other word and it's difficult to communicate more than one major selling idea. Nevertheless, overloaded commercials are very common. They are known as blivots.

Isn't it paradoxical that when TV advertisers want to instill a selling idea they resort to a superimposition of words. In other words, to be remembered it's good to be seen in words—as in print.

Finally, I must mention the seldom used but very titillating print ad that asks you to scratch and sniff the product. I have never resisted becoming involved with this little sensory game and I don't know anybody who has. Unfortunately, there are some ads that smell without scratching.

Those are just some of the reasons why I like print. I speak for no magazine or newspaper, yet I speak for them all. In telling you how great each one of them is numerically, I think they have collectively overlooked the basic virtues they all enjoy.

I could guarantee you this: If somehow print could be viewed as a new medium, you'd see a wave of jaded TV writers and art directors clamoring for print assignments as they once fought for the chance to get into show business via the TV commercial. Print needs that kind of reawakening.

I could write volumes about the effectiveness of TV advertising and maybe someday I will. Call it nostalgia, call it love of the printed word, whatever...this copywriter has seen print go from the most used advertising medium to an underused and misused advertising medium. That bothers me.

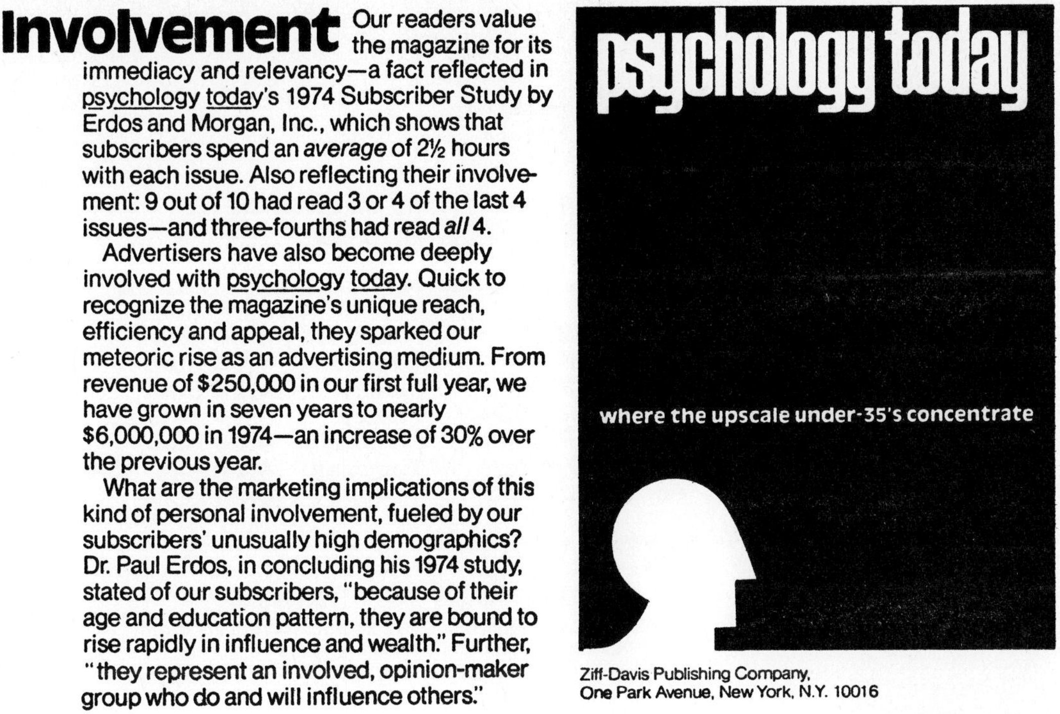

Involvement Our readers value the magazine for its immediacy and relevancy—a fact reflected in psychology today's 1974 Subscriber Study by Erdos and Morgan, Inc., which shows that subscribers spend an *average* of 2½ hours with each issue. Also reflecting their involvement: 9 out of 10 had read 3 or 4 of the last 4 issues—and three-fourths had read *all* 4.

Advertisers have also become deeply involved with psychology today. Quick to recognize the magazine's unique reach, efficiency and appeal, they sparked our meteoric rise as an advertising medium. From revenue of $250,000 in our first full year, we have grown in seven years to nearly $6,000,000 in 1974—an increase of 30% over the previous year.

What are the marketing implications of this kind of personal involvement, fueled by our subscribers' unusually high demographics? Dr. Paul Erdos, in concluding his 1974 study, stated of our subscribers, "because of their age and education pattern, they are bound to rise rapidly in influence and wealth." Further, "they represent an involved, opinion-maker group who do and will influence others."

psychology today

where the upscale under-35's concentrate

Ziff-Davis Publishing Company,
One Park Avenue, New York, N.Y. 10016

FIGURE 6.8
A segment of an advertisement for *Psychology Today* explains why the involvement of *Psychology Today* readers makes it a desirable media choice.

coordinate merchandise on hand with advertising that must be placed weeks ahead of the date on which the advertising will actually appear. Generally speaking, newspapers, radio, and direct mail are considered relatively flexible media. Magazines, network television, point-of-purchase, advertising specialties, and out-of-home media are not.

Cost

One of the most important media characteristics is the cost factor involved in employing them. It is helpful to view cost in two ways: (1) as absolute cost and (2) as relative cost.

Absolute cost is a simple concept. It is the charge imposed for buying a certain amount of time or space in a medium. The significance of this charge becomes apparent when an advertiser compares it with the advertising budget and decides whether the medium is within the realm of fiscal reality or whether it is out of the question. Regardless of how anxious a small advertiser may be to use network television or widely circulated magazines to carry his advertising, the tens of thousands of dollars involved in such a purchase may make such a buy impossible.

Relative cost is different. It introduces such ideas as: What are we

FIGURE 6.7
The intense nature of media competition is revealed in this testimonial (*opposite page*) on the advantages of magazines by an important agency executive. [*Magazine Publishers Association, Inc.*]

197

FIGURE 6.9
The flexibility of
newspaper adver-
tising is shown in
this portion of a
rate card. Other
media may re-
quire weeks or
even months of
lead time in the
placement of ad-
vertisements.
[Eugene Register-
Guard.]

deadlines

Normal Display Advertising
DEADLINES

PUBLICATION DAY	AD DEADLINE
For SUNDAY	Wednesday 4:00 p.m.
For MONDAY	Thursday 4:00 p.m.
For TUESDAY	Friday 4:00 p.m.
For WEDNESDAY	Friday 4:00 p.m.
For THURSDAY	Monday 4:00 p.m.
For FRIDAY	Tuesday 4:00 p.m.
For SATURDAY	Tuesday 4:00 p.m.

ADVANCED DEADLINES

1. Double trucks and color ads 24 hours in advance of normal deadlines, complete with artwork.
2. Holiday deadlines will be distributed as necessary throughout the year.

TABLOID and
REGULAR SECTIONS

accepted for publication under special deadlines arranged with advertising representative.

TV WEEK

Space reservation must be made two (2) weeks prior to publication with complete copy in the shop no less than 10 days prior to publication.

getting for our money in terms of audience quantity and quality? What are we getting in terms of results (benefits to the advertiser)? A common term used to evaluate a medium's audience-reaching capability relative to its advertising rates is "cost per thousand," often abbreviated CPM. The "thousand" employed here may mean a thousand people, thousand homes, or thousand persons within a specific target audience group such as skiers, hang glider enthusiasts, or females between eighteen and thirty-four with incomes exceeding $15,000 per year.

Although cost per thousand is important in selling or buying media for an advertising campaign, it is not always the overriding factor. An elegant or esoteric magazine or expensive television pro-

FIGURE 6.10
The low relative cost of advertising in *The American Farmer* is demonstrated in this advertisement showing the magazine's cost per thousand compared with other farm publications.

gram costs advertisers more, relatively speaking, than a low-quality medium. An exclusive or affluent audience usually brings higher returns to a medium than a lowbrow audience. It is much more expensive to purchase a mailing list of brain surgeons than an equivalent list of taxi drivers because surgeons have more discretionary income to spend.

Another aspect of relative cost involves the relationship between the benefits to be gained by the advertiser and the cost of running the advertising. A postcard sent to prospects that fails to accomplish a stated objective is not only expensive, but an outright waste of money.

A million dollar investment in magazine advertising that reduces other marketing costs and results in many millions of dollars in sales is inexpensive, relatively speaking. Thus, if an advertiser has the money to meet the absolute cost of a media buy, the outlay is not expensive if it does the job intended. By the same token, nothing is cheap if it does not do the job intended. The concept of relative cost is a familiar one in advertising discussions. However, it has ramifications that go beyond the simple media considerations we are concerned with here.

Editorial Environment

A big advantage of some media is the nature of the information or entertainment material that surrounds a buyer's advertising. This quality, called *editorial environment*, is most obvious when applied to magazines, and particularly specialized magazines, but, in a sense, it is applicable to all media.

An advertiser may appreciate greatly the opportunity to place a message in a medium that is pretigious, or authoritative, or respected for its integrity. Naturally, the advertiser feels (or hopes) that some of these qualities will rub off on the product or company advertised. It is not difficult to grasp the idea that an appropriate advertisement placed in *House Beautiful*, *Gourmet*, or *Skiing* magazine enjoys many advantages in terms of its psychological impact on loyal readers of those magazines. Just one of these advantages is the mood of the reader who picks up a specific magazine to read about a particular subject. The advertising often blends in perfectly with the magazine's reading matter and the objective of its readers—to learn something about the subject. See Figure 6.11.

Hallmark greeting cards are often advertised on television in connection with dramatic productions specifically developed to blend with their commercial announcements, as well as to attract a desired audience. For example, a family-oriented Thanksgiving show is the backdrop for sales messages designed to sell Christmas cards.

Advertisements placed in the *Christian Science Monitor*, the *New York Times*, or any other highly reputable newspaper probably enjoy a level of prestige and believability that is higher than the same ads would enjoy in a less-respected medium. To a degree, readers seem to equate a trustworthy editorial policy with a trustworthy advertising policy.

Production Quality

Magazine representatives, for years, have sold advertising space on the strength of magazines' ability to deliver magnificent color and detailed black-and-white reproduction that would authentically display an advertiser's product, or create a mood, in a manner no other

People have been drinking tea out of our cups for 200 years.

We made our first cup for tea-drinkers at Royal Copenhagen in 1775. It belonged to our Design No.1 which we called Blue Fluted. Today, 200 years later, you can drink your tea from a Blue Fluted cup. It is still Design No.1. Blue Flower, equally old, is also very much "alive" and as popular as Blue Fluted.

For extra-special tea-parties, we have a cup, par excellence, in Flora Danica. The first one was made for a Russian Empress when Royal Copenhagen was 15 years old.

The Tranquebar cup, designed by Christian Joachim in 1914, is named after an old Danish colony in India. If you prefer a very modern cup, we would recommend our Blue Line and Domino. Newest of all is Whitepot. Royal Copenhagen has a cup for every occasion.

1. Blue Fluted, full lace
2. Blue Flower
3. Flora Danica
4. Tranquebar
5. Blue Line
6. Domino
7. Whitepot
8. Dagmar
9. Brown Rose
10. Gemina
11. Golden Basket
12. Frijsenborg

Royal Copenhagen has been making history for 200 years.

1775 ≈ 1975
ROYAL COPENHAGEN PORCELAIN
Available at fine stores everywhere and from our shop.
573 Madison Avenue, New York 10022.

FIGURE 6.11
The editorial environment was obviously an important consideration when Royal Copenhagen Porcelain decided to run this advertisement in *Gourmet* magazine.

medium could match. Although the argument has lost some of its impact with the growth of color television, sophisticated newspaper magazine sections, and elaborate direct-mail pamphlets and brochures, magazines are still capable of fine reproduction that can be a strong selling point with some advertisers and media buyers. On the retail level, radio and television stations that offer excellent local programming and production aids in the creation of commercials have a big advantage over stations that do not. According to the Television

Bureau of Advertising, more than 50 percent of the television stations in the United States sell their commercial production services in competition with businesses that specialize in television and radio production.

Permanence

Some media are more durable than others in the sense that they remain before prospects' eyes or within their grasp for a longer period of time. Painted bulletins, for example, may continue delivering the same message to the passing public for a year or more. Monthly magazines are often kept around the house for many months. Weekly newspapers are considered current until a new issue arrives, in contrast to daily newspapers which, characteristically, are read and then discarded. Whatever the case, print media, in general, do offer the reader a chance to study an advertisement or refer back to it, if desired. Broadcast media, on the other hand, give fleeting impressions which cannot be retrieved at the whim of the listener or viewer. This attribute of permanence or durability is of real importance to an advertiser who has a complicated or lengthy message to convey. Retail grocery stores, variety stores, and highly technical industrial companies are examples of advertisers who need a medium that provides a degree of permanence in order that readers may have time to receive the message as it was intended.

Trade Acceptability

This is the degree of acceptance exhibited by retailers, wholesalers, or other intermediaries for a particular medium. It is important when a manufacturer tries to get support for a product along the channels of distribution that the intermediaries be enthusiastic concerning a supplier's advertising. Without such support, a campaign will rarely achieve its full impact or move a maximum volume of products.

Merchandising Cooperation

Years ago, when newspapers first started to feel the competitive pinch from magazines and radio networks for national advertisers' dollars, they developed a system for helping national clients on the local level. They introduced such activities as making calls on retailers handling advertised products to tell them of national advertisers' campaigns in their media. Moreover, they urged retailers to stock up on the advertised products and to tie in with the national advertisers' campaigns. This was to be accomplished by building special store displays of advertised items and by featuring them in their own retail ads—often the same day and, of course, in the same newspaper. Newspaper sales representatives soon learned that an offer of *merchandising coopera-*

tion was a persuasive addition to their regular sales presentations. The practice spread rapidly to other media. Today, some advertisers or their agency media buyers undoubtedly consider merchandising activity when choosing between competing media. The danger here lies in the possibility that a media buyer will choose between competing media on the basis of the free or "at cost" merchandising aid when the decision should be made on the basis of what a medium can accomplish in reaching the proper audience to meet the advertising objectives. But when all other aspects of competing media appear equal, merchandising cooperation can be the factor that tips the scale in favor of one medium over another.

SUMMARY

Media make up the fourth category of businesses that constitute the advertising industry. Through their ability to inform and entertain both mass and specialized audiences, media provide advertisers with the means to reach potential customers with their advertising messages. Advertising, in turn, subsidizes the cost of producing media. Among publications such as newspapers and magazines, it enables publishers to price their media at a cost much lower than would be possible without advertising. It enables the broadcast media—radio and television—to provide their services to consumers free of charge.

Because of the importance of advertising to their existence, most media employ a staff that sells time and space to advertisers or their media buyers. They also employ creative people and a promotion staff to expedite the efforts of their salespeople.

No medium is best. Each one has advantages or combinations of characteristics that make it a viable choice for certain advertisers at certain times. Media sales representatives compete with one another for advertisers' business on the basis of these characteristics. Conversely, media buyers, acting on behalf of advertisers, apply these attributes when deciding which media would work together best in a media mix designed to help meet advertising objectives. Some of the more important considerations used to differentiate media from one another are:

1 *Selectivity.* The ability of a medium to reach a particular audience, based either on the audience's geographic location or on unique traits. These traits may be demographic or psychographic in nature.

2 *Coverage.* The size or nature of the audience a medium can reach. More properly, coverage refers to the degree with which a medium can penetrate a market, that is, homes in an area or persons within a specific group.

3 *Flexibility.* The ease or amount of time required to place an advertisement in a medium, change it, or kill it.

4 *Cost.* In the absolute sense, the charge imposed for buying a certain amount of time or space. In the relative sense, what the medium yields in terms of audience quality and quantity and in terms of results obtained for the money spent.

5 *Editorial environment.* The nature of the information or entertainment material that surrounds a buyer's advertising and how well it serves to meet the advertiser's objectives.

6 *Production quality.* The ability of a medium to reproduce advertising with great fidelity, or, on the local level, to aid clients with the production of their advertising.

7 *Permanence.* The ability of a medium to keep advertisements before prospects' eyes or within their grasp for an extended period of time.

8 *Trade acceptability.* The degree of acceptance a medium can generate among the advertisers' intermediaries—retailers, wholesalers, and other persons working within an advertiser's channels of distribution.

9 *Merchandising cooperation.* A service offered by most media whereby the medium works to generate cooperation among intermediaries in conjunction with an advertising campaign.

QUESTIONS FOR DISCUSSION

1 Describe some of the businesses which make up the media branch of the advertising industry.

2 A number of large, general-circulation magazines, *Look*, *Life*, and the *Saturday Evening Post*, went out of business in the 1960s despite record-high circulation figures. Some observers attributed their failures to the growth of television. Based upon the discussion of the media business in this chapter, how would you explain the demise of these magazines?

3 Media and advertisers are highly dependent upon one another. Explain.

4 Assume you are a media salesperson attempting to sell a cereal firm on using your medium. What would your argument be if you represented a daily newspaper? A television network? A womens' magazine?

5 What is the role of a medium's promotion department?

6 Representative firms are an important arm of the media business. Describe the functions of such a firm and how they fit into the advertising business.

7 Why do you think newspapers dominate total media expenditures? Using the figures in Table 6.1 for *national* advertising only, rank the major media in order of importance. How do you account for the change in the order?

8 Discuss some advertisers to whom you feel editorial environment would be an especially important factor in choosing advertising media.

9 Why is relative cost an important consideration when studying media advertising rates?

10 Visit a local advertising medium, and prepare a brief report on the advertising people working there and what they do.

FOR FURTHER REFERENCE

Barban, Arnold M., Stephen Cristol, and Frank J. Kopec: *Essentials of Media Planning*, Crain Books, Chicago, 1976.

Barton, Roger: *Media in Advertising*, McGraw-Hill Book Company, New York, 1964.

Brown, Lyndon O., Richard S. Lessler, and William M. Weilbacher: *Advertising Media*, The Ronald Press Company, New York, 1957.

Sissors, Jack Z., and E. Reynold Petray: *Advertising Media Planning*, Crain Books, Chicago, 1976.

Television Factbook, Television Digest, Inc., Washington, (irr.) 2 vols., Stations Volume and Services Volume.

World Communications, The Unesco Press, Essex, England, 1975.

CHAPTER 7

TELEVISION AND RADIO

Ninety-seven percent of the homes in America contain at least one television set, and those sets are turned on, on the average, for 6 hours and 15 minutes each day.[1] In addition, 83 percent[2] of all Americans listen to radio every day. Small wonder these electronic media are powerful factors in our society, and important vehicles for carrying advertising messages.

In this chapter, we present, in some depth, both radio and television, keeping in mind that while both are broadcast, or electronic, media, they are very different from one another in many respects and are generally found in intense competition for advertisers' dollars. We shall investigate the unique nature of broadcast media as well as the qualities which differentiate radio and television. As background for an understanding of the makeup of these media we shall discuss the structure of the broadcast industry. Advertisers considering radio and television advertising must make a number of decisions involved with the alternative uses of the media; therefore we shall cover a number of different types of broadcast advertising, as well as the important areas of audiences and programs. Finally, we shall discuss broadcast rating systems and the highlights of rate structures as they apply to the buying of radio and television advertising.

Radio has been an important vehicle for advertising in the United States for about 50 years, television for only half that long. And yet television's rapid growth has lifted it to a position where approximately $3 are spent for television advertising to every $1 for radio. However, when one examines local advertising expenditures, it becomes apparent that radio actually bills more dollars among retailers and other local advertisers than does TV. National advertisers, on the other hand, contribute the bulk of television's advertising revenues.

Late in the 1950s when television-set sales were exploding and advertisers were switching their budgets from radio to television, many advertising experts viewed radio as moribund. Yet in 1974, an astonishing $3.5 billion was spent for the purchase of radios by American consumers, and advertisers spent more than $1.3 billion for radio time.

THE UNIQUE NATURE OF BROADCASTING

Radio and television stations, unlike the print media, rely on waves passing through the air and ground around us to carry their messages. The broadcaster can control the power and direction of his signal (within Federal Communications Commission regulations, at least), but he has no assurance that the messages sent out will take root—that

[1] *Nielsen Television, '74,* A. C. Nielsen & Co., p. 7.
[2] *Radio Facts, 1975,* Radio Advertising Bureau, p. 10.

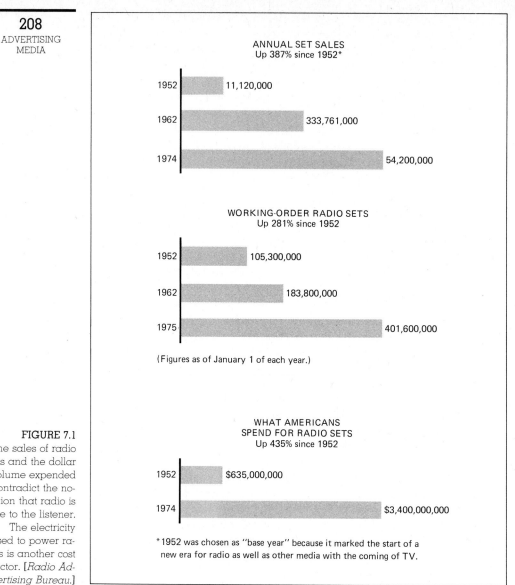

ANNUAL SET SALES
Up 387% since 1952*

1952   11,120,000

1962   333,761,000

1974   54,200,000

WORKING-ORDER RADIO SETS
Up 281% since 1952

1952   105,300,000

1962   183,800,000

1975   401,600,000

(Figures as of January 1 of each year.)

WHAT AMERICANS
SPEND FOR RADIO SETS
Up 435% since 1952

1952 $635,000,000

1974 $3,400,000,000

*1952 was chosen as "base year" because it marked the start of a
new era for radio as well as other media with the coming of TV.

FIGURE 7.1
The sales of radio
sets and the dollar
volume expended
contradict the no-
tion that radio is
free to the listener.
The electricity
used to power ra-
dios is another cost
factor. [*Radio Ad-
vertising Bureau.*]

they will be received. For one thing, the potential listeners or viewers
must turn on a radio or television set. For another, they must have the
set tuned to the proper station, and finally, they must actually listen to
or watch the transmitted message in order to complete the communications process. But once the listener does these things, transmission is
instantaneous. Such is not always the case with print media, some of
which may lie around the house for hours or even weeks before being
looked at or read.

Listeners and viewers turn to radio and television for a multitude of reasons, but the primary purposes are to be entertained or informed. Beyond those reasons, there is the widely accepted idea that many listeners or viewers employ radio and television for background noise when they engage in their day-to-day activities. They value these media simply for their presence. When at home, many people use broadcasting simply for company; students and office workers often use it as a backdrop for other mental activity. In some households TV is even employed as a sitter for children and dogs!

Because broadcasting is employed for many functions and because human tastes vary, there is a demand for a multiplicity of stations and programming. Some listeners look for cultural uplift; others seek light entertainment. Whereas some look for news in depth and analysis of that news, others are more than satisfied with a superficial review of major happenings. Some tune in to Bach and Sibelius, while others tune in to Diana Ross or Elton John. Broadcasters attempt to build their programming to attract an identifiable segment of a total market or city that will, in turn, attract advertisers.

Unlike most printed publications, broadcasting appears to the listening and viewing publics to be free. But this is a misconception. We have already alluded to the billions of dollars spent for radio and television sets each year, not to mention the cost of electricity to power those receivers. Even publicly owned stations are subsidized by tax monies, and the fringe private-subscription stations are sponsored by persons willing and able to provide the contributions to keep these stations airborne. The advertising dollars that support commercial broadcasting are, of course, ultimately paid by the buyers of advertised products, as discussed earlier in this book.

In considering the unique qualities which set broadcasting apart, the word that seems to characterize broadcasting best is "pervasive." Like advertising itself, radio and television are seemingly everywhere in American life. It is not enough to acknowledge that television and radio have reached a saturation level and are found in almost every home in the United States. More than 40 percent of the homes contain two or more television sets, and the average family owns 5.5 radios located in bedrooms, kitchens, living rooms, garages, automobiles, and even bathrooms. A trip to the mountains, the ball game, or beach may bring no respite from the omnipresent portable. Americans are, as radio promotions tell us, "radio-active" and "on the go with radio."

Undoubtedly, one of the reasons for broadcasting's ubiquitous nature stems from the fact that listening or viewing, unlike reading, requires no real effort nor even that the listener be able to read. Although this literacy factor may be of negligible importance in the United States today, in developing nations it is all-important. Those who would communicate with the masses are forced to turn to broadcast media in countries where illiteracy runs high; no other medium can do the job.

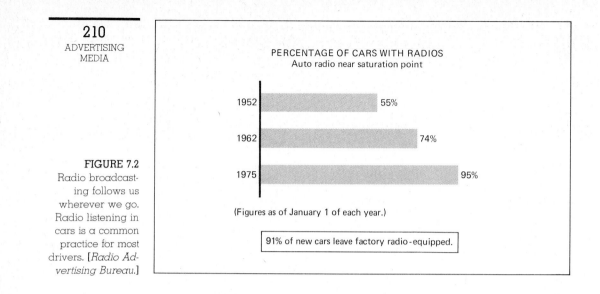

PERCENTAGE OF CARS WITH RADIOS
Auto radio near saturation point

1952	55%
1962	74%
1975	95%

(Figures as of January 1 of each year.)

91% of new cars leave factory radio-equipped.

FIGURE 7.2
Radio broadcast-
ing follows us
wherever we go.
Radio listening in
cars is a common
practice for most
drivers. [*Radio Ad-
vertising Bureau.*]

Another way in which broadcasting is unique is that whether the presentation is taped or live, the listener or viewer has the feeling of another human being's presence. It is instantaneous contact without an intervening medium such as a printed page provides. Thus, the broadcast media claim to be more personal than their printed competitors. In TV, the whole effect is heightened greatly by the combining of sight, sound, and motion, which add realism to the communications act at the same time they make television the ideal medium for demonstration. Radio, on the other hand, is often referred to as a "theater of the mind" where the listener is free to conjure up a personal picture of people, scenes, and even the benefits of advertised goods. In this regard, radio bears a resemblance to print in that reader and listener involvement is often required to provide the mental imagery to accompany the spoken or written word.

Other delineating factors which make broadcasting unique include the following: broadcasting is time-oriented and fleeting, while print is more space-oriented and, relatively speaking, permanent. Broadcasting is nonexpansible. There is a limit to the number of hours in a day, and the number of minutes each station is allowed to broadcast advertising. In contrast, newspapers and magazines have been known to expand to 300 to 400 pages when the need develops. Finally, one might argue that broadcasting is a more competitive business than publishing. Relatively small cities generally have only one daily newspaper, but ten or more radio stations and two or three television stations. Large metropolitan areas will house two to five daily newspapers, but literally a hundred or more broadcast stations. Although thousands of magazines are published in this country, only a few will be directed at the same specific audiences.

FIGURE 7.3
The close personal
relationship be-
tween announcers
or disc jockeys and
regular listeners is
a crucial factor in
the success of
personality-oriented
radio stations.
[*Courtesy of Dan
Nims and KPNW
AM & FM.*]

THE STRUCTURE OF BROADCASTING

The average American, when turning on a radio or television set, has
little realization of the complexities which underlie the presentation of
his or her favorite television or radio program. Taken as a whole,
broadcasting is big business. Its investment in plant and equipment is
prodigious, and the total dollar investment each year by advertisers
had exceeded $7 billion in 1974.[3] In addition, tens of thousands of
employees are engaged in the various aspects of broadcasting which
ultimately make it possible for us to pick up the program of our choice
at almost any hour of the day or night. Figure 7.4 gives a graphic
representation of some of the institutions that make up and affect the
advertising industry. In the following pages we shall elaborate on
some of these businesses, because one cannot truly understand
broadcasting today without some perspective on the industry and how
it came to be as it is.

The Radio Station

The core or basic cell of radio broadcasting is the station, which first
began in the United States, on a commercial basis, in the early 1920s.

[3] *Broadcasting Yearbook*, Broadcasting Publications, Inc., Washington, 1975, p. B-176.

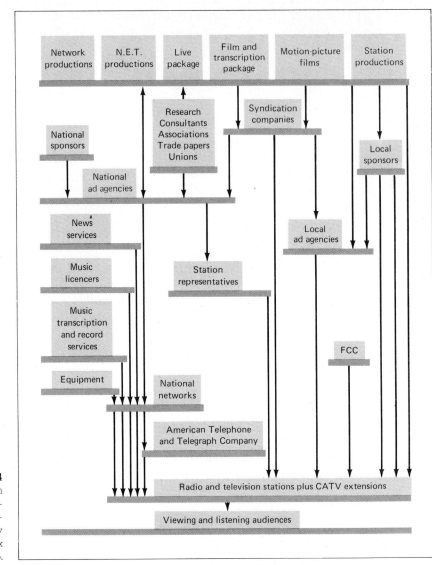

FIGURE 7.4

This diagram
shows the compo-
nents of the broad-
casting industry
and their complex
interrelationship.

By 1922, the Department of Commerce had licensed 30 radio stations. Technological improvements in receivers increased interest in radio as an entertainment device and led to the rapid expansion of America's listening audience. The living room console became a status symbol and, in many homes, the center of family activity. Parents and children would sit around the radio, staring at the box, and sharing their favorite programs, just as they do today with television. Contributing greatly to the improvement in radio programming were radio networks, which provided much higher caliber productions than individual stations could have hoped to produce themselves. News broadcasts, as well as entertainment features, began to appear as part of radio's broadcast services.

By 1931, more than 600 commercial stations were on the air, and radio was firmly established as a part of the American way of life. In the ensuing years, radio programs featuring such stars as Jack Benny, Fibber McGee and Molly, and Edgar Bergen and Charlie McCarthy captured the hearts of America in the evening hours, while Helen Trent, Our Gal Sunday, Ma Perkins, and others provided captivating soap opera fare for daytime listeners.

The power used in transmitting the signal is an important factor in determining the range of reception for a given station. In addition to the amount of power, the antenna system of the station, its frequency on the dial, and various local conditions are important factors in a station's geographical coverage. On the basis of power, there are, essentially, three kinds of radio stations. First, there is the purely local station, with a receiving range of about 25 miles. Second, there is the regional station, which may cover an entire state. The least common type is the clear-channel station. This type of station has lots of power—up to 50,000 watts—and operates on a frequency where no other station is permitted during evening hours.

The majority of American radio stations operate on the principle of amplitude modulation (AM). More than 4,400 AM stations are broad-

FIGURE 7.5
Radio station coverage maps indicate where the station may be received with clarity. Here the solid line indicates the station's best or primary coverage, while the dotted line indicates the secondary coverage area. [*KVI Radio.*]

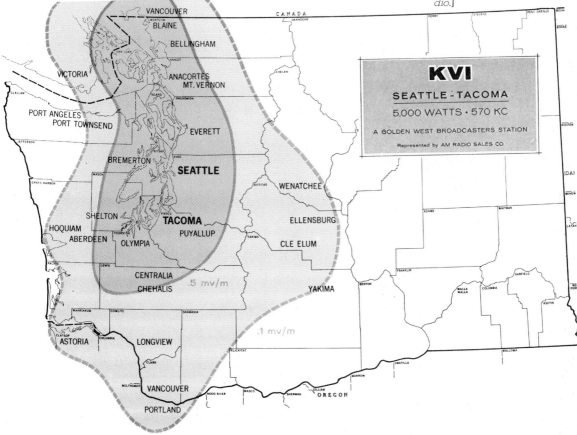

casting in the United States, and an additional 3,593 stations operate on frequency modulation (FM).[4] FM broadcasting has one outstanding advantage over AM. It is practically static-free; thus its signals are received with greater fidelity. Counterbalancing this advantage are two disadvantages: (1) FM broadcasts can be received only on special sets not owned by all Americans. (2) FM signals cannot be received for great distances; thus this type of radio broadcasting has been confined primarily to areas where a large potential audience is available.

The Television Station

Television stations are essentially outgrowths of the radio industry, for when television appeared, many radio station operators moved to secure licenses to operate television stations. This was considered a logical diversification by these managers, who felt that their radio know-how would carry over into the new medium. Moreover, they had an uneasy feeling that television might replace radio as an entertainment and advertising medium, and they wanted to hedge against a change in the business climate.

The station designations in television are called channels, and there are two sets of channel designations in American television. The

FIGURE 7.6

For many years, the use of TV has increased in American households. Recent studies indicate that there may have been a slight decrease in household usage in 1975, however. [*A. C. Nielsen Media Research Division.*]

[4] Ibid.

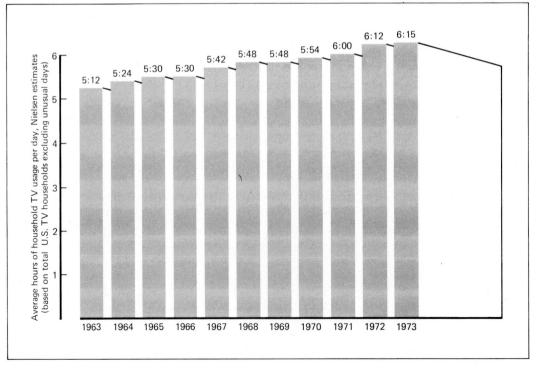

most common is the familiar very high frequency (VHF) station, which uses channels 2 through 13. The other is the ultrahigh frequency (UHF) station, with a channel spectrum running from channel 14 through channel 83. Television stations, regardless of their frequency, transmit two signals at the same time. The video signal comes via amplitude modulation, while the audio signal uses frequency modulation broadcasting. Thus, the sound part of television is comparable in fidelity and range to FM radio.

Station Growth The growth of television in the United States can be illustrated by the increased number of television broadcasting stations. Television was about to become a commercial reality when World War II started. The five stations which the FCC had licensed finally came on the air the year after the end of the war. By 1950, there were 96 stations operating in approximately 50 different geographical markets. In other words, television was still a selective medium from a geographical coverage point of view. The number of commercial and educational stations had climbed to 963 by January 1976,[5] and almost every American home was within range of the signal of at least one television station.

Set ownership kept pace with station starts. In 1950 the number of homes possessing a television set numbered 3.8 million; the figure stood at 68.5 million late in 1974, a penetration rate of 97 percent.[6]

[5] Federal Communications Commission, January 1976.
[6] *TV Basics 18*, Television Bureau of Advertising, 1975.

FIGURE 7.7
Weekly TV viewing by men and women varies according to demographic characteristics such as age and household size and income. Such data are important in the buying and selling of TV advertising. [*A. C. Nielsen Media Research Division.*]

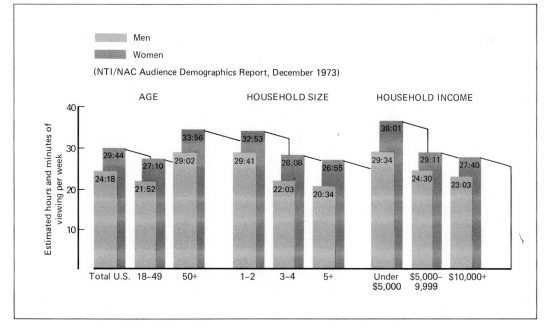

Multiple-set homes now number 28.4 million, or 41 percent of all TV homes. The rate of use of television sets in the home depends to some degree upon family income and the ages of family members. However, on an average, home TV usage rates range from five to seven hours per day.

Because the basic equipment needed to establish a television station is much more costly than that needed for a radio station, it is unlikely that the number of television stations will approach the number of radio stations. Furthermore, since the television signal does not "bend" with the shape of the earth as does the AM radio signal, geographically isolated regions are difficult to reach by regular television transmission.

Expanding TV's Reach Methods have been developed to bring television to these isolated areas. If the market is fairly large, a *satellite station* may be established. This station is similar to any other televi-

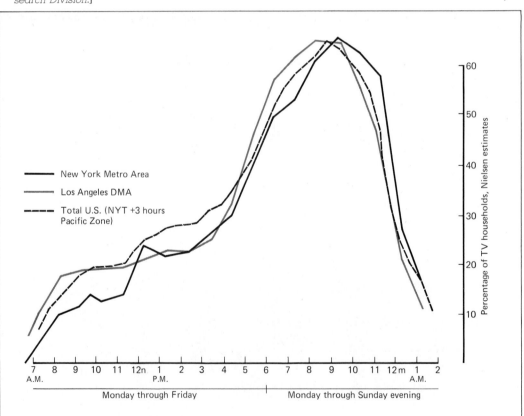

sion station except that in some instances its equipment is incapable of broadcasting local programs. It can, however, by means of *microwave relay*, pick up the programs of a nearby station and transmit them.

Even more common today is the *translator*, which can extend a station's coverage into markets previously impossible to reach, economically, even with a satellite station. In some communities the Community Antenna Television System (CATV) is often used. An entrepreneur erects a high antenna which brings in the faraway signal. The privilege of tapping this antenna by means of coaxial cables piped to the subscriber's home is sold for a monthly fee. CATV, therefore, is sometimes called "cable TV." This idea is also used for apartment houses in metropolitan areas where structural steel acts as a barrier to good reception, or in exclusive housing developments where antennas are not allowed. A total of about 3,200 such cable systems were operating in 1975, serving a subscription list of approxi-

FIGURE 7.9
This comparison of seasonal variations in TV viewing by men and women affects TV advertising sales and, to some degree, the rates charged for time. [*A. C. Nielsen Media Research Division.*]

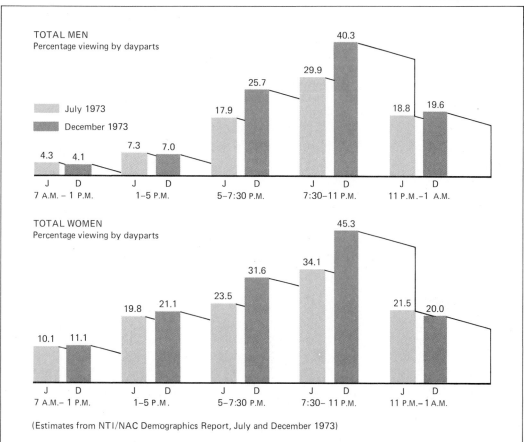

TOTAL MEN
Percentage viewing by dayparts

July 1973
December 1973

	J	D	J	D	J	D	J	D	J	D
	4.3	4.1	7.3	7.0	17.9	25.7	29.9	40.3	18.8	19.6
	7 A.M. – 1 P.M.		1–5 P.M.		5–7:30 P.M.		7:30–11 P.M.		11 P.M.–1 A.M.	

TOTAL WOMEN
Percentage viewing by dayparts

	J	D	J	D	J	D	J	D	J	D
	10.1	11.1	19.8	21.1	23.5	31.6	34.1	45.3	21.5	20.0
	7 A.M.– 1 P.M.		1–5 P.M.		5–7:30 P.M.		7:30– 11 P.M.		11 P.M.–1 A.M.	

(Estimates from NTI/NAC Demographics Report, July and December 1973)

mately 10 million homes. The number of CATV viewers has more than doubled every five years since 1955.[7] The physical limitations of television broadcasting have been overcome in the United States, and more and more communities are receiving television entertainment—and advertising. In 1969 the FCC voted to allow CATV systems to originate commercials at natural intermissions or breaks.[8]

Pay-TV   Another television institution—pay-TV—usually employs the same transmission technique. The basic difference between CATV and pay-TV is program responsibility. Still in the experimental stage, pay-TV generates its own programming—reputed to be of higher quality than the usual TV fare—while most CATV outlets merely feed existing programs as produced by the networks and stations into home receivers of subscribers. Pay-TV's fees are usually assessed on the basis of actual viewing rather than as a monthly rental charge.

Pay-television is designed to permit television viewers to escape from advertiser-sponsored programming. Although it has never been positively established that pay-TV will not carry advertising, as it now stands, the entire cost of programming is borne by subscribers' fees. The pay-TV idea has been tried in several cities. Support by subscribers, both in numbers participating in the plan and in their use of the service after joining the plan, has met with limited success. The most promising and ambitious venture, Subscription Television, Inc., was outlawed by the voters of California in a bitter referendum battle in 1964. Whether substantial numbers of Americans will pay for this kind of home entertainment is still to be ascertained.

Color Television   Early models of sets capable of receiving color signals were very expensive, yet provided poor reception. The number of programs aired for color viewing was insufficient to generate much interest among viewers or advertisers. These obstacles were removed little by little. By 1975, there were more than 48 million homes—71 percent of all TV homes in the United States—with color television.[9] Thus color television is now a standard fixture on the American scene.

Networks

We have already mentioned another important broadcast institution, the network. By furnishing news and entertainment programs to radio and television stations, networks help stations fill their programming

[7] *Broadcasting and Cable Television*, Committee for Economic Development, New York, 1975, pp. 64–65.
[8] *The 4A Newsletter*, American Association of Advertising Agencies, Inc., New York, Nov. 10, 1969, p. 5.
[9] *TV Basics 18*, op. cit.

needs. Because the potential audience of the typical local station is limited, the rates it can charge advertisers are comparatively low. This means that the station is financially unable to present a steady stream of quality programs. Top-flight talent and production are expensive; moreover, they tend to be concentrated in such centers as New York City and Hollywood. The problem of presenting good entertainment which would attract enough viewers to warrant use of the station by national advertisers was solved in part by the development of network broadcasting.

Growth of Networks Shortly after the first commercial radio stations went on the air, several stations banded together for the purpose of simultaneously broadcasting the same program. This was accomplished by sending the program to each station by telephone wire. Broadcasting networks have grown rapidly and now play an indispensable role in American radio and television. Essentially a *network* is a business organization that provides programs to a number of affiliated stations in local markets throughout the nation. These stations agree in affiliation contracts to broadcast the programs furnished by the network. Stations are provided with a varied program schedule, and advertisers who feel they can benefit from national coverage are given an opportunity to tie their commercials to the network programming.

In radio's heyday—before the advent of television—the networks brought the radio listeners of America their entertainment. Network radio was a prosperous advertising medium. Today, however, TV has usurped the national entertainment function of radio, and network

FIGURE 7.10
Behind the scenes in a television station are housed the complex and expensive pieces of electronic equipment that make effective commercial production and transmission possible. [*Courtesy of Larry Cushman and KEZI-TV.*]

FIGURE 7.11
The key to expert production is an expert director. One such expert is shown here carefully coordinating a TV commercial for a local retailer who is on camera in the studio on the right of this control booth. [*KEZI-TV.*]

radio sales account for less than 3 percent of the medium's total advertising revenue.[10]

Networks Today The three television networks—CBS, NBC, and ABC—are all thriving. Their programs are in demand, and their operations are profitable. For example, television time sales in 1974 totaled nearly $5 billion, of which almost one-half was network advertising.[11]

Technically, network television operates somewhat differently from network radio. Instead of using leased telephone wires to send programs to their affiliates, television networks use one of three devices: coaxial cables, microwave relay stations, or in rare cases, direct off-the-air pickups from another affiliate station.

There is still another difference between television and radio networks. In addition to the "big three" networks—CBS, NBC, and ABC—in radio there is one more giant—the Mutual Broadcasting System. Furthermore, in order to serve a broader spectrum of stations, ABC has established some smaller subsidiary networks known as American Contemporary Radio Network, American Entertainment Radio Network, American FM Radio Network, and American Information Radio Network. Thus, it is not unusual to find one city with stations served by each of these ABC organizations. Traditionally, one would rarely have found stations in the same market served by one network system.

There are other, less obvious radio networks that take a variety of forms. Some are ethnically oriented, and one, the Keystone Broadcast-

[10] *Broadcasting Yearbook*, loc. cit.
[11] Ibid.

such as New England or the Southeastern states. Thus, they provide a means of catering to regional tastes and preferences. Every region of the country is interested in its own news and weather developments. In sports, the regional loyalties of football, baseball, basketball, and hockey fans are strong indeed. NCAA basketball, in 1976, was broadcast regionally on Saturday afternoons to meet local interests.

The time differential between the East and West Coasts of our country is another reason for the existence of regional networks. A nighttime program aired at 9 P.M. in New York City will be received on the West Coast at 6 P.M., hardly an equivalent viewing hour. Thus, the Pacific Coast segments of the national networks videotape Eastern programs and air them at more convenient hours for their audiences. Videotape allows immediate playback, whereas film takes many hours to process. The advantage here is that the program can be aired the same day, whereas a filmed version would have to wait until the following day or week in order to fill the same time slot. By using the regional network, stations can time their programs to coincide with listening habits and thus register great listener popularity. Both national and regional advertisers benefit from this system.

3   There are no local networks as there are local stations. Instead the third network classification is the *tailor-made network*, in which a few or many stations join temporarily for a special program. As soon as the special program has been broadcast, the tailor-made network goes out of existence, although it may be re-formed for special purposes. This type of network is especially popular for the broadcasting of sports events, such as professional football or high school basketball tournaments, because interest in various teams is selective by area. Once an advertiser decides that a sports program is a satisfactory vehicle for the promotion of his product, he must decide whether he wants to use an existing network or create a special arrangement for his own purposes. Although the tailor-made network often has trouble clearing regularly scheduled time slots, and must overcome engineering problems, it permits the advertiser to pinpoint his message to the markets he is trying to reach without much wasted coverage. Nevertheless, the tailor-made network is the least used type.

As a general rule, the local television station that is a network affiliate will charge the network approximately 30 percent of its regular hourly time charge for broadcasting network programs. One may ask how the affiliate station can make anything if it sells its time at such a discount. The answer has two parts. First, the costs of airing a network program are very low for the affiliated station. Only a minimum staff is needed, and there are no production or talent charges as there would be if the station produced its own program. Second, the real income for the station comes from the sale of time between network programs or at station breaks. Network programs have high viewership ratings generally, and an advertiser is willing to pay a premium price for a spot which is next to a highly rated program.

The big three TV Networks used to be all you needed. But times have changed.

Today there is a Fourth TV Network serving 13 million consumers in their own language in **Spanish USA.** SIN...the 14 station Network that sells your product in Spanish to Spanish speaking consumers. Makes sense, doesn't it? Surely better than hoping for spillover impressions when you only use the Big Three.

When you use the Fourth Network, your commercial recall will be 2½ times greater. You'll be talking to younger, bigger families who buy more of just about everything.

SIN can help you sell **Spanish USA**...reach more people, more often and more effectively without increasing your television budget. Your results can be spectacular. And we can prove it. Use the Big Three, but add the Fourth Network. You need it.

U.S. SPANISH TELEVISION NETWORK
250 Park Avenue, New York, N.Y. 10017 (212) 697-0585

WXTV New York □ KMEX-TV Los Angeles □ KWEX-TV San Antonio □ WLTV Miami □ KDTV San Francisco □ WCIU-TV Chicago □ KFTV Fresno/Hanford □ KLOC-TV Sacramento/Modesto □ KMXN-TV Albuquerque □ KORO-TV Corpus Christi □ XEWT-TV San Diego/Tijuana □ XEJ-TV El Paso/Juarez □ XHBC-TV Yuma-El Centro/Mexicali □ XEFE-TV Laredo/Nuevo Laredo □ Coming Soon: Phoenix, Denver, Houston.

FIGURE 7.14
The U.S. Spanish Television Network offers advertisers a simple means of reaching a large segment of the American Spanish-speaking population. [*U.S. Spanish Television Network.*]

The Federal Communications Commission

In order for advertising people to work effectively with radio and television, it is important that they understand the constraints within which broadcasters operate. The primary source of these constraints is a governmental agency known as the FCC. Since 1934, broadcasting in the United States has been under the control of the Federal Communications Commission. The FCC not only makes the rules under which broadcasters operate, but is also responsible for licensing each station. These licenses are subject to renewal every three years, and it is this requirement that gives the FCC its muscle.

When a station is launched by a new owner, the owner submits a plan for the direction that station will take. When the FCC makes a decision to grant or reject the application, it takes into account the commitments made by the applicant. One of the angles the FCC people examine is whether the station will be operated in response to the interests and needs of the public. The applicant must pledge a certain amount of public service broadcasting and normally includes a pledge to carry public service advertising as well. Once the license has been granted, the FCC bases license renewals on how effectively the broadcaster has carried out his original pledge. In addition, the public is always told of a station's application for license renewal and asked to testify for or against the renewal application.

Without some form of federal control, broadcasting in the United States would be chaotic. Station signals would overlap, and unscrupulous opportunists would undoubtedly wreak havoc on what is now a fairly orderly system. Despite this, many broadcasters resent some of the governmental interference imposed on broadcasting that is not matched in the newspaper and magazine businesses, protected as they are by the First Amendment to the Constitution.

Beyond FCC regulations, the broadcasters, through their own associations, have additional self-imposed restrictions in the form of the Radio and Television Codes of the National Association of Broadcasters (NAB). These ethical codes have aided greatly in minimizing broadcaster abuses in the areas of both programming and advertising. They relate to matters such as advertising to children, taste, the number of commercial minutes allowed per broadcast hour, etc. Figure 7.15 is a reproduction of a page from an NAB code book. It is inevitable that the FCC casts an eye on how well stations meet their own industry standards when the FCC decides on whether or not to grant a license renewal. This has the effect of obligating broadcasters to abide by codes which otherwise would be simply "gentlemens' agreements."

TYPES OF BROADCAST ADVERTISING

A national advertiser who has decided to embark on an advertising campaign using the broadcast media has a number of decisions to make beyond simply selecting radio or television or a combination of the two. This section deals with the major alternatives and some of the criteria used in determining how to approach a broadcast campaign.

IX. General Advertising Standards

1. This Code establishes basic standards for all television broadcasting. The principles of acceptability and good taste within the Program Standards section govern the presentation of advertising where applicable. In addition, the Code establishes in this section special standards which apply to television advertising.

2. A commercial television broadcaster makes his facilities available for the advertising of products and services and accepts commercial presentations for such advertising. However, a television broadcaster should, in recognition of his responsibility to the public, refuse the facilities of his station to an advertiser where he has good reason to doubt the integrity of the advertiser, the truth of the advertising representations, or the compliance of the advertiser with the spirit and purpose of all applicable legal requirements.

3. Identification of sponsorship must be made in all sponsored programs in accordance with the requirements of the Communications Act of 1934, as amended, and the Rules and Regulations of the Federal Communications Commission.

4. Representations which disregard normal safety precautions shall be avoided.

Children shall not be represented, except under proper adult supervision, as being in contact with, or demonstrating a product recognized as potentially dangerous to them.

5. In consideration of the customs and attitudes of the communities served, each television broadcaster should refuse his facilities to the advertisement of products and services, or the use of advertising scripts, which the station has good reason to believe would be objectionable to a substantial and responsible segment of the community. These standards should be applied with judgment and flexibility, taking into consideration the characteristics of the medium, its home and family audience, and the form and content of the particular presentation.

6. The advertising of hard liquor (distilled spirits) is not acceptable.

FIGURE 7.15
A page from the Television Code of the National Association of Broadcasters.

The Network Approach

Advertisers often turn to the radio or TV networks to carry their advertising when they wish to cover the entire country or a very large geographical section thereof. It is comparable in its coverage to advertising in a large national magazine. There are many different reasons for choosing the network to carry advertising messages, some of the most important of which are:

1 Networks offer an opportunity to air an advertising message through hundreds of local stations at a lower cost than buying the same stations individually.
2 It is much simpler to place advertising through one network than hundreds of local stations.
3 Advertisers have better control over the presentation of their commercials through network broadcasting.
4 Networks provide a single billing for all stations covered.
5 Networks can offer simultaneous coverage with excellent control over time and location of commercials within the network's own programming.

The Spot-Broadcasting Approach

Geographical flexibility is provided to the national radio or TV advertiser through the spot-broadcasting device. There is often some confusion about the term "spot," because it is used in two different ways. Most people think of a broadcast commercial as a *spot*, and it is common to hear advertising professionals apply the same term as a slang expression for a short announcement or commercial. But laypeople fail to realize that the expression is also used by advertising people in a second sense. *Spot broadcasting* is the selection of specific markets and specific stations within those markets. It is an alternative to networks to achieve national advertising objectives; in short, it is *nonnetwork* national broadcast advertising.

Spot broadcasting is particularly suitable for advertisers who have incomplete national product distribution, limited advertising budgets that preclude the use of networks, or fluctuating regional sales patterns. Antifreeze or boat manufacturers fall in the third category because their heavy sales are concentrated in areas with extremely cold winters or locations close to lakes, rivers, or oceans.

Spot television has been described by its promoters as a method of approaching TV advertising that delivers infinitely varying *kinds* and varying *amounts* of advertising pressure *anywhere*, as the advertiser requires it. It always originates from, and is controlled in, the individual market where it is released. Commercials are not "piped through" local stations from the networks. They are originated from each station participating in a campaign.

FIGURE 7.16
Media in secondary markets must sell their market potential to advertisers at the same time they sell their particular stations as the best means of reaching the market. [*KOLN-TV and KGIN-TV*.]

You can't cover Nebraska without Lincoln-Hastings-Kearney

There are two television markets in Nebraska—and they're just about the same size. Omaha, with retail sales of $2,440,821,000, is one. The other is Lincoln-Hastings-Kearney, where retail sales are a robust $1,998,885,000.

Source: SRDS C.M. Data ADI 1/1/75

You can't cover Lincoln-Hastings-Kearney without KOLN-TV/KGIN-TV

In KOLN-TV/KGIN-TV's half of Nebraska, you get one of the largest audience shares in the nation. Total day audience share is 55%. Early evenings (4-6:30) we get 53%, and 55% in prime time (6:30-10 p.m.). We dominate with an 82% share from 10-10:30 at night. That's why you can't cover KOLN-TV/KGIN-TV's half of Nebraska from Omaha . . . unless you are willing to settle for a maximum of 10% prime time ADI share.

Source: ARB Feb., 1975, Total Survey Area.
Rating projections are estimates only, subject to any defects and limitations of source material and methods, and may or may not be accurate measure of true audience.

A Felzer Station

KOLN-TV / KGIN-TV
LINCOLN, NEBRASKA
1500 FT. TOWER
GRAND ISLAND, NEBRASKA
1049 FT. TOWER

Avery-Knodel, Inc., Exclusive National Representative

Spot versus Network Broadcasting In contrast, network broadcasting delivers approximately the same amount of advertising pressure everywhere it goes. It originates from and is controlled at one point—usually New York or Los Angeles. Earlier, we compared network broadcasting to national magazines; now it is apparent that, in the same vein, spot broadcasting is analogous to advertising in local newspapers. The advertiser determines how much advertising he or she wishes to place in each market, the stations on which the advertising is to run, how long it should last, and the time period in which it is to appear in each specific market. Network cannot offer this sort of flexibility, but network still has the advantage of providing a lower cost per station and per household reached—assuming, of course, that the advertiser is aiming for audiences of comparable size.

The spot-broadcasting approach is especially valuable if an advertiser wants to "heavy-up" his pressure against a particular market, rather than treat each market equally. It also allows commercials to be localized in each particular area covered, either by altering the copy or by having it presented by different personalities, each with a special local appeal. For example, a youth-oriented radio commercial could be presented by the outstanding disc jockey in each market covered. Network radio could not provide that sort of creative flexibility.

In 1974, national television advertisers spent approximately $1.5 billion employing the spot-broadcasting approach and slightly over $2 billion on network.[12] In radio the difference was more dramatic. National radio advertisers invested only about $70 million in network radio, but over five times that amount, $380 million, on spot radio.

Program Sponsorship

Most adult Americans think of television broadcasting in terms of specific programs and the sponsors of those programs. We have already stated, however, that radio program sponsorship, as such, disappeared when television swept the country.

Evening network television in the early 1950s was dominated by big advertisers and the weekly programs they sponsored such as "Ford Theatre," "The Texaco Star Theatre," and "The Perry Como Show" sponsored by Kraft. In fact, during the early years of TV, 89 percent of evening network broadcasts were paid for by individual advertisers. During the late 1950s, that figure had dropped to 46 percent as advertisers moved to find compatible cosponsors who would share the mounting costs of TV program sponsorship. Forty-nine percent of the programs in this period were cosponsored,[13] that is, had two or more sponsors.

In 1963–1964, only 16 percent of the prime evening programs enjoyed the luxury of a single sponsor such as Chevrolet's "Bonanza," and 31 percent were cosponsored. By 1975, regular program sponsorship by advertisers was almost unheard of. Even cosponsorship is now rare. Some big advertisers like Timex and Hallmark have moved to sponsoring specials during appropriate seasons of the year, but the vast majority of network advertisers have turned to the participation approach to program sponsorship.

Participation Shows

In the natural evolution of things, the participation program has replaced the fully sponsored show on network television. A *participa-*

---

[12] *Broadcasting Yearbook*, loc. cit.
[13] *Grey Matter*, Grey Advertising, Inc., May 1964.

tion show is one in which a variety of sponsors place commercials within the body of the program, that is, after the first introduction of the program, during breaks, and at the program's conclusion. Contrary to a popularly held idea, the expression "participation" has nothing to do with whether or not members of the studio audience participate in contests or exchange patter with the master of ceremonies.

The term "participation," as we employ it here, refers to advertisers participating in paying for the program as though they were actually sponsors, when, in fact, they have nothing to do with the production of the show itself. This has been a growing trend in network television for many years and has been referred to as the "magazine concept." In this regard, advertisers buy into a network program as they would buy into a magazine. They place their commercials (ads) in an appropriate program (issue) with no responsibility for the details of the program (editorial) content. Advertisers in both cases are concerned, primarily, with the size and buying habits of the audience that a certain program or magazine will attract. "As the World Turns" obviously draws a much different audience than "Meet the Press" or "All in the Family."

Another consideration in program selection is compatibility. How well does the mood or tone of the program coincide with the image of the product the advertiser is trying to sell? Cosmetic advertising blends well with the "Miss America Pageant," Kodak and Campbell's soup with "The Wonderful World of Disney." Conversely, in 1975 when the CBS Network produced a special entitled "The Guns of Autumn," which criticized hunters, some sponsors asked, in advance, that their commercials be removed from the program. Although these advertisers were accused of trying to influence the policy of the network, they maintained that the real problem lay in the mood created among viewers. It is difficult to sell any product when the vehicle used to attract the listeners has infuriated them, or turned them against the companies that they perceive to be sponsors, even though they aren't.

There was a time when one had to point to Johnny Carson's "Tonight Show" or "Wednesday Night at the Movies" for an example of a participation program. Now it is difficult to find a regular network program that isn't of this type.

Announcement Campaigns

Announcement campaigns are a form of local advertising or spot broadcasting. The fundamental difference between these commercials and those within network programs is that these commercial announcements are sold only by local stations or their representatives and are aired *between* regular programs, rather than *within* them. There is little opportunity for the advertiser to identify a product with the show inasmuch as the commercial announcements placed between shows are isolated from the shows themselves. This is viewed by some as a disadvantage.

There is the additional disadvantage inherent in the fact that the break between programs is often a relatively long one with many commercials, station identification breaks, promotional spots for coming programs, etc. It is a fine time for viewers to remove themselves from the television set for a visit to the bathroom or kitchen, or to catch up on a little reading. Lastly, many people are great dial switchers, and it is possible that the announcement will be aired at the moment when thousands of viewers are flipping from one channel to another.

RADIO AND TV PROGRAMS AND THEIR AUDIENCES

Millions of Americans rise in the morning, turn on the radio, if it wasn't already ignited by the alarm that awakened them, shave or shower, and prepare breakfast to radio music or news programs. Millions more tune to the "Today" or "Good Morning, America" shows while eating breakfast. Then they step into the automobile where they are exposed to one of America's 100 million car radios and settle down for the drive to the office, factory, school, or store. Enroute home that evening, again the car radio comes into play, until the workers settle before their television sets for the evening news. Following dinner, television entertainment is America's favorite pastime until it is time for bed. Meanwhile, the homemaker has had the opportunity for radio or television companionship throughout the day.

The programming that attracts these audiences, and the ebb and flow of listeners and viewers from station to station and program to program, is the heart of broadcast time buying and selling.

Radio Audiences

The multitude of radio stations vying for advertising dollars in the United States compete primarily on the basis of audiences attracted because listeners had a personal preference for the particular music or programming that a station featured. This station loyalty is in direct conflict with the nature of television, where most viewers select a program, *regardless of station*, and the idea of listening habitually to one station for its own sake is almost unheard of.

Radio stations vie to develop a style and format that will attract a large number of listeners that advertisers are willing to pay to reach. There are many, many formats available to radio station owners with which you are probably familiar. They represent every point on the musical spectrum from acid rock to heavy classical, including "top 40," the big band sound, contemporary, and others. In addition, some stations are pure news and discussion, whereas others broadcast only "talk programs" with listeners providing the bulk of the entertainment. Some stations are sports-event-oriented, while others concentrate heavily on the personalities of their disc jockeys. All-black, Spanish, or

FIGURE 7.17
Two examples of radio's intense class selectivity. WDEE offers advertisers a chance to reach country music fans in Detroit, while KKSS offers maximum radio coverage of blacks, eighteen to forty-nine years old, in St. Louis.

other ethnic-language stations are common in metropolitan markets.

Advertisers and agency media buyers are vitally concerned with the types and numbers of persons who listen to the various stations. They are also interested in the *availabilities* which a station offers. "Availabilities" refers to the time periods (slots) that a station has available to carry advertising commercials. Radio listenership tends to peak in the morning and evening *drive-time* hours. For this reason, and because of the great demand for these particular times, many stations divide their days among four broad periods: class AAA time, from 6 to 10 A.M.; class AA time, from 3 to 7 P.M.; class A time, from 10 A.M. to 3 P.M.; and class B time from 7 P.M. to midnight. Other variations are arranged to cover early morning and weekend time periods. All these classifications are reflective, of course, of a radio station's ability to attract audiences and, as we shall discuss later, have ramifications for rates charged for commercials.

Television Audiences

Although sponsorship of programs by national advertisers is almost a thing of the past, the program is still the basis of television broadcasting and an extremely important factor in the buying of television time by advertisers.

Programs not only serve to draw large numbers of viewers to particular stations, but also are the determinants of the *type* of person who is attracted to that station during a particular time period. Network television advertisers, like the radio advertisers described above, are interested in the availabilities of commercial time within specific television programs that will deliver large numbers of persons who fall into the advertisers' target-market population groups. A national beer advertiser, for example, might advertise on the World Series telecasts because he wants to reach a significant percentage of males, eighteen to thirty-nine years old—the heart of the beer-drinking public.

Another beer advertiser, one who has only regional distribution, might approach the same advertising problem by purchasing spot announcements during the station breaks on World Series broadcasts. In this case, it would not be feasible for him to buy the entire network on a participation basis, but he would reach the same audience in his own region that the national advertiser would reach. He is highly concerned with "adjacencies," a word used in the broadcasting business to describe the program that a commercial announcement falls next to, or the two shows that it falls between.

Like radio, television viewing by the general public follows definite patterns throughout the day. Again, looking at Figure 7.8 one can see the television viewing audience build fairly steadily throughout the day and peak between 7 and 11 P.M. As the chart reveals, approximately four times as many people watch television in the evening as watch during the noon hour. Furthermore, these flow patterns have significance in terms of the types of persons watching, as well as the number. Mornings and early afternoon are heavily skewed toward full-time homemakers and other stay-at-homes, while late-afternoon hours and Saturday mornings are heavy with children viewers. Working men and women tend to be much heavier viewers in the evening than at any other time during the day, for obvious reasons.

It is important to note that we have been discussing gross audiences of television, that is, all the people exposed to all television sets in use during particular time periods. But no advertiser buys all stations in all markets. Most buy only one or two stations at a time, and these are located in carefully selected markets that offer maximum sales potential. It is at the point of deciding which stations will do the best job that advertisers become particularly concerned with each individual station's program offerings and the numbers and types of people they attract.

Types of Programs

Broadcast advertisers who use programs as vehicles for carrying commercials have a great responsibility. Not only must they be sure that the commercials appearing on their shows are good advertising, but they must be certain that the program is compatible with their products and their overall objectives. They buy time slots on radio or television stations or networks in the same way that they buy a page of space in a newspaper or magazine, but these purchases do not bring a guaranteed circulation. They must also select programs which bring the audiences they want to reach. Thus, advertisers or their advertising agencies must know a great deal about the intricacies of broadcast programming. They must choose the right kinds of programs for their purposes, and the choices are many.

There are many different ways to classify broadcast programs. For instance, the Federal Communications Commission prefers an eight-fold classification: (1) entertainment, (2) religious, (3) agricultural, (4) educational, (5) news, (6) discussion, (7) talks, and (8) miscellaneous. This system is of limited value to the advertiser seeking to place ads within a program format, since his programming is usually in the entertainment category. The subtypes of the entertainment category are numerous: children's daytime programs, variety shows, dramatic performances, audience-participation shows, music, sports, and a variety of other presentations.

An advertiser who decides to sponsor a special has, first of all, the task of justifying the expenditure of a million dollars or more on a one-time-shot advertising expenditure. It is for this reason that firms that have a sales curve heavily influenced by holiday seasons often take this approach. Others, such as Xerox or Gulf Oil Company, may sponsor specials intermittently as a shot in the arm for their sales efforts or as an institutional advertising effort, that is, to improve the environment in which they conduct their business.

A second important consideration facing the sponsor of his own special is the obligation the company faces in being directly responsible for a program worthy of the time of 20 to 30 million viewers. In this light, it is easy to understand why the offerings of firms like Bell Telephone or McDonald's represent some of the best and most worthwhile entertainment found on television.

Sources of Programs

There was a time in the recent past when advertisers and their agencies were highly influential in the development of the programs their companies sponsored. Since regular program sponsorship, in the traditional sense, has ceased to exist, it is now almost exclusively the job of the network or local station to decide what goes on the air and when.

Network and Station Programs   Almost all the programs that we are exposed to stem from a few main sources: the network or station, feature-film producers, or outside packagers. It is fairly obvious to the viewer when a network puts together a news program, a series of ABC broadcasts covering the Olympic Games, or regular documentaries such as "CBS Reports." It is equally apparent that the networks are behind "The Today Show," "Good Morning, America," and "The Tonight Show."

Feature Film   This is the expression employed in broadcasting to refer to regular Hollywood motion pictures that are made available to television stations and networks after the producers have exhibited them in local motion-picture theaters. They are usually offered first to the networks, then to local stations, at a later date, to be broadcast on a rerun basis. A network or station usually runs the same film a number of times before its value is exhausted. Some stations contract with a motion-picture production company such as Paramount or 20th Century Fox for a group of 50 films, to be run at the station's convenience over a three-year period. "Made-for-television" movies may be bought by the networks outright, and after the network has used them fully, made available to their affiliated stations for local rebroadcasting.

Syndication   A third important source of television programs introduces the concept of *syndication*. This refers to the practice of taking a series of successful network television programs and rerunning them on local stations to fill hours not otherwise covered by network programming. In the case of independent (nonnetwork-affiliated) stations, syndicated programs often make up the bulk of all the broadcasting they do. Familiar examples of popular syndicated programs include "Dragnet," rerun on many local stations as "Badge 714"; "Lassie," syndicated as "Jeff's Collie"; "I Love Lucy"; and "Mod Squad". Stations contract for these programs in 13-, 26-, or 39-week blocks and sell advertising time, in and around them, to local and national advertisers.

Television and radio programs are often developed by independent producers and distributors. There are 300 or 400 companies in the business of developing and selling radio programs in the United States and twice that number producing, packaging, and selling television programs. Some shows do not appear first on the networks, but go directly to syndication on local stations. When the "Merv Griffin Show" lost its network slot, he had the initiative to continue producing it as a syndicated show and now enjoys audiences in hundreds of cities across America. Chances are that few viewers are even aware that the program is coming to them on an entirely different basis than it did in the past. The same is true of "The Lawrence Welk Show;" formerly a network program, it is now produced independently and sold to individual stations for presentation to local markets.

Ratings

Most commercial radio and television broadcasting in the United States operates on a rating system. This is a technique for describing the numbers and kinds of people who listen to or view a particular station and the programs on that station. It is the ratings that are largely responsible for television shows being dropped and for new ones being introduced. Ratings also play an important part in the fickle operation of some radio stations that go from one format to another in the never-ending chase to discover a formula that will deliver large audiences to the station and financial success to the station's owner.

Rarely does a week go by that we do not read a news story concerning a television program that is enjoying especially high ratings, or of one whose existence is imperiled by low ratings. The implications of ratings as a measure of success have a strong influence on the television to which American households are exposed for more than 25 percent of every day. And yet the concept of ratings is misunderstood by most viewers.

Television Households   Rating scores begin with the idea of homes with television sets, known as *television households*. These figures may be presented in terms of a city, marketing area, region, or the nation as a whole. It is apparent in the 1970s that households without television are becoming a rarity and that this concept is of less importance than it was in the 1950s when the percentage of homes capable of watching television was growing so rapidly. Today, as reported earlier, about 97 percent of American homes contain at least one television set.

Sets in Use   The research firms that determine broadcast ratings deal next with a dimension of TV audiences called *sets in use*. This expression describes the number, or percentage, of all the homes with television that have a set turned on during a particular time period, with no concern for the station or program to which each set is tuned.

Program Ratings   We now turn our attention to the most prominent of broadcast research concepts, the *program rating*. This simply refers to the percentage of television homes tuned to a particular program. When we read that "Sanford and Son" or "The Six Million Dollar Man" led the rating parade during a particular week, we find that the winning rating is about 24. This means that 24 percent of the TV homes in America tuned to the program. The figure may be projected to the actual number of TV homes, about 70 million, yielding a score of approximately 16.8 million homes. When one considers that large cities may have as many as 10 television stations competing for the viewer's attention, it is understandable that broadcasting executives would be pleased with such a showing, because the rates that stations charge are based, primarily, on the size of the audience of each program.

Share Ratings   Although the subject of ratings will come up again later in this text, two other dimensions of audiences which are measured by research personnel deserve mention at this time. A *share rating*, sometimes referred to as a *share-of-audience* rating, is the percentage of homes in a given area that have their sets tuned to a specific station. Again, this ranking is based only on the homes with sets in use and measures how each station rates against the others in competition for the total viewers' attention. At 2 A.M. there may be only

PROGRAM AUDIENCES

TIME / DAY	STATION / PROGRAM	TELECASTS NO. OF WK	NO. OF ¼ HRS	ADI TV HH RTG	ADI TV HH SHR	METRO TV HH RTG	METRO TV HH SHR	TV HOUSE-HOLDS	WOMEN TOTAL	18-49	15-24	18-34	25-49	25-54	25-64	HOUSE-WIVES TOTAL	MEN TOTAL	18-49	18-34	25-49	25-54	TEENS TOTAL	GIRLS
				1	2	3	4	5	9	10	11	12	13	14	15	16	17	18	19	20	21	22	23
▲ RELATIVE STD-ERROR 25-49%					2	3		10	12	13	18	16	10	11	10	12	12	12	16	11	11	15	13
(1SE) THRESHOLDS 50+%							1	2	3	5	5	4	3	3	2	3	3	3	4	3	3	4	3
8.00P WZZM																							
WED	THATS MAMA	4	8	11	19	8		51	32	17	6	10	15	18	23	30	33	21	14	13	15	16	8
THU	*BARNY MILLER	3	6	8	15	7		38	31	20	10	12	11	13	18	27	35	20	15	10	15	2	1
FRI	KOLCHAK	4	16	7	17	4		32	24	13	7	9	10	11	17	20	24	19	15	9	10	11	7
SAT	ABC SAT MOV	4	40	6	12	5		28	21	15	7	10	10	13	15	16	15	11	6	9	10	9	4
AVG	BARNY MILLER		8	9	17	8		45	33	22	9	14	15	17	22	29	38	23	15	13	17	6	4
WUHQ																							
MON	ROOKIES	4	16	5	10	4		26	24	18	8	12	11	12	15	21	12	7	4	7	8	8	4
TUE	HAPPY DAYS ≠	4	6	4	8	3		18	18	12	8	9	5	7	9	16	12	9	7	6	6	10	3
WED	THATS MAMA	4	8	3	6	2		17	15	11	4	7	8	9	10	11	14	11	7	8	9	6	1
THU	*BARNY MILLER	3	6	4	8	3		21	13	11	4	5	8	10	10	13	15	10	3	10	12	6	1
FRI	KOLCHAK	4	16	2	6	2		12	6	6	2	5	4	4	4	9	6	5	2	5	6	2	
SAT	ABC SAT MOV	4	40	4	7	3		18	15	11	5	8	7	8	9	14	14	11	7	6	6	6	2
AVG	BARNY MILLER		8	4	7	3		19	15	10	5	6	6	9	10	13	14	10	3	10	11	5	1
8.30P WKZO																							
TUE	MASH	3	6	22	43	25		105	84	47	23	30	31	37	52	77	62	39	28	25	29	30	15
FRI	WELL GET BY	2	4	13	29	13		64	54	22	4	15	20	26	38	48	31	15	7	10	17	10	5
SAT	JEFFERSONS	4	8	24	49	26		113	109	49	25	29	30	39	59	87	79	43	27	24	27	26	13
SUN	KOJAK	4	16	19	33	21		86	75	50	31	36	27	33	45	69	68	42	30	25	30	25	17
WOTV																							
TUE	NBC WRLD PRM	4	28	14	26	14		68	53	36	11	21	29	33	39	48	43	29	17	20	25	28	9
THU	BOB CRANE SH	4	8	12	21	13		58	45	26	15	19	14	18	24	34	26	18	9	14	17	13	8
FRI	CHICO-MAN	4	8	18	43	21		84	71	31	15	17	20	28	40	55	60	29	13	19	23	14	10
SUN	SU MYSTRY MV	4	30	20	35	20		92	83	53	21	36	37	44	54	74	75	50	30	36	42	25	9
WZZM																							
TUE	TUE MV OF WK	4	24	10	19	9		47	39	27	13	19	17	20	26	34	25	17	12	13	16	10	6
WED	WED MV OF WK	3	18	11	18	9		51	37	27	13	21	17	20	26	33	34	24	20	17	20	11	5
WED	*BARNY MILLER	1	2	14	21	9		66	40	27	4	19	27	31	37	40	42	26	13	18	18	12	9
THU	KAREN	3	6	11	21	10		53	44	28	14	21	18	19	25	34	32	19	15	11	15	8	6
SUN	ABC SN NT MV	4	32	10	17	9		46	37	23	6	17	20	23	30	31	34	24	16	20	22	14	6
AVG	BARNY MILLER		8	9	17	8		45	33	22	9	14	15	17	22	29	38	23	15	13	17	6	4
WUHQ																							
TUE	TUE MV OF WK	4	23	3	6	3		18	20	14	10	9	7	8	11	15	11	8	4	6	6	9	4
WED	WED MV OF WK	3	18	6	11	5		31	24	19	7	10	13	13	15	22	16	11	8	8	11	6	2
WED	*BARNY MILLER	1	2	3	4	3		13	15	5	5	5		3	7	10	8	6	1	6	6	2	
THU	KAREN	3	6	3	6	2		17	11	8		1	8	9	9	10	8	5	1	5	6		
SUN	ABC SN NT MV	4	32	5	8	4		22	20	16	7	11	10	11	13	15	18	15	11	10	11	5	2
AVG	BARNY MILLER		8	4	7	3		19	15	10	5	6	6	9	10	13	14	10	3	10	11	5	1

TOTAL SURVEY AREA, IN THOUSANDS

two stations broadcasting and very few people with their sets turned on. But a share rating might yield a 70 percent for one station and a 30 for the other. These figures appear respectable enough, but they actually represent the division of a very small number of total homes. Obviously, the program rating is a much more meaningful figure because it represents *all* homes with television rather than just the homes with sets in use at the time of the survey.

Audience Composition   Finally, *audience composition* describes the kinds of people who make up an audience. Such figures consist of demographic data relating to sex, age, race, income level, etc. They may include the buying habits of the audience or psychographic data.

Gross Rating Points   One of the most important changes in the buying and selling of television advertising in the 1970s has been the introduction of the gross rating point (GRP) concept. *One gross rating point* is one percent of the homes with television in a given area. An advertiser or media buyer may decide that the proper saturation for a campaign in one market is 60 gross rating points per week. This might be accomplished by presenting a commercial on three programs with

FIGURE 7.18
This portion of a page from an Arbitron rating book covering the Grand Rapids/Kalamazoo/Battle Creek market shows the ratings and shares of various TV programs as well as demographic data concerning the audiences viewing those programs. Such rating information is vital in the selling and buying of TV time. [*American Research Bureau.*]

ratings of 20 or on ten programs with ratings of 6. The advertiser is primarily interested in how much each station in a market area will charge for this level of saturation.

Sometimes, the media buyer will carry the GRP idea one step further and ask for rates for 60 gross rating points per week, against a target audience with special composition characteristics; that is, the buyer asks for the rate that stations will charge for a certain number of gross rating points where the audience is composed of women twenty-nine to forty-nine years old. The buyer then compares the bids submitted by competing stations and makes a decision accordingly. In this case, the buyer is not so much interested in which programs the commercials appear with, as he is that the commercials reach the most potential customers at the least cost.

BROADCAST RATE STRUCTURES

The men and women who own the broadcast media in the United States, whether those media be radio or TV stations, do so because they feel they can provide a service and make a profit. In establishing the rates charged for advertising in their media, the first requirement is that the advertising income cover station operating costs and provide for some return on the owners' investment. Secondly, rates must be set at a point that reflects the value of the audience and is competitive with other stations' rates.

An advertiser approaches a medium with the hope that an advertising investment will ultimately result in a profit greater than would have been realized had this money been spent in some other medium or not spent at all.

Media rate structures can be an extremely complicated matter, but they are generally based on two factors: the *quantity* and the *quality*—both of the audience and of the advertising messages delivered. It is obvious that a station that delivers an advertising message to 3 million homes can and will charge more than one that delivers the same message to 1 million homes.

The quality factor operating in the establishment of advertising rates has two closely related aspects: the quality of the station or program vehicle itself and the quality, or exclusivity, of the audience it attracts. Better-educated people, by and large, have higher incomes and greater buying power. Their tastes in media, including the stations and programs they listen to or view, tend, to a degree, to be on a more sophisticated plane. An expensively produced television program will be accompanied by higher advertising rates for commercials than a show produced at minimum expense. Similarly, a program that attracts an exclusive audience will probably cost an advertiser more to tie into than a program that attracts an audience of the same size, but

CUME PERSONS—TOTAL SURVEY AREA, IN HUNDREDS												STATION CALL LETTERS	CUME PERSONS—METRO SURVEY AREA, IN HUNDREDS											
TOTAL PERS. 12+	MEN					WOMEN					TEENS 12-17		TOTAL PERS. 12+	MEN					WOMEN					TEENS 12-17
	18-24	25-34	35-49	50-64	TOTAL 18+	18-24	25-34	35-49	50-64	TOTAL 18+				18-24	25-34	35-49	50-64	TOTAL 18+	18-24	25-34	35-49	50-64	TOTAL 18+	
190	35	26		3	70	35	11	7	3	59	61	KASH	180	35	16		3	60	35	11	7	3	59	61
120		9	10	21	46		12	27	15	61	13	KATR	112		9	10	21	46		12	19	15	53	13
283	55	38	6		99	48	4	7	3	62	122	KBDF	283	55	38	6		99	48	4	7	3	62	122
228		19	48	15	88	9	38	31	21	106	34	KEED	210		19	39	15	79	9	38	22	21	97	34
80	20	19			39	22	4	4		30	11	KFMY	80	20	19			39	22	4	4		30	11
69	8	5	6	4	23	10	4	16	3	33	13	KNND	69	8	5	6	4	23	10	4	16	3	33	13
36	7		6		13			12		23		KORE	36	7		6		13			12		23	
21			6		6			12		15		KORE FM	21			6		6			12		15	
41	7		11		18		4	12		23		TOTAL	41	7		11		18		4	12		23	
611	46	65	92	64	278	37	73	93	60	281	52	KPNW	311	29	33	30	43	135	19	27	52	41	153	23
260	7	19	33	10	98	22	36	33	29	152	10	KPNW FM	211	7	19	24	10	89	13	23	33	21	122	
689	74	79	120	59	372	30	82	78	83	300	17	KUGN	599	47	69	99	59	309	30	69	73	74	273	17
198	69	29			98	37	29			66	34	KZEL	120	27	29			56	14	16			30	34
97				9	26		10	16		63	8	KWIL	17								4	3	17	
164	13	15	23	34	100			31	11	64		KXL	26		5		3	15		11			11	
												TOTAL LISTENING IN METRO SURVEY AREA	1594	140	178	153	109	644	129	181	166	138	706	244

FIGURE 7.19

Radio stations prosper or fail on the basis of radio audience statistics like these taken from an Arbitron study of a medium-sized Western market. [*American Research Bureau.*]

with less prestige. For example, a broadcast of the U.S. Open golf tournament draws a relatively small but somewhat exclusive audience composed of a high percentage of top business executives. The charge for advertising on this program would be greater than the charge for an equivalent audience attracted to a wrestling match.

Once basic advertising rates have been set for a radio time period or TV program, there are certain standard variations which occur. The first has to do with the quantity of advertising that a client buys. Just as you buy apples cheaper by the bushel, you can buy spot announcements cheaper in quantity than if you only purchased one or two. In addition, many media are anxious to spread their advertising incomes over long periods of time. Radio and TV stations will allow discounts to advertisers who will buy groups of commercials spread over many weeks or months. The aforementioned variations on advertising rates are often referred to as *bulk* and *frequency rates*, respectively.

One final generalization about media rates—it is common among many media to charge national advertisers higher rates than retail advertisers are charged. Many reasons are given for this (sometimes large) differential. Some say it is because a national advertiser has more to gain; that is, Procter & Gamble can make more money from an ad for Tide detergent than Joe's Shoe Repair Shop can make from a similar advertisement. Others say that inasmuch as agencies deduct 15 percent from media charges, and media representatives deduct

RATE CARD #11 - Effective April 1, 1976

WEEKLY	12x	18x	24x	30x	36x
MONTHLY		40x	60x	80x	100x
YEARLY		400x	600x	800x	1000x

AAA

	12x	18x	24x	30x	36x
:60	14.00	13.50	13.00	12.50	12.00
:30	12.00	11.50	11.00	10.50	10.00

AA

	12x	18x	24x	30x	36x
:60	12.00	11.50	11.00	10.50	10.00
:30	10.00	9.50	9.00	8.50	8.00

A

BTA   3.00

ROS - Pre-emptible

	12x	18x	24x	30x	36x
:60	10.50	10.00	9.50	9.00	8.50
:30	9.00	8.50	8.00	7.50	7.00

DISCOUNTS:

10% contract discounts are earned for:
26 consecutive weeks scheduled or 12 consecutive monthly schedules placed by the 15th of each previous month.

5% contract discounts are earned for:
13 consecutive weeks schedule
6 consecutive monthly schedules placed by the 15th of each previous month.

FIGURE 7.20
This rate card shows the cost of radio commercials for a progressive FM station that features stereo and quadraphonic transmission aimed at a youthful audience. Note the discount available for preemptible spots. [*KEZI-FM.*]

another 10 percent, the media have to charge a higher rate to come out as well on national as they do on local advertising. National advertisers have complained vociferously about this situation, and many media have moved to a "single-rate structure" in order to placate their clients. Broadcasters have been in the vanguard of this trend.

The basic unit for broadcast time sales is the minute or a portion thereof. In both radio and television, commercial lengths tend to follow the same general patterns, although there is no standard offering and stations sometimes differ in what they will accept. Nevertheless, the most common lengths for spot announcements are 10, 30, and 60 seconds. Whereas radio has remained fairly constant in this regard during recent years, television has exhibited some interesting and important trends. Networks carry almost no 10- or 20-second spots. The 60-second spot, which was once the mainstay of network advertising, was only employed 6 percent of the time in 1975. Meanwhile, the 30-second announcement has become the workhorse, used about 80 percent of the time. The 60-second "piggyback" commercials refer to advertisers combining two different products in one 60-second slot. In nonnetwork advertising, the vast majority of spot announcements are of the 30-second variety, with 10- and 60-second commercials following far behind.

A close examination of Figure 7.21, reprinted from *Spot Television Rates and Data* (SRDS), gives you an insight into the rate structure of a typical television station and a clue to some of the complexities involved. This listing covers spot-announcement charges for ABC affiliate WJBF in Augusta, Georgia. It is a relatively simple example, but it reflects some of the basic principles we have discussed. Note that the station management has divided the day into a number of time periods, AA, A, B, and C, and that these periods reflect the size of the potential audience an advertiser may expect to reach. Section I and II designations refer to whether the position the advertiser buys is *fixed*, that is, the commercial cannot be bumped by another, or whether it is *preemptible*, meaning it is subject to being removed from the schedule if the station is approached by a more attractive offer from another advertiser. To be more specific, this listing tells us that we can buy a 30-second spot during prime evening hours, or AA time, for $145. Or we might place the same spot during the morning, Class B time period, for $42.

Below the section on spot-announcement charges in Figure 7.21 is a section entitled "Participation Announcement Programs." This lists the locally produced or syndicated programs that an advertiser may buy into and the rates charged for commercials within these programs. Note that rates vary according to the length of commercials, as well as the time and desirability of the program itself. One would surmise from this listing that "Hee Haw" is by far the most attractive program in WJBF's repertoire.

In contrast to these rather low rates, SRDS quotes prices for 30-second commercials on some leading Chicago stations ranging from $4,000 to $6,000 during the most attractive prime-time periods. But the reader should not lose sight of the fact that the Chicago rates still constitute a better buy in terms of the number of persons reached per advertising dollar.

People unfamiliar with the economies attainable to advertisers in the mass media are appalled by the fact that a 30-second commercial on an outstanding network TV attraction such as the Super Bowl football game, or a presentation of the *Godfather*, costs about $100,000.

W J B F
(Airdate November 26, 1953)

ABC Television Network

Media Code 6 211 0250 8.00
Fuqua Television Inc., Box 1404, Augusta, Ga.
30903. Phone 404-722-6664. TWX 810-755-4023.
1. PERSONNEL
   Chairman of the Board—J. B. Fuqua.
   Pres. & Gen'l Mgr.—John Radeck.
   Vice-President-Sales—Walter Campbell, Jr.
2. REPRESENTATIVES
   H-R Television, Inc.
3. FACILITIES
   Video 100,000 w., audio 20,000 w.; ch 6.
   Antenna ht.: 1,375 ft. above average terrain.
   Operating schedule: 5:55-1 am Mon thru Fri; 6:30-:
   am Sat; 6:30-2 am Sun. EST.
4. AGENCY COMMISSION
   15% to recognized agencies on time charges only.
5. GENERAL ADVERTISING See coded regulations
   General: 1a, 3a, 3b, 3d, 4a, 5, 7b, 8.
   Rate Protection: 10i, 11i, 12i, 13k, 14i, 15, 17.
   Contracts: 20a, 21, 22a, 24a, 27a, 32d, 34.
   Basic Rates: 40b, 41b, 41c, 41d, 42, 43a, 44b, 45a,
      47a, 51, 52.
   Comb.; Cont. Discounts: 60a, 60e, 61c, 62a.
   Cancellation: 70a, 70e, 71, 73a.
   Prod. Services: 80, 83, 85, 86, 87c.
   Affiliated with ABC (primary) and NBC Television
   Networks.
   All rates include a 5% handling charge.
6. TIME RATES
   No. 21 Eff 9/8/75—Rec'd 8/18/75.
   AA—Mon thru Sat 7:30-11 pm; Sun 6:30-10:30 pm.
   A—Mon thru Fri noon-7:30 pm & 11 pm-sign-off;
   Sat 12:29-7:30 pm; Sun 1:59-6:30 pm & 10:30-11
   pm.
   B—Mon thru Fri 6:59 am-noon; Sat 7:31 am-12:29
   pm & 11 pm-sign-off; Sun 11 pm-sign-off.
   C—Mon thru Fri sign-on-6:59 am; Sat sign-on-7:31
   am; Sun sign-on-1:59 pm.
7. SPOT ANNOUNCEMENTS

CLASS AA	—Section—	
	I	II
60 sec	310	280
30 sec	155	140
10 sec	124	112
CLASS A		
60 sec	230	210
30 sec	115	105
10 sec	92	85
CLASS B		
60 sec	180	140
30 sec	90	70
10 sec	75	56
CLASS C		
60 sec	84	60
30 sec	42	30
10 sec	34	24
CLASS D		
60 sec	52	32
30 sec	26	16
10 sec	21	13

Section I—Fixed, non-preemptible.
Section II—Preemptible on 2 weeks' notice.
8. PARTICIPATING ANNOUNCEMENT PROGRAMS
   Rec'd 4/14/75.

	—Flat—	
	Seconds	
MON THRU FRI, PM:	60	30/20
Arthur Smith Show—6:30-7 am	34	17
Today Show—7-9 am	70	35
Morning Rotation—9 am-noon	50	25
PM:		
Afternoon Rotation—noon-4:30	110	55
Trooper Terry—4:30-5	110	55
Mod Squad—5-6	90	45
News—6-6:30	270	135
News—11-11:30	108	54
Tonight Show—11:30 pm-1 am Sun thru Fri	30	15
Saturday Night—11:15 pm-concl	50	25
Vaudeville—7-8 pm Mon	160	80
The Price Is Right—7-7:30 pm Tues	210	105
Hollywood Squares—7:30-8 pm Tues	210	105
Let's Make A Deal—7-7:30 pm Wed	210	105
Candid Camera—7:30-8 pm Wed	210	105
Hee Haw—7-8 pm Thurs	332	166
Nashville on the Road—7-7:30 pm Fri	140	70
Pop Goes the Country—7:30-8 pm Fri	140	70
Lawrence Welk—7-8 pm Sat	140	70
High Chapparal—6-7 pm Sun	90	45
Big Movie—4-6 pm Sun	70	35
Wide World of Entertainment—11:30 pm-1 am	30	15
Early & Late News Combo: Mon thru Fri 6-6:30 pm & 11-11:30 pm. 1 in ea	320	160

Section I—Fixed, non-preemptible.
Section II—Preemptible on 2 weeks' notice.
10. PROGRAM TIME RATES
   Daily 7:31-9:59 pm, 1 hr................................ 900
11. SPECIAL FEATURES

COLOR
Schedules network color, film, slides, tape and live.
Equipped with high band VTR.

BASTIANSEN '75

"...our spot got bumped, huh, J.B.? Well, that's the biz..."

All TV stations offer you rotations in big shows. The problem is, most of them rotate you *too* much. You keep on getting bumped to make room for fixed-rate spots that come in at the last minute, until pretty soon you don't know where the heck you're running.

Well, "that's the biz" at some TV stations.

But that's not the way we do business at WCCO-TV.

When you buy a rotation plan on our station, we won't bump you. So your spots run as ordered. Period.

For more information about this and other business practices that make WCCO-TV different, contact your Peters, Griffin, Woodward representative or our sales staff.

4 WCCO TV
Minneapolis Saint Paul

FIGURE 7.22
This cartoon dramatizes the dangers inherent in buying preemptible time slots on TV stations. Many advertisers are willing to take the risk, however, in exchange for the lower rates such positions afford. [*WCCO-TV.*]

But, again, the cost per person or household reached is less than sending a postcard.

BROADCAST MEDIA ABROAD

Broadcast advertisers devising advertising and marketing strategy in foreign lands face problems that are absent from American domestic planning operations. The first question one might ask is whether the country in which the advertising is contemplated has a broadcasting system that allows commercial advertising. The second question is whether or not the persons the advertiser wishes to reach have access to radio or television sets.

Differing Broadcast Systems

Broadcasting is organized in a variety of different ways in different countries. While it is inevitable that there is some form of government control in every country, the degree of control varies greatly. In countries that operate on a system similar to that of the United States, broadcasters are relatively free to own and manage their stations as they please, providing the operation can be construed to be in the best interest of the public or some significant segment of the public. Most of the broadcasting we experience is done on a commercial basis, with advertising covering the costs. Notable exceptions include educational or public broadcasting stations, as well as a relatively small number of subscription stations, that is, those sponsored by listener contributions.

At the other end of the spectrum from countries whose broadcasting system is similar to the American plan, there are countries where all stations and network facilities are owned outright by the government. These stations may or may not accept advertising. In many cases, when they do accept it, they may lump all commercial time in blocks of solid advertising rather than place announcements within or between programs.

In England, the government has adopted a compromise approach. The British Broadcasting Corporation maintains a network that features programming generally considered of a higher cultural level (some say it is more stodgy) than that of any of the major American networks. Meanwhile, a second system, the Independent Broadcasting Authority, operates an openly commercial network, with programming similar to the American type; in fact, much of the material featured on IBA stations originates in the United States

Switzerland, Poland, Denmark, Norway, and Saudi Arabia are examples of countries with noncommercial television service. But the majority of industrialized countries, such as Russia, Japan, Greece, and France, do permit advertising in conjunction with television broadcasting whether the stations are owned by the government or by independent entrepreneurs.[14]

Brazil, Canada, and Colombia are countries that, like England, offer both commercial and noncommercial television broadcasting. The trend over the years of television's existence has been to move

[14] *Television Factbook*, 1974–1975, no. 44, Stations Volume, pp.106-b–1111-b

toward more commercial stations and programming, primarily because the costs of TV stations and programming are so outrageous.

Set Penetration

Once an advertiser has determined that commercial television announcements are accepted in the country in which he or she wishes to advertise, the next question to be raised is how well the medium penetrates to homes of the country's inhabitants. Although Americans tend to think of television as a medium almost unique to the United States, set coverage has increased throughout the world in dramatic fashion. In the early 1970s there were approximately 54 million TV sets outside the United States, and surveys made in the mid-1970s indicate that the number is now close to 250 million.[15] And these sets are receiving signals from one or more of 3,700 television stations located throughout the world.

The problems with employing radio in multinational advertising are much the same as those described for television. Some countries are wide open to advertisers, some allow no commercial radio advertising, and others offer both commercial and noncommercial radio broadcasting.

According to Merrill, Bryan, and Alisky, the vast majority of the world's population is now, for the first time, within range of both radio and television broadcasting signals.[16] They also point out that now, also for the first time, the majority of the people of the world own a radio. This is highly significant to advertisers of every sort because radio and television transcend literacy barriers and allow communication with people who cannot read. Family-planning commercials, for example, were successfully conveyed by radio in India, to people in regions where illiteracy was appallingly high.

Instantaneous worldwide telecasts of men walking on the moon or of the Olympic Games, whether they are held in Germany, The Soviet Union, or Canada, help dramatize the future possibility of advertisers beaming messages, simultaneously, to potential customers throughout the world.

SUMMARY

Almost every home in America contains one or more radio and television sets. Because these media are so pervasive, they are attractive to advertisers as vehicles for reaching prospects with their commercial announcements.

[15] Ibid., p.1115-b.
[16] John C. Merrill, Carter R. Bryan, and Marvin Alisky, *The Foreign Press*, Louisiana State University Press, Baton Rouge, 1973, p. 16.

In order for broadcast messages to be received, members of the target audience must possess a receiver, turn it on, and listen to or watch the commerical. When these things have been done, communication is instantaneous. Most listeners or viewers employ radio and television as sources of information and entertainment. Some, however, turn them on simply for the company they provide.

Because of the wide variation in human tastes, there is a need for a wide variety of stations and programs; station managers plan their programming to appeal to a significant segment of the population in order that advertisers may be convinced that advertising on the station is a worthwhile investment.

The broadcast industry is composed of three fundamental institutions: stations, networks, and a national regulating organization—the Federal Communications Commission. Stations are the core of the business and are always the sources of the signals we hear or see. Networks often provide the programming the stations broadcast, particularly if the station is a network affiliate. Television stations are much more dependent upon networks for programming than radio stations, which depend on the networks primarily for news and feature material.

National advertisers may opt to take a network approach to their TV or radio advertising campaigns, or they may choose the spot-broadcasting method. Network advertising is simpler and the cost to attain national coverage is less than it would be if one were to choose the nonnetwork approach to national broadcast advertising. But spot broadcasting is much more flexible than the network approach and allows the advertisers to deliver varying kinds and amounts of advertising wherever the advertisers need it, inasmuch as they pick the markets and stations within those markets independently, and are not limited to network coverage or network stations. This is advantageous to an advertiser with spotty product distribution or one who wants to concentrate advertising in particular regions because of geographical variations in sales patterns.

As program sponsorship has diminished in importance in American television advertising, participation shows, in which a variety of sponsors place commercials within the body of a program, have increased in importance, especially among network television advertisers. Announcement campaigns, on the other hand, fall between programs or at station breaks and are sold only by local stations to local and nonnetwork advertisers.

Radio stations attract audiences by developing a particular format or special musical character that will attract a segment of the total radio audience. TV stations generate little loyalty per se, but depend upon specific programs to attract viewers. Advertisers attempt to place their advertising in conjunction with programming appropriate to reaching their potential customers. Most of the programs we see or hear originate from the networks or stations, are Hollywood-type feature films, or are syndicated shows made by networks or independent packagers.

Both radio and television advertising rates are based upon audience sizes or ratings as determined by a number of national rating services. The fundamental rating system is the program rating, which reveals the percentage of TV homes in a given area reached by a particular program. Rating services also attempt to describe the composition of each station or program audience, usually in demographic terms.

The rates that a station charges for commercial time are a reflection of the ratings that it has achieved for its programs or various time periods during the day. Rates fluctuate not only according to the size of the audience but, at times, on the basis of the quality of the audience or the program vehicle itself. The more commercials an advertiser buys from one station or network, the less expensive they become. Most TV commercials today are 30 seconds in length, while radio's most popular commercials are 30 and 60 seconds.

QUESTIONS FOR DISCUSSION

1 In what sense can it be said that radio and television (broadcast media) are unique relative to the other media?
2 Radio and TV stations, networks, and the FCC are the basic institutions that make up the broadcast industry. How do they relate to one another?
3 Describe the basic difference in programming a radio station and a TV station.
4 Discuss, in broad terms, the sorts of decisions a national advertiser must make when embarking on a television campaign. Would these decisions be different if the advertiser were to use radio?
5 What is the basis for judging broadcast rates from the standpoint of the station owner? An advertiser?
6 The term "spot" has been described as a confusing one. Why?
7 What are the main sources of TV programs?
8 What does it mean when a TV program secures a rating of 23? A share rating of 37?
9 Examine a local radio station listing. Try to determine how each station is attempting to attract a viable segment of the local audience.
10 Invite the sales manager of a local TV station to class. Discuss with him the many variables in his rate structure and how he works with advertisers who buy gross rating points.

FOR FURTHER REFERENCE

Barnouw, Erik: *The Golden Web: A History of Broadcasting in the U.S.*, Oxford Book Company, Inc., New York, 1966, vol. II, 1933–1953.

Barton, Roger: *Media in Advertising*, McGraw-Hill Book Company, New York, 1964.

Broadcasting and Cable Television, Committee for Economic Development, New York, 1975.

Broadcasting Yearbook, Broadcasting Publications, Inc., Washington.

Heighton, Elizabeth J., and Don R. Cunningham: *Advertising in the Broadcast Media*, Wadsworth Publishing Company, Inc., Belmont, Calif., 1976.

Land, Herman W., and Associates: *Television and the Wired City*, National Association of Broadcasters, Washington, 1968.

Lucas, Darrell, and S. H. Britt: *Measuring Advertising Effectiveness*, McGraw-Hill Book Company, New York, 1963.

Millerson, Gerald: *The Technique of Television Production*, 6th ed., Hastings House, Publishers, Inc., New York, 1968.

Quaal, Ward L., and Leo A. Martin: *Broadcast Management*, Hastings House, Publishers, Inc., New York, 1968.

Radio Facts: Radio Advertising Bureau, New York, 1975.

Roe, Yale: *Television Station Management*, Hastings House, Publishers, Inc., New York, 1964.

Television Factbook, Television Digest, Inc., Washington, (irr.) 2 vols., Stations Volume and Services Volume.

Wells, Alan (ed.): *Mass Communications: A World View*, National Press Books, Palo Alto, Calif., 1974.

CHAPTER 8

CHAPTER 8

PUBLICATION MEDIA

The excitement inherent in the producing, selling, and buying of advertising is readily apparent in the world of radio and television. Equally exciting are publications, where roaring presses, slick production, compelling deadlines, or simply the idea of working at the "nerve center" of a publishing house holds a fascination for the thousands of men and women engaged in the buying, selling, and producing of advertising. Perhaps the greatest thrill of all is in the discovery of a medium, or an approach, that will do a better, more efficient job of meeting the needs of sellers and consumers than any previously employed. Toward this end, an impressive galaxy of publications is available. In this chapter we shall explore this array in greater detail.

Publication advertising makes use of newspapers or magazines to deliver the advertising message to measurable groups of readers, in combination with news, entertainment, or other editorial content. The degree of a reader's interest in the advertising content of a publication will vary from reader to reader, from advertisement to advertisement, and from publication to publication, but the reader's primary interest is in the information or entertainment provided by the articles or stories, that is, in the editorial pages. Thus a publication's editorial content provides a background of reader interest or acceptance for the advertising message. In many cases, the content attracts certain types of readers who are of special interest to the advertiser, such as skin divers instead of tennis buffs, or graduate students instead of hairdressers.

NEWSPAPERS

A newspaper is typically a daily or weekly publication, containing news and opinion of current events and feature articles. With some exceptions, which we shall refer to later, the newspaper is a local advertising medium, and one of its primary advantages to an advertiser is the intense local coverage or penetration it provides. The word "coverage," in this context, refers to the ability of a medium to reach a certain percentage of homes or prospects in a given area. Because the vast majority of newspapers in America are monopolies in their cities of publication, it is commonplace for a local paper to reach 70 to 80 percent of the homes in a city. Furthermore, 77 percent of all Americans claim they read a newspaper "yesterday."[1] This figure climbs to 88 percent when one considers newspaper readership among college graduates alone.

The typical newspaper in the United States selects its news, its

[1] *Basic Facts about Newspapers*, Newspaper Advertising Bureau, November 1974.

FIGURE 8.1
This console is the cockpit for the technicians who operate the Harris 10-unit high-speed offset press in the background. This multimillion-dollar installation symbolizes the trend away from letterpress newspaper plants in favor of more versatile offset installations. [Eugene Register-Guard.]

features, and the subjects for its editorial opinion with an eye to the needs and interests of people of both sexes and of diverse age, income, and occupational groups within a particular community. It is usually selective geographically rather than qualitatively. The magazine, on the other hand, is selective qualitatively rather than geographically. Most magazines are edited to appeal to the special interests of certain types of people, regardless of where they live. The *San Francisco Chronicle* is published primarily for residents of the San Francisco Bay area—including homemakers, business executives, teen-agers, longshoremen, sports-car enthusiasts, and fishermen. On the other hand, a magazine like *Good Housekeeping* is aimed primarily at homemakers, whether they live in San Francisco, St. Louis, or Savannah. Even the multimillion-circulation magazines with general editorial content for both sexes—such as *Reader's Digest*—are more selective qualitatively than newspapers in terms of average income and educational levels of their respective audiences.

Although there are some notable exceptions to this generalization about the geographical rather than qualitative selectivity of newspapers, the distinction is still useful to advertisers. The *Wall Street Journal* is a newspaper by format, and by frequency of publication. Yet it has a

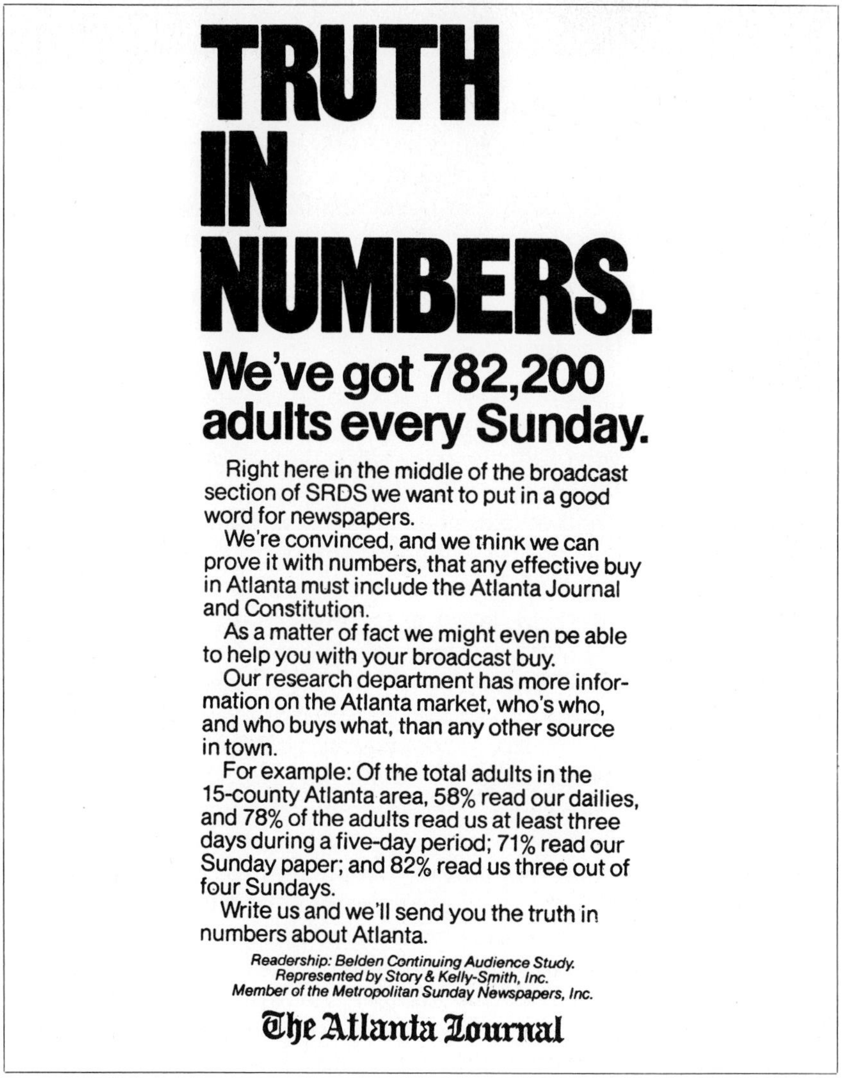

TRUTH IN NUMBERS.

We've got 782,200 adults every Sunday.

Right here in the middle of the broadcast section of SRDS we want to put in a good word for newspapers.

We're convinced, and we think we can prove it with numbers, that any effective buy in Atlanta must include the Atlanta Journal and Constitution.

As a matter of fact we might even be able to help you with your broadcast buy.

Our research department has more information on the Atlanta market, who's who, and who buys what, than any other source in town.

For example: Of the total adults in the 15-county Atlanta area, 58% read our dailies, and 78% of the adults read us at least three days during a five-day period; 71% read our Sunday paper; and 82% read us three out of four Sundays.

Write us and we'll send you the truth in numbers about Atlanta.

Readership: Belden Continuing Audience Study.
Represented by Story & Kelly-Smith, Inc.
Member of the Metropolitan Sunday Newspapers, Inc.

The Atlanta Journal

FIGURE 8.2
Intense coverage of a specific geographical area is a newspaper's biggest advantage. The *Atlanta Journal* conveys this idea in a competitive advertisement placed in the TV Standard Rate & Data book.

national circulation of 1,367,430[2] and delivers a qualitatively selective audience composed largely of executives in business and finance. As an advertising medium, the *Wall Street Journal* is more accurately classified as a business publication and is listed in the business publication edition of Standard Rate and Data Service as well as in the newspaper edition. In a like manner, religious, ethnic, and foreign-language newspapers appeal to special groups of people rather than all the residents in a particular community.

The importance of the newspaper as an advertising medium is

[2] Standard Rate and Data Service, *Newspaper Rates and Data*, June 12, 1975.

indicated by the amount of money invested in newspaper advertising each year (see Table 6.1). In 1975, estimated expenditures for newspaper advertising in the United States exceeded $8 billion. This figure includes only advertising in daily newspapers; yet it represents almost 30 percent of the country's total advertising expenditures for the year. And the particularly local appeal of newspapers—the geographical selectivity they offer advertisers—explains in part why more than $5 out of every $6 invested in newspaper advertising comes from local or retail advertisers.

Classification of Newspapers

In addition to the basic distinction between newspapers which provide broad coverage within a particular community and those which deliver a qualitatively selective circulation that is national or regional, there are two other common methods of grouping or classifying newspapers. One method classifies them by page size or format. The other groups them according to time and frequency of publication and the characteristics of the local markets they serve.

In terms of format or page size, newspapers are divided into standard and tabloid types. Traditionally, the standard newspaper size was approximately 21 inches deep by 8 columns wide, with each column about 2 inches in width. Today, however, the number of columns in a standard-size newspaper may vary from 6 to 9, with different column widths, and page depths may run from 18 to 23 inches. Thus the standard-size newspaper is anything but standard, and the term really means simply a large page, as opposed to the tabloid, or small page. Tabloid newspapers are approximately half the so-called standard size. Most "tabs" are 5 columns wide, and the page measure approximately 10 by 14 inches, but here too there is variation. The page depth of the *Middletown* (New York) *Times Herald-Record*, for example, is 15 inches. Two New York City tabloids, the *News* and the *Post*, have page depths of $14^{1}/_{4}$ and $14^{1}/_{2}$ inches, respectively. Variations in newspaper column widths and page sizes for both standard and tabloid papers present a real problem to the advertiser who wishes to use newspapers in a number of different markets. Oftentimes, printing materials must be adjusted to meet the varying formats.

There is an unavoidable overlap in classifying newspapers according to time and frequency of publication and the characteristics of the markets they serve. By frequency of publication, newspapers fall into two broad groups, dailies and weeklies. However, a daily may be published five, six, or seven days a week, while a weekly may appear once a week, twice a week, three times a week, or only every other week. Generally speaking, the frequency of publication is often a function of the market in which a paper is printed. The *New York Times* publishes seven days a week, while the *Oakridge* (Oregon) *Dead*

FIGURE 8.3
A newspaper advertising sales representative conducts a final check on layout and copy before turning it in to the compositors for production. [Eugene Register-Guard.]

Mountain Echo appears only once a week. Metropolitan papers often reach homes far beyond the city limits, especially with their Sunday editions; for example, more than one-third of the circulation of the *New York Times* and the *St. Louis Post-Dispatch* is outside the primary market areas of the cities in which the papers are printed. Most small dailies, on the other hand, have little circulation beyond their immediate areas.

Small-town and suburban weekly papers are even more highly localized in circulation and editorial appeal. Their content consists largely of local and personal news of the communities they serve, and within these communities they may enjoy a more thorough and careful reading and a longer life than either the metropolitan or small-town daily. However, the cost per reader in weekly newspapers is higher than in dailies, and weekly circulations are usually small. The communities served by weeklies may be independent small towns, suburban areas adjacent to large cities, or even districts within large cities. The *Custer County Chief*, with an audited circulation of 4,574 in Broken Bow, Nebraska, and its environs, is a small-town weekly. The *University District Herald* is a community weekly that provides 22,398 free circulation in a restricted area inside the city limits of Seattle. The growing number of suburban newspapers, competing with metropoli-

In 1975,
the Southern California families most likely to buy a new home or car, throw a party, vacation in Hawaii, invest in real estate or take a flying trip to Europe, are Los Angeles Times families.

They earn more, spend more and add up to the largest and most influential audience in the nation's second-largest market.

Los Angeles Times

1,045,479 weekdays / 1,236,066 Sunday

FIGURE 8.4
Papers in large, competitive newspaper markets tend to pay more attention to the demographic composition of their subscribers than do papers that are monopolies in their home markets. [Los Angeles Times.]

tan dailies on the strength of their coverage of the affluent fringes of big cities, is one of the current trends in the newspaper business.

The shopping newspaper is frequently confused with the free-circulation community weekly. The shopping newspaper is really a form of direct advertising. It contains little news and editorial content, but consists entirely or almost entirely of advertising, and is delivered to homes without charge in newspaper format. Whether a given publication is classed as a community weekly or a shopping newspaper may depend upon the quantity and quality of the editorial content. It may also depend on who does the classifying—the publisher or advertising representative of the paper or someone with a competitive medium.

Newspaper Supplements

A hybrid medium within the newspaper field is the supplement delivered as part of Sunday editions. The familiar comic supplement is a special Sunday section of the newspaper sold to advertisers either on an individual market basis or in multiple market combinations known as "comic groups."

In Los Angeles, the Sunday *Times* distributes its own independent comic section. The *Los Angeles Herald-Examiner*, on the other hand, carries "Puck—The Comic Weekly." "Puck" is a nationally syndicated comic and may be purchased to cover only the Los Angeles market, or it may be purchased to cover 5 West Coast cities, 4 other regional combinations, or—in a national edition—52 papers in 51 cities.

Another type of Sunday supplement, the Sunday magazine supplement, is also delivered to newspaper readers each week at no extra cost. As its name implies, the magazine supplement resembles a magazine in both content and format; it is discussed in the portion of this chapter devoted to magazines.

Tabloid Inserts

Closely related to the concept of newspaper supplements is the technique in which the advertiser provides a newspaper with a tabloid advertising supplement to be inserted into the daily or Sunday newspaper. Commonly called *tab inserts*, these supplements represent another important change in the newspaper advertising business in the last decade. Multiple-page tabloid inserts have become especially popular with discount and variety stores, department stores, and even national automobile advertisers. The advertiser is responsible for printing and shipping the tabloid advertising sections to the various newspapers included in the media buy. The newspaper simply inserts the tab sections into the papers as they come off the press and delivers them within the newspaper in the usual manner. This results in a much

BLACK ENTERPRISE

We deliver 1/3 of all married black male household heads earning $15,000+.

We deliver 2/3 of all single black male household heads earning $15,000.

Our controlled circulation is 175,000.
Total circulation — 200,000.
Total audience — 960,000.

82% of our readers who are male heads of households earn $10,000+.

51% earn $15,000+.

60% are college educated.

40% have professional/managerial jobs.

When you want to influence the influencers

FIGURE 8.5
High-income blacks are the target of *Black Enterprise*, a magazine that is distributed free to the majority of its readers.

more dependable and efficient method of delivery for the advertiser, who formerly had to depend upon makeshift distribution crews to place the advertisements behind screen doors or wedge them behind door knobs. Newspapers generally charge a flat fee for standard 8-page tabloid inserts which equates to the charge the advertiser would have paid had he run the same amount of space at normal black-and-white rates. The use of multiple-page tab inserts increased 68 percent between 1971 and 1975,[3] despite the fact that they have added a "clutter factor" that some newspaper subscribers do not appreciate.

The Newspaper Advertising Department

In a typical daily newspaper, the advertising sales department consists of three subdepartments. One handles only *classified* advertising, so-called because the advertisements are placed in a special section of the paper and arranged by specific products and service classifications for easy reference, much like the yellow pages of the phone directory.

Classified advertising is an important source of revenue for newspapers, but display advertising is of greater importance to most local merchants and national or regional distributors. *Display* advertising is that which is placed on news and feature pages throughout the paper, and uses a variety of space sizes, layout designs, type faces and sizes, and illustrative techniques. Some newspapers also offer an in-between form of advertising called *display classified*, which permits the use of limited display techniques in advertisements that are published in the classified section.

Two subdepartments are concerned with display advertising: the *national*, or *general*, *display* advertising department, which handles advertisements placed by national and regional advertisers, and the *retail*, or *local*, *display* department, which handles the advertising of retail stores and local service organizations. National advertisements emphasize type of product and particular brand. Retail advertisements stress the store as the place to buy and are usually designed to build store traffic as well as to "move" the merchandise advertised.

Newspaper Rate Structure

Most newspapers quote different rates to national and local advertisers and base the rates on different units of space. The local advertising rate is frequently lower than the national rate, allows no commission to advertising agencies, and is subject to appreciable discounts for the amount of space used. The basic unit of space for local advertising is

---

[3] *Basic Facts about Newspaper Advertising*, Newspaper Advertising Bureau, 1974.

How to succeed in New York

It's hard to imagine a successful selling campaign in New York in which The New York Times does not play the dominant part. Because The Times reaches more readers than any other newspaper in the area — both weekdays and Sundays...

...Who are college graduates

...Who hold professional/managerial jobs

...Who earn $20,000 a year or more

That's why, year after year, advertisers have made The Times

...First in total advertising

...First in general advertising

...First in Manhattan department store advertising

...First in classified advertising

...First in financial advertising

...First in real estate advertising

...First in automotive advertising

...First in home furnishings advertising

...First in travel advertising

...First in apparel advertising

...First in liquor advertising

...First in amusements advertising

...And first in advertising in 77 other Media Records classifications as well.

Experience has proved to advertisers that they profit most by putting their money where the money is. It's as simple as that.

The New York Times

For 56 years first in advertising in America's first market.

FIGURE 8.6

The *New York Times* continues to dominate the New York newspaper advertising scene as it has for more than a half century, by convincing advertisers that they should advertise to the more affluent *New York Times* readers.

---

the *column inch*, an area 1 column wide by 1 inch deep. As an example, the standard rate for local advertisers—also called the flat or transient rate—in the *Seattle Times* is $13.79 per column inch. However, a local advertiser can, through volume discounts, reduce this cost by as

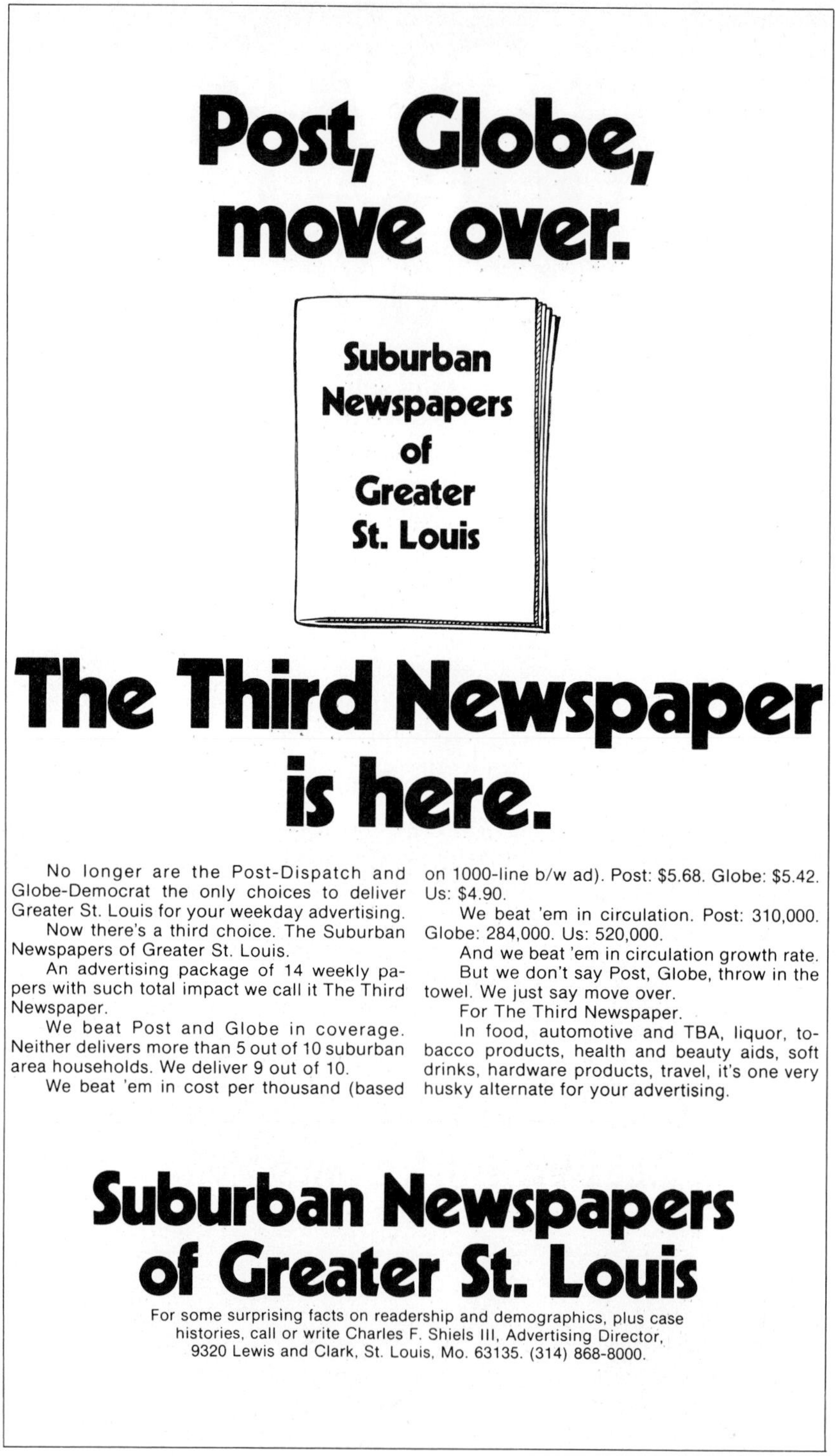

FIGURE 8.7
Fourteen weekly
newspapers surrounding St. Louis
boast a circulation
much larger than
either of the famous St. Louis dailies. This sort of situation exists in
many of the metropolitan areas of
the country. [*Suburban Newspapers
of Greater St.
Louis*.]

Post, Globe, move over.

Suburban Newspapers of Greater St. Louis

The Third Newspaper is here.

No longer are the Post-Dispatch and Globe-Democrat the only choices to deliver Greater St. Louis for your weekday advertising.

Now there's a third choice. The Suburban Newspapers of Greater St. Louis.

An advertising package of 14 weekly papers with such total impact we call it The Third Newspaper.

We beat Post and Globe in coverage. Neither delivers more than 5 out of 10 suburban area households. We deliver 9 out of 10.

We beat 'em in cost per thousand (based on 1000-line b/w ad). Post: $5.68. Globe: $5.42. Us: $4.90.

We beat 'em in circulation. Post: 310,000. Globe: 284,000. Us: 520,000.

And we beat 'em in circulation growth rate.

But we don't say Post, Globe, throw in the towel. We just say move over.

For The Third Newspaper.

In food, automotive and TBA, liquor, tobacco products, health and beauty aids, soft drinks, hardware products, travel, it's one very husky alternate for your advertising.

Suburban Newspapers of Greater St. Louis

For some surprising facts on readership and demographics, plus case histories, call or write Charles F. Shiels III, Advertising Director, 9320 Lewis and Clark, St. Louis, Mo. 63135. (314) 868-8000.

much as 50 percent.[4] The national or general rate, which is rarely subject to such generous volume discounts, provides for a commission to both representative and advertising agency and is quoted in terms of *agate lines* or lines. There are 14 lines to the column inch. In the case of the *Seattle Times*, the national or general rate is $1.35 per line, which is equal to a rate of $18.90 per inch, and the maximum discount for volume reduces this by only 15 percent.[5]

Media that employ two different rate scales for local and national advertisers have what is known as a *dual rate structure*, as opposed to a single rate structure. The dual rate structure is common in the newspaper field and is used by some broadcast media, but a single rate structure is the universal practice with magazines and out-of-home media.

However, all firms which might be considered "local" cannot advertise at the local rate. Many newspapers apply the national rate to wholesalers or jobbers and to advertisers in automotive, financial, transportation, and other specific product or service classifications. The base or flat rates referred to are for black-and-white (b&w) advertisements published *run-of-paper* (ROP)—meaning the position of the advertisement in the newspaper will be whatever is convenient for the publisher. Premium rates are charged for advertisements that use

[4] *Seattle Times* Local Retail Rate Card no. 35, Oct. 1, 1975.
[5] *Seattle Times* General Rate Card no. 54, Jan. 1, 1975.

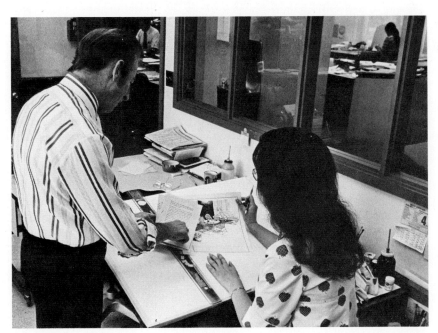

FIGURE 8.8
Artists and copywriters are as much at home in a modern newspaper as in an advertising agency. Those pictured here work on promotion department projects as well as perform creative services for advertising salespeople and their clients. [Eugene Register-Guard.]

color and also for advertisements placed in a specified position, whether in black and white or in color.

Combination rates are a further complication in newspaper rate structure. In some markets, where two papers are owned by the same publisher, the advertiser may buy space in both newspapers at a single combination rate. For example, the only morning paper and the only evening paper in Des Moines, Iowa, are owned by the same publisher. A national advertiser may buy space in the morning *Register* for $1.23 a line or in the evening *Tribune* for $1.17. If the ad runs in both papers within three days, the rate for the combination is only 52 cents a line more than for the morning *Register* alone.[6] This is called an optional combination rate.

The Theoretical Milline Rate   To compare advertising costs among a number of different newspapers, national advertisers have traditionally used a theoretical figure called the *milline rate*. Advertisers are never billed at the milline rate; it is merely a common denominator for calculating the relative cost of advertising in newspapers with different rates and circulations. Specifically, the milline rate is the cost of delivering one line of advertising to an *assumed* 1 million circulation, and it is determined by multiplying the line rate by 1 million and dividing the result by the paper's actual circulation, in this way:

$$\frac{R \times 1,000,000}{C} = MR$$

R = actual or published rate
C = actual circulation
MR = milline rate

For example, the *Des Moines Register* has a line rate of $1.23 and a circulation of 241,403, while the *Des Moines Tribune* has a line rate of $1.17 and a circulation of 102,424.[7] Obviously, although the cost per line is greater in the *Register*, the relative cost per message delivered is less. Using the formula above, we see that the milline rate for the *Register* is $5.10, while that for the *Tribune* is $11.42.[8]

In general, the milline rate goes up as circulation goes down, and the greater the circulation, the lower the milline rate. Since certain overhead and production costs are relatively constant regardless of circulation, milline rates should be compared only between papers in similar circulation ranges. There is no point in comparing the milline rate of the *Los Angeles Times* with that of the Archbold, Ohio, weekly *Buckeye*.

---

[6] Standard Rate and Data Service, op. cit.
[7] Ibid.
[8] Ibid.

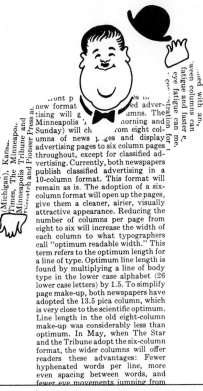

We've replaced our 8 skinny columns with 6 fat ones.

Here's one case where fatter is better. The Minneapolis Star and the Minneapolis Tribune have changed from the old 8 skinny-column format to a new 6 fat-column format, resulting in much cleaner, more readable newspapers. We've gotten rid of a lot of those awkward eye-jumps and hyphens that can make newspapers difficult and tiring to read. Which, of course, means a much more inviting atmosphere for your advertising.

Besides increasing our columns

by 7/16 inch, we've reduced our page width by 1/2 inch. By doing this we've been better able to hold our page rates down, despite the increasing cost of newsprint. So the new 6 fat-column page costs exactly the same as the old 8 skinny-column page. (See our rate listing on this page.) If you'd like more information, we'll be happy to send you a special kit that'll show you how to easily figure out the cost of an ad in the new format and how to convert existing or new ads into the

format. We'll also include a sample newspaper. To get the kit, just send your name and address to: Mr. W. James Van Hercke, General Advertising Manager, Minneapolis Star/Minneapolis Tribune, 5th at Portland, Minneapolis, Minn. 55415. You'll see why fatter is better.

The Minneapolis Star
Minneapolis Tribune

We've got what it takes to reach a great market.

Nationally represented by Cresmer, Woodward, O'Mara and Ormsbee, Inc., Atlanta, Boston, Chicago, Dallas, Detroit, Los Angeles, Minneapolis, New York, Philadelphia, San Francisco

FIGURE 8.9
Standardization of newspaper mechanical requirements for the convenience of advertisers wishing to place an ad in many papers has always been a problem. Perhaps the problem will be solved one day if all papers follow the new trend to a six-column page.

Both milline and actual rates are purely quantitative measurements, of course. The advertiser should evaluate them in relation to such qualitative factors as editorial interest, coverage patterns, and the income, occupation, and buying habit variations of readers. One would not select the lowbrow *New York Daily News* over the *New York*

Times if the advertising strategy were to aim for a well-educated, elite audience, despite the significantly lower milline rate of the *New York Daily News*.

There is a trend today among media buyers to abandon the milline rate as a basis for comparing newspaper costs in favor of the cost-per-thousand (CPM) approach. Because this system was originally a magazine advertising buying technique, it will be discussed in depth under that subject. It is sufficient, at this point, to observe that this system differs from the milline rate in that it focuses on the cost of delivering a 1,000-line or full-page newspaper ad to 1,000 subscribers or homes.

Preferred Positions   Another practice which, although historically important, has fallen from popular use is that of purchasing specific positions within a newspaper at extra cost. For decades newspapers have allowed advertisers to stipulate a page or section in the paper or, a particular location on a page, where they wanted their advertisements placed. When ads appeared in the positions ordered, the advertisers paid a specified premium rate. Advertisers who simply *requested* a certain position did not pay the extra charge even when their requests were granted.

Today, almost all advertising agencies include in newspaper insertion orders some sort of a position request, such as main news, society, or sports section. They often add a request for "well forward" in the paper or section, or "above the fold." Most newspapers honor these requests to the best of their ability, but obviously few advertisements can appear in the front of a given issue, on the first sports page, or on the upper half of a page.

Color in Newspaper Advertisements   While the great majority of newspaper advertisements appear in black and white, color can be employed in newspaper advertising by two different methods. *ROP color* is printed by the newspaper on standard newsprint paper as part of the regular press run. The other method involves preprinted color inserts supplied in rolls and fed into the newspaper during the normal press run, and is generally called Hi-Fi or Spectacolor because the reproduction quality is superior to that of ROP color. Ninety percent of the 1,789[9] daily papers in the United States offer an additional ROP color; 85 percent[10] of them can print advertisements in black plus three colors, or full color. Practically all of them will accept color preprints. Almost all of the country's 641 Sunday newspapers have color capability, but less than 20 percent of weeklies offer one additional ROP color, and very few can supply two or more colors.

[9] *Editor & Publisher Yearbook*, 1975, p. 8.
[10] *Basic Facts about Newspapers*.

The Oregonian \ Oregon Journal

DAILY COMBINATION RATES

RATE PROTECTION

It is the condition of rate card that The Oregonian and Oregon Journal reserve the right to revise their advertising rates at any time upon 60 days notice in writing to holders of contracts and contracts are accepted subject to this reservation. First insertion on contract must be made within 30 days of date of contract. No contract made for a period of more than one year. Contracts must start on 1st day of contract month and end on last day of 12th month.

Black and White (ROP)

BULK RATES when covered by Oregonian contract; combined rate daily OREGONIAN and JOURNAL:

Open, Per Line	$1.68	30,000 lines	$1.56
1,000 lines	1.66	50,000 lines	1.54
2,500 lines	1.64	75,000 lines	1.52
5,000 lines	1.62	100,000 lines	1.50
10,000 lines	1.60	150,000 lines	1.48
20,000 lines	1.58	200,000 lines	1.46

To qualify for the above combination rates, advertisements in both newspapers must be identical in dimensions and copy, and must be published within a seven-day period.

Combination rates are based on OREGONIAN contract rate in effect. Advertisements ordered at the combination rate MUST BE COVERED BY ONE ORDER issued to The OREGONIAN and OREGON JOURNAL in combination and specifying insertion dates in each newspaper within the seven-day period.

Sunday Comics (excluding Puck orders) and Northwest Magazine linage may be added to daily and Sunday Oregonian ROP linage to earn more favorable rate.

There are no combination rates between the Sunday OREGONIAN and the daily JOURNAL.

COLOR (ROP)

	Black and 1 color	Black and 2 colors	Black and 3 colors
1000-1499 lines (min. 1000 lines), extra	50%	50%	50%
1500-2240 lines, extra	35%	45%	50%
Full page, extra	25%	40%	50%

*DISCOUNTS

Full page units only, b/w2c. or b/w 3c.:

6 ads per year	2%
13 ads per year	3%
26 ads per year	4%
39 ads per year	5%
52 ads per year	6%

(*) These discounts are in addition to the regular volume rate discounts

Two and three color rates based on standard process colors. Two colors $50.00 min. extra (each paper) for non-standard inks (non-commissionable). Three colors $75.00 min. extra (each paper) for non-standard inks (non-commissionable).

FIGURE 8.10

This portion of the *Portland Oregonian* and *Oregon Journal* rate card quotes rates for national advertisers wishing to run in both the morning and the evening paper simultaneously. It is a much better buy on a CPM basis than buying either paper alone. [The Portland Oregonian *and* Oregon Journal.]

The use of both ROP and preprinted color advertising in newspapers has increased in the past decade. The merits and the limitations of the use of color in newspapers and other media are discussed later in connection with illustration and design. Here, however, our concern is with the effect of color on newspaper space costs. Each ROP color added to a newspaper advertisement increases the cost of the space, and most newspapers have restrictions on the minimum amount of space for color advertising. Both space restrictions and premium rates vary from paper to paper. Few papers will accept color advertising in space units of less than 1,000 lines, and the premiums charged for color vary from 15 to 30 percent, depending upon the number of colors used.

Although most newspapers will accept preprints at the black-and-white rate, the overall cost of preprints to the advertiser, who must pay for paper, printing, and shipping from a central plant, may exceed the cost of ROP color as much as 60 percent. The importance some national advertisers, especially those in the food and beverage classifi-

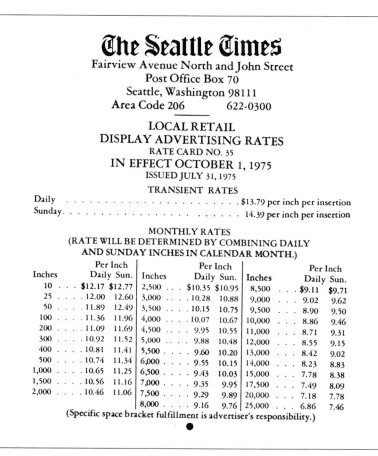

FIGURE 8.11
This section of a *Seattle Times* rate card gives basic rates for retail advertisers. Note that these rates are given in column inches, whereas the national rates offered by the Portland papers are given in agate lines. This is normal practice throughout the country. [Seattle Times.]

The Seattle Times

Fairview Avenue North and John Street
Post Office Box 70
Seattle, Washington 98111
Area Code 206   622-0300

**LOCAL RETAIL
DISPLAY ADVERTISING RATES**
RATE CARD NO. 35
IN EFFECT OCTOBER 1, 1975
ISSUED JULY 31, 1975

TRANSIENT RATES

Daily . . . . $13.79 per inch per insertion
Sunday. . . . . 14.39 per inch per insertion

**MONTHLY RATES
(RATE WILL BE DETERMINED BY COMBINING DAILY
AND SUNDAY INCHES IN CALENDAR MONTH.)**

Inches	Per Inch Daily	Sun.	Inches	Per Inch Daily	Sun.	Inches	Per Inch Daily	Sun.
10	$12.17	$12.77	2,500	$10.35	$10.95	8,500	$9.11	$9.71
25	12.00	12.60	3,000	10.28	10.88	9,000	9.02	9.62
50	11.89	12.49	3,500	10.15	10.75	9,500	8.90	9.50
100	11.36	11.96	4,000	10.07	10.67	10,000	8.86	9.46
200	11.09	11.69	4,500	9.95	10.55	11,000	8.71	9.31
300	10.92	11.52	5,000	9.88	10.48	12,000	8.55	9.15
400	10.81	11.41	5,500	9.60	10.20	13,000	8.42	9.02
500	10.74	11.34	6,000	9.55	10.15	14,000	8.23	8.83
1,000	10.65	11.25	6,500	9.43	10.03	15,000	7.78	8.38
1,500	10.56	11.16	7,000	9.35	9.95	17,500	7.49	8.09
2,000	10.46	11.06	7,500	9.29	9.89	20,000	7.18	7.78
			8,000	9.16	9.76	25,000	6.86	7.46

(Specific space bracket fulfillment is advertiser's responsibility.)

cations, place on high-quality color reproduction in their advertisements is well illustrated by their use of color preprints in newspapers.

Newspaper Services for Advertisers

Most advertising media are interested in the success of their advertisers, and newspapers are no exception. To help national advertisers and their agencies plan effectively, many newspapers conduct periodic studies of buying habits, brand preferences, distribution patterns, retail sales, and other indications of the potential and characteristics of the market areas they serve. They also provide merchandising or sales promotional assistance, such as securing related tie-in advertising from local retailers, encouraging the use of in-store displays, or helping to get adequate distribution. Some newspapers furnish merchandising aid without charge to advertisers contracting for a specified amount of space; others charge for all assistance except advice.

The great majority of small retailers do not have an advertising department, and a surprising number of larger retailers do not have advertising staffs adequate to perform all functions necessary in the planning and the creation of their own advertising. As the retailer's primary advertising medium, newspapers generally provide creative services for local advertisers without charge, although there is a growing trend toward passing some art and production costs to the advertiser. On smaller newspapers, the advertising salesperson frequently writes copy, prepares a layout, and suggests illustration material available from syndicated services to which the paper subscribes. Most metropolitan dailies maintain advertising service departments which are equipped to furnish complete creative services, including original artwork. These departments are not intended to replace the advertisers' own creative departments, however. They were originally conceived to free newspaper sales personnel to sell more space, and to get new accounts into the paper. When a retailer uses the newspaper's creative facility too frequently, a fee may be charged for any major services rendered by the paper.

MAGAZINES

Magazines, the second form of publication advertising, offer the advertiser advantages which in many respects are opposites of those offered by newspapers. The newspaper appeals to all kinds of people within a particular community; the magazine appeals to particular kinds of people in all kinds of communities. The life of an advertisement in a daily newspaper is short—rarely longer than a day. A magazine advertisement continues to "live" and produce results for a week, a month, or even longer. While newspapers are limited in the quality of their ROP reproduction, most magazines of any size or importance offer high-quality paper and printing. At their best, magazines give the advertiser elegant reproduction. The deadline for the insertion of newspaper advertising is usually two or three days in advance of publication. Such flexibility for the advertiser is impossible with a magazine advertisement. Few magazine deadlines are as short as three weeks prior to publication date, and may be as much as two months in advance. The newspaper is primarily a local medium, and the magazine is primarily a national medium.

Regional Coverage by Magazines

Even though we consider the magazine a national medium, this does not mean that the effective use of magazines as advertising media is limited to the advertiser whose product or service is distributed in every one of the 50 states of the Union.

Regional Magazines   The circulation of some magazines has always been restricted to specific regions or sections of the country. For example, *Sunset Magazine* is edited primarily for residents of the Pacific states, including Alaska and Hawaii. Little more than 10 percent of *Sunset Magazine's* total circulation of 1,280,000 is delivered outside these states, and the advertiser may buy the total coverage or either of three sectional editions within the total. *Southern Planter*, a century-old agricultural magazine, concentrates 97 percent of its circulation in 13 South Atlantic and South Central states.

Regional Editions   And among magazines which in the past offered only broad national coverage, there is today a strong trend toward making special editions available to the manufacturer who advertises different brands in different geographic areas or whose marketing efforts are limited to certain regions or sections of the country. The editorial content of each regional edition remains essentially the same, but the advertisements on some pages vary in different geographical locations. *Newsweek*, for example, offers advertisers a choice of 39 different metropolitan city editions, 14 regional editions, and a number of special editions focusing on specific interest or vocational groups. *Newsweek's* Los Angeles edition delivers 200,000 circulation and the Detroit edition 75,000. But the availability of regional editions is not limited to magazines with huge multimillion national circulation figures. *Bride's Magazine*, with about 300,000 circulation, publishes a special edition delivered only to the Eastern market. *TV Guide* currently offers the maximum in geographical selectivity among magazines with a national circulation of 19 million that can be broken down into 89 different metropolitan editions.

Split-Run Editions   In many cases, when the magazine is not published in regional editions, special arrangements may be made for

Ms.
salutes the
liberated
advertisers!
May their
tribe
increase.

I am a liberated advertiser

Thanks to them, Ms. has grown 18% in advertising pages in the past six months.

In the year of the cut-back dollar, that's not a contribution to the cause. That's business. Our liberated advertisers—men and women—have their eyes wide open.

They're sensitive to the changing market, recognize the changing woman and know where to find her. They have freed themselves from old prejudices, reached beyond the conventional to a new appreciation of who could and would buy.

They have brought us their automobiles & insurance, travel & credit cards & cosmetics, cameras & book clubs, liquor & corporate campaigns.

If Ms. now has a range of advertising no other woman's magazine ever dreamed of, our advertisers are enjoying success in a new market they never dreamed of.

If you've seen TGI, you know our 1,700,000 Ms. readers have better educations, live in higher income households,

and hold more managerial/professional jobs than women who read Time, Newsweek, or any other woman's magazine.

These are the women interested in and capable of responding to the advertisers who can reach them.

Our advertisers can. They have a feeling about what should be said to women, how women want and expect to be treated. Ms. readers recognize and reward this.

A few years ago, this kind of advertising to women was a radical notion.

Today in Ms. you can be as radical as McDonnell Douglas. Or Mobil. Or Volkswagen. Or Chevrolet, or Bristol-Myers, or AT&T, or Diners Club, or Almaden, or Dunlop.

Our liberated advertisers are not so much ahead of the times as with it.

In Ms., you, too, can be a liberated advertiser and win your button.
Call: Robert Friedman, West Coast Sales Representative (213) 988-4541
Write: R. J. Friedman Assoc., Inc.
5643 Lemona Ave., Van Nuys, Calif. 91411

It is their time and we are their magazine.

FIGURE 8.12
Ms. magazine salutes advertisers who use the magazine's pages to reach almost 2 million women readers with advertising that *Ms.* says was formerly confined to male audiences.

Mightier than Maude.

**When <u>Newsweek</u> plus <u>Time</u> can deliver
a larger audience than Maude can,
it's time to rethink television.**

What can be mightier than Maude?

It's not Phyllis. Or The Six Million Dollar Man. It's not even a TV show. It's Newsweek plus Time—one of the strongest media buys you can make today: efficient, effective, and highly selective. Ask your media planning experts.

Newsweek, to start with, reaches an audience of 19 million adults—a rating of 13.6.

And that's just Newsweek.

Add Time and you get an unduplicated audience of 32 million adults and a rating of 22.7—larger than that of Maude, Phyllis or The Six Million Dollar Man. When you confine it to men 18 to 49 the rating jumps to 30.7. Which beats any regular prime-time TV series.

Yet you can buy Newsweek at a cost per thousand for men 18-49 that's actually less than that of the average prime-time show. And you can even buy the Newsweek plus Time combination at a cost per thousand that's comparable—particularly when you consider the quality of the audience.

Here the picture gets still brighter. With Newsweek plus Time—or Newsweek plus Sports Illustrated or Business Week—you zero in on people you just can't reach that efficiently with television alone.

As study after study shows, newsweekly readers are younger, better educated, more affluent. They do more. They buy more.

And, something else we suspect is true, they're more receptive to what a good, persuasive ad is saying. Because it's seen within the informative context of a newsweekly—instead of flashing by during a break in the entertainment on TV.

These days, with rising costs and limited availabilities, a lot of advertisers are having some second thoughts about television.

If you're among them, remember: the ratings point to the newsweeklies.

For the advertiser whose budget is limited, Newsweek, with its lower cost per thousand, is the more efficient. But consider the advantages of both. Newsweek plus Time.

It's a mighty big buy.

Newsweek

split-run insertions—insertions in which two or more products with different regional distribution patterns cooperate in sharing the same space, each advertiser paying for the share of total national circulation actually delivered into his region. The end result of both methods of using only that part of a publication's total national circulation which fits the marketing plans of the advertiser is the same. However, when regional editions are available, the advertisers can buy any edition without including the others, just as they might buy *McCall's Magazine* without buying *Redbook* even though both are published by the same company. Split-run coverage, on the other hand, often requires special arrangements with the publisher in order to provide other advertisements for the portion of national circulation which the regional marketer cannot use.

Selecting Coverage The tendency of national magazines to offer advertisers regional as well as national coverage is increasing and promises to minimize one of the traditional disadvantages of the magazine as an advertising medium—lack of geographical selectivity.

The first factor an advertiser must consider in the selection of newspapers is the importance of the local market covered by the paper. If the geographical area covered by a newspaper is of little or no importance, all other considerations—circulation, frequency of publication, rates, color availability, reproduction quality, and merchandising support—are immaterial. On the other hand, the first question to be answered about a magazine is "Does this magazine reach the kind of people who are the best prospects for our product?" If the answer is "no," there is little need to investigate the availability of regional coverage, rates, or mechanical requirements.

The Newspaper Magazine Supplement

The comparison of newspapers and magazines explains the dual nature of the newspaper *magazine supplement*. Some magazine supplements to Sunday newspapers, such as the *New Orleans Times-Picayune* tabloid rotogravure section "Dixie," or the "This World" section of the Sunday *San Francisco Examiner and Chronicle*, are locally edited. Other magazine supplements—*Family Weekly, Parade*—are syndicated or are produced by a publishing company which makes copies available in finished form as inserts for Sunday newspapers in different cities. Some locally edited supplements can be bought as groups of markets; others are sold only individually. Syndicated Sunday magazines are sold only in groups, but the groups themselves have different market profiles. *Parade*, for example, is distributed currently in 109 markets, and may be bought in 5 regional groups; *Family Weekly* goes into more than 307 smaller markets, such as Klamath Falls, Oregon, and Bowling Green, Kentucky.

Whether locally edited or syndicated, the content and format of the magazine supplement resemble a magazine more than a newspaper. It enjoys a longer life than the newspaper. Most magazine supplements are printed by the gravure process and offer greater color fidelity and finer reproduction than the ROP sections of the papers which distribute them. Their deadlines for advertising copy—their time

FIGURE 8.14
Chicago magazine and *Texas* monthly are typical of the many exceptions to basic concepts learned by advertising students. One is a city magazine, the other a magazine with statewide distribution. While geographically selective, they maintain magazines' prime characteristic—they reach a selective audience.

flexibility—are those of magazines. But here the similarity stops. The magazine supplement does not select its readers from particular kinds of people in all kinds of communities. It is delivered automatically to all kinds of readers in a particular community with the newspaper that serves that community; it provides intensive coverage of a local market or a group of local markets.

Classification of Magazines

As advertising media, magazines may be grouped or classified in several different ways. By page size, they may be divided into the four groups listed in Table 8.1.

Magazines Grouped by Page Size   The majority of magazines use the 3-column × 140-line page, and today very few represent the older "standard" size. Unless an advertiser cannot adequately present his message in the smaller space, page sizes are relatively unimportant except to art directors concerned with the visual impact of a particular design. The relative visibility or attention value of a full page in a magazine is the same whether the page is $9^3/_8 \times 12^1/_8$ inches (large) or $4^5/_{16} \times 6^1/_2$ inches (pocket). Advertisers who wish to present a message that cannot be easily accommodated on a small page are finding they can do an effective job by using several consecutive pages in the same issue. For example, Uniroyal, Inc., once ran 40 consecutive full-page color advertisements in the *Reader's Digest*.

   The trend in the 1970s has been to reduce the size of magazine formats from *large* to *flat* dimensions. *Seventeen* and *McCalls* have both made this switch, apparently to reduce paper costs and to reduce production costs for advertisers who face extra engraving charges when their ads run in different-sized magazines.

Magazines Grouped by Frequency   Another way of classifying magazines is by frequency of publication—whether they are issued weekly, biweekly, monthly, semimonthly, bimonthly, quarterly, or semiannually. Monthly magazines are by far the largest group, with weeklies second. The other five categories account for a relatively small number of the total. For some advertisers—those marketing a product with

TABLE 8.1

CLASSIFICATION	MAGAZINE	APPROXIMATE PAGE SIZE
Large	*Ebony*	4 col. × 170 lines
Flat	*Time, Seventeen, The New Yorker, Newsweek*	3 col. × 140 lines
Standard	*National Geographic Magazine*	2 col. × 119 lines
Small or pocket	*Reader's Digest, R. N. Magazine, TV Guide, Jet*	2 col. × 85 lines

seasonal appeal or attempting to establish a new product as rapidly as possible—publication frequency may be an important consideration. For example, an advertiser aiming at the Christmas gift market can deliver 12 advertisements to readers of a weekly such as *The New Yorker* between the first week in October and Christmas. In the same period of time, that same advertiser can deliver only three advertisements in a monthly such as *Holiday*.

Magazines Grouped by Editorial Appeal   The most important method of classifying magazines is in terms of the editorial appeal or the type of readership they attract. Classified by editorial appeal, magazines fall into three broad groups: consumer magazines, business publications, and farm publications—and each of these three is further divided into subgroups of more specific appeal.

1   *Consumer magazines.* A common subgrouping of consumer magazines, for example, separates them into general appeal and special-interest appeal. The former offers its readers a diversified editorial content, while the latter focuses its content on more restricted and more specific subjects which appeal to people with a special interest. A typical example of general consumer magazines is the *Reader's Digest*, which appeals to both men and women, to varying age, occupational, income, and educational levels, with a wide assortment of editorial content. On the other hand, the special-interest appeals of *Ski, Car & Driver*, and *Better Homes and Gardens* are indicated by the very names of the magazines.

The weakness in this general- versus special-appeal classification is that there is a degree of special appeal in almost all so-called general consumer magazines, and it is difficult to draw even a very wobbly line between the two groups. *Harper's Magazine, The New Yorker*, and *Grit* are all classified by Standard Rate and Data Service as magazines of general editorial content. But the editorial appeals of the three differ widely. *Harper's Magazine* features a definite appeal to the intellectual. *The New Yorker* attracts a more worldly, "sophisticated" audience. *Grit*, by its own definition of editorial flavor, is "designed to fill small-town needs, to satisfy small-town tastes and interests." In format, *Grit* resembles a tabloid newspaper more than a magazine, and its 1,321,978 circulation[11] concentrates on families with average incomes living in towns of less than 2,500 population.[12] On the other hand, 40 primary trade areas account for 71 percent of *The New Yorker's* circulation. Subscribers have median family incomes of over $20,000. Ethnic publications like *Ebony* and *Jet* are usually classed as special-interest magazines. Although they contain general editorial content, they are specifically aimed at black readers.

[11] Publisher's statement, June 30, 1974.
[12] Standard Rate and Data Service, *Consumer Magazine and Farm Publication Rates and Data*, Mar. 27, 1975.

A new syndicated study proves that people pay more attention to advertising in PLAYBOY than to advertising in any other major medium.

Traditional media research tells you the number and characteristics of people who read a given magazine, watch a specific television show, listen to a certain radio station.

What it doesn't tell you is whether these folks are paying attention to the advertising to which they're being exposed.

However, the answer to that rather significant question is now available—in a new study called *Media Insight*, which rates various media in terms of their effectiveness in gaining male attention for the advertising they carry.

Media Insight demonstrates quite dramatically that PLAYBOY generates more attention for the advertising it carries than does any other major medium measured—print or broadcast.

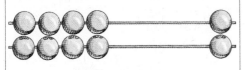

8 OUT OF 10.

Indeed, nearly eight of ten readers, on an over-all basis, pay attention to the advertising in PLAYBOY. (And in specific categories, the percentages climb even higher.) Contrast this with other mass-circulation magazines:

PLAYBOY	**79.1%**
National Geographic	70.1
Sports Illustrated	61.7
Reader's Digest	60.9
U.S. News	57.6
Esquire	55.1
Time	50.4
Newsweek	46.7
TV Guide	34.6

In comparing PLAYBOY with television programming, the same superiority exists:

PLAYBOY	**79.1%**
Real Life TV Adventure Shows	58.6
Sunday Afternoon Pro Football	57.5
Baseball (local broadcasts)	50.5
ABC's Wide World of Sports	47.8
Pro Golf Telecasts	46.9
Weekly TV Drama Series	45.5
Game/Quiz Shows	40.9
Adult Comedy Series	39.1
Late Night Movies	34.2

And when we compare PLAYBOY with newspapers and with radio, the same dominance holds true:

PLAYBOY	**79.1%**	
Daily		
Newspapers	65.3	
Sunday		
Newspapers	63.8	
FM Radio (more than 1.5 hrs/day)		65.0
FM Radio (0.5 hrs/day or more)		63.1
AM Radio (more than 1.5 hrs/day)		60.5
AM Radio (0.5 hrs/day or more)		56.8

How do the media you now have on your list compare with PLAYBOY? How many people whom you think you're reaching are you *really* reaching? And influencing?

If you're selling automobiles, you'll want to ponder the fact that auto ads in PLAYBOY will gain greater attention than in any other major medium.

If you're selling beer, wine or cigars, you'll be heartened to know that PLAYBOY will provide your advertisement the attention of better than eight out of ten readers, once again a far greater attention factor than offered by any other major medium—print or broadcast.

FIGURE 8.15

Playboy takes a nontraditional approach—claiming that *Playboy* advertising gets more attention than advertising in other media. [Playboy.]

The variety of magazines with definite special appeals and highly selective readerships is illustrated by the number of different classifications of consumer magazines in the Standard Rate and Date Service publication *Consumer Magazine and Farm Publication Rates and Data.* After eliminating newspaper supplements, directories, and general-appeal listings, 51 classifications remain, ranging alphabetically from "airline inflight" to "youth" magazines. The effectiveness of special-interest magazines as media does not rest entirely on their ability to deliver selective audiences. In addition to appealing to special groups, the editorial content of a magazine influences the mood of the reader, and the influence may be in favor of an advertiser's product. For example, Katherine Jones may read both a women's service magazine and a newsmagazine. When she reads *Better Homes and Gardens,* her thoughts are naturally directed toward her home and her family. When she reads *Newsweek,* her thoughts are directed away from her home and family. The advertiser may well ask which line of thought leads more directly to the product advertised.

2 *Business publications.* A business publication is designed to appeal to a particular group, classed either by type of occupation or position or by kind of business or industry. In terms of both number of

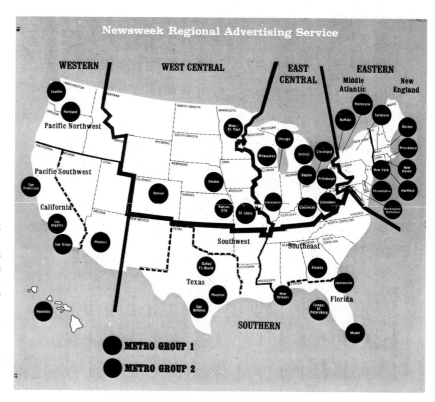

FIGURE 8.16
Regional and metropolitan editions of some magazines give advertisers an opportunity to combine the prestige of a national magazine with an upper bracket audience and tight geographical selectivity.

We turn down thousands of non-management applications every year.
(Result: a concentrated circulation of over 630,000 top decision makers that really means business.)

Business Week
A McGraw-Hill Magazine

FIGURE 8.17
Some magazines
refuse subscrip-
tions to people
who would dilute
the specialized na-
ture of their audi-
ences. Here *Busi-
ness Week* ex-
plains its policy in
a trade ad aimed
at advertisers.
[Business Week.]

publications and number of advertisers using them, the business
magazine group is larger than the consumer and farm groups combined. However, because circulations are usually smaller and page
rates lower, the dollar volume of business publication advertising is
about 70 percent that of consumer magazines.

The advertiser who wishes to reach an occupational group, such
as advertising people or woodworkers, can do so through the pages of
magazines such as *Advertising Age* and *Woodworking & Furniture
Digest*. Standard Rate and Data Service lists business publications
under 159 different occupational or industrial classifications, some of
which include as many as 20 different magazines.

Regardless of the classification, readers of business publications are looking for news and information that will help them on the job, not entertainment. As a result, well-edited business publications have high reader acceptance, and there is a direct correlation of interest between editorial and advertising columns, since both offer the readers possible solutions to current problems of their industry or their type of work. Subscriptions are often paid by the company instead of the individuals, and a single copy is frequently routed to a number of employees.

A large and important group of business publications consists of *professional magazines* read by men and women in recognized professions such as medicine, architecture, education, and law. The readers of professional magazines, like the *Journal of Marketing, Architectural Forum*, and *Journal of the American Medical Association*, are not primarily interested in ways to cut costs or increase profits but in new technical developments in their professions. And they do not usually purchase the products and services advertised to them; instead they recommend them to their patients or clients.

A second subgroup of business publications is accurately called *trade magazines*. These magazines are concerned with merchandising or marketing operations and circulate to dealers, jobbers, and distributors. *Supermarket News* is an example of a trade publication in the food field; *Men's Wear* is read by wholesalers and retailers of men's clothing.

A third subdivision is *institutional magazines*. The editorial content of this group is aimed at the particular problems of hospitals, hotels, and other institutions or service organizations. *The Modern Hospital* and *Hotel and Motel Management* are examples.

Industrial publications, a fourth subgroup in the business magazine field, are edited for the manufacturing and production side of business. *The Iron Age* and *Factory* are examples. Industrial magazine advertisers are commonly manufacturing or service companies advertising their products or services to other manufacturing companies.

The fifth and final classification of business publications is the *general business* or *executive magazine*, designed to appeal to men or women in executive or managerial positions in all types of businesses and industries. *Business Week, Fortune*, and *Dun's Review and Modern Industry* are general business magazines. And by editorial content, newspapers like the *Journal of Commerce* and the *Wall Street Journal* clearly belong in the general business publication category.

Business publications may be either horizontal or vertical in coverage of the field and in reader interest. The *horizontal publication* attracts readers in similar positions of responsibility in many different types of business. *Vertical publications*, on the other hand, are edited for people at all levels of responsibility within a single industry. General business or executive periodicals are horizontal in coverage; that is, they seek to reach executives regardless of their fields of endeavor. *Factory* is horizontal, covering plant managers, engineers, and other supervisory personnel, regardless of whether they manufacture electric motors, automobile tires, or furniture. *Advertising Age* is vertical, edited for all types of persons employed at any level in the advertising business.

3 *Farm publications*. A farm publication is a business publication concerned with farming. But it may be something more. Some farm publications are family magazines, because agriculture is a family enterprise as well as a business to be operated at a profit. A farm or ranch is not just a place of business; usually it is also the home of the farm family. Many farm and ranch families read the same consumer

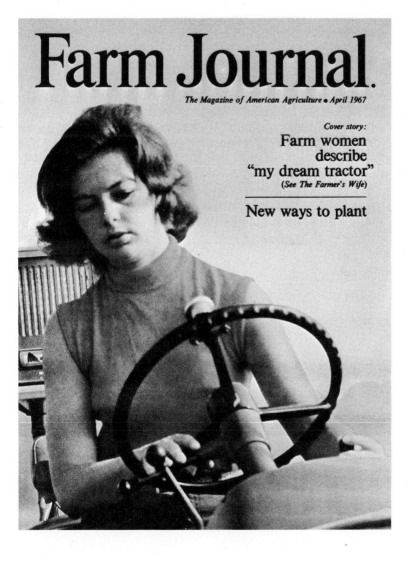

FIGURE 8.18
Farming is a family affair as this magazine cover suggests. Thus, farm publication advertising is more broadly based than some of the more technical business publications. [Farm Journal.]

magazines their city cousins read. But the farm magazine supplies them with ideas and information they are unlikely to get from other communications media, and it receives high reader interest from the family members. *Successful Farming* is a national farm magazine with over 800,000 circulation whose stated editorial policy is to deal "entirely with the business of farming and farm family ,management."[13] So unique is the farm publication category that it is afforded a large special section in the *Consumer Magazine* volume of Standard Rate and Data Service.

Since both climatic conditions and crop production are quite different for the North Carolina farmer and the North Dakota rancher, and since the problems of the egg producer and the grape grower are not the same even though both live in California's Napa Valley, farm magazines tend toward either regional or specialized vocational coverage. Regional farm magazines may circulate in several states or in only one. *The Progressive Farmer* concentrates more than 1 million circulation in 16 South Atlantic and South Central states—an arc of rural coverage extending northeast from Texas to Delaware.

Specialized farm publications focus on the problems of a particular type of farming or ranching such as fruit growing or livestock or poultry raising. They provide less editorial content of interest to the entire family than general farm magazines. *Poultry Tribune* and *Hoard's Dairyman* have subscribers in every state and many foreign countries. Naturally, the distribution of this circulation tends to follow the geographical pattern of the type of farming covered. Many small farm publications do not have their circulations audited by circulation verifying services such as ABC, BPA, or VAC, and the advertiser must depend on the publisher's statement or a crystal ball for circulation figures.

Magazine Rate Structures

Originally, because there were no local and few retail advertisers in national magazines, the single rate structure was standard. Advertising rates are quoted in units of pages, quarter pages, and agate lines. These rates include a commission to advertising agencies (15 percent) and representatives (10 percent).

Color Premiums   Color reproduction is available in almost all leading magazines, including those in the business or farm fields. Premiums charged for color are by no means uniform, even among magazines in the same appeal classification or circulation range. A two-color page in *Playboy* costs $40,425,[14] approximately 25 percent

---

[13] Standard Rate and Data Service, *Consumer Magazine and Farm Publication*, op. cit.
[14] *Playboy* Rate Card no. 26, April 1975.

GENERAL ADVERTISING RATES

SPACE UNITS	BLACK & WHITE	TWO COLOR (Black & One Color)	FOUR COLOR
Full page	$5,400	$6,650	$7,900
Two columns	3,675	5,030	6,200
Half page horizontal	3,330	4,690	5,775
One column	1,830	3,290	4,330
Half column	920	—	—
COVERS			
Second cover	—	—	$ 8,640
Third cover	—	—	7,900
Fourth cover	—	—	9,170

SPECIAL RATES

A. Split runs: available in 9 geographical areas, or combinations of these areas totaling full national distribution, in black-&-white space or in black imprinting on four-color pages.

Cluster Splits, and True Alternate Splits also available. Details and charges for press changes on request.

B. Retail and Book rates available on request.

C. Condé Nast Group: Rates and discounts on request for orders covering MADEMOISELLE, Vogue, Glamour, and House & Garden.

D. Bleed accepted in color, black & white, and on covers, at an additional charge of 20%. No charge for gutter bleed in double-page spread.

FIGURE 8.19
A portion of a rate card for *Mademoiselle* magazine. Note the premium required for full color over black-and-white ads and the special rates for split runs and bleed pages.

more than a black-and-white page, and a four-color page 40 percent more. In *Reader's Digest*, an advertiser can buy a two-color page for $56,170,[15] 6 percent more than black and white, and a four-color page for a premium of 20 percent. In publications with small circulations four-color reproduction may increase the space cost as much as 70 percent. Minimum space requirements for full color will vary also; *Rolling Stone* requires a full page, while *McCall's* will accept one-

[15] Standard Rate and Data Service, *Consumer Magazine and Farm Publication*, op. cit.

twelfth of a page in four colors.[16] Discounts for volume or frequency of insertions are the rule rather than the exception among magazines of all types.

Magazine Cost per Thousand The standard method for comparing magazine advertising costs focuses on the cost of delivering one full-page black-and-white ad to 1,000 homes (or in the case of business publications to, for example, 1,000 engineers or 1,000 airplane pilots). The formula for applying this technique is:

$$\frac{R \times 1,000}{C} = \text{CPM}$$

R = rate for one page, black and white
C = actual circulation
CPM = cost per thousand

Applying this method, a magazine with a basic black-and-white page rate of $11,000 and a circulation of 2 million would have a cost per thousand of $5.50. But a magazine with only 40,000 circulation and a rate of $640 per page would have a CPM of $16. As with the milline rate for newspapers, the cost per thousand for magazines usually goes up as the circulation goes down. In many cases, however, an advertiser is justified in absorbing the higher relative cost because of the qualitative selectivity of the magazine; that is, waste circulation is minimized. If the product is bought only by artists, advertising funds are invested more wisely in a magazine that reaches 40,000 artists at $16 per thousand than they would be in a publication read by 5 million people of all kinds, even though the ad might reach more artists in the second magazine and the cost per thousand for the latter publication might be as low as $2.83. The key in this case, of course, is the cost per thousand *prospects*.

A peculiarity of magazine rate structure is the circulation guarantee. Rates are tied to a specific quantity of circulation called the *rate base*. Any excess of copies over the guaranteed rate base is considered a bonus for the advertiser. If the circulation falls below the guarantee, the advertiser will receive a pro rata refund on his advertising in the magazine.

Preferred Positions for Magazine Advertisements The page size of magazines and the greater uniformity in size and shape of advertisements make the problems of position in magazines simpler than in newspapers.

Neither position on the page nor position of the page within the publication is of great importance to the magazine advertiser, even though certain pages are considered *preferred* or *premium positions*.

[16] Ibid.

In today's economy, Good Housekeeping's efficiency is more important than ever.

HOW MANY 4-COLOR BLEED PAGES CAN YOU BUY FOR $308,880?	TOTAL FEMALE IMPRESSIONS
Good Housekeeping — 12 PAGES	196,416,000
Ladies' Home Journal — 9.6	158,510,000
McCall's — 9.4	159,795,000
Family Circle — 8.3	137,808,000
Woman's Day — 9.7	168,240,000
Better Homes & Gardens — 7.2	124,201,000

HOW MANY 4-COLOR BLEED PAGES CAN YOU BUY FOR $161,622?	TOTAL FEMALE IMPRESSIONS
Good Housekeeping — 6 PAGES	98,208,000
Ladies' Home Journal — 4.7	79,255,000
McCall's — 4.6	88,775,000
Family Circle — 4.2	68,904,000
Woman's Day — 4.8	84,120,000
Better Homes & Gardens — 3.6	70,972,000

HOW MANY 4-COLOR BLEED PAGES CAN YOU BUY FOR $84,402?	TOTAL FEMALE IMPRESSIONS
Good Housekeeping — 3 PAGES	49,104,000
Ladies' Home Journal — 2.3	31,702,000
McCall's — 2.2	35,510,000
Family Circle — 2.1	34,452,000
Woman's Day — 2.4	33,648,000
Better Homes & Gardens — 1.9	35,486,000

Source: 1974/75 Simmons Study. Latest announced rates and discounts (regular).
Pages rounded to nearest full page to compute total female impressions.

FIGURE 8.20
Good Housekeeping builds a case for itself with a Simmons study showing its advantageous relative cost when compared with competitive women's magazines.

Because of its extra exposure, the back cover of a magazine (and, of course, the front cover, which is sometimes available in business publications) is always considered a premium position and commands a higher rate than inside pages. Inside covers are also usually classed as preferred positions, and in most magazines carry a premium rate somewhat lower than that for outside covers.

With the exception of covers, the most important consideration in the position of a magazine advertisement is probably its relation to editorial content, particularly in "departmentalized" publications such as *Better Homes and Gardens*. Because of reader interest stimulated by editorial content, a food manufacturer prefers to have his advertisement in the section of a women's magazine devoted to recipes and food preparations rather than with ideas for home decoration or gardening. Even in magazines with general editorial content, the advertiser stands to gain readership if his copy appears next to a feature of unusual interest. However, studies of direct inquiries received from advertisements in national magazines indicate that differences in returns attributable to differences in location are moderate, except for cover positions.

Magazine Services for Advertisers

The fundamental difference in the editorial appeal of newspapers and magazines is reflected in the marketing and merchandising assistance each type of publication offers advertisers. Except in competitive newspaper cities, newspaper market studies concentrate on the buying habits and other characteristics of a heterogeneous group within the geographical area the paper covers, while magazine studies tend to focus on the attitudes, opinions, and buying behavior of different income, sex, and occupational groups regardless of geographical location. Such studies, especially those of industrial and professional magazines, can be valuable aids in planning a manufacturer's marketing and advertising operations. In addition, many magazine publishers will collect market data of special interest to a specific advertiser more rapidly and with less expense than other research sources.

Magazines do not supply the elaborate creative service furnished local advertisers by newspapers, but most have departments that will assist in the preparation of folders, special letters to distributors and retailers, counter cards, and other merchandising material. Few magazines offer any merchandising or promotion material without charge or without a sizable purchase of space. Some consumer magazines have merchandising specialists in certain trade or product classifications, such as department stores or men's apparel, and some will send representatives to sales meetings to help present advertising plans to wholesalers, retailers, and the advertiser's own sales organization.

Sources of Publication Information

When advertisers or media buyers seek information on print media, they probably turn first to Standard Rate and Data Service. But by most buyers' standards, the information found there, while valuable, is incomplete—it does not provide the in-depth information sophisticated buyers require to make sound decisions.

The second important source of information about a newspaper or magazine is the publication itself. Through salespeople and representatives, a raft of information is available ranging from relatively simple rate cards to elaborate brochures describing in great detail both geographical markets and audiences covered by specific publications. Oftentimes these also include comparative figures on competitive publications.

The third and most prominent group of print media information sources are the private research firms who compile, primarily for their own subscribers among media, agencies, and clients, in-depth reports on such matters as advertising linage placed in leading newspapers and magazines, and incredibly detailed profiles of media audiences that far transcend SRDS's simple circulation figures. Included in this group of research organizations are such well known names as Media Records, Inc.; W. R. Simmons and Associates; Leading National Advertisers, Inc.; and Target Group Index, commonly known as TGI.

Through services like these, a media buyer can learn such information as: What accounts are running how much advertising in which newspapers or magazines? How do the psychographic and demographic profiles of the readers of one newsmagazine differ from those of another newsmagazine? What is the most efficient magazine to buy to reach female skiers between eighteen and thirty-five years old? Which newspaper in a two-paper market carries the bulk of the retail book advertising? The list could go on, for the information now available to advertisers and their advertising agency media buyers is extensive. This explains, in part, why it was said earlier in this book that advertising has its scientific aspects and also why the computer is playing a larger and larger role in agency media buying activities.

Printed Media Abroad

In our discussion of printed advertising media, we have naturally focused on the characteristics of these media in the United States. The qualities we have stressed and the distinctions we have drawn cannot be extended to apply to the same media in other countries. Literacy levels, for example, will obviously have a direct effect on the efficiency of printed media of any kind.

In the United Kingdom, an advertiser who wants to reach the whole country with a print advertisement thinks automatically of the national newspapers. Once a day, they penetrate to the most remote corners of the country. By using only one of them an advertiser can spread his or her message at least to some people, if only to a small minority, in each area.[17]

---

[17] Colin McIver, "Formulating Media Strategy for Foreign Markets," in S. Watson Dunn (ed.), *International Handbook of Advertising*, McGraw-Hill Book Company, New York, 1964, p. 133.

The availability of data on foreign publications (and other major types of media as well) has been greatly improved by Standard Rate and Data Service's extension of its operations overseas. Today, media rate and data directories are available from SRDS for England, France, Italy, West Germany, and Mexico, each published in the language of the country of issue. *British Rates and Data* is a monthly publication. *Tarif Media* (France) and *Medios Publicitarios Mexicanos* are quarterlies. *Dati e Tariffe Pubblicitarie* (Italy) and *Media Daten* (West Germany) are issued bimonthly.

International Publications

The growth of international marketing and international advertising has stimulated the development of international publications. One of the pioneers in the field is the Paris edition of the *New York Herald Tribune*, an eighty-five-year-old institution purchased in 1967 by the *New York Times* and *Washington Post* organizations. Now called the *International Herald Tribune*, the paper is published in Paris and boasts a circulation of over 116,000.[18] It is written in English, and the majority of its subscribers live outside France in Europe, Africa, and the Middle East. *Newsweek* and *Time* both present a variety of choices in overseas editions. *Time*, for example, offers more than 60 different editions going into 185 countries. Advertisers may purchase any combination of these editions or all of them if they prefer. Ninety percent of the readers of *Time* International are not United States citizens.

The Goliath of international periodicals is the Goliath of United States magazines—*Reader's Digest*—with over 110 foreign advertising editions and 12 million circulation.[19] Published in 13 languages, the foreign editions of *Reader's Digest* compete successfully not only with such international publications as *Time* and *Newsweek*, but also with local foreign media. It is the magazine of largest circulation in Canada, Spain, South Africa, and six Latin American nations, and second or third in six more, including Brazil, Chile, France, and Italy. More than 80 percent of the advertising in the international editions of *Reader's Digest* originates outside the United States.

On another plane, the Hearst Corporation publishes *Cosmopolitan en Espanol* with a circulation of 332,000 for Spanish-speaking women in Mexico, the Caribbean, and central and South America. In the fashion field, Condé Nast publishes special editions of *Vogue* in Australia, England, France, and Italy. If an advertiser is interested in reaching potential customers traveling to or from foreign locations, he may choose to place his messages in one or more *inflight magazines*. Outstanding among these media is *Clipper*, the magazine ed-

---

[18] *Editor & Publisher Yearbook*, p. 428.
[19] Advertisement for *Reader's Digest* International, Standard Rate and Data Service, *Consumer Magazine and Farm Publication*, op. cit.

ited for Pan American World Airways passengers. *Clipper* claims a circulation, that is, "on-board readers," of close to 1 million; the audience is described as "decision making executives and affluent world tourists."[20]

The United States business press has been less successful than consumer publications in establishing overseas editions. One reason is that the circulation of business publications is not large enough to support the multiple language translations featured by *Reader's Digest*. English, however, seems to be developing into the international language of business and technology. McGraw-Hill's *International Management* publishes in Spanish for Latin America and depends upon an English edition to reach Europe, Africa, and Asia. *Engineering Construction World*, published in New York, follows a multilingual digest policy for both editorial and advertising content, with condensed translations in Italian as well as German, French, and Spanish.

International Railway Journal reaches 112 countries, with its English text accompanied by summaries of key articles in French, German, and Spanish. *Iron Age Metalworking International* uses the same sort of digest approach, plus multilingual picture captions and headlines, to reach its international audience. In addition, it offers to split-run advertising by language communities in order to serve advertisers who wish to insert preprinted advertising pages. Thus, an advertising insert in French can be delivered only to readers in France, Belgium, Luxembourg, Haiti, and former French colonies in Asia, Africa, and the Middle East. In like manner, preprints may be directed to Spanish-, German-, and English-language circulation areas.

SUMMARY

One of the major categories of print media is publication advertising, which includes newspapers and consumer and business publications, as well as farm magazines.

With few exceptions, newspapers offer advertisers intensive coverage of the homes in a particular geographical area, but little class selectivity. Newspaper advertising costs and deadlines are highly flexible, but newspaper advertisements are short-lived. The bulk of newspaper advertising revenue comes from retail and classified advertising, but national advertisers also find newspaper advertising valuable in meeting certain campaign objectives. Thus, newspapers garner the largest single share of the total advertising dollars spent in the United States each year.

Newspaper supplements such as comic sections, Sunday magazine sections, and tabloid inserts broaden the flexibility of newspapers and enhance the medium's value to advertisers.

[20] Standard Rate and Data Service, *Consumer Magazine and Farm Publication*, op. cit.

Newspaper advertising space is usually sold to retailers by the column inch and to national advertisers by the agate line. An agate line is a unit of space 1 column wide and $1/14$ of an inch deep. Fourteen of these lines equal one column inch. At the retail level, newspaper advertising is usually subject to attractive bulk or frequency discounts. Under a single rate system national advertisers may also benefit from similar discounts, but this practice is still relatively rare. Rates may also vary when an advertiser employs color or demands a guaranteed position in the paper.

While a newspaper appeals to all sorts of people within a particular community, the magazine appeals to particular kinds of people in all kinds of communities. It is this ability to reach homogeneous groups that makes magazines so attractive to advertisers. In addition, magazines offer excellent reproduction possibilities and extended exposure of the advertisers' messages.

Although magazines are usually viewed as a medium which gives national coverage, there are regional magazines, regional editions of national magazines, and split-run possibilities which give the medium geographical flexibility.

Magazines may be classified in many different ways, by the size of the page, by frequency of publication, and by editorial appeal, that is, consumer magazines, business publications, and farm publications. Business publications are a complex group which include professional magazines, trade magazines, general business magazines, institutional magazines, and industrial publications.

Magazine space is generally sold at rates based on pages, quarter pages, or agate lines. As in the case of newspapers, premiums may be charged for color or special positions within the magazine.

The most important sources to which media buyers turn for information on magazines are Standard Rate and Data Service, the magazine itself, and private research firms who sell detailed information concerning magazine audiences, advertising linage, and other relevant data.

American advertisers who market products or services abroad may employ foreign newspapers or magazines, or they may buy space in the international editions of American publications. In areas where literacy is high, these print media may prove very effective. Standard Rate and Data Service again comes into play as the prime source of information available to media buyers charged with purchasing space for advertising abroad.

QUESTIONS FOR DISCUSSION

1 What are the fundamental differences between newspapers and magazines as they would be viewed by a media buyer?

2 A newspaper advertising department has a fairly complex organizational structure. Discuss the primary subdepartments' functions and the "back-up" departments that help service the needs of newspaper advertisers.

3 Newspapers continue to dominate the American advertising scene in

terms of total advertising dollars invested. Why does this situation exist? Would you expect the dominance of newspapers to continue in future years?

4 It has been stated that all magazines, even those with the biggest and broadest circulations, are "class-selective." Explain.

5 Compare the rate structures of newspapers and magazines.

6 Explain, without using the formula, what the cost-per-thousand concept reveals to a media buyer. How does it differ from a milline rate?

7 Why do you think some people are confused by whether or not magazines offer geographical selectivity?

8 Salespeople for newspaper magazine supplements claim they offer an advertiser the best advantages of both media. Why?

9 Select a particular magazine and discuss why you believe some of its advertisers selected that medium to carry its advertising.

10 How do vertical and horizontal business publications differ? Cite examples of each.

FOR FURTHER REFERENCE

Barton, Roger: *Media in Advertising*, McGraw-Hill Book Company, New York, 1964.

Brown, Lyndon O., Richard S. Lessler, and William M. Weilbacher: *Advertising Media*, The Ronald Press Company, New York, 1957.

Ferguson, James M.: *The Advertising Rate Structure in the Daily Newspaper Industry*, Prentice-Hall, Inc., New York, 1963.

Gaw, Walter A.: *Advertising Methods and Media*, Wadsworth Publishing Company, Inc., San Francisco, 1961.

Gill, Brendan: *Here at the New Yorker*, Random House, Inc., New York, 1975.

Kobre, Sidney: *Development of American Journalism*, Southern Illinois University Press, Carbondale, 1969.

McClure, Leslie W., and P. C. Fulton: *Advertising in the Printed Media*, The Macmillan Company, New York, 1964.

Medill School of Journalism, Northwestern University: *Magazine Profiles: Studies of Magazines Today*, Evanston, Ill., 1974.

Merrill, John C., Carter R. Bryan, and Marvin Alisky: *The Foreign Press*, Louisiana State University Press, Baton Rouge, 1973.

Peterson, Theodore: *Magazines in the Twentieth Century*, 2d ed., The University of Illinois Press, Urbana, 1964.

Wolseley, Roland E.: *The Changing Magazine: Trends in Readership and Management*, Hastings House, Publishers, Inc., New York, 1973.

Wood, J. P.: *Magazines in the United States*, The Ronald Press Company, New York, 1971.

CHAPTER 9

DIRECT ADVERTISING AND POINT-OF-PURCHASE ADVERTISING

291
DIRECT
ADVERTISING
AND POINT-
OF-PURCHASE
ADVERTISING

When an advertiser or media buyer selects an advertising medium, it is like a golfer selecting the right club. Each medium, like each golf club, should be considered and selected in terms of the needs of the situation in which it is to be used. While the bigger media and the longer clubs have their applications in the user's strategy, each club or medium, regardless of size, is indispensable in its place. The finest driver is of little value on the green or in a sand trap. By the same token, neither network television nor a multimillion-circulation magazine can substitute for some of the less glamorous media available to advertisers involved in the intense competition that characterizes marketing today. These forms of advertising, often referred to as *collateral* or *collateral media*, are explained in this and the following chapter. While they are usually employed as supplementary buys to other media in an advertiser's media mix, one should be aware that to some advertisers they may represent the most important media in their advertising campaigns.

Unlike the media discussed earlier, most of which are termed "measurable media," those we now approach do not lend themselves easily to accurate record keeping.

DIRECT ADVERTISING

The terms "direct advertising," "direct-mail advertising," and "mail-order advertising" are frequently confused. *Direct advertising* includes all forms of printed advertising delivered directly to the prospective customer, instead of indirectly as part of a newspaper or magazine. It may be handed over the counter of a retail store, distributed from door to door, delivered by messengers, passed out to people on the street, or sent through the mail. If it reaches the reader by mail, it is *direct-mail advertising*. *Mail-order advertising*, on the other hand, does not refer to the channels through which the message is delivered, but to a method of product distribution. When the advertising message is designed to consummate the sale of the product by mail, without the aid of intermediaries or personal, face-to-face selling, it is mail-order advertising—sometimes referred to as direct marketing. To secure orders by mail, the message may be delivered by direct advertising, direct-mail advertising, publications, or any other mass communications medium.

The Selectivity of Direct Advertising

The almost universal use of direct advertising, and particularly direct-mail advertising, is due to its ability to deliver messages to selected groups of prospects who are difficult to reach economically through other mass communications media. For example, with direct advertising, the service station operator can concentrate his messages only on car owners who live in his immediate neighborhood. Moreover, the Ford Motor Company, through its advertising agency, J. Walter Thompson Company, once created a special direct-mail campaign addressed only to women owners of Plymouth and Chevrolet cars. No other major medium can offer an advertiser both the geographical and the qualitative selectivity possible with direct advertising.

The Flexibility of Direct Advertising

Another important advantage of direct advertising is its flexibility—in format, in size, in color, and consequently in cost. Direct advertising may be as simple in form as a leaflet or postal card or as impressive and comprehensive as a Sears, Roebuck catalog. Letters are perhaps the most widely used of all direct advertising forms. They offer the advertiser an opportunity to personalize the message, and are frequently used in conjunction with other kinds of direct advertising material. Postal or mailing cards provide relatively inexpensive direct-mail advertising, well suited to short, direct messages such as the announcement of a sale to charge customers by a retail store.

Other commonly used forms of direct advertising are leaflets, folders, broadsides, booklets, brochures, and house organs or company publications. A *leaflet* is a simple folder. A *broadside* is a giant

FIGURE 9.1
Creative flexibility is one of the outstanding characteristics of direct-mail advertising. Note the variety of shapes, sizes, and production techniques, including the use of die cuts and three-dimensional techniques. [*Direct Marketing Advertising Association. Photograph by John Briggs.*]

293
DIRECT
ADVERTISING
AND POINT-
OF-PURCHASE
ADVERTISING

FRITZ S. HOFHEIMER, INC.

MAIL ADVERTISING and SALES PROMOTION SPECIALISTS
88 THIRD AVENUE   MINEOLA, N.Y. 11501

FSH

PHONE: 516-248-4600
CABLES: EVRIADRESS
SINCE 1878

Qty	Description	Price
16,000	MUSIC TEACHERS (College)*	40.00 M
28,565	(High School)	37.50 M
12,000	(Private—Schools & Individuals)	40.00 M
7,000	Musical Instrument Dealers*	35.00 M
794	California	37.50
185	Connecticut	20.00
207	Florida	22.50
150	Georgia	17.50
370	Illinois	27.50
202	Indiana	22.50
265	Massachusetts	25.00
355	Michigan	27.50
182	Minnesota	20.00
170	Missouri	17.50
258	New Jersey	25.00
516	New York State	32.50
283	New York 5 BOROS	25.00
200	North Carolina	25.00
463	Ohio	30.00
99	Oregon	15.50
465	Pennsylvania	30.00
311	Texas	27.50
154	Washington State	17.50
228	Wisconsin	25.00
135	MUSICAL Instrument Importers	22.50
330	Instrument Manufacturers	30.00
33,500	MUSICIANS (Professional)	35.00 M
1,441	(Accordion)	45.00 M
4,500	(Drums)	40.00 M
2,670	(Guitar)	40.00 M
4,600	(Saxophone)	40.00 M
2,900	(Violin)	40.00 M
121	Mustard Manufacturers	22.50
402	MUTUAL Casualty Insurance Cos.	30.00
1,996	Fire Insurance Cos.	40.00 M
104,000	Fund Owners (Minimum 3,000)*	30.00 M
561	Funds	40.00
503	Savings Banks	30.00
137	NAIL Manufacturers	22.50
44	(Wire) Mfrs.	15.00
1,346	NAMEPLATE Manufacturers	40.00
56	NAPHTHALENE (Crude) Mfrs.	40.00
41	(Refined) Mfrs.	13.50
164	NAPKIN Manufacturers	27.50
108	(Paper) Mfrs.	18.50
32	(Sanitary) Mfrs.	10.00
4,000	Narcotics Enforcement Officers	45.00 M
369	Addiction Treatment Agencies	30.00
14,618	NATIONAL ADVERTISERS (Newspapers)	40.00 M
2,115	(Poster)	40.00 M
2,072	(Premium Programs)	40.00 M
3,516	(Radio & TV)	40.00 M
5,904	NATIONAL ADVERTISERS' Advtsg. Mgrs.	40.00 M
16,401	Presidents	35.00 M
9,461	Sales Managers	40.00 M
4,200	NATIONAL Associations	35.00 M
4,200	Associations' Secretaries	35.00 M
11,080	NATIONAL & State Assns.	35.00 M
11,080	& State Associations' Secretaries	35.00 M
33	NATIONAL Parks	10.00
263	Parks & Landmarks	25.00
71	Parks Catering Concessionaires	15.00
191	Parks Concessionaires (all kinds)	25.00
1,632	NATURAL Gas Companies*	35.00 M
180	Gas Pipe Line Cos.	30.00
3,050	Gas Pipe Line Executives	40.00 M
940	Gasoline Producers	50.00
49	History Publications	12.50
14	History Societies	10.00
275	Naturopaths	40.00
	Nautical Instrument Makers	25.00
3,191	Naval Architects & Marine Engineers*	35.00 M
12	Naval Yards (U.S.)	10.00
128	Navy Post Exchanges	18.50
799	Navy Prime Contractors	40.00
419	NECKWEAR Jobbers	40.00
113	Manufacturers (Women's)	22.50
64	NEEDLE Manufacturers	15.00
3,070	NEEDLEWORK Retailers	40.00 M
1,116	Retailers (Department Stores)	35.00 M
373	NEGRO Clubs & Associations	30.00
109	Colleges	18.50

Qty	Description	Price
1,874	NEGRO Funeral Directors	40.00 M
172	Newspapers	25.00
67	Organizations (National)	15.00
224	Publications	28.50
146	Weeklies	22.50
2,684	Neon Sign Makers	40.00 M
162	Net & Netting Mfrs.	25.00
2,900	Neurological Surgeons see Doctors*	
1,290	Neurological Surgeons (Leading)	45.00 M
2,292	NEW YORK CITY Officials (Major)	40.00 M
14,500	Officials & Dept. Heads	32.50 M
3,402	NEWS Editors (Radio)	40.00 M
546	Editors (TV)	37.50 M
26	Magazines	10.00
61	Picture Syndicates	15.00
200	Services	25.00
269	Syndicates	30.00
2,137	Newsdealers Retail (PROPER)	40.00 M
262	California	25.00
103	Illinois	16.50
202	Massachusetts	22.50
69	Michigan	13.50
168	New Jersey	17.50
202	New York	25.00
99	Ohio	14.50
235	Pennsylvania	25.00
94	Texas	14.50
86	Washington State	14.50
1,014	Newsdealers Wholesale	45.00 M
297	Newsletter (Financial) Publishers	27.50
3,241	Newsletters	40.00 M
14,618	NEWSPAPER Advertisers	40.00 M
1,224	Advertisers (Largest)	45.00 M
1,618	Editors (Dailies' Chief)*	40.00 M
1,082	Editorial Writers	40.00 M
261	Feature Syndicates	27.50
181	Feature Syndicate Editors	27.50
110	Industry Publications	25.00
455	Librarians	30.00
840	Photographers	45.00
388	Representative Firms	32.50
1,771	Newspapers (Dailies)*	35.00 M
139	California	14.50
47	Florida	10.00
80	Illinois	12.50
95	Indiana	12.50
45	Massachusetts	10.00
54	Michigan	10.50
53	Missouri	10.50
31	New Jersey	9.50
86	New York	12.50
98	Ohio	12.50
53	Oklahoma	10.50
127	Pennsylvania	14.50
113	Texas	13.50
206	NEWSPAPERS—DAILIES (Top Rated)	22.50
1,081	(Circulation of 10,000 or MORE)*	35.00 M
478	(Circulation of 25,000 or MORE)*	32.50
1,220	(Circulation of 25,000 or LESS)*	35.00 M
1,438	(Evening)	32.50 M
65	(Foreign Language)	13.50
296	(Morning)	27.50
7	(Negro)	8.50
276	(Offering Split Runs)	25.00
669	(Offset Printed)	35.00
1,140	NEWSPAPERS (College) & Magazines	40.00 M
53	(German Language)	15.00
60	(Jewish)	14.50
172	(Negro)	25.00
477	(Shoppers' Free)	35.00
33	(Spanish Language)	12.50
561	(Sunday)	35.00
255	NEWSPAPERS Permanently retained in Library of Congress	25.00
655	Currently received in Lib. Congress	40.00
7,382	Newspapers (Weeklies)*	32.50 M
109	Alabama	14.50
17	Alaska	7.50
56	Arizona	10.50
123	Arkansas	15.00
480	California	26.50
124	Colorado	15.00

FIGURE 9.2

This page from a mailing-list catalog illustrates the highly selective nature of direct advertising. Lists range from 26 million people who make mail-order purchases to a single corrugated-fiberboard coffin manufacturer. [*Fritz S. Hofheimer, Inc.*]

folder, sent as a self-mailer or enclosed in an envelope, and used primarily when the dramatic impact of size seems needed. *Booklets* have the pages bound together rather than folded; they are designed to carry longer messages than folders or broadsides can carry, and they are made for reference use rather than for a one-time impression. Booklets are often used for catalogs, technical manuals, and price lists. A *brochure* is to a booklet what a broadside is to a folder—an elaborate booklet, planned to impress the reader with the prestige of the advertiser and the importance of his story.

House organs or *company publications* may seem to fall outside our definition of direct advertising material since they contain editorial matter—news or entertainment. However, instead of having an independent editorial staff provide a separate background for his message, the advertiser prepares the entire content of the house organ. Therefore, it is usually classified as direct advertising. Whether it is an internal house organ (published for employees) or an external house organ (published for dealers, stockholders, or customers), the sole aim of the publication is to further the interests of the company by providing channels of communication for group relations.

The variety of sizes, shapes, and formats of direct advertising material is limited only by the ingenuity of the advertiser, by the advertising budget, and—in the case of direct-mail material—by postal regulations. Die cuts, odd folds, unusual dimensions, gadgets—such as coins, pins, mirrors, or keys—and specially designed, three-dimensional packages as containers for the advertising message are used in direct-mail advertising to capture the receiver's initial attention and interest.

DIRECT-MAIL ADVERTISING

It is often said, almost to the point of becoming one of the leading advertising myths, that the general public dislikes direct mail and that direct-mail advertisers have a real problem even getting addressees to open their envelopes.

Hope S. Roman, director of the United States Postal Service's Market Research Division and a prominent marketing and advertising research specialist, has stated that almost 80 percent of direct-mail recipients read the direct-mail advertising they receive.[1] Roman also reveals that, according to U.S. Postal Service surveys, close to three-fourths of all adults receiving direct mail have a favorable attitude toward it.

Paradoxically, Roman's biggest complaint, from a consumer point

[1] Hope S. Roman, "Do Consumers Love Mailers?" *Direct Marketing*, October 1975, pp. 64, 66.

of view, is that direct-mail advertising concentrates on middle-class Americans, eliminating a full 30 percent of the population who receive none at all. This, she contends, is unfair to lower income groups who might benefit from direct-mail offers that feature lower prices than some neighborhood stores.

295
DIRECT
ADVERTISING
AND POINT-
OF-PURCHASE
ADVERTISING

Postal Classes

Postal rates and regulations are important to direct-mail advertisers, because they affect the cost of delivering their messages. Rates and regulations are subject to change, of course, and the wise user of direct mail will check regularly with a postmaster or with a supplier who specializes in the preparation of direct-mail material before planning a direct-mail campaign. There are four postal classes, three of which may be used by the direct-mail advertiser. First-class mail carries the highest rate except airmail parcel post. It is required for typewritten or handwritten communications. Second class is reserved for newspapers and magazines with paid circulations. Fourth class is parcel post. Third class covers all other mail. Third class mail must be so marked on the mailing wrapper, or left unsealed to permit postal inspection. Bulk mail is a special classification of third class that takes an even lower rate, and applies to a minimum of 200 identical pieces, or 50 pounds of them, bundled together. The sender must pay a fee for the permit required to use bulk mail.

First- and third-class mail accounts for all direct-mail advertising, except occasional specialties or samples sent by parcel post. The advertiser's choice between first and third class must be determined by considering a number of different factors—including the product or service the advertiser wishes to promote, the type of prospect he wishes to reach, the corporate or product image he wishes to create, and the available budget. First class is faster, enjoys more prestige, and is more costly. Third class is more economical, but slower, less impressive, and likely to get less attention.

Mailing Lists

Both the quantity and the quality of direct-mail circulation are determined by the mailing list the advertiser uses. Ideally, a mailing list should include only those people who are in a position to purchase, or influence the purchase of, the product or service. It should be accurate in the spelling of names, titles, and addresses, including the zip codes. And it should be free of duplication and "deadwood." People are mobile. They move to different residences, change jobs, get married, and die. Direct-mail experts estimate that the average turnover, or obsolescence, in mailing lists is as high as 25 percent of the names each year.

A list of names and addresses does not necessarily constitute a ready-made source of prospects. Advertisers still have the responsibility of determining who the best prospects are. Many factors affect the desire and ability to buy. When advertisers have decided which persons they wish to try to sell, they have a choice of building their own mailing lists or buying names from firms that specialize in furnishing lists of people classified according to certain characteristics such as occupation, income, product ownership, or special psychographic factors, including the propensity to buy by mail. Sources for building a mailing list include rosters of present customers; reports from the sales staff; inquiries received from periodical or broadcast advertising; city, business, or professional directories; tax lists; and other public records. The important considerations are that the list be accurate and appropriate.

Problems of Direct Mail

Two major disadvantages are inherent in the use of direct-mail advertising: first, it is often difficult to secure and maintain an appropriate mailing list, and second, it has a relatively high cost per recipient. Large-circulation magazines or newspapers, for example, will deliver full-page advertisements, supported by editorial content of interest to the reader, to millions of homes at a cost per reader that is a fraction of the cost of the postage on a postal card. The total cost of a direct-mail piece, of course, includes the postage plus the cost of the paper, printing, addressing, and handling. On the average, this cost would approach 12 to 15 cents, depending on the number mailed, even for a run-of-the-mill postcard. These costs have been escalating severely over the past five to ten years, and no end is in sight.

ADVERTISING SPECIALTIES[2]

Another form of direct advertising is *advertising specialties*, sometimes called "remembrance advertising." It consists of products which bear the name and address or slogan of a business firm and which are given away free by the advertiser to present and prospective customers. The advertiser hopes to create a feeling of goodwill, and hopes that the receiver of the gift will do business with the firm in the future, although the item is given on a "no-obligation" basis. Industry estimates place the annual sales volume for advertising specialties at close to 1 billion dollars.

[2] Some of the materials for this section were obtained from a pamphlet, *Specialty Advertising*, by Walter A. Gaw, Specialty Advertising Association, Chicago.

297
DIRECT
ADVERTISING
AND POINT-
OF-PURCHASE
ADVERTISING

Theodore Levitt of the Harvard Business School stresses that specialty advertising can provide reinforcement for other forms of business communication done by a company. Furthermore, according to Levitt, specialty advertising is both a good attention getter in a competitive arena and less pushy than some other media.[3] The idea of employing specialty items to act as reminders or reinforcers is one which has been getting a great deal of attention in recent times. Although creative people may not be able to pack the persuasive content of a printed advertisement or a TV commercial into a specialty item, Levitt believes there is value in reminding prospects of previous advertisements through the use of specialty items.

If the prospective customer finds the specialty useful in carrying out a daily routine of work, household duties, or just living, the advertiser's message is exposed every time the item is used. Thus, it is hoped, the name of the advertiser will be implanted in the prospect's mind, and when a need arises for the advertiser's product or service, the brand name will be recalled and a sale will result.

Types of Advertising Specialties

The advertising specialty industry classifies its many-item offerings into four main categories: calendars, novelties, matchbooks, and executive gifts.

Calendars Many of us carry a small calendar in our purses or wallets. We have others on desks and in different rooms of our homes and offices. Calendars are ubiquitous—seemingly everywhere. It is estimated that more than a third of the money spent annually for advertising specialties goes into the purchase of calendars. The total number printed annually is said to exceed the population of our country.

The calendar advertiser must face two important decisions. First, one must select a design and illustration that is appropriate and attractive to the target audience. If the intention of the calendar is to promote a family-oriented product such as a pizza parlor or a soft drink, the illustrations must fit the home environment. This suggests reproductions of landscapes, animals, children, or humorous situations. Some advertisers feel that a sports orientation or a bit of cheesecake is appropriate for a masculine audience. However, Brown and Bigelow, the country's leading calendar producer, reports that sexy calendars rate low in popularity compared with patriotic themes, nature scenes, and such. Many calendars omit the illustration in favor of recipes, almanac notations, or space for daily memoranda. Whether

---

[3] "The Reinforcers," reprinted from *Media Decisions* by the Specialty Advertising Information Bureau.

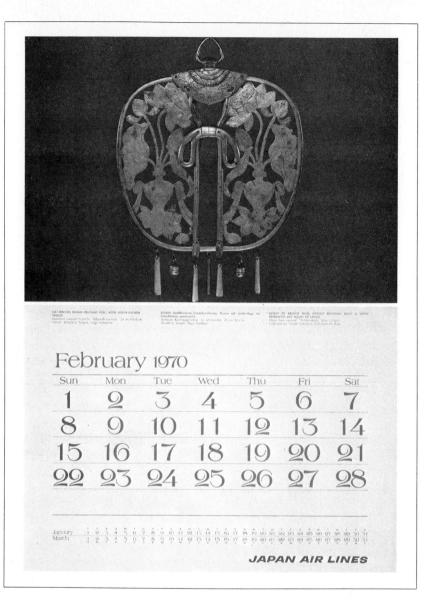

FIGURE 9.3
Full-color repro-
ductions of antique
Japanese art with
descriptions in En-
glish, German,
and French project
the image of Japan
Air Lines' world-
wide service to in-
ternational travel-
ers.

the value of the calendar to the recipient is aesthetic or functional, the
key is that it have value to the prospect and that he or she will be
willing to display it.

A second challenge facing calendar advertisers is the matter of
their physical distribution. Oftentimes they are distributed in the
advertiser's place of business, but this system has the drawback of only
reaching current customers. No new prospects are touched. They can
also be distributed door to door or by mail—a system commonly used

by national calendar advertisers—but this can involve considerable expense due to mailing list, postage, and other delivery costs.

299
DIRECT
ADVERTISING
AND POINT-
OF-PURCHASE
ADVERTISING

Despite the problems involved, many business executives continue to favor calendars as part of their advertising programs. Tradition, itself, furthers the idea, and customers expect them once the idea has been established. Fortunately, if handled correctly—if they are well designed and efficiently distributed—calendars are an effective, inexpensive way to keep the advertiser's name before the public every day of the year. This can be important to airlines and insurance companies, as well as to mortuaries, plumbers, and automobile repair shops. Although extensive coverage of vast numbers of homes may prove prohibitive due to the high cost per thousand for calendar advertising, the frequency and continuity of exposure, as well as the audience selectivity of calendars, are outstanding advantages.

Novelties The great variety of advertising novelties is staggering. The pen or pencil many of us use is the gift of some advertiser. Many ashtrays reach smokers through the compliments of a favorite cafe or filling station. Key rings, bottle openers, balloons, swizzle sticks, memo pads, thermometers, and rulers are a few examples from the long list of inexpensive, mass-produced novelties used in advertising.

FIGURE 9.4
This array of novelty items represents the thousands available to advertisers who employ remembrance advertising as part of their total advertising program. [*Specialty Advertising Association.*]

The novelty advertiser faces problems similar to those encountered with calendar use. One must take precautions to see that the distribution system reaches *prospects*, and that the novelty is *appropriate*. Appropriateness is not so much a matter of design, however, as it is one of use. The gift should be closely related to the advertiser's business or the prospect's personal interests. Personalized golf balls are hardly an enduring reminder if the prospect isn't a golfer. An appropriate advertising specialty for a filling station could be a key ring, for every time a driver starts his car, the name of the station would flash into his consciousness. On the other hand, a key ring might not do a good job for a dairy. An ice-cream scoop should be more effective. A fuel-oil dealer would find a wall thermometer an effective advertising device, and so on. The novelty user should keep appropriateness in mind when choosing an item.

FIGURE 9.5
A coordinated specialty program for a Midwestern credit union combined calendars, coloring books and crayons, ball-point pens, and key chains. [*Specialty Advertising Association.*]

Another thing a novelty advertiser must check into before selecting a particular kind of novelty is the degree of saturation of similar items in the marketing area. Fads develop in advertising novelties, and for a while every merchant in town may be giving away ball-point pens. At that point it would be advantageous to switch to felt- or nylon-tipped pens if the price is not prohibitive. If full impact from the use of novelties is to be realized, the advertiser must select an item that is, in fact, novel.

301
DIRECT
ADVERTISING
AND POINT-
OF-PURCHASE
ADVERTISING

Matchbooks Although matchbooks are not technically a novelty item, they are another useful advertising specialty. Manufacturers who wish to give wide, repeated exposure to their messages can have them printed on matchbooks; the books are then usually distributed through retail outlets of all varieties. The person who gives them away may pay a small part of the cost of the matchbooks, but ordinarily the advertiser absorbs the entire cost. Many retailers distribute matchbooks containing their own advertising. Hotels sometimes use them to enhance their images, while some hotel chains go a step further and pass out matchbooks advertising hotels in the chain other than the one at which the recipient is staying.

Calendars, novelties, matchbooks, and other advertising specialties are sold by sales representatives just as other advertising media are. These salespeople work to develop creative approaches which incorporate the use of one or more of their specialty items; then they call upon prospective advertisers to try to sell their programs.

Executive Gifts When the potential business to be garnered from one buyer is appreciable, the "remembrance" factor tends to become more crucial for the manufacturer or business firm. Reliance on an inexpensive trinket is replaced by the power of a more costly gift. The principle involved is the same: the item is given in anticipation of future business, although specialty advertising people are quick to point out that it is also a means of expressing friendship during a holiday season or saying "thank you." The difference is a matter of degree. The key ring is supplanted by a genuine leather, personalized key case, or the ball-point pen by a fine desk set. Advertising slogans or advertiser identification may be eliminated completely or held to an absolute minimum on the more prestigious items. The word "novelty" is no longer fitting, and the industry has coined the phrase "executive gift" to describe the more expensive specialty. Jewelry, watches, pen sets, sporting goods, cocktail sets, leather goods, luggage, and the like find their way to key executives. Frequently liquor and food specialties are on the gift list. It has been reported that 70 percent of the companies in the United States give business gifts.

As the potential gain is greater, so is the cost. Executive gifts are expensive; if they were not, their impact would be lessened. Further-

more, it may take a fairly elegant item to find a place in an executive's pocket or office. The seller who uses them takes a calculated risk; one has no assurance that business will result from the gift. There is, however, a more serious risk involved, namely, a moral one. As the value of the gift increases, the line between a simple act of gift giving and commercial bribery becomes fuzzy. No one can object on moral grounds to the giving of a ball-point pen worth 29 cents. Such a gift would not influence a buyer to make an uneconomical purchase of any consequence. Would the receipt of a desk set worth $150 change an attitude? The sense of obligation might be intensified, to say the least.

This matter becomes even more touchy when the gift goes not to the owner of the business but to a paid executive. The executive's duty to his or her employer is to make purchases advantageous to the employer. Nothing should be placed in the way to color buying decisions among competitive offerings. The point is that the seller who uses executive gifts is treading on thin ice. As a matter of fact, some corporations have regulations against the receipt of such gifts, as do most governmental agencies. Moreover, the Revenue Act of 1962 removed any gift valued at more than $25 from its status as a tax-deductible business expense, thereby placing a constraint upon the practice of executive gift giving.

Once a certain indefinable dollar value is reached, an item is no longer classifiable as an advertising specialty; it becomes an executive gift. At this point, it is no longer fair to consider the item as an advertising expenditure, although such gifts are often paid for out of the advertising budget.

POINT-OF-PURCHASE ADVERTISING

The ultimate purpose of most advertising is to persuade the prospect to buy a particular product. Ideally, the result of advertising impressions

FIGURE 9.7
A glance at a supermarket interior readily reveals why advertisers have difficulty placing point-of-purchase materials—it's a highly competitive activity. [Chain Store Age.]

received over a period of time is that the prospect moves from an attitude of complete ignorance about the product to a state of awareness and interest, followed by acceptance, then preference and purchase. Print and broadcast media help to create a favorable attitude while the prospect is at home. The influence of radio, outdoor, and transportation advertising follows when a would-be buyer leaves home. When the prospect arrives in the marketplace, the moment of truth has arrived for the advertiser. Here the prospect decides either to buy the advertiser's brand or not. There is, however, one last chance to influence that decision: point-of-purchase (POP) advertising.

In the case of advertisers who sell *impulse items*, that is, those purchases we make without preplanning, POP represents an opportunity to suggest to people not only that they buy gum, but beyond that, that they buy *Wrigley's* gum.

Principal Forms of Point-of-Purchase Advertising

"Point of purchase" is used as a collective term to describe a variety of advertising devices. Two alternative names sometimes used among retailers are "dealer displays" and "point-of-sale" advertising, but we believe the consumer viewpoint is better expressed by the term we have chosen for use in this book. *Point-of-purchase advertising* is defined as "promotional materials situated in, on, or immediately adjacent to retail distribution points, designated to build traffic for the retailer, register advertising impressions, redirect in-store traffic, and actually sell merchandise."[4] The variety of POP appears infinite, as a trip to the supermarket will reveal. The volume, while officially unmeasurable, is estimated at more than $2.5 billion per year, according to the POP Advertising Institute.[5]

Signs *On-premise signs* are discussed in Chapter 10 along with other forms of outdoor advertising, but they also qualify as point-of-purchase advertising. They furnish the bridge between external advertising presented outside a store and efforts exerted internally. In effect, these stores say, "Here is a place to buy that brand you saw advertised." The Coca-Cola Company, whose signs adorned storefronts across the country for generations, employed this technique to beckon passing motorists or pedestrians into any establishment that sold Cokes.

Window Displays In certain types of retailing, store location is extremely important. A location may be selected by a retailer because it is a convenient spot for consumers; that is, it is near a concentration of potential customers. This would apply to a corner grocery store or a boat shop at a lake resort. A second basis for selecting a location may

[4] William W. Mee, "How Point-of-Purchase Is More Efficient as an Advertising and Sales Medium," *Media/scope*, September 1963, pp. 55–56.
[5] "POP Volume Up in '75," *Advertising Age*, Mar. 15, 1976, p. 4.

305
DIRECT
ADVERTISING
AND POINT-
OF-PURCHASE
ADVERTISING

FIGURE 9.8
On-premise signs work to bridge the gap between national advertising and point-of-purchase advertising or the product itself.

be that a sizable volume of pedestrian traffic passes the spot. If the merchandise sold is the variety that might stop a hurrying passerby when it is properly displayed in a store window, then high pedestrian traffic is obviously an important consideration in site selection. A toy store and a high-fashion outlet are obvious examples.

Window displays slow the pace of a passing consumer long enough to entice him or her into the store to look further—or that is the thinking, at least, of retail merchandisers. Thus, the display should be striking and timely. It is the face that the store presents to the passing public.

Window displays are an important part of the store image in the consumer's mind. Therefore, retail managers should give serious thought to what they have in their windows; displays should meet sales objectives and be imaginative; they should be changed frequently; and they should be topical. Some firms hire professional POP display specialists to install their window displays. Occasionally, national advertisers such as liquor companies will pay these specialists to install the display in a retail outlet—with the owner's approval, of course.

Wall Displays   Once the consumer enters the store, another type of point-of-purchase advertising may influence the buying decision. Posterlike ads, promoting a nationally advertised brand, may be affixed to the walls of the store. Soft-drink manufacturers have used window and wall displays a great deal. Behind the counters of the cafes and snack bars of America, colorful messages urge the purchase of a particular brand of soft drink. Often these signs carry the same theme as the other media. For instance, the wall display may be a miniature version of the manufacturer's outdoor posters. The advertising impact is made just before the consumer says, "I'll have _____ brand." Breweries vie for display space in taverns and retail stores with elaborate, often animated and illuminated signs which embellish such establishments in whatever numbers management will permit. Proof of their attractiveness is found in their ubiquitous appearance on the walls of college dormitories and fraternity houses, as well as private rumpus rooms.

Display Cards   A considerable amount of point-of-purchase advertising is placed on various sizes and shapes of cardboard. These display cards may be as elaborate as life-size cutout models which stand on the selling floor, or may be as simple as reproductions of a magazine advertisement. Display cards may be used as part of a window display, or they may be used inside the store as *counter cards*. They perform the function of silent salespeople, for the message tells consumers why they should buy the product, and often features some special offer currently available. It is common for magazines to provide reprints of magazine ads affixed to display cards for use on store counters. These are often offered free, or at cost, as part of a magazine's merchandising cooperation. Sometimes these cards have recipes or coupons attached.

Merchandise Racks and Cases   An effective point-of-purchase device is the rack or case. Not only are consumers presented with a message about the product, but they see the merchandise itself. A good example of this form of POP is the candy rack designed and placed by Life Savers. This rack presents a collection of candy offerings in a case which fits near the cash register where impulse buying is highest. As shown in Figure 9.9, the rack is designed in a stair-step fashion so that all items can be seen; however, the best spot is reserved for Life Savers.

Merchandise racks for bigger items are placed on the floor instead of on the counter. Greeting-card companies place such cases in retail outlets; cards are displayed attractively, and an ample reserve stock is stored below. Typewriters, leather goods, rug samples, and baby food are just a few of the many product classifications for which manufacturers have designed attractive racks and cases in order to secure good spots on the retailer's floor and to catch the consumer's attention as he or she is shopping. Another development is the display shipping carton which may be cut or opened to become a display rack. Successful marketers like Campbell Soup Company furnish supermarket operators with cartons which can be shelved without removing the cans, a great labor-saving device.

Shelf strips, pennants, plaques, ceiling streamers, mobiles, decals, window banners, and end-aisle displays are among the miscellaneous forms of point-of-purchase advertising in common use.

Occasionally the retailer takes the initiative in point-of-purchase advertising by designing and placing a display on the store premises. Certainly this is true for the department store that has a special display budget and personnel charged with the display function. Small-scale retailers may emphasize display in their operations, but their efforts may be confined to the crude lettering of "specials" on butcher paper on store windows. The responsibility for the creation of point-of-purchase advertising reposes in the hands of the manufacturer of nationally advertised brands because intermediaries expect the manufacturer to create acceptance for the product. In this sense, these manufacturers are the users of POP, but the place of use is the retail outlet. Therefore, the retailer is also a user of the technique.

Point-of-Purchase Advertising Strategy

A manufacturer decides to include dealer displays in his communications for one or both of two major reasons. First of all, the purpose of point-of-purchase advertising is to promote buying at the retail level. The goal is to continue the flow of advertising impressions right down to the time of purchase. The consumer is informed that the brand is

FIGURE 9.9
A counter rack can work wonders at increasing impulse purchases when properly placed in a store. It may contain competitive products as well as those of the advertiser. [*Beech-Nut Life Savers, Inc.*]

FIGURE 9.10
Display racks such
as this one for
L'eggs have
helped revolution-
ize the marketing
of stretch hosiery.
[*L'eggs.*]

stocked at the particular retail outlet. A reminder is furnished which brings back previous advertising impressions. Thus, when a woman college student goes to her favorite specialty shop in search of the "right" swimsuit, several brand names are in her consciousness, including White Stag, Cole of California, and Jantzen. Although style will be the dominant factor in her choice, attractive displays will help her to make a choice and will reassure her that her choice is a wise one by providing new evidence of superiority. Obviously, the manufacturer who has secured the most display cooperation from the retailer has a distinct advantage.

309

DIRECT
ADVERTISING
AND POINT-
OF-PURCHASE
ADVERTISING

The second important reason manufacturers use dealer displays moves us again into the fascinating merchandising concept known as *impulse buying*—unplanned purchasing. Point-of-purchase advertising may be used to remind or persuade consumers to buy products they had not intended to buy when they entered the establishment. For example, we are paying our check at a restaurant and take one of the 3-cent mints which are displayed near the cash register. Or we are walking down the street when the odors from a popcorn stand come our way, and so we buy a bag of popcorn. Spur-of-the-moment purchases are part of everyone's buying pattern.

What is little realized is the extent to which we make unplanned purchases or buy goods on impulse. The movement toward self-service retailing has accentuated impulse buying. Studies of consumer buying habits in supermarkets, for instance, show rather conclusively that half of the purchases made in these establishments are not planned. The customer may enter the store with a "want list" in hand, but it is more than likely a short one. Moving up and down the aisles, the customer's eye rests on certain items or displays, and he or she takes a mental inventory of the cupboard at home and decides whether or not to purchase. In this situation, the importance of POP in the sale of goods bought on impulse cannot be overestimated.

The current trend in marketing and merchandising toward self-service has brought to the fore three principles which are crucial for the manufacturer. One, the package must be attractive to the consumer's eye and must stand out against a galaxy of competing brands. In fact, the most important form of point-of-purchase advertising is the package itself. Given a good package, the next condition needed if the product is to succeed in self-service stores is good shelf position. Where the brand is placed—high, low, or hand level—is extremely important to the total sales rung up by a brand on the store's cash registers. Shoppers are not prone to stretch or bend over to reach a particular brand if acceptable substitutes are in easy reach. Thus, the manufacturer tries to get the retailer to give his brand preferential shelf position.

Given a good package and good shelf position, the consumer's decision to buy hinges largely on a favorable attitude toward the brand. Prior experience in using the product is an important factor, as is the advice of acquaintances, and advertising plays a key role in preselling the product. Frequent messages have created favorable or unfavorable impressions. Often, however, consumer attitudes toward several competing brands are approximately the same. Thus, the brand which makes the best impression—at the point of purchase—makes the sale. It behooves the manufacturer of any product bought on impulse to back the brand at the retail level with effective POP if he wishes to prosper.

Problems in Point-of-Purchase Advertising

The manufacturer who decides to use point-of-purchase advertising is presented with a number of knotty problems. We next explore these problems and attempt to show the retailer's attitude toward them. The close interrelationship of the manufacturer, POP, and dealers is crucial to the successful use of this medium.

Creativity Every type of advertising has creative problems which must be solved. The advertising must be tailor-made to do the job it is expected to do. Thus, the objectives of advertising and the means designed to achieve those objectives cannot be separated. Manufacturers expect their point-of-purchase advertising to establish their brand at the point of sale and to stimulate impulse buying. The principal technique involved in designing POP materials for establishing the brand is to adapt ideas and themes from the brand's current campaign in other media—magazines, newspapers, television—and reproduce them on signs, counter cards, and the like. Here the design problem is not too great, although the display must be designed with the importance of the product to the retailer in mind. Overly large or inappropriate materials simply will not be used.

When the primary purpose of the display is to stimulate impulse buying, the creative problem is different. If possible, the actual product should be incorporated into the display in such a way that it will be easy for the consumer to act—to choose a magazine or a roll of film, to select a greeting card, and so on. Although the design of POP is not within the normal range of advertising agency responsibilities, some agencies do create such advertising. Occasionally the advertising department of the manufacturing firm does the job. However, this task is most frequently handled by a specialized firm, expert in the design and production of cardboard, plastic or metal signs, decals, showcases, and the like. It is important, therefore, that close coordination exist between the manufacturer's advertising department, the advertising agency, and the point-of-purchase specialist.

Placement Even if the dealer display is superb in its design and well coordinated with the overall advertising program of the advertiser, the materials will do no good unless they are properly used in retail

311
DIRECT
ADVERTISING
AND POINT-
OF-PURCHASE
ADVERTISING

FIGURE 9.11
This "Carousel of
Sound" display by
Motorola helped
the company and
its retailers dem-
onstrate and sell
the Motorola 4
Channel Sound for
Cars.

outlets. In many ways the most vexing question in the management
of POP is "How can we persuade dealers that they should use our
displays in their stores?" There is only so much window, wall, floor, and
counter space in the retailer's store. This space is valuable, and
ordinarily the store owner wants to use it for stocking and displaying
actual pieces of merchandise. Retailers are under constant pressure,
however, to use the point-of-purchase advertising of countless manufacturers. Thus, the placement problem is troublesome for the merchant as well as for the manufacturer. Essentially, the retailer must be
convinced that it is advantageous to use the display materials, that is,
that it will increase product turnover and profits.

But the possibility of fast turnover does not ensure immediate
acceptance of a company's display materials. More than likely, competing products carry equally good margins or can be expected to sell
equally well if they are given proper promotion in the retail outlet. At
this point two forces come into play. One is the influence of trade
advertising. In various trade journals, the retailer is exposed to

arguments for the use of the manufacturer's POP. The second force is persuasion by the members of the manufacturer's field selling force, and for decades, a vital part of this persuasion was friendship with retailers. With the advent of large-scale retailing, however, the importance of friendship or good rapport as a motivating factor has been lessened. A technique of securing dealer cooperation has supplanted friendship to a large degree, namely, the system of paying the retailer a "display allowance" for permitting the placement of dealer displays in a store.

As an example, the manager of a grocery store is approached by a representative of a leading spice company. The spice company has designed a new display rack for use in grocery stores of this particular type and size. The sales rep asks for permission to place the rack, and the merchant replies, "What's in it for me?" After discussing the increased sale of spices that will result from proper display, the company representative finally states that the spice company will pay the merchant $10 a month or give a 5 percent discount on each case purchased if the manager permits placement of the rack in the store. The rack, of course, prominently displays the brand name of the manufacturer and provides a convenient display for the consumer.

It should be noted that certain legal problems arise when promotional allowances are used. Under the Robinson-Patman Act, discussed in Chapter 20, these allowances must be equally available, on a proportional basis, to all competitors stocking the product. Thus, the manufacturer who uses this method to place POP materials must be certain that all competing intermediaries have the opportunity to accept such an offer.

Waste All advertising has a problem of waste, since no medium is completely successful in reaching only immediate prospects. In the case of POP there is great opportunity for inefficient use. First, there is the problem of unused display material. Obviously, all manufacturers cannot place upon their sales force the burden of seeing that their point-of-purchase advertising is installed in every possible outlet. There is a real distribution problem, and it is often solved by mailing the display piece to the retailer or by asking the wholesaler to distribute it to customers. Much of this display material never leaves the back room, and considerable amounts of money ranging from 10 cents to $20 per item are wasted.

A second source of waste is misuse or short-term use of the materials. Many retailers, left to their own resources, use POP materials ineffectively. They put a display in an out-of-the-way corner of the store or in a window which commands little traffic. Such use is little better than nonuse.

Some point-of-purchase advertising pieces, such as cardboard signs, are designed to be used for only a few weeks, whereas other pieces, such as metal or plastic signs, are made to be useful for many years. Regardless of which category we consider, a source of great waste in the medium is the removal of a display before its normal life has expired. Often a retailer will remove a display piece if it appears that it does not increase the sale of the product. The merchant may find another manufacturer who will bid a higher price for the space. Only a binding contract for a specified time period, accompanied by close policing on the premises, will prevent some retailers from removing a display. Occasionally small merchants, in a desire to be agreeable, will allow every sales representative who comes along to place displays in a store. Thus, a display erected one day may come down the next if another salesperson commandeers the space.

A third source of waste in point-of-purchase advertising is closely related to misuse. It involves the improper selection of retail outlets. Stores generating the lowest sales volume are often the most willing to use POP materials, especially if a "deal" or cash allowance for a display is involved. When a display is placed in a store where potential sales do not equal the cost involved, it is obviously a poor investment for both the manufacturer and the retailer. When the placement of POP materials is in the hands of trusted sales representatives or independent display specialists, this waste is minimized.

Faced with the waste factor in the use of POP materials, advertisers may consider charging retailers for the displays. Historically, this approach has not proved very successful. Retailers who are hard to convince that they should place display pieces in their stores will be impossible to deal with when they are asked to pay for them.

SUMMARY

Direct advertising and point-of-purchase advertising are vital elements in the advertising strategies of many manufacturers and retailers despite the fact that these media may not receive the lion's share of most advertisers' budget allocations. To some advertisers, however, these media may represent the primary means by which communication with potential customers is accomplished.

Direct advertising is defined as any printed material delivered directly to potential customers without the use of an intervening medium such as radio, newspapers, or magazines provide. Direct advertising enjoys broad usage because of two outstanding characteristics. Properly used, it is highly selective and eliminates the waste normally connected with the more broadly based media such as television and newspapers. Secondly, direct advertising is outstanding in its flexibility—in format, color, and cost. Thus the selection of a direct advertising piece may vary from a simple postcard or letter to a huge catalog, calendar, or specialty item.

The most prominent form of direct advertising is direct mail. Direct mail is

313

DIRECT
ADVERTISING
AND POINT-
OF-PURCHASE
ADVERTISING

an extremely efficient way of reaching prospects without waste circulation, but there often is a problem in securing and maintaining an appropriate mailing list. The cost of using direct mail is high in the relative sense, that is, in terms of the cost per thousand persons or homes reached.

Advertising specialties, another form of direct advertising, are products of small unit value upon which are placed the name and address, or the slogan, of the advertiser. The items are given away, free of charge, to present or prospective customers in anticipation of future business. The four main types of specialties are calendars, novelties, matchbooks, and executive gifts. Advertising specialties are found in the media mixes of most advertisers and serve as "remembrance advertising" for their sponsors.

Point-of-purchase advertising is promotional materials located in or around retail establishments. The power of POP lies in its ability to persuade and remind potential customers of a particular product or service at the point of sale. POP is the last opportunity an advertiser has to speak to prospects before a purchase is made. Another important function of point-of-purchase advertising is to stimulate impulse sales by reminding shoppers of latent wants and needs. These unplanned purchases are commonplace among such items as light bulbs, razor blades, stockings, and magazines.

Although POP advertising is sometimes used as the only medium in an advertising campaign, it is used primarily to back up national campaigns in publication or broadcast media.

QUESTIONS FOR DISCUSSION

1 Most direct advertising is of the direct-mail variety, but a significant share is not. Using the text's definition of direct advertising, how many examples can you think of?

2 Direct mail is described as a medium with almost universal appeal to advertisers. Review its prime attributes and explain how it might be useful to (a) a small specialty shop; (b) a national health insurance company.

3 Differentiate among the following: direct advertising, direct-mail advertising, and mail-order advertising.

4 Bring to class two direct-mail advertisements and discuss (a) why you think the advertiser included you in the mailing, (b) how you got on the mailing list, (c) whether you normally open direct-mail advertising.

5 Why do many package-goods advertisers use point-of-purchase advertising?

6 Name a number of impulse items whose sale might be affected by the use of point-of-purchase advertising.

7 Name an advertising specialty item you have encountered that you feel was an especially good tie-in with the product being sold.

8 What is the strategy behind the sending of executive gifts? Discuss the ethical problems involved.

9 What are the basic problems encountered in the use of point-of-purchase advertising?

10 Both direct-mail and specialty advertising campaigns register high cost-per-thousand ratings when compared with other mass media. Why do advertisers spend so many dollars in these media when they could reach more people for less money through broadcast or print media?

315
DIRECT
ADVERTISING
AND POINT-
OF-PURCHASE
ADVERTISING

FOR FURTHER REFERENCE

Association of National Advertisers: *Advertising at the Point of Purchase*, McGraw-Hill Book Company, New York, 1957.

Barban, Arnold M., Stephen M. Cristol, and Frank J. Kopec: *Essentials of Media Planning*, Crain Books, Chicago, 1976.

Cook, Harvey, R.: *Selecting Advertising Media*, Small Business Administration, Washington, 1969.

Direct Mail Manual, Direct Mail/Marketing Association, New York, 1975.

Francisco, L. Mercer: *The More You Show, the More You Sell*, Prentice Hall, Inc., Englewood Cliffs, N.J., 1961.

Herpel, George L., and Richard A. Collins: *Specialty Advertising in Marketing*, Dow-Jones–Richard D. Irwin, Inc., Homewood, Ill., 1972.

Hodgson, Richard S.: *The Dartnell Direct Mail and Mail Order Handbook*, 2d ed., The Dartnell Corporation, Chicago, 1974.

Luick, John G., and William L. Zeigler: *Sales Promotion and Modern Merchandising*, McGraw-Hill Book Company, New York, 1968.

Maguire, John T., and John D. Yeck: *Planning and Creating Better Direct Mail*, McGraw-Hill Book Company, New York, 1961.

Mayer, Edward N., Jr.: *How to Make More Money with Your Direct Mail*, Printers' Ink Books, New London, Conn., 1956.

Michman, Ronald D., and Donald W. Jugenheimer: *Strategic Advertising Decisions: Selected Readings*, Grid, Inc. Columbus, Ohio, 1976.

Sissors, Jack Z., and E. Reynold Petray: *Advertising Media Planning*, Crain Books, Chicago, 1976.

Stone, Bob: *Successful Direct Marketing Methods*, McGraw-Hill Book Company, New York, 1976.

CHAPTER 10
OUT-OF-HOME AND OTHER MEDIA

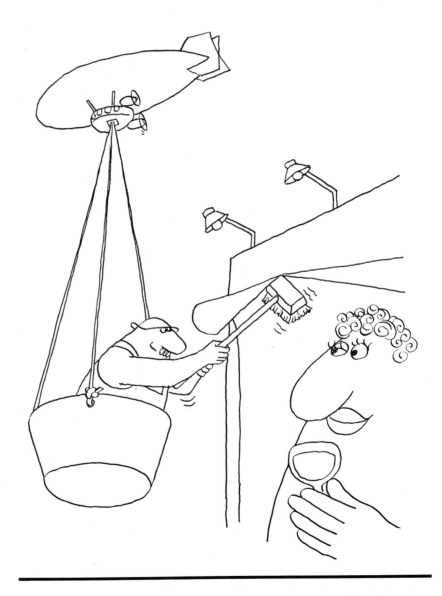

In preceding chapters, we have presented, in some depth, the story behind a number of different media—why they seem appropriate for some advertisers at particular times and how one goes about employing them. In concluding this survey of media in the present chapter, you will learn something of the workings of a group which has become known as *out-of-home media*, along with a few miscellaneous advertising vehicles which, while less intrusive in our daily lives than major publications or broadcast advertising, are nonetheless important to advertisers who find them efficient methods of reaching their target audiences.

Early in this book, it was noted that signs outside a merchant's building and along the routes followed by traders of the ancient world were the earliest means of mass communications. Today, out-of-home media, sometimes referred to as traffic or position media, represent modern refinements of this ancient method of delivering messages to large groups of people. The fundamental difference between out-of-home media and other media discussed earlier is that, while other media seek out prospects in their homes or offices, out-of-home media depend upon people, or traffic, passing the location of the medium. The unique advantage inherent in this approach is that it provides an advertiser with an opportunity to choose the location as well as the timing of the message. In effect, it enables one to reach consumers at a critical moment in the pattern of buying behavior—when they are en route to a store or any other point where purchase decisions will be made.

Modern out-of-home media include outdoor advertising in several forms, nonstandardized signs, and transit advertising placed on public and private transit vehicles and in rail, bus, and air terminals. In the analysis of how more than 30 billion advertising dollars are spent each year, there is no specific category for out-of-home media. However, we do know that the organized outdoor industry accounts for approximately $400 million each year, while nonstandard signs and transportation advertising are lumped together in the big "miscellaneous expenditure" category.

OUTDOOR ADVERTISING

Among out-of-home media, the dominant subtype is *outdoor advertising*. This term presents a neat problem in definition. At first blush, one might think that any and all advertising which is presented out of doors would fall into this classification, including billboards; store signs; ads on the outside of trucks, buses, and taxis; skywriting; etc. However, such is not the case, for outdoor advertising, as the term has come to be used by advertising people, has a special meaning.

In common parlance, outdoor advertising is often called billboard advertising. We all know what billboards are. They dot commercially zoned city streets and the landscape along the highways, advising us of the products of manufacturers and the services of many local businesses. The first use of this advertising method probably was in the promotion of theatrical performances. The "bill" was placed where the passersby could see it on a board, fence, or wall; thus the word "billboard" came into use. With the coming of the automobile and the highway system, a natural evolutionary process brought the outdoor poster to the roadside.

But not all the posters encountered on the streets and highways of America are included in the technical definition of outdoor advertising. Only those signs which meet certain standards established by the Outdoor Advertising Association of America (OAAA) are so classified. The standards imposed by this trade association deal with the size, design, and method of construction of those billboards which are called either *posters* or *painted bulletins*. Roadside and on-premise devices which are not standardized are in turn called *signs* by the industry.

Basic Types of Outdoor Advertising

The workhorse of the standardized outdoor industry is the poster. More than three-fourths of the national outdoor sales volume is realized by

FIGURE 10.1
Barn signs are favorites with nostalgia buffs but are dying rapidly in the face of pressure from environmentalists.

this form. Traditionally, the most popular size has been the *24-sheet poster*. The standardized structure is built in such a fashion that the advertising message to be placed upon the board (posted) fits into a copy area 104 inches high and 234 inches long. The message is framed by a border which remains part of the structure. Incidentally, the term "24-sheet poster" dates from the time when it required 24 individual sheets of paper to fill the board. With modern printing presses, more of the message can be printed on one sheet of paper; thus, only 10 sheets have to be pasted on the typical 24-sheet poster today.

The outdoor industry is busy developing new structures as part of its joint standardization program. The goal is to present outdoor advertising which is attractive to the public, as well as efficient and durable. The old wooden board has almost disappeared. The frame today is more likely to be made of plastic or metal.

Another aspect of the industry's program aimed at meeting new needs has been the development and rapid acceptance of the 30-sheet poster. In this case, the copy area has been increased 25 percent over the 24-sheet poster. The copy area is 115 inches high and 259 inches long. Faster flow of traffic and increased competition for the motorist's

Poster Panel

FIGURE 10.2
The two basic types of standardized outdoor advertising are posters and painted bulletins. These illustrations give some perspective to their relative sizes. [*Institute of Outdoor Advertising.*]

Painted Bulletin

attention have combined to provide a need for this poster with its greater impact. It is replacing the 24-sheet poster as the standard in the industry. Meanwhile, bleed posters which utilize all the space within the poster frame and measure 125 by 272 inches are gaining popularity.

Poster panels may be illuminated or regular (nonilluminated). Where night traffic is relatively high, it is often desirable to expose the outdoor message for several additional hours each day. This is done by providing light on the poster until around midnight. The need is obviously greatest in metropolitan areas, and the ratio of regular and illuminated posters in a community depends upon the nocturnal habits of its residents and visitors.

Two minor variations of the poster form are the 6-sheet and 3-sheet posters. The former is called a junior panel and is in reality a miniature 24-sheet poster used in congested areas where space is at a premium. The 3-sheet poster is designed to reach pedestrian traffic on downtown streets; it is frequently used for theater advertising.

FIGURE 10.3
Note the difference in the space afforded the 24-sheet poster (top) versus the 30-sheet (bottom). The 30-sheet is rapidly becoming the standard. [*Foster and Kleiser.*]

Painted displays constitute the second major form of outdoor advertising. Instead of being printed on sheets of paper, the message content is painted. If the advertisement is placed on a sign similar to but larger and more streamlined than the structure used for posters, it is called a *painted bulletin*. This is the most common variety of painted display and the only one that falls within the outdoor advertising industry definition of an approved painted display unit. Painted bulletins are rectangular in shape—usually measuring 14 by 48 feet. They are commonly illuminated and, like posters, may be embellished with extensions that protrude from the top, bottom, or sides. It is also possible, but not common these days, to arrange for some form of animation on a painted bulletin such as a wagging tail on a dog. When a painted bulletin bears a border, it is referred to as a *picture-frame bulletin*. But when it appears as a bleed design with no frame at all, it is termed a *royal facing*.

Buying Outdoor Posters

In the print media, the unit of purchase is an area of space—a page, a column inch, or an agate line. In broadcasting, advertising is purchased by the minute or fraction thereof. Outdoor advertising is purchased in accordance with a system that incorporates both space and time. The outdoor advertising industry has expedited the use of the medium by convincing all outdoor plant operators that they should concentrate on a single set of specifications in selling their posters. Thus, all plants feature the same 24- or 30-sheet panels described earlier. Furthermore, the standard time period for renting space on boards is the 30-day unit.

Intensity is one more standard employed in the buying and selling of outdoor posters. In most markets, according to the Institute of Outdoor Advertising (IOA), poster panels are now sold by the month in packages of *gross rating points*. A 100-GRP package in the outdoor business provides enough panels to deliver *in one day* a number of consumer exposure opportunities equal in size to all (100 percent) of the population of the market in which the panels appear. A 50-GRP package will deliver just half as many exposure opportunities, and a 25-GRP buy is exposed daily to an audience equal to one-quarter of the population.[1]

Most outdoor plants adopted the GRP selling approach in 1973. Some, however, have clung to the more traditional "100-showing" concept. They sell poster panels to advertisers in packages called *showings*—a 100 showing includes enough panels to assure exposure of the advertiser's message to 100 percent of the mobile population of a city in *a 30-day period*. A 50 showing would ultimately expose almost

[1] *The First Medium*, Institute of Outdoor Advertising, New York, 1974.

Hardly anybody knew her name, until she appeared in Outdoor.

Shirley Cothran

Miss America 1975

Photo by Hess Studio, Atlantic City, Miss America Photographers

We've long believed that Outdoor can outperform other media in getting across a message to the public. But we needed a way of proving it.

So last year we decided to see if our medium, by itself, could increase public awareness of the name of Miss America 1975.

We approached the Outdoor companies with our plan, asking them to donate space not already sold or earmarked for public service announcements.

They gave us 10,000 panels — or about $1.5 million worth of Outdoor at the going rate.

Our poster (above) was to go on display for two months beginning January 1, 1975. But before it did, the Outdoor companies sponsored a series of studies to determine public awareness of Miss America's name prior to posting.

Random-sample surveys were conducted during November and December 1974 in 44 metropolitan markets by 25 colleges and universities and 12 independent research organizations (names furnished on request). Over 15,000 adults were asked: "What is the name of Miss America 1975?"

Only 1.6% of the respondents gave the correct answer. Hardly anyone knew her name, despite her having been crowned on the sixth-ranked TV special of the year, her appearances on five other major network TV shows, her inter-

How we improved awareness of Miss America's name.

16.3%

1.6%

BEFORE OUTDOOR   AFTER OUTDOOR

views on scores of local radio and TV programs, and articles about her in national magazines and hundreds of newspapers.

Then the posters went up — an average #75 showing in the markets tested. And in February and March 1975, a second wave of over 15,000 interviews was conducted by the same research teams. *This time, 16.3% of the respondents knew who Miss America was.*

That's a 10-fold increase in awareness. Projected nationally it would mean that Outdoor had communicated a new and difficult name to more than 20 million adults.

Through a two-month posting, Outdoor made Shirley Cothran the best-known reigning Miss America in history.

Why were we able to do such an outstanding communications job? Because no other medium can match Outdoor's performance in the area of reach plus frequency.

In a single month, according to Simmons, a #100 Outdoor showing will reach 89.2% of all adults in a typical market an average of *31 times each.* At the lowest CPM around.

Outdoor's edge in building awareness is just one reason it's America's fastest-growing medium. Like to know how this edge can work for your product or service? Call us at (212) 755-4157 or write to Mel Grayson at IOA, 625 Madison Avenue, New York, N.Y. 10022.

Outdoor... the Outdoer

Institute of Outdoor Advertising

as many people but at a slower rate and with much less frequency during the month the display is posted. As with any medium, the mere fact of "exposure" does not necessarily mean that the person involved saw or read the message. In print media it simply implies "open eye to visible advertisement."

It is important to note that the size of the market determines the cost and number of boards involved in achieving a level of 100 gross rating points, or a 100 showing. In Hornbeak, Tennessee (population 315), it may be possible to achieve complete coverage for $85 with just one poster panel. But it would be called a 100-GRP package. So would the purchase of 498 panels in Los Angeles, California, where the advertiser would reach millions of people at a cost of $85,506 per month.[2]

Discounts are offered buyers of outdoor posters in much the same way they are offered by other media. They are generally given for purchases extending over a period of months, especially in cold climates when the somewhat less desirable winter months are included. The message (known as *paper*) on a panel may be changed every month at no extra charge if the buyer wishes and provides the new paper. It is the responsibility of the plant operators to see that the paper is always in presentable form. If the paper tears, or if the copy is defaced by vandals, new paper is installed free by the plant owner.

Buying Painted Bulletins

The arrangements for advertising on painted bulletins are entirely different from posters. Inasmuch as paint is much more durable than poster paper and much more costly to apply, the usual length of time for an installation is one year. Because there are so few painted bulletins in a community and they are purchased so sparingly by advertisers, each position is selected individually. There is no such thing as a 100-GRP buy in the world of painted bulletins. Of course, advertisers have the option of changing their copy more than once a year, but at their own expense. Refurbishment of an existing advertisement, on the other hand, is the responsibility of the plant. Although it is the custom to hand-paint bulletins, new processes now make it possible to print the larger designs on paper without sacrificing the gloss or reflective quality of paint. In large national campaigns, this may afford advertisers an opportunity to save money and, if generally adopted, will yield greater flexibility in making copy changes at more frequent intervals.

It is possible for an advertiser with limited means to buy one painted bulletin and then have it moved from one location in a city to other locations for extended time periods. This gives viewers the impression the advertiser has purchased a number of different locations. It also extends the reach of the message.

[2] *1976 Metro Market Rate Card*, Foster and Kleiser (Metromedia, Inc.).

FIGURE 10.4
This test (*opposite page*) was conceived and executed in order to prove that outdoor advertising can get a message across to the public. [*Institute of Outdoor Advertising*.]

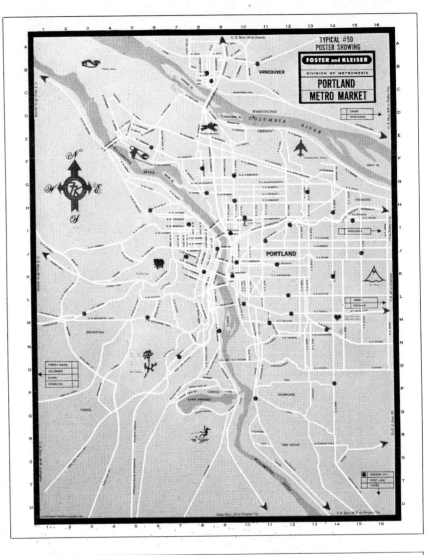

FIGURE 10.7
These pictures record the complete cycle of one multivision sign. [*Oscar Mayer, Inc., and Foster and Kleiser.*]

A more common, but expensive, alternative, is to participate in what outdoor salespeople call a "rotary plan." Under this arrangement, a buyer may purchase three painted bulletins in a central city area, each featuring a different message. Then every month or two, bulletin number one is moved to site two, bulletin two to site three, and so on. The movement involved in these foregoing examples is possible because the painted advertisements are placed on metal panels that can be installed or removed from a bulletin very easily.

Despite the high cost of painted bulletins—often costing thousands of dollars per month—they have proved popular with large local advertisers, and the outdoor industry boasts dozens of national advertisers who believe in the value of the medium.

Industry Organization

The outdoor advertising industry is primarily a local business operation. It consists of more than 700 individual firms which own poster and painted-display locations in some 15,000 American communities. In a few market areas there are competing firms operating, but generally there is a monopoly situation. There are also chain organizations operating outdoor businesses in several different marketing regions. In the years since 1960 the industry experienced several mergers and consolidations of outdoor plants, particularly in major markets. Today, for example, Foster and Kleiser, originally a Pacific Coast firm, is now a division of Metromedia and operates outdoor plants in Illinois, Ohio, Texas, Michigan, and New York, as well as California and the Pacific Northwest.

The local outdoor operator's business, as stated earlier, is called a *plant*. The most obvious part of the plant consists of the structures upon which the messages are placed, that is, the poster panels and painted displays. The owner of the plant erects these structures on land which the company owns or leases; employees see that the messages are posted and changed. Office work and painting work are done in the shop of the firm, and poster paper is stored there. The sales force works out of this headquarters, as do the crews which keep the boards in good repair and the grounds surrounding them landscaped and neat.

Whereas national advertising provides the bulk of outdoor business, probably one-fourth of the business of a typical outdoor plant is derived from local advertisers—department and specialty stores, hotels, cafes, financial institutions, and the like. As in the case of any medium serving local advertisers, the outdoor firm may have to perform various duties in the creative realm for its local clients. For example, outdoor firms employ art directors to design both posters and painted displays. These duties are usually performed by advertising agencies for national advertisers.

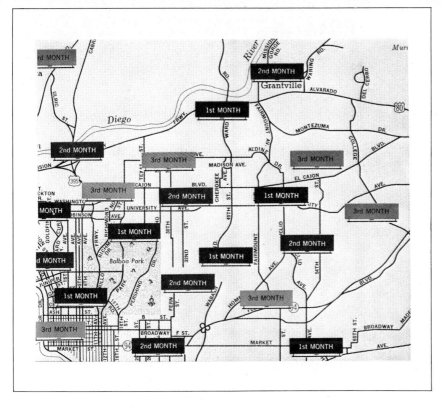

FIGURE 10.8
This map segment illustrates how rotating bulletins circulate in the San Diego market. Bulletins are moved at 30- or 60-day intervals. [*Foster and Kleiser.*]

One point should be stressed. In addition to paying the plant operator for placing the messages, the advertiser pays for paper, artwork, and printing. When boards are filled throughout the country, the production cost is as low as $13 on a per-unit basis, as costs are spread over many units. However, the small firm, which uses a limited number of boards, finds the cost per unit as high as $125 in the case of posters. The monthly charge for painted displays includes the cost of painting the bulletin.

In the quest for a practical way to use outdoor advertising, the local advertiser often employs the cooperative advertising technique. Under this approach, the national manufacturer furnishes the paper for the poster and the name of the local retailer is bannered at the bottom of the message. The two then share the costs of renting the boards on some agreed-upon basis, such as 50-50.

Outdoor Advertising Locations

One of the most intricate phases of outdoor plant operations is in the area of real estate. Not only must the potential advertiser be convinced

ROTATING PAINTED/PRINT BULLETIN RATES

SPACE RATES

MARKET	UNIT COST PER MONTH *PAINTED	UNIT COST PER MONTH **PRINT
SOUTHERN CALIFORNIA		
Los Angeles	$1250	$1188
Los Angeles Airport	$1450	$1378
Los Angeles Freeway	$1450	$1378
San Diego	$1000	$ 950
NORTHERN CALIFORNIA		
San Francisco Bay Area	$1200	$1140
Sacramento	$ 950	$ 903
CHICAGO		
Chicago	$1250	$1188
Expressway (18' x 61')	$2000	NA
NEW YORK		
New York	$1800	$1710
PACIFIC NORTHWEST		
Seattle—Tacoma	$ 850	$ 808
Seattle—Tacoma Airport	$1050	$ 998
Portland—Salem	$ 850	$ 808
OHIO		
Cleveland	$1025	$ 974
Cleveland Airport	$1275	$1211
Cincinnati	$ 850	$ 808
HOUSTON		
Houston	$ 750	$ 750
DALLAS		
Dallas — Ft. Worth	$ 750	$ 750
Dallas — Ft. Worth Airport	$ 950	$ 950

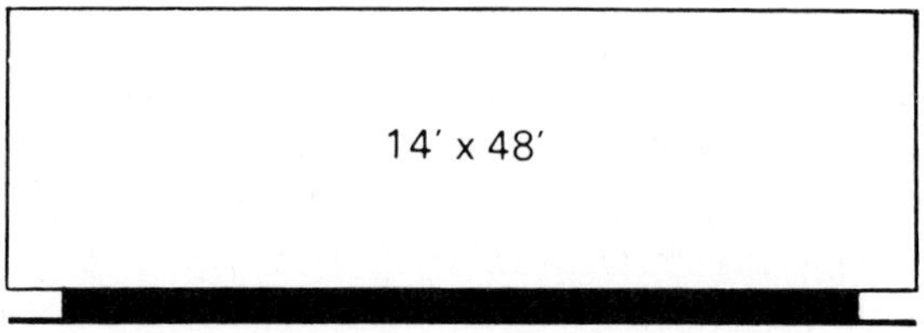

14' x 48'

*Base rate, 12-month contract.
**Print bulletin service available on minimum 12-month contracts.
All space prices quoted are subject to change without prior notification.

FIGURE 10.9
Rotating bulletin advertisements may be painted or preprinted on paper. This rate card indicates the relative cost in various United States markets. [*Foster and Kleiser.*]

of the value of the outdoor medium to his marketing goals, but he must be shown that a specific plant can deliver his message effectively. This can be done only if boards are located in places where traffic passes and where they can be seen. The plant owner must study his area constantly in order to be alert to shifts in population, changing traffic patterns, and new road and street construction. Owners must lease or buy sites for structures that can deliver the exposures desired by their advertiser clients.

What constitutes a good location for a poster or painted display? The formula has many variables. The Traffic Audit Bureau (TAB) has been studying this problem since 1934 and has developed useful techniques for measuring the total circulation of a plant and what is called the *space position value* of individual locations. The procedure is briefly as follows: a number of boards constituting a showing is chosen, and total traffic counts are made for each structure in the showing. The counts are made on a sampling basis, and the figures are expanded to daily estimates. These raw figures are reduced by making allowances for the average portion of passing traffic unlikely to see the individual posters. The biggest factor here is the prevalence of angled panels which can be seen only by traffic flowing in one direction.

The circulation figures, however, are quite general and do not reflect the worth of individual locations in a precise manner. The value of a particular location as a site for an outdoor advertising panel also depends on the overall visibility of the site. Several factors affect this visibility, or space position value:

1 *The length of approach.* The longer the panel is visible, the more effective the location, other things being equal.

2 *The speed of travel.* The slower the traffic passing the spot, the greater the opportunity to see and read the message.

3 *The angle of the panel.* The closer to head-on the approach is to oncoming traffic, the better the site. The worst location is one parallel to traffic.

4 *The proximity to other panels.* Preferably a panel should be alone. If joined with others, the one closest to the road has the best chance of being seen. Too many panels, too close together, lead to viewer confusion.

TAB gives numerical weights to each of these factors and arrives at an individual rating for each particular location. Obviously, a plant operator uses similar criteria in the search for new locations. Whereas a newspaper or magazine sells total circulation as a reason for advertising in the publication, and a radio or television station sells audience, outdoor operators must sell circulation—effective circulation—of a different kind, namely, the total amount of traffic passing their posters in such a way that the messages can be seen by the potential audience. Advertisers often "ride a showing," either before signing a contract to use a plant's services or afterward to see what they are getting for their money.

Outdoor circulation and newspaper and magazine circulation are not the same. In the outdoor medium the exposure of the message is duplicated many times. The poster usually remains unchanged for 30 days, and many a passerby may see the message nearly every day. A publication advertisement, on the other hand, is seen only when the reader looks at the newspaper or magazine which contains the ad.

In preparing circulation reports, TAB performs a function for outdoor which is similar to the function the Audit Bureau of Circulations performs for magazines and newspapers. TAB is also active in gathering evidence of the value of outdoor advertising as far as total coverage, impact, effectiveness, and the like are concerned.

Industry Associations

Before passing on to the uses of outdoor advertising, the reader should become acquainted with three other organizations working within the framework of the industry. The first is the trade association of the standardized outdoor medium, the Outdoor Advertising Association of America. Like any trade association, it is interested in promoting the use of its services. It is the driving force behind the standardization of the structures erected by the industry. In addition, OAAA represents the outdoor industry in legislative halls and handles the public relations program for the industry.

Another organization, the National Outdoor Advertising Bureau (NOAB), is cooperatively owned and used by some 200 advertising agencies. It handles much of the work involved in the creating, placing, buying, billing, supervising, and checking of outdoor advertising, and thus frees the staffs of the respective agencies for planning activities. NOAB also helps evaluate the performance of individual plants in carrying out the advertising programs of the clients of the various agencies. The Institute of Outdoor Advertising rounds out the trio. Formed in 1965, IOA is concerned with three activities in the field of outdoor advertising—research, creativity, and information dissemination.

The Uses of Outdoor Advertising

Early users of outdoor advertising were manufacturers of automotive, petroleum, tobacco, food, and beverage products. These product categories are still featured on outdoor posters, but many more items have been added to the list. An analysis of the top 100 advertisers in the United States revealed that about half of the group used outdoor advertising in their media mixes. We are interested in the question, "Under what circumstances does a national advertiser use outdoor?"

National Advertisers More than likely a national advertiser uses outdoor as part of an overall campaign which includes other advertising media. Often a slogan is developed to tie the campaign together and to provide prospects with something easy to remember. A short slogan so developed can be integrated into a program of outdoor showings which will permit repetition of the slogan frequently and economically.

It is common for outdoor advertisers to feature products which are associated with highway use. Their message is delivered while the prospect is in the process of making buying decisions. Oil companies, tire manufacturers, battery makers, and the like are prime examples. Hotels, motels, and restaurants use outdoor boards on traffic routes leading into the city, and airlines buy poster showings and painted bulletins on highway approaches to airports.

Another group of advertisers who find outdoor useful are the makers of extremely well-known, impulse-purchase products. There is no pressing need to explain the product to potential users; everyone knows about it already. The purpose in advertising for such companies is aptly expressed in the phrase "keeping the company name before the public." Outdoor provides an excellent medium for this reminder advertising. Coca-Cola and Wrigley's chewing gum illustrate the point.

In recent years outdoor has come to fill a new need. With the growth of self-service merchandising, particularly in the food field, manufacturers have been deprived of the help of the salesperson's recommendations. Advertising has been called upon to fill the gap by preselling the customer—if the prospect is exposed to the advertising just prior to making the actual purchase, the advertiser has a better chance of being remembered. Thus, many food manufacturers now try to place outdoor messages near big supermarkets in an attempt to make an impression on potential customers. Morton's Salt and Best Foods are examples.

These uses of outdoor advertising certainly do not exhaust the possibilities of the medium. Outdoor can be a relatively low-cost form of advertising, and small-budget advertisers may select the medium as their vehicle for reaching prospects. It is argued that small-budget advertisers can appear big by concentrating their budgets in outdoor.

Local Advertisers Local advertisers usually expect a more immediate response to their advertising than national advertisers do. Their primary goal is to reach people as they move about a community and persuade them to trade at the advertiser's place of business. If the tourist is an important factor in the business, posters or painted bulletins are placed at the approaches to the city. Restaurants, hotels, motels, shopping centers, garages, and service stations are good examples. If the town is a shopping center for farmers and small-town residents, the operators of department stores, specialty shops, theaters, and bowling alleys use outdoor messages to urge patronage. Furthermore, especially in the large metropolitan region, the residents of one area are like tourists or out-of-town visitors when they are driving around the city; therefore outdoor may influence them. It should be noted that local advertisers are more inclined to use nonstandardized signs than national advertisers. This point is discussed below in the section on signs.

Regulation of Out-of-Home Advertising

Few media, save television, have been exposed to the critical pressure that out-of-home advertising has endured in the last two decades. The primary area of critical attack has been on aesthetic and environmental grounds although some voices have been raised in objection to outdoor for traffic safety reasons. In general, the furor caused by these criticisms has been a setback to the industry and has resulted in the removal of thousands of posters and signs from America's roads and highways.

The most telling damage to the industry has been wrought by the Federal Aid Highway Act of 1958 and the Highway Beautification Act of 1965. These congressional acts made it advantageous, financially, for states to limit billboards along freeways and primary road systems by providing federal highway fund bonuses or penalties in connection with construction grants to individual states.

Surprisingly, the organized outdoor advertising industry has been reasonably supportive of these regulations, feeling that they were designed to strike primarily at the jerry-built and irresponsibly placed signs constructed by individuals rather than those built in accordance with the organized industry's ethical guidelines. It appears, at this time, that the users of nonstandard signs are, in fact, the big losers in this campaign to clean up our highways and that the organized industry will, in the long run, be strengthened. Nevertheless, environmental pressures have resulted in the removal of thousands of displays, for which, incidentally, the owners have received compensation from the government.

NONSTANDARDIZED SIGNS

We are all exposed to countless signs every day that fall outside the organized outdoor advertising framework. Not all are unnattractive or decrepit, but many are truly eyesores. Some are erected by sign companies operating outside the organized industry; some are built by amateur or itinerant sign painters who may sell as well as erect their own handiwork. Independent businesses may create signs in their back rooms or install signs supplied by the manufacturers they represent. Regardless of source, these signs fall into two main categories: roadside and on-premise signs.

Roadside Signs

Roadside signs are similar in function to regulation posters and painted bulletins, but they lack some important qualities. Categorically speaking, they lack uniformity or standardization; they are often placed in a careless, hit-or-miss fashion; and they are found in abundance leading to tourist traps such as mangy private "zoos," hot-dog stands, or souvenir shops.

Nonstandard signs are primarily the realm of local advertisers—retailers and service firms such as gas stations, motels, and restaurants—who have regarded them for years as the primary link between their establishments and passing motorists. In light of this real need by roadside entrepreneurs, highway officials have constructed official highway exit signs revealing the location of such tourist necessities as gas, food, and lodging. In some areas they have gone one step further and allowed entrepreneurs to place business logos on highway department signs—for a fee, of course.

New Trends in Highway Advertising

The need of businesses to communicate with motorists, and especially tourists, in order for those businesses to survive in the face of strong government regulation of outdoor advertising of all types, has led to innovations which technically fall within the realm of out-of-home advertising. We shall discuss briefly two examples that typify this response to the need for tourists to have information as they drive down the highway and the desire of businesses to achieve survival through meeting those needs.

FIGURE 10.10
An example of a neat, well-maintained roadside sign. Rock City promoters had formerly employed painted barns to draw tourists to this attraction. [*Rock City*.]

FIGURE 10.11
Many states now
sell listings on
signs such as this
as a replacement
for roadside signs
of a more commer-
cial nature.

Information Centers   There is a strong movement in states across the country to establish tourist rest facilities to relieve the tedium and discomfort of long-distance driving. Aware of the desire of travelers to know something more of available establishments than is conveyed by a "gas-food-lodging" sign, one firm, Travel InfoCentres, Inc., has secured franchises from state governments to establish travel information centers at rest-stop locations along major highways. See Figure 10.12.

These centers, usually built in the form of attractive gazebos, provide the resting tourist with information on local points of interest, plus tasteful advertisements covering motels, service stations, restaurants, and camping facilities in the area and off the road ahead. This information is presented colorfully on attractive backlighted panels, easy to read day or night. Advertisers may buy a simple listing or a large display ad, depending upon their assessment of the value of such a medium.

Travel Directories   A second example of the ingenuity of business people in the face of changing times is National Advertising Company's new Travelaide directory and map publication. The function of this medium is almost exactly the same as those discussed above. The form is entirely different. Travelaide maps, too, were born of the pain caused to many businesses by the government's regulation of roadside signs and the new trend among gasoline companies to abandon the practice of providing free road maps to all who request them.

Travelaide's solution to these problems is to provide a group of maps in brochure form covering a particular region or portion of the country. Integrated with the maps is a directory of establishments

FIGURE 10.12
Travel InfoCenters are one means resort and restaurant owners have to tell tourists of the merits of their establishments. [*Travel InfoCenters of Oregon, Inc.*]

whose services might be of benefit to travelers along any particular route. These listings, or ads, are arranged in the chronological order in which a tourist or business person driving along a particular highway would reach them. Rates are charged advertisers in accordance with the amount of space they use and whether or not they wish to have their listings set in a contrasting color. It is assumed, of course, that motorists will carry these directories in their cars for easy reference, and this constitutes the justification for classifying Travelaide directories as out-of-home media.

On-Premise Signs

The open road is not the only place where signs are useful. Hardly any business fails to tell potential customers of its existence by means of on-premise signs. Movie theaters have their brilliant marquees. Department stores blaze their name upon the skyline with multistory signs. Service stations inform the approaching motorist that a particular brand of gasoline is sold at their pumps. The plastic sign, brightly illuminated at night, is the most popular on-premise sign these days.

On-premise signs are an integral part of the business image

FIGURE 10.13

A column cut from
a Travelaide map
book demonstrates
how this company
has moved to fill
the void created
when signs are
banned from high-
ways.

UTAH

ARIZONA STATE LINE To IDAHO STATE LINE

15

MILEAGE FROM/TO
UT./AZ. STATE LINE

0	UTAH/ARIZONA STATE LINE
8	St. George

ST. GEORGE. N-13

ATKIN'S SUGAR LOAF CAFE. Varied family menu, popular. AAA. 6 a.m. - 11 p.m. 309 E 100 N. Most cr. cards.

FOUR SEASONS MOTOR INN. Luxury lodging featuring the "Golden Pheasant". Gourmet fare served in your private alcove. Coffee shop, lounge, 2 pools. 1 blk off Exit. Ph. (801) 673-4804. Outstanding!

10	Bus. I-15—St. George—Santa Clara
18	UT. 15—Hurricane

TO HURRICANE. N-13

EL CHAPARRAL BEST WESTERN MOTEL. 30 deluxe rooms with color TV, dd phones, queen & kings. Rest. & coffee shop. Near Zions Park. Res. Ph. Coll. (801) 635-4647.

32	UT.17—Toquerville—Hurricane—Zion Park
51	REST AREA
66	UT. 130—Bus. I-15—Cedar City
68	UT. 14 East—Cedar City &
	UT. 56 West—Newcastle

radiating from every retail outlet. Thus, they should be carefully designed to reflect the character of the business, and they should be placed where they can be readily seen by prospective customers. Often companies spend large amounts of money urging patronage, and then fail to make it easy for their potential customers to locate their places of business. Identification is the primary purpose of on-premise signs. In addition to this function, such on-premise signs as the familiar "reader boards" that allow change of copy are used to promote bargains or help convey the store's personality.

TRANSIT ADVERTISING

The third category of out-of-home media to be considered is transit advertising, which is similar in function and method of operation to standardized outdoor advertising. Instead of relying on passing traffic for its principal circulation, however, transit advertising depends upon consumer usage of commercial transportation facilities—buses, airlines, trolleys, subway and commuter trains—and upon pedestrians viewing the advertising from the street. This dual role that transit advertising boasts is explained by the fact that it is really two media in one, with a number of variations in each of its forms.

Transit advertising volume is currently running at an annual rate of about $39 million. This is small compared to some of the media discussed in this section, but transportation advertising has enjoyed steady increases in recent years which suggest that the industry, at least in metropolitan areas, is healthy. While the total investment in transit advertising may not be impressive, the investments by some national advertisers have been a strong testimonial to the medium's worth. In recent years, for example, financial institutions, oil companies, other media, beverages, and food products have been leaders in the field.

Transit advertising builds its case on the fact that there are 7 billion individual rides on public transportation systems each year. Add to this the fact that the majority of women passengers are on shopping trips and one begins to understand the value of the medium.[3] In addition to these facts, certain trends in the United States have worked to strengthen the position of transit operations and transit advertising.[4] Foremost among these has been the environmental movement, which, combined with the energy crisis of the early 1970s, has increased the social pressure to leave the automobile at home and use public transportation systems. Other beneficial trends include increased federal support for the transit industry in recent years, allowing for larger and better transit systems. A more efficient standardization program for transit advertising has made it easier for national advertisers to buy the medium. Furthermore, the volume of riders has increased faster than space rates, making transit advertising's cost-per-thousand exposure ratio one of the most attractive among all media.[5] In the advertising business, transit advertising is generally viewed as consisting of three forms: *car cards* (inside the vehicle), *traveling displays* (outside of the vehicles), and *station posters* and *displays*. Each of these forms offers a variety of possibilities as discussed below.

Car Cards

At one time, car cards accounted for the vast majority of transit advertising revenues. Today, however, they are secondary to the traveling display advertisements found on the exteriors of transit

---

[3] Conversation with Joseph Palastak, executive director, Transit Advertising Association, January, 1976.
[4] Letter from Rosemary Boss, Public Information Coordinator, Lane Transit District, January, 1976.
[5] Ibid.

FIGURE 10.14
A jeweler, a restaurant, and a brewery all find transit advertising beneficial to their sales efforts. [*Washington Transit Advertising.*]

vehicles, accounting for only 10 to 15 percent of total transit advertising income.[6]

Just what are car cards? They are the small advertising messages found in the overhead racks and in other interior locations of buses, streetcars, subways, and trains. The industry has been standardized somewhat as outdoor advertising has been. The trade group behind these efforts is the Transit Advertising Association. The size of car cards has been standardized at a height of 11 inches and a length of 28 or 56 inches. However, a special 22- by 21-inch interior card is rapidly becoming a standard, also.

The car-card message is often coordinated with that appearing in the advertiser's other media buys. This is understandable, for the purpose of the car card is very much akin to that of the outdoor poster, namely, to provide a reminder to persons on their way to the market. In this case potential customers are not driving their own automobiles but are riding a commercial vehicle. Thus, the time of exposure is lengthened from an average of 5 seconds to an average of 20 or 30 minutes, and the audience is a captive one in a very real sense. These conditions permit a longer message and make car cards an effective medium for the advertiser who wishes to reach the commuter or the shopper using commercial transportation to get to work or the downtown shopping district.

Some astute advertisers take advantage of the unique nature of transit advertising by adapting their advertising copy directly to the medium. Alka Seltzer has suggested on a car card in the New York subway that the product would be an appropriate remedy for the miseries suffered by the subway rider. A famous fish restaurant in Hoboken, New Jersey, places car cards directing riders to the restaurant which is situated across the street from the last stop.

Buying Car Cards In the sale of transportation advertising the standard unit is a *full service* or *run;* this means that every vehicle operated by the transportation company will carry one of the advertiser's car cards. Half service or quarter service may be purchased. The cards are placed by a firm similar to the outdoor plant. Contracts made by the firm and the transportation company give the firm exclusive rights to place car cards in the vehicles. Usually the standard time period agreed upon by the advertiser and the transportation advertising firm is the same as in outdoor, that is, 30 days or multiples thereof.

Traveling Displays

This form of transportation advertising is really a hybrid between the car card and the outdoor poster. It is an advertising message placed on

[6] Ibid.

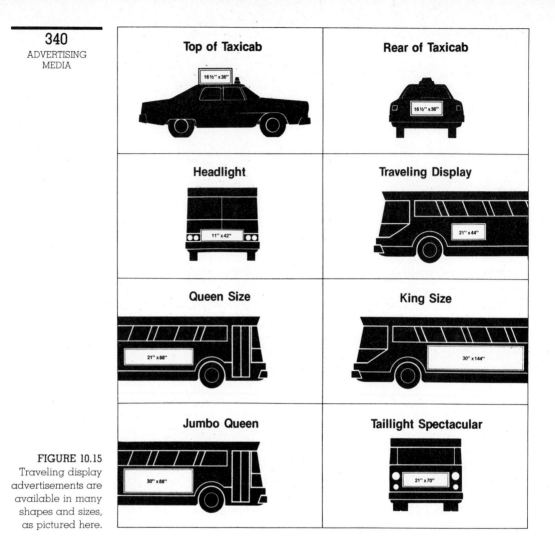

FIGURE 10.15
Traveling display
advertisements are
available in many
shapes and sizes,
as pictured here.

the exterior of a bus or streetcar. Thus, as the vehicle makes its rounds
about the city, the message is exposed to motorists, pedestrians, and
persons waiting for buses and streetcars.

The size of traveling display advertisements have, like car cards,
been standardized. (See Figure 10.15.) The most popular dimensions
today have a height of 21 inches; the length is most commonly 44 or 88
inches. "King-size" displays measuring $2\frac{1}{2}$ by 12 feet are available in
many markets. Rates vary by the size of the display and the number or
percentage of a transit system's vehicles that carry a particular
campaign. Purchases are ordinarily contracted for 30-day periods.

Station Posters and Displays

Essentially, station (terminal) posters are a form of the outdoor posters studied earlier except they are smaller in size and are found in bus and subway stations and railroad terminals. Their role as advertising media is precisely the same as other forms of transit advertising.

More important today than station posters are the standardized display units found in dozens of metropolitan rail and bus terminals and more than 100 airports in the United States. Similar installations are available at air terminals throughout the world—London, Paris, Berlin, Rome, Tel Aviv, Tokyo, and Mexico City, to name a few.

SOME MISCELLANEOUS MEDIA

Human ingenuity being what it is, there are few aspects of life that have not been commercialized in one way or another. Alert entrepreneurs have found ways to attach advertising messages to almost everything we see, including garbage cans, automobiles, tires, motorcycles, T-shirts, racing drivers' clothing, blimps, and even Frisbees. No text could, or would want to, touch on every conceivable medium. However, a few relatively important media that did not fit smoothly into previous portions of this book deserve brief mention because, for some advertisers, they are important.

Advertising on Film

Photography touches advertising at many points. The most obvious are in the realms of print advertising illustration and, of course, television, where 16- or 35-millimeter film is as vital to commercial production as videotape. These production techniques will be discussed further in subsequent chapters; our focus here is on the use of cinematography as it is used by advertisers who produce their own films to meet advertising and public relations objectives.

Once an advertiser has decided to use films as an advertising medium, he must decide where to run the films. He may choose to show them in regular movie houses, in his factory, to his dealers, or to the general public in places other than movie houses, including retail stores by means of closed-circuit television. Only theater or drive-in showings are comparable to other advertising media in so far as a charge is made for presenting the film. Nontheatrical showings, such as plant, school, or service club presentations, are actually public relations activities, and we shall not include them in our discussion here.

Some movie theaters and drive-ins in the United States show

advertising films on their screens. Of course, the preview of coming attractions is advertising by the theater itself, but we are considering the messages of other businesses, sometimes called *trailers*. Ordinarily, these messages are shown between the presentations of the main feature, that is, at the time of the short subjects and the previews. They are usually 45 seconds or 1 minute long, although in rare cases, some are longer. Not only do theaters limit the length of advertising messages, but most restrict the number shown at one time to three.

Though the medium is older than television, the messages are similar to the TV commercial in format and style. It is claimed that films are superior to television as an advertising medium because the larger screen and better projection equipment present a more powerful message to the viewer. Somewhat counterbalancing this advantage is the fact that since the television program comes free to viewers, they may have a more tolerant attitude toward the TV advertising message. It is the price of admission, so to speak. Some patrons of movie houses, on the other hand, resent the showing of advertising messages. They feel that they have paid their money for entertainment and do not want to be part of a captive audience for advertising. And it is impossible, of course, for theater advertising to approach the potential coverage of TV. Film advertising is most effective and most widely used in areas where the impact of television has not been great. Thus, theatrical showings are more numerous in other parts of the world than in the United States.

Who uses the medium and why? The users consist of both local merchants and manufacturers of nationally advertised brands. They use the medium because of its geographical and audience selectivity. Rates are ordinarily based upon audience size and ticket prices. The rate per exposure is not low, but the viewer is almost certain to see the message. The rate quoted is for a one-minute message, and the charge is based on an average weekly attendance figure for the past three or six months.

National advertisers can select the geographical area where they wish their messages to go. Farm-implement firms can tap agricultural areas, and ski-equipment manufacturers can hit areas near ski resorts. Furthermore, selection can be made on the basis of income groups and other classifications. Each theater has its own personal characteristics. It is very local in nature even though the featured movie is shown throughout the nation. The roster of national users includes milk companies, dog-food manufacturers, automobile manufacturers, and the marketers of beverages and cosmetics.

Many of the local dealers who place films in movie houses are dealers for automobiles, farm implements, and similar products. More than likely their messages appear as part of a cooperative advertising program with the manufacturer. Other local users are various service establishments, such as jewelry stores, insurance agencies, and dry cleaners. Logical users are the advertisers catering to the after-theater business—cafes, ice-cream parlors, etc. To solve the national advertiser's problem of selecting theaters and scheduling films, a number of firms specialize in this kind of work.

Cinema advertising, as in-theater advertising is called in international circles, is relatively more important in many countries of the world than it is in the United States. This importance springs, in part, from the fact that motion pictures still remain one of the world's major forms of entertainment. The impact of in-theater advertising throughout the world seems to vary in inverse proportion to the degree of development of competitive media in any given nation. Thus, the higher the socioeconomic development of a country, the less importance this medium assumes in relation to other media. With the spread of television broadcasting and set ownership throughout the world, cinema advertising has declined in importance; however, it seems likely that the medium will always be used to reach selective markets and that it will continue to be especially important in countries where television commercials are not permitted.

Advertising in Directories

Directories are valuable sources of information for people who wish to locate something with a minimum of effort. The information sought may be a street address, a person's occupation, or the name of a firm which manufactures a certain item or retails it in a given community. The proprietors of the various directories often sell advertising space which is interspersed among the listings in the directory. This practice makes it possible to sell the directory for a nominal price or, in some instances, to give it away free. At the same time the advertiser has an opportunity to call special attention to a product or service at a time which may coincide with the prospective customer's search for such a product or service.

The Yellow Pages   The most familiar directory is contained in the yellow pages found in the back of the telephone book in most communities or in a separate book in larger cities. About 6,000 classified directories are published annually in the United States; Canada offers about 500 more. Although every business telephone is automatically listed in the classified directory, the telephone company tries to get the business to emphasize its listing, either by having its name printed in boldface type or by showing a display advertisement on the appropriate page. For either of these services, the firm must pay. For example, a quarter-page ad in a directory for a medium-sized city (400,000) costs from $1,500 to $1,600 per year.

Whether a local business should expend advertising funds for special treatment in telephone directories depends largely on the role

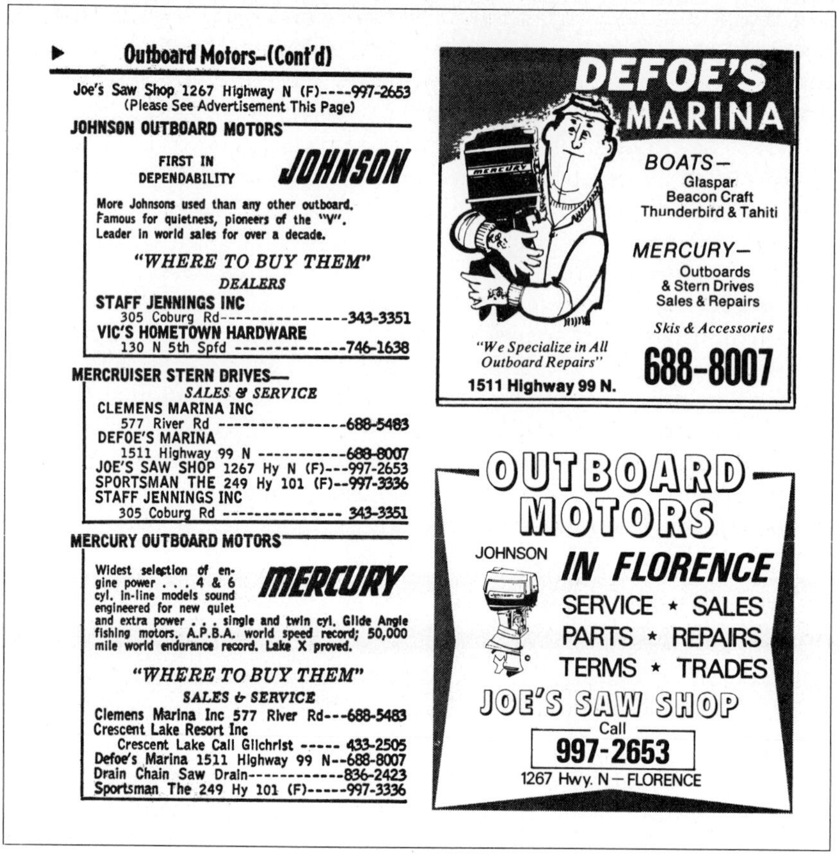

Outboard Motors–(Cont'd)

Joe's Saw Shop 1267 Highway N (F)----997-2653
(Please See Advertisement This Page)

JOHNSON OUTBOARD MOTORS

FIRST IN DEPENDABILITY
JOHNSON
More Johnsons used than any other outboard. Famous for quietness, pioneers of the "V". Leader in world sales for over a decade.

"WHERE TO BUY THEM"
DEALERS

STAFF JENNINGS INC
305 Coburg Rd----------------343-3351
VIC'S HOMETOWN HARDWARE
130 N 5th Spfd --------------746-1638

MERCRUISER STERN DRIVES—
SALES & SERVICE
CLEMENS MARINA INC
577 River Rd ----------------688-5483
DEFOE'S MARINA
1511 Highway 99 N -----------688-8007
JOE'S SAW SHOP 1267 Hy N (F)---997-2653
SPORTSMAN THE 249 Hy 101 (F)--997-3336
STAFF JENNINGS INC
305 Coburg Rd --------------- 343-3351

MERCURY OUTBOARD MOTORS

Widest selection of engine power . . . 4 & 6 cyl. in-line models sound engineered for new quiet and extra power . . . single and twin cyl. Glide Angle fishing motors. A.P.B.A. world speed record; 50,000 mile world endurance record. Lake X proved.
MERCURY

"WHERE TO BUY THEM"
SALES & SERVICE
Clemens Marina Inc 577 River Rd---688-5483
Crescent Lake Resort Inc
Crescent Lake Call Gilchrist ----- 433-2505
Defoe's Marina 1511 Highway 99 N--688-8007
Drain Chain Saw Drain------------836-2423
Sportsman The 249 Hy 101 (F)-----997-3336

DEFOE'S MARINA
BOATS—
Glaspar
Beacon Craft
Thunderbird & Tahiti
MERCURY—
Outboards
& Stern Drives
Sales & Repairs
Skis & Accessories
"We Specialize in All Outboard Repairs"
1511 Highway 99 N.
688-8007

OUTBOARD MOTORS
JOHNSON
IN FLORENCE
SERVICE ★ SALES
PARTS ★ REPAIRS
TERMS ★ TRADES
JOE'S SAW SHOP
Call
997-2653
1267 Hwy. N—FLORENCE

FIGURE 10.16 A portion of a page from a classified telephone directory illustrating three basic types of listings: firm listings, trademark headings, and display advertisements. [*Pacific Northwest Bell Telephone Company.*]

the telephone plays, or can play, in the business. For some firms, directory advertising is a primary medium. Such types of business depend to a great extent on the customer who reaches them by phone. The need for the service they offer may be infrequent; thus their name or phone number may not be known. The plumber is a good example. When a pipe springs a leak, the need is sudden and urgent. What could be simpler than to go to the yellow pages and look for the phone number of the nearest plumber?

When the nature of the business is less urgent and the purchase pattern is one of shopping around before buying, there still is a case for advertising in telephone directories, as many people use the phone as a shopping device. By calling all appropriate businesses, the consumer can decide which stores can be visited with some likelihood of shopping success. One telephone company survey revealed that 74 percent of the adult population over 20 years of age use the yellow pages during a 12-month period. Thus, this form of advertising is an important supplemental medium for the vast majority of local businesses.

Many national advertisers list the names of local dealers in telephone directories. The idea behind the use of the medium in this fashion is to lessen brand switching by consumers. If interest in a product is aroused by advertisements in print or broadcast media, followed by the consumer locating the local dealer in the classified pages of the phone book, the chances of the consumer going directly to one of the dealers and buying the advertised product are increased.

Other Directories   As far as advertising in other kinds of directories is concerned, prospective advertisers must decide whether the directory will have any significant distribution and fill a need for their users. If so, they must ascertain whether that distribution taps a potential market for their business. Many consumer directories are not too worthwhile as advertising media because they fail on these scores.

Sellers of industrial products find directories useful in their advertising mixes. The industrial guide is succinctly explained in the following quotation:

> In industry the modern directory answers one or more of these questions: Who makes what, and where is he located? Who offers what service, and where can I find him? If sufficient description of the product or service accompanies the listing of sources, it is a directory. If a mere listing of sources by name and address is given, it is more properly described as a roster.[7]

Probably the best-known directory serving the industrial market is the *Thomas Register of American Manufacturers*, which the publisher claims is the most widely used advertising medium in the United States.[8] In addition to general industrial directories, the vertical directory is confined to designated industries and the functional directory to selected functions or technical skills. *Post's Paper Mill Directory* is an example of the vertical directory, while *Data Processing Yearbook* illustrates the functional variety. Regional directories and those of association membership complete the list. Our general observations concerning correct use of consumer directories apply for industrial directories.

Donation Advertising

Local and national firms alike are constantly solicited by the representatives of different organizations who want businesses to "advertise" in promotional devices, such as charity-ball programs, trade-union newspapers, and church bulletins. Some of these publications may offer a little advertising value, but in most instances they are worth-

[7] Donald A. Dodge, "The Case for Directory Advertising," *Media/scope*, July 1964, p. 47.
[8] Ibid.

SALES BEGIN WITH A KNOCK AT THE RIGHT DOOR

When only reliable information will do, depend on the source the experts do. Top salesmen depend on The Standard Directory of Advertisers to direct them to the right door to make the sale.

"The Advertisers Redbook," published in two editions, Classified and Geographical, provides all necessary data for selling to the 17,000 listed companies and their agencies, doing national and regional advertising. 80,000 executives are listed by title for direct contact. The Classified Edition arranges companies in 51 classifications for contact by line of business. The Geographical Edition shows companies by state and city for territorial contact. A pocket size Geographical Index comes as a cross reference with the Classified Edition. The Monthly Supplement, issued 9 times a year, is a cumulative updating of changes in advertiser companies, advertising agency appointments and newly advertised products.

When making a sale depends on knocking on the right door . . . depend on the Standard Directory of Advertisers to get you there.

FIGURE 10.17
The *Standard Directory of Advertisers* and the *Standard Directory of Advertising Agencies* are two of the basic reference books used by people in the advertising industry. [*National Register Publishing Co.*]

For those of you
who hunger
after culture.

FIGURE 10.18
Sometimes program advertising can fit well into an advertiser's media mix. This yogurt advertisement appeared in a concert program, *Playbill*, at Lincoln Center in New York. The creative theme fits the medium to perfection. [*Dannon Yogurt.*]

less. Thus, the business person should consider them in their true light—as charitable donations or public relations. Money spent on these devices should not be charged to the advertising budget. Yet these contributions often act as an appreciable drain on the funds available for advertising in many concerns. It is not unusual, for example, for a medium-size department store to spend more than $10,000 in a single year on such questionable ventures. This issue must be faced squarely and handled candidly if the business intends to give advertising a chance to prove its worth.

Correctly charging these expenses to the public relations account rather than to the advertising account in the company books does not, however, dispose of the matter. Theoretically, one might state that no business firm should participate in these schemes, as they are of little value to the contributor. In a practical sense, however, this is easier said than done. Often pressure is applied by the organization either in a subtle way by promising the advertiser goodwill in the community or occasionally by outright coercion. The turndown process is a delicate one. The company using an advertising agency may make it the scapegoat by stating that all advertising decisions are made by the agency. Big firms may delegate the responsibility to one executive who may devote a considerable part of his or her time to weighing the various appeals and demands made on the firm. Small businesses must handle the matter themselves, face to face with the delegation, many of whom may be among their best customers. The practice is

FIGURE 10.19
Plastic shopping bags are an example of the myriad of media available that are not treated in detail in this text. It behooves advertisers to be alert to new ideas and changing modes of communication.

costly in time and money. Once a decision to "advertise" has been made, regardless of the motivation, the advertisement should be taken seriously. Steps should be taken to design an effective advertisement, for it will influence the mental picture of the firm held by some small segment of the general public.

SUMMARY

This chapter describes out-of-home media and other miscellaneous forms advertisers use to convey advertising messages. Despite the relatively small amounts of money invested in these media, each one is used as a primary medium by some advertisers who find them especially useful in meeting specific advertising objectives. Most of them are used by important national advertisers as "backup" or secondary media to reinforce campaigns run in television, magazines, newspapers, and radio.

Out-of-home media include outdoor posters (billboards), painted bulletins, and on- and off-premise signs of all descriptions. However, the posters and painted bulletins are the mainstays of the outdoor advertising industry primarily because they are part of a well-organized business that has made giant strides in standardizing its offerings. As a result, advertisers can purchase outdoor advertising space in almost any region of the country, confident that their advertisements, or *paper*, will fit the panels purchased and that they will receive a fair allocation of boards relative to those that other advertisers receive.

The standards that have accomplished this system are the 24- and 30-sheet poster and the new gross rating point system for selecting boards that outdoor plant owners have recently adopted. Outdoor plant operators sell boards in packages known as 100 gross rating points, 100 showings, or portions thereof.

Other signs that we see along our roads and highways are primarily individual efforts that, for the most part, follow no standardized specifications. Although some of these signs are respectable in both concept and design, many are not, and much of the public distaste for outdoor advertising stems from these disreputable eyesores.

On-premise signs are those located on the property of a retail store or service establishment. They are used to identify a place of business or the products or services offered therein.

Out-of-home advertising fills the gap between all of an advertiser's promotional activities and the location of the actual sale of a product. Outdoor reminds potential customers of products they may wish to buy and, in some instances, guides them to the point where a purchase may be made.

Federal regulations covering the outdoor advertising industry have resulted in the removal of thousands upon thousands of outdoor posters and signs. But this governmental action has, in a sense, strengthened the organized industry by eliminating many of the disreputable signs that have hurt the industry's cause for decades.

Transit advertising was developed to accomplish essentially the same functions as outdoor advertising, that is, to reach potential customers on the way to markets or shopping centers. The most important categories of transit advertising are car cards, traveling displays, and station, or terminal, posters and displays.

Car cards are generally, but not always, located above the heads of bus, train, or subway passengers. They offer many of the benefits of outdoor advertising but offer a much longer period of exposure and therefore may bear a more complex advertisement or message. Traveling displays are carried on the outside of transit vehicles and have much wider exposure than car cards, but, again, the message, while more broadly broadcast, must be kept brief. Station posters are simply small outdoor posters located inside public transit stations. They are confined for the most part to our major metropolitan cities.

Cinematography is important to advertisers who wish to advertise in motion-picture theaters. These commercials provide maximum impact to short commercials among a group of viewers who are quite homogeneous. The geographical selectivity of this medium is outstanding, but the cost per thousand limits its use either to national advertisers who want to tap audiences located in particular regions or to local retail establishments.

The main vehicle for directory advertising is the yellow pages of our telephone directories. The great value of directories is that customers tend to turn to them in their hour of need.

Donation advertising is a constant threat to a well-planned advertising budget. It generally involves little-known media with low circulations and astronomical cost-per-thousand figures. Such expenses, if necessary, should be charged to public relations.

QUESTIONS FOR DISCUSSION

1 What are the basic, underlying needs of advertisers that are fulfilled by out-of-home advertising?
2 Referring to the question above, how might these needs differ for national and local or retail advertisers?
3 Name and define each category of outdoor advertising.
4 Standardization is the key to the success of outdoor advertising. Being as specific as you can, what are standards that exist today?
5 Explain the difference between a buy of 100 gross rating points and a 100 showing.
6 What is the difference between an outdoor poster and a painted bulletin?
7 Describe the various facets of transit advertising. Name any advertisers you can who use this medium, and discuss why you think they find it a profitable buy.
8 Discuss in class your uses of the yellow pages, and poll the group as to whether they find this a useful medium to consumers.
9 As the owner of a retail store you are constantly beseiged by individuals trying to sell you advertising in church bulletins, union and lodge publications, etc. How would you handle this situation? Try to be as realistic as possible in your discussion.
10 You have now been exposed, in some depth, to more than a dozen advertising media representing thousands of individual media companies throughout the nation. Discuss how you think these media are able to survive in such a competitive field.

FOR FURTHER REFERENCE

Advertising in Motion, Transit Ads, Inc., San Francisco, 1975.
Cook, Harvey R.: *Selecting Advertising Media*, Small Business Administration, Washington, 1969.
Essentials of Outdoor Advertising, 2d ed., Association of National Advertisers, Inc., New York, 1958.
The First Medium, Institute of Outdoor Advertising, New York, 1974.
Houck, John W. (ed.): *Outdoor Advertising: History and Regulation*, University of Notre Dame Press, Notre Dame, Ind., 1969.

Nelson, Roy Paul: *Design of Advertising*, 2d ed., Wm. C. Brown Company Publishers, Dubuque, Iowa, 1973.

Outdoor Advertising Manual, Foster and Kleiser (Metromedia, Inc.), 1967.

Sissors, Jack Z., and E. Reynold Petray: *Advertising Media Planning*, Crain Books, Chicago, 1975.

FOUR

ADVERTISING MESSAGES

The advertising media discussed in Part Three serve as vehicles for carrying advertising messages to customers and prospects. Part Four explores the creation of these advertising messages. This section deals with the communication aspect of advertising, and each chapter explains ways that advertisers can increase the communication potential of their advertisements.

Chapter 11 reviews how people act in their respective roles as consumers. The fundamentals of consumer behavior are extremely important to the creator of advertising messages, for ads should convey information and ideas in terms which are readily understood and accepted by their intended receivers. The more ad makers know about the purchase-consumption process, the more effective will be their messages.

Basic techniques employed in writing the words of the advertisement—the activity known as "copywriting"—are given in Chapter 12. Because illustrations, as well as words, communicate information and ideas, the use of art in advertising is the focal point of Chapter 13. A simplified explanation of the mechanical production of both print and broadcast advertisements follows in Chapter 14. Taking these elements—an understanding of consumer behavior, copywriting, art direction, and the production of advertisements—and blending them together should mean that the basic instrument in advertising, the advertisement itself, will be capable of establishing efficient and effective communication between buyer and seller.

CHAPTER 11
CONSUMER BEHAVIOR AND ADVERTISING

When cultivating markets, the producer seeks people who have the ability to pay for the product, who possess the power to make the buying decision, and who are capable of deriving satisfaction from the product. This satisfaction may spring from its actual personal use or from the purchase for use by others. Mary Jones gets satisfaction from using her washing machine because it is a time-saver for her, while the satisfaction she gets from buying Wheaties comes from the pleasure its purchase gives her son Billy.

How people derive satisfaction from products is important when manufacturers and advertisers are making decisions about the scope of their products or markets in our complex economy. Basically, manufacturers try to satisfy consumer wants and needs. But how do they know what consumers want and how do they know what facets of their product are most appealing? Producers and advertisers need to understand the basic forces that shape human behavior within the context of the marketplace. Many of the social sciences, notably psychology and sociology, provide such basic knowledge about consumer desires. The body of knowledge which has been developed on this topic is called *consumer behavior*. In this chapter we analyze some of the basic motivations of people as consumers. In real life, these insights concerning consumer behavior are used to construct models which enable marketing people to plan their strategies. After a survey of these ideas, we show how they are used in an advertising campaign.

THE IMPORTANCE OF THE BEHAVIORAL SCIENCES IN ADVERTISING

Any academic discipline that deals with characteristics of human behavior can be labeled a "behavioral science." Some persons have claimed that marketing belongs in the behavioral sciences, and it is certainly vitally concerned with buyer behavior. The usually accepted disciplines of behavioral science include anthropology, economics, linguistics, political science, psychology, and sociology. Although all have made important contributions to our knowledge of how and why people act as they do, the two that have provided the most direct assistance to advertisers are sociology, the study of humans in relation to society, and psychology, the study of humans as individuals. Both viewpoints are important and are combined in social psychology. Advertising, like politics and diplomacy, is one of the sociopsychological arts.

The importance of psychology to advertisers was soon recognized.

In the October 1895 issue of *Printers' Ink*, the editor made this suggestion to his readers:

Probably when we are a little more enlightened, the advertisement writer, like the teacher, will study psychology. For however diverse their occupations may at first sight appear, the advertising writer and the teacher have one great objective in common—to influence the human mind.

At the time *Printers' Ink* published this editorial, a psychologist at the University of Minnesota, Harlow Gale, was engaged in laboratory experiments "to find the mental processes which go on in the minds of consumers from the time they see the advertisement until they have purchased the article advertised." Gale considered advertising an entirely new field for psychological work, and "one of great and increasing importance."[1]

Before the twentieth century was four years old, the 1895 recommendation-prediction of *Printers' Ink* was given form and substance in a book by Walter Dill Scott, then director of the psychological laboratory at Northwestern University and later president of the same university. The title of Scott's book was *The Theory and Practise of Advertising*, and the subtitle described the content as "A Simple Exposition of the Principles of Psychology and Their Relation to Successful Advertising."[2]

Fifty years after the publication of the works of Gale and Scott, sociologists and anthropologists became interested in advertising. Pierre Martineau, research director of the *Chicago Tribune* at the time, supported the pioneering work into social class conducted by Professor W. Lloyd Warner of the University of Chicago in the 1950s. Martineau popularized Warner's scholarly findings in addresses before professional marketing and advertising groups, and finally in his book, *Motivation in Advertising*.[3] Burleigh Gardner, along with his associate Sidney Levy, was investigating the role of cultural considerations in the marketing process at the same time. These studies were the forerunners of the academic discipline which is known as *consumer behavior:* the study of those activities dealing with the buying of products and the reasons for such action.

Consumer psychologists are interested in the behavior of masses of consumers rather than the behavior patterns of single individuals. Four principal areas of interest are (1) decision making in the market-

[1] Harlow Gale, "On the Psychology of Advertising," *Psychological Studies*, July 1900, pp. 39–69.
[2] Walter Dill Scott, *The Theory and Practise of Advertising*, Small, Maynard and Company, Boston, 1903.
[3] Pierre Martineau, *Motivation in Advertising*, McGraw-Hill Book Company, New York, 1957.

place, (2) changes in attitudes and behavior of consumers, (3) influence of time and uncertainty, and (4) studies of group belonging.[4]

Many models, each attempting to explain how humans behave in their role as consumers, have been developed in the last 20 years. In these models of consumer behavior, two extreme positions are held. At one end of the spectrum is the *stimulus-response model*, as derived from the behaviorist school of psychology. Believers in this model state that "exposure to advertising virtually guarantees that the consumer will respond in a manner desired by the advertiser, even if this is against the consumer's best interests."[5] In other words, the consumer can be manipulated at the will of the seller. We do not believe this to be true today, if it ever was.

At the other extreme, the consumer is believed to be sovereign. Underlying this model of consumer behavior is the assumption that the consumer is "an individual with a highly developed cognitive filter fully capable of admitting only those stimuli which are felt to be pertinent. Non-pertinent stimuli . . . are screened through selective attention, comprehension, retention and response."[6] The advertiser, consequently, "must adapt to the basic dispositions of the consumer, and behavior change results when the basic dispositions are either

[4] Carl M. Larson, Robert E. Weigand, and John S. Wright, *Basic Retailing*, Prentice-Hall, Inc., Englewood Cliffs, N.J., 1976, p. 57.
[5] James F. Engel, "Advertising and the Consumer," *Journal of Advertising*, no. 3, pp. 6–7, 1974.
[6] Ibid., p. 7.

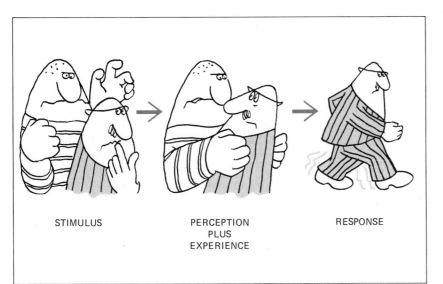

STIMULUS   PERCEPTION   RESPONSE
                     PLUS
                  EXPERIENCE

FIGURE 11.1
Learning involves an association between a stimulus and a response. The individual's perception influences the response to any stimulus, whether internal or external.

favorable or at least neutral with respect to the suggested change."[7] In other words, consumers react to the offerings of the marketplace in ways that they believe are in their own best interests. We hold this to be a correct view of marketplace reality—so important that it deserves elaboration in the following sections.

Cognitive Psychology[8]

The cognitive school of psychology is oriented toward the human's *desire to know.* The underlying notion of this approach is that behavior is a function of *cognitions* (knowings) which are nothing other than ideas, bits of knowledge, values, and beliefs held by the individual. One authority describes cognition as "those processes by which any sensory input is transformed, reduced, elaborated, stored, recovered, or used."[9] Cognitive structures and processes provide two functions: (1) "They are *purposive* in that they serve the individual in his attempt to achieve satisfaction of needs," and (2) they are "*regulatory* in that they determine in large measure the direction taken in the consumer's steps toward his attempt to attain the satisfaction of his initiating needs."[10]

The following quotation sums up nicely the cognitive psychology view of human behavior:

> The human organism, and especially the focus of our inquiry, the consumer, is a sensory-processing and data-gathering organism. His behavior stems from his goal striving and his aspirations. He is not so much driven to acts of choice by his goals and aspirations. Consumers *learn*—they modify their behavior over time. What was sufficient cause or *motivation* for behavior in one situation may for numerous reasons no longer be interpreted or *perceived* as sufficient justification for action or similar action in a subsequent situation. Thus, it can be seen that motivation, learning, and perception lie at the core of the consumer cognitive processes.[11]

In advertising terms, the consumer is looked upon as a thirster for knowledge—for cognition. Producers try to find out more about individuals themselves and about the products they use or may consider using in their daily lives. The consumer is a solver of problems; to do this, information is needed. Advertising is one source of such information, and to be effective, advertising must be presented in proper psychological terms.

[7] Ibid.
[8] Based in part on Rom J. Markin, Jr., *Consumer Behavior*, The Macmillan Company, New York, 1974, pp. 110–113.
[9] U. Neisser, *Cognitive Psychology*, Appleton Century Crofts, New York, 1967, p. 10.
[10] Markin, op. cit., p. 112.
[11] Ibid., p. 113.

FIGURE 11.2
Advertisers operating under the theory of cognitive dissonance realize that people are receptive to messages that reduce dissonance and reject those that are contrary to their opinions or beliefs.

Consumer behavior is usually explained by identifying and studying those factors which influence all human behavior. Traditionally, those factors are classified into two broad groups: (1) social or group influences and (2) individual influences. We start with social influences first because we believe the overall culture and societal setting in which the individual is embedded should be understood before looking at the influence of individual differences. However, two additional psychological concepts—cognitive dissonance and defense mechanisms—are first examined.

The Theory of Cognitive Dissonance

An extremely important cognitive idea was articulated by Leon Festinger in his book *A Theory of Cognitive Dissonance*.[12] People sometimes act in ways that are inconsistent with their knowledge or opinions. The basic assumption in Festinger's theory is that individuals attempt to maintain consonance, or consistency, between what they know or believe and what they do, or between two different attitudes. Hence they attempt to avoid situations or communications that are dissonant or inconsistent with opinions or beliefs. Moreover, such

[12] Leon Festinger, *A Theory of Cognitive Dissonance*, Harper & Row, Publishers, Incorporated, New York, 1967.

dissonance or lack of consistency stimulates individuals to behavior aimed at achieving consonance. In other words, when dissonance exists, an individual will try to reduce this disequilibrium by changing behavior, or if behavior cannot be changed, opinions will be.

This psychological process, called *dissonance reduction*, explains why we often see someone trying to justify his or her actions. Studies indicate that people who have recently bought a new car tend to be higher-than-average readers of advertisements about the particular make of car they have just purchased. They seek additional justification for the large investment made; they want information that will confirm the wisdom of their decision. Since we are constantly exposed to new communications, it is possible that a certain degree of dissonance must be continually reduced by all of us, either by acting on the new information or by rejecting it and thus confirming previous attitudes. The special significance of Festinger's theory to advertising is that people will be quite receptive to messages that help reduce dissonance, and correspondingly resistant to ones that might increase it.

Defense Mechanisms

Another important psychological concept for the advertiser is that of *defense mechanisms*. These are devices used unconsciously to protect ourselves from frustration or anxiety. Four types are featured below: repression, sublimation, compensation, and rationalization.

Repression is the denial of a motive, or a goal, or a barrier—anything involved in an anxiety situation. Put another way, repression is a method of dealing with motivational conflicts by excluding from conscious awareness thoughts or feelings that cause pain or shame. It may take the form of convenient forgetting, or it may go deeper and become self-deception about the very existence of a motive or goal. While this does not resolve the conflict, it does relieve the anxiety. Sex is a motive frequently repressed. So is aggression. There are few permissible forms of direct aggression against members of one's own group, but a variety of "indirect" aggressions are acceptable, such as golf tournaments, or football games, or the keen competition of academic accomplishment.

Sublimation is the use of a substitute activity to satisfy a motive. This is essentially a Freudian concept, and believed by Freud to be particularly related to the sex urge. According to Freud, when the sexual motive cannot be directly gratified because of internal conflicts or external obstacles, it may be satisfied by channeling the urge into art, music, religion, or some other socially acceptable activity. Some psychologists have gone so far as to claim that all forms of effort can be broadly classified as sublimated sexual drive, but such a broad view of sublimation is debatable. It is doubtful that biological motives can be

I keep coming back to the Rock

5 out of every 10 new Prudential policies go to people who already have a piece of the Rock.

Today, many people are discovering that as their life changes, they don't have to change life insurance companies. Whatever insurance need you might be facing—whether it's building cash-value security, or an income for when you're not working anymore—you can get the help you need with a piece of the Rock, Prudential Insurance. Talk to a Prudential representative. Find out why more people come back to Prudential for another piece of the Rock than ever get started with most other life insurance companies.

Come to a company that people come back to. ⬤ **Prudential** *Security and Service since 1875.*

FIGURE 11.3
This ad may well reduce dissonance among present policyholders. The message, of course, also provides a rational reason for insurance prospects to pick the company doing the advertising.

satisfied by substitute activities. Still, the general idea that tensions may be relieved by substituting one type of response for another is well founded.

Compensation is a familiar term in its sense of something that is equivalent to or makes up for a loss or privation, as in workmen's compensation laws, for example. The psychological meaning is similar: a defense mechanism that enables us to overcome, or make up for, feelings of inadequacy or inferiority. Like sublimation, it involves a substitute activity for a frustrated motive. Unlike sublimation, however, there is no implication of sexual frustration. Instead, compensation refers to offsetting failure or the loss of self-esteem in one activity by efforts in another area of endeavor. We may compensate for feelings of inadequacy by buying a flashy car, by wearing diamonds and mink, or by assuming a dictatorial attitude toward subordinates. On the other hand, some of the great thinkers were probably directed toward scholarship as a compensation for feelings of social inadequacy.

Rationalization is a defense mechanism in which the individual explains his or her behavior by substituting benign motives for less acceptable real ones. Rationalization thus lets us gratify behavior without having to take the blame for it. Such self-justification is prevalent in any society. A traditional example is the fox who rationalized that the grapes he couldn't reach were sour anyway. The rationalization may be objectively true—the grapes may actually be sour—but the reason given for the behavior is still self-deceptive.

A retailer may rationalize his failure to sell a product by claiming that the manufacturer's advertising is poorly conceived or inadequate. In like manner, a consumer may rationalize a decision not to buy a product by saying, "It's not a good value," or "I just can't afford it," when the real reason is that he doesn't believe it will enhance his prestige in the eyes of his associates. Research among women shoppers indicates that stores with the highest prices are often reported as the ones which offer the "best bargains" and the "best values." A man may buy an expensive sport jacket largely to satisfy a need for superiority or distinction and rationalize the purchase by telling himself that the imported British tweed is a "better value." It may well be a better value to him, too, but not necessarily in terms of money.

These principles as found in cognitive psychology, in Festinger's *A Theory of Cognitive Dissonance*, and the concepts implicit to defense mechanisms are helpful in the planning and creation of advertising programs. Using cognitive psychology, we develop a working philosophy or model of consumer behavior to which the advertising message should be adapted. Messages should take into account the idea of dissonance. Skillfully constructed advertisements may have common defense mechanisms as part of their appeal to consumers.

SOCIAL AND CULTURAL INFLUENCES ON CONSUMER BEHAVIOR

Human behavior is purposeful. As we experience needs, we seek to satisfy them. The pattern of interrelated motives and attitudes that determine our responses is acquired largely from groups, beginning with our early learning in the primary group of the family. If an advertisement is to reinforce or change a consumer's attitude, the action or response desired must conform to the standards of his or her group. If group approval is lacking, the suggested action is not likely to take place. On the other hand, if strong group approval for a particular action is present, this is the action we are most inclined to choose from many otherwise equally desirable.

Culture

Strong influences on consumer behavior come from the culture in which people live. Culture represents the ideas, values, attitudes, artifacts, and symbols governing the behavior of a member of the group; it determines many of the responses that individuals make in given situations.[13] Thorstein Veblen, in his book *The Theory of the Leisure Class,* first aired the idea that social influences can affect how people spend their money.[14] His thesis revolved around the idea of "conspicuous consumption," which meant that people of wealth bought products not so much for their utilitarian value, but to impress other people with the purchaser's exclusiveness and individuality. Since Veblen's time, many economists and other observers of American life have studied cultural patterns and espoused various explanations on how culture does affect our spending of money—consumer behavior, if you will.

Out of the various cultural influences operating upon us as individuals emerges a personal *value system. Values* define what is expected and desired by the consumer; values predispose him or her to certain behavior. Every person goes through a long socialization process wherein "the impact of family, culture and groups shape and affect our personal values of standards."[15] One common value standard observed by Markin is that "Americans in general value goods"; furthermore, "their core values all have, to differing degrees, a consumption orientation."[16] Accepting these generalizations as true, there are other facets of value systems and the effect of culture upon them which need to be known if product and promotional programs are to be designed to fit into consumers' value systems.

The role of materialism and acquisitiveness, as well as the symbolic versus the utilitarianism of goods, as cultural factors in our society has been discussed and debated for a long time. That our society's standards of value are undergoing rapid and drastic change is common knowledge. The marketer must be listening to the right

[13] Larson et al., op. cit. p. 78.
[14] Thorstein Veblen, *The Theory of the Leisure Class,* The Macmillan Company, New York, 1899.
[15] Markin, op. cit., p. 120.
[16] Ibid., pp. 120–121.

drummer if the marketing and advertising program is to stay in step with the target market's way of thinking.

More than 20 years ago, Martineau identified eight cultural trends of special interest to advertisers:[17]

1 A growing desire to be identified with youth

2 The urge to be different or distinctive in tastes, within certain limits of conformity

3 A trend toward informality and casual living

4 A greater sophistication in behavior

5 Changed concepts of sex roles, of what is "masculine" and what is "feminine"

6 An active search for adventure, for new experiences

7 An increased desire for leisure that provides an outlet for creativity

8 The wish to be modern, or not to be old-fashioned

Martineau's observations of the 1950s are interesting to compare with present-day conditions. Since that time we have gone through the traumatic days of the Vietnam War and the hippie and counterculture movements, all of which brought changes in American cultural standards. In the early 1970s another observer of American life-styles, Daniel Yankelovich, noted five major social trends operating in our society, each altering consumption patterns. The five trends, along with selected manifestations of each trend, are:

1 "Psychology of Affluence" trends, including physical self-enhancement; personalization; physical health and well-being; new forms of materialism; social and cultural self-expression; personal creativity; meaningful work.

2 "Quest for Instant Change" trends, including the "New Romanticism," novelty and change; adding beauty to surroundings; sensuousness; mysticism; introspection.

3 "Reaction against Complexity" trends, including life simplification; return to nature; increased ethnicity; increased community involvement; greater reliance on technology; away from bigness.

4 "Anti Puritanical Value System" trends, including pleasure for its own sake; blurring of the sexes; living in the present; more liberal sexual attitudes; acceptance of stimulants and drugs; relaxation of self-improvement standards; individual religions.

5 "Trends Associated with the Emerging Generation," including greater tolerance of chaos and disorder; challenges to authority; rejection of hypocrisy; female careerism; familism.[18]

[17] Martineau, op. cit., pp. 157–162.

[18] Daniel Yankelovich, "What New Life Styles Mean to Market Planners," *Marketing/ Communications*, June 1971, pp. 38–45, as excerpted from David J. Schwartz, *Marketing Today*, Harcourt Brace Jovanovich, Inc., New York, 1973, pp. 170–171.

Now in the last half of the 1970s, there is talk of a reaction setting in with a return to an era similar to that portrayed in the movie *American Graffiti*, which shows less political concern and more emphasis upon materialism and fun by young people. Prediction of where our society is headed is not our task at this point; instead our goal is to dramatize how volatile that society is and how important it is for the advertiser to know what values are held by the consumers with whom communication is desired. Advertising specialists, when operating in their professional capacities, cannot indulge in value judgments on the desirability of cultural changes taking place in our society. The job of the

Clairol knows what it's like to have a family you can be proud of.

We've got a family, too. A big one.
We've got hair coloring for bringing out even more of your natural beauty.
We've got detanglers and conditioners for making your hair more manageable.
We've got electric hair setters, styling brushes, skin cleaners, and makeup mirrors.
Not to mention cosmetics, shampoos and hair relaxers.
And we've taken the time to develop and nurture each one of them to work best for you.
To us, they're more than just a line of hair products— they're a family we've put together with care and pride.
Kind of like yours.

© 1973 Clairol Incorporated

FIGURE 11.4
A beauty-aid manufacturer seeks to sell to the black subculture through print ads which appeared in such black-oriented media as *Essence*. [*Copyright Clairol Incorporated.*]

advertising specialist is to recognize these changes in order to plan creative and effective communication with people who accept new values.

One principle of good communication is that the audience should be defined as clearly as possible—the "mass" divided into smaller parts so that we don't try to talk with everyone at once. The most elementary way to divide society is to look at American *subcultures*. By far the largest such grouping is our black population, which consists of approximately 22 million people who constitute 92 percent of the nation's nonwhite population. Blacks are concentrated in urban areas of the nation, which, in one way, makes communication with them easy. Their cultural heritage is different from many segments of the United States populace, because they have different language patterns. Special advertising media exist for marketers who wish to sell to members of this minority, and sometimes different creative strategies must be implemented. On the other hand, as blacks and members of other ethnic groups move up the economic scale, there is evidence to indicate that typical American middle-class values may take over, in which case regular media and appeals are indicated.

Social Class

A more logical way to divide the population into manageable groupings is found in the *concept of social class*. A *social class* is a group of the population whose members hold comparable positions in the socioeconomic system and who hold generally similar attitudes, beliefs, and value systems. Warner, in a classic study, broke the population of the United States into six social classes.[19] The accompanying table summarizes each group, along with a short description of its membership and its relative proportion of the total population.

GROUP	MEMBERSHIP	PERCENTAGE
Upper-upper	Aristocracy	0.5
Lower-upper	New rich	1.5
Upper-middle	Professional and managers	10.0
Lower-middle	White-collar workers	33.0
Upper-lower	Blue-collar workers	40.0
Lower-lower	Unskilled workers	15.0

A person's attitudes, beliefs, and value system are influenced by the group, or social class, in which he or she resides. For example, upper-lower-class men prefer baseball as a spectator sport, while hockey is patronized by the upper-middle and higher classes. Furthermore, each class sets different priorities for the spending of its discre-

[19] W. L. Warner et al., *Social Class in America*, Harper & Row, Publishers, Incorporated, New York, 1960.

VOLVO CREATES A WORKING CAR FOR THE LEISURE CLASS.

Even those who can afford life's luxuries must occasionally carry them home. A fact apparently of minor concern to practically every prestige car maker in the world. They've shown a dramatic lack of interest in station wagons.

The Volvo 265 overcomes this oversight. It can be likened to a limousine with the world's largest trunk. But unlike most limousine drivers, the Volvo chauffeur gets more consideration than his cargo.

The front seat cushions raise, lower and tilt. The seat backs recline. The area at the small of your back adjusts from "soft" to "firm."

Air conditioning and automatic transmission are standard equipment, of course.

Driving is silent, smooth and effortless.

Steering and braking are power-assisted. And a fuel-injected, light alloy, overhead cam V-6 provides ample performance for the most sporting driver.

Quite naturally, a car this generously endowed does not come cheap. But when you think about it, Volvo does offer extra incentives for paying the price.

All the things we've put into the Volvo 265. And all the things you'll be able to.

VOLVO 265
The car for people who think.

FIGURE 11.5
An interesting class appeal is made by a car manufacturer. [*Copyright 1976, Volvo of America Corporation.*]

tionary income, with blue-collar workers opting for recreation vehicles and white-collar workers preferring more intellectual items, including books, records, and theater tickets. These preferences are not so much a result of differing levels of income, for the two groups may receive the same size paychecks; it is a matter of how each group wishes to spend its money. In the early 1970s, union wages and the recession caused the earnings of blue-collar and white-collar workers to become equivalent, but buying patterns are still quite distinct. Spending income for "appropriate" purposes results in the class member receiving acceptance by his or her peer group; deviation from acceptable norms may lead to rejection by the group. Obviously, advertisers can benefit greatly in their communication efforts if the social class of target markets is known.

Because an important belief in our society is that of egalitarianism—that everyone is equal—the concept of social class is repugnant to many of us. We prefer to associate the concept with medieval days of nobles and serfs. With social mobility a relatively common phenomenon in our society, families are not necessarily locked into one social class from generation to generation, and people in one class aspire to moving to a "higher" status group and may even emulate the consumption patterns of that group.

Reference Groups

It should be remembered that it is quite natural for individuals to act in a manner associated with their status in life, or with statuses to which they aspire. This self-awareness leads us to identify ourselves with certain reference groups. A *reference group* is any collection of people that helps to shape the attitudes and behavior of an individual. These groups can be formal in nature, as found in church, fraternal, and social organizations, or informal, such as friendships. Such groups usually adopt certain objects as symbols. Therefore, these objects become desired by group members. The advertiser might find the opposite situation equally important—how to reject identification with individuals or groups of lower status, and the symbols that represent them. Our choice of a university, a profession, an automobile, or a restaurant can be strongly influenced positively or negatively by status and prestige identification.

Opinion Leaders

Katz and Lazarsfeld developed a concept dealing with the role of opinion leaders.[20] Their theory contends that an opinion leader can influence other consumers in making buying decisions about products. They believe that opinion leaders exist at all levels of society and function in a "two-step" flow of communications where the opinion leader gets the information from the media, including advertising, and passes it along to the opinion followers in the leader's sphere of influence. A practical problem in putting the theory into action is that it

[20] Elihu Katz and Paul F. Lazarsfeld, *Personal Influence*, The Free Press of Glencoe, Ill., Chicago, 1955.

"The brokerage house of E.F. Hutton & Company is a firm with which I have had close and pleasant relationships for four decades. They have been helpful and their service has been good."
— *J. Paul Getty*

When E.F. Hutton talks, people listen.

FIGURE 11.6
One of the world's richest men, certainly an opinion leader in the field of financial affairs, endorsed a brokerage firm. This print advertisement was developed from a television campaign which the advertiser ran successfully earlier.

is very difficult to locate opinion leaders, and the leader for one product category often is not for another one. For example, Joe Smith, a fullback on the football team, is an authority on rock music, whereas Ed Jones, captain of the chess team, is an expert on stereo equipment or movies. Furthermore, restaurants become the "in" place in a city because celebrities patronize them. Isolating appropriate media vehicles to reach opinion leaders is difficult. More research is needed on the subject before the theory can be widely adopted in the development of advertising strategy.

The Family

Most of the attitudes which we hold were developed within the context of our immediate family. Attitudes are formed by parents and other family members not only toward God, country, motherhood, sex, and politics, but also toward products, brands, and retail outlets. Certainly, the influence of each family member is important when products for family use are being purchased. Recently the relative influence of the husband and of the wife in the purchase of various consumer durables, such as homes and automobiles, has received much attention. Advertisers need to be aware of these influences when disseminating information about their products. For example, it is quite possible that automobile manufacturers have underestimated the importance of the woman's influence when a new car is being chosen. Certainly, changing standards of women's role in society would impact on such decisions. Where once the decision of buying a new car was wholly the prerogative of the man, the woman, who now drives the automobile and may well be making the payments for it, will have a strong voice in the decision.

Two other important interpersonal variables influence consumer behavior: the concepts of *family life cycle* and *life-style*. Whereas social class, reference groups, and opinion leadership come out of cultural and nonfamily group relationships, these two concepts are largely derived from the influence of the family.

Family Life Cycle Life cycle deals with the way that attitudes, behavioral dispositions, and expressive movements change over time. Every individual over his or her lifetime passes through various stages of growth. The famous soliloquy delivered in Shakespeare's *As You Like It* enumerated seven in number. The individual normally possesses certain attitudes and beliefs and holds values appropriate to where he or she is at each stage of life. Similarly, the individual's behavior as a consumer is, to a degree, determined by his or her position in the cycle of life. Advertisers need to be conscious of the normal mind sets encountered along the continuum of life.

The *concept of a family life cycle* is more important to marketing and advertising planners. A typical household passes through four stages: family formation (years 20 to 34); peak income (35 to 49); discretionary spenders (50 to 64); and retirement (65 plus).[21] Another important group, of course, is the singles market, which amounts to 15 million households—9.3 million females and 5.7 million males living alone or with nonrelatives—contrasted with 46.8 million husband-wife units.[22] The kind of products needed are determined largely by the family's life cycle. For instance, in early married years, the emphasis is upon the accumulation of consumer durables; children bring the need for more housing. Advertising strategy calls for timing of messages to target groups at the right stage in the cycle. Talking about the purchase of a home to young bachelors, or even newlyweds, is largely

[21] *Grey Matter*, vol. 46, no. 6, p. 3, 1974.
[22] Ibid., p. 4.

a waste of advertising dollars. After the birth of a child, however, such communication is well received, even sought by the new parents.

Life-Style "Life-style" is a term and concept still in the process of being defined. In many ways it is closely akin to individual differences; yet whole families adopt life-styles, and family influence in their creation is high. The term describes a distinctive mode of living, or to turn the phrase around, a "style of living." The concept goes beyond the broad characterizations that result from a person's social class. Life-style variables describe how people go about their daily routines. Some authorities put the emphasis on how people allocate their time, rather than how they spend their money, although the two are interrelated in many instances. What is important to individuals is reflected in their actions. Thus, we may see two people who are in the same social class and who possess the same demographic characteristics, yet lead very different lives. Such popular descriptions as "swinger" and "straight" cover greatly divergent life-styles.

"Psychographics" is a term closely related to the concept of life-style and is often confused with it. One definition of the term is:

> Psychographics is a quantitative research procedure which seeks to explain why people behave as they do and why they hold their current attitudes. It seeks to take quantitative research beyond demographic, socioeconomic and user/non-user analysis, but also employs these variables in the research. Psychographics looks into three classes of variables, of which life-style is one. The others are psychological and product benefits.[23]

Psychographics, or life-style research, can be extremely useful in the development of advertising strategy and copy. It provides data beyond dealing with such demographic variables as age, sex, and income or studies of consumer attitudes about the product and its use. Psychographics gives creative people in advertising a feel for the life-styles pursued by members of the target market for the product. When Schlitz Beer felt there was a need to freshen its advertising campaign in 1968, a life-style research found that the heavy beer drinker could be described as:

> . . . a dreamer, a wisher, a hero worshiper. He goes to the tavern and has six or seven beers with the boys. . . . To talk with this man where he lives, in terms he respects and can identify with, we must find for him a believable kind of beer he inwardly admires.

The major life style patterns that emerged indicated that the heavy beer

---

[23] Emanuel Demby, "Psychographics and from Whence It Came," in William D. Wells (ed.), *Life Style and Psychographics*, American Marketing Association, Chicago, 1974, p. 28.

drinker was a risk taker and a pleasure seeker, at least in fantasy. . . . More than the nonuser, the heavy user tended to have a preference for a physical and male-oriented existence . . . the life style data showed . . . an enjoyment of drinking, especially beer, which was seen as a real man's drink.[24]

Schlitz built a campaign around the imagery of the sea to dramatize the adventure of one of the last frontiers. The focus was on the life-style of the men of the sea, men who lived their lives with "Gusto." The campaign communicated with members of the target market in terms of their life-styles as related to the product category of beer. Schlitz's share of the beer market increased, and the "Gusto" theme was continued until 1976.

In sum, the advertising strategist attempts to learn as much as possible about the social and cultural influences playing upon the members of the target market. These insights combine to permit better communications.

THE IMAGE OF THE PRODUCT AND THE BRAND

The behavioral concepts that we have already discussed are not only important to the creation of advertising messages which will stimulate favorable rather than unfavorable responses from consumers. Any phase of marketing can utilize them, because what the modern consumer buys is more than the end product of certain raw materials processed to certain specifications. What the consumer wants and buys is a package of symbols appropriate to his or her self-image. This package of symbols is known as the *image* of the product, and it is considerably broader than the physical combination of many ingredients. The image of a product includes not only the picture the consumer has of the intrinsic qualities of the product, but also all the ideas he or she has about it—the sort of people who use it, the kind of stores that sell it, the character of the advertisements about it, the "personality" of the firms that make it—in other words, the total of all the stimuli received by the buyer that are related to the product. This bundle of product attributes is referred to as the *product image*. We measure the worth of a product to us in terms of values that result fundamentally from the interreaction of perception, learning, and motivation. We may see a book on advertising that is a bargain and can be a useful supplement to our study, but if added knowledge of advertising is an unimportant goal, we will probably buy a couple of T-shirts or a stereo album instead.

---

[24] Joseph Plummer, "Applications of Life Style Research to the Creation of Advertising Campaigns," in Wells, op. cit., pp. 164–165.

You only go around once in life.
So grab for all the gusto you can.
Even in the beer you drink.
Why settle for less?

When you're out of Schlitz,
you're out of beer.

Schlitz

© 1970 Jos. Schlitz Brewing Co. Milwaukee and other great cities

FIGURE 11.7
The Schlitz
"Gusto—You Only
Go Around Once"
campaign is
shown in this print
advertisement. Tel-
evision, however,
was the dominant
medium used in
the total campaign
for the beer.

Most advertisers and marketers are more concerned with *brand image* than with product image. Their basic problem is not to increase the sales for a generic product, such as neckties or toothpaste, but to sell a particular brand of necktie or toothpaste in competition with other brands of the same type of product. The concept of product image is useful when considering the relative inherent interest two different products, such as automobiles and dishwashers or television sets and life insurance, offer consumers. The concept of brand image helps explain why two products that are technically identical are purchased by different types of people for different reasons: why, for example, soap A is preferred by young college women, while soap B, which has the same essential ingredients, is preferred by women over forty. Economist John K. Galbraith says that there is no such phenomenon as identical products, or the "undifferentiated market," in the modern economy of monopolistic competition:

> If the number of sellers is small, they will always be identified as distinct personalities to the buyer. And although their products may be identical, their personalities will not and cannot be. There is always, accordingly, a degree of product differentiation.[25]

This economist's viewpoint is underscored by advertising practitioners. A decade ago one large advertising agency cautioned advertisers with these words:

> Because of the great and growing similarity of products and multiplicity of strong brands, it is vital to build a distinct brand personality and engrave a sharply defined brand image on the consumer's consciousness.[26]

Building meaningful product and brand images for consumer goods involves the use of the concepts of consumer behavior. Certainly the images appeal to the consumer's desire for information, and attitudes and beliefs about products are useful bits of information. Advertising is a vehicle for building bridges between the consumer's self-image or self-perception and product and brand images. Purchase and consumption activities are generally nothing more than an exercise in matching images.

CONSUMER BEHAVIOR AND THE COMMUNICATION PROCESS

Basic Elements in Mass Communications

When the consumer is viewed as an information-processing, decision-making entity, it is important to understand how needed information reaches him or her. In other words, how does the information communicated reach the consumer? We have seen how the behavioral

[25] John K. Galbraith, *American Capitalism*, Houghton Mifflin Company, Boston, 1956, p. 43.

[26] *Grey Matter*, Grey Advertising, Inc., New York, November 1968, p. 8.

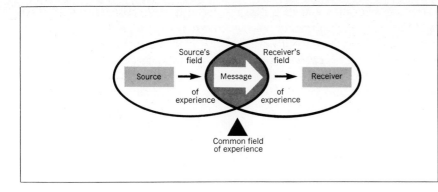

FIGURE 11.8
Effective communication requires a field of experience common to both sender and receiver. Advertisers must translate product information into the language of the customer.

sciences help producers and advertisers to understand buying behavior. Psychological theories are equally valuable in analyzing advertising as a form of mass communications. Essentially, the process of communication includes three elements: a source; a message; and a destination, or receiver, for the message. In personal or direct communications, the source is an individual; the message may be a speech, a gesture, or some other sign or signal; the receiver may be either another individual or a group—students in a classroom, a lecture audience, or the other 10 members of a football team. In mass communications, however, the source is not in direct contact with the receiver, and the receiver is always a group—or more precisely, an *aggregation*—rather than another individual. Thus, mass communications requires a fourth element—a mechanism or medium, such as a newspaper, magazine, outdoor poster, or broadcast station—to deliver the message simultaneously to many persons. The message may take the form of ink on paper, motion-picture film, electronic impulses, or paint on metal.

As we shall see later, it is important to visualize the real receiver of mass communications as the individual member of the group reached by the mass medium—the reader of a particular newspaper, the motorist who passes a certain outdoor poster, someone listening to a radio newscast or watching a television program. In advertising communication, the message becomes a stimulus designed to obtain a certain response from the receiver—the purchase of a product or the acceptance of an idea.

Special Problems of the Advertiser

This elementary source-medium-message-receiver analysis is inadequate, however, if we are to understand some of the basic problems of mass communications that are of particular significance to the advertiser. Even in direct or personal communications, the source or sender must be capable of transmitting signals that the receiver is able to receive. There is obviously little or no communication if the students in the back of the room cannot hear the instructor's voice. But it is not enough for the receiver to be able to see or hear the message. His or her reception must be psychological as well as physical. The receiver must perceive and be able to understand what is seen or heard.

In certain personal situations, communication can be quite complete with a soundless gesture. The symphony director's baton says "fortissimo" (very loud) to the members of the orchestra as effectively as if the word appeared on a screen in 4-foot letters. Although the new recruit will not understand the sergeant's arm signal, the trained soldier will. In both examples, a field of experience common to both sender and receiver assures understanding of the message. But the advertiser and the consumer do not have this close relationship. One of the primary problems in the creation of advertising is the translation of news and information about the product from the language of the advertiser into the language of the consumer.

Another problem the advertiser must face, which is not inherent in all types of communication, is lack of *feedback*. When we talk with a person face to face, or even when we address a group, it is possible to get an impression of how successfully our message is being delivered. The receivers may ask questions about points which are not clear to them. And even though they do not talk back, their actions or expressions can indicate whether the message is being received. A yawn from the audience, for example, is a signal that the information is not getting through. In this way, interpersonal communication is usually a two-way process.

Most advertising, however, is one-way communication. The prospect, or the receiver of the message, has no opportunity to ask questions or even to indicate to the advertiser whether the message has been received. Instead of "feeding back" reactions, the page is turned or the channel is changed. The advertiser may subsequently find through research or through sales reports that all too few people received the message, but this is not known at the time the advertiser is actually trying to communicate. The nonpersonal nature of the presentation through mass communications media prevents two-way communication. To overcome this obstacle, the advertiser must attempt to anticipate the audience's reaction when exposed to the message.

Interference is another problem the advertiser must cope with. To a degree, interference is present in all forms of communication; even when two completely sympathetic friends are conversing in a soundproof room, distractions or interruptions will be present—a fly speck on the wall or the squeak of a chair under shifting weight. Interference to advertising messages can come from many sources. The phone rings while we are reading the newspaper. The traffic light turns red when we are listening to the car radio. The baby cries, and mother leaves the television set. But the greatest interference to advertising is not external interference, but internal interference that is inherent in all the media of mass communications. This internal interference takes the form of other messages competing for the attention of the reader, the listener, or the viewer—not only news and entertainment, but advertising messages being transmitted by other advertisers.

Three Requisites for Effective Communication

Lack of feedback, interference, and translation of advertiser language into consumer language are important problems in advertising, but they do not alter the basic requirements for successful advertising. For any idea to be transmitted effectively from source to receiver, whether the source is personal or nonpersonal, the message must meet these three qualifications:

1 It must be so designed and delivered as to gain the attention of the receiver.

2 It must use signals that are understood in the same way by both source and receiver.

3 It must arouse needs in the receiver and suggest some way of satisfying these needs that is appropriate to the receiver's group situation when moved to make the desired response.[27]

These three requirements are often combined to form the first rule of effective communication: *know your audience.* This rule applies equally to direct or personal communications and to indirect or mass communications. It applies equally to residents of the white, middle-class American suburb and to the growing black, Puerto Rican, or Mexican-American inner-city audiences in urban areas. A lecture that will hold the attention and interest of graduate students in marketing is not likely to hold the attention and interest of sophomore English majors or the members of the Eastlake Garden Club. In the same way an advertisement designed to stimulate increased use of long-distance telephone service among business executives is unlikely to be an efficient means of increasing long-distance telephoning among families or for personal reasons.

In personal, face-to-face communications, the fundamental rule, know your audience, may be comparatively easy to apply, although in a surprising number of instances it seems to be ignored, and the ladies of the Eastlake Garden Club get the same lecture as the graduate students in marketing. For the advertiser, who never enjoys the luxury of a captive audience like the marketing class or the garden club, the task is both more difficult and more important.

[27] Adapted from Wilbur Schramm (ed.), *The Process and Effects of Mass Communications*, The University of Illinois Press, Urbana, 1954, p. 13.

FIGURE 11.9

Pantyhose is promoted through a rational approach. The ad is highly informative in nature.

Consider for a moment the advertiser's problem in gaining the audience's attention. Unlike the marketing students and members of the garden club, the advertiser's audience is not conveniently gathered in a room waiting for the message. All the advertiser can do is make the message available through newspapers, television, or some other mass medium, and hope that prospects will select it from the vast volume of other advertisements, entertainment, and information competing for their attention. None of us can possibly receive all the communications to which we are exposed. The ones we select are those which quickly provide a cue—an illustration or a headline, for example—that relates to our needs and interests at the time of exposure.

Obviously signs that are not meaningful to the intended receiver provide no such cue, nor will interest be held to complete the balance of the message unless the sender is in tune with the receiver. This is one of the problems faced by the advertiser who tries to communicate with prospects whose culture is unfamiliar. Even when the language is the same, the meaning of words may be quite different. In England, for example, the "hood" of a car means the top, and what we call the hood is the "bonnet." We should also realize that the meaning of a message is not merely the combined meanings of the words used. In an oral communication, such as a brief radio announcement, meaning is conveyed by the timing, the pattern of emphasis, the intonations, and the quality of the announcer's voice. Even in a purely verbal printed mass communication, such as a newspaper advertisement without illustrations, the reader derives meaning from the size of the ad, the size and design of the type, the position of the ad on the page, and the page within the paper. So we should, as Schramm says, "visualize the typical channel of communication, not as a simple telegraph circuit, in which current does or does not flow, but rather as a sort of coaxial cable in which many signals flow in parallel from source toward destination."[28]

[28] Ibid., p. 10.

FIGURE 11.10
The same product is promoted by the same manufacturer using an emotional appeal.

Particularly significant for the advertiser is the third requirement of effective communication—suggesting need or *want* satisfaction that is appropriate to the group situation of the receiver.

Two Additional Models of Communication

Many models, in addition to the Schramm model, have been designed to help clarify the communication process. Two particularly insightful models for the student of advertising are (1) the Hierarchy of Effects Model and (2) the Transactional Process Model.

The Hierarchy of Effects Model Lavidge and Steiner think of advertising as a force which must move people up a series of steps,[29] starting from being unaware of the product's existence, on to its actual purchase. The positive steps in the model are shown in Table 11.1.

The first two positive steps in the chain, "awareness and knowledge, relate to *information* or *ideas*." The next two steps, "liking and preference, have to do with favorable *attitudes* or *feelings* toward the product," while the final two steps, "conviction and purchase, are to produce *action*—the acquisition of the product." These three advertising functions compare to the classic psychological model which divides behavior into three dimensions: (1) cognitive—intellectual, mental, or "rational" state; (2) affective—"emotional" or "feeling" state; (3) conative or motivational—"striving" state, treating objects as positive or negative goals. The point is made that "the actions that need to be taken to stimulate or channel motivation may be quite different" depending on whether knowledge is being produced or favorable attitudes created.

The Transactional Process Model In this model, the individual is viewed as "an information-processing machine, who presented with some new information, tries to absorb and deal with it as effectively as possible and alter his behavior accordingly."[30] There are six behavioral steps through which the individual must pass if he or she is to be effectively persuaded: presentation, attention, comprehension, yielding, retention, and behavior. The model is explained in these words:

> A message designed to affect a consumer's behavior in a certain manner may or may not succeed in being *presented* to him. If it is, he may or may not *attend* to this message. If he does, the question then arises as to

[29] Robert J. Lavidge and Gary A. Steiner, "A Model for Predictive Measurements of Advertising Effectiveness," *Journal of Marketing*, pp. 59–62, October 1961. All quotes in this paragraph are from this source.

[30] From *Consumer Behavior* by Thomas S. Robertson. Copyright © 1970 by Scott, Foresman and Company, Glenview, Ill. All material in this paragraph from page 46. The model is attributed to William J. McGuire. Reprinted by permission.

TABLE 11.1
LAVIDGE AND STEINER'S
HIERARCHY OF EFFECTS MODEL

RELATED BEHAVIORAL DIMENSIONS	MOVEMENT TOWARD PURCHASE	EXAMPLES OF TYPES OF PROMOTION OR ADVERTISING RELEVANT TO VARIOUS STEPS
CONATIVE The realm of motives. Ads stimulate or direct desires.	PURCHASE ↑ CONVICTION	Point-of-purchase Retail store ads Deals "Last-chance" offers Price appeals Testimonials
AFFECTIVE The realm of emotions. Ads change attitudes and feelings.	PREFERENCE ↑ LIKING ↑	Competitive ads Argumentative copy "Image" ads Status, glamour appeals
COGNITIVE The realm of thoughts. Ads provide information and facts.	KNOWLEDGE ↑ AWARENESS	Announcements Descriptive copy Classified ads Slogans Jingles Sky writing Teaser campaigns

SOURCE: Robert J. Lavidge and Gary A. Steiner, "A Model for Predictive Measurements of Advertising Effectiveness," *Journal of Marketing*, p. 61, October 1961.

whether he has *comprehended* it as intended by the advertiser. The fourth and fifth steps in the chain are whether he will *yield* to what he has understood, and if so, whether he will *retain* "this new behavioral inclination." If these five steps in the chain are successfully completed, the final one remaining is whether or not the consumer will *behave* according to this inclination (i.e. act in a manner intended by the original message).

These models attempt to show that advertising moves people along a kind of continuum of performance, starting the consumer with an inoculation of basic information, moving him through the process of creating interest in and favorable attitude toward products, ending ultimately in a stage of commitment or action. There is no one "right" model, as is shown in our discussion of copywriting and art direction later in this section of the book.

FORCES SHAPING INDIVIDUAL CONSUMER BEHAVIOR

By our emphasis upon the social influences on consumer behavior we do not mean to imply that individual influences thereon are not important. It is dangerous to think of behavior as activated by a single motive rather than a combination of different motives. Usually a complex of motives, some positive and some negative in effect, which are in turn strongly influenced by attitudes, especially in terms of the specific goal response, are present.

You might consider the purchase of a portable typewriter, for example, because of a desire to save time in preparing class projects or reports, or because you want the recognition or feeling of superiority that might come with high grades, or because you believe you could make money typing papers for others, or because of a combination of all three motives. At the same time, you might postpone the purchase or decide not to buy the typewriter because a desire to save money, or a need for appetizing food and drink, or both, overcomes the combination of motives pulling you toward the purchase. And if the motives in favor of the purchase win, the brand you buy and where you buy it will be influenced by your attitudes toward the manufacturer and the retailer.

Nor should an advertiser or marketer view either buying motives or attitudes as static forces. Despite the universal nature of certain motives, their relative strengths within the total complex of motivation vary, not only among groups of people, but even within the same individual at different times and under different circumstances. If we have just finished an appetizing dinner, our need for food and drink is obviously dormant. The strength of a motive and the manner in which we seek to satisfy it changes from time to time and from place to place.

A critical question, left unanswered in this discussion, is whether behavior results from internal mind sets, such as attitudes and motives, or whether individual behavior is largely affected by the situation in which the individual finds himself. Separate schools support each point of view. It is important, therefore, to know the major concepts explaining the psychology of the individual, as they may help to explain how advertising affects consumer behavior.

Sugar Free Dr Pepper will taste even better after you try on last year's bathing suit.

Some people drink Sugar Free Dr Pepper just because they like it. But a lot more people drink it because it tastes great and there are only two calories per serving.

And no matter how much you drink, it doesn't leave an unpleasant aftertaste.

So when you get up the courage to try on last year's bikini, have a nice cold Sugar Free Dr Pepper handy.

Put on the suit, peek in the mirror and quickly take a sip. Then look in the mirror again and take another sip.

Notice how Sugar Free Dr Pepper tastes better and better every time you look in the mirror?

Just keep sipping, watch what you eat and pretty soon you'll start looking better and better too.

Sugar Free Dr Pepper. You can drink a lot of it.

FIGURE 11.11
The desire to be liked underlies this ad for a diet soft drink.

Motivation, Perception, and Learning

Most behavioral scientists agree that three concepts fundamental to an understanding of human behavior are motivation, perception, and learning. *Motivation* is all those conditions of inner striving described as needs, drives, wants, urges, motives, and the like. For our purposes, then, a *motive* is a state of tension or disequilibrium within the individual that activates or moves his or her behavior toward an objective or goal. Such motivation may be conscious or unconscious; individuals are not always aware of the motives that channel their behavior, but the behavior is always purposive, or goal-directed, nevertheless. Hunger and thirst are examples of goal-directing motives universal among both humans and lower animals.

Since behavior is purposive action, it is strongly influenced by the individual's environment. All knowledge of the world is derived through sensory stimulation, or the response of sense organs to light, sound, and similar stimuli. The complex process of selection, organization, and interpretation of these stimuli is called *perception*. Another way of describing perception is the process of discrimination among the stimuli which collectively constitute the world or the environment of the individual. As such, perception is a process that intervenes between sensory processes and behavior.

Much of the perceptive process depends on *learning*, a relatively permanent change in behavior that results from past experience. In addition to everything taught in school or out, practically all behavior except that resulting from physiological change, such as sleep, growth, or disease, has been learned. Many behavioral scientists consider learning the most important concept in understanding human behavior. Basically, the learning process involves an association between a stimulus and a response, or between two stimuli, and most associations are formed when the individual is motivated in some way. Because perception is strongly dependent on learning and motivation is an important aid to learning, we can see how the interrelation of these three psychological concepts is fundamental to understanding human behavior.

FIGURE 11.12
The appeal in this outdoor poster for life insurance is to the desire people have to care for loved ones.

TABLE 11.2
LIST OF SOCIALLY ACQUIRED MOTIVES

1 The desire to obtain group approval and conform to their standards.
2 The desire for superiority over others, for extra achievement.
3 The desire to control material objects, to master and control the environment.
4 The desire to be liked, admired, respected, and wanted, for social acceptance.
5 The desire for economic security, to avoid want and deprivation.
6 The desire for play, for diversion and amusement.
7 The desire to care for loved ones, the parental need.
8 The desire for health, to maintain one's physical body in good repair.
9 The desire to acquire information, to learn.
10 The desire to acquire material objects for ownership or possession.
11 The desire to investigate in order to satisfy curiosity.
12 The desire for convenience, to achieve comfort.
13 The desire for personal accomplishments, for self-realization.
14 The desire for group preservation, to sustain and maintain economic, political, religious, and social structures.
15 The desire for dependability, for reliability.

SOURCE: Richard M. Baker, Jr., and Gregg Phifer, *Salesmanship, Communication, Persuasion, Perception*, Allyn and Bacon, Inc., Boston, 1966. p. 336.

Classifying Motives Some motives stem directly from physical or organic needs of the individual, and their satisfaction is essential to physical well-being. Most psychologists include hunger, thirst, temperature regulation, sex, and breathing as drives which are physiological in nature.

Motives which are not directly related to physical needs are called various names including "learned," "social," or "psychogenic" motives. The desires for security and for achievement are acquired from the individual's environment and experience and are good examples of learned or socially derived motives. Hunger is physiological and thus is "unlearned." All human beings have the hunger motive regardless of age or the culture in which they live. Cleanliness, on the other hand, is a trait that is learned or acquired and does not exist in little boys or in the adult Australian bushman. Some people say the trait is overemphasized in the American culture.

Many lists of social motives have been compiled by behavioral scientists. One concise list, suggested by W. L. Thomas, an eminent sociologist, is restricted to four wants, or "wishes": for new experience, for response, for belonging, and for recognition. A list designed by Baker and Phifer contains 15 socially acquired motives, as shown in Table 11.2.

One classification of drives that has received wide acceptance was that of Abraham H. Maslow. Ranking them in a hierarchial fashion, with the first-mentioned holding highest place, Maslow delineated five drives as being important to humans:[31]

[31] A. H. Maslow, *Motivation and Personality*, Harper & Row, Publishers, Incorporated, 1954.

1 *Self-actualization.* The desire to know and understand

2 *Esteem and status.* The desire for reputation

3 *Belongingness and love.* Wanting acceptance by others

4 *Safety.* The need for security, protection, order

5 *Physiological survival.* The need for oxygen, food, water

One additional list may be useful. James Bayton believes that psychogenic needs can be sorted into three broad categories:[32]

1 *Affectional needs.* The needs to form and maintain warm, harmonious, and emotionally satisfying relations with others

2 *Ego-bolstering needs.* The need to enhance or promote the personality; to achieve, to gain prestige and recognition, to satisfy the ego through domination of others

3 *Ego-defensive needs.* The needs to protect the personality; to avoid ridicule and "loss of face"; to prevent loss of prestige; to avoid or to obtain relief from anxiety

The advertiser has little opportunity to use the physiological needs in his or her work. Food is advertised but rarely on the elementary message that it will prevent starvation. On the other hand, most advertising messages should strive to show consumers how the product will fulfill one or more of their socially acquired needs. George Gallup, the public opinion pollster, has also studied advertising for half a century. He contends that advertisers "have concentrated far too much attention on the product and far too little on the need the product satisfies."[33]

Perception

The perception process starts when an individual receives a stimulus through one of the five senses—such as hearing a noise or smelling an aroma. Repeated stimuli can cause a predictable response, based on the capacity of the human memory. For example, a truck driver stops at red lights as a type of learned behavior.

If we consider any sensory input to behavior as a stimulus, and any definable output of behavior as a response, we have a rudimentary explanation of basic behavioral patterns, but one that is wholly inadequate to clarify normal adult behavior. First, we must keep in mind that a stimulus is not necessarily an external phenomenon, like a

[32] James Bayton, "Motivation, Cognition, Learning: Basic Factors in Consumer Behavior," *Journal of Marketing,* vol. XXII, p. 282, January 1958.

[33] George Gallup, "How Advertising Works," *Journal of Advertising Research,* p. 8, June 1974.

THE $60 DIFFERENCE

The Heritage craftsman guides the dowels into place, extends the curve of the arm to the back and sets the basic design. When a chair, or any piece of furniture, takes its shape from its frame and not just the bulge of its padding, only more money can buy it.

You might be able to buy a chair that looks like one from this pair for about $260. But you won't be buying the same chair or one that's even close. As time will tell when the springs go their own way, the fabric pulls away from a welt and your chair loses the comfort and the looks you bought in the showroom. Upholstered in this elegant cut velvet, one of these Heritage swivel base lounge chairs will cost you about $320. Or $60 more than its look-alike. Cut to form the basic design of

this chair alone, the parts of the frame were carved or cut and locked into one solid unit. The springs it supported were tied to the frame and to one another. Then the Heritage upholsterer stretched, shaped and stitched layer on layer of batting over the lines set down by the frame. By the time the fabric was fitted, the contours of the chair were true to the frame, the final repeat of the basic design. The higher price on this chair, or any other piece of furniture

we make, buys something that only more money can buy. Whether it's our concern for the support that holds the lines and ensures the look of a chair. Or the way we'll take the time to bring a wood to its fullest beauty by hand... because no machine or shortcut method can match it. When you see work like this, you'll find the Heritage name. Stitched on the platform under the cushions of this pair of Heritage chairs. Burned inside the drawers of a mahogany

Heritage lowboy. Stitched under the cushions and swinging on a hangtag from a crushed velvet Heritage sofa. If you would like to know more about Heritage and see how it could fit into your home, send two dollars for a Heritage catalog collection and room planning kit to Dept. HG-9-67, Heritage Furniture Company, High Point, North Carolina.

HERITAGE
A division of Drexel Enterprises, Inc.

FIGURE 11.13
Quality of product is the basic theme of a furniture advertiser.

beam of light on the retina of the eye, or an advertisement on television or in a magazine. The term includes internal physical changes, such as an accelerated heartbeat, or the presence of a virus in the respiratory system. Second, we must remember that the individual's interpretation of any stimulus depends on perception and learning, processes which intervene between sensory input, or stimuli, and the output of behavior, or response. Third, we should not make the mistake of thinking of behavior as activated by a single motive; more often than not, the individual is driven by a combination of several motives. The behavior we describe as marriage may be traced to a combination of such motives as the biological sex urge, a desire for comfort, and a desire for social approval, to name only a few possibilities. The purchase of a new auto might well involve the urge to be superior, the need for social approval, and the desire for more comfort or convenience.

It should be clear that not every signal or cue sent out by an advertiser is fully and accurately received or digested. There is a great deal of selectivity going on in the process of perception. A popular word in the lexicon of the consumer behaviorist is *selective perception*. This means that the "human mind is highly selective with regard to what signals are allowed to contribute to the learning process."[34] Three kinds of selectivity occur:

1 *Selective exposure*. The customer attempts to encounter only those media and messages that are important to him and consistent with his deeply held values and beliefs.
2 *Selective perception*. The customer will "see" or "hear" certain signals and not see or hear others.
3 *Selective retention*. The retention and forgetting rates will differ among incoming signals.[35]

In other words, the advertiser must design a message that the consumer will be willing to receive, or else he or she will use the filter each individual possesses to avoid the message's impact.

Reinforcement and Habit

Reinforcement and habit are phases of the learning process of particular interest to the marketer or advertiser. When achievement of the goal results in satisfaction or gratification of the motives activating the behavior, the result is *reinforcement*, and when the same needs are aroused later, the individual will tend to repeat the same process to achieve the same goal. If brand X provides you with a high degree of satisfaction, when the same motives arise at a later date you will have a tendency to buy brand X again. Moreover, effective advertisements for brand X will act as secondary reinforcements, increasing the odds of your choosing brand X.

Continued reinforcement tends to reduce the importance of thinking in behavior patterns until ultimately the connection between stimuli and responses becomes practically automatic. The result is *habit*, an important timesaving response, which does not depend on decision-making mental activity for either its formation or its execution. Thinking may even interfere with habit performance.

---

[34] Larson et al., op. cit., p. 73.
[35] Ibid.

The weaker the motivational forces that may be satisfied by a product, the greater the chance that the product will be a habit purchase. This psychological concept is often of considerable importance in the analysis of brand preferences. Strong motivation may lead to the purchase of a type of product; yet the selection of the particular brand may result from habit. The main (or "preponent") motive activating the purchase of a soft drink may be a strong, biogenic thirst, but the individual's order for a "Coke" may result from continued reinforcement that has reached the habit stage. The strength of such habit behavior depends on the degree to which the individual will persist in it after it has ceased providing satisfaction.

Learning Theories and Advertising

Steuart Henderson Britt claims "that learning theorists and experimentalists have contributed practical and testable methods of behavior-influence that are relevant to marketing communications."[36] For example, he indicates that "a dichotomy exists between *intentional learning* and *incidental learning*," with the latter having important implications in the promotional aspects of marketing, for "most advertising messages are presented to people who either are doing something or relaxing."[37] This fact obviously has significance for the writer of advertising copy.

There is some general agreement on how people learn, regardless of whether it is "a concept, a message, information about a brand, or even such things as typing and bicycle riding."[38] Learning is slow at first, but with repetition it increases rapidly until a plateau is reached, after which it slows down again. With more repetition, a new plateau may be reached.[39] Thus, an important question for the media planner is how many exposures the target audience should receive. Research into the matter is inconclusive, but Kassarjian believes that "the massive repetition of an advertisement may be sufficient to induce the consumer to buy the product advertised."[40] This introduces the obverse side of learning, *forgetting*, and the intriguing question of the *decay of advertising effects*. If the earlier learning involved reinforcement or rewards, the fact would have an effect on the decay rate. There is evidence that after several repetitions, or fewer if the ad is memorable, forgetting is not complete for many years and even many decades.[41] Sometimes a so-called sleeper effect takes place wherein there is

[36] S. H. Britt, "Applying Learning Principles to Marketing," *MSU Business Topics*, Spring 1975, p. 5.
[37] Ibid., pp. 5–6.
[38] Harold H. Kassarjian, "Applications of Consumer Behavior to the Field of Advertising, *Journal of Advertising*, 1974, vol. 3, no. 3, p. 11, 1974.
[39] Loc. cit.
[40] Ibid., p. 12.
[41] Loc. cit.

actually a lack of decay of a learned response after an advertising campaign has ended and the consumer is no longer exposed to the message.[42] The effects of advertising messages may be difficult to eradicate; passage of time alone is not sufficient. The argument for corrective advertising, discussed in Chapter 20, is based upon this premise.

Opinions, Attitudes, Beliefs, and Prejudices

"Opinions," "attitudes," "beliefs," and "prejudices" are terms which describe learned tendencies to respond favorably or unfavorably to certain situations, persons, or objects. All involve the positive or negative classification of stimulus objects in relation to the individual's experience and goals, or the making of value judgments that accept or reject stimuli. Such preferences may involve rational or intellectual processes, but they always include emotional reactions: they are friendly or unfriendly; respectful or disrespectful; "I like" or "I don't like." The research technique of psychographics, as discussed earlier, is particularly useful in ferreting out opinions, attitudes, beliefs, and prejudices.

A woman who buys her apparel from the same dress shop year after year and the man who buys the same kind of golf ball are said to have favorable attitudes toward the shop and the brand of golf ball. Institutional advertising has as its purpose the stimulation and reinforcement of such long-range, favorable attitudes toward the advertiser. The following example explains the importance of the relationship between attitudes and drives, or motives:

> Some stimulus . . . makes the individual aware of the fact that he is hungry. Such a drive, however, does not function by itself; he almost always has no generalized craving for food but seeks a particular kind more or less in accordance with his everyday existence. He wants food, but an attitude-induced drive must also be satisfied. The goal response—the eating of the food—is then determined both by the hunger drive and the accompanying attitude. As an individual, he will be completely satisfied only when the tension produced by both drives is reduced.[43]

A prejudice is merely a negative attitude, and while it is possible to distinguish between attitudes, opinions, and beliefs in terms of their generality or the intensity of feeling involved, these distinctions are relatively unimportant except to psychologists and sociologists. There are no hard-and-fast boundaries for the terms, so that one person's opinion may be another person's attitude and still another person's belief.

[42] Loc. cit.

[43] Leonard W. Doob, *Public Opinion and Propaganda*, Henry Holt and Company, Inc., 1958, p. 29. Reprinted by permission of Holt, Rinehart and Winston, Inc.

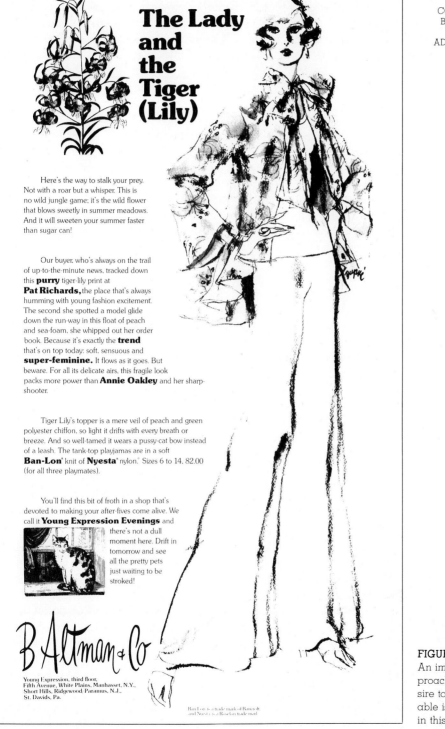

The Lady and the Tiger (Lily)

Here's the way to stalk your prey. Not with a roar but a whisper. This is no wild jungle game; it's the wild flower that blows sweetly in summer meadows. And it will sweeten your summer faster than sugar can!

Our buyer, who's always on the trail of up-to-the-minute news, tracked down this **purry** tiger-lily print at **Pat Richards,** the place that's always humming with young fashion excitement. The second she spotted a model glide down the run-way in this float of peach and sea-foam, she whipped out her order book. Because it's exactly the **trend** that's on top today: soft, sensuous and **super-feminine.** It flows as it goes. But beware. For all its delicate airs, this fragile look packs more power than **Annie Oakley** and her sharp-shooter.

Tiger Lily's topper is a mere veil of peach and green polyester chiffon, so light it drifts with every breath or breeze. And so well-tamed it wears a pussy-cat bow instead of a leash. The tank-top playjamas are in a soft **Ban-Lon'** knit of **Nyesta'** nylon.' Sizes 6 to 14, 82.00 (for all three playmates).

You'll find this bit of froth in a shop that's devoted to making your after-fives come alive. We call it **Young Expression Evenings** and there's not a dull moment here. Drift in tomorrow and see all the pretty pets just waiting to be stroked!

B Altman & Co

Young Expression, third floor,
Fifth Avenue, White Plains, Manhasset, N.Y.,
Short Hills, Ridgewood, Paramus, N.J.,
St. Davids, Pa.

Ban Lon is a trademark of Bancroft
and Nyesta is a Rosedon trademark

FIGURE 11.14
An image approach to the desire to be fashionable is employed in this retail ad.

The person charged with creating advertising messages needs, thus, to know that the mass audience to which the advertiser wishes to communicate consists of individuals who possess motivations, who perceive and learn and hold opinions, attitudes, beliefs, and prejudices. All these factors make the communication task a difficult one.

SUMMARY

Planning effective advertising requires a knowledge of the behavioral sciences. The insights of psychology and sociology provide an explanation for the communication process between the advertiser and the consumer and for the reasons consumers will favor one product over another or make their buying decisions. What makes humans think and act is a complex question; therefore, the advertiser should know the basic principles guiding people in their roles as consumers, which is best explained by psychological and sociological research and theories.

All humans have a desire to know, and in the role of consumer, an individual is actually an information processor who uses accumulated data to assist in problem solving. The presence of defense mechanisms and cognitive dissonance may modify such behavior.

Social and individual influences determine consumer behavior. Culture provides a significant influence upon such actions, for it leads to the development of personal value systems which in turn determine how people view products. The social class to which an individual belongs also affects the symbolic value that products may possess for him or her. Reference groups, opinion leaders, and especially the family are other sources of group influence upon a person's behavior. Within the family its own life cycle and its life-style are additional influencing forces. Anyone designing mass communications messages needs to know as much as possible about these social and cultural influences upon members of the target audience. If the message does not fit into the audience's collective value system, there will be no communication. Furthermore, products and brands have images which must be matched with the self-images of consumers.

Individual differences among consumers are caused by motivations, perceptual levels, and learning ability. Actions of consumers are affected by a number of needs, drives, or motives. Some of these are physiological; others are psychogenic or acquired. Lists of needs or wants are useful in providing a check sheet of the more common consumer desires or buying motives when an advertiser seeks to reach a specific market segment. How the consumer perceives a situation is also important, for through selective perception a message may be filtered out from the potential receiver's consciousness. Advertising, as a piece of information, should be constructed with the laws of learning in mind. Opinion, attitudes, beliefs, and prejudices are also forces to be taken into consideration. Moreover, the consumer's mental state about the product influences what message is suitable for effective communication to the target audience.

QUESTIONS FOR DISCUSSION

1 What is the difference between social influences and individual influences on consumer behavior? Which is the more significant? Why?

2 When we say that the marketer seeks people "who are capable of deriving satisfaction from the product," what does this mean? Why is it of importance to someone creating advertising messages for the marketer?

3 Contrast the philosophies of the "behaviorist" and "cognitive" schools of psychology. Which do you subscribe to? Why?

4 Describe a personal experience where the theory of cognitive dissonance seemed to be operating.

5 Name three social trends which you discern to be emerging in American life today which will be of critical importance to advertising plans and strategies in the future.

6 Explain the influences of the following on the behavior of consumers: culture, social class, reference groups, opinion leaders, and the family.

7 Explain the concept of life-style. Cite specific examples where advertisers appear to be employing the concept in their current advertising strategies.

8 Take each of the five steps in Maslow's hierarchy of needs model and explain the role of advertising at each stage.

9 What is "selective perception"? Cite a personal example of its operation, possibly by a friend or a member of your family.

10 If you were planning a campaign for (a) make-up for thirty-five-to-forty-five-year-old women, (b) stereo equipment, (c) ski equipment, what aspects of consumer behavior do you feel would most influence the purchase of these items?

FOR FURTHER REFERENCE

Berelson, Bernard, and Gary A. Steiner: *Human Behavior: An Inventory of Scientific Findings*, Harcourt, Brace & World, Inc., New York, 1964.

Engel, James F., David T. Kollat, and Roger D. Blackwell: *Consumer Behavior*, 2d ed., Holt, Rinehart and Winston, Inc., New York, 1973.

Kassarjian, Harold H., and Thomas S. Robertson: *Perspectives in Consumer Behavior*, rev. ed., Scott, Foresman and Company, Glenview, Ill., 1973.

Katona, George: *Psychological Economics*, Elsevier, New York, 1975.

Markin, Jr., Rom J.: *Consumer Behavior: A Cognitive Orientation*, The Macmillan Company, New York, 1974.

Robertson, Thomas S., *Consumer Behavior*, Scott, Foresman and Company, Glenview, Ill., 1970.

Schramm, Wilbur (ed.): *The Process and Effects of Mass Communications*, The University of Illinois Press, Urbana, 1954.

Walters, C. Glenn: *Consumer Behavior: Theory and Practice*, Richard D. Irwin, Inc., Homewood, Ill., 1974.

Wells, William D. (ed.): *Life Style and Psychographics*, American Marketing Association, Chicago, 1974.

CHAPTER 12

ADVERTISING COPYWRITING

Given a basic understanding of our product or service, and knowledge of our intended media audiences (in terms of both demographics and psychographics), we can focus on the techniques, processes, and skills involved in creating effective advertising messages. First, however, we must have a clear conception of what "creativity" really is.

The creative writer—poet, novelist, playwright—takes well-known words and phrases and develops a fresh, often brilliant manner of presentation. Thus, a household pet, plus a hazy weather condition, in the hands of a Carl Sandburg turns into the classic: "Fog comes on little cat feet. . . ." And while anyone who so desires might write about revolution, there is only one Charles Dickens and one *Tale of Two Cities*. Creativity may also be expressed through painting or music. Even a child can draw a picture of a smiling woman, but Leonardo da Vinci's artistic talents produced the *Mona Lisa*; likewise, the creative genius of Anton Dvorak displayed simple "impressions of America" in the masterpiece we know as the *New World* Symphony.

In each of these cases, the creator's purpose was self-expression. Similarly, when a student is assigned a creative writing or art project, he or she gives imagination free rein and lets ideas come together as they will. The purpose is to achieve a tangible representation of what the mind's eye can already see—or hear—or feel; and in most cases, the author aims to create in others an understanding of and appreciation for his or her artistic output. By translating ideas and impressions into poems, pictures, or other works, each composer gains personal satisfaction and creates enjoyment for others who come in contact with his efforts.

DISCIPLINED CREATIVITY

Creativity in advertising most assuredly draws on "pure" writing talents, but, as should be obvious by now, the nature of the business demands a certain kind of discipline not found in creative writing circles. Granted, every writer, no matter what his field, is expected to be adept at spelling, grammar, and punctuation, and to be familiar with current idiomatic expressions. Successful advertising, however, requires knowledge of overall marketing environments and awareness of consumer learning abilities; creativity in advertising, therefore, must be *disciplined* creativity.

The advertising copywriter must still write with a purpose—but this time it is to achieve *clients'* objectives, instead of his own. Self-expression gives way to expression of features or attributes of particular products and services—presented in psychological terms with which the ultimate audience can identify. In other words the copywriter translates the *selling points* of a client's product or service into *benefits* for those selected consumers whom the advertiser has chosen to reach through one or more of the mass media.

In this case, the "creativity" involved is really the opposite of pure freedom of imagination. As the copywriter creates, he or she builds messages according to specific plans, to fulfill specific objectives. In the words of research practitioner Alfred Politz, advertising creativity:

> . . . has to follow rules which are guided by a well-defined purpose, by an analysis of the thoughts supplied by imagination, by a selection of the useful ones which meet the purpose. The analysis and the final arrangement of surviving ideas is impossible without the employment of our logical faculties.[1]

Certain "checks" must therefore be placed on the free rein ordinarily assumed by the creative person writing purely in accordance with inspirations of the moment. For example:

1 The "communication" check (will the intended ad achieve its assigned persuasive task and thereby help sell its product?)
2 The "image" check (is the proposed message in line with the existing or desired advertiser image—in terms, for example, of ecological concerns, product safety, or company dependability, and will it be legally and ethically sound?)
3 The "audience" check (is the proposed message on target with regard to audience predispositions?)
4 The "media" check (will the intended ad be able to do its job memorably, believably, and convincingly, given inherent time or space limitations, and is it feasible in terms of production facilities and cost?)

Note well that these checks need *not* be considered *restrictions* on advertising creativity! Nowhere in today's society is it more necessary for writers to be allowed creative freedom than in advertising, where the mass media daily—hourly—devour new ideas with insatiable appetites. As long as copywriters are *disciplined* in the marketing and behavioral spheres relevant to their particular advertising situations, they are free to run the creative gamut—from Prudential's "Piece of the Rock" to Pillsbury's Doughboy.

THE NATURE OF IDEAS

It is important to point out that while *imagination* is an innate human quality, truly creative ideas are not often easy to find. Advertising

[1] Alfred Politz, "Creativeness and Imagination," *Journal of Advertising*, vol. 4, no. 3, p. 14, Summer 1975.

copywriters must be *doers* as well as *thinkers*. They participate—soak up as much of life as they possibly can—for their work demands a heavy reliance on background and prior experiences (a movie or play, a symphony or song, a trip or an accident, a day on the farm, a walk through the park, even a visit to a local tavern) for help with advertising ideas. They study products from the inside out and from top to bottom. They scrutinize intended audiences (wants and needs, likes and dislikes, media and shopping habits) and the competition (products and ads) in painstaking detail. They read and watch, listen and remember, analyze and experiment until they find the "right" words to express the theme, or concept, or idea which is the beginning of a message or series of messages.

Creativity, then, is almost always based on a systematic, logical accumulation of *facts* that forms the foundation on which insight and ingenuity can build. Both heredity and environment do contribute to creative talent, but effort and motivation are important forces in its cultivation. In "creating," we associate known facts (or factors: people, objects, issues, events) with one another in order to develop unique relationships. Or, as veteran advertising man James Webb Young has long maintained, creativity is the combination of existing elements in new and unexpected ways.[2] Or as John Matthews, chairman of the Plans Board of Draper Daniels, notes:

> Many times the most creative thing you can do in your advertising is not to create something new—but to utilize something so old you may have forgotten you had it. Not to discover, but to uncover; not to innovate, but to renovate; not to seek new horizons but to capitalize on an element which is right under your nose waiting for you to recognize its potential.[3]

Remember, though, that no matter how original an idea may be, it must be related to reality or help solve a problem to be considered creative. Clearly, in any case, fact gathering must precede writing; all the "magic of words" a copywriter is able to employ will not produce a successful advertisement if the facts about products or prospects are incomplete or false—or if the evaluation of them is inaccurate or superficial.

DIGGING FOR FACTS

Before proceeding further, we should clarify what the word "facts" ought to mean to an advertising copywriter. Definitely, a fact is something that has actual existence, an event. It is a fact that we are

[2] James Webb Young; *A Technique for Producing Ideas*, Crain Communications, Inc., Chicago, 1960, pp. 25–41.
[3] John E. Matthews, "A Two-Course Survey of 'Creative Country,'" *Journal of Advertising*, vol. 4, no. 2, p. 15, Spring 1975.

reading this book. It is a fact that the words we read are set in 10 point Memphis Light type. These are *absolute* facts. The copywriter is concerned with absolute facts. Is the price $2.95 or $3.95? Is the fabric Dacron or nylon? Does this engine deliver 105 or 150 horsepower at 3,000 rpm?

But many of the "facts" which are important to the writer of advertising are not so easy to substantiate by observation or test. Is it really a fact that the initial impetus for the purchase of an automobile comes from the husband in two out of three families, as suggested by a 1958 study?[4] We can't be sure. As the introduction to this particular study carefully states, the findings cannot be projected to the total population because of the inadequate size of the sample. (Moreover, are family car-buying patterns the same today as they were in 1958?) Nevertheless, lacking evidence to the contrary—or the time and money to complete a study which is statistically projectable to the entire market—the copywriter must make use of the "facts" he or she does have. Nor does fact gathering or research necessarily provide final answers. What it does is reduce the probability of error. As Charles K. Ramond summed up the function of his department when he was manager of advertising research for Du Pont:

> Research cannot substitute for judgment. Research is fundamentally an aid to the decision-making processes. It is simply a technique for minimizing the area in which pure judgment must act.[5]

The mechanics of the copywriter's fact gathering can be quite complex, involving extensive market and psychological research methods, or they may be rather simple. In retail-department-store advertising, for example, the copywriter is usually furnished a "fact sheet" about the merchandise by the buyer in charge of the department. Frequently this fact sheet and an examination of the merchandise give the writer enough data to prepare effective retail copy. If not, the copywriter must be prepared to dig for additional facts.

Whether the copy is aimed at a local retail market, a national consumer market, or a special group of industrial prospects, the copywriter needs to explore a number of different areas in looking for information about the product and the prospects for it. While some areas are more important than others in specific copy assignments, the answers to certain basic questions are needed to write effective copy for almost any product and any form of advertising. Twelve such basic fact-gathering questions—six about the product itself and six about the people who use it—are worthy of consideration now.[6]

---

[4] Daniel Starch et al., *Male vs. Female*, an exploratory depth interview study, Fawcett Publications, Inc., New York, 1958, p. 108.

[5] Quoted by permission from a speech delivered at the annual conference of the Advertising Research Foundation, New York, Oct. 2, 1958.

[6] The authors are indebted to Charles L. Whittier's *Creative Advertising*, Holt, Rinehart and Winston, Inc., New York, 1955, chap. 5, pp. 56–60, for the basic approach to these questions. By permission of Holt, Rinehart and Winston, Inc.

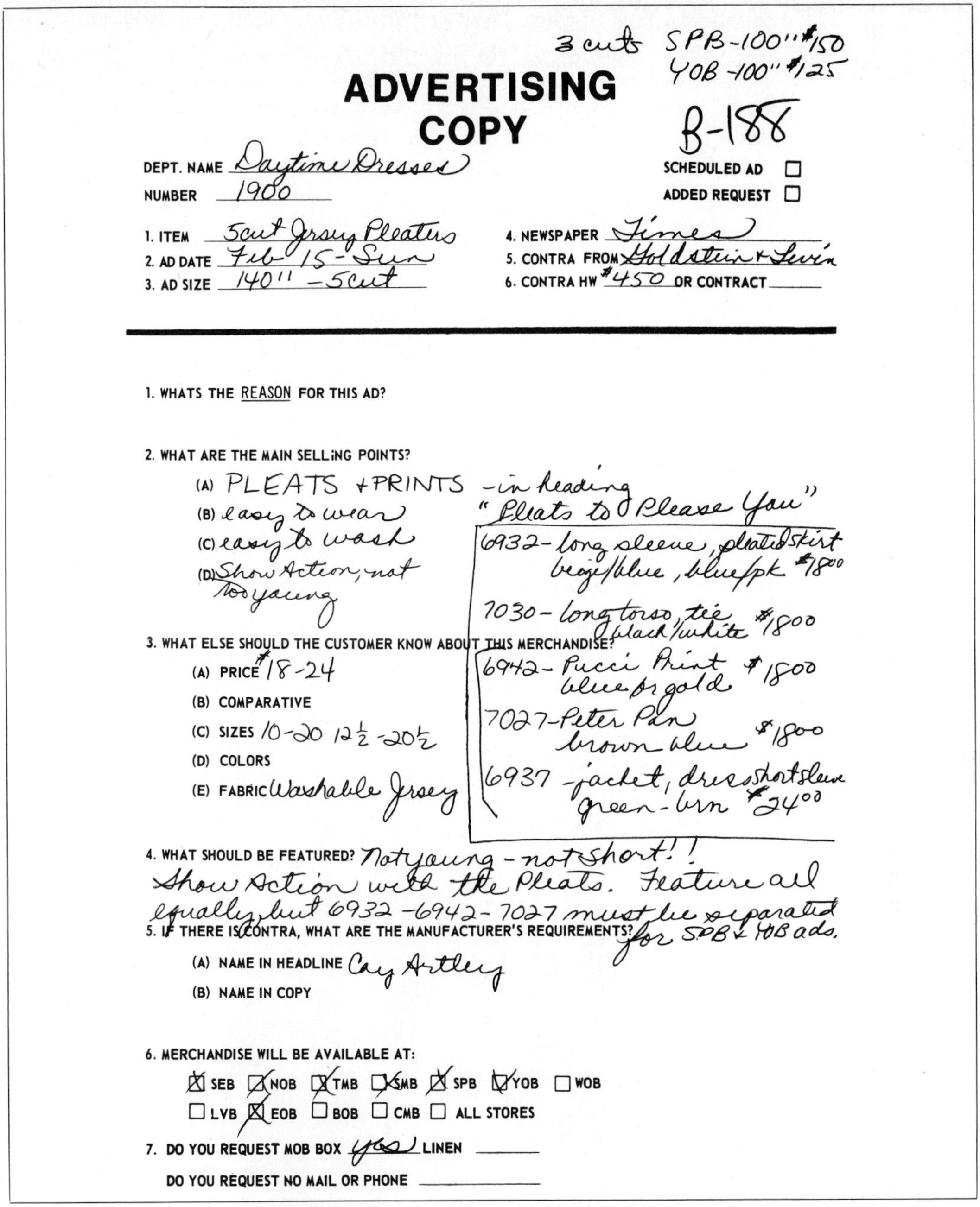

ADVERTISING COPY

3 cuts SPB-100" #150
YOB-100" #125

B-188

DEPT. NAME *Daytime Dresses*
NUMBER 1900

SCHEDULED AD ☐
ADDED REQUEST ☐

1. ITEM 5 cut Jersey Pleaters
2. AD DATE Feb 15 – Sun
3. AD SIZE 140" – 5 cut

4. NEWSPAPER *Times*
5. CONTRA FROM Goldstein & Levin
6. CONTRA HW #450 OR CONTRACT _____

1. WHATS THE <u>REASON</u> FOR THIS AD?

2. WHAT ARE THE MAIN SELLING POINTS?
   (A) PLEATS + PRINTS – in heading "Pleats to Please You"
   (B) easy to wear
   (C) easy to wash
   (D) Show Action, not too young

   6932 – long sleeve, pleated skirt beige/blue, blue/pk $18.00
   7030 – long torso, tie black/white $18.00
   6942 – Pucci Print blue & gold $18.00
   7027 – Peter Pan brown blue $18.00
   6937 – jacket, dress short sleeve green – brn $24.00

3. WHAT ELSE SHOULD THE CUSTOMER KNOW ABOUT THIS MERCHANDISE?
   (A) PRICE $18-24
   (B) COMPARATIVE
   (C) SIZES 10-20 12½-20½
   (D) COLORS
   (E) FABRIC Washable Jersey

4. WHAT SHOULD BE FEATURED? Not young – not short!! Show Action with the Pleats. Feature all equally, but 6932 – 6942 – 7027 must be separated for SPB & YOB ads.

5. IF THERE IS CONTRA, WHAT ARE THE MANUFACTURER'S REQUIREMENTS?
   (A) NAME IN HEADLINE Cay Artley
   (B) NAME IN COPY

6. MERCHANDISE WILL BE AVAILABLE AT:
   ☒ SEB ☒ NOB ☒ TMB ☒ SMB ☒ SPB ☒ YOB ☐ WOB
   ☐ LVB ☒ EOB ☐ BOB ☐ CMB ☐ ALL STORES

7. DO YOU REQUEST MOB BOX yes LINEN _____
   DO YOU REQUEST NO MAIL OR PHONE _____

FIGURE 12.1
On standard forms called *fact sheets*, department stores give copywriters information needed to prepare an ad. [*The Bon Marche, Seattle.*]

Essential Facts about the Product

What Is It Made Of? The ingredients or raw materials that go into a product may be a source of effective sales ideas. For years the Stroh Brewery has made good use of the fact that Stroh's beer is fire-brewed. The slogan "Brewed with pride for 200 years" has called attention to the element of quality. The Campbell Soup Company has attracted a significant segment of the market to its "chunky" varieties through its claim that the soups are "so chunky you'll be tempted to eat 'em with a fork." And who can doubt the effectiveness of McDonald's famous (though heretofore highly unorthodox) product description: "Two-all-beef-patties-special-sauce-lettuce-cheese-pickles-onions-on-a-sesame-seed-bun"!

Even the absence of certain ingredients or components may contribute to effective selling points. Mr. Coffee advertisements proudly proclaim: "No oils, no sediment, no bitterness."

Services, of course, have ingredients or raw materials just as products do. The facilities, equipment, personalities, and performance of a service organization are what the service is made of—the "raw materials." One of these in the Delta Air Lines service is frequent and convenient scheduling of flights to and from popular destinations:

She's all you expect Japan to be.

Japanese womanhood blossoms with a 1,200 year-old tradition of gracious personal service. Come with us to any of 35 great cities around the world and experience what we mean. You'll be pampered like never before. For what other airline hostess ever had such an auspicious background? Or such a tradition to uphold?

JAPAN AIR LINES

Fly JAL around the world. 24 countries. 35 cities. For reservations see the worldwide airline of Japan, or your travel agent.

FIGURE 12.2
Services, like products, have "ingredients" that distinguish them from competitors. Here Japan Air Lines dramatizes the tradition of gracious personal service as a benefit enjoyed by its passengers. [Botsford/Ketchum, Inc.]

"Delta is ready when you are." Greyhound has used "Leave the driving to us" to emphasize carefree bus travel, and the Avis auto-rental system turned a negative attribute into a positive one by stressing its goal to "try harder" to please customers (to make up for the fact that its business was not the largest in the field).

How Well Is It Made?   The same cavity-fighting ingredient, stannous fluoride, goes into a number of different toothpastes. But Aim puts that fluoride in the form of a gel so it can "spread good taste faster." Or a company might refer to its design and development without actually naming ingredients at all. Turtle Wax has made particularly good use of radio by "dramatizing" that "*nothing* [rain, hail, sleet, or other hazards] can crack the turtle's back." Finally product construction or composition may be indicated through focus on sheer "value" or end result. Johnson & Johnson's baby shampoo expanded its market from children to entire families with its "Gentle enough to use every day" promise.

What Does It Do?   Almost any product may provide more than one satisfaction for the user. A new all-weather topcoat will keep us warm on chilly days and dry on wet ones. The weatherproofing may reduce pressing bills, and the design and fabric may be such that the coat does not go out of style quickly or show wear as soon as other topcoats. It may improve our appearance and bring admiring comments from friends.

It is the copywriter's task to determine the primary satisfaction or need the product fills and not allow lesser ones to obscure it. An automatic dishwasher may improve the appearance of a kitchen, and it may result in more sanitary dishes and glassware, but the primary reason for owning one is to make a recurrent household chore easier. Thus, the Drackett Products Company advertises its Mr. Muscle oven cleaner as the one which "self-scours overnight—while you sleep." And Tide detergent, which *could* center creative efforts around an attractive price, an easy-to-handle-and-store container, or a reliable company name, chose instead to speak directly to consumers' demands with "Gets out the dirt kids get into."

How Does It Compare with Competition?   Few if any products can be rated as the unqualified best in the total field of all products with similar uses. A product that possesses certain advantages is also likely to possess certain disadvantages. Furthermore, what may be a strong advantage to one type of user may be unimportant to another. The advertising writer must determine which of the advantages the product offers against competition are most important to the particular segment of the market at which the advertising is aimed, and what evidence there is to support these claims. One washing machine may

There are more than 375 Saab dealers nationwide. Overseas delivery available. Luggage area of all 3 cars measured by volume.

This Saab gives you durable construction like Volvo,

the luxury of a comfortable interior like Audi,

and more luggage room than Volvo and Audi put together.

FIGURE 12.3
In this ad, Saab tells its product story through the technique of side-by-side comparison. [*Cox & Co., Inc.*]

The WagonBack by Saab. Like our other Saabs, the WagonBack comes with such standard features as front wheel drive, rack and pinion steering, roll cage construction and power assisted four wheel disc brakes.
    Unlike any other car in its class, the WagonBack converts from a 5 passenger sedan (with rear seat up) to 53 cu. feet of pure station wagon (with rear seat down). Over 6 feet of flat floor room.
    In short, it's a sedan when you want it and a wagon when you need it.

It's what a car should be.

have an agitating action which will clean badly soiled clothes more thoroughly and more quickly than another machine that is designed differently but sells at the same price. The first machine may be hard on delicate fabrics; however, parents of young children might prefer it. Parents with older children or people with no children might find the second washer more satisfactory. The copywriter should talk to people who sell the product and people who use it and get their opinions on the product features that are most important.

Some product categories (for example, headache remedies or deodorants) feature side-by-side comparisons in their ads and commercials. Laboratory tests are often cited to support one brand's claim of superiority over specified others. Such practices are legal today if handled with restraint.

Advertising copy need not mention competing products by name, but may simply compare *uses*, as advertisements for Contac cold capsules have done. "Six, or three, or one" says the copy—"six tablets [two every four hours], three doses of liquid cold medicine [one every four hours], or just *one* Contac." On the other hand, a well-known pantyhose manufacturer sums up competitors' efforts with a memorable: "Gentlemen prefer Hanes."

How Can It Be Identified? The majority of marketing problems involve the creation or stimulation of selective rather than primary demand. Even when a new type of product is launched, the need or desire for which must be developed, the innovator strives to create a preference for his brand as well as for the new type of product, for he will rarely enjoy exclusive production for long. Competitors are quick to enter new and promising markets. In a few advertisements—notably those of the agricultural cooperatives responsible for the marketing of an entire crop under many different labels or brands, or the campaigns of all-industry associations or franchised monopolies—primary demand is the sole objective, and brand identification is unimportant.

With other products and services, however, it is the copywriter's responsibility to provide adequate product identification in the advertisement and to tell the reader how the product can be identified at the point of purchase. The objective, of course, is to make substitution difficult. In some cases this may be accomplished with nothing more than an illustration of or reference to the package or the trademark. Thus, Chicken of the Sea advises "Ask any mermaid," and, hence, reminds its media audiences to look for the mermaid pictured on its cans. Or "Ho, ho, ho," sings the TV jingle: "The little blue jug is Dynamo!" (Dynamo detergent).

In other cases, where the product is a component part, or a subordinate product or process, more careful instructions are needed. Thus Du Pont closes its advertisements for Dacron with suggestions such as "Ask for Enro shirts with Dacron. You'll like the way you look."

Some ads must do more than tell the prospect how to identify the product at the point of purchase. The writer must tell how to identify the point of purchase itself. Unless the advertisement is for a product which is on sale at every drugstore, supermarket, and restaurant cashier stand, such as cigarettes, gum, or candy bars, it may fail to accomplish its objective if it does not tell the reader where to buy the product. Everyone knows that Chevrolets are sold by authorized Chevrolet dealers, but many people may not know that the Opel is sold by Buick dealers. Cosmetics can be purchased in drugstores, variety stores, specialty shops, department stores, and even "food" stores. The copywriter should know where the brand is sold and let the audience know.

How Much Does It Cost?   In almost all retail advertising, price is an essential element in the copy and is given display emphasis in proportion to its strength as a sales point. In much national advertising, at least in the United States, it is difficult to quote retail prices because they vary from area to area and frequently from store to store. Nevertheless, the copywriter should know the recommended retail price of clients' products (and of competitive products), and should be able to give prospects some idea of price range or cost. If a specific product costs more than competitive ones, there must be a reason why people will pay more for it—a reason that may be used to attract other buyers.

Essential Facts about the Prospects

Is It Used by Men, Women, or Both?   In most instances, women buy their own foundation garments and shaving cream is used by men. Both men and women use deodorants, drive automobiles, watch television, and drink Coca-Cola. The advertising writer needs to find out whether the product is used by men, women, or both, and if by both, which sex accounts for the larger share of the market.

What Age Group Dominates?   Current studies indicate that young adults are more likely to drink beer than are older people. Children are certainly the big users of popsicles and bubble gum, but they are unlikely prospects for shares in mutual investment funds or air travel to South America. Men over sixty are poor prospects for retirement income insurance. They may have a strong desire for this insurance, but it's too late for most of them to accumulate the income they want. Both sexes and all ages are prospects for record albums, but if the particular album happens to be rock music, the copywriter will do well to aim the message at high school and college students. Ten-year-olds are rarely prospects for portable typewriters, but in another five years, as they get into high school, they will be good typewriter prospects. As people change in age, they change in needs and in desires.

Is Income a Critical Factor?   Traditionally income levels have been an important consideration in determining who are prospects for products or services. The basis for this was not only the ability to pay for the product, but the assumption that income was a prime determinant of social status, and hence of purchasing preferences. While it is true today that few men with incomes below $25,000 a year are likely to buy a $5,000 diamond dinner ring, and few upper-income women buy cosmetics at variety stores, the significant changes in our society that are mentioned in Chapters 1 and 2 have made income a far less important determinant of consumer profiles than formerly.

Today, Department of Labor statistics show that large numbers of blue-collar families enjoy larger incomes than many white-collar families and even some professionals. And although 23 million American homes still show an income of less than $9,200 (the "low budget standard of living" level established by the Bureau of Labor), most of them *do* own television sets.[7] In fact, A. C. Nielsen figures indicate that *95 percent* of households in the United States earning less than $10,000 a year have at least one television.[8] Finally, one home in five in this country shows annual earnings of less than $5,000.[9] (Who is to say that the physical need for food and clothing is any more "pressing" than the psychological need for televised entertainment?)

Obviously, the desire for certain products, or the degree of satisfaction they deliver to users, does not necessarily parallel either total or disposable income. Although the relation of income to buying habits cannot be ignored, it may well be the least important factor for many products.

Does Occupation Affect the Purchase? It is obvious that certain vocational groups are of primary importance in the creation of trade, industrial, professional, and agricultural advertising. There are few prospects for seed corn who aren't farmers and few prospects for log-loading equipment who aren't in the lumber trade.

But differences among occupational groups may produce quite different market potentials for consumer products also. Refinery workers are better-than-average consumers of gum and chewing tobacco, because they cannot smoke on the job. Lawyers, doctors, and bankers prefer more conservative clothing than persons in the sales or entertainment fields. Sales representatives and sales engineers are better prospects for hotel or motel rooms than dentists, doctors, bankers, or college professors. But the effect of occupation is not restricted to the use that is made of the product.

There is a close relationship between occupation and social status, and the symbols of social status may vary widely among different occupations. The successful salesperson or young lawyer who entertains customers or clients may consider beer a negative status symbol; the construction superintendent, the teacher, or the supermarket manager may attach no social symbolism whatever to beer.

---

[7] 1975 Survey of Buying Power, Sales Management, July 21, 1975, p. A-29.
[8] As reported in *TV Basics 18*, Television Bureau of Advertising, New York.
[9] 1975 Survey of Buying Power.

Educational levels may also be important factors in determining the best markets for certain products. Proprietary medicines are purchased most frequently by people of limited education. Books and classical record albums appeal most strongly to better-educated families.

Who Influences the Purchase?   Some buying decisions are made by one person. Few of us consult anyone when we buy a candy bar, a package of gum, or a soft drink. A woman may ask for X brand of nylons or select a box of Y detergent from the supermarket shelf without considering the preferences, if any, of others in her family. On the other hand, if she is the wife of a dairy farmer, her choice of Y detergent may be influenced by her husband's preference for Y to clean his milking equipment. The breakfast cereal she buys is probably the brand little Johnny and Jane like best, and the coffee she drops into the market cart may be one her husband prefers.

While the husband in most cases is responsible for the purchase of life insurance, especially in middle- and lower-income families, studies indicate that a high percentage of the decisions to buy are influenced by the wife. Although, most often, the wife is the actual user of household appliances, such as refrigerators, ranges, and dishwashers, the husband and wife jointly make the buying decision. Secretaries don't buy office typewriters, but they may influence the boss's choice. Purchasing agents buy lubricants and forklifts for industry, but their buying may be strongly influenced by the chief engineer or the general manager. It is not enough for copywriters to know who buys the product. They must also know who influences the actual buying, and to what extent.

What Other Characteristics Identify the Best Prospects?   This last question is an open-end query for other possible common denominators that will help define potential buyers. For example, where people live obviously affects how they live and the products they use. Homeowners are better prospects for power mowers than apartment or mobile-home dwellers, whereas residents of Minnesota, Michigan, or Montana are better prospects for snow tires and antifreeze than people who live in Florida, Arizona, and California. On the other hand, people close to supplies of fresh fruit, vegetables, or fish are generally not heavy users of canned or frozen varieties; those living great distances away, however, must rely on such packaged items. These examples seem very obvious. But most of us tend to overlook the obvious as we search for the remote. As Justice Oliver Wendell Holmes once remarked, "We need education in the obvious more than investigation of the obscure."

A particular product, or brand, may enjoy much greater use among certain religious, racial, or nationality groups than among others, and such demographic factors as age, occupation, sex, or income may have little significance. A manufacturer of tomato products had established almost universal acceptance for his catsup, but in launching a new tomato paste his primary advertising effort was aimed at families of Latin extraction, because Italians, Spanish, and Portuguese have used tomato paste as a cooking ingredient for generations.

Or consider the fact that the city of Des Moines, Iowa, ranks 109 in the nation in drugstore sales, but 76 in sales of general merchandise. Miami, Florida, ranks 24 in sales of general merchandise, but 14 in the sale of furnishings.[10] Chapter 11 noted that demographic criteria have become less clearly defined through greater affluence and changing social values; hence, it has become increasingly important for the creator of advertising to discern psychographic patterns of attitudes and interests to which a specific product appeals.

An important warning, too, on gathering facts about prospects comes from Burton Durkee, advertising consultant and former vice-president of J. Walter Thompson Co. Durkee says such facts should be constantly updated (as often as information is available), and at least annually. Look, Durkee suggests, for changes in age groups, for changes in income and spending patterns, and particularly for changes in the characteristics of users and owners.[11]

ANALYSIS OF SELLING POINTS AND BENEFITS

Once the copywriter has collected all possible data about the product and the people who buy and use it, his or her role changes from fact gatherer to analyst. The next step is to develop from these facts a set of selling points and benefits.

A selling point for a product, generally, is a characteristic of the product itself which can contribute to the satisfaction of a need or desire of the buyer. A benefit, then, becomes the satisfaction received from purchase or use. *However, from a creative point of view, any relevant factor may form the basis of a selling point or benefit.* It is up to the copywriter to select the most valuable product "feature," or "value," or other item, and mentally match it with its "other half." For instance, suppose "ingredient X" is a detergent's most outstanding property. If it is used as a selling point, the idea might become: "Because this detergent has ingredient X (selling point), you get the satisfaction of whiter, brighter clothes (benefit)."

Or if it is used as a benefit, we could have: "Because of the extra

[10] *Spot Radio Rates and Data*, vol. 57, no. 10, Oct. 1, 1975.
[11] Burton R. Durkee, *How to Make Advertising Work*, McGraw-Hill Book Company, New York, 1967, p. 26.

time and special effort that went into this detergent's research and development (selling point), it now gives you the cleaning properties of ingredient X (benefit)." It all depends on how the copywriter chooses to present the sales message.

How are specific advertising appeals (selling points *and* benefits) selected from the (often long) list of potentials? First, the copywriter must remember that one of the most important functions he or she can perform for an advertiser is the creation of campaigns from the outside in—looking at the product through the eyes of *prospects* and seeing it as something *they* may willingly buy, rather than as something the advertiser must sell. Second, the copywriter notes that people are not interested in the advertiser's product per se; they are interested in the *rewards* the product promises—the values it holds in terms of want or need fulfillment. Tom Dillon, president and chief executive officer of Batten, Barton, Durstine & Osborn, maintains that:

> If an advertisement does not communicate how a product or service answers the prime prospect's problem, it is like an automobile with square wheels. It may be beautiful, entrancing, memorable, and a triumph of creative skills . . . but it will not function![12]

Charles L. Whittier, former creative vice-president of one of the largest American advertising agencies, suggests the copywriter use a checklist of basic advertising appeals or benefits the product may deliver. While it does not include all the wants buyers seek to satisfy, Whittier found this list of 10 questions a practical guide in his own creative work:

1 Will the product make the purchaser feel more important?
2 Will the product make the purchaser happier?
3 Will the product make the purchaser more comfortable?
4 Will the product make the purchaser more prosperous?
5 Will the product make the work easier for the purchaser?
6 Will the product give the purchaser greater security?
7 Will the product make the purchaser more attractive? Or better liked?
8 Will the product give the purchaser some distinction?
9 Will the product improve, protect, or maintain the purchaser's health?
10 Will the product appeal to the purchaser as a bargain?[13]

Many products promise more than one benefit, and many advertisements offer more than one basic advertising appeal. A new reading lamp may make the buyer more comfortable by providing better light, add some distinction to the home and so to the owner, and

---

[12] Tom Dillon, "The Triumph of Creativity over Communication," *Journal of Advertising*, vol. 4, no. 3, p. 10, Summer 1975.
[13] Whittier, op. cit., pp. 62–72.

at the same time appeal as a bargain because of relative price. However, the copywriter must analyze product selling points and the benefits they support and focus the message around one or two that are stronger than others in order to provide a central selling idea for the advertisement.

UNIQUE SELLING PROPOSITION

Development of this "central idea," or what is often called a *unique selling proposition*, is one of the copywriter's most difficult tasks. The USP (as it is often abbreviated) originated at the Ted Bates advertising agency in the early 1940s; as its famous originator, author, and agency vice-president, Rosser Reeves, has indicated, however, it has been picked up by hundreds of agencies and has spread from country to country. Unfortunately, it has also become a very *misused* concept; frequently, it is applied loosely and without understanding to slogans, clever phrases, unusual pictures or sound combinations—in short, to almost anything deemed "different" in copy, layout, or production. We hope our interpretation of the USP will come close to the one intended by Rosser Reeves, but every student of advertising creativity must ultimately develop his or her own.

A USP, Reeves claims, gives leverage to an advertising campaign—that extra tug that pulls consumers over the line of indecision or confusion to specific product preference, and then to brand loyalty. Now consider the three words individually.

"Unique"

"Unique" refers either to a unique feature of the brand itself (for example, only V-8 has this unique combination of eight vegetables in one juice) or to a claim not currently being made by competing brands (even though they could if they so desired!). Klear floor wax provides an example of this latter case with its long-used claim: "Dries clear as glass, never yellows." Note that Bravo floor wax does not yellow floors either! (We shall come back to this example shortly.)

It is important to point out that today's Federal Trade Commission does require substantiation of advertising claims, and may take issue with anything presented as "unique." Some copywriters feel that regulation tends to stifle advertising creativity; in any case, the challenge to create effectively *around* such laws is often monumental.

"Selling"

"Selling refers to sales value. The claim—whatever it is—must be strong enough, important enough, relevant enough, believable enough to convince consumers that it is in their own best interests to try the brand in question. Consider vegetable juice again, and suppose that V-8 had been developed by a person named Valdimir Van Vaulkenburg! Unique? Certainly—but the consumer's reaction will merely be: "So what? Who cares?"

There is no *sales value* in the name Vladimir Van Vaulkenburg. Even if he represented a well-known company, it is doubtful in this day and age that consumers would buy his juice without some idea of its taste and/or nutritional value. On the other hand, Chapter 11 discussed a number of factors which do motivate consumers today, such as health, convenience, and the desire to care for loved ones; these are the kinds of qualities copywriters should latch onto and develop in the food and beverage line.

"Proposition"

"Proposition" refers to a promise: that if the consumer buys a certain product, with the unique feature or claim attached (selling point), he or she will receive a specific benefit. In other words, the USP *matches a selling point with a consumer benefit, and does so in a unique way.*[14]

Now let us return to the floor-wax example. It is a fact that neither Klear nor Bravo (both made by Johnson Wax) will yellow floors. Also, both dry "as clear as glass." But *only Klear* has made that claim in that specific way. Klear's ability to dry clear (selling point) is matched with the benefit of worry-free, yellow-free floors, and the "glass" idea helps express the promise in a unique fashion. Advertisements for many years (in both magazines and television) have featured shining glass and sparkling decor along with the Klear sales message—a "beauty" theme for the homemaker interested in entertaining.

Conversely, advertising positioned Bravo floor wax quite differently. Research showed that working women with large families needed shiny floors that were easy to care for—ones that would not require a rewax job every time a child spilled a glass of milk (especially since Mother was tired after a long day away from home). So Bravo took "durability" as its selling point, "ease of maintenance" as its benefit theme, and the unique expression became: "So tough, you can wash it with detergent, and it comes up shining."

The point is, again, that Klear is tough, too! It withstands detergent, too! But Bravo zeroed in on the claim *as a USP*, while Klear stayed with the beauty treatment. The products became positioned (thanks to advertising) in consumers' minds as ones that fulfilled two different needs. One was primarily for beauty, and the other was primarily for ease of maintenance, although it was well known that Bravo gave a pretty shine and Klear was not hard to care for (secondarily). Here is an excellent example of advertising which caters to the divergent life-

[14] Rosser Reeves, *Reality in Advertising,* Alfred A. Knopf, Inc., New York, 1961, pp. 46–49.

styles discussed in Chapter 11. On the basis of physical composition alone, either Klear or Bravo would have been suitable for either group. Each of the two USPs, however, zeroed in on a separate set of audience wants and needs in terms of floor wax.

By now, the reader should begin to appreciate the complexity of this creative tool; USPs are difficult to grasp and apply—but they make or break most advertising campaigns. They are really so crucial to creative (and overall communicative) success that they should pretty well *fill* their respective advertisements. A maxim for copywriters is: one solid USP per ad—and if "additional" selling points and benefits are included, they had best be *few* in number and relatively *minor* in importance. (Otherwise, they overpower the USP.)

COPY DEFINED

Before proceeding further, it is important to note that the copywriter is equally concerned with *what* to say and show in an advertisement and *how best* to say and show it.

In a restricted sense, "copy" refers to typewritten material which is to be set in type for printed media or spoken by announcers or personalities for broadcast transmission. So the copywriter is often pictured as the person who writes the *words* for an advertising message.

Today, except for the classified columns of newspapers, few advertisements rely on words alone to deliver their messages. Printed advertisements make their impression through words *and* pictures, which support and supplement each other. Radio employs sound effects and music as well as words. Television combines the elements of both printed advertising and radio and adds another dimension—motion.

A broader meaning of the word "copy" includes all the elements in an advertising message, either printed or broadcast. In this sense, copy for a newspaper advertisement includes not only the reading matter—headlines, subheads, picture captions, slogans, and body copy—but also pictures, trademarks, borders, and other illustrations or visual symbols. Copy for a TV commercial includes not only the words to be spoken by the characters in the script but music, sound effects, illustrative material, and action and camera cues.

When we think of "copy" as all the elements that are to be included in the finished advertising message, the function of the copywriter and the techniques of writing advertising appear in their proper perspective. Whether the design for a particular advertisement starts from an illustration idea which is explained or amplified by words or whether the design begins with an idea expressed in words, which is dramatized and supported by illustration, the copywriter is concerned with every element that will appear in the complete message.

VISUALIZATION AND THE COPYWRITER

To the audience a printed advertisement or broadcast commercial appears as a complete unit—a combination of verbal and graphic signs or symbols that work together to present the USP. If the copywriter is to write words that are effective, he must think in terms of pictures, sounds, and movements which may accompany these words, and he must think of the complete advertisement as the audience will see or hear it. He must *visualize* it in final form as he writes the copy.

Visualization and Layout

The term "visualization" is an elusive one. Writers, artists, and production personnel all "visualize" in creating an advertisement, but "visualization" is often confused with "layout" in the print media. True visualization, however, is concerned with the *creation* of an idea, whereas layout deals with the *arrangement* of the various elements—headlines, illustrations, trademarks, firm name, and main text or body copy—to deliver the idea effectively. In suggesting the composition or the situation for the key illustration that dramatizes the theme of the ad, the artist is visualizing. In arranging this illustration with supporting illustrations and verbal elements in the form of the finished ad, he or she is making a layout—a blueprint for the printer. Visualization is a step that must precede the design step of layout, and must either precede the actual writing of the words or take place more or less simultaneously.

Some copywriters work simultaneously with typewriter and pencil, writing to develop the theme and drawing "rough-roughs" or "thought sketches" to help convey ideas for graphics to the artist.

Visualization and Commercials

In visualizing for radio, the copywriter uses two methods to stimulate the listener to evoke his or her own images: scene-setting and word-painting. In scene-setting, familiar sounds or comment immediately create the scene in the listener's mind. The ping of the pump-island bell and the sound of an automobile engine stopping, for example, create a filling station scene. Word-painting is a subtle and exacting art, in which the writer relies upon both the literal meaning and the emotional connotations of words to evoke mental images.

While radio communicates by sound alone, television is primarily a visual medium. The television writer is less concerned with verbal

POSITIONS OFFERED

COPYWRITER WANTED IN SAN FRANCISCO

$12,000

. . . and more to come if your ideas break through the ho hum level. Must think visually, have an organized mind - - and desk. No committee to contend with. Agency is national, well-heeled and growing. Resume to Box 7 R 420, Classified Depts., 4041 Marlton Ave., Los Angeles, Calif. 90008.

FIGURE 12.4
This classified advertisement for an agency copywriter is an example of the importance of visualization in copywriting.

symbols than either the radio or the print copywriter, and the real test of a TV commercial is whether the video alone can deliver an effective message. If the full impact of this unique combination of sight, sound, and motion is to be realized, however, the creation of a television commercial calls for a greater variety of skills than the creation of any other type of advertisement. TV writers must not only *visualize pictures*, but also think in terms of *movement*. An understanding of the stage and motion-picture studio and the techniques of television production is even more important than a knowledge of graphic arts processes is to the print writer.

COPY STRUCTURE

Now the copywriter is really ready to get to the job of "wordsmith." In essence, the structure of good advertising copy is the same as the structure of any good sales or promotional presentation.

Returning to the Hierarchy of Effects Model presented in Chapter 11, we can chart the progress of advertising copy communication through the six stages:

Awareness. Gaining prospects' attention to the product and its sales message

Knowledge. Presenting the USP in a clear and interesting manner so prospects will understand and accept it

Liking. Relating the message to prospects' own life-styles, making it relevant and believable

Preference. Developing desire for the specific brand advertised (and for its promised benefit)

Conviction. Convincing prospects that it is in their own best interest to buy

Purchase. Motivating prospects to act in the manner intended by the advertiser—physically, in some cases, and mentally or emotionally in others (since sometimes the "sale" is in terms of an idea rather than a physical product)

Although there will probably never be any pat formula for ideal copy, these six steps constitute a handy guide for the copywriter. They provide a convenient means of orienting a message toward its prospects and of identifying the responses which it should stimulate.

Of course, not all advertisements require a *detailed* inclusion of all six parts. Some ads and commercials accomplish their objectives with a very simple structure because the product, the desires it satisfies, and the pattern of distribution and purchase are simple. A 10-second television spot for a soft drink, for example, may contain only the first and last part (awareness and motivation to purchase), combined into a single sentence or slogan. Nor should we think of a "comprehensive advertisement" as one that employs hundreds of words; it all depends on the specific communication goal we are asked to achieve, and on the facts and facilities at our disposal.

Hierarchy of Effects in Print

At this point, the copywriter faced with creation of a newspaper or magazine advertisement can concentrate on ways of meeting the model's requirements. And usually—though not always—the most important copy element is the headline idea; for if it fails in its function—to attract its prospects to the message and product—the remaining parts of the ad are wasted (barely even seen). Creative personnel who place great importance on the illustrations in printed ads may take exception to this statement, claiming that the reader's eye is more often caught by a picture than by the words above or below it. Any argument over words versus pictures as attention-getting devices in advertisements is fruitless and overlooks the correct viewpoint toward advertising copy—the broad concept that copy consists of verbal and graphic symbols working together. The headline idea is not limited to the words in large type that appear above or below the main illustration. In some effective advertisements a dramatic or provocative photograph provides the "grabber," unaccompanied by a verbal headline. But the majority of advertisements rely on both words and illustrations for the primary attention-getting device.

The fact that a simple change in the wording of a headline can

Downtown OREGON

In the heart of Oregon City you can fish for salmon at Willamette Falls—only 20 minutes from downtown Portland. Spectacular ocean beaches are only an hour away. So is year 'round snow atop the rugged Cascades. A short drive over fine highways will take you from big-tree forests to wide open Old West range country or broad, green valleys. It's an uncrowded country — 96,000 square miles big and beautiful. Oregon is so conveniently arranged by nature that you are never more than minutes away from something new. You can relax in luxury at modern resorts or rough it in style at superb state parks. To change the scene to suit your pleasure, simply move 50 to 100 miles in any direction. That's the way it is here— the fastest fun in the West. Come see for yourself, soon.

Relax in a State of Excitement...OREGON

MAIL COUPON OR WRITE TODAY
Travel Information, Highway Dept., Salem, Oregon 97310
Please send me free booklet, **Oregon — Cool Green Vacationland,** 32 pages, in full color.

NAME _____
ADDRESS _____
CITY _____
STATE _____ ZIP _____

FIGURE 12.5
An excellent example of the concept of the headline idea. In this full-color magazine advertisement, neither the illustration nor the verbal headline conveys a complete thought alone, but together they present an arresting promise. [*Cole & Weber, Inc.*]

increase the efficiency of an advertisement by several hundred percent clearly illustrates the importance of the headline idea. For example, the following two headlines were compared in a split-run test in which all other elements in the two advertisements remained the same:

1 NEW JOBS ARE OFFERED IN TELEVISION STATIONS
2 TELEVISION COURSES FOR $11.50 PER WEEK

Headline (1) returned six times as many orders as headline (2), or six times the value for an identical investment in advertising space.

Headlines Perhaps the most important element of content in the headline idea is *selectivity:* the headline must serve to signal or "cue" those who are dieting that a low-calorie dessert message is directed specifically to them. That example may seem obvious, but it is not as easy to understand why an ad for a product used by "everyone" (such as soap or toothpaste) should not strive to attract "eveyone's" attention. But as John Caples, former vice-president of Batten, Barton, Durstine & Osborn, has said: if your attention-getting device tries to appeal to everybody by simply shouting "Hey, everybody!" you may fail to attract the very people who might be interested in buying your product. Copywriters must not inflate readership or listening or viewing audiences by attracting curiosity seekers at the expense of losing customers.[15]

In certain instances, a *question* may make an effective headline: "Need a hair drier that dries *without* frizzing?" Or perhaps: "Have you checked your energy IQ today?" At other times, an *invitation* is more on target: "Treat yourself to convenience and good taste."

In addition to selecting key prospects, the headline idea should make them aware of the promise Samuel Johnson described as the "soul of an advertisement." Sometimes it is in the form of a *command:* "Don't miss your chance to save!" while a simple statement of fact also has merit: "Eight essential vitamins in each crunchy serving."

Finally, "news flashes" may be just as important in advertising as they are in a purely journalistic sense: "Introducing a delicious one-step cake and frosting mix" (which could be *exactly* what key prospects have been waiting for!).

There are no right or wrong words, lengths, or "forms" for effective headlines. Copywriters must take care, however, to avoid calling attention to their *ads* per se (a condition known as "adiness"), instead of to their products and real sales messages. (How many times have you described an ad or commercial to a friend—and found you had forgotten the brand advertised!) Each headline must relate clearly and specifically to the intended audience *and* to the rest of the advertisement (product and USP).

Transitional Copy If a headline has already suggested a product's value to the consumer, the job of a subheadline is easy, if necessary at all. Sometimes, however, subheads (and also picture captions) may help convert reader interest into product knowledge by expanding or amplifying the main headline idea. They are especially helpful when the headline only "indirectly" refers to the real sales message. For example, if a headline advises: "Don't read this ad," a subhead proves extremely helpful: "Unless you'd enjoy having younger-looking skin!"

---

[15] John Caples, *Making Ads Pay*, Harper & Row, Publishers, Incorporated, New York, 1957, pp. 3–4.

FIGURE 12.6
In this small space
advertisement, the
headline idea
carefully selects
the specific market
segment that will
be interested in
the products of-
fered.

Body Copy In stimulating liking and preference for a given product, body copy must *develop* the benefit-promise, *explain* product features and values, and *support* claims—logically and convincingly. Most effective advertisements use a combination of two basic types of writing: *emotional* reason why and *rational* reason why. The first is mainly *subjective* and the second mainly *objective*, but both must provide compelling "reasons why" the consumer should spend hard-earned dollars for the product (and brand) advertised.

Proof of claims, to enhance conviction, may come from descrip-

It takes a good egg
to make mayonnaise real,
to make mayonnaise rich,
to make mayonnaise Kraft.
Because you've got to break some eggs
to make a real mayonnaise.

At Kraft we do.

FIGURE 12.7
In some cases,
brief, simple copy
may be all that is
needed to deliver
a message effec-
tively. This adver-
tisement doesn't
even use a tradi-
tional headline.
[*Kraft Foods.*]

tions of how the product works or is made, facts and figures from test results, a brief case history on performance, testimonials, quotations from experts, and guarantees. Or it may take the form of sensory appeals and invitations to the reader to "see for yourself" or "try it for a week and feel the difference."

The extent to which the rational or the emotional appeal should be used varies with the type of product and the buying motives of prospects. More stress is usually placed on emotional appeals in consumer advertising than in industrial, trade, or professional advertising. Copy for convenience or style goods makes greater use of emotional appeals than copy for durable goods, such as building materials, refrigerators, or water heaters. But emotional appeals need to be handled with care; if overdone, they destroy the credibility of the entire advertising message.

The Closing Idea All efforts to establish awareness, knowledge, liking, preference, and conviction are designed for the sole purpose of persuading the reader to act: to accept an idea, change an attitude, agree with a proposition, visit a store, ask for a brand name, or react in any of a host of other ways—and thereby take a big step toward ultimate purchase of the product advertised.

Because an advertisement, unlike a personal sales call, is one-way communication, its closing efforts must supply all information, directions, and motivation necessary for the buyer's action. In addition, it must make that action appear as *easy* as possible, and present a final "stimulus" as well. Interest in the product may be keen, and the desire for attainment of benefits intense, but if the ultimate action required is too difficult a process, the consumer will rarely make the effort.

Generally, there are two types of "calls to action" in advertising copy. The first was clearly illustrated by street vendors such as Molly Malone, who cried out for immediate sales: "Cockles and mussels . . . alive, alive-o!" This form of advertising, asking potential customers to "buy now," or "do it today," later became known as *hard-sell* (or direct-action) advertising—regardless of whether or not it included the "shouting" or "browbeating" often associated with this technique. Unfortunately, because so many direct-action advertisements do feature a fast talker or supersalesperson, the term "hard sell" is often erroneously associated with anything loud or pressured.

The second call to action is known as *soft sell* (or indirect action), and asks readers to "remember a name," "keep an idea in mind," or "think about buying" sometime in the future. Often, this form of ad "send-off" is judged preferable by consumers asked to choose between the two. Just as often, though, people "like" (and identify with) the advertisements which speak to their own needs and predispositions—regardless of any direct or indirect call to action.

In any case, examples of ways to ease readers into action include (1) providing a coupon (to reduce cost); (2) emphasizing convenient accessibility (available at a nearby location—address or directions supplied); (3) urging immediate compliance (to take advantage of limited quantities or short-lived "sales"); (4) offering early-bird-shopper specials; (5) noting easy buying terms (possibly even mail and phone orders—with clear addresses and/or telephone numbers included); and (6) reminding readers of special reasons for buying (birthdays, anniversaries, graduations), and, hence, offering *excuses* for buying as well as fulfillment of needs.

Hierarchy of Effects in Broadcast

Commercial messages on radio—combinations of words, music, and sound effects—can develop "mind pictures" bounded only by the extent of their listeners' imaginations. Radio gives the copywriter complete freedom of time and place, and unlimited forms and amounts of physical activity. Television combines sight, sound, and motion to approximate face-to-face selling better than any other medium. The TV advertiser can, in effect, come into a viewer's home, chat with the viewer personally, display products actively over musical background, and stimulate sales by demonstrating ease of purchase.

On the other hand, both radio and television, as "entertainment" media, present advertising copywriters with the challenge of keeping the urge to entertain under control. It must always be secondary to the application of sound selling principles and to the development of a solid USP.

In broadcast, unlike print, the copywriter controls the direction of attention. There is no page to scan, no chance to reread selected lines or to spend extra time studying a given caption or illustration. Once the listener or viewer has chosen to "tune in" or "become aware," the copywriter can focus attention exactly where the advertiser wants it. A problem here, however, revolves around the fact that *listening* and *watching* usually require less effort than reading. And so we all tend to get careless in our listening and viewing habits—to take them for granted. We "hear" with only half an ear—and "watch" without really seeing or comprehending. Our attention to these media is often divided (while we are busy cleaning or repairing, cooking or eating, even talking, writing, or paging through a magazine or newspaper).

No "Headlines" in Commercials   What does it all mean to copywriters? First, certainly, they have to work *extra* hard to gain attention. "Unexpected" words or actions sometimes prove effective stoppers: "When was the last time you *dyed* . . . with bright, color-fast results in clothing or bedspreads?" Or picture an animated soda-pop can that "flips its lid" and begins a furious "fizzing" action as its contents fill a frosty glass. The copy begins: "*Watch out*—for the new, sparkly soda pop that keeps on fizzing." Since such unusual beginnings may jar listeners or viewers somewhat, the copywriter sometimes uses them to zero in on the target audience.

Some broadcast writers will argue for an "establishing" shot or sound at the beginning of a commercial—a scene-setter which orients viewers or listeners to the "environment" of the forthcoming message. Indeed, if viewer attention can be snagged in the first few seconds with material which sets the stage for USP development, there is no need to jump immediately into the sales pitch.

Another school of thought, however, maintains that the USP may begin effectively in the opening moments—in a suspenseful atmosphere, for instance, which motivates the audience to stay with it. Again, no one "rule" applies in every case. A careful analysis of product and sales message, audience, competition, and available media resources *must* precede creative decisions; and adiness must be avoided in broadcast as well as print. Gaining awareness is as vital in one medium as another, for once the audience is gone (tuned out, visiting the refrigerator, or switching channels), it rarely, if ever, comes back.

Knowledge and Liking Simple commercials generally hold interest best. Long lists of items or sets of figures bore radio audiences, and TV scenes whose actions do not parallel lines of copy exactly prove confusing. (Research has shown that maximum recall is obtained when audio and visual elements say and show the same thing at the same time).[16]

Repetition, of both product name and USP, is essential in commercials since messages are perishable (*and* very short—the "standard" length of commercials in both radio and TV today is 30 seconds). Studies have also shown that repetition *with variation* enhances both retention and interest.[17] Thus copywriters need to concentrate on saying and showing the same thing different ways, so that audiences do not become bored by redundancy.

Developing Preference and Conviction As is true in print, both rational and emotional "reasons why" are used in commercials to demonstrate how and why claims are true, valuable, and relevant to selected audiences. Radio commercials assume any of six basic formats in developing desire for a particular product or service:[18]

1 *The straight sell.* A clear, simple presentation of product benefits, with emphasis on product differentiation. Overselling, however, can antagonize prospects.
2 *The educational.* More rational than emotional in appeal, and frequently used for corporate or institutional messages.
3 *The testimonial.* Credibility is the secret here. The endorser may be a

---

[16] Thomas Fredrick Baldwin, "Redundancy in Simultaneously Presented Audio-Visual Message Elements as a Determinant of Recall," unpublished Ph.D. dissertation, Michigan State University, 1966.
[17] Carl I. Hovland, Irving L. Janis, and Harold H. Kelley, *Communication and Persuasion*, Yale University Press, New Haven, Conn., 1953, p. 247.
[18] Adapted from Robert L. Hilliard, *Writing for Television and Radio*, Hastings House, Publishers, Inc., New York, 1962, chap. 3. See also 2d ed., 1967, pp. 73–83.

celebrity, the star of a dramatic program, or an ordinary person with whom the viewer can easily identify.

4 *The humorous.* Humor is entertainment, and it holds audiences. But humor is also both elusive and fragile. Be sure the commercial contains real comedy material, and is delivered by people who know how to be funny.

5 *The musical.* This may be instrumental with the message delivered straight, or the singing commercial. Despite criticism from both laypeople and experts like David Ogilvy, musicals are effective when well done.

6 *The dramatization.* This narrative technique is particularly effective to present a problem that can be solved by the product—the brief "boy meets girl, boy loses girl, boy gets girl with product" playlet.

To these six basic formats should be added one more, the integrated commercial. An integrated commercial is one that has been carefully designed for a particular program, and it is less common than it was in the days of network radio shows featuring big-name performers. The integrated commercial is delivered without a noticeable break with program content. Today the integrated commercial is often ad-libbed by a station announcer or personality who has been supplied with a simple fact sheet about the product.

These six formats might also be applied to television, but the visual rather than aural character of television suggests different, though somewhat overlapping, classifications. The straight sell, dramatization, and testimonial formats are visual interpretations of the same arrangements in radio. So is the integrated commercial, although in TV this is more often referred to as the "personality" format, which emphasizes fame and the following of the television star who presents the product message in his own individual style.

Two commercial formats peculiar to television are the so-called song and dance, or production commercial, and the demonstration technique. The song-and-dance productions are really sight, sound, and motion presentations of radio's musical format, requiring peak professional performance in both the visual and aural areas, and are usually possible only for advertisers with mass budgets aiming at mass audiences.

Creative advertising professionals agree that the demonstration format is the one that best utilizes television's unusual potentials. Hanley Norins, creative director for the Young and Rubicam agency, calls television "the fast, fast medium," and says:

> The words "demonstration" and "simple" . . . are the keys to effective television commercials.[19]

[19] Hanley Norins, *The Compleat Copywriter*, McGraw-Hill Book Company, New York, 1966, pp. 149, 151, 152.

Wainwright stresses the importance of simplicity with this warning:

> Commercials can be so loaded with frills that the message becomes buried under the glitter and glamour of a tiny motion picture epic. A true selling commercial requires the writer to have a logical, disciplined, orderly mind. He must think first of the problem and eventually determine the solution.[20]

Demonstration can, of course, be combined with dramatization, testimonial, personality, and even song-and-dance formats. If the product lends itself to demonstration, failure to make use of such an opportunity is difficult to justify.

Calling for Action   Both direct and indirect calls to action are used in commercials—although radio tends to feature hard sell more often than television does. The reason is usually that radio is more locally oriented and commercials are more apt to stress hurry-up sales, limited offers, and other "time" considerations.

One word of caution here: copywriters should avoid using lengthy addresses and telephone numbers on radio—and to some extent on TV; although the visual channel *is* helpful in this regard, messages are so short that it is questionable whether viewers really have time to "take notes." Some possible alternatives to giving the actual number might be: "check your yellow pages for the store nearest you"; "located on the corner of Elm and Main Street"; or "across from the Varsity Theater."

BUILDING BLOCKS OF STYLE

Advertising copy style refers to the mode of presentation characteristic of advertising writing as distinguished from letter writing, magazine article writing, editorial writing, or formal English composition. Learning how to write advertising requires more than an understanding of the techniques involved. It requires practice in these techniques and constructive criticism of this practice, just as learning to play the violin or piano requires practice and criticism. Writing advertising is a difficult art; Aldous Huxley has said it requires more skill than any other form of creative writing.

Although this chapter cannot teach how to write, a brief discussion of style in advertising copy is necessary if we are to have any practical

---

[20] Charles Anthony Wainwright, *The Television Copywriter*, Communications Arts Books, Hastings House Publishers, Inc., New York, 1966, p. 90.

understanding of advertising copywriting. Also, it should be useful to persons who do not plan a career in advertising, but whose business position may require an appraisal of creative advertising effort.

Truth and Believability

Despite careful adherence to disciplined creativity, occasionally a copywriter's claims for a household cleaning agent may appear to be mere "product puffery." Homemakers need only try the product once, however, before discovering the ad's exaggeration, and ensuing copy for the same item—though highly "creative" in nature—falls by the wayside as far as potential customers are concerned. On the other hand, advertising which is accurate to the last detail is of little value if it is not believable. Even if a medication is someday discovered for instant cure of the common cold, advertising creative strategy will have to center around some very clearly laid persuasive tracks; otherwise, consumers' deep-rooted skepticisms regarding cold remedies may prevent acceptance of the advertising message.

We should be aware, however, that *literal* truth or falsity is not much of an issue in advertising today; the rise of consumerism and resulting government regulations have pretty well taken care of that problem. What we are concerned with is truth *as perceived by the consumer* (often called believability). Without it, advertisements have not got a chance for successful communication. William Blake's famous warning still holds: "A truth that's told with bad intent, beats all the lies you can invent!"

A special tip to broadcasters is to beware putting too much of a sales message in the mouths of "real people" engaged in dialogue. Somehow, it all just seems to come out sounding artificial—rehearsed—canned (unless handled by *very* experienced writers and acting talent). Believability is often best served by letting an announcer or TV commercial presenter handle the heart of the sales story.

Readability

More than 60 years ago, Sir Arthur Quiller-Couch lectured his students at Cambridge on the importance of making their writing readable:

> All reading demands an effort. The energy, the goodwill which a reader brings to a book is, and must be, partly expended in the labor of reading. . . . The more difficulties, then, we authors obtrude on him by obscure or careless writing, the more we blunt the edge of his attention.[21]

[21] Sir Arthur Quiller-Couch, *On the Art of Writing*, G. P. Putnam's Sons, New York, 1916, p. 292.

People buy books to read what the author has written. But people do not buy advertisements at all, much less buy them to read what the copywriter has written. Easy reading is of greater importance in advertising than in business reports, news, editorials, or literature. With the tremendous increase in mass communications media and in the number of communicators, the competition for the reader's attention is many times as great as it was when Quiller-Couch stressed the importance of writing that is easy to read.

We can extend "readability" to include "listenability" and "viewability." A conglomeration of voices, sound effects, and musical fanfare can make a radio commercial impossible to comprehend; and televised scenes which are too "busy" block understanding and lose viewers. "Readable" ads and commercials speak to consumers on their own levels and in their own terms. They make liberal use of the "you attitude"—because people like to be addressed in the second person [you, your(s), and you're].

After all, as John O'Toole, president of Foote, Cone & Belding, points out:

> Advertising isn't about products, it's about a person's life and how a product can fit into that life to make it better. This is advertising designed to get into someone's heart, not under his skin.[22]

Simplicity and Human Interest

Reduced to the simplest common denominator, the readability of copy depends on simplicity and human interest. The degree of simplicity and human interest varies according to audience and product or service, but any writing is more readable when it uses words that are familiar and personal, sentences that are short and uncomplicated.

Contemporary readability experts like Flesch and Gunning emphasize the importance of simple, colloquial language, but such basic guides to readable writing are not new. They were stressed by Quiller-Couch, by Herbert Spencer, by Thomas Wilson in 1560 in his *Arte of Rhetoricke*, and by the Apostle Paul in biblical times. Paul said:

> Except ye utter by the tongue words easy to understand, how shall it be known what is spoken? For ye shall speak into the air.[23]

Ideally, copy should contain no words that stop the reader's flow of thought. The word "obtrude" in the quotation from Quiller-Couch on

[22] John E. O'Toole, "Are Grace Slick and Tricia Nixon Cox the Same Person?" *Journal of Advertising*, vol. 2, no. 2, p. 34, 1973.
[23] I Cor. 14.9.

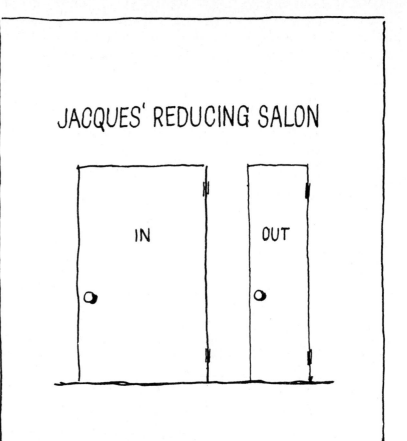

JACQUES' REDUCING SALON

IN   OUT

A strong simple selling idea . . . dramatically presented

If "Jacques" existed, we'd hire him. Because he practices what we preach. Brilliant simplicity. Not that we always meet our standards. But that's what we shoot for every time out in the advertising for Instant Maxwell House, Prell, Schick Shavers, IBM, Pream, Western Union, to drop just a few of our favorite names.

B&B
BENTON & BOWLES, INC.

FIGURE 12.8
The importance of simplicity in advertising copy is the theme of this advertisement for a well-known advertising agency. [*Benton & Bowles, Inc.*]

page 424 is an example. Perhaps "obtrude" was a familiar word to students of literature at Cambridge 60 years ago. But it is hardly a word to use in a message to business executives, homemakers, or students in America today. It would stop the flow of thought quite successfully. Sometimes unfamiliar or complex words are necessary, because they describe a new ingredient, a new process, or a new design. But if they are explained in simple terms immediately, they need not stop the flow of thought. If, for example, it seemed necessary to use the word "obtrude" in an advertisement, a skilled copywriter would say something like this: "The more difficulties, then, we authors obtrude, or force, on him. . . ."

The use of the familiar word is particularly important in connection with technical terms which may be everyday language to the maker of the product, but which will make reading hard and meaning obscure for the public. Most major kitchen and bathroom appliances and equipment have vitreous finishes. But ask your friends to tell you what "vitreous" means, and you'll see why advertising copy will be more effective if it describes the finish as having a "surface hard as glass." The latter is not only easier to read, but also clearer, more graphic, and more persuasive.

Good style in advertising copy is specific about *who, what, when, where, why,* and *how.* It relies on words that are concrete and tied in with the experience of the readers it wants to interest and motivate into action.

Clichés and Superlatives

In a critical study of advertising messages published in 1952, William H. Whyte, Jr., pointed out that the effectiveness of much advertising copy was greatly reduced by the use of clichés, stock expressions, and superlatives.[24] Clichés and exaggerated stock expressions block communication in much the same way that abstract and general terms do. Expressions like "world's greatest," "medically proven," and "extra value" have been used so much they have lost the power they had originally to create an image for the receiver. Superlatives may cause the FTC to label the advertising misleading, and in any case are unbelievable.

Whyte's warnings are more important today than when he voiced them almost 25 years ago. In 1969, the Grey advertising agency published this comment on clichés and superlatives:

> It is becoming increasingly obvious that people today are wary of advertising which assumes the consumer is gullible. Shopworn gimmicks are rapidly losing their power to persuade. . . . A growing number of consumers in our affluent society have more realistic, mature attitudes about the role of material things in life. More literate, better educated, they have also become increasingly skeptical about product claims. Thus, effective advertising reflects a new, more modest attitude about products and portrays with greater candor the role they play in people's lives. The superlatives once thought essential to the lexicon of salesmanship are being replaced in good advertising copy by a more colloquial tone of voice, even to the point of engaging in understatement.[25]

But it is easy to overgeneralize about clichés and stock expressions. A cliché becomes a cliché to begin with because it is a useful tool

[24] William H. Whyte, Jr., "The Language of Advertising," *Fortune*, September 1952.
[25] *Grey Matter*, Grey Advertising, Inc., June 1969, pp. 1, 2.

FIGURE 12.9
Advertising profes-
sionals have long
recognized the
danger of using
superlatives in ad-
vertising copy. This
is one of a series
of advertisements
published more
than 65 years ago
by Lord & Thomas,
predecessor to the
Foote, Cone &
Belding advertis-
ing agency.

Lord & Thomas Creeds

No. 1. Exaggeration

Men whose opinions are effective are men of moderation.

Instinct discounts superlatives. And the discount often goes too far—to the article's injustice.

Adjectives callous credulity.

Blatancy does not command respect.

Over-statement, in reaction, creates commensurate resistance.

Some things may be the best of their kind in the world. But it is pretty hard for finite minds to know it. And harder still for cynical minds to believe it.

Modesty, by its very rarity, commands attention. And by its fascination wins.

Too much effort makes men think that your selling task is hard.

Remember how the expression "Morgan & Wright Tires are Good Tires" stood out amidst the bombast of its time.

What advertising phrase was ever more effective than the simple words "It Floats"?

with which to communicate. However, not all stock expressions are clichés. Some retain interest and emotional appeal long after their novelty has worn off. The purchases men and women make every day indicate perhaps better than readership studies the interest people may have in things that are *new, easy, reliable,* or *safe.* Sometimes, too, the cliché can't be avoided any more than the abstraction can. Attempts to replace it with fresher words may end in confusion or an awkward wordiness. A clear stereotype is better than obscurity, no matter how fresh the wording of the latter.

The Importance of Connotation

As an interpreter, the writer of advertising is concerned with both the denotation, or the literal meaning, and the connotation, or indirect implication, of words. A word can produce a positive or negative response quite apart from its literal meaning, and different people may associate a different connotation with the same word. "Substitute" is an example of a word with a negative connotation to most people.

Literally, this noun means a person or thing acting or being used in place of another. But the idea which it has been used to express most often—the substitute quarterback, avoid substitutes—has given the word a connotation of inferiority or cheapness. To the college professor, a "theory" is a systematic statement of principles; to the average person, a "theory" is a guess or an impractical idea.

Author and educator David Berlo insists that "meanings are in people, not in words." Here is yet another reason copywriters must get to *know* their audiences before starting to write for them.

Every Word Should Work

Good advertising writing is "tight" writing. It contains no stuffing, no padding, no empty words or phrases. It does not say "in terms of plant maintenance, BXB saves...." It says "in plant maintenance BXB saves...." Good copy does not say "this is an improvement which...." It says "this improvement...." In *The Elements of Style*, William Strunk says:

> Vigorous writing is concise. A sentence should contain no unnecessary words, a paragraph no unnecessary sentences, for the same reason a drawing should contain no unnecessary lines and a machine no unnecessary parts. This requires not that the writer should make all his sentences short, or that he should avoid all detail and treat his subjects only in outline, but that he make every word tell.[26]

Veteran copywriter Hal Stebbins offers this comparison:

> A good surgeon and a good advertising writer have this in common: *the art of quick exposure*. They make every stroke count.

National advertisers frequently invest $40,000 for a single page of advertising in a magazine. Very few of the ads contain as many as 400 words of copy. The cost per word of copy is $100, and the importance of making every word count is rather obvious. Bernbach gives this advice to advertising writers:

> Everything you write, everything on a page, every word, every graphic symbol, every shadow should further the message you're trying to convey.[27]

But conciseness should not be confused with brevity. While

---

[26] William Strunk, Jr., and E. B. White, *The Elements of Style*, 2d ed., The Macmillan Company, New York, 1972.
[27] Denis Higgins (ed.), *The Art of Writing Advertising*, Advertising Publications, Inc., Chicago, 1965, p. 17.

increased competition for the prospect's attention emphasizes the need for greater use of graphic symbols as well as copy that is tightly written, this does not mean that "people just won't read long copy." The length of copy is a matter of structure rather than style, assuming the writer knows how to use words effectively. Three important factors affect the length of copy. First, the character of the unique selling proposition—the simplicity or complexity of the message itself. Second, and closely related to the first, is the objective of the advertisement. Third is the interest to prospects that is inherent in the product.

Short copy is more likely to be effective when the product has low inherent interest and little differentiation, and when the advertiser is primarily interested in favorable brand awareness. Package goods like facial tissues, snacks, or soft drinks are examples. When the product or service is one that will be bought thoughtfully or cautiously, long copy is often necessary to build confidence, present believable advantages, and persuade the prospect to buy.

SPECIAL CREATIVE PROBLEMS

Before leaving this chapter we must consider a few special copywriting concerns at the local level. In Chapter 4, the objectives of retail advertising are explained, and true retail advertising is distinguished from local advertising. But while most retail advertising is local, there is a considerable volume of local advertising that differs from true retail, and the problems faced in their creation differ.

Retail versus Local Advertising

The true retail advertisement—for a department store, a specialty shop, or a supermarket—is part of a continuing series that presents a parade of different merchandise that is either new or offered at a special price. Retail advertisements in newspapers enjoy a degree of directed readership not unlike the yellow pages of the telephone directory. People "shop" the advertisements of department stores and food chains to see what new merchandise is offered and what bargains they can find. On the other hand, a national advertisement has no such preconditioned audience to search it out; it must create its own attention.

When local advertising is not a continuing series of announcements of interesting new merchandise or special price offers, it is not true retail advertising, and the creative problems are closer to those of national advertising than to retail advertising. Many local advertisers, particularly in service areas, fall into this classification. Fuel dealers, hotels and motels, restaurants, insurance agents, firms handling building supplies or office equipment, and banks are examples of local advertisers who do not have a ready-made audience with advance interest in what their advertisements will say. Generally, people do not "shop" the advertisements of banks. Most banks offer essentially the same services at the same prices, fees, or rates. Creating a series of effective advertisements for a bank requires the same strategy used for the national advertiser. Each advertisement must reach out and stop the reader by promising to tell an interesting story. (It is interesting to note, however, that *some* bank ads today seem to feature special incentives, such as gifts for opening new accounts, so that people *will* begin to "shop" these ads.)

The local advertiser must develop a headline idea that arrests the attention of the transient reader. The retail advertiser can count on the logotype, the new merchandise, or the price appeal to bring directed readers into the ad—and thus into the store. An illustration of the product, usually a weak method of visualization for the national advertiser, is one of the most effective forms for the retail advertiser, and it is probable that illustration carries the major communicative burden in a retail advertisement.

Some stores, especially large department stores, create much of their own advertising art. Others rely mainly upon illustration material furnished by manufacturers or upon mat service organizations which supply monthly books of seasonally timed illustrations available in mat form to both advertisers and newspapers. Both illustration sources can save the advertiser time and money, but in both cases the material usually carries no exclusive right of use and is unlikely to be as relevant or as distinctive as artwork created for a specific advertising message or a particular store personality.

Essentials of Retail Copy Since retail copy is essentially information about what the store has for sale, it should be simple, direct, and specific. The advertisement should describe the product, give the price, and tell the reader where and how to buy it. The buying directions should include not only the store name and address, but also the location of the department in which the item can be found—the "floor line," such as "Young Modern's Shop, Fourth Floor." If the store has more than one location, the advertisement should indicate at which ones the merchandise is available. If mail or phone orders are accepted, the advertisement should say so, and mail-order addresses or coupons and phone numbers to call should be given.

Although most retail copy leans toward the informative, and should be direct and specific, this is no excuse for dull, trite retail advertisements. Every retail advertisement tells two stories: the story of the merchandise and the story of the store. Even the most direct selling retail copy will, intentionally or not, reflect the store's personality, and to this extent all retail advertising is institutional. Research indicates that shoppers become rather expert in evaluating the personality or character of department stores from the physical appearance of their advertising, even when the store is an unfamiliar one in a strange city.

The Image of the Store   Retail advertising should strive, by choice of words, illustration, and layout design, to establish a distinctive style which identifies the store and continues to reinforce the store image in the minds of customers. The layout of a retail advertisement is the most important symbol of store personality. Advertisements packed with different items are symbolic of stores—or "budget basements"—that attract all kinds of people with bargain merchandise. As the main appeal shifts from price to prestige to attract people with higher levels of taste and income, layouts have increased white space and present a more orderly and more sophisticated appearance.

The headline and text treatment of retail advertising should expand on the impression created by the overall design. And while the body copy should complete the information about the advertised merchandise, it should not necessarily supply all the information the prospect needs in order to arrive at a buying decision, as is sometimes claimed. In its simplest concept, retail advertising says, "Buy this at *my* store." But the primary objective of retail advertising, whether direct selling or institutional, is to build store traffic—to get customers to the store to buy either the product advertised or other merchandise.

Fashion Advertising

For many the word "fashion," like the word "propaganda," has particularly negative social connotations. It is associated with concepts of conspicuous waste developed by Thorstein Veblen more than 70 years ago. But while fashions are capricious, transitory, and emotional, they provide the foundation from which both convention and customs emerge. Later students of society, like Max Lerner, have observed that fashions are an index of social change, and Prof. John Mertes, in a study of the literature of fashion, concludes that:

In an open society, fashion becomes a prod toward progress.[28]

Most fashion advertising is definitely feminine. Despite the success in the apparel field of such male couturiers as Cassini, Christian Dior, and Yves St. Laurent, many retailers still believe it takes a woman to buy, sell, or advertise fashion merchandise. There are probably no more male fashion copywriters than female sportswriters. Yet the broad objective of fashion advertising is no different from that of any

[28] John E. Mertes, "Fashion: A Prod toward Progress," *Business and Economic Dimensions*, June 1970, pp. 12–18.

other retail advertising. It is aimed at creating store traffic. And while retail copy in general should be simple, direct, and specific, these basic guides to copy style cannot be extended to fashion copy without modification.

There are two quite different types of fashion advertising: the high-style or high-fashion advertising most often seen in magazines like *Vogue, Harper's Bazaar*, or *The New Yorker*, and the volume-fashion advertising of department stores and apparel shops. High-fashion advertising aims at people who wish to feel they are making or establishing style, and the primary appeal is one of prestige. Volume-fashion advertising, on the other hand, reaches the people who want to be assured that they are good judges of good fashion, and who wish to be in style rather than ahead of it. In a way, high-fashion copy stimulates primary demand, as for "the slim, shaped-line suit," while volume-fashion copy stimulates selective demand for a specific suit at a specific store. Mention of price and details of colors, fabrics, and workmanship are definitely secondary in high-fashion copy, and may even be omitted completely. Volume-fashion copy should include price and such details as fabric, color, and sizes, as well as answer questions that may be in the prospect's mind, such as washability or durability. Both types of fashion copy should have a light, gay tone, rely heavily on illustration to convey mood as well as design, and carefully avoid overworked adjectives and words or phrases prospects might consider passé. Fashion must be fresh and new to be fashion.

Local Copy Calls for Local Flavor

Even retail copy that is not in the fashion classification can be written in a sprightly manner that will add much to the stimulation of interest and desire. The close relation between store and customer makes it easier to inject a personal tone into retail than into national copy. Copywriters who live in the same community as their readers should understand the local point of view and be able to write with a local flavor for either true retail or local advertisements.

This discussion of special creative problems in retail and local advertising has been basically in terms of the newspaper medium, the medium which receives the major portion of the budget of local or retail advertisers. They use other media successfully, of course—outdoor, direct mail, transit, radio, and television. More than half the nation's food chains use local radio to deliver repeated messages to consumers at low cost, and retailers of all types are increasing their use of both radio and television. Whatever medium the retailer or local advertiser chooses, the basic principles for the creation of successful newspaper advertising can be applied within the limitations and possibilities of the particular medium.

SUMMARY

Advertising creativity is disciplined creativity, channeled in such a way that clients' communication objectives are achieved through mass media messages. Copywriters work with ideas, which come from carefully gathered and analyzed facts about products and prospects.

Product information includes physical composition of the product itself, as well as notes on how well it is made, what it actually does, how it compares with competing brands, and how it may be identified. Information on prospects includes factors such as sex, age, income, occupation, and place of residence.

One of the copywriter's most difficult tasks is the development of a unique selling proposition—the unique matching of selling point to benefit. But only after that task is accomplished can real ad development take place.

"Copy" includes all the elements in an advertising message—and the copywriter's job includes writing words *and* "visualizing" pictures, sound effects and music for radio, and televised action. Successful ads and commercials are often built around the Hierarchy of Effects Model, but may be presented in a variety of formats.

Effective copy *style* calls for both literal truth and believability in advertisements, and for words and graphics which are "readable" in print, and easily understood in radio and TV. Simplicity and human interest are important requirements in all media, but clichés and exaggerations tend to block effective communication. An appreciation for the connotation of words is also valuable, since different audiences may perceive different meanings from the same message.

Special creative problems include retail and local advertising, as well as advertising in the area of fashion.

QUESTIONS FOR DISCUSSION

1 Disciplined creativity lies behind all successful advertisements. What does that term mean to the copywriter? What disciplines other than those mentioned in this chapter appear important to you?

2 Explain how ideas are formed and what kinds of factual materials are most helpful, calling on your own experiences for reference.

3 Differentiate between a selling point and a benefit using several different examples.

4 Find an ad in a popular magazine and explain how the Hierarchy of Effects Model was applied to copy and layout.

5 Name several ways radio and TV commercials "gain attention." Which do you think are the most effective? Why?

6 Consider a recent purchase you have made. Who and/or what led you to make that purchase? Name as many different people and stimuli as you can remember.

7 Describe the elements which make up a sound piece of copy. Do they differ between print and broadcast media? Why?

8 Differentiate clearly between local and retail advertising.

9 Why do you think believability is often hard to achieve in advertisements?

10 Give an example illustrating how different connotations for the same word might lead to legal difficulties in advertising.

FOR FURTHER REFERENCE

Adams, Robert (ed.): *Creativity in Communications*, BP Trading Limited, the Netherlands, 1971.

Book, Albert C., and Norman D. Cary: *The Television Commercial: Creativity and Craftsmanship*, Decker Communications, Inc., New York, 1970.

Burton, Philip Ward: *Advertising Copywriting*, 3d ed., Grid, Inc., Columbus, 1974.

Caples, John: *Making Ads Pay*, Harper & Row Publishers, Incorporated, New York, 1957.

————: *Tested Advertising Methods*, 4th ed., Prentice-Hall, Inc., Englewood Cliffs, N.J., 1974.

Higgins, Denis (ed.): *The Art of Writing Advertising*, Advertising Publications, Inc., Chicago, 1965.

Hilliard, Robert L.: *Writing for TV and Radio*, 2d ed., Hastings House, Publishers, Inc., New York, 1967.

Norins, Hanley: *The Compleat Copywriter*, McGraw-Hill Book Company, New York, 1966.

Osborn, Alex: *Applied Imagination*, rev. ed., Charles Scribner's Sons, New York, 1963.

Wainwright, Charles Anthony: *The Television Copywriter*, Hastings House, Publishers, Inc., New York, 1966.

Whittier, Charles L.: *Creative Advertising*, Holt, Rinehart and Winston, Inc., New York, 1955.

CHAPTER 13
ADVERTISING DESIGN

The emphasis placed on verbal communication in the preceding chapter should not lead us to underestimate the role of graphic elements in all advertising messages except those delivered by radio. Drawings, photographs, and moving pictures usually convey an idea more quickly than words can. Moreover, the arrangement of such elements in combination with verbal symbols—the design of the total advertisement—can add to or subtract from the responses the message seeks to stimulate.

Draper Daniels, chairman of the board of his own advertising agency, put it well when he noted that:

> The best advertising is a combination of words that make pictures in the mind and pictures that make words in the mind.

> [And great ads] are usually strong, simple words and arresting obvious art combined in a fresh and surprising manner.[1]

But this chapter should not be approached with apprehension because one isn't an artist or can't draw a straight line. It isn't necessary to be an artist or a connoisseur of art to understand the basic principles of design and visual communication, any more than it is necessary to be a skilled writer to understand the basic principles of verbal communication that must be applied by the copywriter.

DESIGN VERSUS LAYOUT

The term "design," like "creativity," is both overused and often misunderstood. As a noun, design is both an arrangement of parts and the plan behind the arrangement that produces a desired unit or structure. As a verb, design applies to any human activity concerned with organizing (arranging, displaying) elements in a manner which achieves some specific purpose.[2]

The word "layout" is an advertising colloquialism; it is a condensed way of saying "laying out the elements of an advertisement within specific space limitations." The term is most specifically applied to the design of a newspaper, magazine, outdoor, or transit advertisement. In planning direct advertising and point-of-purchase material, which usually require a three-dimensional presentation of the message, the layout is called a *dummy*. In the creation of television commercials, the layout is referred to as a *storyboard*—a series of

[1] Draper Daniels, *Giants, Pigmies, and Other Advertising People*, Crain Communications, Inc., Chicago, 1974, pp. 253–254.
[2] Roy Paul Nelson, *The Design of Advertising*, 2d ed., W. C. Brown Company Publishers, Dubuque, Iowa, 1973, p. 102.

pictures or frames which coincide with the audio or sound script. Regardless of the specific term used—rough, sketch, visual, "comp," dummy, or storyboard—all refer to the same thing, a drawing of some kind that simulates the finished advertisement.

Like an architect's drawing, the layout for an advertisement serves as a sort of "blueprint." Its function is to assemble the different parts of the advertisement—illustrations, headlines, body text, advertiser's signature, and the like—into a unified communication of the advertiser's message. In all but the very simplest form, layouts present these elements in the same size, shape, position, and proportion as desired in the final ad. Hence, the layout gives both those who have created the advertisement and those who will pay for it a good idea of how the ad will appear in publication.

Like the architect's drawing, it offers an opportunity for modification or approval before actual construction or production begins. And finally, the layout, like the architect's plan, provides specifications for estimating costs as well as a blueprint for engravers, typographers, and other craftsworkers to follow in producing the ad to specifications.

LAYOUT STAGES

Some designers begin with *thumbnail* layouts—miniature sketches (even "doodles") often only one-quarter the size of the desired ad. From such preliminaries may come the one design deemed worthy of further development.

The second stage (or the first, if thumbnails are omitted) is the *rough* layout—an actual-size layout in which headlines and subheads are lettered in (and type styles approximated), artwork and photographs are drawn, and the position and extent of copy is indicated with ruled parallel lines. As the rough presentations become more true to form, the layout stage may be called *finished*, although it is far from ready for publication. Students in advertising layout classes, as well as many retail advertisers, direct-mail users, and even clients of advertising agencies, work somewhere in the rough-to-finished area.

A *comprehensive* layout (or "comp") gets additional polish; in fact, it is considered "perfect" in every detail. Important clients paying thousands of dollars for magazine ads usually demand comps before giving approval. Photographs are pasted in and copy actually set. If offset lithography is involved, or plates of the entire ad required, a *paste-up* or *mechanical* is prepared (camera-ready work); this stage, however, is actually a step beyond our discussion of layout.[3]

[3] Ibid., pp. 79–80.

FIGURE 13.1
An ad without white space, and one which superimposes copy not just *over* the illustration but actually "inside" it. The result gives added impact to the sales message. [*Foote, Cone & Belding.*]

PRINCIPLES OF DESIGN

As we saw in Chapter 12, headline ideas do not necessarily require verbal headlines; nor do all advertisements utilize graphic elements or art. As a matter of fact, *all* layout elements (headlines and subheads, picture captions and blurbs, illustrations and product packages, body copy and coupons, trademarks and advertiser logotypes) appear in today's ads with varying degrees of frequency.

Basic design principles, however, demand thoughtful consideration regardless of the number or nature of specific units involved; all must, in the end, form a single effective communication message. The following five principles of "good composition" are important to anyone concerned with creation or evaluation of advertisements.

Balance

Designers point out that balance is a fundamental law of nature. It occurs when equal weights or forces are equidistant from a reference point, or when a light weight is placed at a greater distance from the reference point than a heavy one. A familiar example of the principle is the child's teeter-totter or seesaw. The board will stabilize in a horizontal position when two children of equal weight are equidistant from the fulcrum, or when a light child is farther from the fulcrum than a heavy one.

In a layout, the reference point or fulcrum is the optical center of the advertisement. The artist always begins with a given area—a magazine page 7 inches wide by $10^{3}/_{16}$ inches deep, for example. All the elements must be kept within this space. The optical center of the advertisement is a point approximately one-third of the distance above the physical center, or two-thirds of the distance from the bottom; it is the reference point that determines the balance of the layout.

The weight of a layout element is affected by both size and intensity of color or tone. Two units have the same weight if both size and color value are equal; a small element may be equal in weight to a large one of lighter shade or less intense color value.

When the weight of all elements on both sides of the vertical center line is equal, the layout has formal or symmetrical balance. When the equilibrium is the result of placing elements of different weights at different distances from the optical center, the layout has informal or asymmetrical balance. Most artists agree that formal balance (with nothing "unusual" or unexpected about it) is less interesting than the more dynamic, informal composition. Some suggest that the primary value of formal balance lies in its suggestion of dignity, conservatism, and dependability—attributes desirable in the creation of corporate images for financial institutions, for example. While the lively pattern of informal balance is exciting and provides an opportunity for effective display of a number of different elements, there is much to be said for the direct simplicity of formal balance when an interesting illustration can deliver the headline idea.

Proportion

The principle of proportion is another fundamental of good composition. Proportion is closely related to balance, since it is concerned with

Remember when you were in such a hurry to grow older?

At the time, thirteen seemed like a silly age. It was so...*young*.

And since growing up was taking so long, you decided to hurry nature along, and become Very Mature instantly.

As it turned out, the years didn't need any hurrying at all. The girl above trying to look like a Woman is *now* a Woman—and probably wondering, like yourself, how she got there so fast.

You can't postpone the future.

If all that time can fly by so fast, imagine how quickly the *next* several years will pass.

That's why we'd like to urge you to get ready for them.

And that's where Metropolitan Life can help.

We don't just insure your life. We help insure your future.

Let's say you're planning to send your children to college someday. If you take out your own Metropolitan policy, that can help pay for it.

Or maybe you've chosen a career instead, and you have an eye on a business of your own someday. Your Metropolitan insurance can help make that possible, too.

And, of course, men aren't the only people who retire. Women do, too. Your Metropolitan insurance can help make a secure retirement possible, too.

In fact, two out of every three dollars we pay out in benefits go to *living* policyholders to help pay for their future.

**She who hesitates
pays higher premiums.**

At Metropolitan Life, we insure over forty million people. We've been helping people prepare for the future for 107 years. But while much has changed over that time, one fact about personal life insurance is always the same:

The sooner you begin, the less it costs every year.

See your Metropolitan representative. Soon.

Because the future gets closer every minute.

❄ Metropolitan
Where the future is now

FIGURE 13.2
The reference point that determines the balance of a layout is the optical center, approximately one-third of the distance above the physical center. Here the reflection of the girl's eyes in the mirror, the focal point of the advertisement, is placed at the optical center. [*Metropolitan Life*.]

the division of space among layout elements for a pleasing optical effect. But good proportion in an advertisement also requires placing the desired emphasis in terms of size, shape, and color on each element. If the successful delivery of a message depends greatly on an unusual illustration, this element deserves space and position in

FIGURE 13.3
Balance in
layout does not
mean that the fin-
ished advertise-
ment will have a
cold, formal ap-
pearance, as this
delightful, infor-
mally balanced
advertisement
shows. [*Gardner
Advertising Com-
pany, Inc.*]

proportion to its importance. If the major appeal is the price of the
product, then price should be given display value that is proportionate.

As a rule, *unequal* dimensions help create lively advertising
design; conversely, when distances between elements are equal, or
when the layout is exactly half color, half noncolor, or half copy, half
illustration, the advertisement tends to become monotonous.

Contrast—for Emphasis

Contrast, of course, means variety. It gives life to the entire composition
and adds emphasis to important elements. The advertiser wants the ad

to stand out from competitive advertisements, and wants the most important elements in the ad to attract the most attention.

Contrasts come in a variety of useful forms, among them sizes, shapes, colors, and "directions" (for example, a vertical tree, a horizontal pavement, an arched rainbow), and may involve any of a layout's elements—not just illustrations.

Eye Movement

Movement is the principle of design that carries the reader's eye from element to element in the sequence desired for effective communication of the advertising message, just as the structure of advertising copy leads the reader step by step from initial attention, through interest and desire, to action, as explained in Chapter 12. "Eye direction" and "sequence" are two other terms for the same principle, and the layout artist accomplishes it in several different ways. Mechanical eye direction relies upon such devices as pointing fingers, lines, or arrows deliberately to push attention from unit to unit. Sequence direction takes advantage of established reading patterns, such as the tendency to start at the top left corner of the page and read generally on a diagonal line to the lower right corner. The eye also moves somewhat naturally from large items to small, from dark units to light, and from color to noncolor.

A more subtle method is suggestive direction by means of movement within illustrations. The curve of the model's figure, for example, leads the eye from headline to body copy, or the direction in which the model is looking causes the reader to look in the same direction.

Also, if a sales story is told in comic-strip sequence, readers will very likely follow it in the intended order. Care should be used not to direct the reader's eye out of the advertisement, of course, particularly in newspaper or magazine advertising that is less than full-page size.

Unity

Some artists consider unity, or harmony, the most important of all design principles. While it is necessary to consider each element as a separate unit in striving for balance, proportion, contrast, and eye movement, the complete layout should be constructed so that component parts are combined as a single unified composition. To use the comparison with architecture again, attention should not be attracted to doors, windows, gables, or chimney pots; all these structural details should melt into one harmonious impression of the complete building. Some of the common methods of securing unity in layout are the use of consistent typographical design; the repetition of the same motifs, such as an affinity of shape for different elements; the overlapping of elements; the use of a border to hold the elements together; and the avoidance of too much white space between elements.

Two questions generally arise here. First, do the demands for unity

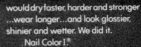

Revolution!

Until now..."doing" your nails could be their undoing.

Dry, split, cracked, chipped, peeling or discolored nails...dry cuticles and finger tips...could be caused by harsh chemicals in nail cosmetics.

But...Germaine Monteil® has staged a revolution.

And, to do it, we had to change the system.

We had to invent a nail cleanser that would remove polish without drying, bleaching or staining your nails. We did it.

We had to invent a cuticle conditioner that would strengthen your outgrowing nail while it softens your cuticle. We did it.

We had to invent a base coat that would actually smooth ridges and imperfections without drawing natural oils and moisture from your nails. We did that, too.

And we had to invent a nail enamel that would dry faster, harder and stronger ...wear longer...and look glossier, shinier and wetter. We did it.

Nail Color I.®

And we did it in 24 fashionable cream shades with three sophisticated, transparent topcoats.

To complete our revolutionary movement we also invented the first civilized bottle for nail enamel. Angled so it's virtually tip-proof and so the brush never hangs high and dry. And with a double seal to prevent thickening and evaporation.

Join this revolutionary movement toward healthier looking, lovelier nails.

See your Germaine Monteil Beauty Consultant...at your favorite department or specialty store...everyday.

Also, sign The Beauty Register®...to qualify for free samples and the chance to make purchases at very special values. Sign up when you drop in...to join the Nail Color I revolution.

Germaine Monteil

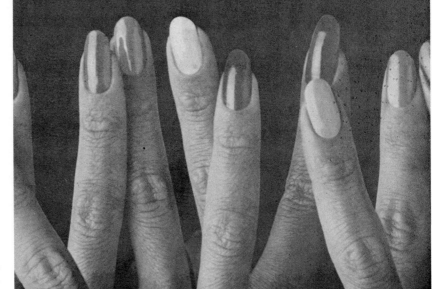

FIGURE 13.4
The design principle of movement, or eye direction. Here the fingers carry the reader's eye through the logotype to the copy. Notice that even the product itself is "pointed" to the headline. [*Tatham-Laird & Kudner Advertising.*]

and contrast in fact conflict with each other? While they may appear to operate at cross-purposes, they can actually function quite smoothly together—if the artist strives for "balance" here, too, as well as in the layout overall. Unity contributes orderliness to elements—a state of coherence or of "belonging" together. And properly placed, contrasting sizes, shapes, colors, and directions can flow together beautifully.

A second question concerns white space and its role in a layout. Sheer "nothingness" (blank space) can be a very significant part of an overall pattern. It can lend prestige to a product (setting it off from the rest of the ad), make any illustration more prominent, and make blocks of copy easier to read. Conversely, too much white space (or white space at the wrong spot) can throw a layout off balance, or detract from a claim of "low-cost" items or "bargain-basement" sales.

ADVERTISER OBJECTIVES AND IMAGE

In discussing disciplined creativity in Chapter 12, we noted that an advertisement must fulfill a specific communication objective while furthering the existing or desired company or brand image. There are styles of design, type, and illustrations that are appropriate in one situation and quite inappropriate in another. There are even styles of layout that seem to violate many basic principles of good design; yet they are effective as advertisements because they are appropriate to—or in harmony with—the image of the product or the firm.

While a layout is essentially an art or design procedure, the designer must never forget that the composition is not an end in itself. It is being prepared for a purpose, and that purpose is simply the communication of an idea. If the basic appeal of an advertisement is "bargains," the function of the layout design is to suggest bargains—not the designer's appreciation of fine art.

William Golden, the late creative director of advertising for CBS Television Network, warned commercial artists of the important difference between art with a capital "A" and advertising design:

> To regard the blank rectangle on a layout pad with the same attitude that the abstract painter confronts his blank canvas is surely a pointless delusion. The printed page is not primarily a medium for self-expression. Design for print is not Art. At best it is a highly skilled craft. A sensitive, inventive, interpretive craft, if you will, but in no way related to painting.[4]

[4] William Golden, "The Visual Craft of William Golden," in John S. Wright and Daniel S. Warner (eds.), *Speaking of Advertising*, McGraw-Hill Book Company, New York, 1963, p. 224.

GET ONE THING MORE
THAN COMPUTERIZED ACCURACY:

BULOVA

THIS NAME.

BULOVA
ACCUQUARTZ

SA

These watches are as accurate as miniature computerized quartz crystal movements can make them. They are as dependable as *we* are (and *we've* stood the test of time for 100 years now).
They can be seen in a variety of styles, from $150 to $2500, at fine jewelry and department stores.

BULOVA ⬢ ACCUQUARTZ® WATCHES

WHAT THE VISUAL ELEMENT SHOULD CONTRIBUTE

Every element in advertising layouts and television storyboards must pay its own way and contribute to effective communication of an idea. The great majority of print advertisements use some form of illustration (a practice readily justified in terms of increased attention), and of

SEAGRAM'S CROWN ROYAL, BLENDED CANADIAN WHISKY. 80 PROOF. SEAGRAM DISTILLERS CO., N.Y., N.Y.

Have you ever seen a grown man cry?

(a)

FIGURE 13.6
Three major con-
tributions of photo-
graphic illustration
are (a) realism
[*Warwick, Welsh &
Miller, Inc.*],
(b, *page 448*) im-
mediacy [*Batten,
Barton, Durstine &
Osborn, Inc., for
General Electric
Company*],
and (c, *page
449*) shock effect
[*Doyle, Dane,
Bernback, Inc.*].

course, while some television scenes contain no spoken message, they
are by nature visual. Well-conceived illustrations and moving pictures,
however, do more than just attract attention. They may amplify and
speed up each step in the communication process, help shape the tone
or atmosphere of entire ads and commercials, and convey abstract

This thimble can hold enough fuel to run the average home for seven months.

One answer to our long-range energy needs is no bigger than your fingertip.

Nuclear fuel.

Put to work inside a General Electric reactor in a nuclear power plant, 3 pellets of uranium dioxide can produce enough steam to make nearly 48 hundred kilowatt-hours of electricity.

Enough to run the average home for about seven months.

It would take 330 gallons of fuel oil to make the same amount of electricity. (About half the residual fuel oil consumed in this country is burned to make electricity.)

This is important.

Our need for electricity will double in the next twelve years or so. With oil and natural gas in short supply, we are going to have to rely more and more on nuclear power. And also our ample supplies of coal.

Coal and nuclear fuel. We have good supplies of both. Enough to provide hundreds of years of electricity. But no one fuel can do the job alone. We need to use *all* our natural resources wisely and efficiently. And continue to look for new ways to make electricity.

Because a country that runs on electricity simply can't afford to ever run out.

Three pellets equal 330 gallons of oil.

Nuclear plants produce 8% of our electricity.

Progress for People.

GENERAL ⊛ ELECTRIC

FIGURE 13.6
(*Continued*)

(*b*)

concepts—such as prestige, beauty, and faith—which are next to impossible to deliver quickly and clearly with words.

In addition, carefully planned visual sequences may stimulate reader or viewer *participation*, and, hence, enhance interest. Recent ads for Camel cigarettes, for example, ask readers to "pick out the Camel smoker" from a picture of people representing different interest

©AMERICAN TOURISTER, WARREN, R.I.   SIMULATED SITUATION BASED ON ACTUAL INCIDENT.

"Dear American Tourister: You got hit by a tornado."

On April 3, 1974, the following happened.

A tornado slammed into an Alabama trailer court, demolishing Wilfred Gileau's house trailer and everything in it.

On April 4, 1974, the following happened.

Under piles of wreck and rubble, Wilfred Gileau found the one thing the tornado hadn't destroyed. His American Tourister. It was a little scuffed, a little scraped, but in good working order.

Mr. Gileau was amazed. And frankly, so are we. Because we don't build American Touristers to do things like ride out tornados.

When we take the toughest materials we can find to mold our cases, and wrap each case with a strong stainless steel frame, and put in nonspring locks designed not to spring open on impact, we do it for just one reason.

So that year after year and mile after mile, your American Tourister will go through all the everyday perils of everyday traveling.

We don't intend American Touristers to survive tornados.

We do intend them to survive your next trip to Wichita.

FIGURE 13.6
(*Continued*)

(*c*)

groups and life-styles. Or television commercials for various types of insurance often call upon the viewer to "put yourself in this situation" or "imagine how you would feel if . . ." and then proceed to illustrate an automobile accident, a house fire, or the death of a loved one.

The value of such audience participation is clear; psychologists have long maintained that it aids learning far more than does "passive reception" of a message. And learning—along with understanding—leads not only to retention but also to application of knowledge gained in the marketplace.[5]

Print: Photographs or Drawings

Print illustrations can be produced by either photography or drawing. The latter method is referred to as art, but creative photographers are just as much artists as their colleagues who work with pen or brush. A number of different drawing techniques—or media, in the artist's vocabulary—are available to the advertiser, and each has a distinctive character which recommends it for certain uses. Drawings done with pen and ink, crayon, or the dry-brush technique result in clean, hard lines of solid black and white. Paintings and wash drawings—a black-and-white brush technique similar to watercolor painting—produce varying tonal gradations from black through shades of gray instead of solid blacks and white.

Photographic art, like pencil and wash drawings, contains a depth of tonal values and is usually reproduced by halftone photography, although it is possible to make line reproductions from such continuous-tone artwork by using processes described in Chapter 14. In many cases, it is not easy to decide whether photographs or drawings per se will make the best illustrations. Photographs can usually be eliminated from consideration, of course, when the subject of the illustration existed only in the past and was not photographed or not adequately photographed. While it may be physically possible to recreate the personality of Socrates or the stark drama of Valley Forge with photography, as motion pictures do, for printed advertising it is usually more effective and less expensive to rely on the artist's skill with brush or pen. The same applies to events which may happen in the future, such as manned space stations, with maintenance crews for spacecraft in orbit.

In most circumstances, however, photographs can be secured economically, quickly, and easily. An amazing variety of "stock" photographs, catalogued by subject classifications, are available from news services, private collections and libraries. The New York Public Library, for example, has a huge collection of more than 6 million photographs of every conceivable subject. The disadvantage of stock photos is that they are available to everyone, and are therefore often overused, although exclusive use rights for a limited time may sometimes be purchased at extra cost. Their main advantage, of course, is economy, both in money and in time. An advertiser might spend weeks and thousands of dollars sending a photographer to get photos of an

[5] Steuart Henderson Britt, "How Advertising Can Use Psychology's Rules of Learning," *Printers' Ink*, Sept. 23, 1955, pp. 74–80.

Nature made strawberries without artificial color, flavor, or preservatives.

Bama makes strawberry preserves the same way.

7¢ off any size jar of Bama jams, jellies, or preserves.

BAMA
STRAWBERRY PRESERVES

NO ARTIFICIAL FLA

MR. GROCER: Borden will redeem this coupon for face value of coupon plus 5¢ for handling when submitted as part payment for any size jar of Bama Jams, Jellies or Preserves. Any sales tax must be paid by consumer. Invoices showing purchase of sufficient stock to cover coupon must be shown on request. Coupon void in any state or locality where taxed, prohibited or restricted by law. Coupon may not be assigned or transferred by you. Good only in the U.S.A. Cash value of 1/20 of one cent. For payment, mail to Borden, Inc., Box 1720, Clinton, Iowa 52732. GOOD ONLY ON BAMA JAMS, JELLIES OR PRESERVES. ANY OTHER USE CONSTITUTES FRAUD. LIMIT ONE PER FAMILY. OFFER ENDS DECEMBER 31, 1976.

BORDEN

Bama. Natural fruit flavor at a down-to-earth price.

B-9384-S-FC

Store coupon

FIGURE 13.7
This advertisement shows both the realism which photographic art can convey and the value it can contribute to the overall sales message. [*Tracy Locke Advertising & Public Relations, Inc.*]

eruption from Hawaii's famous Kilauea volcano, when the exact picture desired is already in the files of a library, or could be supplied by a commercial stock photo firm for a $25 fee. This particular shot might be obtained without cost from the publicity departments of air lines or bureaus concerned with the promotion of tourist travel to Hawaii.

Many art directors feel that photography is something more than just another art technique. Although it is not accurate to say that the camera always tells the truth, there is an obvious realism to a photograph that adds to its impact and its conviction value. If testimonials or case histories are a part of the advertisement, illustrating them with photos provides an element of authenticity and believability that strengthens the entire message. There is also a sense of immediacy in photographic illustrations, and so the reader becomes personally involved with the situation. Also, we should remember that people are accustomed to receiving news by means of photographs and so are likely to accept the photograph as news—one of the three important elements of content for a headline idea.

Finally, the camera is a superb medium to get the most out of a fantastic or off-beat situation. The very fact that a fanciful or "impossible" picture is presented with the instrument of realism—the camera—gives it more punch than if it were obviously the product of an artist's imaginative hand.

We should not get the impression from this list of advantages offered by photographs that the skillful application of pen and brush techniques is obsolescent. The only limitations on the effect or impression which can be delivered by a drawing or painting are the skill and imagination of the artist. He does not have to find the right models or right setting for his picture, as the photographer must. He can see them in his own mind and can create the exact personalities, expressions, positions, and moods he wants. He has more leeway to develop a distinctive atmosphere or a personal style than the photographer, and this can be quite important in getting attention as well as in building the "image" of the advertiser.

Also, it is easier to emphasize or dramatize parts of a product or details of design or construction with drawings. Most photos in which structural detail is important are actually modified by retouching, a painstaking process in which an artist uses a brush to refine details or change tone values of the original photo. Finally, photographs cannot provide the degree of distortion or exaggeration so essential in cartoons or comic-strip characters.

Television: Live Action or Animation

Any moving picture in which living performers (human or animal) appear is generally thought of as "live action." On the other hand, animation consists of drawings of characters and backgrounds which appear to move in a realistic manner—and may be presented in three basic ways. The first involves *limited* movement and is known as *limited animation*; it is a money-saver which can still be an effective creative tool.

The second involves very *refined* movement (often including lip movement) and is called *full animation*; it is often associated with Walt Disney productions. The third combines animation and live action in such a way that cartoon figures are *superimposed* over a scene with

If you can put $1,500 a year away for retirement, and qualify, we can help you do it tax-free.

New York Life's Personal-Pension Policies.

Until just recently, if you worked and your employer didn't set up a retirement plan for you, you probably wouldn't have one. There was no tax incentive for you to put money aside for later years.

But the new Federal pension law has changed all that.

Now you can put 15% of your annual income, up to a maximum of $1,500, into your own retirement plan—and deduct some or all of it on your Federal income tax return.

If your husband or wife has earned income and qualifies, he or she can start a separate plan. Together you may be able to put away $3,000 a year—and pay no tax on principal or interest until you retire.

All you need is a specially designed New York Life retirement annuity or endowment policy.

Unlike some retirement plans, a New York Life policy guarantees you and your spouse a monthly retirement income for as long as either of you lives. And you can even elect, in advance, to have us pay the premiums if you become disabled.

What's more, a New York Life endowment policy provides insurance protection for your family.

Personal pension. It's just one of the ways that your New York Life agent can help you protect your family and your future. See him or her soon.

We guarantee tomorrow today.

New York Life Insurance Company, 51 Madison Avenue, New York, New York 10010. Life, Health, Disability Income, and Group Insurance, Annuities, Pension Plans.

FIGURE 13.8
It would be difficult, if not impossible, for photography to treat this advertisement's subject as distinctively as the drawing does. [*New York Life Insurance Company.*]

live talent. All three are excellent methods for presenting a product as the "star" of a commercial. Product identification is easy, and action is a natural. Clinical psychologists have found that the human eye is attracted to movement; animate both product and USP and it is not hard to hold viewer attention.

Usually, animation takes viewers into a kind of fantasyland—a world of beautiful maidens, knights in shining armor, and animated characters who are absolutely invulnerable to any of life's realities. Fantasy commercials look like they are easy to write; actually, they are among the most difficult. The danger of adiness is tremendous, whereas the task of creating credible, memorable brand differentiation is monumental. Still, fairy tales and dreamworld techniques *may* create genuine product enjoyment by association.

Of course, live-action demonstration can also prove a superb means of proving how and why claims are true—and, hence, of enhancing both credibility and memorability. On the other hand, imagination can get out of hand in this area, too. Fairfax Cone, retired chairman of the board of Foote, Cone & Belding, put the matter in perspective when he said: "What I object to is foolishness in advertising: such as a woman rushing across a lawn into the face of a television camera and suddenly disappearing from view to act out the name 'Open Pit' barbecue sauce."[6] Here we have an excellent example of what might be called an advertising charade. It makes no promise, has no real significance to consumer needs, and really does nothing whatsoever to demonstrate brand characteristics or superiority.

WHAT A PICTURE SHOULD PICTURE

Whether advertisers use photographs or drawings, live action or animation, they must decide what *ideas* the pictures are intended to convey or amplify. The simplest method of visualization is a shot of the product, and it is used frequently (especially in retail advertising). But unless the product is unique or has high raw pulling power for some reason, this may be a weak visual technique. We don't buy the product; we buy an image of the product or what the product will do for us. Consequently, it is usually more effective to show the product in a setting or against a background that suggests the image or shows the product in a particular context. Many attention-getting pictures do not show the product at all, but instead dramatize a benefit derived from the use of the product or a need which the product satisfies. An advertisement for a service, such as life insurance, telephone, or transportation, has no product to see and no product to illustrate.

Product Settings

Although there is probably an unlimited number of different "settings" in which a product might be featured in both print and broadcast

---

[6] Fairfax Cone, *The Blue Streak*, Crain Communications, Inc., Chicago, 1973, p. 175.

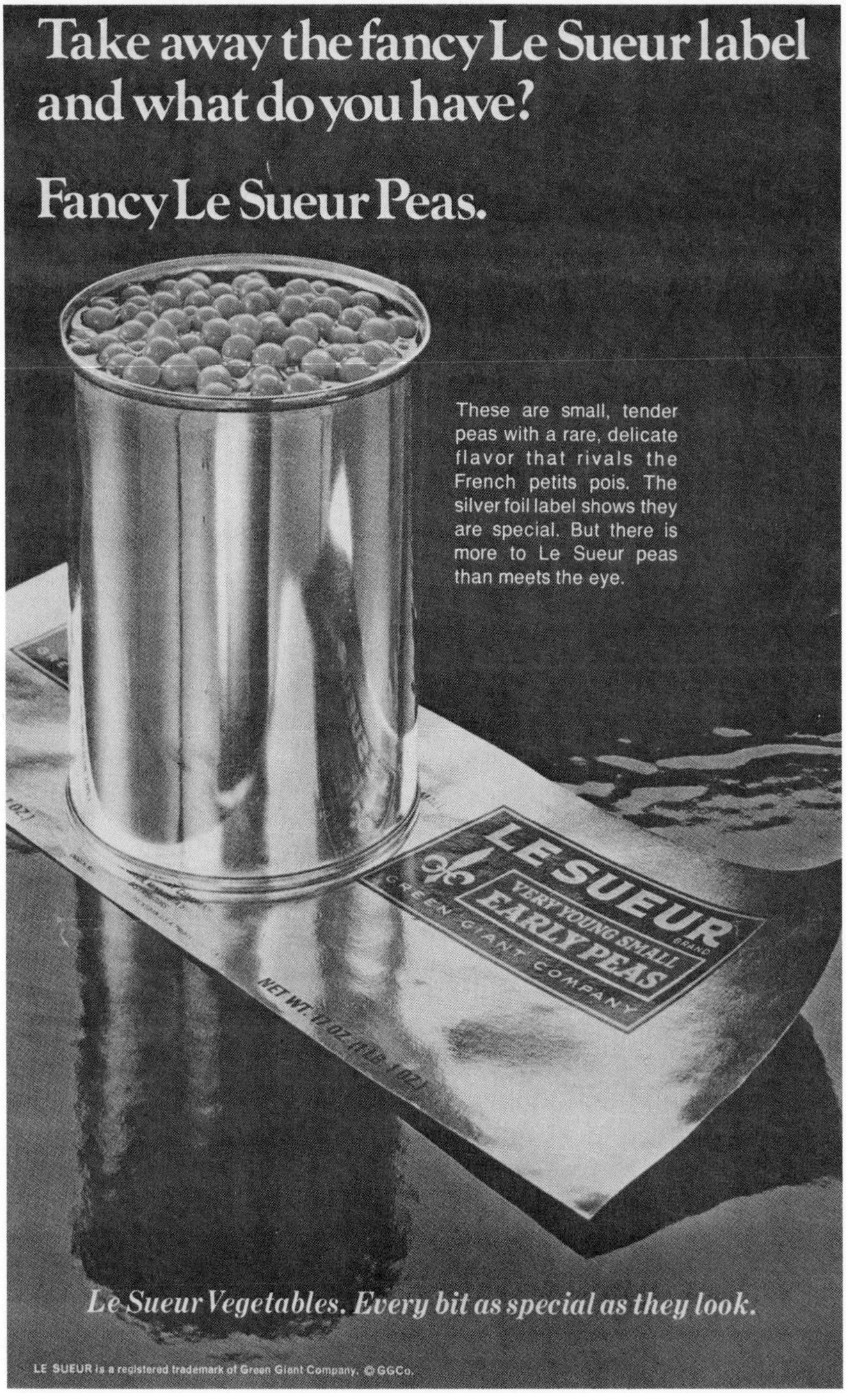
Take away the fancy Le Sueur label and what do you have?
Fancy Le Sueur Peas.
These are small, tender peas with a rare, delicate flavor that rivals the French petits pois. The silver foil label shows they are special. But there is more to Le Sueur peas than meets the eye.
LE SUEUR
BRAND
VERY YOUNG SMALL
EARLY PEAS
GREEN GIANT COMPANY
NET WT. 17 OZ. (1 LB. 1 OZ.)
Le Sueur Vegetables. Every bit as special as they look.
LE SUEUR is a registered trademark of Green Giant Company. © GGCo.

FIGURE 13.9
Even an illustration of the product alone can be effective when that product is distinctive or has high inherent interest for intended readers. [*Leo Burnett Company.*]

media, it may be helpful to consider a few basic ones using one specific product. Suppose a copywriter for a dishwashing detergent decides on the following USP: "Scrubbing power to make dishes sparkle, with a skin conditioner to leave hands soft."

Preliminaries to Product Use   In a "preliminaries" setting, we might well find an illustration of product composition—a behind-the-scenes glimpse of the actual ingredients in the detergent which result in clean dishes and smooth skin. The bulk of the visual message in a television commercial here might, similarly, feature development of the detergent's cleansing properties (in a test laboratory, for example), and the addition of skin-softening ingredients (perhaps right through the packaging process, so that viewers could see both elements combined in box or bottle).

Product in Use   The same USP in a product-in-use situation could be emphasized through a simple side-by-side comparison with a competitor's detergent, or through two separate pictures: one which clearly showed grease-cutting suds attacking dirty dishes, and the other which showed the skin conditioner soothing a pair of hands. In television, cameras might take viewers "underwater" to examine firsthand the reason why the USP is true; while food stains took a beating, hands would not—and the audience might observe various emollients soaking into skin during the wash-and-rinse process.

Result of Product Use   Third, plans might call for a result-of-use story—placing the same USP in still a different framework. Now the scene pictured would be "aftereffects": soft hands for an evening's date—after the dishes are done. Time-lapse photography in television might compare two sets of hands over a period of days or weeks: dry, rough skin following use of harsh detergents, and smooth, soft skin thanks to the advertised brand.

Incidentals to Product Use   Last, the "tough-on-stains-but-mild-on-skin" message could be told with reference to incidentals—the easy-to-handle (in one or several situations) container which holds the product, the variety of colors and fragrances available (to suit different personalities), or the selection of sizes and prices (for a range of family sizes and needs).

HOW TO CHOOSE

What the context of a picture (either "still" or "moving") should be depends on a number of considerations. Important among these are the nature of the product and of competitive strategies, the audience to which the message is aimed, the medium used, and the objective of the advertisement, as well as the function of the pictures themselves. If the function of a particular illustration is to provide the visual element in the attention-getting headline idea, the content and composition may be quite different from an illustration designed to add believability or conviction to the same message. For example, a static graph may effectively illustrate the results of tests presented as evidence of the efficiency of a product, but the same illustration would be unlikely to stop a reader turning the pages of a newspaper or magazine.

Some products, too, are inherently more interesting than others and are susceptible to a more direct visual presentation. The readers of business publications, who are looking for information, will be attracted by nuts-and-bolts illustrations which would be skipped by the more casual consumer magazine reader bent primarily on entertainment—or by the homemaker shopping the pages of the local paper. When the objective of an advertisement is to complete the sale, as in mail-order advertising, the kind and number of illustrations may differ greatly from those used in an advertisement planned to create or reinforce a corporate image.

It has been said that there is a great difference in the attention-getting and interest-holding power of pictures of certain subjects. Studies have been made which indicate, for example, that pictures of children attract more attention from adults of both sexes than pictures of animals or natural scenery. Advertisers, however, cannot measure the value of an illustration in the abstract; they must consider it only as a specific visual contribution to the message. The question is not whether pictures of children are high in attention and interest, but whether a picture of children promises the reader or viewer an interesting story about the product. In other words, can a picture of children be related quickly and believably to the idea the advertiser is trying to communicate. The first criterion to apply to advertising graphics, then, is relevance.

Relevant and Incongruous Graphics

Relevancy should not be confused with congruity. To say that the first qualification for an advertising illustration is relevancy simply means that it should have traceable and significant connection with the idea the advertisement attempts to deliver. An illustration can be relevant and at the same time be incongruous or have inconsistent and inharmonious parts. A picture of a baby will probably have high intrinsic attention value, but it is an irrelevant illustration if used over the headline "This new cassette recorder has a built-in condenser microphone." There is no traceable or significant connection between the idea in the illustration and the idea in the words.

The incongruous-but-relevant, or "offbeat," illustration, on the

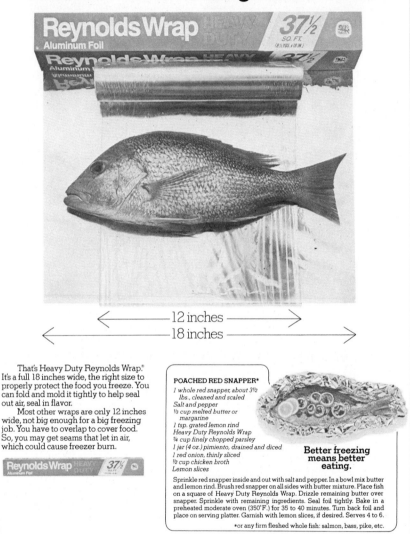

The best wrap for freezing is also the best size for freezing. It's 18" wide.

Reynolds Wrap Aluminum Foil HEAVY DUTY 37½ SQ. FT.

← 12 inches →
← 18 inches →

That's Heavy Duty Reynolds Wrap.® It's a full 18 inches wide, the right size to properly protect the food you freeze. You can fold and mold it tightly to help seal out air, seal in flavor.

Most other wraps are only 12 inches wide, not big enough for a big freezing job. You have to overlap to cover food. So, you may get seams that let in air, which could cause freezer burn.

Reynolds Wrap Aluminum Foil 37½

POACHED RED SNAPPER*
1 whole red snapper, about 3½ lbs., cleaned and scaled
Salt and pepper
⅓ cup melted butter or margarine
1 tsp. grated lemon rind
Heavy Duty Reynolds Wrap
¼ cup finely chopped parsley
1 jar (4 oz.) pimiento, drained and diced
1 red onion, thinly sliced
½ cup chicken broth
Lemon slices

Better freezing means better eating.

Sprinkle red snapper inside and out with salt and pepper. In a bowl mix butter and lemon rind. Brush red snapper on all sides with butter mixture. Place fish on a square of Heavy Duty Reynolds Wrap. Drizzle remaining butter over snapper. Sprinkle with remaining ingredients. Seal foil tightly. Bake in a preheated moderate oven (350°F.) for 35 to 40 minutes. Turn back foil and place on serving platter. Garnish with lemon slices, if desired. Serves 4 to 6.

*or any firm fleshed whole fish: salmon, bass, pike, etc.

(a)

FIGURE 13.10
Dramatizations of (a) the benefits derived from product use [*Reynolds Aluminum*] or (b, opposite page) the losses incurred from nonuse [*Avis Rent A Car System, Inc.*] are widely used, highly effective visualization techniques.

other hand, provides an arresting effect that has been the basis for many successful advertising campaigns. As art director Stephen Baker says:

> The logical way of displaying merchandise is to show it where it belongs: the typewriter on the desk, the car on the highway.

"There now, that didn't take long, did it?"

Name? Address? Company? Zip? Compact? Mid-size? Method of payment? Give up?

Avis does not want you to go through this.

That's why no one can get you a car faster than Avis, once you make a reservation with your free Wizard Number.

And on the return trip, no one can get you out and on your way quicker.

We're the Avis System, renting all make automobiles, featuring those engineered by Chrysler.

More importantly, we're the people of Avis, trying harder and caring more.

And part of trying harder and caring more, is renting faster.

(b)

Put these objects where they are least expected and the result can be a stopper. The background need not be selected for its shock value alone; it can emphasize a sales point in a very real way. The office typewriter placed in the midst of a profusely blooming flower bed would underline the headline, "The World's Most Beautiful Typewriter." A picture of an automobile parked *inside* a fancy hotel dining room might go nicely with the caption, "Distinguished people take their car wherever they go!"

When handled photographically, the incongruity of a situation has even more impact. The realism of the photography combined with the implausibility of the situation makes the reader look twice—or more often.[7]

Like anything else that promises greater return, the use of an incongruous illustration involves greater risk than does a more direct approach. It can fail miserably if it is not skillfully handled. What the well-executed incongruous picture does, of course, is suggest to the readers that there must be a story about this picture—a story they want to find out more about. Particularly in consumer advertising, the illustration should not merely repeat what the headline words say. If readers can take in the entire story at a glance, they have no reason to stay with the ad any longer. Advertisements for some products do tell the story at one glance. Often when the product is a low-cost shopping-list item, the "story" can be told completely and quickly by illustrations, almost without words.

Television pictures can provide real curiosity—even suspense—through carefully selected scene composition. Suppose, for example, that a commercial opens with a close-up shot of a person crying. Attention is aroused: is someone hurt? Sick? Frightened? Then the camera pulls back slowly—and we see the person is peeling onions! Or a device as simple as a door may provide both intrigue and sales value if opened cautiously (over appropriate music or sound effects) to take viewers "through the door of investment opportunity" or "into the house of appliance values."

On the other hand, a careless use of visuals may lead to "vampire video"—scenes totally unrelated to the product or USP at hand. These are shots which literally feed on the commercial vehicle (hence, the name "vampire"), to serve purely selfish ends (usually artistic whims of producers). Unfortunately, these same scenes are often brilliantly witty, highly memorable, and thoroughly enjoyed by audiences. At times, such commercials win "creativity" awards, too—and receive the praises of trade and lay persons alike. With no audience recall of product name, however—and no application of the "content" to any sales message—*disciplined* creativity has gone out the window. (And often, the campaigns prove disastrous at the cash register.)

COLOR VERSUS BLACK AND WHITE

Only an occasional local television commercial is still produced in black and white (to save expense). In the print media, however, the issue is an important one. Although basic principles of layout design

[7] Stephen Baker, *Advertising Layout and Art Direction*, McGraw-Hill Book Company, New York, 1959, p. 175.

and picture composition remain the same for both color and black and white, the decision to use color—and how much color—affects the development of copy and art and complicates the graphic arts processes required to reproduce the finished printed advertisement. The mechanical production of color advertising is explained in Chapter 14. In this chapter we shall consider color as it affects the design, rather than the production, of the advertisement.

Except for such simple applications as printing in one color on paper stock of another color for a direct advertising piece, the addition of color to advertisements may materially increase costs. Periodicals charge a higher rate for color advertisements than for the same amount of space in black and white. Art in color is more expensive than comparable black-and-white art, and mechanical production costs are also higher. Nevertheless, some advertisers are willing to pay the premium for color for a number of reasons. Color adds attention value; helps emphasize more important elements; presents the product or situation with a realism or an atmosphere impossible in a black-and-white ad; provides a better identification of product, brand name, and trademark; and endows the advertisement with a feeling of quality and prestige. In certain situations, the use of color may be essential if the advertisement is to make the desired impression on the reader. For example, trying to convey the "appetite appeal" of catsup on a hamburger in a black-and-white ad is difficult, if not impossible. For some examples, turn to the color insert. Also, readers have come to expect color in certain instances, and are disappointed (or otherwise negatively impressed) when an ad fails to comply.

For most advertisers, however, the question is not this simple. Certainly the use of color is hard to justify per se on the grounds of added attention value, since readership scores for black-and-white advertisements often exceed those for color advertisements on a cost-ratio basis. What the advertiser must decide is whether, within the limits of a specific advertising budget, the extra cost for color is justified for the particular product, the advertising objectives in mind, and the media to be used.

Most of us would probably agree that food and travel advertisements, as well as ads for rugs, fabrics, and fashions, can usually benefit greatly from color. On the other hand, messages designed to promote a particular brand of accident insurance or a new banking service may not demand color for effective communication. In fact, they might benefit from the feeling of "stark realism" (or the atmosphere of a "news documentary") created through the use of black and white.

Color in Newspaper Advertisements

The advertiser can put color into newspaper advertisements in two different ways. One is through the use of preprinted color inserts, which are furnished to newspapers in rolls and fed into the regular newspaper presses along with the locally printed editorial and advertising material. One of these methods is called Hi-Fi color. In this the advertisement must be designed as though it were on wallpaper, because the rolls are cut into page-size sections and there is no control on exactly where each cut is made. Thus each section in the roll must be a complete message. Spectacolor is the other form of preprinted newspaper color advertising. While it eliminates the disadvantage of the continuous wallpaper effect and permits full-page ads to appear as separate units with their own margins, it requires special equipment to process the preprinted rolls, which relatively few newspapers have. Newspaper magazine and Sunday comic sections, whether nationally or locally produced, also provide color advertising, but these supplements are more logically classed with magazines than with newspapers, as outlined in Chapter 8.

The second opportunity for color advertising in newspapers is ROP, or run-of-paper, color, which has increased in importance in recent years and comes closest to justifying the added cost on straight extra-attention value. Since the great preponderance of both advertising and editorial content in newspapers appears in black and white, any additional color supplies an element of contrast and distinction that makes the message stand out from competition. As the use of color increases, however, its attention value must decrease.

Also, a typical surcharge or premium for one additional color in ROP newspaper advertising ranges from 15 to 20 percent, with a 1,000-line space unit the minimum acceptable. Two or three colors (black plus three colors, or "four-color") cost from 20 to 30 percent more than black and white, and frequently such an advertisement may not be possible in units of less than a full page.

If an advertiser can deliver a message effectively in 420 or 770 lines of space, he or she must decide whether the additional initial attention, realism, atmosphere, identification, or prestige to be received from the use of color will make it worth buying more space at a premium of 15 or more percent. Perhaps one clue can be found in the advertising of one of the largest consistent users of newspaper space—department stores—most of which rely on black-and-white advertisements except for special promotions.

Color in Magazine Advertisements

In magazines, particularly national consumer publications, much of the editorial art and many of the advertisements are in color, and black-and-white space may be overwhelmed by color competition unless presented very dramatically. Furthermore, the quality of reproduction and the realism obtainable from color in magazine space is considerably greater than is possible with the coarser screens and rougher paper stock used by newspapers, as is explained in Chapter 14. Finally, both brand identification and prestige are more important objectives for most national advertisers than for retail or local advertisers. Typical minimum space units for two-color magazine advertisements are 85 to 170 lines; half pages are common as the minimum for full color. Surcharges for color vary widely. In some small-circulation magazines, the premium for four colors will run as much as 50 percent above the black-and-white rate. Currently, one multimillion-circulation consumer magazine charges 35 percent more for a four-color page than for a black-and-white one, while another multimillion consumer magazine charges only 10 percent more for a four-color page than for one in black and white.

Color in Out-of-Home, Point-of-Purchase, and Direct Mail Advertisements

In outdoor and transit advertising, there is no additional space cost for color, and the added costs of production for color are more than justified by increased attention and visibility in most cases. This is particularly true of outdoor, with its fixed position and moving audience. Point-of-purchase material and direct-mail advertising make wide use of color to attract initial attention, which is a very important objective. In both cases, the only added cost is in the printing process.

Color Characteristics and Dimensions

In addition to such specific advantages as increased attention value, realism, prestige, emphasis, and identification of package, brand, or trademark, colors have a symbolism of their own which can contribute to the communication process. Most of us know that certain colors, for example, are *warm* and that others are *cool*. Blues and greens, perhaps from their association with the sky, the sea, trees, and grass, are cool, restrained colors. Red and orange, at the other end of the color spectrum, are warm colors suggesting fire, passion, action, and excitement. Yellow is a bright, cheerful color, implying warmth without heat. Regardless of the symbolism or psychological impact of added color in advertisements, the layout artist must consider its use just as he or she would consider the use of an additional illustration or more white space. Color is another physical element of layout, and if the result is to incorporate the basic principles of good design, the artist must understand the dimensions of color.

To convey the suggestions of colors in advertising copy or in face-to-face communication, we often use such terms as "avocado," "ruby," or "tangerine." In the design of a product, its package, or its advertising, however, we need a more accurate means of classifying colors if we are to get the results desired.

Without getting into complexities which properly belong in the field of color theory rather than advertising art and layout, we should understand the essential principles artists use to identify colors. To begin with, although light is the source of all color, the artist works with pigment color, rather than light color. For example, the three primary light colors, from which all others are derived, are green, red-orange, and blue-violet. The artist's primary pigment colors are red (magenta), blue (blue-green), and yellow. From these the artist produces such secondary colors as purple by mixing the primary red and blue, or orange by mixing yellow and red pigments. A mixture of all three primary pigments neutralizes each of them, and tends to produce black if the primaries are equally strong and brilliant.

The artist identifies colors in terms of three qualities or, technically, measures color by three dimensions. These are hue, value, and chroma. *Hue* is the basic identity of color, the quality that distinguishes one color from another, such as blue from green, red from orange, or red-orange from red-purple. Pink, however, is not a hue, but only a tone or tint of red—a basic color neutralized by the addition of white. To change one hue into another, we must alter its fundamental nature, such as making blue into green by adding yellow.

Value is the lightness or darkness of a hue, the quality that distinguishes pink from red, for example. We can increase the value of a hue by adding white and decrease the value by adding black without changing the hue. Adding white to blue results in a lighter tint and adding black produces a darker shade, but in neither case do we change the basic "blueness." Value is the only dimension that distinguishes neutral or achromatic pigments—blacks, grays, and whites—from one another.

Chroma refers to the purity of a hue, its intensity in terms of saturation, or the strength or weakness of a color. When we change the value of a color by adding black or white, we also change its intensity or chroma. The pink we make by adding white to red has a higher value than the original red, but it also has less chroma or intensity because its proportion of pure color is smaller. We can also change the chroma without changing the value by mixing a gray of the same value with the hue pigment. The more gray we add, the lower the chroma or intensity becomes, but the value remains constant.

DESIGN SUGGESTIONS FOR DIFFERENT MEDIA

Many of the principles of good composition apply to almost all major media. It may be helpful, however, to examine a few graphic considerations in terms of individual media characteristics.

Newspapers

To grasp the primary problem in the design of newspaper advertisements, we need only to turn the pages of our local paper. The advertisements are stacked from the lower right corner up to the upper right, and across to lower left. Here is competition for attention raised to the *n*th power—competition not only with other advertisers, but with the news of the day. The typical reader moves through this pandemonium of communications at a rapid pace, skipping from item to item and page to page while eating breakfast, riding the bus to work, or waiting for dinner.

The most important design principle in newspaper layout is contrast. Big space and ROP color are applications of this principle, but hardly the most economical ones for the majority of advertisers. A distinctive border may help an advertisement stand out from the mob; so may the large dark areas of photographs, or good-sized illustrations of any type. Perhaps the most effective method of assuring the contrast that will call attention to a newspaper advertisement is the generous use of white space—a "white fence" to separate one property from all the other properties on the page. Informal or asymmetrical balance, with the elements so arranged that each touches only once on any of the four sides, and touches at unequally spaced points, is a layout treatment that makes maximum use of white space for contrast. Both structure and suggestive direction should be carefully planned to be sure that the reader will not be directed out of an ad to an adjacent competitor—either editorial or advertising.

Magazines

For magazine advertisements, the designer can count on more leisurely readership, and even upon rereading, since magazines, unlike newspapers, are rarely read in one sitting. Nor do magazine advertisements face the intense competition so typical of newspaper advertising. Magazine advertisements are almost never "buried" by other ads above and alongside; space as small as one column inch is almost always next to reading matter. Also, what competition there is tends to be based more on quality than quantity.

Because of better quality of paper stock and finer reproduction processes used in magazine production, the designer of a magazine advertisement has more freedom in approach and in technique, especially in the use of color, than the designer for newspapers. The selective audience characteristic of most magazines enables the layout artist to focus the presentation more directly toward the mood and interests of a particular group. A sophisticated, high-style layout and art treatment which is out of place in a business publication or an outdoor magazine can be very effective in *Vogue* or *The New Yorker*.

Television

Many effective television commercials capitalize on this medium's "action" capabilities and thereby provide viewers with great visual variety. (After all, if the TV sales message is mainly in the audio channel, over dull, repetitive shots, it might as well be a radio spot; and even if the visual material is vital, if it appears in relatively "still" form, it might as well be in a magazine.) A good rule of thumb is: let *something* move in every shot (camera, product, people, special effects); or as has often been said: in television, if something does not move, the viewer will.

Intricate features do not belong in television graphics, because the TV camera simply cannot pick them up. A machine with a hundred tiny moving parts is better "demonstrated" on the printed page. Also, visual sequences in television must flow naturally, logically, and believably throughout. If transitions are too abrupt, confusion often results; and if they are drawn out too long, bored viewers will tune out. Of course, there is a "willing suspension of disbelief" on the part of viewers—and so a prepared cake mix can be popped into the oven in one scene and pulled out in ready-to-eat form in the next. Still, copywriters must take care not to exploit viewer trust through nonsense gimmicks and camera tricks.

Outdoor Advertising

No medium relies more heavily on the pictorial method of communication than outdoor advertising. Here is advertising in its simplest and most direct form, without news or entertainment of any kind to attract initial attention and interest. Moreover, the audience is moving past the advertisement at a distance, and the message must be delivered clearly and completely in five seconds or less. The simplicity that is always desirable in layout becomes a vital principle with outdoor—simplicity not only in the sense of relatively few design elements that are orderly arranged for unity, but also in terms of the idea itself.

The Outdoor Advertising Committee of the Association of National Advertisers recommends that layouts for outdoor posters contain not more than three elements, with one element dominating the space. Five or six words of copy are considered ideal, and eight the maximum—exclusive of trademark or logotype. The value of silhouette illustration instead of front or full-face view is recognized by most poster designers, because the total illustration should stand out from the background as a mass that is readily identifiable from a distance.

Simplicity in outdoor design applies especially to typography. Simple lettering, somewhat heavier than average in weight, is highly desirable; ornamental or script lettering should be avoided because of poor legibility. Bright, warm colors contrasting with cool ones provide greater visibility, and the effective carrying power of the design may be further increased with fluorescent ink or paint. The selection of colors must almost always be a compromise between combinations that are best for visibility and those that are essential for identification or desirable for realism or psychological suggestion. Color visibility seems to depend less on contrasts in hue than on contrasts in value. Red and green combinations have poor visibility; blue or green and white have medium visibility. Combinations of yellow and black are the easiest to read at a distance—as is seen in traffic safety signs.

Transit

The problems of designing transit advertising are comparable to those of outdoor. Again we have a "pure" advertising medium, without

SEE THE LANDSCAPE THAT INSPIRED THE LANDSCAPE.

France. Known throughout the world for great artists and great art. And known by great artists for its breathtaking light and magnificent countryside.

For as much as you will appreciate French museums, châteaux, and cathedrals, you'll discover one of the greatest masterpieces in France is the country itself.

On a "Fly-Drive" tour, you can fly to Paris the French way on Air France, and see the treasured works of the masters. Then drive to the country and see the works of nature that inspired them.

Or you can tour the country in the comfort of the French Railroads, without cramping your legs or your wallet.

And you'll see why the world's greatest artists, poets and dreamers made France their home. Or wished that they could.

The French Government Tourist Office, Box 477, New York, N.Y. 10011

Please send me the information about your "Fly-Drive" tours. Quickly.

Name_____

Street_____

City_____

State_____ Zip_____

France

PLATE 1

This collection of color plates illustrates how color can enhance the effectiveness of advertising. France seeks to increase tourist travel by use of a Van Gogh painting in this magazine advertisement. Only print media are capable of such fine reproduction quality. [*French Government Tourist Office and Needham, Harper & Steers.*]

(MUSIC THROUGHOUT)

SONG: It's the real thing ...

It's the real thing.

ANNCR: (VO) Ever notice the taste of food

onto a bottle of ice-cold Coca-Cola?

That's no accident,

PLATE 2

This photoboard of a 30-second television commercial makes the point that the featured soft drink is a good companion to food. The commercial features the "It's the real thing" theme used by Coca-Cola for several years. (This advertisement was developed by The Coca-Cola Export Corporation for overseas use.)

in the back of your mind.

What you're hoping to find ...

seems to get a little bit better

when you're holding

that's the real thing. Coke.

SONG: ... is the real thing.
Coca-Cola is Coke.

PLATE 3
The same soft drink is advertised in magazines as part of a well-coordinated advertising campaign. Note the similarity of this ad to the seventh frame of the television commercial shown in Plate 2. (This advertisement was developed by The Coca-Cola Export Corporation for overseas use.)

We separate the cream from the milk

And the milk from the bottle. And the bottle from the background. We do offset color separations. That's all we do. That's why we're the best at what we do. Call us. Write us. We're ready to serve you.

Litho Masters, Inc.

PLATE 4
Lithographers are important special-service groups who aid in the preparation of effective advertisements. Using a high-quality print ad, this lithography company dramatically demonstrates how its services can contribute to that goal. [*Litho Masters, Inc.*]

PLATE 5

Food manufacturers benefit greatly when their products can be shown as the consumers will see them in the household kitchen. This ad also provides the cook with useful information. [*Young & Rubicam New York and General Foods Corporation.*]

PLATE 6

These two examples of out-of-home media dramatize the impact that can be created by this form of advertising. The Sunkist message is on a standard outdoor board, whereas the zoo message is on a painted bulletin. Note how the snake configuration extends beyond the regular dimensions of the sign. [*Foster & Kleiser, Sunkist, and the San Diego Zoo.*]

PLATE 7
These three examples of point-of-purchase advertising employ color to attract the attention of consumers in the retail store. [*Point-of-Purchase Advertising Institute.*]

news or entertainment to attract readers. While the audience for car cards inside buses or trains is not an audience in motion, and the message can thus be longer than an effective outdoor message, each card faces tough competition from many other cards displayed close together, and simplicity should be a prime design objective. Because the audience of traveling displays on the outside of buses is usually in motion, and the message itself is in motion, both layout and copy for traveling displays should be even simpler and more easily visible than for outdoor posters.

THE TEST OF A GOOD LAYOUT

We have made the point that good advertising writing is tight writing—writing that contains no stuffing, no padding, no empty words or phrases. Every word works to tell the message. The same principle can be applied to advertising design. Nelson gives this advice to students:

> When you have arranged your elements into a good layout—when you have designed your ad—see whether you can remove any one of your elements without hurting the ad's balance, its proportion, its unity. If you find your ad doesn't suffer from having lost an element, you might well question its basic structure.[8]

This advice can also be applied to visual portions of a television commercial. A physically attractive presenter might win viewer attention, but his or her *removal* (to an off-camera "voice-over" position) might better focus that attention on the product and sales message. Likewise, relevant action in a TV commercial helps speed development and comprehension of the advertiser's message. On the other hand, irrelevant "gimmicks" can result in little more than viewer disgust—and both mental and physical tune-out. An increasingly larger segment of the buying public grew up surrounded by television commercials, and no longer find them "fascinating" as such. Only scenes crucial to the unfolding of the USP should be included.

Some experts even claim that an effective commercial is one which *would be a disaster without the advertised brand*. In other words, if a competitor's brand would fit in its place, without changing the image the message creates, the commercial is a communication failure in terms of its USP. (The USP, of course, is *supposed* to give some kind of "unique personality" to one specific product.) As an example, consider the animated Raid insect spray can. A long series of TV commercials has featured insect "culprits" engaged in varying activities. Then, at a crucial point in each commercial, they are "surprised" by a Raid attack and, immediately thereafter, destroyed. If we tried to

[8] Nelson, op. cit., p. 43.

place a competing product, such as Black Flag, into Raid's role in the commercial, however, the message would fall apart. The personality *belongs* to Raid, and the play on the *word* "raid" clinches it.

THE IMPORTANCE OF CONTINUITY IN DESIGN

Regardless of the media used by an advertiser, the designer should strive for a continuity of design that will relate each advertisement to the preceding one in the series and produce a cumulative impression to attain fully the objective of the advertising campaign. This task can be accomplished in a number of different ways: the same format may be retained (such as picture caption in print, or song and dance in television); a distinctive graphic treatment may be used; or a celebrity or unusual model or character may be employed throughout the series. A certain amount of continuity is realized with nothing more original than the identical logotype or jingle in each ad or commercial.

And continuity should not be limited to a series of advertisements for a single medium. Newspaper ads should have enough family resemblance to magazine, television, and other messages for each to aid the others in building the desired image. The same principle should be extended to include the design of packages, point-of-purchase materials, and even the firm's letterhead.

SUMMARY

Illustrations and layout design in print, and moving pictures in television, work together with words to deliver advertisers' sales messages. Layout stages range from thumbnail sketches, through rough, actual-size layouts, to polished comprehensives. Basic layout elements include headlines, illustrations, body copy, and logotypes, and are developed in accordance with five principles of design: balance, proportion, contrast, eye movement, and unity.

No layout, however, is an end in itself. Rather, it is prepared to achieve a specific communication task; and the overall impression created by the finished advertisement must be in harmony with the image of its product or firm. Similarly, television commercials should involve viewers with the USP and take care to avoid irrelevant entertainment and distractions.

Print illustrations may include both photographs and drawings, and TV commercials both live action and animation. The products advertised may appear in varied settings, depending upon the specific medium, desired audience, and objectives.

Nearly every television commercial on today's airwaves is produced in color, but a number of print advertisements still appear in black and white. The reasons are usually financial, though some advertisers justify added costs on the basis of extra-attention value.

Finally, regardless of the medium used or the visual techniques selected, we must strive for design continuity throughout a campaign.

QUESTIONS FOR DISCUSSION

1 What are the specific functions of an advertising layout?
2 Balance, contrast, and eye movement are three principles of design. Discuss three different ways each of these principles may be achieved in layouts.
3 Select a product, a service, and a store. Then explain how "white space" in an ad for each of them might be used for different purposes.
4 Describe a current television advertising campaign which does a good job stimulating "audience participation" in commercials.
5 What advantages do photographs offer as advertising illustrations? When would you prefer to use drawings?
6 Discuss two advantages and two disadvantages of the use of animation in television commercials.
7 Name the four basic settings in which an advertised product may appear. Then find an example of each from either print or TV.
8 Color increases the cost as well as the attention value of advertisements. Give three situations in which the added cost for color may be justified on grounds other than added attention.
9 Differentiate clearly between hue, value, and chroma.
10 Compare and contrast the need for "simplicity" in print ads, outdoor posters, and television commercials.

FOR FURTHER REFERENCE

Antebi, Michael: *The Art of Creative Advertising*, Reinhold Book Corporation, New York, 1968.

Bach, Robert O. (ed.): *Communication: The Art of Understanding and Being Understood*, Hastings House, Publishers, Inc., New York, 1963.

Ballinger, Louise Bowen, and Raymond A. Ballinger: *Sign Symbol & Form*, Reinhold Publishing Company, New York, 1972.

Coe, Barbara Davis: *Advertising Practice: Analytic and Creative Exercises*, Prentice-Hall, Englewood Cliffs, N. J., 1972.

Garland, Ken: *Graphics Handbook*, Reinhold Publishing Company, New York, 1974.

Hurlburt, Allen: *Publication Design*, Reinhold Publishing Company, New York, 1971.

Lem, Dean Phillip: *Graphics Master*, Dean Lem Associates, Los Angeles, 1974.

Nelson, Roy Paul: *The Design of Advertising*, Wm. C. Brown Company Publishers, Dubuque, Iowa, 2d ed., 1973.

Schlemmer, Richard M.: *Handbook of Advertising Art Production*, Prentice-Hall, Inc., Englewood Cliffs, N.J., 1966.

CHAPTER 14
PRODUCTION OF PRINT AND BROADCAST ADVERTISING

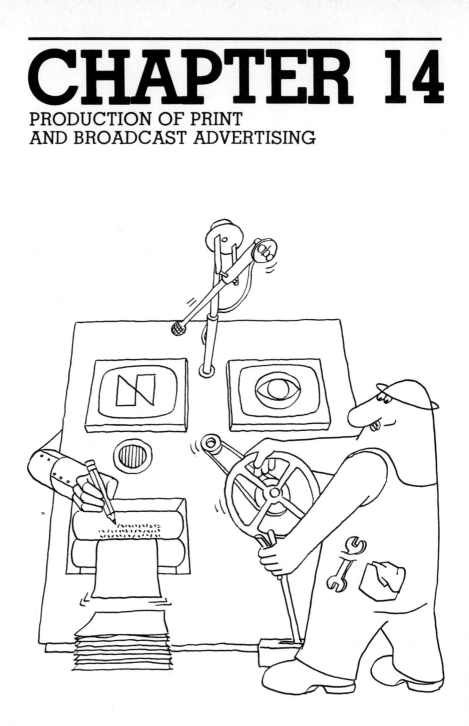

471
PRODUCTION
OF PRINT
AND
BROADCAST
ADVERTISING

Before an advertiser's message can be delivered to prospects, both verbal and visual symbols must be processed or produced in forms that suit the mechanical or electronic requirements of the medium. The basic requirements of print and broadcast media are naturally quite different, and will be considered separately.

MECHANICAL PRODUCTION IN PRINT MEDIA

Mechanical production cannot be viewed merely as a terminal procedure in the creation of a printed advertisement. If the possibilities and limitations of production methods are not considered early in the creative effort, costs may be excessive and the effectiveness of the advertisement impaired. For example, a copywriter needs to tell his story in fewer words for a half-page ad than for a full-page ad, at least if the same relative emphasis is to be maintained between verbal and illustration elements. If the advertisement is to appear in color, the selection of selling points and benefits to be presented specifically by words may not be the same as those emphasized in a black-and-white advertisement. The type of medium that will deliver the message and the printing process it employs can affect the choice of illustration material and even of layout design. Small photographic illustrations may be quite effective with high-quality magazine printing, but quite ineffective on the coarse paper generally used by newspapers.

Once the advertiser has approved the copy, layout, and finished art for an advertisement, however, the translation of these symbols into the mass communication of a printed advertisement involves a series of graphic arts operations. If printing is to be done by the photographic process of offset lithography, the magazine or newspaper is usually supplied with a paste-up, or what is often called "camera-ready copy." Line artwork and reproduction proofs of type (proofs adequate to produce good photographic negatives) are rubber-cemented into position exactly as they are to appear in the final printed version. Photos and other continuous-tone art (that is, art that has not been screened) are usually submitted separately to the photographer, who photographs them through a screen and then strips them into position with the line negatives. These stripped-in negatives are used to make the offset printing plates.

On the other hand, when printing is done by letterpress, the design and size of type are selected or specified, and the typographer sets type to fit the layout; type proofs are returned to the advertiser or agency for approval. Artwork for illustrations or other graphic elements is sent to the engraver with instructions on the kind of engraving to be made, with size, screen, and other specifications. Engraver's proofs are made, approved, and sent with the engravings to the typographer, who assembles them in a form with the type, following the design of the layout or "printer's blueprint." Proofs of the completed advertisement are then pulled for final approval or corrections, and printing plates, or mats (matrices) of them, are prepared for delivery to the media.

Exact steps, of course, and their sequence will vary with the kind of advertisement and the medium. A local advertiser planning an all-type ad may send typewritten text and layout directly to the newspaper. No engraver is involved, and the newspaper functions as typographer and compositor supplying proofs to the advertiser for approval.

These printing processes and others will be detailed shortly. Regardless of the medium or method of printing, however, each successive production step should be carefully proofed, both for accuracy and for quality of reproduction.

BASIC PRINTING METHODS

The four printing processes in most common use by advertisers are letterpress, gravure, offset (lithography), and screen printing. Most newspapers and magazines today print by offset, and this process is also widely used for outdoor posters, point-of-purchase displays, and direct-mail advertising. Perhaps the most familiar examples of gravure printing are such newspaper magazine supplements as the Sunday book review and magazine sections of the *New York Times*. Some national magazines also print by gravure; others use both gravure and letterpress in the same issue. Screening is used for smaller runs of all types of posters, transit advertising, displays, and printing on cloth, metal, plastics, and other special surfaces.

Letterpress

The basic principle of all four printing processes is the same—the transfer of an inked image from one surface to another. The method of transferring the image differs in each of the four, however. The term "letterpress" describes the method this form of printing uses; the image or letters to be transferred are actually pressed into the paper by raised, or relief, surfaces which carry the printing ink.

Gravure

The process used in gravure printing is the reverse of letterpress; the design to be printed, instead of being raised above the rest of the printing plate, is cut down or engraved into the plate. When the plate is

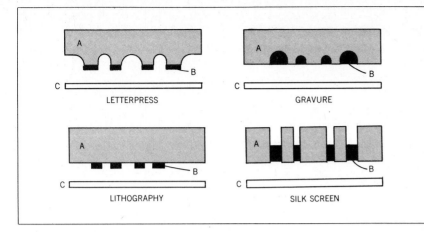

FIGURE 14.1
These diagrams illustrate the basic principles of the common printing processes: "A" represents the printing plate or screen; "B" is the printing ink; and "C" is the surface on which the image is to be printed.

inked and wiped clean, ink is retained in the depressions that form the image and is transferred from them to the paper. Gravure is also called intaglio, from the Italian word "intagliare," to engrave or carve. In copper-plate or steel-plate engraving, the method is used to print wedding invitations, stamps, and currency. The high-speed commercial form of intaglio printing used to produce newspaper supplements, magazines, and direct advertising material is known as rotogravure.

Offset

In offset, the image is neither raised above the plate nor cut down into it. This process is "planographic" printing, or printing from a flat surface. It sounds mysterious, but the principle is a simple one based on the fact that oil and water do not mix. The image takes the form of a greasy coating on the printing plate. The plate is then dampened or flushed with water. The greasy image repels the water, but the blank portions of the plate retain it. When the plate is inked with an oily ink, the moist blank portions of the plate repel the ink; the greasy image, however, retains it for transfer to a rubber blanket or roller which in turn transfers (or offsets) it to the paper. This textbook and its cover were printed by offset.

How to Choose

Once a specific newspaper or magazine has been selected as an advertising medium, the advertiser is, of course, restricted to the printing process used by that publication. Still it may be helpful to examine the three printing processes just described, according to four basic criteria important to all advertisers, in order to compare their advantages and disadvantages. Then we'll consider screen printing.

	OFFSET	LETTERPRESS	GRAVURE
Cost	Cost of metal plates lowest, but complete new plates must be made if corrections needed	Metal plates cost more than offset, but less waste (no delay in obtaining water/ink balance)	Expensive copper cylinders; economical only in production of 100,000 or more
Appearance	High quality; fine screen highlights even on rough surface	More body and brilliance; inks glossier; less problems with metallic inks	Rich effects, especially on cellophane, acetate, metallic foils
Paper stock	Sensitive to moisture changes; acute problems in paper curl and dimensional instabilities	Best-quality printing; works well with special stock: paper suitable for Bibles	May use softer paper than offset or letterpress, but thereby fails to reproduce in sharp detail
Quantity	Small runs are ideal (low paper cost); even large jobs are reasonable, especially with *web* offset.	Almost no limits on number of impressions, but small, simple runs more expensive than offset	Ideal for long runs on periodicals and catalogs, or package wraps

Screen Printing

Some graphic arts purists claim the screening process, or "serigraphy," is not real printing, but advertisers have learned that it deserves to be ranked with offset, letterpress, and gravure as a major method of producing printed advertising. The process functions on the stencil principle and requires no printing plates. A special screen stretched tightly in a frame is placed over the surface on which the image or message is to be printed. A stencil, prepared by hand or photographically, is used to block out areas which are not part of the desired image, and rubber rollers, or squeegees, force the printing ink through portions of the screen not covered by the stencil to reproduce the desired image. (*Note:* Printing stencils are generally made of nylon or stainless-steel mesh; formerly, they were made of silk, and the process was widely known as "silk screen.")[1]

Although screening was originally suitable only for flat-color reproduction, tonal values resembling those in lithography are possible with photographically produced stencils. It is primarily a "hand"

[1] Kenneth Roman and Jane Maas, *How To Advertise*, St. Martin's Press, Inc., New York, 1976, p. 100.

process, but fully automatic presses are available. Since no printing plates are necessary, as required in letterpress, gravure, or offset, screening can be used economically in far smaller quantities than other processes. Moreover, it will print on any surface of any thickness, from bottles and 55-gallon oil drums to sweatshirts. It can be used efficiently in combination with other processes and when time or cost limitations or an unusual printing surface makes other processes impractical.

475
PRODUCTION
OF PRINT
AND
BROADCAST
ADVERTISING

THE ART OF TYPOGRAPHY

Regardless of the printing process used, the words in the typewritten text of an advertisement must be either lettered by hand or set in type. Hand lettering is usually restricted to headlines and other display elements; it is used to create an effect felt to be unattainable with conventional type. The word "type" means either a rectangular block of metal with a letter or character in relief on its upper surface or the image of these letters or characters printed on paper.

Typography is the art of selecting and arranging type in order to deliver the printed message most effectively. In advertising, the art of typography focuses on two primary objectives: first, that the selection and arrangement of type be inviting to the eye and easy to read; second; that it be appropriate to the message itself. Readability is influenced by spacing between words, lines, and paragraphs, as well as by type size and style. But whatever the type, it should not call attention to itself (adiness); the reader must be attracted, *through* the type, to the product and sales message.

Of course, the design of type can convey meaning to the reader quite apart from the meaning of the words it forms. Some type designs look rugged and masculine; others are light and feminine; still others say "new, modern" or "old-fashioned" or "bargains" almost as surely as if they spelled out the words. A type that is feminine or old-fashioned in the headline below an action photo of a new earth-moving machine detracts from the impression of rugged new equipment created by the illustration.

How Type Is Set

The most common method in use today for setting type is machine setting. An operator uses a keyboard similar to that of a typewriter to select the letters, and the machine either casts these letters in the form of metal type or arranges them on film or paper suitable for photographing. Thus machine-setting methods produce either metal type from which one can print directly or images on film or paper which the platemaker can transfer to metal printing surfaces. The latter method is known as *photocomposition*.

Machine Setting Machine-set copy can be produced on any of four different machines. Linotype and Intertype machines cast a full line of type, a slug, at a time. The Monotype system produces individual characters, and the Ludlow machine, which also casts a whole line simultaneously, is used mainly for display type or headlines. Slug-composing machines are faster than the Monotype, and the slugs are easier to handle than individual characters. But corrections can be made more easily with the individual characters cast by Monotype, and it is practical for composing lines of irregular widths. Linotype composition is less expensive than Monotype and is used by most periodicals. The more flexible but more costly Monotype method is preferred by publishers of technical books, which may have many corrections after type is set and which require variations in spacing around equations or tables. It is widely used also in advertising copy for both ease of correction and variable line widths.

Photocomposition Photocomposition, sometimes called *cold type*, is increasing in use, particularly for offset and gravure printing, but also for the typography of advertisements to appear in publications that print by the letterpress process. Among the advantages claimed for photocomposition are improved sharpness and clarity, greater choice of type sizes, and faster production at lower cost.

Machines for photocomposition are similar in construction to those used for "hot-metal" typesetting, except the metal-casting mechanism

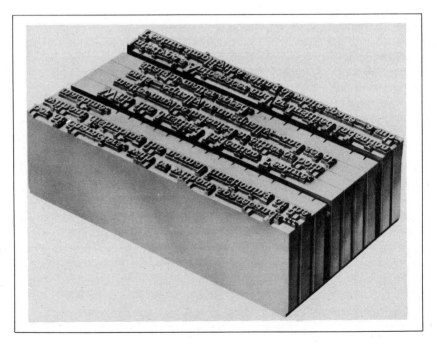

FIGURE 14.2
Linotype and Intertype machines cast a one-piece line of type of predetermined length of molten metal. [*Intertype Company.*]

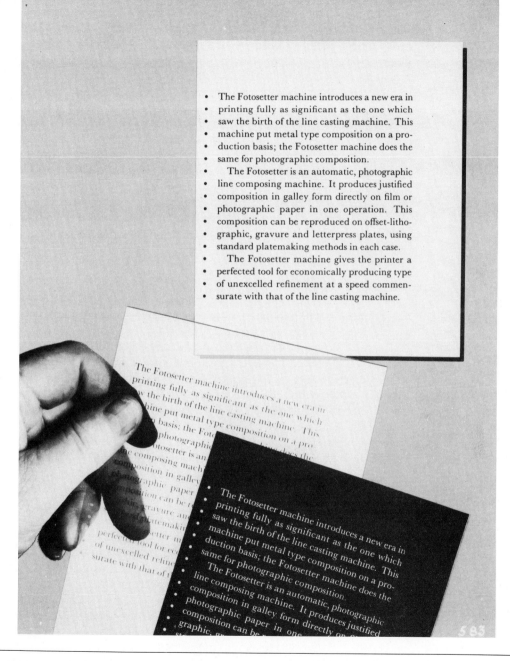

FIGURE 14.3
Photocomposition, or cold type, uses machine methods to produce typographic
composition on either film or paper. [*Intertype Company.*]

is replaced with a camera device that produces lines of type on film or sensitized paper rather than in slugs of metal.

Nonmetal, or cold-type, composition can also be produced by such equipment as the IBM Executive typewriter, the VariTyper, and the Justowriter. The IBM Executive is an electric typewriter with characters that vary in width, as they do in metal type; a *w* is given more space than an *i*, for example. Thus, unlike familiar typewriters, the IBM machine automatically provides proportional spacing and, in addition, is available with a variety of type faces. Both the VariTyper and the Justowriter are typewriterlike machines that also produce images on paper rather than photographic film, and both are more versatile and more expensive than the IBM. Justowriter furnishes proportional letter spacing and automatic word spacing to provide an even right-hand margin. VariTyper also does both, and in addition, its type is instantly changeable from one design to another. All three types of machine offer speed and economy impossible with conventional typesetting methods, and are widely used for catalogs, direct advertising materials, and house organs.

Type Structure and Measurement

The anatomy of every piece of type, regardless of size or letter design, includes a face, a body, shoulders, and feet. The face is the design of the letter or figure which we see printed. No two faces are exactly alike, and each is distinguished by its name and its size. The type we are reading now is named *Memphis Light;* its size is described as *10 point*.

The point system of measuring type is confusing to the average person because it is different from our common way of measuring by inches, but it is no more difficult to grasp than the metric system. Any measurement is based on an arbitrary standard, and this basic standard in typography is the *point*. The point is a measurement of type height only, and for practical purposes 72 points equal 1 inch. Thus 12 points equal $1/6$ inch, 18 points equal $1/4$ inch, 36 points equal $1/2$ inch, and so on.

The point measurement does not reflect, however, the size of a single letter. The point actually measures the height of a line of type, and it is the distance from the bottom of the descenders, or tails, of *g, j, p, q,* and *y* to the top of the ascenders of *b, d, f, h, k,* and *l.* As a result, a 72-point (pt.) capital letter *M* is slightly less than an inch in height, and a lowercase 72-point *m,* which has neither ascenders nor descenders, is considerably less than an inch high. On the other hand, a line of 72-point type—composed of a variety of letters—will measure 1 inch, and 6 lines of 72-point type will measure 6 inches in depth.

The width of a single letter of type depends on both the proportions of the letter and the design of the particular type face. In any design, for example, the letter *m* will obviously be wider than the letter *n*.

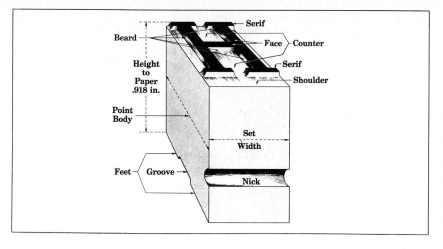

FIGURE 14.4
This piece of type, for the letter H, shows all parts of its anatomy, from its face and shoulders to its body and feet. [*American Type Founders Co., Inc.*]

The unit of measurement for width of lines or depth of blocks of type is the *pica*, or pica-em. The terms are synonymous; the unit equals ¹⁄₆ inch (and so 12 points are equal to 1 pica). Printers also use the pica as a general unit of measurement for illustrations or other layout elements. The total depth of a newspaper or magazine advertisement, however, is usually measured in agate lines or column inches, as mentioned in our discussion of newspaper rates in Chapter 8.

When lines of type would be too close together for easy reading or for the airy, open effect desired, they are separated by thin strips of metal called *leads*—pronounced as we pronounce the name of the metal "lead." The following example shows lines of type of the same size (12 point) and design (Caledonia) set without leading (set "solid") and with 2-point leading—leading one-sixth the type size. We can see how much more open and readable the leaded text is. The same effect can be accomplished by using type that has an extra amount of shoulder to separate the characters vertically. Thus, 12-point type with an extra 2 points of shoulder, called "12 on 14," provides the same separation as 12 point that is 2-point leaded.

FIGURE 14.5
The point system measures the height of a line of type—the distance from ascenders to descenders.

Chances are, when you bought your present washing machine, you expected it—like your car—to grow old and run down. There wasn't much you could do about it, so you thought. But today it's possible for your old washing machine . . .

12 point Caledonia

Chances are, when you bought your present washing machine, you expected it—like your car—to grow old and run down. There wasn't much you could do about it, so you thought. But today it's possible for your old washing machine . . .

12 point Caledonia, 2-point leaded

To provide the necessary space between words in a line or at the end of a paragraph, the compositor uses blank pieces of metal known as *quads* or *spaces*. It is also desirable at times to space between letters of type to produce a pleasing display effect. The example that follows shows a headline set with and without letter spacing.

HOME STYLE TOMATO JUICE

HOME STYLE TOMATO JUICE

Type Designs Classified

The character or personality of type results from the design of the letters and figures, and this design also affects the readability of the type. The *Graphic Arts Production Yearbook* lists more than 1,000 different type faces which are in common use today, and typographers are continually developing new designs. Fortunately, this overwhelming variety of faces can be classified into relatively simple groups, and a knowledge of the essential characteristics of type designs which fall into each group will serve the purpose of anyone who does not intend to be a specialist in advertising production.

For our purpose, a practical way to classify type is by four races, as an anthropologist might classify people according to four basic racial stocks—the Caucasoid, Mongoloid, Negroid, and Australoid groups. The four races of type which are fundamental in modern typography are the *roman*, the *block letter*, the *script*, and the *ornamental*. Let us consider the distinguishing features of each of these races.

These words are set in roman.

This race is derived from the lettering chiseled into monuments in the

A font of 6-pt. Century Expanded

ABCDEFGHIJKLMNOPQRSTUVWXYZabcdefghijklmnopqrstuvwxyz1234567890,.;:?¢@*&%$

Examples of sizes in the Caslon New type series

a a a a a a a a a **a** ᴀ ᴀ ᴀ ᴀ ᴀ ᴀ A A A **A** A

Six variations of the Caslon family

Caslon   **Caslon Condensed**

Caslon Italic   **Caslon New**

Caslon Bold   Caslon Old Face

Examples of the four basic races of type

1. Roman.
    a. Old style   Caslon Old Face
    b. Modern   Bodoni

2. Block letter.
    a. Sans-serif   **Spartan**
    b. Square serif   **Stymie**

3. Script.
    a. True script   *Bank Script*
    b. Cursive   *Coronet Light*

4. Ornamental
    a. Text   𝔊𝔬𝔲𝔡𝔶 𝔗𝔢𝔵𝔱
    b. Miscellaneous   P. T. Barnum, **Hobo**, **STENCIL,**

FIGURE 14.6
Examples of a font of type, different sizes in the same design, variations in a family of type, and the four basic races of type.

days of the Roman Empire, and it probably includes a larger number of designs than any of the other three groups. The two most distinguishing characteristics of roman letters are the small lines, or "serifs," that cross the ends of the main strokes and the variation in the thickness of strokes. One of the main virtues of roman type is its versatility within a single type family, providing contrasting effects without a basic design change. The other outstanding advantage of the roman race is legibility; no other group of designs is so easy to read, especially in smaller sizes.

These words are set in block letter.

Type designs in this group differ from the roman faces in two ways. First, the strokes forming the letters do not vary, but remain a uniform thickness throughout. Second, they either lack serifs (sans serif), or the serifs have the same weight and thickness as the main strokes of the letters (square serif). The absence of serifs and/or the uniform weight of all strokes makes the block-letter group less easy to read than roman faces, particularly in the small sizes used for text passages or body copy. The simple, clean lines of block-letter type, however, give it a modern feel or tone that is desirable in much advertising layout, and it is widely used.

These words are set in script.

The script group includes a number of type designs that resemble handwriting, and like much handwriting, script faces leave something to be desired in legibility. True script letters appear connected or linked together, as though made with a continuing stroke of a pen. In the other variety of script, the letters are not joined together; these faces are called cursives or cursive scripts. Because script generally is less easy to read than roman or block letter, it should be used with great care in advertising even when a feminine or formal effect is an important typographic objective.

These words are set in ornamental type.

The last of the four basic races of type faces includes a large number of designs which cannot be classified in any of the other three groups. In spite of marked differences in appearance, these faces are all essentially ornamental, decorative, suggestive of other times and other cultures. While the uses of ornamental type are limited, the advertiser who wishes to create unusual effects can select appropriate type from a surprising range of eccentric designs.

In addition to being able to recognize the four basic races of type and understanding what is meant by a family of type, we should be familiar with the terms "series" and "font." A series of type is all sizes of an identical design; within the Caslon family of the roman race the Caslon New series includes sizes from 6 to 48 points. A font is a complete proportionate assortment of capital and lowercase letters and figures of a single size and single design; the more frequently a character is used, the more pieces of that character the font includes.

483
PRODUCTION
OF PRINT
AND
BROADCAST
ADVERTISING

Fitting Copy and Type

Type, of course, must fit into the amount of space indicated for it in the layout. The larger the type size, the more space a given number of letters or words will require. But the number of characters that can be accommodated in a line of a certain length will vary with different designs of the same size of type. For example, both lines of type below are the same length—15 picas, or $2^1/_2$ inches—and both are set in 12-point type. The second line, set in Century Bold Condensed, accommodates seven more letters than the first line, which is set in Century Bold of the same point size.

The quick brown fox jumps over the

The quick brown fox jumps over the lazy dog.

The most accurate method of fitting type to layout, or copy fitting, is by means of type charts or tables that show the number of capital and lowercase characters per pica or per inch for different faces and sizes. Newspapers and printers supply advertisers with such copy-fitting guides for the type kept in stock. More comprehensive tables are available from type founders and manufacturers of typesetting machines such as the Linotype. For rough preliminary fitting of copy to type or type to copy, the "square-inch method" is commonly used. This method consists in counting the number of words and dividing this total by the number of words per square inch that can be set in type of various sizes, according to tables like Table 14.1.

While it is wise to leave the exact specification of type to an expert typographer, anyone who creates or evaluates advertisements should be familiar with a few fundamentals that affect the readability and

TABLE 14.1
APPROXIMATE NUMBER OF WORDS
PER SQUARE INCH

TYPE SIZE	WORDS
6 pt., solid	47
6 pt., leaded 2 pt.	34
8 pt., solid	32
8 pt., leaded 2 pt.	23
10 pt., solid	21
10 pt., leaded 2 pt.	21
18 pt., solid	7
18 pt., leaded 2 pt.	6

appeal of elements set in type. *Italics*, for example, are harder to read than vertical letters. Lines set all in capital letters are harder to read than capitals and lowercase letters, and italic caps are even more difficult than vertical ones. Lines of type that are either too long or too short make hard reading. The larger the type size, the longer the line can be without becoming difficult. A handy guide to maximum line length is 60 lowercase characters. We should strive for simplicity and should not use too many different type faces in one advertisement. All the contrast and variation for emphasis needed in most advertisements is actually available from a single family of the better type designs.

THE PRODUCTION OF GRAPHIC ELEMENTS

Engraving, or photoengraving, processes are not restricted to the production of illustrative or art material only. They are also used to produce text material in combination with illustrative elements, and even text alone, as in the photocomposition of type.

Basically, however, the production of graphic elements involves camera-and-chemical methods of reproducing images which are not composed—as type is—of standard, movable units. Handlettered headlines, for example, consist of words. The same words can be set in standard units of movable type, either by hand or by machine. But because the advertiser desires an effect not easily obtainable with type, the words are executed as a piece of artwork, that is, shot with a camera to make a negative. The negative then is stripped into the type and a plate is made. Finally, there is the transfer, by a photochemical process, to a suitable surface for printing.

Line and Halftone Engravings

Two different photoengraving processes are used in the preparation of artwork for letterpress printing. The first and simplest is the line engraving or line plate. The line plate reproduces only two tones, solid black and solid white. If continuous tones from solid black through grays to white—like the varying tones of a photograph or wash drawing—are desired, the halftone-engraving process is used. This produces the intermediate shades of gray by breaking up the varying tone values of the picture into minute dots of different size, each dot becoming a separate surface carrying printing ink. Whereas the line cut prints from solid lines or areas, the halftone prints entirely from dots, with the darker areas formed by large dots and the lighter ones by small dots.

The same basic photochemical techniques are used in the production of both line and halftone engravings, but in the halftone process the original artwork is photographed through a screen. The screen, which is made of glass or plastic film, has hundreds of very fine parallel lines crossing one another at right angles; this mesh effect

65-line screen

110-line screen

133-line screen

150-line screen

FIGURE 14.7
The more dots per square inch in a halftone, the finer the reproduction. The four sections of this illustration are reproduced from left to right in successively finer screens, from 65-line to 150-line. Refer to Figure 13.7 to see how this photo was used in an actual ad.

breaks up the image of the artwork into dots on the negative film. The more lines a screen has to the square inch, the finer the screen, and the sharper and clearer the details of the printed reproduction.

While a coarse screen may be less expensive than a fine one, the major factor governing their use is the smoothness of the paper on which the halftone will be printed. On coarse, rough paper, a fine-screen halftone will smudge in printing because the ink collects in the smaller spaces between the dots. The rough paper used by most newspapers restricts the halftones they can use to 85 lines or less. A magazine using a smooth, coated stock, however, will accept 110- or even 150-line halftones. Still finer screens are used in the photographic processes of transferring images to cylinders for either gravure or offset lithography, with satisfactory results on paper with a soft finish.

COLOR PRODUCTION OF PRINT ADVERTISEMENTS

Normally, if an advertisement is to appear in color instead of black and white, a separate press impression is required for each color, regardless of the printing process. In recent years, however, newspaper and magazine advertisers have had a choice of paper stock, also; hence, the color green, for example, may be *added to* an otherwise black and white ad (through a separate printing process) or the black type and illustrations may appear *on green paper.*

Returning for a moment to letterpress printing, and assuming plans call for an advertisement to appear in black and red, we find that two different plates are required. One will carry the black impression, and the other will carry the elements to be printed in red. If the advertisement is printed by gravure or offset lithography, the advertiser provides no plates. Color separation negatives are furnished to the printing firm or are made there from camera-ready artwork; these are then transferred to separate press plates or cylinders, each of which carries a different color of ink.

The advertisements we see in complete natural color—or "full color"—are usually printed from black and three primary pigment colors described in Chapter 13. By mixing the primary yellow, red, and blue pigments in proper proportions, we can produce a range of intermediate or secondary hues, such as violet, brown, or green. This is the principle of the four-color process of printing. Separate halftone plates are made for each of the three primary pigment colors and black. Superimposed printing of these four plates with transparent inks "mixes" the primary pigments and results in a color-blended image with all the hues and values of the original full-color artwork. The usual color sequence in printing is yellow first, red next, then blue, and black last. The black plate is called the key plate; it strengthens the depth and detail of the other plates, provides neutral shades of gray, and usually carries the text matter.

To make four-color process plates, the engraver photographs the original full-color artwork four times, each time using a filter that eliminates all but the desired color in the resulting negative. These are called color-separation negatives. From each of the four negatives the plates for letterpress, lithography, or gravure—or the stencils for screen printing—are made in the same way that a plate is made for black-and-white reproduction, although more hand finishing is required. The printing press shown in Figure 6.4 is a web-offset press capable of printing four-color advertising.

BROADCAST PRODUCTION

Radio and television productions become deeply involved with drama and the other performing arts. Their very nature makes them more susceptible to creative manipulation than some of the more prosaic operations encountered in getting advertisements into print. Unfortunately, the glamour and excitement which are often associated with broadcast production may sometimes overshadow the fact that it can be as technical and demanding in detail as typography and photoengraving.

Radio Commercial Production

Commercials are broadcast either live or transcribed, and in either case, radio production methods are simple and inexpensive compared to television production. Often the equipment involved is no more complex than a tape recorder. The ad-libbed integrated commercial is an example of live broadcasting. Straight sell and educational formats may also be broadcast live from typed copy at less cost than recording them. The delivery will naturally vary from announcer to announcer, and there is always the possibility of errors, or "bloopers." Transcribing commercials on tape, however, is preferred by most advertisers, because it permits establishing tone and timing through rehearsals, and eliminates the possibility of bloopers. Costs of an effective transcribed music-and-voice radio commercial can be as little as $400. When station talent is used, costs may be zero, as in the case of local or

487

PRODUCTION
OF PRINT
AND
BROADCAST
ADVERTISING

AS RECORDED -- 4/30/76

D'Arcy-MacManus & Masius
200 East Randolph Drive.
CHICAGO, ILLINOIS 60601

Radio Continuity

ACE HARDWARE
ACCOUNT
Corporate Fall
PRODUCT
"Homecoming Float"
TITLE
:30
LENGTH
AH-115-30
SCRIPT NUMBER
5/10/76 Rev: #1
DATE R76-85013

MUSIC	UP & UNDER THROUGHOUT
CONNIE (PACE TO MUSIC)	Hi, I'm Connie Stevens. Homecoming days are going on now, so come on over to Ace.
	Whatever you need for your home this fall, remember Ace is the place.
	Lots of bargains all through the store.
	Paint, appliances, power tools, your Ace Man's got 'em all.
	He can save you money on national brands during homecoming days.
MUSIC	UP FOR END LINE
CONNIE (SINGS)	ACE IS THE PLACE
	WITH THE HELPFUL HARDWARE MAN.

FIGURE 14.8
In this script for a transcribed 30-second radio commercial, the celebrity presenter's lines are combined with music to create the advertiser's image of friendliness. [*D'Arcy-MacManus & Masius.*]

retail newspaper advertisements created by the paper's display staff.

In a sound-only medium, casting can prove crucial; inflection, vocal emphasis, and pacing are often as important as the actual words in communicating a sales message. Also, there is a warmth and "companionship" quality inherent in radio that wise copywriters use to full advantage. Friendly (sometimes well-known) voices can enhance both credibility and memorability of a message.

Sometimes, a jingle (words set to music) will fill most or all of the commercial; and sometimes a quieter musical background simply helps maintain the smooth flow of spoken copy. Libraries of such "stock" music (and also sound effects) are readily available in many cities. Originally composed scores may be produced by major recording studios or local radio stations.

Television Commercial Production

Like radio, television messages can be transmitted either live or transcribed. Live broadcasting involves action and sound as it takes place in the studio at the moment of transmittal, and is rare today; rather, transcribed commercials normally appear on either film or tape.

Film About 80 percent of commercial shooting on behalf of national advertisers is done on 35-millimeter film.[2] (For small stations which do not have 35-millimeter projection equipment, 16 millimeter prints may be prepared; virtually all stations have videotape equipment, however, and often prints are made on videotape instead of film, with better quality as a result.)

Film production lends itself to repeated telecasting, and to spot telecasting in a number of different markets. It can also be edited before airing, and performers, especially "stars," prefer film commercials (to anything done live) because they can be produced at convenient times. Finally, film offers greater opportunities for realism and action by shots on location and "chase sequences," plus greater variety in sets and in camera and electronic effects. Repayments to actors and actresses, however, under codes of the Screen Actors Guild and the American Federation of Television and Radio Artists, for repeated telecasting of commercials, are now made regardless of whether the shooting is on film or videotape.

Videotape Locally produced spots are almost all recorded on videotape.[3] This tape is a continuous plastic ribbon coated with magnetic

---

[2] Arthur Bellaire, "Nat Eisenberg Tells Agencies: Videotape Commercials Merit More Consideration," *Advertising Age*, May 5, 1975.
[3] Ibid.

NEW
MIGHTY DOG
from Carnation
"BRANDING IRON"

Pure beef.
Only new MIGHTY DOG . . .

from Carnation has it. All other
canned dog foods contain by-products.

But New MIGHTY DOG is . . .

pure beef — no by-products.

No wonder it smells good.

And tastes better than any other
dog food.

With vitamins and minerals for
complete nourishment.

And single-serving cans that end
left-overs.

Get new MIGHTY DOG.

Pure beef — no-by-products.

FIGURE 14.9
An example of a 30-second TV commercial for
nationally advertised Mighty Dog canned dog
food. Notice actual visualization, in addition to
audio copy. Each static scene here represents
approximately three seconds of actual "moving
picture" time. [*Carnation and Erwin Wasey,
Inc.*]

particles, and looks like audio tape enlarged about eight times. Like film, it records both sound and video simultaneously, with the audio track running as a narrow strip on the edge of the wider video track. Both tracks can be erased and rerecorded separately, and the tape can be edited and spliced in the same manner as audio tape. It can record in color as well as monochrome.

Videotape offers the advertiser all the advantages of film transcription plus some that are unique. Tape transcriptions can be played back immediately without the time-consuming developing necessary with film. Both visual and sound can be rerecorded while performers are still on the set, instead of requiring another shooting session. The production quality is superior to film, and on viewers' receiving sets it is virtually impossible to tell a videotape telecast from one that originates live. Last-minute changes in either audio or video can be made quickly because the tape is easily erased. The initial cost of tape is considerably less than film and processing, and it can be fully or partially erased and used again. Even more important, perhaps, are the savings in man-hours, both in shooting and in editing. With the development of compact, moderate-priced recorders, the overall flexibility of tape and its lower costs make it possible for local advertisers to use the television medium with creative potential impossible by either film or live telecast.

Of course, we must also note that film and videotape may be combined in a single commercial. An example might be an in-studio videotaped message dealing with a furniture sale; a filmed insert might take viewers on a trip through the furniture factory.

FIGURE 14.10
Videotape equipment in a television station. The lower cost of tape and its economy in both shooting and editing have increased the creative potential of TV for local advertisers. [*KOMO-TV, Channel 4, Seattle.*]

FIGURE 14.11
This is a TV script for a 30-second locally videotaped commercial for a Cincinnati bank. Instead of pictures, video *instructions* are included. Terminology includes MLS (medium long shot, generally from the knees up) and MS (medium shot, from the waist up, as opposed to a close-up, which might feature just a face or hand). TRUCK is a camera movement, CUT is an electronic switch between cameras, and SUPER refers to superimposition of the indicated line of copy over the existing shot—in this case, a shot of the commercial presenter. [*Stockton-West-Burkhart, Inc.*]

Stockton · West · Burkhart · Inc.   **TELEVISION CONTINUITY**

STATION
CITY
DATE & TIME
PROGRAM   Check Cashing
ADVERTISER   The Central Trust Company, N.A.   (VTR–CT–74–18...CUT #5)

ORDER NO. T-6958
PROGRAM NO.
PAGE NO. _____ OF _____
LENGTH :30
DATE TYPED 8/30/74

VIDEO	AUDIO
1. OPEN ON AN MLS OF LANSING SITTING BEHIND AN EXECUTIVE-TYPE DESK. AS HE TALKS, GRADUALLY TRUCK AROUND TO A SIDE SHOT & THEN MOVE IN SLIGHTLY AS HE ADJUSTS TO A MORE PERSONAL, MORE CASUAL RELATIONSHIP WITH THE VIEWER. SUPER ACROSS BASE FOR 3 SEC: ROBERT LANSING TALKS ABOUT CENTRAL CARD.	R. LANSING: A bank is only as good as its service. Right? So why get a lot of static when you want some of your money and you're in a branch where no one knows you? That won't happen if you have a Central Trust checking account...and the new Central Card.
2. HE REMOVES CENTRAL CARD FROM HIS BREAST POCKET OF CARD CASE & SHOWS IT TO CAMERA.	Your Central Card and personal code number instantly identify you as a preferred customer in _any_ Central Trust banking Center.
3. CUT TO DIFFERENT ANGLE SO THAT, INSTEAD OF A TASTEFUL OFFICE SETTING BEHIND HIM WE NOW SEE, AGAINST AN INFINITY BACKGROUND, A TELLER'S POSITION & TELLER & CUSTOMER APPROACHING. TO ONE SIDE--OR BEHIND SET--IS GIANT MOCK-UP OF CENTRAL CARD. HE INDICATES THIS (AS CUSTOMER HANDS A CHECK & HIS CENTRAL CARD TO THE TELLER) WITH A NOD OF HIS HEAD.	And that's only one of the time-saving conveniences you get with Central Trust...and Central Card.
4. CUT TO MS OF LANSING STANDING BESIDE CARD MOCK-UP AGAINST LIMBO BACKGROUND, & SUPER ACROSS BASE: INSTANT CHECK CASHING...AND A _LOT_ MORE ONLY AT CENTRAL TRUST.	Why settle for less?

Production Techniques

Just as there are two different television production methods, so also are there two different basic techniques used in commercial production: live action and animation. Live action should not be confused with live broadcasting, since a live action commercial may be broadcast live or transcribed on film or tape.

The live action technique uses real people as performers and conveys realism that isn't possible with animation. The dialogue style of live action has performers on the screen, talking to each other or the audience, and is particularly adaptable to testimonials, dramatizations, and the personality commercial. The narrative style of a live action commercial is usually less expensive than dialogue, and is most frequently used with off-screen voices to demonstrate the product in use or its benefits.

Animation is the basic principle of motion pictures in reverse. In animated film or tape production for television, the inanimate objects are changed slightly in position while the transcribing camera is stopped. When the series of separate shots is projected at normal speeds, the result is the same sort of action delivered by the motion-picture camera.

Cartoons are perhaps the best-known form of animation, and certainly one of the best-liked commercial techniques. They provide opportunities for fantasy that cannot be equaled with live action production, and at the same time offer a visual distinction that identifies exclusively with the advertiser. While cartoon commercials rate high in viewer interest and low in production cost compared to live action, they may easily lose credibility. Generally they are most effective for impulse-purchase products. When combined with a follow-up of live action, in which real people present reason-why copy, cartoons may be very effective for more serious purchases.

Stop motion and photo animation are techniques used to animate the inanimate, or to bring the product to life and make it dance, walk, or disassemble itself. Refrigerator doors open and close by themselves, soft-drink bottles uncap themselves, and packages unwrap themselves to disclose the contents. Like cartoons, stop motion can personalize the product, and at the same time lend an intriguing effect to demonstrations, as when accessories attach themselves to a vacuum cleaner without human hands. Again, as with cartoons, support by live action is wise if realism and believability are important to the advertiser's television message.

There is a fair amount of experimentation today in the area of computerized animation on videotape. One such system "describes" the desired scenes on IBM punch cards and feeds them into a computer which is instructed to "move" the objects involved in specific ways. Actions can be speeded up or slowed down, and colors can be altered at will. In addition, objects can grow, shrink, or be changed in any other way with a great deal of realism.[4]

TWO FUNDAMENTALS OF ADVERTISING PRODUCTION

Two of the most important fundamentals of advertising production apply to all printing processes, whether in color or in black and white, and to broadcast techniques as well. Both are simple, nontechnical essentials of good production practices; yet both are often overlooked or ignored. The first is that it costs more—considerably more—to make changes in print advertisements after they have once been delivered to the typographer, engraver, printer, or publication. Corrections should be made before copy starts on the first step of mechanical production. Changes should be made while the text is in typewritten form, not after the words have been set in type.

The same rule applies with even greater force to art elements.

[4] "Animation through Computer Offered as New Ad Technique," *Advertising Age*, Mar. 17, 1975, p. 58.

Major changes in illustrative material cannot be made after the engraver has photographed it; we can't change a photograph of a man on a horse to one of a woman pushing a baby carriage. All we can do is get the woman and the baby carriage and shoot a new picture. Minor changes can be made in finished art, or even in engravings, but it will save a lot of time and money if even minor changes are made before finished art is prepared.

Audio and videotaped commercials may be rerecorded, of course, if changes are desired, but cast and crew must be recalled at additional cost, and sometimes a special scene is next to impossible to reestablish. (Consider, for example, a concert, ballet, or circus performance.)

The second fundamental of good production practice is that we must learn to communicate with graphic arts and studio production specialists and rely upon the expert in a particular area if we are not experts ourselves. When the material for an advertisement or commercial is ready for production, we should have a fairly clear-cut idea of what the message has been designed to accomplish. If we communicate our ideas to production experts, they not only will understand what we want, but will probably be able to suggest ways of improving the end result. We have a better chance of avoiding misunderstandings and of realizing our objectives if our wishes are stated in writing. In most advertising agencies, it is a firm policy that no production work may be started until it is covered by a written order or memorandum.

When estimates for printing are prepared, we should be sure that they include all the costs. A common error, for example, occurs in estimating folders or other direct-advertising pieces. Dummies and text copy are submitted to several printers for competitive bids, and the printers' bids are used as cost estimates for the job. A printer's bid, however, may or may not include all the costs involved. As an example, it is regular practice for a printer to assume that he will be furnished complete artwork or engravings, and costs for such materials will not be included in his estimate.

Similarly, there is a big difference between using prerecorded "stock" music in a radio or TV commercial and composing a whole new selection (or even a jingle). And, of course, the same "characters" are much more expensive when played by Hollywood stars than they are when played by "unknown" talent. The best practice is to use a standard form that includes all possible items for production estimates. No one job is likely to require all the elements listed, but checking off each one is the sure way to include all charges.

LAW OF THE UNATTAINABLE TRIAD

The wise advertiser realizes that the production of all advertising is governed by the "law of the unattainable triad." Production focuses on

493
PRODUCTION
OF PRINT
AND
BROADCAST
ADVERTISING

three objectives—price, speed, and quality—but it is impossible to be sure of getting all three in the same production job. A tight budget may make low cost the prime objective. If so, the advertiser gets competitive bids from reliable suppliers or studios, or seeks out firms which for one reason or another are willing to do the work at less than standard rates. The latter course of action often results, in the end, in costs that are actually higher than necessary.

Unanticipated but immediate special competitive threats or marketing opportunities can make speed the most important requirement of production. If brand A launches a special merchandise offer in 14 key markets, it may be necessary for brand B to meet this threat immediately with a new newspaper campaign. If the campaign is to be successful, mats must be shipped in less than half the time normally allowed for their production. This can be and is done frequently, but it is almost always done at costs that are considerably above normal. Likewise, television film crews can always work overtime to shoot a commercial ahead of schedule, but union wages may double.

In many cases, fine-quality reproduction is the essential aim of magazine advertising production. If an advertisement is to present an image of quality or excellence for a product or a firm, the typography, engraving, and printing should be as fine in quality as the copy and artwork. Less-than-fine production contradicts the advertising message that attempts to convey distinction or quality. So does sloppy sound production in a radio commercial—or music hastily composed or selected to meet a deadline.

A skilled production specialist can get top quality at a reasonably low price—but he or she will almost certainly sacrifice speed. The only reason a quality printer, engraver, or radio sound specialist will cut the price is to take a job that can be done in spare time—and that means he or she cannot be rushed. Or the expert can buy low price and fast delivery at a sacrifice of quality. Low price and fast delivery mean cut corners somewhere; the time needed to produce fine work and meet the price and speed requirements is simply not available. And when fast delivery is combined with fine quality, bills are likely to be as much as 50 percent higher to cover overtime. So anyone concerned directly or indirectly with the production of ads and commercials should remember the law of the unattainable triad and decide which of the three objectives—quality, speed, and price—is the most important in each individual case. In this business, as in many others, compromise is one of the keys to success.

SUMMARY

Mechanical and electronic production of advertisements and commercials both involve complex processes demanding serious considerations of time and cost, selection of paper stock or transcription processes, and overall quality. Basic printing methods include offset, letterpress, gravure, and screen printing, and each has its advantages and limitations. Likewise, different styles of type have different "personalities" and are used to achieve separate objectives.

Readability is affected both by type size, measured in points and picas, and by spacing, as well as by type style. Actual setting of type is handled either by machine or by the process of photocomposition.

Ads which appear in full color are usually produced through the process of four-color printing. Primary yellow, red, and blue pigments can be mixed to form a range of secondary hues, while black is added to strengthen the depth and detail of other colors.

Radio and television commercials are broadcast live or (more commonly) on audiotape or videotape or film. Music and sound effects may enhance a sales message, as can "character" voices, animated products or other elements, and celebrity presenters. Sometimes, jingles are used to aid memorability, and televised scenes shot "on location" often increase credibility and the feeling of "realism."

A fundamental rule in communicating effectively with production experts is to give them complete information about requirements and objectives—and the best way is in writing. Sometimes, standard forms or checklists for estimating production costs help make certain that nothing has been overlooked. Costs increase when ads or commercials must be redone to correct errors.

Regardless of its form, every production job is subject to the law of the unattainable triad. Production specialists can combine fine quality with low cost, but not in a hurry. They can combine fine quality with rapid delivery if premium costs are no object. Or they can get production done in a hurry and at low cost, but quality is almost sure to leave something to be desired. Consequently, one of the most important decisions the advertiser must make about any production job is whether the prime objective is to keep down costs, get fine quality, or have the material delivered quickly.

495
PRODUCTION
OF PRINT
AND
BROADCAST
ADVERTISING

QUESTIONS FOR DISCUSSION

1 What are the basic distinctions between the four races of type?
2 Explain the term "photocomposition." Is its use in printing decreasing or increasing? Why?
3 Explain the point and pica systems for measuring type.
4 Explain how a jingle in a radio commercial can prove both advantageous and disadvantageous to communication of a sales message. Then do the same for celebrities in television commercials.
5 Distinguish between the halftone and the line plate and the uses to which each is put.
6 Name three advantages of videotape over film in the production of television commercials.

7   The text describes four different printing processes. What basic principle is common to all four? What are the fundamental differences between the four methods?

8   Identify the following lines of type. Then rank them in decreasing order of readability: (*a*) HOW READABLE IS THIS? (*b*) ***HOW READABLE IS THIS?*** (*c*) How readable is this?

9   Pick out two television commercials and indicate which one you think was more expensive to produce. Discuss several reasons why.

10 Explain the law of the unattainable triad.

FOR FURTHER REFERENCE

Arnold, Edmund C.: *Ink on Paper*, Harper & Row, Publishers, Incorporated, New York, 1963.

Herdeg, Walter (ed.): *Film and TV Graphics*, Hastings House, Publishers, Inc., New York, 1967.

Melcher, Daniel, and Nancy Larrick: *Printing and Promotion Handbook*, 3d ed., McGraw-Hill Book Company, New York, 1966.

Millerson, Gerald: *The Techniques of Television Production*, 6th ed., Hastings House, Publishers, Inc., New York, 1968.

Nelson, Roy Paul: *The Design of Advertising*, 2d ed., Wm. C. Brown, Dubuque, Iowa, 1973.

Pocket Pal, A Graphic Arts Production Handbook, 11th ed., International Paper Company, New York, 1974.

Roman, Kenneth, and Jane Maas: *How to Advertise*, St. Martin's Press, Inc., New York, 1976.

Rosen, Ben: *Type and Typography: The Designer's Type Book*, Reinhold Publishing Corporation, New York, 1963.

Schlemmer, Richard M.: *Handbook of Advertising Art Production*, Prentice-Hall, Inc., Englewood Cliffs, N.J., 1966.

Stevenson, George A.: *Graphic Arts Encyclopedia*, McGraw-Hill Book Company, New York, 1968.

Turnbull, Arthur T., and Russell N. Baird: *The Graphics of Communication*, 2d ed., Holt, Rinehart and Winston, Inc., New York, 1968.

FIVE

FIVE

PLANNING AND MANAGING
THE ADVERTISING CAMPAIGN

Advertising is a business activity which, like any business, must be skillfully managed if maximum returns are to be achieved. Preceding parts of this book show what advertising is, where it fits into the marketing process, what the characteristics of the various advertising media are, and what effective advertising messages are. Part Five ties these elements together and explains how advertising programs are built and managed.

Business management is often described as consisting of three principal activities: planning, organizing, and controlling. How these activities are carried out in managing advertising programs is described by means of an integral part of every advertising program, the advertising campaign. Thus, Chapter 15 explains how campaign planning precedes action, while Chapter 16 highlights the importance of research to accurate advertising planning.

There are four critical decision points in advertising management:

1 How much should be spent for advertising?
2 What types of advertising media should be used?
3 What kinds of advertising messages should be run?
4 Has the campaign been successful?

In Chapter 17 we learn how budgetary matters are handled, and in Chapter 18 the equally important media selection decision is explored. The need for careful coordination of advertising with other elements of the promotional mix is given in Chapter 19. Because all advertising decisions are influenced by laws, Chapter 20 is devoted to that topic. All of the elements discussed in Part Five are influential in the evolution of a campaign.

CHAPTER 15
ADVERTISING PLANNING

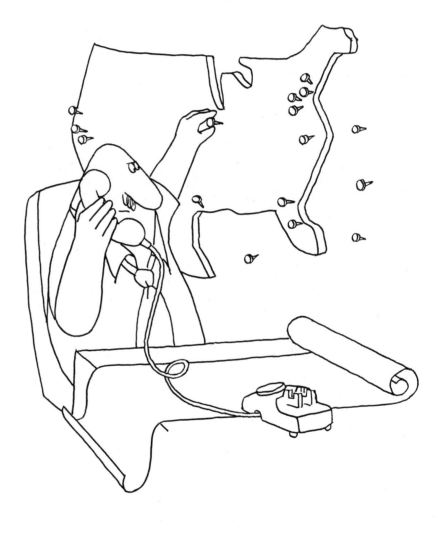

Advertising programs are a major subunit of many firms' marketing efforts. Advertising is the critical communication arm for those marketing organizations. And advertising programs, whose planning, organizing, and controlling are important responsibilities of management, also have a basic unit, which is known as the *advertising campaign*.

The term "campaign" has long been used to describe battle maneuvers in warfare. Today the term is applied to many systematic efforts including the election of political officers, the raising of money for charities, and the persuasion of people to buy airline travel, automobiles, pop records, or a myriad of other products and services. One definition of campaign is *a unit of effort to accomplish a set of objectives*. Thus, an advertising campaign might be described as *a unit of product information distributed to accomplish a set of objectives*. When A&P changed leadership in the mid-1970s, the first advertising run by the new supermarket management was designed to overcome a price-cutting, low-quality image created in consumers' minds by previous advertising whose theme was WEO—"Where Economy Originates." Ads were headlined, "The Time Has Come to Put Price and Pride Together Again," and the campaign was in the nature of a turnaround maneuver. This chapter examines the decision-making processes involved in implementing an advertising campaign.

It might be revealing to superimpose the analogy of a game of darts over the advertising decision-making process. Delivering an advertising message to a specific target group entails many of the same problems and opportunities found in hitting the bull's-eye. First, the target must be located: How far away is it? What is it made of? What areas of the target yield the most points (payoff)? Second, the dart thrower must assess the atmospheric conditions existing in the area between him and the target: Is there any wind, or other distorting factors? Third, the dart itself should be well designed with aeronautical adaptability if the target is to be struck with sufficient velocity to make an impression on the target and for the dart to stick in it. Fourth, with this kind of information, the dart thrower can then position himself in such a manner that each toss of the dart hits the mark easily and economically. Fifth, after each toss, the dart thrower determines where the dart hit and corrects the next effort in order to come closer to the bull's-eye. In the following sections, we shall apply the skill needed to hit the bull's-eye to the creation of a successful advertising campaign. The prerequisites for an effective advertising program will be explained first, and then we shall examine the basic areas of campaign planning.

502

PLANNING
AND
MANAGING
THE
ADVERTISING
CAMPAIGN

PREREQUISITES FOR AN EFFECTIVE ADVERTISING PROGRAM

Advertising is only one of the basic elements in the marketing program of most firms. Thus, underlying an effective advertising program—or advertising campaign—is a sound marketing plan which considers and determines the interrelationship of all the elements of the marketing mix. Basic marketing plans may remain effective for a period of years and provide a foundation for several advertising programs and a number of different advertising campaigns. Nevertheless, progressive marketing managers recognize the dynamic nature of markets and view market planning as a continuous process. Our emphasis is on planning by the national advertiser.

Any marketing plan should be under constant review and evaluation. A marketer can control the product and its distribution, as well as the promotional efforts designed for it. However, all of these operate in an environment of forces beyond his or her control—general business conditions, governmental actions, social and cultural forces, and, of course, the actions of both direct and indirect competitors. Therefore, such management analysis systems as PERT are employed to help solve the problems of evaluating and controlling the marketing plan. PERT, an acronym standing for program evaluation and review technique, helps to identify all inputs into the marketing system, to establish lead times and completion dates, and to simplify the coordination of all elements. It cannot update itself, however, or establish degrees of urgency for different activities. Both of these are management responsibilities. Employment of the computer has made this type of decision making easier, as is explained later on in Part Five.

THE SIX BASIC AREAS IN CAMPAIGN PLANNING

When a national advertiser plans an advertising campaign, several essential steps are taken. The infinite number of problems which have to be considered can be grouped into six areas, involving six planning steps:

1 Analyzing the market

2 Determining advertising objectives

3 Establishing the budgetary and control systems

4 Developing advertising strategy for:

   a Selecting media

   b Creating messages

5 Coordinating advertising with other promotional and marketing methods

6 Evaluating results

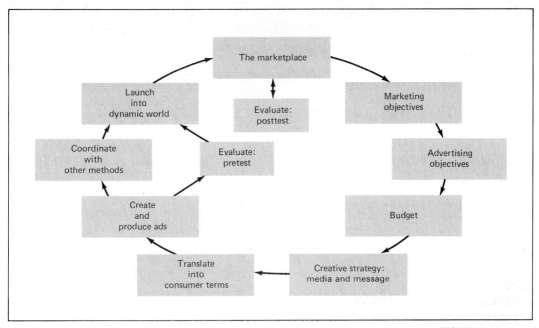

FIGURE 15.1
Advertising decisions and activities flow from the marketplace back to it. [*Based in part on a chart devised by Kenneth Hollander, Atlanta.*]

These six planning steps are not necessarily taken in precise sequential order. Decisions at each step impinge on decision making at other levels. The nature of the advertising message, for example, may influence the choice of media. The investment required in media in order to make an adequate impression compared with competition can be a major factor in arriving at the advertising budget. In actual practice, the first five of these basic planning steps may be under consideration simultaneously. The first two steps—analyzing the market and determing advertising objectives—are very closely interrelated and, more importantly, must precede the other steps. Results cannot be measured, of course, until after the campaign has started.

Analyzing the Market

The advertiser's overall marketing plan provides the basis for a current analysis of the target market and a projection of market conditions when the campaign actually appears. Such information as the total industry volume over the past 10 years, the advertiser's share of industry sales, as well as the shares of competitors, the legal constraints placed on the product category, and the role of foreign competition should be determined. These factors of demand, competitive response, and legal constraints are highly important in planning future action. Equally significant are conditions within the firm itself,

504
PLANNING
AND
MANAGING
THE
ADVERTISING
CAMPAIGN

*The best way
to unearth a new
and interesting
advertising campaign
is to dig into the
interesting facts
about the product itself.
And the agency
which digs deepest
usually comes up
with the most pay dirt.*

YOUNG & RUBICAM, *Inc., Advertising*

NEW YORK · CHICAGO · DETROIT · SAN FRANCISCO · LOS ANGELES · HOLLYWOOD · MONTREAL · TORONTO · LONDON · MEXICO CITY · FRANKFURT · SAN JUAN · CARACAS

FIGURE 15.2
The first step in planning an advertising campaign is an analysis of the market for the product.

including the extent of the firm's financial and production capabilities. If a company mounts a campaign which is very successful, the factory might not be able to meet the demand for the product. Similarly, if there are not enough dollars available to make an impact in the national market, the plan must be structured to include regional markets only to the extent that available funds will permit.

In 1971 Lever Brothers decided to develop a new toothpaste, which became its Aim brand. An analysis of the market at that time yielded some very interesting data. The dentifrice category accounted for annual consumer sales of $460 million. Procter & Gamble entries held a 45 percent share of that market, Colgate followed with 28 percent, Lever with 17 percent, and all other brands, a little over 9 percent. When analyzed by advertising appeals, it was discovered that 64.9 percent of toothpaste was sold through a therapeutic appeal (cavity prevention) and 25.8 percent was sold through a cosmetic appeal (winning smile), with 9.3 percent using other approaches to the market. Procter & Gamble's two brands, Crest and Gleem, were both in the therapeutic section of the market, Colgate had a brand in each section—Colgate in the therapeutic segment and Ultra-Bright in the cosmetic area. Lever's two brands, Close-Up and Pepsodent, were both in the cosmetic portion. It was obvious that the opportunity was for another entry into the therapeutic segment where 65 percent of sales resided, and Lever Brothers did not have an entry. The company formulated a new product, which they believed to be superior to Crest, and then developed an advertising campaign designed to give consumers an alternative to Crest, as well as diminishing that brand's domination of the dentifrice market.[1]

Of course, Lever Brothers did a more thorough analysis of the dentifrice market than this short paragraph can relate. But from the marketing plan that was created to bring about the introduction of the new brand, it was easier to create an advertising plan which would make the marketing plan a success.

Probably the most critical decision made when the market is analyzed is to define clearly the *target market* for the product. Essentially this is an exercise in segmentation. A careful balancing of organizational capability with the opportunities which exist in the marketplace is sought. Once it is known for whom the product is designed, advertising campaigns can be built to reach these people. Of course, in some instances, conditions warrant a mass-market orientation which aims at nearly everyone. However, generally speaking, *the* market is broken up into several smaller segments or parts. Thus, Lever Brothers did not go after the entire dentifrice market with its new brand, Aim, but tried instead to aim for segment using toothpaste for therapeutic reasons. Obviously, that in itself was a heavy assignment; nevertheless, it was more likely to succeed than if the campaign had been aimed at the total toothpaste market. By 1975 Aim held a 10 percent share of the total market for toothpaste.

Going back to our dart game, the market is similar to the game of darts and the target group can be compared to a section of the target board.

[1] This paragraph is based on a paper delivered before the Eastern Annual Conference of the American Association of Advertising Agencies, Nov. 19, 1974, by Charles Fredericks, Executive Vice President, Ogilvy & Mather, Inc.

Great news for mothers of cavity-prone children!

Most children don't brush properly or often enough. That's why the dental scientists at Lever Brothers invented a new fluoride dentifrice called Aim. If you have children, read on:

Case history of a cavity-prone family:

Mr. and Mrs. K. of New York City have two children, aged 10 and 12.

The children brush with a fluoride toothpaste, but still seem to get more than their fair share of cavities.

Mrs. K. worries that the children may be eating too many sweets without her knowledge. Mr. K. suspects that the children say they brush, but actually don't.

Neither parent questions the effectiveness of their fluoride toothpaste. "It's been around so long, it must be good." But still, cavities occur. A typical situation in a cavity-prone family.

New Aim dissolves faster than ordinary paste.

Dentists talk about something called "dispersal rate." This refers to the speed at which

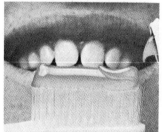

a toothpaste dissolves and spreads across the surfaces of your teeth.

Aim has an unusually fast dispersal rate.

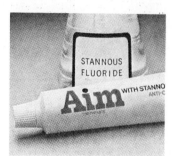

You see, Aim not only contains stannous fluoride. It is also a gel—a clear blue gel that disperses faster than any fluoride paste, in your regular brushing time.

Less abrasive—less likely to wear down enamel.

In order to clean teeth, all toothpastes must be somewhat abrasive. That's how they remove decay-causing matter from the tooth surface.

But if they're too abrasive, they can scratch or wear down the protective enamel coating.

If your children are already cavity-prone, you don't want this to happen.

Aim's gel formula is less abrasive than the great majority of toothpastes. That includes the leading fluoride paste you probably use now.

A special flavor for children.

The dental profession has long stressed that the most effective way to fight cavities is by better brushing.

Even the leading fluoride toothpaste can't do its best if a child brushes too briefly or too infrequently.

That's why, in designing new Aim, the formula was enhanced by flavoring compounds known to be especially appealing to children. The results were astounding:

In tests with 1,300 children, Aim was preferred more than 2 to 1 over the leading fluoride toothpastes.

Ask your dentist about Aim.

Add it up: the precise amount of stannous fluoride recognized as effective by dental authorities in preventing tooth decay. Lower in abrasion. The taste children preferred more than 2 to 1. And a faster dispersal rate to spread faster on the teeth.

Like any dentifrice, Aim can be of significant value only when used conscientiously in a program of good dental care and regular

professional visits. But if you are the mother of a cavity-prone child, you owe it to yourself and your family to ask your dentist about Aim.

Take Aim against cavities!

FIGURE 15.3
The Aim brand was introduced to consumers by ads such as the magazine ad shown. A therapeutic appeal was used for the new toothpaste.

Determining Advertising Objectives

This second step in advertising planning is actually inseparable from the analysis of the marketing situation. Both activities must be finished before decisions on budget and strategy can be made or before coordination and evaluation of the campaign are possible. Advertising objectives were already discussed briefly in Chapter 4; however, inasmuch as many campaigns falter because clearly defined, specific objectives are lacking, the point is now emphasized again.

Planning starts with the objectives of the business and by means of a trickle-down process. These broad corporate objectives lead to a statement of marketing objectives which in turn help determine advertising objectives. We recognize that advertising is a tool of marketing, and that recognition often leads to the phrasing of advertising objectives in terms of ultimate marketing goals, such as "increasing our share of the market." If the results of an advertising campaign are to be evaluated, however, advertising objectives must be clearly distinguished from marketing objectives. Moreover, because few advertising campaigns, and even fewer marketing plans, are restricted to the accomplishment of a single goal, the different advertising objectives should be carefully classified in terms of immediate importance.

Some years ago a management consultant, named Russell H. Colley, emphasized this point of separating marketing objectives, for which advertising is not the sole or even the primary cause, from advertising objectives. He further recommended that objectives—broad, long-range aims—be distinguished from goals—immediate, short-range objectives that are specific as to time and degree. These examples illustrate his point:

Objectives:
Marketing: To sell products
Advertising: To create brand preference for products
Goals:
Marketing: To achieve 12 percent of total industry sales in the product category in 1980
Advertising: To establish a 20 percent preference for brand A among Y million consumers in 1980[2]

For a specific example, consider the case of American Motors when introducing its Buyer Protection Plan. The company might well have used the following objective: "To establish a reputation for product quality and service dependability for its automobiles." The related advertising goal would then be: "To register the name Buyer

[2] Adapted from Russell H. Colley, *Defining Advertising Goals for Measured Advertising Results,* Association of National Advertisers, Inc., New York, 1961, p. 6.

508

PLANNING
AND
MANAGING
THE
ADVERTISING
CAMPAIGN

Protection Plan and its program elements in the minds of at least 60 percent of all current Chevrolet, Ford, and Plymouth owners within 90 days after the program's introduction." This goal is specific, quantified, and measurable. It also provides the maker of the advertising message with a specific direction.[3]

Before the advertising executive can develop any specific strategies for use in a current advertising campaign, these questions of objectives and goals must be settled. The portion of the total marketing effort to be carried by advertising must be established, and these responsibilities in terms of specific communication tasks or goals must be defined. Short-term communication goals should not be attained at the sacrifice of long-range objectives. For example, advertising that might successfully "increase awareness of new product A among housewives in 1977" could detract from the advertiser's brand or corporate image, thus seriously affecting accomplishment of long-range marketing objectives, or even the ultimate corporate objective of making a profit.

The final responsibility for determining long-range advertising objectives and short-term goals rests with the management of the advertising firm. Such managerial personnel have control of the marketing organization charged with carrying out the objectives set down, as well as the budget which provides the wherewithal for doing so. Nevertheless, the most productive decisions result from an effective partnership between advertiser and agency. Ideal objectives desired by management may have to be modified because of the lack of sufficient funds. Or desirable time slots for spot TV commmdercials may not be available, and the job that advertising is expected to do may have to be redetermined.

Winning in darts is equivalent to reaching your sales objective in marketing. In advertising, the objective is to contribute to marketing's goal of making more sales than competitors.

Establishing the Budgetary and Control Systems

To control the use of funds in a large corporation, management assigns a specific amount of money to various departments. A budget is a plan that is used to allocate this amount to each department. Within the advertising budget (that amount allocated for all advertising costs) different products, different markets, different media, and different time periods may each receive a share of the total. To determine the budget, estimates of the cost of each task are taken into consideration.

The budget should be carefully distinguished from the advertising appropriation, which is essentially a lump sum, often arrived at arbitrarily. Although arbitrary appropriations are common in advertising, this approach toward deciding what to spend for advertising is undesirable. Such appropriations are often unrelated to objectives, thus making it difficult to determine whether advertising is being employed efficiently.

One should keep in mind that any budget is only a plan; an advertising budget is only a plan for financing certain future advertising operations. Even though budgets are established to cover a specific period of time, usually a year, they should be constantly reviewed in terms of changing marketing situations, just as the total marketing plan should be under constant review and evaluation. Shifts in distribution patterns, competition, changes in production capacity, and other elements in the marketing situation may require changes in advertising objectives with consequent adjustments in the advertising budget. Flexibility is a key factor in a realistic budget. The establishment of a contingency fund within the budget is desirable, thus permitting rapid response to changed conditions.

Deciding how much to spend on advertising is one of the most perplexing problems faced by many corporate managers. It is difficult to measure what advertising does to profits, or even to sales volume, in most marketing situations. Therefore, the key factors in determining the optimum size of an advertising fund are the experience and judgment of management. This is a specialized kind of business creativity which is founded upon a philosophy toward advertising's role. Some managers think of advertising only as a current cost of doing business and as a cost that is more easily trimmed or eliminated than many others which appear on a firm's operating statement. This attitude tends to dilute the success of the advertising program, for almost any advertisement performs a dual purpose. It does help to produce immediate sales, and in this function, is rightly viewed as a current operating expense. But it also contributes to the image of the product or brand and the image of the advertiser, builds goodwill, creates acceptance for future products, and consequently serves as an investment toward future profits. When advertising is thought of as an investment, the likelihood of the company mounting a carefully planned advertising program is greatly enhanced. Furthermore, the chances of advertising being made a scapegoat in periods of reentrenchment are lessened. Advertising is more than a stimulant to immediate sales. It should be looked on as a capital investment, just as an investment in a new piece of manufacturing equipment is.

Deciding Strategy Issues

Objectives describe the intent of the advertising; once they are laid down, it is time to develop appropriate strategies to bring about their accomplishment. Strategy issues arise in two major areas of

510

PLANNING
AND
MANAGING
THE
ADVERTISING
CAMPAIGN

MOTHER: Oh my yes, Crayola Crayons are definitely important to me . . .

we're very particular about the toys our children have, and drawing is such a good challenge for them.

And you know, they're such a good value . . . the big box especially seems to last and last.

When it's new Steven will spread out all the colors and just rearrange them—for hours!

FIGURE 15.4
This storyboard for a television commercial portrays how a crayon manufacturer advertised to parents. A different approach was used in reaching children, another important segment of the market for the product.

FATHER: They have to be *Crayola* Crayons, too.

I picked up the wrong kind once—we finally had to throw 'em out.

advertising: (1) selecting media and (2) creating ads. Each area is discussed individually below, but first, what is meant by the term "advertising strategy"?

"Strategy," a military term, translates from the Greek to literally mean "generalship."[4] A specific strategem can be described as "an

---

[4] This paragraph is adapted from *White Paper I: A Point of View on Advertising Strategy*, McCann-Erickson, Inc., New York, 1972, pp. 2–4.

ingenious design for achieving an end." Thus, a strategy is results-oriented. Furthermore, being "ingeniously designed," "it must go beyond a summation of facts and objectives to that *creative insight* leading to a more effective way to sell the product."[5] One additional quotation may help to illuminate this point:

> Advertising strategy is creativity applied to knowledge for the purpose of finding the most effective way of achieving an end. We believe that advertising strategy must encompass the totality of what a product or service is, and how it is sold to the consumer. It embodies the product's and service's reason for being; it is the product's most important property; it is the differentiating principle that the product embraces. Strategy welds all of the marketing factors into a cohesive unity that will achieve the end.[6]

In other words, creativity is applied to the advertising objective, and a design for achieving an end is developed.

Selecting Advertising Media

Identifying the members of a target market, as determined in the analysis of the market, provides the grist for the development of a creative media strategy. In a simplified way, the media selection process can be described as matching media vehicle audiences with the media habits of persons in the target-market group. Although media selection may involve considerable use of scientific techniques and computer hardware, there remains a lot of art, or creativity, in the designing of an effective media plan.

The budgets established by advertising managers are spent for the use of media that have been selected by the advertising agency. The costs of time and space in media usually absorb the major portion of any advertising budget. Decisions on what types of media to use, and what specific media within these types, call for the kind of specialized skill and experience that is the backbone of agency service—the knowledge of how to create and deliver advertising messages efficiently.

What is sought in media selection is the delivery of effective advertising messages to the greatest number of prospects (people in the target market) at the lowest possible cost. That assignment is complicated by the many variables which affect the ability of any medium to communicate a particular advertising message, of which cost, coverage, merchandising possibilities, and the nature of the message are the most important. No one type of medium can be thought of as being better than all others, and few advertisers rely on a single type of medium. All types, and all specific media within these

[5] Ibid., p. 2.
[6] Ibid., p. 3.

"I read
The Houston Post."

Women prefer the Post above all of the nine daily newspapers in the Houston A.D.I. With a choice of seven evening newspapers and two morning newspapers, more Houston women read the morning Post than any other newspaper. Between the two *Houston* newspapers the Post has 45,000 more readers daily than the evening Chronicle among women between the ages of 35 to 49. And in terms of *total* audience the Post is read by 60,000 more adults daily than the Chronicle!

For the best reach of the Houston market...and especially women...play it safe and pick the morning Houston Post. Additional demographic data on the readership of Houston newspapers is available from Branham/Moloney, Inc., or The Houston Post National Advertising Department.

Source: M/A/R/C Continuing Newspaper Readership Study, 12 months ending December 31, 1972.

types, offer advantages and disadvantages. The media buyer seeks to find the right combination for a particular advertiser at a particular time.

Advertising media are similar to the dart, for they carry the message from the sender to the receiver. Some darts in the game are better balanced and thus are more likely to score well. Some advertisers choose media more precisely than competitors and also score better with their advertising.

Creating Advertising Messages

The Association of National Advertisers holds that the value of an excellent advertising message may be 10 or more times greater than a mediocre message. This is true whether the measuring stick is in terms of consumer attitudes, preference for the product, or final sales results. In general, every advertiser pays the same amount for similar time or space in advertising media; thus message content provides an opportunity area where dollar maximization can operate. Superior messages mean greater return on dollars spent for advertising.

The creation of the advertising message, like selecting and scheduling of media, is one of the primary functions of the advertising agency. The two tasks must be closely interrelated, if not actually undertaken at the same time. Often the process of creating effective advertising is aided by devising a creative blueprint which can be derived from the answers to the following questions:

1 What business goals do we seek to accomplish?
2 What kind of persons do we now sell to? What kind of persons should we sell?
3 How does that person now think, feel, and believe about our product, our company, and our competition?
4 What do we want that person to feel, think, and do?
5 What key thought can we put into that person's mind to make him think, feel, and believe or do that?
6 What tone of voice will get that person to hear and believe us?[7]

One of the important principles of copywriting is to emphasize or concentrate on a certain selling idea or theme. This principle deserves special attention in campaign planning.

The Campaign Theme Every advertising campaign should have a basic theme which reflects the campaign objective. This theme should appear in every advertisement. In this way, each advertisement

[7] Wright and Bostic, op. cit., p. 940.

FIGURE 15.5
An advertisement for a newspaper (*see opposite page*) contains a description of its audience so that advertisers may be persuaded to use the paper as a vehicle when attempting to reach the target market for the product.

514

PLANNING
AND
MANAGING
THE
ADVERTISING
CAMPAIGN

supports every other advertisement in achieving the desired results, just as each separate copy element supports the central sales idea of a single advertisement. The theme may or may not incorporate the whole USP as this concept was explained in Chapter 12. Without a basic theme to furnish continuity and focus, an advertising campaign becomes little more than a collection of unrelated messages. The advertising of Coca-Cola provides an excellent example of the use of the campaign theme. The firm changed to its theme "It's the real thing" in 1969 in order to make Coke advertising contemporary with the American scene at that time. The theme was used until 1976, when the "Coca-Cola Adds Life to . . ." theme was introduced. Thus, we see that well-chosen themes can last for long periods of time, but their use should be carefully monitored and changed when circumstances warrant.

The importance of choosing the correct campaign theme is dramatized by the experience of Lever Brothers with their number one product in the heavy-duty liquid detergent category, Wisk.[8] In 1950, the company management concluded that the firm would not be able to make any impact on Tide's leadership in the detergent field with a powdered formulation. Research people were put to work developing a liquid laundry product which was launched in 1956 with $20 million of advertising support. When national distribution was completed in 1957, the product accomplished a conversion rate of one in twenty-five instead of the hoped-for goal of getting one household in eight to switch to the liquid detergent. Sales were disappointing. The advertising approach was something like "try it, you'll like it." The consumer apparently didn't feel that was enough reason to change. Heavier rates of advertising yielded no significant increase in sales of the brand. Then, in 1967, a copywriter at Batten, Barton, Durstine, and Osborn (BBDO), the agency for the Wisk brand, hit upon the "Ring around the collar" copy execution. This theme exposed a need that the product satisfied well. The consumer need for stronger general cleaning was clearly addressed, and within eight years sales for the brand had tripled without any increase in advertising. Wisk is now in third position in the total laundry detergent category and number one in the liquid detergent group. This success story is particularly dramatic when one realizes that the laundry detergent product category is a large, crowded, and mature market that grows only 2 percent per year.

The shaft of the dart is similar to the campaign theme; it remains constant for a long period of time. When the dart no longer sticks in the board, the point, or tip is changed. In advertising the copy point, or headline, is changed so that the message will remain in the mind of the prospect.

---

[8] Based on "Packaged Goods: An Industry Profile," *Madison Avenue*, September 1975, pp. 19–20.

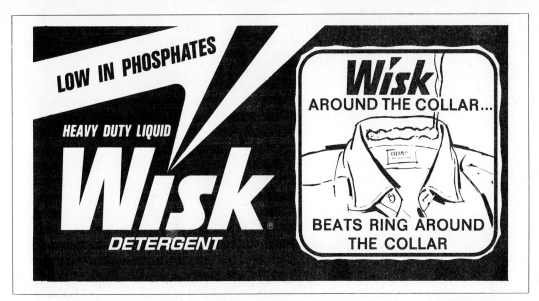

FIGURE 15.6
This car card employs the "Ring around the Collar" theme. Most of Wisk's advertising, however, is presented via the television medium.

Coordinating Advertising with Other Promotional and Marketing Methods

Advertising, to be fully effective, needs active support from the channels of distribution and from other nonadvertising components of the marketing organization. The responsibility for securing such cooperation rests with the advertiser. If the advertising program is to be successful, such elements as production, delivery, and inventory must be integrated with the advertising plan.

Personal selling by both the advertiser's own sales force and by intermediaries is an essential ingredient to a total marketing success. What is sought in this area of advertising planning is to get maximum cooperation from distributors, dealers, and salespeople. The effort to get this cooperation is referred to as *merchandising the advertising*. What the term means is that the advertising program is sold to the advertiser's own sales force and to dealers in his products. The burden of that sales message is the story of how the advertising directed at prospects will make the jobs of these salespeople and dealers easier.

Merchandising the Campaign to the Advertiser's Own Sales Force

The effectiveness of a strong consumer-oriented advertising program can be multiplied appreciably if the advertiser's salespeople know the specific objectives behind the campaign, as well as such information as the size of the advertising budget, media being used, and when and why. Field troops perform better if they know why they fight and what support is being given their efforts by artillery and

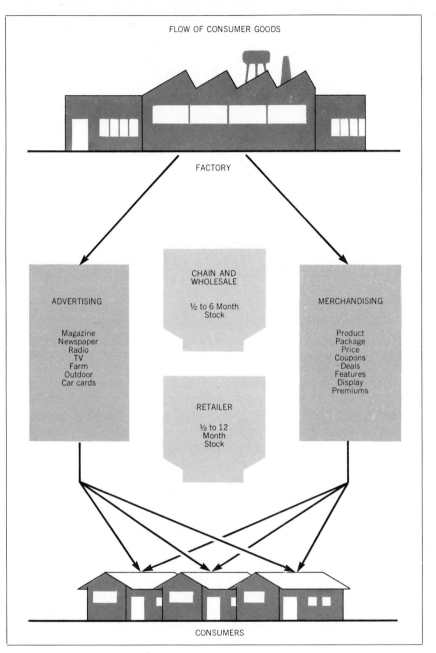

FLOW OF CONSUMER GOODS

FACTORY

ADVERTISING

Magazine
Newspaper
Radio
TV
Farm
Outdoor
Car cards

CHAIN AND
WHOLESALE

½ to 6 Month
Stock

MERCHANDISING

Product
Package
Price
Coupons
Deals
Features
Display
Premiums

RETAILER

½ to 12
Month
Stock

CONSUMERS

FIGURE 15.8
Every advertising
campaign must be
coordinated with
other marketing
and promotional
efforts. [*A. C. Niel-
sen Company.*]

airpower. A salesperson can do a better job if fully informed about the
advertising that paves the way for and supports the person's selling
efforts.

518

PLANNING
AND
MANAGING
THE
ADVERTISING
CAMPAIGN

Merchandising the Campaign to Dealers   Some advertisers believe that dealer cooperation is not needed if the company's consumer advertising is powerful enough to pull the product through the channels of distribution. This school of thought holds that the retailer exerts little or no influence on the consumer's choice. Supermarkets and other self-service establishments are given as examples. While it is true that clerks in these stores do little or no personal selling and in some instances stores are almost forced to stock highly advertised products, alert marketers are not content to have the retailer "stock" the product. Such marketers want the retailer to give their products good display, to provide advantageous shelf position for their products, and to promote the products within the store's advertising. Thus, products which have the greatest consumer demand—such as Coca-Cola—consistently supplement their powerful consumer programs with well-executed promotional effort at the retail level.

In addition to merchandising the advertising to salespeople and dealers, the advertising program should be coordinated with other elements of the marketing mix. For instance, a high-quality, premium-price policy for the product calls for dignified advertising, whereas bargain pricing indicates the need for busy, almost hectic appearing messages. There should also be consistency with the sales promotion and public relations efforts of the firm and its advertising.

Evaluating Advertising Results

All previous steps in campaign planning must have been undertaken, at least partially, before the results of advertising can be evaluated. As soon as the campaign materializes, it can be subjected to testing within a simulated marketing environment. The results then are used to correct the format of the advertising message, or to adjust expectations from the actual expenditures for the campaign. This process, called *pretesting*, is done before—and may influence—the buying of media and the creative steps yet to come. Pretesting is a research technique which determines the reaction to advertising by a representative sample of the target market before a full commitment is made. The goal of pretesting is to eliminate errors or weaknesses in program design before considerable sums of money are invested in the effort.

The most prevalent form of evaluation, however is *posttesting*. This is done only after a full commitment to a creative approach and a schedule of media has been made. The objective is to ensure that future campaigns will be more effective. Underlying posttesting is the idea that we can learn from our past mistakes—and also our successes.

Advertising testing can be isolated to the advertisement or any of its elements, such as the headline idea, basic theme, or illustrative treatment; such evaluation is actually copy testing. Furthermore, the underlying concept or "proposition" behind the advertising may be placed under the microscope. Similarly, the value of a particular kind of medium may be assessed. A whole series of research techniques, as explained in the next chapter, are available when this step gets under way. Actual testing is carried out by the advertising agency or by an independent research organization. Advertising as a science has come a long way through these testing methods, but the methods are not a substitute for the creative skill which is the essence of good copywriting or imaginative media selection.

If the advertiser maintains a continuous watch over results while a campaign is in progress, a weakness in any phase of the planning—the campaign theme or the dealer program, for instance—may become soon apparent. The campaign can then be strengthened quickly by making changes in the plan.

After the campaign has run its course, an attempt to see what returns have been received for the money spent should be made. Except in the case of the mail-order advertiser, determining the campaign's effect on sales is difficult. Even when relatively sophisticated experimental methods are employed to measure the effectiveness of advertising, the effect of advertising tends to be understated.

Execution of the Advertising Program

Planning of the advertising program is the joint responsibility of the advertiser and the advertising agency. The carrying out of the plan—its execution—is nominally the responsibility of the agency, with the advertiser's role largely one of review and control. The execution phase in one area is frequently in progress while planning is still being discussed in another. For instance, copy is prepared and submitted with rough layouts before specific media plans are approved. There is a need, therefore, to coordinate the planning and execution phases of the program. The situation may call for a number of rolling adjustments when some execution decisions require a reexamination of earlier plans.

SUMMARY

Good planning leads to better efficiency, and effective advertising is built with a sound advertising plan as its foundation. Essentially six areas are involved when an advertising campaign is being designed.

The first step is analyzing the market. Every advertising plan is the child of the marketing program for the firm, and knowledge of market conditions, competitive forces, legal restraints, and international considerations is vital to the advertising planning process. Defining the target market, with which the advertising will strive to communicate, is at the core of this step.

520

PLANNING
AND
MANAGING
THE
ADVERTISING
CAMPAIGN

The second step involves setting down objectives for the campaign. Objectives should be specific, for a stated period of time, and set down in terms that can be measured after the campaign is finished. Once it is known what advertising is to accomplish, the third step is deciding how much money will be needed to achieve the objectives. A budget is arrived at, and control methods are set up to ensure that the money is spent efficiently.

Two strategy issues constitute the fourth step in campaign planning. With the target market firmly in mind, two closely interrelated decisions are made: (1) the advertising media to be used and (2) the creative approach to be employed. Media selection involves weighing the advantages and disadvantages of the various media against the objectives set and the budget available for the campaign. The creative blueprint is designed with the campaign theme at its heart.

Advertising must be coordinated with other marketing and promotional activities to maximize the return from the effort and money expended on the advertising campaign. Two forms of evaluation are pretesting of the program's creative and media elements and posttesting the campaign after it has run its course. The execution of the program should also be carefully coordinated with the various phases of the planning activity.

QUESTIONS FOR DISCUSSION

1 What are the major steps followed in planning an advertising campaign? Is there any set order in which these steps are to be taken? Explain.

2 List the principal kinds of information needed for a complete analysis of the marketing situation.

3 Why is defining the target market such an important element in the planning of advertising programs? Using real or hypothetical examples, illustrate your answer.

4 Select a current advertising campaign running in a consumer-oriented magazine and write a set of objectives for it similar to the one laid out for the AMC Buyer Protection Plan described in this chapter. This statement must, of necessity, be imaginary but will show understanding of the concept of setting objectives.

5 What is the role of the budget in the planning process of the advertising campaign? Is an appropriation preferable to a budget? Explain.

6 What are the four principal variables affecting the ability of any advertising medium to communicate a particular advertising message?

7 What is a creative blueprint? What questions must be asked to gather the relevant information to permit its construction?

8 How does coordination as an activity fit into the planning of advertising? Into the execution stage of advertising?

9 From current advertising campaigns, choose two themes which seem to be particularly effective and explain why they are effective.

10 How is advertising evaluated? Is the evaluation process effective? Why or why not?

FOR FURTHER REFERENCE

Bogart, Leo: *Strategy in Advertising*, Harcourt, Brace & World, Inc., New York, 1967.

Barton, Roger (ed.): *Handbook of Advertising Management*, McGraw-Hill Book Company, New York, 1970.

Britt, Steuart Henderson (ed.): *Marketing Manager's Handbook*, The Dartnell Corporation, Chicago, 1973.

Jones, Bob: *The Business of Advertising*, Longman Group Limited, London, 1974.

Morgan, Eric A. G.: *How to Do Business in Branded Goods*, Longman Group Limited, London, 1972.

Nicosia, Francesco M.: *Advertising, Management, and Society*, McGraw-Hill Book Company, New York, 1974.

Obermeyer, Henry: *Successful Advertising Management*, McGraw-Hill Book Company, New York, 1969.

Quera, Leon: *Advertising Campaigns: Formulation & Tactics*, Grid, Inc., Columbus, Ohio, 1973.

Simon, Julian L.: *The Management of Advertising*, Prentice-Hall, Inc., Englewood Cliffs, N.J., 1971.

Stansfield, Richard H.: *Advertising Manager's Handbook*, The Dartnell Corporation, Chicago, 1969.

CHAPTER 16
RESEARCH FOR ADVERTISING PLANNING

We learned about the creation and physical production of advertisements and commercials in Chapters 12 to 14. A great deal of effort, however, is expended on planning before ads are created. Furthermore, effective planning and execution of advertising strategies depend upon the availability of sound, relevant information which helps to answer such questions as "What should the 'unique selling proposition' be?" "Who are the prime prospects for the product?" "Are they aware of its existence?" Do prospects read magazines, listen to the radio, or watch television?"—the list could be extended indefinitely. In advertising today, many of these questions can be answered by research.

An important function of marketing and advertising research is to gather information needed for the development of the advertising campaign. Prior to campaign development the market is analyzed to decide what kinds of things need to be known about the target market for the product. The behavioral research techniques discussed in Chapter 11 are useful in predicting consumer attitudes.

The thrust of this chapter is confined to the use of research in the development of the creative strategy underlying the campaign and the measurement of its effectiveness. This area is generally known as *advertising research*. Before turning specifically to that subject, however, an overview of the research process is desirable.

RESEARCH OVERVIEW

No need for advertising existed before the Industrial Revolution because sellers met face to face with buyers and, therefore, knew their customers intimately. Similarly, there was no real need for research into the market. Only after buyers and sellers became separated geographically was there a desire and need for market information. As business developed, the gap continued to widen, with even more intermediaries separating sellers and buyers. The feedback of information provided by market research became a valuable tool which enables sellers to satisfy the needs and wants of consumers.

The gathering of such information, now known as *market research*, went through an evolutionary process responsive to the needs of its own marketplace. When the Census of the Population of the United States was commenced in 1790, it became the first source of information about the scattered American market. In 1890 a system of punched cards was developed which permitted more speedy tabulation of census data; more information could then be gathered by field interviewers. In the 1925–1940 period the emphasis in market analysis shifted to the individual consumer, and rather sophisticated sampling

524

PLANNING
AND
MANAGING
THE ADVERTISING
CAMPAIGN

techniques were developed to facilitate the data-gathering process. In the 1940s another shift in emphasis occurred with the firm's impact on markets receiving attention in addition to an understanding of the composition and operation of specific markets. The advent and growing availability of large-scale digital computers in the 1960s made the once burdensome manipulation of market data vastly quicker and more economical.[1]

Market Research and Advertising Research

The American Marketing Association defines market research as "the systematic gathering, recording, and analyzing of data about problems relating to the marketing of goods and services."[2] Such research is carried on "to guide managers in their analysis, planning, implementation, and control of programs to satisfy customer and organizational goals."[3]

Most sizable business firms maintain a marketing research department as an integral part of the company's marketing organization. The research department assists the advertising manager in the gathering of market data and helps in sifting through and classifying the material, which is then fed to the advertising agency to use when discharging its primary functions of creating and placing advertising.

Information already existing within the company, *internal data* such as sales figures and customer lists, is tapped first. However, available data in most situations are insufficient for accurate decision making; therefore, additional research is undertaken. *External data* can be added to the store of information necessary for thorough planning. *Secondary data*, the results of other researchers' efforts, should be brought together, assessed, and added to the company's inventory of marketing data.

If additional data are still needed, a program of original research is instigated. The overriding research constraints of time and money are felt most heavily at this point. The search for *primary data* can be conducted by the firm's own marketing research department, by the advertising agency's research people, or by special-service groups established to perform such tasks.

Although marketing research plays a significant part in product formulation, packaging, new-product introductions, and advertising copy, we shall be specifically concerned here with its influence on advertising copy. Marketing research when directed at the advertising copy decision is usually called *advertising research*. It should thus be

---

[1] Based on Gerald Zaltman and Philip C. Burger, *Marketing Research*, The Dryden Press, Inc., Hinsdale, Ill., 1975, pp. 4–6.
[2] Committee on Definitions, Ralph S. Alexander, Chairman, *Marketing Definitions*, American Marketing Association, Chicago, 1963, pp. 16–17.
[3] Zaltman and Burger, op. cit., p. 8.

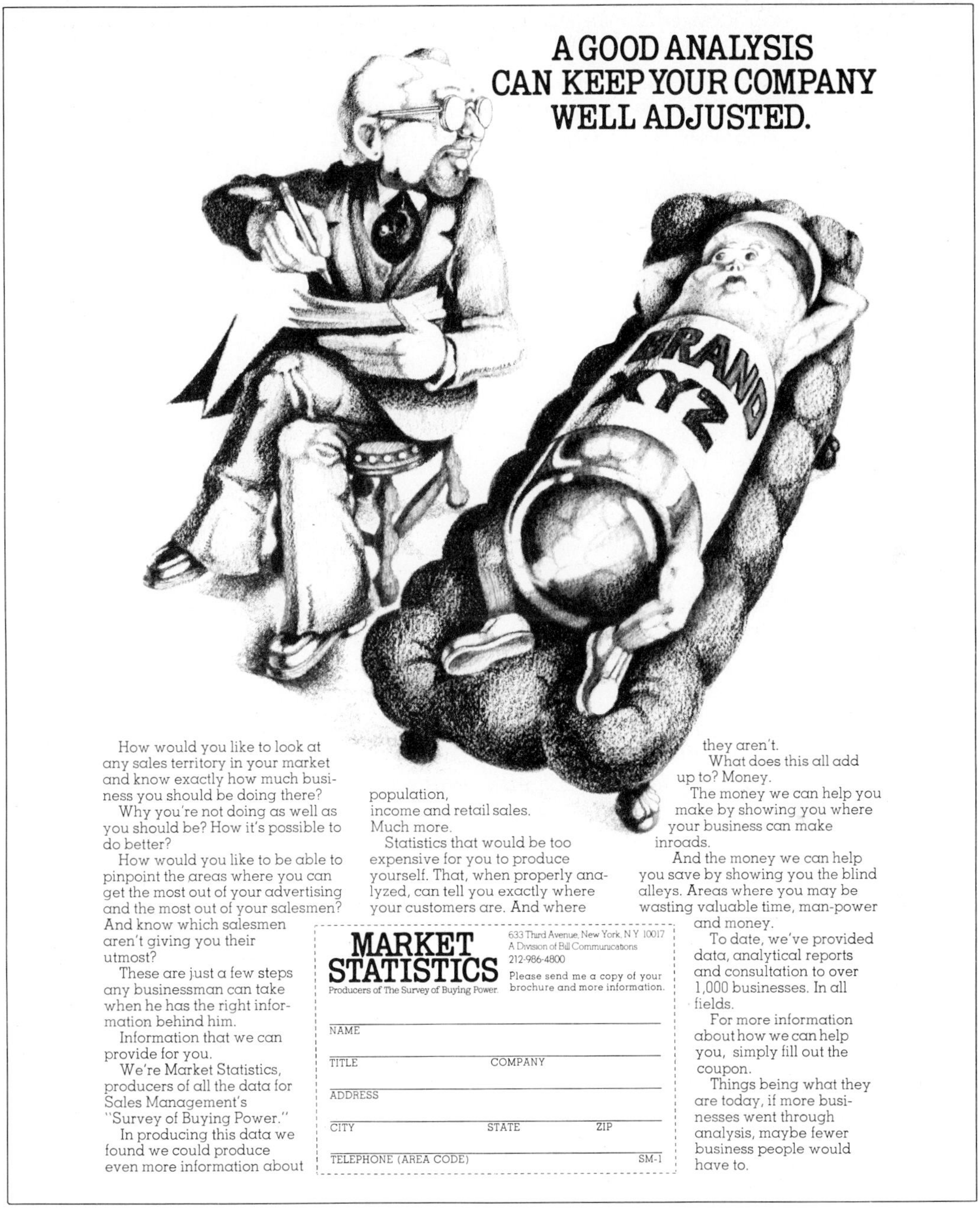

FIGURE 16.1

Special service groups supply research data and analysis to advertisers as is demonstrated in this ad.

clear that advertising research is actually a subsystem of the marketing research process. Furthermore, information gathered through marketing research is used by the advertiser and the advertising

526

PLANNING
AND
MANAGING
THE ADVERTISING
CAMPAIGN

agency when engaged in campaign planning. Another area important to the advertising process, *media research*, is discussed briefly in Chapter 18.

One business executive describes advertising research as the "big apple" of the marketing research field.[4] For one reason, more money is spent for this part of the market research field than for any other area. Since advertising is the "primary interface between business and the public, . . . it is no wonder that business is so concerned with doing sensible advertising research."[5] Holbert also points out that advertising research is the final test of all the efforts to produce and market the product that has gone before. His thinking is capsuled in these words:

> It is an absolute necessity to be thinking of the advertising, the advertisability, and the research on the advertising as the final product of all that is done in researching the product or service all along the way. The earlier that advertising (and advertising research) is integrated into the process of product and research planning, is regarded seriously, and is looked at in many early rough forms, the better the process will go. If it isn't, it may not go at all.[6]

Distinctions have been drawn between market research and advertising research. The first type of information, it is said, is concerned with the description and measurement of a particular market, whereas advertising research evaluates the impact of advertising messages on the market. By this distinction, a study of the days in the week when consumers purchase their groceries would be market research. A study of their readership of grocery advertisements in newspapers would be advertising research.

Rather than attempt to place market research and advertising research in two separate pigeonholes, a more practical approach for either the creation or the management of advertising is to think in terms of advertising *and* market research. Both types of information are needed, and the same basic techniques are used to collect and interpret both types of information. Advertising research, as for all forms of research, is based upon certain fundamental principles which are explained in the following survey.

RESEARCH FUNDAMENTALS

Through research an investigator attempts to arrive at precise answers to precise questions. "Precise" is a relative term, and in areas involving

---

[4] Neil Holbert, *Advertising Research*, American Marketing Association, Chicago, 1975, p. 1.
[5] Ibid.
[6] Ibid., p. 2.

human behavior the variables are more difficult to identify and to quantify than in the case of the physical and biological sciences. Research is used to reduce the area of uncertainty in which judgment and experience must operate to the point where one of several alternatives can be chosen with confidence. Marketing involves selling to people, an undertaking not nearly so predictable as other business activities such as production lines or accounts. On the basis of market research, decisions can be made, not with certainty, but with probability. Like many branches of science, market research attempts to quantify the unknown so that educated guesses can be made.

Marketing research employs several steps based on the scientific method. First, facts are assembled; second, some kind of order is imposed on the facts; third, a hypothesis is generated; and fourth, a theory results. The essence of this research approach is lodged in the principle of the *hypothesis*—a tentative theory or supposition adopted to guide the researcher—plus the employment of procedures that permit either proving or disproving the hypothesis. Thus, the validity and reliability of any research depend primarily on two criteria. First is the reliability of the researcher—whether his or her viewpoint is objective, rational, and free from bias. Second is the extent to which basic scientific procedures, such as the historical, experimental, or analytical methods and the generally accepted techniques developed in such relevant fields as statistics, psychology, and sociology, are employed. The more specialized terms *"validity"* and *"reliability"* in research is discussed later in this chapter.

Five Basic Steps in Research Procedure

Five steps can be used to analyze a market research problem. Different authorities classify and describe the basic procedure of marketing and advertising research in different ways, but most will agree that a full-scale investigation includes these steps: (1) defining the problem; (2) collecting secondary, or available, data; (3) collecting primary, or original, data; (4) compiling and collating data; and (5) interpreting the findings.

Marketing research specialists, with an eye perhaps to the practical application of research projects, often include two other steps: (6) presenting the results and (7) applying the conclusions, or follow-up. Important as these operations are, they seem to be less concerned with actual research procedure than with ways to increase the utility of a research project. Effective presentation of the results of an investigation is a problem in communications techniques rather than research procedure, and applying the conclusions drawn from research involves the management decision which the project itself was planned to aid.

528

PLANNING
AND
MANAGING
THE ADVERTISING
CAMPAIGN

Defining the Problem   The problems of advertising research are the problems of advertising itself, but searching for an answer to such a general question as "Why is brand X outselling our brand?" involves not one but several research projects.

Part of the answer may come from research conducted at the retail level, which shows the movement of both brands through retail outlets, stock levels, relative shelf position and display, and other indications of what is happening to both products in distribution channels. But such a study tells us nothing at all about the people who are—or are not—purchasing our brand and brand X. This will require a separate research project, one designed to probe the habits and actions and, in some cases, even the ethnic orientation of the consumer instead of the retailer.

Part of the answer may also be found in studies of the effectiveness of advertising media used, in tests of advertising appeals, or in investigation of a number of other areas which exert positive influence on the sales curve. Just as the broad, general marketing objective "to increase sales" should be refined in terms of such specific advertising goals as "to establish 20 percent preference for brand A among Y million housewives in 1980," so the broad, general questions posed as research problems should be rephrased as specific, workable hypotheses. Good answers are the replies to good questions, and if the problem is not clearly and specifically defined, research is off to a bad start.

One respected marketing researcher holds that defining problems can be more important than finding solutions:

> If we would represent ourselves more as problem-definers than as problem-solvers, the chances are we would solve more problems "because' if a researcher is only an order-taker and a client an order-giver, the research may well focus on the wrong problems.[7]

FIGURE 16.2

The wide variety of secondary data available to advertisers is illustrated in the table on the opposite page. This page from a volume of *Standard Rate & Data Service* shows that $93.5 billion of the nearly $120.5 billion total United States food store sales come from 334 metropolitan areas. The dollar volume share of each is also given.

Collecting Secondary Data   Gathering all information pertinent to the problem that is already available either from the internal records of the advertiser or from external sources is the second step in research procedure. Sales records, for example, should show the geographical distribution of buyers, seasonal fluctuations, high-volume outlets, and a wealth of other information that may have a bearing on the problem. And questions that confront a specific advertiser for the first time may have already been answered in published reports available from departments of federal or state government, advertising media, advertising agencies, universities, foundations, chambers of commerce, and trade associations.

Informal investigation—discussions with executives and salespeo-

[7] Emanuel H. Demby, *Marketing News*, June 6, 1975, p. 8.

State, Standard Metropolitan Statistical Areas (SMSA's), county and city estimates are developed exclusively by Market Data division of SRDS.

Metro Area Food Store Sales, Rank

January 1, 1974 to January 1, 1975

Rank		($000)
1	New York, N. Y.-N. J.(1)	6,068,461
2	Los Angeles-Long Beach(2)	4,589,118
3	Chicago(3)	3,864,762
4	Philadelphia, Pa.-N. J.(4)	2,915,588
5	Detroit(6)	2,460,514
6	San Francisco-Oakland(5)	2,138,671
7	Washington, D. C.-Md.-Va.	1,841,144
8	Boston (Official S.M.S.A.) (7)	1,628,890
	Boston-Lawrence-Haverhill-Lowell (county basis)	1,910,401
9	Nassau-Suffolk, N. Y.(1)	1,604,202
10	Pittsburgh	1,545,234
11	Dallas-Fort Worth	1,454,251
12	Houston(9)	1,381,317
13	Cleveland(8)	1,353,971
14	St. Louis, Mo.-Ill.	1,337,582
15	Newark, N. J.(1)	1,299,767
16	Baltimore	1,185,733
17	Atlanta	1,078,239
18	Minneapolis-St. Paul, Minn.-Wis.	1,023,871
19	Seattle-Everett(11)	979,909
20	Miami(10)	947,553
21	Anaheim-Santa Ana-Garden Grove, Calif.(2)	902,100
22	Milwaukee(13)	850,918
23	Cincinnati, Ohio-Ky.-Ind.(12)	840,027
24	Tampa-St. Petersburg	800,038
25	Kansas City, Mo.-Kans.	788,691
26	Buffalo	765,909
27	Denver-Boulder	745,224
28	San Diego	742,340
29	Riverside-San Bernardino-Ontario(2)	676,647
30	San Jose(5)	671,024
31	Portland, Ore.-Wash.	627,907
32	Indianapolis	609,953
33	Phoenix	609,464
34	New Orleans	605,531
35	Providence-Warwick-Pawtucket (Official S.M.S.A.)	577,130
	Providence-Warwick-Pawtucket (county basis)	562,777
36	Rochester, N. Y.	575,365
37	Columbus, Ohio	574,432
38	Louisville, Ky.-Ind.	534,538
39	Sacramento	521,974
40	Nashville-Davidson	510,536
41	Dayton	508,369
42	Hartford (Official S.M.S.A.)	506,198
	Hartford-New Britain-Bristol (county basis)	592,081
43	Fort Lauderdale-Hollywood(10)	494,484
44	Birmingham, Ala.	485,648
45	Memphis, Tenn.-Ark.-Miss.	485,115
46	Toledo, Ohio-Mich.	474,179
47	Albany-Schenectady-Troy	470,822
48	San Antonio	450,961
49	Jacksonville, Fla.	421,506
50	Northeast Pennsylvania	405,561
51	Oklahoma City	404,064
52	Greensboro-Winston-Salem-High Point, N. C.	399,513
53	Norfolk-Virginia Beach-Portsmouth, Va.-N. C.	396,307
54	Gary-Hammond-East Chicago, Ind.(3)	387,636
55	Allentown-Bethlehem-Easton, Pa.-N. J.	385,996
56	Akron(8)	381,495
57	Syracuse	374,862
58	Salt Lake City-Ogden	364,952
59	Richmond, Va.	363,868
60	Wilmington, Del.-N. J.-Md.(4)	349,265
61	New Brunswick-Perth Amboy-Sayreville, N. J.(1)	347,517
62	Jersey City, N. J.(1)	345,253
63	Orlando	344,276
64	Grand Rapids	339,997
65	Youngstown-Warren	331,816
66	Tulsa	318,973
67	Charlotte-Gastonia, N. C.	313,500
68	New Haven-West Haven (Official S.M.S.A.)	306,692
	New Haven-West Haven-Waterbury-Meriden (county basis)	578,323
69	Greenville-Spartanburg, S. C.	304,906
70	Springfield-Chicopee-Holyoke (Official S.M.S.A.)	304,848
	Springfield-Chicopee-Holyoke (county basis)	318,787
71	Bridgeport (Official S.M.S.A.)	303,814
	Bridgeport-Stamford-Norwalk (county basis)	628,055
72	Long Branch-Asbury Park, N. J.(1)	301,327
73	Honolulu	297,003
74	Flint	290,195
75	West Palm Beach-Boca Raton	286,519
76	Omaha, Neb.-Iowa	285,504
77	Knoxville	275,641
78	Paterson-Clifton-Passaic, N. J.(1)	270,869
79	Canton	267,026
80	Chattanooga, Tenn.-Ga.	263,608
81	Fresno	263,569
82	Harrisburg	249,132
83	Wichita	245,251
84	Beaumont-Port Arthur-Orange	236,762
85	Raleigh-Durham	234,504
86	Tacoma(11)	227,269
87	Oxnard-Simi Valley-Ventura, Calif.(2)	[illegible]
88	Worcester (Official S.M.S.A.)	217,937
	Worcester-Fitchburg-Leominster (county basis)	360,728
89	Fort Wayne	214,614
90	Mobile	213,936
91	Lansing-East Lansing	213,146
92	Peoria	207,563
93	Tucson	206,711
94	Des Moines	204,683
95	Bakersfield	201,664
96	Binghamton, N. Y.-Pa.	198,123
97	Davenport-Rock Island-Moline, Iowa-Ill.	197,778
98	Utica-Rome	194,365
99	Lancaster	194,238
100	Stockton	193,114
101	Corpus Christi	190,909
102	Baton Rouge	186,463
103	Newport News-Hampton	185,851
104	York, Pa.	185,506
105	Albuquerque	184,400
106	Stamford (Official S.M.S.A.) (1)	183,176
107	Spokane	182,891
108	Lexington-Fayette	178,842
109	Huntington-Ashland, W. Va.-Ky.-Ohio	178,723
110	Lakeland-Winter Haven, Fla.	177,707
111	El Paso	174,762
112	Huntsville	173,967
113	Las Vegas	172,889
114	Evansville, Ind.-Ky.	172,700
115	Charleston, W. Va.	172,343
116	Trenton(4)	171,698
117	Austin	170,780
118	Charleston-North Charleston, S. C.	170,013
119	Melbourne-Titusville-Cocoa, Fla.	168,311
120	Duluth-Superior, Minn.-Wis.	167,282
121	Waterbury (Official S.M.S.A.)	166,758
122	Little Rock-North Little Rock	165,092
123	Erie	164,900
124	Columbia, S. C.	162,013
125	South Bend	159,638
126	Reading	158,413
127	Shreveport	158,331
128	New London-Norwich (Official S.M.S.A.)	158,179
	New London-Norwich (county basis)	148,636
129	Kalamazoo-Portage	157,903
130	Lorain-Elyria(8)	155,846
131	Santa Rosa	155,042
132	Jackson, Miss.	154,453
133	Santa Barbara-Santa Maria-Lompoc	152,638
134	Madison	151,868
135	Poughkeepsie	149,445
136	Lawrence-Haverhill (Official S.M.S.A.) (7)	149,112
137	Rockford	148,284
138	Appleton-Oshkosh	148,004
139	Augusta, Ga.-S. C.	145,128
140	Macon	144,511
141	Portland, Maine (Official S.M.S.A.)	142,940
	Portland, Maine (county basis)	154,206
142	Vallejo-Fairfield-Napa, Calif.(5)	141,320
143	Daytona Beach	141,201
144	Johnstown, Pa.	139,374
145	Ann Arbor(6)	136,295
146	Montgomery	135,306
147	Pensacola	134,396
148	Eugene-Springfield	131,647
149	Savannah	131,058
150	Salinas-Seaside-Monterey, Calif.	130,929
151	Hamilton-Middletown, Ohio(12)	127,173
152	Galveston-Texas City(9)	126,213
153	Roanoke	125,468
154	Wheeling, W. Va.-Ohio	124,884
155	Lima	124,811
156	*Kingsport-Bristol, Tenn.-Va.	124,660
157	Modesto	122,795
158	Salem, Ore.	118,665
159	Columbus, Ga.-Ala.	118,230
160	Saginaw	117,019
161	Visalia, Calif.	113,861
162	Atlantic City	113,719
163	Norwalk (Official S.M.S.A.) (1)	110,700
164	Topeka	109,986
165	Springfield, Ohio	109,662
166	Racine(13)	108,191
167	Lowell (Official S.M.S.A.) (7)	107,899
168	Lubbock	106,620
169	Muskegon-Norton Shores-Muskegon Heights, Mich.	105,765
170	Colorado Springs	104,917
171	Steubenville-Weirton, Ohio-W. Va.	104,493
172	Amarillo	102,841
173	Battle Creek	102,150
174	Sarasota	102,130
175	Springfield, Ill.	100,779
176	Yakima	98,787
177	Waco	97,212
178	Asheville	96,952
[illegible]	Danbury (Official S.M.S.A.)	[illegible]6,110
180	Parkersburg-Marietta, W. Va.-Ohio	95,826
181	Terre Haute	95,680
182	Santa Cruz	94,708
183	Cedar Rapids	94,411
184	Brockton (Official S.M.S.A.) (8)	89,954
	Brockton (county basis)	191,504
185	Longview, Tex.	89,889
186	New Britain (Official S.M.S.A.)	89,719
187	Green Bay	88,843
188	McAllen-Pharr-Edinburgh, Tex.	87,942
189	Fall River (Official S.M.S.A.)	87,565
190	Altoona	87,361
191	Lynchburg	86,147
192	Jamestown, N. Y.	85,679
193	New Bedford (Official S.M.S.A.)	85,509
	New Bedford-Fall River (county basis)	248,655
194	Reno	85,017
195	Biloxi-Gulfport	84,634
196	Mansfield	84,195
197	Springfield, Mo.	83,522
198	Fort Smith, Ark.-Okla.	82,611
199	Fort Myers, Fla.	81,933
200	Vineland-Millville-Bridgeton, N. J.	81,758
201	Gainesville, Fla.	80,883
202	Anderson, Ind.	80,426
203	Petersburg-Colonial Heights-Hopewell	79,897
204	Lincoln	79,594
205	Champaign-Urbana-Rantoul	79,345
206	Brownsville-Harlingen-San Benito, Tex.	78,681
207	Fayetteville, N. C.	77,881
208	Jackson, Mich.	77,522
209	Bangor, Maine (county basis)	77,202
210	Janesville-Beloit	76,054
211	Williamsport, Pa.	75,273
212	Boise City, Idaho	75,190
213	Waterloo-Cedar Falls	73,259
214	Elkhart	73,062
215	Manchester (Official S.M.S.A.)	72,234
	Manchester-Nashua (county basis)	126,374
216	Lake Charles, La.	71,921
217	Killeen-Temple, Tex.	71,773
218	Bremerton, Wash.	71,394
219	Abilene, Texas	71,230
220	Tuscaloosa, Ala.	70,978
221	Wichita Falls, Tex.	70,954
222	Anderson, S. C.	70,526
223	New Castle	69,219
224	Richland-Kennewick, Wash.	68,960
225	Florence, Ala.	68,588
226	Kenosha	68,477
227	Decatur, Ill.	68,256
228	Muncie	67,315
229	Newark, Ohio	67,291
230	Pittsfield (Official S.M.S.A.)	67,162
	Pittsfield (county basis)	99,260
231	Bay City, Mich.	66,700
232	Lebanon, Pa.	66,610
233	Pueblo	66,120
234	Odessa	65,793
235	Texarkana, Tex.-Ark.	65,261
236	Wilmington, N. C.	65,238
237	Sioux City, Iowa-Neb.	64,173
238	Hagerstown, Md.	63,675
239	Provo-Orem, Utah	63,171
240	Eau Claire, Wis.	62,841
241	Burlington, Vt. (county basis)	62,510
242	Tyler, Tex.	62,195
243	Fargo-Moorhead, N. D.-Minn.	62,079
244	Lafayette-West Lafayette, Ind.	62,048
245	Nashua (Official S.M.S.A.)	61,758
246	Danville, Ill.	61,655
247	Elmira, N. Y.	60,876
248	Fayetteville-Springdale, Ark.	60,239
249	St. Cloud, Minn.	59,782
250	Clarksville-Hopkinsville, Tenn.-Ky.	59,522
251	Burlington, N. C.	59,403
252	Bristol (Official S.M.S.A.)	58,619
253	Cumberland, Md.	57,685
254	Rocky Mount, N. C.	57,451
255	Medford, Ore.	56,983
256	St. Joseph, Mo.	56,922
257	Kankakee, Ill.	56,911
258	Monroe, La.	56,630
259	Anniston, Ala.	56,618
260	Sherman-Denison	56,477
261	Danville, Va.	56,444
262	Jackson, Tenn.	55,424
263	Tallahasse	55,294
264	Charlottesville, Va.	55,251
265	Alexandria, La.	54,939
266	Panama City, Fla.	54,809
267	Anchorage	54,501
268	Gadsden	54,477
269	Billings	54,282
270	Florence, S. C.	53,900
271	Kokomo	53,449
272	Bellingham, Wash.	52,272
[illegible]	Watertown, N. Y.	51,926
274	Fitchburg-Leominster (Official S.M.S.A.)	51,292
275	Sheboygan	51,234
276	Sandusky, Ohio	51,099
277	Portsmouth, Ohio	51,003
278	Rome, Ga.	50,871
279	Owensboro	50,505
280	Fond du Lac, Wis.	50,136
281	Clarksburg, W. Va.	50,029
282	Lafayette, La.	49,730
283	Lewiston-Auburn (Official S.M.S.A.)	48,801
	Lewiston-Auburn (county basis)	57,090
284	Albany, Ga.	48,792
285	Bloomington-Normal, Ill.	48,435
286	Decatur, Ala.	48,260
287	Wausau, Wis.	48,116
288	Fort Collins, Colo.	47,968
289	Pascagoula-Moss Point, Miss.	47,953
290	Bloomington, Ind.	47,589
291	Laredo	47,574
292	La Crosse	46,759
293	Richmond, Ind.	46,712
294	Marion, Ind.	46,700
295	San Angelo, Texas	46,301
296	Dubuque	46,158
297	Joplin, Mo.	45,765
298	Pine Bluff, Ark.	45,690
299	Great Falls, Mont.	45,354
300	Sioux Falls, S. D.	45,337
301	Athens, Ga.	44,140
302	Meriden (Official S.M.S.A.)	43,707
303	Greeley, Colo.	43,455
304	Midland, Texas	43,405
305	Victoria, Tex.	43,303
306	Fort Pierce, Fla.	43,099
307	Valdosta, Ga.	43,073
308	Paducah, Ky.	42,341
309	Houma, La.	42,326
310	Rochester, Minn.	42,242
311	Iowa City, Iowa	40,285
312	Lawton	39,591
313	Hutchinson, Kans.	39,183
314	Missoula, Mont.	38,251
315	Quincy, Ill.	38,145
316	Hattiesburg, Miss.	38,076
317	Midland, Mich.	37,856
318	Columbia, Mo.	36,542
319	Dothan, Ala.	36,284
320	Meridian, Miss.	35,346
321	Pocatello, Ida.	35,262
322	Idaho Falls	35,217
323	Lewiston, Ida.	34,879
324	Bowling Green, Ky.	34,634
325	*Johnson City, Tenn.	33,843
326	Santa Fe	33,621
327	Rapid City, S. D.	33,563
328	Bryan-College Station, Tex.	33,124
329	Hot Springs, Ark.	30,921
330	Salina, Kans.	30,596
331	Enid, Okla.	30,268
332	Casper, Wyo.	25,190
333	Grand Forks, N. D.	24,580
334	Manhattan, Kans.	22,921
	Total Metro Areas	93,560,185

(1) New York-Newark-Jersey City, N. Y.-N. J.-Conn. Consolidated Area ... 9,231,505
(2) Los Angeles-Long Beach-Anaheim, Calif. Consolidated Area ... 6,393,357
(3) Chicago-Gary, Ill.-Ind. Consolidated Area ... 4,252,398
(4) Philadelphia-Wilmington-Trenton, Pa.-Del.-Md.-N. J. Consolidated Area ... 3,436,551
(5) San Francisco-Oakland-San Jose, Calif. Consolidated Area ... 2,951,019
(6) Detroit-Ann Arbor, Mich. Consolidated Area ... 2,596,809
(7) Boston-Lawrence-Lowell, Mass.-N. H. Consolidated Area ... 1,975,855
(8) Cleveland-Akron-Lorain, Ohio Consolidated Area ... 1,891,312
(9) Houston-Galveston, Tex. Consolidated Area ... 1,507,530
(10) Miami-Fort Lauderdale, Fla. Consolidated Area ... 1,442,037
(11) Seattle-Tacoma, Wash. Consolidated Area ... 1,207,178
(12) Cincinnati-Hamilton, Ohio-Ky.-Ind. Consolidated Area ... 967,200
(13) Milwaukee-Racine, Wis. Consolidated Area ... 959,109

(*) Effective October 9, 1975 Johnson City-Kingsport-Bristol became an official S.M.S.A. This table does not reflect the change. See the Metropolitan Area Definition page and the Tennessee and Virginia state tables for current information.

U. S. TOTAL FOOD STORE SALES—$120,466,131(000)

ple for the company and talks with wholesalers and retailers—is useful in evaluating the importance of hypotheses developed for the preparation of the campaign.

Examination of available data and of the results of informal interviews with people who have some knowledge of the product and its market is sometimes referred to as the *situation analysis*. This step in research procedure takes place more or less concurrently with the first

530

PLANNING
AND
MANAGING
THE ADVERTISING
CAMPAIGN

step—defining the problem. It helps redefine the problem, develops possible hypotheses, and provides a background for the planning of the next step—the collection of primary, or original, data. It may even show that planning original research can be an expensive and time-consuming procedure and that the chances of getting valid and reliable answers to a problem are sometimes slim indeed.

The usefulness of secondary data is definitely limited, of course, by two important factors. The first is possible bias. The study may be an effort to prove or document a particular point of view rather than an attempt to provide accurate, objective information. Both advertising agencies and advertising media perform research, and both have an obvious interest in how much is invested in advertising and where it is invested. The second factor is the possibility that the data are obsolete. Since markets are dynamic, a research report may be completely objective and still not reflect conditions applicable to today's problem.

Collecting Primary Data   If existing information does not supply an adequate guide to decision making, the advertiser must look for answers elsewhere. Original research must be conducted. There are three standard or traditional methods of collecting primary data, and they may be used singly or in combination: (1) direct observation, (2) experimentation, and (3) the survey or questionnaire.

The *observational method* involves just what the label suggests: a person or a machine watching and recording an activity. The Nielsen Audimeter is a machine that uses the observational method to collect information on the viewing habits of television audiences.

The *experimentation method* requires some type of test operation. If the problem involves a new package design, the actual package may be distributed to stores in a test market, and its movement compared with that of the old design in a control market. A manufacturer who is considering a change in price or a premium offer may use the experimentation method to test the reaction to the price change or premium in restricted market areas before applying them in the total market.

The *survey or questionnaire method* is perhaps the best known and most popular method of securing original research data. It involves asking questions in order to get firsthand information from individual respondents—from a sample of consumers who use the product, retailers who sell it, or any other group which may play an important part in the success of an advertising campaign.

In all three methods, basing the research findings on a sample of the universe is a recognized practice. In research terminology, "universe," or "population group," applies to *all* the units under investigation, such as all black families living in Chicago, all persons holding American Express credit cards, or all independent druggists in California.

Compiling and Collating Data Before conclusions can be drawn from original research, it is necessary to edit and tabulate the findings and critically compare their indications with those of existing data. Editing, or careful examination of the reports, serves two important purposes. First, it eliminates errors by either correcting or rejecting inaccurate or doubtful replies or records. In spite of careful planning, some respondents may have misinterpreted certain questions, or the mechanical recording devices may have made errors or failed to operate properly. Second, editing prepares field reports or questionnaires for tabulation by standardizing responses reported in a variety of ways. For example, in reply to the question "How long (in *months*) have you used product X?" some respondents may answer "One-and-a-half years." Instead of discarding the answer as incorrect or doubtful, the field report editor will convert it into the standard units—18 months.

Compiling or tabulating the results involves counting and summarizing the statistical conclusions from all the reports not rejected. Tabulation may be done by data processing equipment, or if only a small amount of information is required, it may be done by hand, using standardized counting sheets. Regardless of the method of tabulation, statistical conclusions do not result automatically. A mere summary of the data, even when presented in neat tables or colorful charts, is likely to be meaningless. A good summary calls for both skill in statistics and imagination to establish significant relationships between different groups of facts and the objectives of the research.

Interpreting the Findings The statistical conclusions arrived at in the data-compiling step are not the objective for which the research was undertaken, of course. They are merely evidence to be evaluated and interpreted in terms of alternative courses of action if the research is to aid the decision-making process. The computer's capacity for handling fantastic volumes of data with incredible speed has materially refined the decision-making process, but it has not eliminated the need for judgment and experience. A statistical summary is the end of the *inductive* process—the process of drawing general conclusions from a number of controlled experiments or investigations. The interpretation is *deductive* logic—the drawing of sound inferences from the statistical generalizations.

Straight thinking is necessary if the recommendations are to be both logical and practical. To be logical, they must, of course, be adequately supported by the statistical data. To be practical, logical recommendations must often be modified to suit a particular advertiser in a specific situation. A logical recommendation might call for the use of full-color ROP newspaper space in all markets, but if the advertiser does not have sufficient funds for such an investment, a practical recommendation might modify this to include only the dozen most important cities.

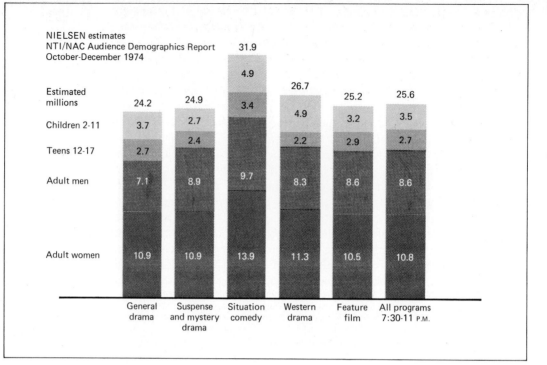

NIELSEN estimates
NTI/NAC Audience Demographics Report
October-December 1974

Estimated millions

Children 2-11

Teens 12-17

Adult men

Adult women

	General drama	Suspense and mystery drama	Situation comedy	Western drama	Feature film	All programs 7:30-11 P.M.
Total	24.2	24.9	31.9	26.7	25.2	25.6
Children 2-11	3.7	2.7	4.9	4.9	3.2	3.5
Teens 12-17	2.7	2.4	3.4	2.2	2.9	2.7
Adult men	7.1	8.9	9.7	8.3	8.6	8.6
Adult women	10.9	10.9	13.9	11.3	10.5	10.8

FIGURE 16.3
Research results can be clarified, and communication accelerated, with graphic presentation of data. These bar charts show the share of audience for different prime-time TV program formats by children, teens, and adult men and women groupings. [*A. C. Nielsen Company.*]

Much of the effectiveness of a research project depends on the form in which recommendations are presented to management. This is a problem in communications rather than marketing or advertising research, and such basic principles as brevity, clarity, and consideration of the audience to which the recommendations are made are as important here as they are in the creation of advertising copy.

FUNDAMENTALS OF PRIMARY DATA GATHERING: QUANTITATIVE RESEARCH

The third step in the research process possesses several elements which are hard for the student to understand. Therefore we shall expand our discussion at this point to cover these topics in detail.

Sampling Theory

Nearly every form of research employs sampling. When the medical doctor extracts a vial of blood from the patient's body, sampling is being done. The 2 or 3 ounces of blood that are analyzed represent the condition of all the blood, and this helps the doctor diagnose the patient's illness. The theory of sampling is derived from the mathematical theory of probability—the laws of chance—and it provides the researcher with a reliable means of getting the maximum amount of information for a minimum expenditure of time and money. If the sample is to be relied upon, however, it must meet two basic requirements: it should be representative and it should be adequate.

A sample is representative if it reflects the pertinent characteristics of the larger group, or population, from which it is drawn. If the particular population that is relevant to the specific problem is not carefully defined early in the project, the sample may be representative of the wrong population. Households—a single individual or any group of persons living together and pooling their resources—make up a population commonly sampled for studies of consumer spending. But if the study involves products like beer, soft drinks, or tobacco, bought in substantial quantities by such nonhousehold persons as members of the armed forces or students, households obviously do not provide a representative sample. In addition, the sampled population almost always differs from the total relevant population, merely because it is restricted to those willing to cooperate, and this may be important in evaluating the results.

If a sample is to be considered adequate, it must be large enough to give us confidence in the stability of the characteristics it reflects. The larger the sample, the less the probability of variation from the true nature of the universe. The question that must be answered is "How accurate do we want to be?" Statisticians use the term "sampling error" or "sampling tolerance" to refer to the limits of accuracy in projecting sample figures or percentages to the total population. Formulas used to calculate sampling error have been determined, but they are too complicated for our discussion here.

Once an acceptable sampling error is established, then an adequate sample is the minimum size necessary to produce results within this range. But there are other sources of inaccuracy in research besides sampling error. No increase in sample size can compensate for inaccuracy that results from an unrepresentative sample or from faulty questionnaire design or poor interview methods.

Sampling Methods

The two most commonly used methods of sampling in marketing and advertising research are (1) probability sampling and (2) quota, or judgment, sampling.

Probability Sampling   In the probability method, each unit of the universe has a known or equal chance of being selected, and the chance of any unit's being selected is unrelated to the subject or

534

PLANNING
AND
MANAGING
THE ADVERTISING
CAMPAIGN

purpose of the study. Simple random sampling is one form of probability sampling. The most important characteristic of the probability method is that the variance between the characteristics of the sample and the true characteristics of the universe can be accurately estimated mathematically. Stratified sampling is often done when the probability sampling method is being employed. The total universe is first divided into two or more parts, or strata, and then a sample is drawn from each of the strata. For example, a total universe of 21,000 college students might be divided into four "subuniverses," consisting of 8,000 freshmen, 6,000 sophomores, 4,000 juniors, and 3,000 seniors. If 5 percent of the names from each of these four strata were selected at random, we would have a stratified probability sample of 1,050 proportionate in class standing to the total enrollment of 21,000. The sample would be representative.

Quota Sampling   Quota sampling, which is sometimes called judgment sampling, is a method of sampling in which interviewers look for specific numbers of respondents with known characteristics. For instance, a marketer seeking to sell a new razor to college men may be able to learn all that needs to be known from interviewing 300 men with heavy beards from the 21,000 students on the campus. Considerable freedom is left to interviewers in the selection of respondents to fit these specifications. Despite the restrictions on the choice of respondents, interviewers are expected to select a random sample within the universe of respondents that fits the criteria established for the sample. In reality, however, interviewers tend to select those who are easiest to interview—and each member of the universe does not have an equal chance of being selected. This is the main difference between quota sampling and probability sampling.

Despite this weakness, the quota method continues to be popular in marketing and advertising research as a means of maximizing research dollars. It is likely to be both faster and less expensive than probability sampling. Also, in recent years, considerable attention has been given to ways of reducing the interviewer or respondent-selection bias. Nor is it always practical to apply probability selection techniques to the problem under study. If considerable cooperation is required from individual respondents to complete interviews, probability sampling may be difficult if not impossible. Where speed and economy are more important than precise results, quota sampling continues to be used with satisfactory results.

To sum up, haphazard or unsystematic sampling methods are to be avoided in any research project. In situations where the use of probability sampling techniques is impractical or where speed and economy are greater considerations than precision, quota sampling is the answer. But if a precise answer is required, along with an estimate of the extent of probable error, a probability sample is mandatory.

Methods of Getting Responses from the Sample Group

Most original information secured during marketing and advertising research is obtained (1) through questionnaires mailed to individuals or (2) by telephone or (3) by face-to-face interviews with consumers. The information-gathering phase is highly critical to the research process. Determining which data-collection method to use is based on consideration of relative costs, sample size, type of respondent, nature of the information sought, time available, and desired accuracy. The advantages and limitations of each of the three major methods follow. The discussion assumes the need for an adequate and representative sample.

Mailed Questionnaires Mailed questionnaires are more economical than face-to-face interviewing, particularly when the respondents are widely dispersed geographically. People who are inaccessible to either personal and telephone interviews can be reached by mail. As the questionnaire can be filled out at the respondent's convenience, more time will likely be devoted to providing the information. The method is slow in generating responses, partially because of delays in mail service.

Many people are unable or unwilling to answer questionnaires without probing or stimulation from an interviewer. Extensive or complex questionnaires usually yield poor results when mailed. Furthermore, the respondent's interest in the subject under investigation has a direct effect on returns; thus mailed questionnaires are not usually an effective research tool for any but a highly selective group of respondents, such as college deans, ceramic engineers, or advertising managers of large companies. The fact that many people receive large quantities of impersonal mail means that the mailed questionnaire competes for the receiver's attention. The number of completed questionnaires can be increased by a covering letter relating the study to the respondent's interests. An assurance that replies will be kept anonymous and the inclusion of a return-addressed postage-paid envelope also help enhance the response rate.

Telephone Interviews Large numbers of responses in a short time and at relatively low cost can be produced through telephone interviewing. Moreover, the method permits the reaching of respondents at specific times of the day; this is an important consideration in the study of radio and TV listening habits. Obtaining information on age, economic status, occupation, and other important respondent data by telephone is sometimes difficult. Securing cooperation through telephone inquiries is not easy, partly because the interview approach has been wrongly used as an entry approach for various selling schemes. The telephone method is often confined to studies involving rather

536

PLANNING
AND
MANAGING
THE ADVERTISING
CAMPAIGN

CONFIDENTIAL QUESTIONNAIRE

For a survey relating to the needs and purchases
of Metropolitan Milwaukee families to be compiled by

THE MILWAUKEE JOURNAL

A VERY LARGE SHOPPING BAG FILLED WITH PACKAGES OF GROCERY ITEMS and other merchandise is yours **FREE** *for filling in this questionnaire.*

To get this bag of grocery products you must answer the questions herein and have your husband or the man of the house answer those questions regarding his purchases. Questionnaires will be accepted from single persons or widows who maintain households. All replies are confidential and names are not released for any purpose.

Your household address was selected at random as one of a few in your locality to give us household data representative of your community. Even if you live alone your reply is important. Answer any questions that apply. Without your questionnaire our survey will not be representative of your area.

You must be accurate in your answers and an adult member of the family must bring the questionnaire to the Survey Dept. of The Milwaukee Journal.

THE SURVEY DEPT. IS LOCATED AT **918 N. 4TH ST.** *IMMEDIATELY SOUTH OF THE JOURNAL BUILDING*

The questionnaire must be returned BEFORE OR BY the due date specified below in red type.

Your co-operation will be appreciated and will help make possible publication of the nationally known "Consumer Analysis of the Metropolitan Milwaukee Market."

THE MILWAUKEE JOURNAL
SURVEY DEPARTMENT

B 2373

INSTRUCTIONS

1. Each major question should be answered YES or NO with an "X" or other checkmark. Give brand names only for items which you have bought within SPECIFIED time periods. If your answer to the main question is NO, do not answer any of the subquestions.

2. PLEASE do not guess in answering this questionnaire. LOOK UP THE BRAND NAME if you don't remember it. In each case list the brand you, yourself, BOUGHT LAST.

3. IF YOU DO NOT KNOW THE BRAND NAME, AND CAN'T FIND OUT, WRITE "DON'T KNOW" ON BRAND LINE.

4. Some questions ask for quantity purchased. This should be the total quantity of this type of product you have bought within the SPECIFIED time period.

5. Please write plainly. Use ink or typewriter if possible.

6. Do not return this questionnaire by mail.

7. The completed questionnaire must be returned to the Survey Office of The Milwaukee Journal, IN PERSON, by an adult member of this household.

B 2373

| Name | Your Street Address | City, Town or Village | Zip | Telephone No. |

You will receive a large shopping bag of grocery products if you fill in this questionnaire and bring it to The Journal Survey Dept. no <u>later than</u> **FRI., OCT. 10, 1975**

30 The Survey Office Hours Are 9 a.m. to 8 p.m., Monday Through Friday; 9 a.m. to 5 p.m., Saturday and Sunday

FIGURE 16.4

The first page of a mailed questionnaire is shown. The probability method of sampling was used; respondents were offered a reward for cooperating. The questionnaire was returned in person and checked by interviewers. [The Milwaukee Journal.]

simple questions and a relatively small amount of information. Another limitation to the method is that in many markets a significantly large number of telephones are unlisted in directories and thus are not likely to be included in the universe being sampled; however, the use of random digit dialing has tended to reduce this factor.

Personal Interviews The most reliable means of collecting the maximum amount of information from a representative sample is through the face-to-face or personal interview. The questionnaires can be longer and more complex. The interviewer can stimulate responses that are both complete and accurate by employing skilled observation and probing, by encouraging the respondent, and by repeating questions. Furthermore, the representativeness of the sample can be well controlled with personal interviews, and the researcher has a control over responses.

Face-to-face interviewing, of course, is more costly than other methods. Some respondents, such as high-level business executives, are difficult to contact. The personal bias of individual interviewers can affect results. The reliability of face-to-face interviewing depends on the skill and integrity of interviewers, which makes the selection, training, and supervision of these persons a significant factor. Recently, personal interviewing has declined in use because it is difficult to get (1) interviewers to do door-to-door interviews and (2) respondents to answer their doorbells.

FIGURE 16.5
A trained interviewer meets with six women in a focus group session. They are discussing attitudes toward consumer household products. [*Wainwright, Spaeth & Wright, Inc., Chicago.*]

538

PLANNING
AND
MANAGING
THE ADVERTISING
CAMPAIGN

Questionnaire Design

The results of interviewing, regardless of the method employed, depend directly upon the questions asked. Designing a good questionnaire requires skill and great care, and the task is not subject to the statistical principles which guide sample design. Leading researchers claim the greatest errors in survey results are due to the wording of questions. Asking the right question in the right way is an art more than a science.

Technically speaking, a questionnaire is a form which the respondent fills in, while a "schedule" refers to a series of questions used in face-to-face or telephone interviews wherein the answers are entered by the interviewer rather than by the respondent. In face-to-face interviewing an "interview guide" may be employed; it consists of a list of topics to be covered. The interviewer possesses considerable freedom with respect to the order in which the questions are asked and the language used in posing them.

Questions on the schedule and the questionnaire are either "open" or "closed." Closed questionnaires are phrased in such a fashion that they permit only a relatively small number of alternative answers which may be included in a checklist on the form. An example is: "Do you smoke cigarettes?" It has only two possible answers—"yes" or "no." Open-end questions—ones to which the responses cannot be anticipated specifically—are also used extensively. A question like "Why do you buy X brand shaving cream?" does not, for instance, permit advance classification of answers.

In constructing a questionnaire, schedule, or interview guide, certain basic principles should be observed:

1 Questions should be stated in such a way that their meaning is clear to respondents. Generalities and ambiguity can destroy the reliability of results.

2 General questions should be asked before more detailed ones, and the order of questions should be logical, with related ones grouped together.

3 Questionnaires should not be too long, for as the patience of the respondent is taxed, willingness to cooperate diminishes and careless answers and excuses for not answering develop.

4 Questions which suggest or direct the answer—"leading questions"—should be avoided, as should any words with strong favorable or unfavorable connotations that will bias responses.

5 Well-constructed questionnaires contain some questions designed specifically as cross-checks on the validity of answers to more critical or key questions, unless adequate verification is available from observation or previously recorded data.

6 Questionaires should be pretested in actual use on a subsample of

respondents before being used in full-scale research. The purpose is to make sure that the questions are being interpreted as intended by the question designer.

QUALITATIVE RESEARCH

Even when questions are so skillfully designed that there is no danger of misinterpretation by respondents, the research may not get valid answers simply because the respondent is either unable or unwilling to provide them. This is especially true when the questions are directed at explanations for a respondent's behavior, or the "why" of attitudes and actions. Because it may be even more important for the advertiser to know *why* consumers buy his or her product than to know when or where it is bought, a variety of indirect methods of research are used in the attempt to answer the question "why" in marketing and advertising research. These methods are known collectively as *qualitative research*.

The survey research which we have been discussing up to this point was labeled as quantitative research, which can be described as "research which provides information to which numbers can be applied."[8] The following quotation nicely defines qualitative research:

> Qualitative research is usually exploratory or diagnostic in nature. It involves small numbers of people who are not usually sampled on a probabilistic basis. . . . In qualitative research no attempt is made to draw hard and fast conclusions. It is impressionistic rather than definitive.[9]

Qualitative research methods generally fall into two categories: intensive and projective. Intensive techniques include depth and focus group interviews, whereas projective techniques include such devices as Thematic Apperception Tests (TAT), role playing, cartoon completion, and word association. The goal of both techniques is to probe beneath overt behavior and verbalized responses—to find answers to why-type questions.[10]

Intensive Techniques

Depth Interviews An unstructured conversation is at the heart of this technique. The interviewer meets with the respondent on a one-to-one

[8] Danny N. Bellenger, Kenneth L. Bernhardt, and Jac L. Goldstucker, *Qualitative Research in Marketing*, American Marketing Association, Chicago, 1975, p. 2.
[9] Peter Sampson, "Qualitative Research and Motivational Research," in Robert M. Worcester (ed.), *Consumer Market Research Handbook*, McGraw-Hill Book Company, Ltd., London, 1972, p. 7.
[10] Paragraph based on Bellenger et al., op. cit., p. 2.

540

PLANNING
AND
MANAGING
THE ADVERTISING
CAMPAIGN

basis for an hour or more. The immediate goal is to get the consumer talking freely about attitudes toward the marketing situation under investigation. Ultimately, the goal is to interpret the underlying motivation involved in the buying process—"to get at 'true' rather than 'surface' answers to why-type questions."[11]

Depth interviews reveal more precisely the feelings of one individual to a larger extent than can be determined in a group interview. In other words, there may be a degree more precision in the responses. Major limitations lie in the difficulty of getting skilled, qualified interviewers with the consequent expense that the method entails. Depth interviews are also very time-consuming in data gathering and in their interpretation; thus, in most instances, group approaches are employed.

Focus Group Interviews   Research, like all human activity, has its fads and fashions. The "popular" research technique today is undoubtedly the focus group interview, sometimes called the group depth interview. Growing out of psychiatric group therapy, focus group interviews are "based on the assumption that individuals who share a problem will be more willing to talk about it amid the security of others sharing the same problem. It offers a means of obtaining in-depth information on a specific topic through a discussion group atmosphere which allows an insight into the behavior and thinking of the individual group members. Rather than using a structured question-and-answer methodology, the procedure is to encourage a group to discuss feelings, attitudes, and perceptions about the topic being discussed."[12]

The procedure is rather simple. A small group of 8 to 12 homogeneous consumers, often homemakers, are brought together for a period of $1\frac{1}{2}$ to 2 hours. Under the guidance of a moderator who is often a professionally trained psychologist, the participants are encouraged to engage in conversation about the topic under investigation. The technique has been employed in such decision areas as new-product prototype testing, package change, advertising strategy change, and advertising copy formulation.[13]

A whole body of guidelines concerning how the group should be chosen, who should participate, and so forth has developed in the field. It is generally agreed that the moderator's skill in leading the group is the critical factor for success when focus group interviewing is being conducted. It is difficult to predict at this point in time how extensively the technique will ultimately be used in marketing and advertising research.

[11] Ibid., p. 30.
[12] Ibid., p. 7.
[13] Ibid., p. 8.

Projective Techniques

Projective techniques are another way to gather information which is difficult to secure by direct questioning. Projection, to the psychologist, is noncommunicative behavior, and a projective technique is any method of interpreting noncommunicative behavior, or of determining attitudes and needs people will not or cannot express. All the specific projective techniques operate on the principle of presenting the respondents with an ambiguous or vague stimulus—a picture, a sentence, a word that is abstract or incomplete. The respondents are asked to describe what the stimulus suggests to them, and their responses disclose to a skilled interpreter the information the respondents either cannot or will not supply in answer to direct questioning.

Among the projective techniques that have been used successfully in advertising and marketing research are word association, sentence completion, and picture response. *Word association* and *sentence completion* are accurately described by their names. In the first, individuals are given a series of words, one at a time, and asked to respond with the first word that comes to mind. In sentence completion, respondents are asked to complete a series of incomplete statements.

The picture-response technique is an adaptation of the Thematic Apperception Test and the Rosenzweig Picture-Frustration (P-F) Study, both used in clinical psychology. The individual is shown an illustration which may be interpreted in a number of different ways and asked to tell a story about the picture or to interpret the feelings and actions of people in the picture. For example, when shown the illustration in Figure 16.6, women were asked to tell what they thought the woman in the picture was saying.

The use of projective techniques requires a high level of cooperation from respondents, and special skills in interpretation of responses, and poses difficult sampling problems. They are costly and time-consuming in comparison with direct approaches, and also are difficult to quantify. Though less publicized than a few years ago, they have proved valuable in uncovering hypotheses which in turn may be tested by more conventional, quantitative methods.

RESEARCH INTO THE CREATIVE ASPECTS OF THE ADVERTISING CAMPAIGN[14]

Although other facets of advertising are often included in the sphere of advertising research, its very heart is what has been called *creative*

[14] The basic structure and some of the concepts discussed in this section were drawn from: *The Advertising Man's Guide to Creative Research*, a professional publication of Richard K. Manoff, Inc., Advertising, New York (Daniel Lissance, editor), 1974.

FIGURE 16.6
Projective techniques are an indirect approach to gathering information that may be difficult to obtain by direct questioning. This illustration is an example of the picture-response variety as used in a study of air travel. [*Fawcett Publications Inc.*]

① *Imagine that this husband and wife have their choice of traveling by plane, automobile or train on their next vacation trip. What would he be saying about his preference? What would she be saying about her preference?*

research. This term is descriptive of "research as it applies to the development and evaluation of the agency's creative product, i.e., its ads and commercials."[15] Thus, we use the term "creative research" as it is applied to the creation of advertising. In other words, our focus is on the advertising message. Every advertising campaign can be thought of as having three distinctive stages in its life cycle, and research is done at each stage. The three stages of creative research are:

1 Developing copy strategy
2 Pretesting individual advertisements
3 Evaluating the cumulative effects of advertising campaigns

Developing Copy Strategy

The importance of choosing an appropriate copy theme and concept to serve as the foundation of the advertising campaign has been stressed earlier in this book. Many potential copy platforms are generated at the agency. Each idea is considered within the background of information about the product, the market, and the motivations of consumers. One specific idea must be chosen as the basis of the *right* copy strategy for the campaign. Three common procedures can be used to help in this selection process: analysis of competitive appeals, individual depth interviews, and focus group interviews.

[15] Ibid., p. 2.

Analysis of Competitive Appeals   The first step is to look at the primary and secondary appeals that are being made for other brands in the product category. In some instances, investigation will reveal that a particular appeal is so strongly identified with a competitive brand that its use would only strengthen the position of the original

FIGURE 16.7
This page from *Reader's Digest* has been "Starched." The "noted," "associated," and "read most" scores have been reported, by sex, for the entire ad. In addition, four other elements of the ad were ranked: the paper cola container in the illustration, the headline, the body copy, and the logo. [*Courtesy of Starch Inra Hooper.*]

544

PLANNING
AND
MANAGING
THE ADVERTISING
CAMPAIGN

user of that appeal. In other words, the appeal has been *preempted*. The hope is that a suitable appeal will be isolated which is not firmly identified with another brand and is thus available for adoption by the brand. The Ad-Files service of Daniel Starch & Staff provides tear sheets of magazine ads which are grouped by product category and brand. Creative approaches used in the past and their relative success insofar as readership scores are concerned can be obtained from the service.

Individual Depth Interviews   Moving from secondary sources, the researcher can employ the techniques of qualitative research to learn about consumer attitudes toward products and their advertising.

Focus Group Interviews   This technique has supplanted individual depth interviews to a large extent in modern advertising research. From the tapes of these meetings a number of tentative creative strategy alternatives are developed. Such labels as "selling propositions" and "copy concepts" are sometimes used for these hypotheses.

Selection of an Appeal   Obviously the list of alternatives must be narrowed to one strategy, believed most likely to accomplish the advertising objectives. The alternatives may be measured against previously established criteria, such as importance of features, believability of claim, exclusiveness, or informativeness.

In some way, the alternatives should also be brought before present or prospective customers to obtain their input into the evaluative process. A host of research techniques, including paired comparisons, simple rankings, semantic differential tests, ranking scales, and multivariate analysis, are available at this stage of research. In sum, there are many methods of testing copy concepts; each has its advocates, and each method can yield useful insights when a choice of creative strategy alternatives is to be made.

Pretesting Individual Advertisements

After the creative strategy alternative has been chosen, copy personnel in the advertising agency set about to translate the strategy into advertisements. Again many alternative approaches will be developed, and research should be employed to choose the one to be actually used in communicating with consumers. The research goal is to determine which execution of the copy concept is most productive. Criteria, of course, must be set and choices then made among various available research approaches. Our discussion of these is divided in two parts: for print advertising and for television advertising.

Print Advertising   There are three major methods of pretesting print advertisements: consumer-jury tests, portfolio tests, and dummy magazine tests. In *consumer-jury tests*, respondents are shown various alternative ads and asked to rank the ads or to answer questions about the content of the advertisements. From this method consumer preferences can be learned, as well as the believability, memorability, or comprehensibility of the various ads being scrutinized.

In the *portfolio test*, test ads are interspersed among other advertisements and editorial matter in a book something like a photo album. Groups of consumers are shown the portfolio, and respondents in a matching sample are shown the same portfolio without the test ad. Afterward, questions are asked to determine the recall of the advertisement being tested.

When the *dummy magazine approach* is employed, an actual magazine is used in place of the portfolio. Test ads are stripped into the magazine, which is left with respondents for a period of time, after which they are questioned about the recall of advertising in the magazine. Two syndicated readership services, Gallup & Robinson and Daniel Starch & Staff, provide pretest services for firms wishing to learn about their proposed magazine advertisements.

Television Advertising   Pretesting commercials is more complex than for magazine advertisements because the production costs of commercials are so much higher than for most print advertising. For instance, if a finished commercial costs $20,000 to make and a collection of five different commercials is to be tested, an investment of $100,000 is made before a decision on which to use is made. This situation has been alleviated somewhat by the development of the *animatic film*, which is simply a film of storyboards with a sound track attached. When well done, such devices yield test results nearly as satisfactory as if a finished commercial were used in the test.

Two different environmental situations are available for the testing of television commercials. The first is under artificial or forced viewing conditions. Under this condition, one approach is the *captive audience* method, wherein selected respondents are invited to a theater for the purpose of previewing a television show. Data are gathered at the beginning and the conclusion of the show. Shifts in attitudes toward, or preference for, the brands featured on television commercials being tested during the showing provide the measuring stick for the commercials. High-scoring executions are then used in regular advertising schedules. One special-service group employing this technique is McCollum/Spielman Co. Audience Studies (ASI), also active in this field, measures audience reactions second-by-second during the entire showing.

546

PLANNING
AND
MANAGING
THE ADVERTISING
CAMPAIGN

Another approach is the *in-home projector*, or "black box," method. Test commercials are run on a 16-mm projector in the respondent's home with questions asked before and after exposure to the commercials.

A third approach, the *recruited natural environment* method, is gaining popularity because instead of measuring attitudes, it focuses on actual consumer behavior. Respondents are contacted in a real-life setting, such as in a shopping mall, and asked to view commercials in a trailer set up like a theater. Respondents are asked questions about products, shown the commercials, and given a packet of coupons which permit the purchase of products featured on the commercials at price reductions. A matched sample of consumers who have not viewed the television commercials, are given a similar packet of coupons. The differential in redemption rates between the two groups is attributed to the impact of the television commercials. Tele-Research, Inc., makes this method available to advertisers.

The second environmental situation available for the testing of television commercials is *exposure under normal viewing conditions*. Other names for this approach are "on-air" and "in-the-market" testing. In this test the commercials being tested are substituted for regular commercials on established programming. While this may be done at the network level, it is more common to air these commercials in a local market. The commercial is "cut in" where another commercial would normally run, and later a sample of respondents is interviewed by telephone about the test commercial. Burke Marketing Research, Gallup & Robinson, and Television Testing Company (TTC) are well known in this field; however, a host of similar services is available for the advertiser wishing to test commercials under normal viewing conditions which do not have the artificiality of the forced exposure.

Evaluating Campaign Effectiveness after the Fact

Research can contribute to the evaluation of message effectiveness even after the advertising has been completed. The value in measuring effectiveness after the fact is that it can help make future advertising better. The money has been spent, the advertising either did do its assigned job or failed to do so. This kind of research has little value unless we learn from past failures—and past successes.

There are two ways that advertising can be assessed after it runs: (1) on an individual advertisement basis and (2) for an entire advertising campaign. *Posttesting* is the name given to the first type; it is discussed separately for print advertising and for television advertising as was done for pretesting.

Posttesting of Print Advertising   This facet of advertising research is characterized by two well-known syndicated readership services: *Starch Readership Reports* and *Gallup & Robinson Magazine Impact Studies.*

Starch is the most widely used syndicated research service found in advertising today. Magazine readers are classified into groups (expressed in percentages) of those who remember seeing a particular advertisement, those who associated the sponsor's name with the advertisement, and those who read half or more of its copy. Starch labels these categories: "Noted," "Seen-Associated," and "Read Most." Figure 16.7 shows a magazine page with "Starch" scores indicated. This rating service is provided for most consumer magazines, for ads of half-page or more size. Research is also done for selected business and industrial publications. An added value of this service is that various advertising campaigns can be compared over rather long periods of time, as well as readings given on individual advertisements. The company also can provide advertisers with qualitative data, gathered through depth interviews, from *Starch Reader Impression Studies.*

Starch's major competitor, Gallup & Robinson (G & R), uses a different, and probably more rigorous, method in gathering data from magazine readers. Where Starch interviewers turn magazine pages while asking respondents the questions outlined above, G & R interviewers first ask the respondent to recall and describe advertisements from the closed issue of the magazine. The advertiser's name is the only clue given to aid recall. Additional questions probe the respondent's memory of the sale message. Three levels of effectiveness are then indicated: "Proved Name Registration" (PNR) score—which gives the percentage of readers who remembered the ad and proved its recall by describing the ad; "Idea Playback Profile"—a measure of sales message recall; and "Favorable Buying Attitude" score—which measures message persuasiveness.

The magazine advertiser can get a good reading on individual advertisements through these services. Furthermore, by careful analysis and tracking over periods of time, successive campaigns should improve in effectiveness. With many buyers of the service sharing the heavy costs of field interviewing involved, the information is available at a relatively reasonable cost. Thus, advertisers get information that would be too expensive to obtain on an individual firm basis.

Posttesting of Television Advertising   The services listed as providing pretesting of TV commercials are also engaged in their posttesting. Gallup & Robinson with its *Total Prime Time (TPT) Studies* is again active in this field of advertising research. A sample of television viewers is asked to trace their viewing pattern for the previous

548

PLANNING
AND
MANAGING
THE ADVERTISING
CAMPAIGN

evening. Recall of commercials is probed as to sales points and persuasiveness. Two scores—"Commercial Recognition" (CR) and "Proved Commercial Registration" (PCR)—are reported for every commercial broadcast during prime viewing hours. Additional qualitative information is given to buyers of the service. Many other syndicated services are available in this field, and custom-made studies are also common.

Evaluating the Cumulative Effect of Advertising Campaigns

This stage of advertising research is less developed than the other stages; consequently, less use of quantitative techniques is present. Because each advertising campaign is unique in its stated objectives, measuring the effectiveness of a given campaign must be done against those objectives. That is why we earlier stressed the importance of stating objectives in terms that are specific in time and character and that are expressed in measurable form. In this stage of advertising research there is at least one source of economical syndicated research data, Ad-Tel. Ad-Tel maintains a consumer panel whose members are subscribers to cable TV. The research firm can control the commercials reaching the consumers in the sample group; half of the panel homes are beamed the message undergoing testing, while the others receive a different commercial on their sets. Panel members also keep a diary of the products purchased every week; it can then be determined if seeing a particular television commercial had any impact on sales or not.

Expensive custom-made research is prevalent for advertisers seeking to measure the cumulative effect of their advertising. The usual research design employed is the *baseline*, or *benchmark*, study. A reading of the variable to be influenced by advertising, such as awareness of the brand, is taken prior to the campaign, and another is made at its conclusion. Probably the most commonly used measure is awareness, which has the advantage of being relatively simple to measure. Either people are aware of the brand, or its benefits, or they are ignorant of it; research can disclose the fact of the matter. Other measures may include understanding, belief, interest, persuasion, and sale. Although the last condition is the ultimate goal of nearly every advertising campaign, it is hard to attribute a sale to an advertising campaign due to the difficulty in separating the multiple influences bearing on the purchase of a product. This stage of advertising research leaves many unanswered questions and presents an opportunity area for advertising researchers of the future. When better ways of determing whether an advertising campaign has worked as desired are developed, more efficient advertising should follow.

HOW RESEARCH CONTRIBUTES
TO BUSINESS SUCCESS: THE STATE FARM
INSURANCE COMPANIES CASE[16]

Blair Vedder, chairman of the board of Needham, Harper and Steers (NHS) Advertising, related in a talk before the Advertising Research Foundation how advertising research was used over a 20-year period to guide a client's advertising. Although State Farm Insurance Companies have been an NHS client since 1939, the story really begins in 1945 when American business emerged from World War II.

In the 1940s State Farm became the leading auto insurance underwriter in the United States. Low rates was its primary consumer benefit. Allstate, a subsidiary of Sears, entered on the scene in the early 1950s and immediately became an effective competitor. Attitude research showed that State Farm was perceived as a rural company interested mainly in insuring farmers' cars. Sales projections made in 1953 showed that Allstate would overtake the company by 1957 or 1958. It was realized that a change in State Farm's advertising direction was in order.

A study of prospect attitudes made in 1954 revealed that State Farm was thought to provide inferior claim service and that it was too small, with insufficient resources to cover policyholder claims. A multipage insert was run in *Life* magazine telling the full story of the company's history, size, record with claims, and so forth. The company's share of market accelerated rapidly, and State Farm became a "true believer" in the value of consumer attitude research. A consumer probe conducted three years later showed there was no longer any doubt about the size of the company and its resources. Advertising had done its job.

The research did show, however, that people felt large companies are cold, impersonal, and insensitive to their customers. This finding posed a tough communications challenge, namely, how to show State Farm as a giant in its industry, selling insurance at low rates, yet as a company interested in its policyholder's well-being. Jack Benny, a well-known comedian of the era whose act revolved around his stinginess, was chosen as spokesman for the company. Benny presented the saving and service selling points with a light touch. Allstate struck back with its "Good Hands" theme delivered by Ed Reimers, a professional announcer, as spokesman. Significantly, Allstate was outspending State Farm in advertising by margins as high as 50

[16] Based on Blair Vedder, "Like a Good Neighbor, Research Was There," *1975 ARF Midyear Conference Proceedings*, pp. 39–41. Copyright 1975 by the Advertising Research Foundation.

550
PLANNING
AND
MANAGING
THE ADVERTISING
CAMPAIGN

percent a year, a fact which added importance to the need for effective advertising by State Farm.

Further research at the time showed that the two competitors were confused in consumers' minds due to the name similarity between the firms. Therefore, State Farm changed its communications goal in order to minimize the confusion without losing the saving message, delivered in a warm and friendly tone.

In 1965, 10 years after the *Life* insert, State Farm led Allstate by $200 million in earned premiums, which was Allstate's size when the battle began. In 1965 the automobile industry faced a new environment characterized by large underwriting losses. Obviously the search for new business was halted, and the emphasis shifted to retaining the better policyholders already in the fold. Now the advertising objective became one of keeping the company name before these policyholders. Radio was selected as the vehicle, and various comedians delivered the message.

Early in the 1970s conditions changed again, and aggressive selling returned. The rate advantage previously held by State Farm had largely disappeared, and new research revealed that consumers were less interested in cost and more concerned with service from their insurer. One finding was that people's primary interest was in buying insurance from an agent who was *knowledgeable*, was *available*, and could be *counted on* when help was needed. Inasmuch as State Farm had 10,000 agents, it was in a good position to meet these expectations. Thus, in 1971, the "Like a Good Neighbor, State Farm Is There" campaign was created. The promise was communicated first through film dramas and later by using a real-life agent as the star and spokesman of the message. State Farm is the undisputed leader in car insurance today; the company is also the largest homeowners' insurance company and a fast-growing life insurance underwriter.

The State Farm case shows how research and advertising creativity interplay. People's concern over the various product attributes changes over time, and the continuous tracking of these shifts has permitted the company to continue to prosper because its communication with customers and prospects has had continued relevance for them.

MANAGEMENT OF ADVERTISING RESEARCH

A recent survey of 172 advertisers of consumer goods reveals that approximately 60 percent of the firms use advertising research, and another 15 percent plan to do so. In accordance, an average of 1.4 percent of the 1974 advertising budget was spent for advertising research. Thirty-seven percent of the research was done by outside organizations, thirty-five percent by the advertiser's employees, and twenty-eight percent by an advertising agency.[17]

These statistics give an idea of the magnitude of the advertising manager's responsibility respecting advertising research. First of all, a decision has to be made whether to use research as a management tool. This idea may have to be sold to the top management of the firm; certainly the fact that three-fourths of the firms surveyed either do or plan to use advertising research means that doing so may well be a competitive necessity.

Once the decision to employ advertising research has been made, two other questions appear: "How much should be spent for the activity?" and "Who should do it?" The first question is very difficult to answer, as the field is somewhat short of guidelines. Experts have long advocated that a minimum of 1 percent of the advertising budget should be spent for advertising research. If this norm is accepted, the advertising manager may have an appreciable amount of money to spend as wisely as possible.

Getting the most return from that expenditure often depends on the correct choice concerning who should do the research. There is no easy answer to this question. Sometimes circumstances dictate the choice. If the advertiser has a relatively small budget, funds are insufficient for the in-house approach. That route may also be undesirable because employees frequently do not feel completely free to speak frankly when their research findings run contrary to the opinions of superiors.

The greatest objectivity is to be found in outside organizations, although they may be inhibited by the desire to get repeat business. Use of these sources of research is clearly indicated when the kind of data they provide coincides precisely with those data needed by the advertiser, for such data will usually be provided more cheaply and are likely to be more accurate.

The advantage of using the advertising agency is speed, and the researcher is usually closer to the problem, especially when copy execution is the area of investigation. On the other hand, the agency has a vested interest in the work that is being researched and also suffers from the limitations inherent in the client-agent relationship. Commonly, an advertiser will end up with a combination of all three sources of advertising research, with each acting as a sort of check on the others' efforts.

The advertising manager should become conversant with research methodology in order that he or she can make a judgment

---

[17] Data from *The Gallagher Report*, Dec. 2, 1974.

552

PLANNING
AND
MANAGING
THE ADVERTISING
CAMPAIGN

about whether the advertiser is getting full value for research dollars spent. Advertising research counsel, no matter what the source, should not be accepted on faith. The buyer of advertising research should demand evidence of the following three characteristics:

> *Reliability.* Using the same technique, do you get answers from test to test and from group to group that are of the same magnitude except from expected statistical fluctuations or is the technique so tenuous that you will get wildly different answers from administration to administration?
>
> *Discrimination.* Do all the ads or commercials seem to score the same or is there a "sensitivity," a sort of range in scores so that at least you may be able to guess at some clear winners and clear losers?
>
> *Validity.* Does the technique do what it says it does? Can it really "predict" (at least a little bit) marketplace winners? Is it in line with what other smart people are doing and writing about? Does it seem like a sensible sort of thing to ask people about, and so forth?[18]

One last point: The advertising manager must be careful not to become a captive to the research syndrome. A healthy skepticism toward research findings must be held at all times, viewing them as informational inputs which help make it possible to arrive at decisions with some facts. Research should help stimulate creativity in advertising, not stifle it. It must be realized that a certain antipathy exists between research people in advertising and those who actually create the ads. This point of view is expressed cogently by William Bernbach, an all-time great among copywriters and a cofounder of the Doyle Dane Bernbach advertising agency, in this quotation:

> Research can tell you what people want, and you can give it back to them. It's a nice safe way to do business, but who the hell wants to be safe? Small companies these days can't afford to run just competent advertising—the big guys have competent advertising, too, and a hundred pages to your one. Anyway, advertising isn't a science, it's a persuasion. And persuasion is an art.[19]

Fortunately, the schism between these two activities hardly exists today in many agencies. Thus, we see the Wells, Rich, Greene, agency, highly respected for its creative advertising, claim in its promotional literature that all of its work is based on "research, research, research."

[18] Holbert, op. cit., p. 16.
[19] Martin Mayer, *Madison Ave., USA*, Harper & Row Publishers, Incorporated, New York, 1958, p. 68.

SUMMARY

Advertising campaign planning should be based on as many facts as possible. Pertinent information is sifted out of the marketplace through the tools of modern research. Advertising research is needed as the geographical distance between producers and consumers widens. Reliance is made upon data gathered by researchers within the company and from outside firms. Similarly, secondary and primary data are employed.

Marketing research covers investigations into all the many facets of the marketing process, while advertising research, a subsystem of marketing research, deals with the message and its dissemination. Creative research, the focus of this chapter, deals with the question of how to make advertisements, either singly of as part of campaigns, more effective.

Advertising research, as with all research, employs certain research fundamentals. The five basic steps used to gather data are defining the problem, collecting secondary data, collecting primary data, collating the data, and interpreting the data. A sample population is used in advertising research to save both time and money. The principal ways of sampling are the probability and the quota methods. The sample is chosen to represent the entire market. Respondents from members of the sample may be obtained through personal interviews, telephone queries, and mailed questionnaires. When motivational answers are desired, focus groups and projective techniques are brought in to supplement quantitative findings.

Creative research, which delves into the message itself, is conducted at three stages in the campaign: (1) when copy strategy is being formed, (2) when individual advertisements are pretested for relative effectiveness, and (3) when the effects of the whole campaign are assessed. The goal during the first stage is to isolate a copy approach around which to build a campaign. In the second stage, which is true copy testing, the execution of the strategy decided upon during the first stage is measured. Testing after the advertising has run, called posttesting, as well as evaluating the total effect of a specific campaign, is done during the third stage. In other words, advertising research can first help in deciding what to say and through the creative research even how to say it. Testing will tell if what was said was communicated and understood as planned. At each level a number of syndicated services provide useful information at reasonable costs, although special-purpose studies may be also needed.

The advertising manager does not need to be a research specialist, but must have a good understanding of research methodology. Typically, the manager must decide if, and when, research is needed; how much to spend for research; and who should do the research. When deciding if research is sound, evidence of its reliability, discrimination, and validity must be obtained. Research should not, however, become a panacea, but rather should be

554

PLANNING
AND
MANAGING
THE ADVERTISING
CAMPAIGN

viewed as an aid to decision making. Research, if used properly, is especially helpful to creative people when in the process of making advertisements.

QUESTIONS FOR DISCUSSION

1 What appears to be the copy themes used in the current television advertising for State Farm and Allstate automobile insurance? What is the reason for the present approaches?
2 List any secondary data that a motor home manufacturer might use to shape the firm's advertising approach. Is this advertising research or marketing research?
3 What are the five basic steps in a full-scale "information-gathering" project?
4 How do you know if advertising research results are accurate?
5 Do people answer questions truthfully? What implications does this have on questionnaire and interview design? Do the above questions imply the answer desired?
6 How does an advertisement supply its own feedback?
7 Within the company, what information presently exists that should be used in aiming the product's advertising for efficiency?
8 Do industrial-products manufacturers need more or less advertising research than consumer-goods manufacturers? Why?
9 Explain the difference between marketing research, advertising research, and creative research.
10 Should a bank ad be factual or humorous? How do you know?

FOR FURTHER REFERENCE

Advertising Research Foundation: *Electronic Test of In-Home TV Viewing among Those Families Who Fail to Respond to Doorbell*, New York, 1968.

Boyd, Harper W., Jr., and Ralph Westfall: *Marketing Research: Text and Cases*, 3d ed., Richard D. Irwin, Inc., Homewood, Ill. 1972.

Buzzell, Robert D., Donald F. Cox, and Rex V. Brown: *Marketing Research and Information Systems*, McGraw-Hill Book Company, New York, 1969.

Cox, Keith K., and Ben M. Enis: *The Marketing Research Process*, Goodyear Publishing Company, Inc., Pacific Palisades, Calif., 1972.

Green, Paul E., and Donald S. Tull: *Research for Marketing Decisions*, 3d ed., Prentice-Hall, Inc., Englewood Cliffs, N.J., 1975.

Haskins, Jack B.: *How to Evaluate Mass Communications*, Advertising Research Foundation, Inc., New York, 1968.

Holbert, Neil: *Advertising Research*, American Marketing Association, Chicago, 1975.

Lucas, Darrell B., and Steuart Henderson Britt: *Measuring Advertising Effectiveness*, McGraw-Hill Book Company, New York, 1963.

Luck, David J., Hugh G. Wales, and Donald A. Taylor: *Marketing Research*, 4th ed. Prentice-Hall, Inc., Englewood Cliffs, N.J., 1974.

Ramond, Charles: *The Art of Using Science in Marketing*, Harper & Row, Publishers, Incorporated, New York, 1974.

Simon, Julian L.: *The Management of Advertising*, Prentice-Hall, Inc., Englewood Cliffs, N.J., 1972.

Wheatley, John J. (ed.): *Measuring Advertising Effectiveness*, Richard D. Irwin, Inc., Homewood, Ill., 1969.

Zaltman, Gerald, and Philip C. Burger: *Marketing Research: Fundamentals and Dynamics*, The Dryden Press, Hinsdale, Ill., 1975.

CHAPTER 17
THE BUDGET DECISION

With annual advertising expenditures in the United States totaling in the neighborhood of $30 billion, and increasing yearly, the decision on how these dollars are spent is not to be taken lightly. This chapter is a discussion of the various ways advertising dollars are allocated. The 25 leading national advertisers in 1974 are listed in Table 17.1. It is not difficult to believe that when Procter & Gamble gets ready to commit nearly one-third of a billion dollars for advertising, top management participates in the decision. The A/S (advertising to sales) ratios given reveal another dimension to the advertising spending picture. For instance, Sterling Drug, Inc., ranks seventeenth on the list with an expenditure of $85 million; however, this amount is more than 15 percent of the company's sales volume. Several other firms on the list have ratios nearly as high. For these companies, advertising is an extremely vital force in the success of their marketing endeavors; to a degree, advertising is their product, for without these relatively high levels of expenditure, it is not likely the companies would continue to prosper. In many instances, advertising is the single largest marketing expenditure, and total advertising expenditures of all American companies today are nearly one-half of reported net profits and come close to equaling total dividend payments. The budget decision, always important, is crucial where advertising plays a major roll in the firm's marketing mix.

As soon as the current market is fully evaluated and the advertising objectives for the campaign are set, the next order of business is deciding the level of advertising support needed. This decision clearly affects strategy decisions. When media choices are being made, the size of the advertising budget often acts as a limiting factor. The reason is that the major expenditure in a typical advertising program is the purchase of media time and space. Certain elaborate techniques in advertisement creation, such as preparation of four-color print ads or TV commercials, which involve high production costs, may also be out of the question. Logically, if budgetary constraints eliminate certain media alternatives, the creative advantage of these media is not available.

By the same token, certain media, when chosen as components of an advertising program, automatically prescribe that a minimum amount of money has to be budgeted. To spend too little on a TV campaign, for example, means that the impact on target audiences will be insufficient and the total advertising investment will be ineffective. A continuous dialogue, therefore, must exist when media and message strategy decisions are being made on the one hand and the budget is being allocated on the other. These critical decisions cannot be made independently; a high level of interdependence is present at every stage of advertising campaign planning.

558

PLANNING
AND
MANAGING
THE ADVERTISING
CAMPAIGN

TABLE 17.1
LEADING NATIONAL ADVERTISERS IN 1974

COMPANY	MILLIONS OF DOLLARS	ADVERTISING TO SALES RATIO
Procter & Gamble Co.	$325.0	7.3
General Motors Corp.	247.0	0.9
Sears, Roebuck & Co.	220.0	1.7
General Foods Corp.	189.0	6.9
Warner-Lambert Co.	156.0	14.3
Bristol-Myers Co.	150.0	9.4
American Home Products Corp.	135.0	8.8
Ford Motor Co.	132.0	0.6
Colgate-Palmolive Co.	118.0	10.7
United States government	110.8	N/A
R. J. Reynolds Industries	102.0	2.3
American Tel. and Tel. Co.	96.5	0.4
Heublein Inc.	95.6	6.4
Int'l. Tel. & Tel. Corp.	92.2	1.8
Chrysler Corp.	86.2	1.1
Lever Bros.	85.0	12.7
Sterling Drug, Inc.	85.0	15.1
RCA Corp.	84.0	1.8
Richardson-Merrell Inc.	83.5	14.5
Philip Morris, Inc.	81.0	2.7
General Electric Co.	80.0	0.6
American Cyanamid Co.	76.0	4.3
Gillette Co.	75.0	6.0
Norton Simon Inc.	75.0	5.4
Coca-Cola Co.	74.4	3.0

SOURCE: *Advertising Age*, June 30, 1975, p. 56.

ADVERTISING AS AN INVESTMENT

Two important, somewhat philosophical, attitudes are important to the success of advertising programs. Management should, first of all, look at advertising from the prospective customer's point of view. Second, management must think of advertising as an investment because a greater return is then likely to result from the expenditure of funds for advertising. Investment in a capital asset may cause more goods to be produced and sold—likewise, an effective advertising campaign may also increase sales.

The accountant lists advertising as a business expense, and the Internal Revenue Service accepts such handling for income tax purposes. Business managers are traditionally charged with the controlling of expenses and the cutting of costs. Thus, when the income statement of a company is being reviewed, the chief executive may well decide that the expense from advertising should be reduced, or even eliminated. This action, taken in the belief that good managerial initiative is being exercised, does not bode well for the role of advertising in the company's future, nor, quite possibly, for the future of the company itself. Viewing advertising only as a cost is a narrow attitude and not usually a sound one.

Considering advertising as a capital investment rather than a current expense is supported by Joel Dean, a leading business economist. Dean states that advertising is an investment which can be defined as "an outlay made today to achieve benefits in the future," whereas a current expense is "an outlay whose benefits are immediate." Therefore, it is reasonable to think of advertising as an investment just like a capital asset since both will provide larger returns in the future. Regardless of bookkeeping practice or tax treatment, Dean states:

> Promotional investments do have unusual characteristics, different from many other investments that now fight for funds in the capital budget. However, these traits . . . do not destroy the essential investment character of the promotional outlays.[1]

We agree that advertising expenses, like all other expenses, should be carefully scrutinized for wastefulness. A great deal needs to be known, however, about the results being derived, or failing to materialize, from advertising before a reduction or elimination is in order. Advertising must stand or fall on its own merits after a careful consideration of income and outgo factors and should not be made a scapegoat in periods of retrenchment for the firm. A cut in advertising budget in periods of recession brings an inevitable trade-off in future sales.

Unsound or capricious treatment of advertising funds is not likely when the dollars spent for advertising are thought of as an investment in the creation of future customers as well as the retention of present ones. The tendency to consider advertising as a necessary evil begins to disappear, and the urge to spend funds quickly—so that "more important" business can be transacted—is curbed. Planned advertising expenditures result, and advertising is then looked upon as "building a consumer franchise" for the advertised brand in addition to being a source of direct returns. David Ogilvy once said, "Every advertisement is a long term investment in the image of a brand." When advertising's contribution to the long-term future of the firm is recognized and respected, effective advertising is more apt to emerge.

THE ADVERTISING BUDGET-MAKING PROCESS[2]

Devising a budget—and the advertising budget is no exception—forces people to face realities and to plan. Neither task is pleasant for most

[1] Joel Dean, "Does Advertising Belong in the Capital Budget?" *Journal of Marketing*, October 1966, pp. 15–21.
[2] This section is based in part on Richard J. Kelly, *The Advertising Budget*, Association of National Advertisers, Inc., New York, 1967. Quoted material is from this source.

560

PLANNING
AND
MANAGING
THE ADVERTISING
CAMPAIGN

of us, and yet the rewards from dealing with conditions realistically and from planning future action are great. Another reason advertising executives find the advertising budget troublesome is that it involves the financial side of the business; advertising managers must deal with accountants and controllers. And the two groups hold different attitudes toward advertising and its role in the business and how company funds should be used. Furthermore, they speak different languages. Communication is difficult because both groups tend to use specialized terminology. Nevertheless, controllers and other company officers charged with financial responsibilities must understand the presentation made on behalf of the advertising budget if they are to approve its provisions.

What Is a Budget?

A budget is "an expression in dollars and cents of the forward plan of any activity, and budgeting, in essence, is nothing more than planning." It is only natural that the terms "budget" and "plan" are often used interchangeably in advertising circles. However, the concepts should be kept separate in our thinking. The following statement should help:

> The advertising plan typically includes a large body of information embracing sales goals, product facts, marketing information, competitive situation, creative platforms and rough examples of copy treatment. It sets forth marketing and advertising strategies, copy and media recommendations for implementing that strategy, and plans and schedules which define the timing of the campaign.

> The advertising budget is the translation of an advertising plan into dollars and cents—it is the "price tag." In its most elementary form, it states the amount of proposed advertising expenditures and informs company management of the anticipated cost of executing the advertising plan. It serves as a decision-making tool in the top-management process of allocating available funds to the various functions and activities of the company.

Anyone concerned with developing an advertising budget must observe two fundamentals of budgeting. One, the budget must be constructed within the financial capabilities of the company. Two, it must contain specific details on the allocation of funds to specific operations. Only when this is done can the budget perform its "single most important purpose . . . as the cornerstone for an effective budgetary control system." The actual budgetary process consists of four steps: preparation, presentation, execution, and control.

Budget Preparation

The advertising budget is planned and prepared by the advertising manager, or a similar person in the advertiser's employment. Agency personnel often do much of the planning work. One study indicates that only 21 percent of all national advertisers receive no agency assistance on budgetary matters.[3] The previous chapter outlines how research people provide information and insight for decisions dealing with product formulation, packaging, advertising copy, new-product introductions, and media selection. Marketing research, on the other hand, has pretty much stayed away from the important issue of how much to spend for advertising.

Determining the size of the future advertising appropriation is the first step in preparing the advertising budget. Once this figure has been set through the use of the somewhat unsophisticated methods described in the next section of this chapter, budget specifics must be established. The total advertising pie is cut into slices, and the total budget is allocated among the various media and advertising functions. The budget must be allocated among different market segments, time periods, and geographical areas. This is done largely on the basis of market potential within the segments, periods, or areas.

Presentation and Approval of the Budget

The presentation of the budget is a sales job. The advertising budget, as developed by the head of the advertising department, is subject first to approval either by the president, or chief executive officer, of the firm (in approximately 70 percent of the cases for consumer goods) or by the vice-president of marketing (30 percent).[4] The corporation's executive or financial committee is also involved in the final approval process. These executives act as a watchdog group over company funds; paring down requests for money is one of their prime responsibilities. This situation, coupled with the fact that every department in the typical business firm feels its own activities are of paramount importance, means that compromises will often have to be made. Adjustments in advertising budget requests are common.

The final budget for advertising should be evaluated in conjunction with the sales forecast. Since advertising is employed to make sales, this budget must be compatible with sales goals. Although the advertising agency may provide the advertising manager with visual materials and moral support, getting the advertising budget approved is the advertising manager's responsibility and one important test of his or her competence.

[3] *The Gallagher Report*, December 1974.
[4] Ibid.

562

PLANNING
AND
MANAGING
THE ADVERTISING
CAMPAIGN

Budget Execution

Each year the appropriation is used up in execution of the advertising. Administration of advertising spending is a somewhat routine activity. Purchase of advertising time and space is the primary task, and the advertising agency handles the job. The costs of advertising production, such as making television commercials, can also be significant elements in the overall expenditures for advertising; these are also incurred by the agency on behalf of the client. The advertising manager, therefore, should monitor these expenses to make certain that advertising dollars are spent in an economical manner. Periodic checks to determine whether media discounts are being taken and that special services are being purchased at competitive rates help to bring about this efficiency in the use of advertising funds.

An important duty of the advertising manager during the advertising program execution stage is to make sure that the marketing situation has remained unchanged. When critical changes do occur, it is vital that the budget have enough flexibility to permit program changes. One device which facilitates such action is the *contingency* account. Many companies include a reserve for contingencies in their advertising budgets. When the practice is followed, some set part, such as 15 percent, of the budget as approved by management is set aside in a "service account." These dollars are then available for the covering of cost fluctuations and also for items not already worked into the planned advertising program because they were not anticipated at budget time.[5]

Control of the Budget

Ascertaining whether advertising expenditures coincide with the schedule set down in the advertising budget is one important control function. A procedure must be established which brings information about current expenditures to the attention of the advertising manager. These reported expenditures are then compared with the advertising plan. If the budget calls for expenditures of $100,000 during July, the advertising manager must be sure that no greater amount is actually spent. Planned expenditures and actual expenditures must run parallel if the budget is to serve as a control.

Protecting the budget from uses other than advertising is another vital responsibility of the advertising manager. Because advertising is closely related to many other business functions—personal selling, merchandising, sales promotion, packaging, sampling, and public relations—it is often difficult to state clearly which department should bear certain charges. For example, should the cost of free samples be charged to the advertising or sales budget? Should a charitable gift be

[5] See "Contingency Accounts," in Ovid Riso, *Advertising Cost Control Handbook*, Van Nostrand Reinhold Company, New York, 1973, pp. 22–23.

handled as an advertising or public relations expense? Should production or advertising bear the cost of redesigning the product package? Department heads commonly fight to obtain larger budgets; almost all departments want more money to carry on their operations. If the argument for a larger budget is lost, there is another route to achieving the desired end, namely, to get other departments to pay expenses which are beneficial to the department escaping the charges. This process is sometimes called *budget attrition* and dramatizes the need for clarifying which budget is to be charged.

Making such determinations is not always a simple matter. Certain expenses are obviously chargeable to the advertising budget: media charges, advertising department expenses, and advertising production costs. Some charges are almost universally excluded: annual reports, scholarships, house organs, product research, coupon redemption costs, recruitment advertising, factory signs, product publicity, and premium handling costs. There exists, however, a gray area wherein such charges as the following may or may not be made against the advertising budget: advertising aids for salespeople, financial advertising, dealer-help literature, point-of-sale materials; catalogs for dealers, test-marketing programs, cost of contest entry blanks, mobile exhibits, packaging consultant fees, and consumer contest awards. In these instances, the decision is a matter of company policy or executive judgment. The advertising manager, acting as trustee of the advertising budget, must see that the advertising department does not bear the penalty of misplaced charges. This viewpoint is capsuled in this quotation:

> Guarding the budget against the marauders from other departments is almost as difficult as getting it in the first place.[6]

One pithy summary of what is involved in advertising budget control is to be found in this three-sentence formula: "Get it. Guard it. Milk it." The advertising manager needs to be persuasive in order to get an adequate number of dollars in the advertising budget. Steps need to be taken to guard against those hard-won dollars being used up for nonadvertising purposes. Finally, the dollars should be spent as efficiently as possible.

SPECIFIC METHODS OF DETERMINING
THE ADVERTISING APPROPRIATION

Advertising appropriations are determined in a variety of ways. Adherents of each method fervently believe their own approach is best. The truth of the matter, however, is that no one method is ideal for

[6] Fred Decker as quoted in ibid., p. 13.

564

PLANNING
AND
MANAGING
THE ADVERTISING
CAMPAIGN

all situations. Advertisers should, therefore, be aware of all major approaches in their search for an appropriate budget decision model. Among national advertisers, three major methods predominate: (1) the fixed-guideline approach, (2) the task method, and (3) subjective budgeting.

The Fixed-Guideline Approach

When the advertising budget is determined by the fixed-guideline approach, a formula is used. Basically, there are three varieties available, of which the percentage-of-sales method is by far the most widely used. Some firms employ the unit-of-sales variation, while the third method uses advertising expenditures of competitors as the guide.

Percentage-of-Sales Method The procedure in the percentage-of-sales method is to apply a stated percentage to the sales volume figure, and the advertising appropriation appears automatically. Nothing could be simpler. Management of the firm determines what percentage figure is to be used. It is usually based upon (1) the industry average or (2) what the company has spent in the past for its advertising. The chosen percentage is applied either to the sales volume achieved during the previous year (past year's sales approach) or to the sales level anticipated for the current year (planned sales approach).

The percentage-of-sales method has a major shortcoming: little attention is given to the specific advertising needs of the individual firm. If the chosen percentage is based upon industry averages, the advertiser's situation may not be average. Companies vary a great deal in their relative share of market; some companies are dominant in their field; others are quite insignificant in the overall supply picture for the generic product. Moreover, firms employ different marketing systems to reach customers. Thus, an individual company may need to do more—or less—advertising than the average of the industry.

The same basic principle carries over when the firm's own experience is chosen as the measuring stick. Conditions change, and advertising expenditures should change with them. Moreover, there is the question whether the percentage should be applied to the previous year's sales or planned sales. The former method can lead to too little or too much advertising, depending on whether sales are increasing or declining. The latter method, while sounder, is filled with problems of sales forecasting, among other things.

In essence, the philosophy underlying this method is faulty. It is based on the premise that advertising results from sales, while the converse—that sales result from advertising—is sounder thinking. Nevertheless, the percentage-of-sales method continues to be popular with many advertisers. Sheer force of habit provides one explanation. Moreover, management may use the method because of its simplicity, and because it relates advertising expenditures directly to sales. When advertising changes from a fixed cost to a variable cost, management feels that advertising costs can be controlled more easily. If sales decline, advertising expenditures decline, and vice versa. However, the interaction between sales and advertising is ignored. Management is lulled into believing that it has this important problem under control when, as a matter of fact, it does not. Use of this method is an indicator that money is budgeted by routine and probably spent in the same way.

Sometimes the percentage-of-sales method is used to bring a degree of stability to an industry. If all firms in the industry use the same percentage as their base, the volume of advertising done by each firm is directly proportional to its relative position in the industry. Thus, advertising loses some of its power to change share-of-the-market relationships. Of course, the creative selling power of different advertising campaigns is still a means of bringing about such market changes.

The percentage-of-sales method can be used most effectively by companies which face the same conditions year after year. Some public utilities are in this situation; the companies operate in static industries where there is little reason—including product differentiation through advertising—for buyers to change from one seller to another. Few firms, however, are so situated. For this reason, the percentage-of-sales method should be supplanted or supplemented by a different method.

Unit-of-Sales Method   A variant of the percentage-of-sales method is the unit-of-sales method, which is more precisely labeled the "fixed-dollar-unit-expense method." A specific dollars-and-cents amount is allocated to the advertising budget for each unit produced instead of applying a stated percentage of the sales figure to the advertising budget. Otherwise the two methods are practically the same. The method can be illustrated by looking at cooperative marketing organizations and their advertising budget procedures. For instance, members of the Washington State Apple Commission assessed themselves at the rate of 14 cents per hundredweight in 1975; this figure is roughly $6\frac{1}{2}$ cents per box of apples. Application of this formula resulted in a budget of $2.3 million.

Often this budget method is called the assessment method. Among other users of the unit-of-sales method are the major car manufacturers. Each automobile produced is allocated an advertising charge, and advertising programs are often revamped when sales are greater—or less—than planned. The unit-of-sales method has the same basic weakness as the percentage-of-sales approach to budgeting; the

566

PLANNING
AND
MANAGING
THE ADVERTISING
CAMPAIGN

seller's *need* to advertise is not weighed carefully. Of course, the unit-of-sales method can be incorporated with some variant of the task method, to make certain that funds are sufficient to meet the needs of advertising. The trouble is that often the amount of the assessment becomes traditional, and the advertising program is not designed to meet dynamic marketing problems.

Competitors'-Expenditures Method   Advertisers who base their advertising budgets on what competitors are doing may adopt one of two points of view. Some attempt to match competitive expenditures, while others strive to spend more than their competitors. In the first instance, advertising is viewed as a defensive device; the ruling thought is to advertise only as much as competition requires. This defensive strategy is as poor in advertising as it is in war. The second attitude often springs from a deep-seated competitive spirit that tries to outdo competition on the basis of sheer volume of advertising.

Neither approach is sound, however, for the advertising task facing one firm is not the same as that of its competitors. While the amount of competitive advertising may affect the market for an individual advertiser's products, matching or exceeding competitive expenditures cannot be relied upon as a sure way of developing a satisfactory advertising budget.

The Task Method

The search for a budget method which would help develop more positive management attitudes toward advertising expenditures has been going on for a long time. Most budget methods fail to treat advertising as a vehicle for achieving business objectives. Advertising is viewed either as a cost or as a result of sales instead of as an investment or the cause of sales. The task method, sometimes called the objective method, was developed with one purpose in mind: to use advertising to further the smooth functioning of the marketing process. Most major national advertisers claim to be users of the task approach. The task method involves four basic steps.

Defining the Task   The first step taken in implementing the task method is to identify the objectives that advertising is to achieve. The number and variety of objectives that can be set down for advertising are practically endless, as we discussed in Chapter 4. For example, some sellers use advertising primarily as a means of getting leads for their sales force or to arouse enough interest among prospects that they will be moved to send for additional information about the advertised product.

The sellers of encyclopedias often use advertising to stimulate inquiries. Let us assume that the Eureka Encyclopedia Publishing

Company has a permanent sales force of 100 members. The company would like to see its salespeople sell—on an average—100 sets annually. Furthermore, let us assume that one call in five develops into a sale. If the only source of leads is inquiries from people who have been exposed to company advertising, 50,000 inquiries will be needed (100 salespeople × 100 sets sold annually = 10,000 sets; 10,000 sets × 5 inquiries per sale = 50,000 inquiries). The advertising objective is to secure 50,000 inquiries from consumers.

A more typical task is the achievement of a specific level of brand awareness for the product among a group of consumers. The task is then expressed in communication terms. Other advertisers, such as those engaged in the direct-response business, may phrase the task in terms of actual sales. Advertising, of course, does not carry the entire burden in the achievement of most business objectives. For the moment, however, we shall put aside the real-life problem of specifying the relative role of advertising in the marketing mix and continue with our step-by-step explanation of the task method.

Determining the Type and Quantity of Advertising The truly difficult part of the task method lies in this step, for at this stage the most efficient and effective means of satisfying the objectives must be worked out. The problem is that there is no exact way to predict expected returns from advertising. An advertiser may decide that consumer magazines in general, and *Reader's Digest* in particular, are the best ways to reach the market for the advertising product. That media selection process is not easy in itself, as the next chapter will amplify, but the question of how much advertising is needed is much more complex. "How many full pages in four colors in *Reader's Digest* are needed to obtain 50,000 inquiries for the encyclopedia marketer?" is a very hard question to answer with any precision. While the task method is often considered the most scientific budget method, successfully determining the type and quantity of advertising depends largely on the practice of the art of advertising, although the techniques for evaluating advertising effectiveness can help the advertising decision maker. Clearly defined objectives, however, make the measurement of advertising effectiveness somewhat easier and more accurate.

Determining the Cost of the Advertising Program The third step in the task method is more mechanical than the first two steps. The addition of estimates of various costs, including media and production charges, is a matter of simple arithmetic.

Determining Whether the Program Is Affordable Once a cost figure is reached, management must decide whether the company is financially able to make such an expenditure for advertising. The totality of the costs is evaluated within the profit and loss structure of the brand

568

PLANNING
AND
MANAGING
THE ADVERTISING
CAMPAIGN

FIGURE 17.1
One principle of
advertising bud-
geting is that the
amount of money
available for ad-
vertising deter-
mines what media
can be used. [*Re-
produced from* Ad-
vertising Age *by
permission.*]

"I had heard they were cutting their advertising budget."

and company. If the funds are simply not there, a rational decision can be made respecting which objectives are to be sacrificed or modified in order to reduce the budget to viable dimensions. By use of the task method, the decision can be based upon greater amounts of factual information, for the very acts of establishing the objective and deciding the kind and quantity of advertising needed to achieve it require intensive fact gathering. Moreover, clearly stated objectives supplant prejudices and snap judgments in the budget-making process.

Other Considerations   The task method possesses at least one important limitation, which is pointed out by Bogart in these words:

> The task method of budgeting arose in a prebroadcast era. This method afforded the advertiser a considerable degree of freedom because of the variety of ways in which print media can be scheduled. In an epoch of large-scale expenditures on network television, the task method loses a good deal of its flexibility. The advertiser who is considering the possible buy (or "participation" buy) of a network "package" (of combined program production costs and air time costs) has only a yes or no choice as to his

participation. The inflexibility of these media costs is incompatible with the task method theory that the advertiser should spend whatever is needed to do a particular job.[7]

One further comment is important. The task method builds up while most methods break down the budget. That is to say, in the task method the various needs for advertising and their costs are totaled and the advertising budget emerges. In the breakdown method, a total is determined first and funds are then allocated to different advertising functions and media. Because the buildup approach forces management to set realistic objectives for advertising and fosters an attitude which regards advertising as a long-term investment, the task method has much to contribute when sound advertising budgets are being designed.

Subjective and Other Methods of Budgeting

Most advertisers probably use either one of the fixed-guideline methods or the task method when setting budgets for advertising programs. At least very few executives will admit that such an important decision is made on a subjective basis. Nevertheless, it is quite likely that the subjective method is used more than is admitted, especially by smaller firms. One variety is called the *arbitrary method*, or put less elegantly, the "gut" method. When this approach prevails, management states, "We will spend X dollars on advertising next year." The budget is arbitrarily set without any analysis of the tasks of advertising, the funds available, or any other considerations. The amount of the budget is set because it feels right to the decision maker.

The *"what-can-be-afforded" method* is better strategy than the arbitrary method, for at least some rational process is involved. The method, like the percentage-of-sales and the unit-of-sales method, may emerge from a conservative advertising philosophy: the goal is to closely control advertising expenditures.

The what-can-be-afforded method may, on the other hand, be used for the aggressive employment of advertising. This use of the method calls for advertising expenditures which are related either to company profits or to company assets. Management may decide to spend 20 percent of company earnings for advertising or to use 10 percent of the liquid assets for the advertising program. If management is too conservative, this approach may not yield enough to accomplish the advertising task. Moreover, the decision is left to the whim of management, and general business psychology may be the ruling factor rather than the needs of the business.

---

[7] Leo Bogart, *Strategy in Advertising*, Harcourt, Brace & World, Inc., New York, 1967, p. 27.

570
PLANNING
AND
MANAGING
THE ADVERTISING
CAMPAIGN

Some advertisers feel every cent they can get their hands on should go into advertising. The *"go-for-broke" method* is essentially the what-can-be-afforded method taken to its optimistic extreme. The users of the method had sublime faith in the ability of advertising to sell products. For example, when the "halitosis" theme was first developed for Listerine around 1922, Gerard Lambert, who was general manager, sold the go-for-broke method to the Lambert Pharmacal Company management. The following quotation explains his approach:

> At that time we were spending about $100,000 a year on advertising Listerine. I made the board a proposition. If they would let me spend $5,000 more each month, cumulatively—that is, $5,000, then $10,000, and so on—I would resign if I couldn't show an additional net profit for each month of at least $5,000. . . . By 1938 our expenditures for advertising were above $5 million a year.[8]

Radically different products with wide potential demand may be successfully advertised in this manner. The shortcoming of the method, of course, is that it is risky. If this approach to the budget is used by unsophisticated advertisers, it is possible that advertising can become a great gambling adventure in which funds are spent willy-nilly. Moreover, early sales success, which seems to indicate an unlimited market for the product, may turn out to be merely a temporary fad or the prompt action of an interested—but small—market segment. This method of budget making should be employed only in rare circumstances—and then by persons who recognize that it is highly speculative.

With the *"mail-order" method* the budget is set by the costs needed to obtain sales or inquiries through advertising. Once results are no longer paying for advertising charges, advertising is discontinued.

The *"profit-planning" method* attempts to relate advertising expenditures to desired profits rather than to desired sales volume. The basic premise is that the results obtained from advertising can be precisely measured. Increased units of advertising are added to the advertising program until the marginal return from the last unit does not equal the marginal cost. This is fine in theory, but since advertising effectiveness cannot be weighed precisely in most cases, the method is of limited practical use. One other limiting factor is that advertising is rarely used as the sole means of securing sales. Once marginal returns are weighed against marginal costs for several factors, the process becomes bogged down with complex mathematical calculations.

FIGURE 17.2
The "go-for-broke" approach was employed to determine the advertising budget for this "classic" advertising campaign (*opposite page*). Listerine's ability to "cure halitosis" was the theme of the campaign.

[8] Gerard B. Lambert, "How I Sold Listerine," *Fortune*, September 1956, pp. 111, 168. (From *All Out of Step*, Copyright © 1956 by Gerard B. Lambert. Reprinted by permission of Doubleday & Company, Inc., New York.)

Often a bridesmaid but never a bride

EDNA'S case was really a pathetic one. Like every woman, her primary ambition was to marry. Most of the girls of her set were married—or about to be. Yet not one possessed more grace or charm or loveliness than she.

And as her birthdays crept gradually toward that tragic thirty-mark, marriage seemed farther from her life than ever. She was often a bridesmaid but never a bride.

That's the insidious thing about halitosis (unpleasant breath). You, yourself, rarely know when you have it. And even your closest friends won't tell you.

Sometimes, of course, halitosis comes from some deep-seated organic disorder that requires professional advice. But usually—and fortunately—halitosis is only a local condition that yields to the regular use of Listerine as a mouth wash and gargle. It is an interesting thing that this well-known antiseptic that has been in use for years for surgical dressings, possesses these unusual properties as a breath deodorant.

It halts food fermentation in the mouth and leaves the breath sweet, fresh and clean. Not by substituting some other odor but by really removing the old one. The Listerine odor itself quickly disappears. So the systematic use of Listerine puts you on the safe and polite side.

Your druggist will supply you with Listerine. He sells lots of it. It has dozens of different uses as a safe antiseptic and has been trusted as such for half a century. Read the interesting little booklet that comes with every bottle. —Lambert Pharmacal Company, Saint Louis, U. S. A.

FIGURE 17.3

Different products experience different sales patterns, as these charts reveal. The retail advertisers will want advertising messages for hosiery, vacuum cleaners, children's shoes, and luggage to coincide in time with the buying of such products by consumers. (Numbers indicate percentage of year's sales done each month.) [*Bureau of Advertising, American Newspaper Publishers Association, Inc.*]

THE USE OF COMPUTERS AND QUANTITATIVE METHODS IN THE BUDGET PROCESS

On the routine side of advertising budgeting, computers play an important role, primarily in the area of control. Once the final budget is established, it is placed on the computer, and such items as invoices, costs, and commitments can be fed into the machine. Printouts which tell whether things are progressing on target are then available to the advertising manager. Ready access to such information permits adjustment of the advertising program to changing conditions, provided such flexibility has been built into the budget.

The computer, along with specially designed quantitative models, has been useful in the allocation process, especially in helping to decide which media to use. How models are employed in media selection is discussed in Chapter 18. Our concern at this point is whether mathematical models can be employed to help decide how

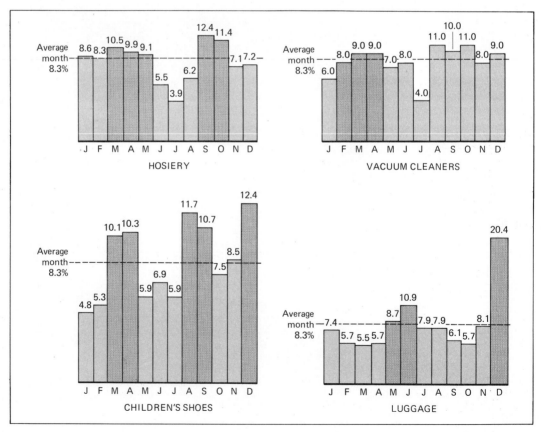

much money should be spent for advertising. That opportunity is more one of future prospects and hopes than present reality. The challenge has been perceived, and substantial experimentation is already under way in this area. The models developed so far have encountered two serious problems: (1) the information required is often unobtainable at reasonable cost; and (2) the models make budgetary recommendation based on the assumption that advertising is the only variable, and interdependencies within the marketing mix are ignored.[9]

Because the bulk of the work is confidential, it is not available to other advertisers and students of advertising. The firm which finances the experimenting naturally keeps the information secret in order to enhance its competitive advantage. Fortunately, however, one advertiser, Anheuser-Busch, Inc., has agreed to release the results of 15 years of advertising research, part of it dealing with budgeting.[10] Two college professors were commissioned by the company to apply management science research procedures to the marketing area of the firm and to oversee the implementation of their recommendations. One prime area of attention was advertising expenditures.

Budweiser beer, the principal brand of Anheuser-Busch (A-B), was marketed in 198 geographic areas. The company president was constantly asked to provide increased advertising support for these markets on the premise that increased sales would follow. He asked the researchers to develop a model aimed at determining what amount should be spent on advertising. An interesting experiment was run during calendar year 1962. Eighteen areas were chosen on a random basis, and adequate control areas were selected. In six test areas advertising expenditures were reduced 25 percent; in another six, the amount was unchanged; and in the third group of six markets, advertising was increased 50 percent. Two important marketing variables, the amount spent on sales effort (salespeople) and the amount spent on point-of-purchase sales displays and signs, were held constant in these areas. Price could not be controlled because of varying competitive pressures. Every month an observation was made in each market area.

The results of the experiment left A-B executives incredulous. They could easily believe that a 50 percent increase in advertising might well yield a 7 percent increase in sales, which it did for the relevant market areas. However, a 25 percent reduction of advertising pro-

[9] James F. Engel, Hugh G. Wales, and Martin R. Warshaw, *Promotional Strategy*, 3d edition, Richard D. Irwin, Inc., Homewood, Ill., 1975, p. 228. See pages 217 to 229 of the Engel book for a comprehensive discussion of the application of quantitative methods to the promotional budget.
[10] Russell L. Ackoff and James R. Emshoff, "Advertising Research at Anheuser-Busch, Inc. (1963–68)," *Sloan Management Review*, Winter 1975, pp. 1–15; also see their "Advertising Research at Anheuser-Busch, Inc. (1968–74)," *Sloan Management Review*, Spring 1975, pp. 1–15.

574
PLANNING
AND
MANAGING
THE ADVERTISING
CAMPAIGN

duced a 14 percent increase in sales in the pertinent market areas. More elaborate tests were conducted in 1963 and 1964 with the results confirming those obtained in the first experiment. Advertising reductions of 15 percent were tried in many marketing areas; later on the reduction was raised to 25 percent, and the number of markets involved was gradually increased. The advertising expenditure per barrel of beer was ultimately stabilized at 80 cents, whereas it stood at $1.89 when the research was initiated, a 58 percent reduction. Budweiser sales increased from approximately 7.5 million to 14.5 million barrels, and its market share increased from 8.14 to 12.94 percent in the years running from 1962 through 1968. We are conditioned to think that increased advertising expenditures automatically lead to increased sales and brand share. However, it is possible, as this case example illustrates, for an advertiser to be spending more than is necessary. Money saved from unnecessary advertising goes directly to company profits. Ackoff and Emshoff explored many other areas of the advertising decision, including the timing of advertising, the effectiveness of various media, advertising message content, and beer-drinking behavior patterns. The lesson to be learned from this case example is that the management sciences have much to offer the advertising decision maker, who should welcome and foster such experimentation.

SUMMARY

As one of the six major steps in planning an advertising program, setting the budget holds a unique place. On the one hand, no other steps can take place—no other decisions can be made or implemented—without money being budgeted to them. However, on the other hand, the size of the budget depends largely on the content of these other decisions; collectively they add up to the funds required in the advertising budget.

Advertising is a cost of doing business and should be carefully scrutinized for waste; nevertheless, the expenditure should be thought of in broader, more fundamental terms—as an investment in the future of the enterprise. Immediate returns are important, but not nearly as much as payoff over the long term. Holding this philosophy leads to sounder advertising decisions.

Like all budgets, the advertising budget is a basic management technique for planning and controlling operations. It is a financial tool which is concerned with future operations. In its development four stages are present. The first stage is its preparation, in which the advertising manager marshals the case for sufficient dollars to achieve objectives set down for the advertising program. The advertising manager then presents ("sells") the plan to higher levels of corporate management, whose approval is needed if implementation of the plan is to occur. This step involves considerable negotiations and adjustment among marketing and financial executives of the firm.

Once the budget is established, it is executed. In this third stage the advertising agency has the primary responsibility, as it buys the media which are the major components of most advertising budgets. The advertising manager is concurrently observing the marketing scene to ascertain whether any changes are needed in the program. To facilitate such adjustments, every advertising budget should contain a contingency account which will permit flexibility in spending patterns. The fourth stage is concerned with control of the budget. The advertising manager watches to make certain that the monies are spent as planned and that purchases are made on an economical basis. Furthermore, the budget should be carefully guarded to see that its use for nonadvertising activities is prevented.

The size of the advertising budget can be determined in three basic ways: by the fixed-guidelines approach, by the task method, and by subjective methods. Fixed guidelines include the percentage-of-sales, unit-of-sales, and competitive parity methods. All tend to overlook the specific task which advertising has to perform for a given company at a specific point of time; however, these methods are realtively simple to employ. The task method is oriented to objectives with the budget evolving from the job to be done by advertising; its major stumbling blocks rest in the hard question of how much advertising is needed to accomplish a specific task. Subjective methods are least desirable, as they often possess little logic, being dependent upon the arbitrary opinion of the executive.

The computer is helpful in the routine management and control of the advertising budget. Management science is just beginning to help advertising managers with the difficult "how much to spend for advertising" question. It is anticipated that in future years a more scientific approach will be possible and that, consequently, the advertising budget-making process will become more efficient.

QUESTIONS FOR DISCUSSION

1 How does the advertising budget-making process relate to (a) setting advertising objectives, (b) the media selection decision, (c) the creative strategy decision?
2 Will the budget decision become more demanding in the years to come? Why?
3 Can the philosophic stance that advertising should be viewed as a long range investment be explained by an analogy to one's personal life? Outline such an analogy.
4 Does the budget-making process involve the executive's ego in any way?

576

PLANNING
AND
MANAGING
THE ADVERTISING
CAMPAIGN

What kind of attitude should the advertising manager have toward the process?

5 What are the key problems encountered at each of the four steps in the advertising budget-making process? Are some more serious than others? Which, in your opinion, provides the most serious obstacle?

6 Explain "budget attrition."

7 What are the strengths and weaknesses of the fixed-guideline methods of advertising budgeting?

8 If the task method is so desirable, why is it not in universal use? What needs to be done before adoption of the method is likely?

9 Is there any situation where any of the subjective methods of determining the advertising budget may be justified?

10 From current professional or trade journals, find an article explaining the use of a model, similar to the Budweiser example, in advertising budgeting. Write a short summary of the article.

FOR FURTHER REFERENCE

Barton, Roger (ed.): *Handbook of Advertising Management*, McGraw-Hill Book Company, New York, 1970.

Bogart, Leo: *Strategy in Advertising*, Harcourt, Brace & World, Inc., New York, 1967.

Buell, Victor P.: *Changing Practices in Advertising Decision-Making and Control*, Association of National Advertisers, Inc., New York, 1973.

Engel, James F., Hugh G. Wales, and Martin R. Warshaw: *Promotional Strategy*, 3d edition, Richard D. Irwin, Inc., Homewood, Ill., 1975.

Ennis, F. Beaven: *Effective Marketing Management*, Association of National Advertisers, Inc., New York, 1973.

Hurwood, David L., and James K. Brown: *Some Guidelines for Advertising Budgeting*, The Conference Board, New York, 1972.

Morgan, Eric A. G.: *How to Do Business in Branded Goods*, Longman Group Limited, London, 1972.

McNiven, Malcolm A.: *How Much to Spend for Advertising*, Association of National Advertisers, Inc., New York, 1969.

Stansfield, Richard H.: *Advertising Manager's Handbook*, The Dartnell Corporation, Chicago, 1969.

CHAPTER 18

CHAPTER 18

PLANNING THE MEDIA STRATEGY

With the market situation analyzed, advertising objectives determined, and the budget set, the time for media and message strategy decisions has arrived. A sound media strategy is important to the overall success of the advertising program for two reasons: (1) media charges are the largest cost in most advertising budgets, and (2) well-designed advertisements are dependent, if they are to be truly successful, on where and when they are placed. "Effective advertising is saying the right thing in the right medium at the right time."[1] Being in the right medium at the right time is the result of sound media decisions. Media strategy decisions, therefore, fall into two groups: Selection of the medium (the "where" decision), and the timing of its appearance (the "when" decision). The decisions about place and time involve media planning and media buying.

MEDIA PLANNING

Media planning may be defined as "the process of designing a course of action that shows how advertising time and space will be used to contribute to the achievement of marketing objectives."[2] In carrying out a media planning program the essential steps in advertising planning are followed with objectives, strategies, and tactics all serving to define the purpose of the campaign.

Before the media plan can be worked out, certain information is gathered and analyzed. The basis of sound media selection is dependent upon (1) the people or market to be reached—the target market—and (2) the nature of the message to be disseminated to that target group. Through market research, facts about prospects are accumulated and generalized into a *consumer profile*. This consumer profile, along with the basic copy strategy and copy requirements as modified by any need for seasonal or geographical emphasis and taking into account the size of the advertising appropriation, is then analyzed. This analysis is followed by a matching of the audience characteristics of various media with the market profile and by an evaluation of the adaptability of the physical format of the media to the copy requirements. Finally, through the exercise of judgment concerning the dimensions of coverage, reach, frequency, continuity, and ad size, the media plan emerges.

The primary responsibility for choosing media usually rests with

[1] Donald G. Hileman, "Changes in the Buying and Selection of Advertising Media," *Journalism Quarterly*, Summer 1968, p. 279.
[2] Arnold Barban, Stephen M. Cristol, and Frank J. Kopec, *Essentials of Media Planning*, Crain Books, Chicago, 1975, p. 1. Credit was given by these authors to Roger Barton, *Media in Advertising*, McGraw-Hill Book Company, New York, 1964, p. 19.

580

PLANNING
AND
MANAGING
THE ADVERTISING
CAMPAIGN

the advertising agency. The advertiser may wish to pass upon the media plan, but the basic thinking is usually performed by agency specialists.

Three decisions are made during the media selection process: (1) the general type of medium is chosen—newspapers, magazines, television, radio, or out-of-home; (2) classes within the chosen type are picked—network or spot television, women's magazines or shelter magazines; (3) a specific media "vehicle" within the chosen class of the preferred type is selected—*Family Circle*, or *McCall's*, or *Good Housekeeping*.

Key Factors Influencing Media Planning[3]

Three major forces are weighed when media decisions are being made: (1) marketing conditions facing the advertiser, (2) the level of competitive advertising efforts, and (3) specific media considerations.

Marketing Conditions

Marketing plans of the advertiser influence advertising plans, and media plans are likewise affected by what the firm hopes to achieve in the marketplace through the use of advertising. Brilliant creative strategy can fail because marketing conditions are not right. And, of course, the marketing plan determines the size of the budget available for media buys. Furthermore, the basic nature of the market—its size, its location, and its qualitative characteristics, such as sex, age, socioeconomic features, and educational background, does make an impact on the media plan. In addition there are four other facets to take into consideration when assessing marketing conditions: product characteristics, distribution channels, promotional strategy, and the nature of the advertising copy.

Product Characteristics   Because the product possesses certain characteristics, the use of certain media may be denied for its advertising. For example, the television industry refuses liquor advertising, and legislation prevents the advertising of cigarettes on radio and television. In other instances, the presence of a product characteristic may virtually require that one advertising medium be employed as its status coincides, say, with the product's image. For example, ads for luxury jewelry are rarely placed in the broadcast media. Print media are used to convey the message. In other words, product characteristics are weighed carefully and matched against what impressions of those characteristics are conveyed by various media.

[3] Based upon a combination of Lyndon O. Brown, Richard S. Lessler, and William M. Weilbacher, *Advertising Media*, The Ronald Press Company, New York, 1957, pp. 283–354, and Barban et al., op. cit., pp. 5–27.

Distribution Channels Most products can be promoted through any type of medium; the choice depends upon factors other than product characteristics. If the product is distributed locally or regionally, national media, in the absence of local or regional editions or networks, are out of the question. Advertisers of nationally distributed products, on the other hand, can choose between national media or a combination of local media.

Often overlooked are the reactions of intermediaries toward various types of media. If the advertising is aired on television where the store manager can actually see the commercials in the role of viewer, the feeling that customers must be seeing the advertising is generated. Other retailers may believe that a "prestige" medium should be used to promote the product. Furthermore, such seemingly mundane matters as the size of the retail margin (markup) may affect whether the manufacturer can reasonably expect promotional support from channel members. The distribution system employed for the product can dictate whether the manufacturer must use a great deal of advertising or whether the promotional burden should logically rest with the retailer. The media planner, therefore, needs to be firmly grounded in the distribution patterns used in marketing the advertised product.

Promotional Strategy A synergism or interdependence should exist between the various parts of the promotional mix—personal selling, advertising, sales promotion, and public relations. Suppose an advertiser wishes to sponsor a contest to promote the sales of the product to consumers. Such sales promotional devices must be advertised aggressively if they are to be successful. If the contest is devised in response to a sudden need for additional promotional effort, a flexible medium, such as newspapers or radio, which takes advertising copy on relatively short notice, may be the best choice. However, if the contest is part of a long-range program designed to enhance the prestige of the product, the ad may be run in consumer magazines or on network TV.

In Chapter 3 we discussed the importance of "positioning the product"—obtaining a place for the product in the mind of the prospect—to marketing success. Media choices are important in product positioning because the use of one medium connotes one attitude about the product, whereas another medium presents a different view. Furthermore, a positioning strategy against the leading brand in the field may dictate the avoidance of the same media that the frontrunner is employing

Nature of the Advertising Copy The advertising message itself provides the last major determining factor when media choices are made. Campaign themes may be designed for universal use, that is,

582
PLANNING
AND
MANAGING
THE ADVERTISING
CAMPAIGN

they may be adaptable to almost every advertising medium. Or themes may be created to suit specific media. Slogan-type campaigns of soft-drink advertisers illustrate the universal approach, whereas animated-cartoon or demonstration themes of household cleaning aids are more effective on television.

Competitive Advertising Efforts

An important goal of most marketing programs is the improvement—or retention—of the seller's share-of-market position. Advertising, of course, is only one force used to achieve this goal, but it is a more apparent gauge of competitive activity than the work of a competitor's sales force or distributive organization. It is more difficult to find concrete information about these two areas of competitive activity. Thus, it is easy to attribute the success of a competitor to the advertising program employed, and competitors, therefore, watch one another's advertising expenditures closely.

The philosophy of matching a competitor's advertising may carry over into media planning. A business executive may not want to spend the same amount of money as competitors, but may wish to spend it in the same way. If the industry leader is using television, other firms may adopt the medium. There is a considerable amount of fad and fashion in the use of advertising media. An advertising agency must recognize the emotional forces involved when it is making media recommendations to a client.

Advertisers have personal media preferences, and these preferences may enter the media selection equation. While current practice carries the sanction of implied success—others wouldn't be using the medium unless it were yielding good results—such reasoning ignores the fact that advertising needs are not uniform. Follow-the-leader tactics may change advertising efforts from investments to speculations.

Media Considerations

Advertising media possess certain dimensions which affect the media decision. When media objectives are being established, these factors exert an impact: (1) size of the budget; (2) special requirements to be found in the media concepts of reach, frequency, continuity, and dominance; (3) discount structures of the various media; (4) cost efficiency of alternative forms of media; and (5) availability of media to advertisers.

Total Available Dollars Scientific media planning is aimed at expending advertising dollars where they will make the greatest possible impact. The smaller the advertising budget, the more crucial the media

FIGURE 18.1
(*Opposite*) The various advertising media compete aggressively for advertising dollars. Media data are included in the sales message.

How to spend $2 million on tv to remain practically anonymous.

The average tv viewer sees over 600 commercials in a 10 day period. Read how to catch his attention in the middle of it all.

Easy. Let's say you're the number 2 or 3 brand in your product category.

You may be sinking 2 million — or more — into an ingenious tv plan. Your commercials are dynamite. Yet the sales of brand number 1 go up, up, up — while you're lucky if you can hold your own.

What happened?

Brand misidentity is what happened. The Starch Atlanta Study, for instance, showed less than 32% of the viewers remembering commercials seen that very evening. (And of these, 25% *misidentified* the advertiser!)

Tv can be scarey for some advertisers.

People see a commercial for your Brand #2.

They may even remember it.

But they end up asking for Brand #1.

Today's utter avalanche of tv commercials (about 80% more on the air than 10 years ago) is what has created this problem.

And unless you're the guy with the biggest avalanche, it's *your* problem.

But we've got an answer.

It's two-fold.

First, when you advertise to the 43,000,000 adults who read The Digest every month, you're reinforcing your tv message with one out of every three adults in America. The very *best* adults, from a marketer's standpoint.

Second, well over one third of our readers (16,000,000) are light tv viewers. They watch an average of 27 minutes per day of prime time (Simmons). So even the biggest tv budget in the world is going to keep you all but anonymous to this huge, better-educated, better-able-to-buy group.

Use horse sense.

Obviously, tv's important to a lot of advertisers.

But equally as obvious, it just makes good sense to sock some of your tv money into The Digest.

Where you're in instant touch with our 16,000,000 light tv viewers ...and reinforcing your message with another 27,000,000 Digest readers who do like tv.

Doesn't your product deserve the cleanest shot it can get?

Doesn't it deserve The Digest?

Reader's Digest — WORLD'S BEST SELLER — **The visibility book.**

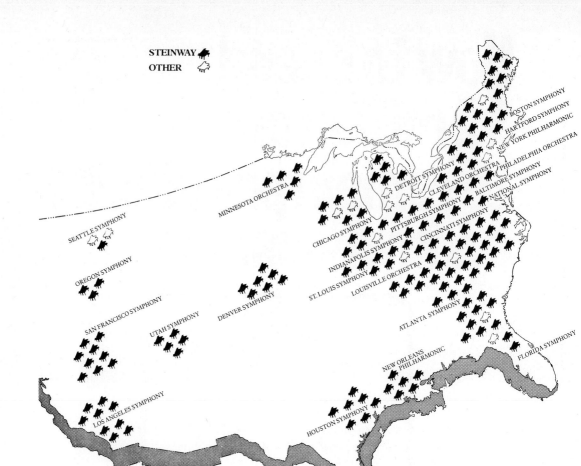

STEINWAY 🐗
OTHER 🐑

DETROIT SYMPHONY
CLEVELAND ORCHESTRA
MINNESOTA ORCHESTRA
BOSTON SYMPHONY
HARTFORD SYMPHONY
NEW YORK PHILHARMONIC
PHILADELPHIA ORCHESTRA
BALTIMORE SYMPHONY
NATIONAL SYMPHONY
PITTSBURGH SYMPHONY
CINCINNATI SYMPHONY
CHICAGO SYMPHONY
INDIANAPOLIS SYMPHONY
LOUISVILLE ORCHESTRA
ST. LOUIS SYMPHONY
ATLANTA SYMPHONY
FLORIDA SYMPHONY
NEW ORLEANS PHILHARMONIC
HOUSTON SYMPHONY
LOS ANGELES SYMPHONY
SAN FRANCISCO SYMPHONY
UTAH SYMPHONY
DENVER SYMPHONY
OREGON SYMPHONY
SEATTLE SYMPHONY

FIGURE 18.2
The manufacturer of expensive pianos will obviously wish to "skim the market," trying to reach the relatively few prospects for the product wherever they might live. This ad appeared in *Atlantic Monthly, Harper's, The New Yorker, Smithsonian*, and *Music Clubs Magazine.*

OF THE PIANO SOLOISTS SCHEDULED TO PLAY WITH MAJOR U.S. ORCHESTRAS
DURING THE 1975-76 CONCERT SEASON, THE GREAT MAJORITY
WILL PLAY THE STEINWAY PIANO.

STEINWAY & SONS

selection decision. Large-budget advertisers may be able to stand some waste in their advertising programs, but small-budget advertisers must wring every ounce of selling power from their advertising. A very small budget, however, makes this task difficult. The budget of every advertiser places an upper limit on the amount of advertising that can be created and used, and it prescribes what media the advertiser can afford. An advertiser with an advertising budget of $250,000 cannot buy a series of full-page advertisements monthly if the page rate in the chosen magazine is $40,000. A limited budget freezes out many media choices for the advertiser. The same principle, of course, applies to all advertisers in varying degrees.

Reach, Frequency, Continuity, and Dominance   When media objectives are developed, these four criteria must be taken into account. Decisions about the reach of the advertising and its frequency are usually decided simultaneously, as they closely interact. *Reach*, which is related to the concept of coverage, is the number of people who are exposed to the message at least one time during a stated period of time (usually four weeks). *Frequency* is the number of times the members of the target audience are exposed to the advertising message. When the advertiser wants a high rate of reach, many media vehicles are likely to be employed. When the orientation is toward frequency, a limited number of vehicles is generally used with many repetitions of the message being the keystone of the plan.

Media scheduling attempts to balance the twin objectives of reach and frequency. The combination of these two characteristics has led to the concept of the *gross rating point*. GRP is a value assigned to "the gross weight of a given media effort against a defined demographic target.[4]

The continuity of a medium is another factor to consider in media planning. *Continuity* of advertising can mean many things; for instance, it relates various advertisements in an advertising program to one another. This is important because isolated ads generally make little impact. Continuity in the creative effort is brought about by the advertising theme, copy style, layout, etc. Continuity in media usage is also desirable. Audiences should be exposed to the message in a regular pattern over a period of time long enough to achieve the marketing objectives set for the campaign. At this point, we shall use continuity to evaluate the timing of the advertising.

A trade-off exists in the reach-frequency decision and if considerations of media continuity are added to the equation, an analogy can be drawn to the "unattainable triad" of advertising production discussed in Chapter 14.[5] The following quotation explains what is involved in the trade-off:

> If the advertiser is willing to take a periodic hiatus during the campaign period, the budget will allow both reach and frequency to be enhanced during each flight of advertising. Conversely, since a steady flow of media

[4] Barban et al., op. cit., pp. 50–51.
[5] Ibid., p. 51.

586

PLANNING
AND
MANAGING
THE ADVERTISING
CAMPAIGN

dollars is needed to support continuous advertising, a continuous schedule limits the opportunity to maximize reach or frequency during any portion of the campaign period.[6]

A somewhat related media concept is that of dominance. Webster defines *dominance* as "superior to all others." In the case of advertising dominance, superiority is measured in many different ways. The concept is explained by Bogart as media's "third dimension," which he describes as the "size or length of the message unit."[7] Thus, full-page advertisements are considered more dominant than half pages and usually serve as a determinant of true reach as opposed to potential reach.

The designer of a media plan must weigh these various qualities, and when available funds are limited, the decision maker must decide where to cut corners. Should the advertiser reduce coverage and try to reach only a part of the potential market? Should advertising be done less frequently? Should the drive for dominance be curbed by abandoning full-page advertisements? The retailer has the special problem of weighing the need for frequent advertising against the principle of selling when customers are buying. Correct decisions are arrived at only after deliberation, experimentation, and constant study. Various combinations should be tried and carefully evaluated in order to develop better media combinations.

Media Discounts An advertiser may elect to concentrate advertising in a few media because of the discounts which are given to advertisers who use specific media frequently. Generally speaking, this factor in media selection is considered after the type and class of media have been chosen. Although few national advertisers use only one medium, let alone one class of media, we shall assume, for purposes of illustration, that such is the case. An advertiser has decided to use women's magazines as the prime advertising vehicle. Normally the advertiser will then divide the media budget among the major publications in the field, say, *Family Circle, McCall's*, and *Good Housekeeping*. Advertisements may be scheduled in each magazine every other month throughout the entire year. After the media buyer examines the rate cards, he or she realizes that substantial savings will result if monthly insertions are placed in only one of the three publications. The money saved by this maneuver can be used to enhance readership through better-quality ads. For instance, color can replace black and white, or larger space units can be used. Dominance of the advertiser's message in one magazine is more likely.

[6] Ibid., pp. 51–52.
[7] Leo Bogart, *Strategy in Advertising*, Harcourt, Brace & World, Inc., New York, 1967, p. 145.

Continuity and frequency of advertising are increased. On the other hand, coverage or reach is lessened. And although there is considerable duplication of readership among many closely related media, this duplication actually increases the frequency of advertising impressions with the duplicated audience. Thus, the media buyer must weigh the possible gains and losses before final media selections are made.

Media Cost Efficiency   Often advertisers attempt to reduce the media selection process to one simple question, "How much audience do I get for every dollar spent?" They compare the total audience with costs, and using the resulting figures as a base, choose the most efficient medium. They ignore qualitative factors and play a "numbers game." The marketers of some mass-consumed products may find this "cost-per-thousand" approach satisfactory, but audience characteristics are usually more important than sheer numbers. Cost-efficiency figures may be useful, however, when all other considerations seem to balance out. For example, if two radio stations appear to reach the same kind of people, the station which delivers the largest audience per dollar is obviously the better buy.

Media Availability   The availability of time or space may determine media choices. This factor is extremely important in television. Often advertisers cannot use the medium because a suitable time slot is not available. Sometimes advertisers who have not planned to use television in their current advertising program change their plans when a good time availability is presented to them. The same principle applies to other media. During hot political campaigns, for instance, candidates occasionally find that their opponents have already contracted for prime radio and television time and outdoor space. The built-in expansibility of publications makes availability a much less important factor in printed media than in broadcast or traffic media.

MEDIA DECISION TOOLS

Where does the media planner turn when data about marketing conditions, competitive advertising efforts, and media characteristics are desired? We have already discussed, in previous chapters, such information sources as Standard Rate and Data Service, Audit Bureau of Circulations, and the broadcast rating services. There are several other major sources of media information which are discussed in the following section. The list is not complete; new services are constantly being developed, adding to or replacing existing sources. Therefore a comprehensive listing is not feasible. Experienced media decision makers will be able to add to these suggestions.

588

PLANNING
AND
MANAGING
THE ADVERTISING
CAMPAIGN

Information about Market Conditions

Information on market conditions is closely guarded by business executives; thus easy-to-tap data are hard to come by. The federal government issues a wealth of pertinent statistics. However, by the time of publication they are often too old to be used in business planning. And there is a need for considerable sifting and analysis before decisions can be based upon such raw data. Thus, the advertiser's marketing research department and various independent marketing research firms may all be called upon to generate this kind of information—using available published data and the techniques of business intelligence to do so.

For the marketer of consumer products the *Survey of Buying Power*, published annually by *Sales Management* magazine, is an invaluable tool. This volume of nearly 1,000 pages contains sections which give (1) data on county-city populations and incomes, plus data on farmers and their incomes; (2) data on county-city retail sales; (3) rankings and summaries by counties, cities, metropolitan areas, regions, and states; (4) special Canadian data. Essentially the publication gives important data about retail sales, population, and effective buying income. Market data of a similar nature now also appear in the various editions of SRDS. Every three months *Sales Management* also makes a quarterly retail sales forecast and periodically publishes other market data in its regular semimonthly issues. Advertisers who are trying to allocate their advertising dollars according to market potentials often find these data very useful. Another excellent service is the *Media Market Guide*, which provides quarterly data on physical dimensions, population profiles, and media opportunities for the top 100 United States markets.

Information about Competitive Advertising Efforts[8]

The media planner needs to know how much competitors are spending for advertising. Equally important is information about where they are spending their advertising dollars; just what are their respective media mixes? Such information would be impossible for the individual advertiser to gather; fortunately specialized services operate to furnish the data to advertisers wishing to purchase them from these collection agencies.

One important service, LNA (Leading National Advertisers), is perhaps the best known of the competitive data services. LNA analyzes every advertisement in 86 consumer magazines and 3 national newspaper supplements, as well as tear sheets from over 1,500 regional editions of magazines per year. It is estimated that the service monitors

[8] Based in part on *Media Decisions*, August 1975, pp. 58–60, 100, 102, 104.

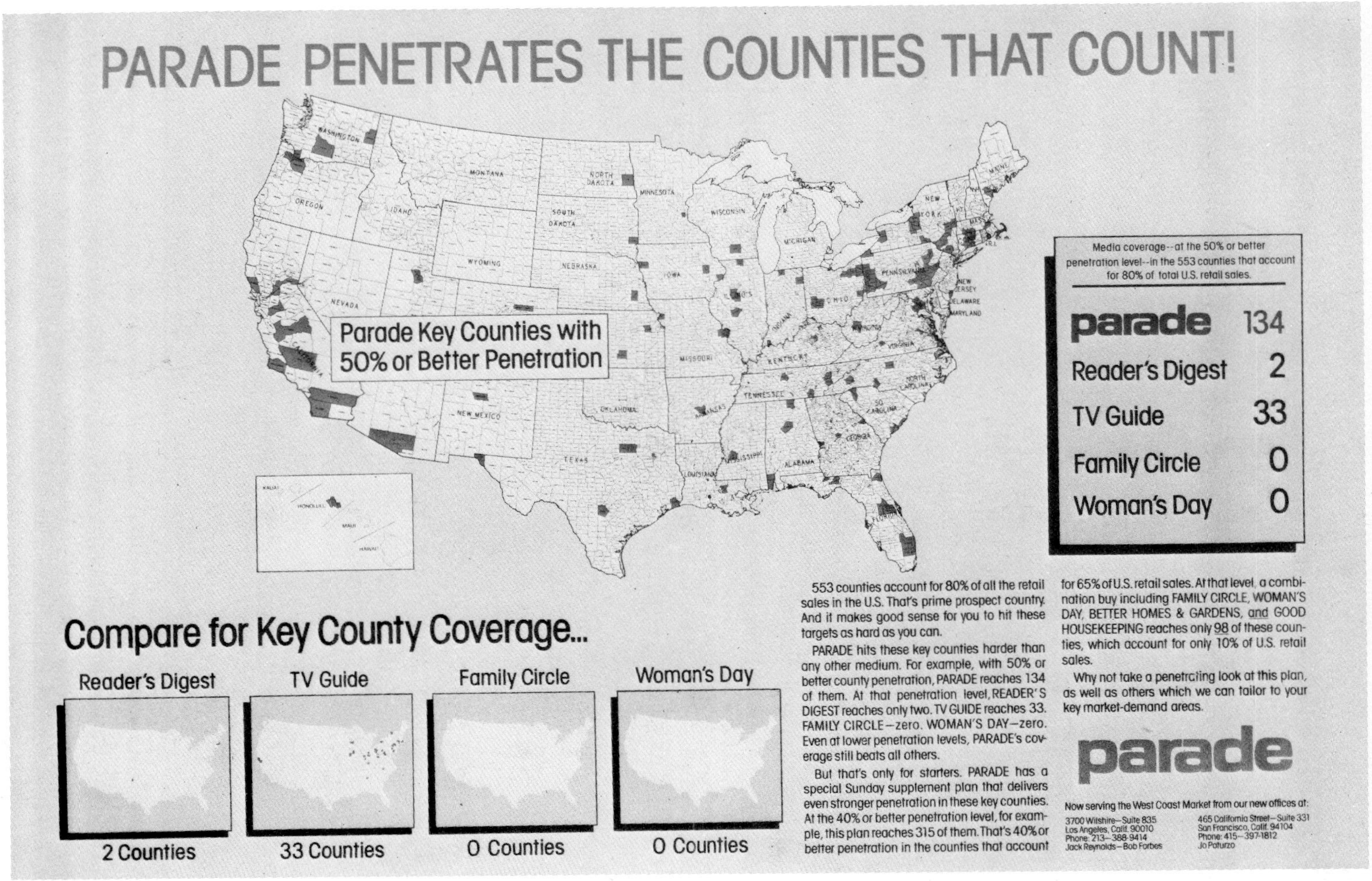

PARADE PENETRATES THE COUNTIES THAT COUNT!

Media coverage—at the 50% or better penetration level—in the 553 counties that account for 80% of total U.S. retail sales.

parade	134
Reader's Digest	2
TV Guide	33
Family Circle	0
Woman's Day	0

Parade Key Counties with 50% or Better Penetration

Compare for Key County Coverage...

Reader's Digest
2 Counties

TV Guide
33 Counties

Family Circle
0 Counties

Woman's Day
0 Counties

553 counties account for 80% of all the retail sales in the U.S. That's from prime prospect country. And it makes good sense for you to hit these targets as hard as you can.

PARADE hits these key counties harder than any other medium. For example, with 50% or better county penetration, PARADE reaches 134 of them. At that penetration level, READER'S DIGEST reaches only two. TV GUIDE reaches 33. FAMILY CIRCLE—zero. WOMAN'S DAY—zero. Even at lower penetration levels, PARADE's coverage still beats all others.

But that's only for starters. PARADE has a special Sunday supplement plan that delivers even stronger penetration in these key counties. At the 40% or better penetration level, for example, this plan reaches 315 of them. That's 40% or better penetration in the counties that account

for 65% of U.S. retail sales. At that level, a combination buy including FAMILY CIRCLE, WOMAN'S DAY, BETTER HOMES & GARDENS, and GOOD HOUSEKEEPING reaches only 98 of these counties, which account for only 10% of U.S. retail sales.

Why not take a penetrating look at this plan, as well as others which we can tailor to your key market-demand areas.

parade

Now serving the West Coast Market from our new offices of:

3700 Wilshire—Suite 835
Los Angeles, Calif. 90010
Phone: 213—386-8114
Jack Reynolds—Bob Forbes

465 California Street—Suite 331
San Francisco, Calif. 94104
Phone: 415—397-1812
Jn Petruno

FIGURE 18.3

A newspaper supplement publisher stresses that the featured medium reaches key markets better than some competitive vehicles.

590
PLANNING
AND
MANAGING
THE ADVERTISING
CAMPAIGN

over 150,000 ads each year, recording space size, color, bleed, magazine, issue, brand advertised, and the division of company doing the advertising. LNA supplies its data to the Publishers Information Bureau (PIB), which issues monthly and semiannual reports; the latter are entitled *Leading National Advertisers* and contain media expenditure data for all national advertisers investing $100,000 or more annually. LNA also provides data on competitive expenditures in the out-of-home medium.

BAR (Broadcast Advertisers Report) is active in the fields of network and spot television and network radio broadcasting. Broadcast material is collected on audio tape, from which information is transcribed into sequential listings of commercials by brand, station, time, length of commercial, and program. Computations are then made leading to estimates of expenditures for the respective media. LNA and BAR combine their data for quarterly and yearly *Multi-Media Reports*.

RER (Radio Expenditure Reports) traces the use of spot radio by brands; the compiled data are issued by the Radio Advertising Bureau on a quarterly basis. Data are obtained directly from stations using a sample of 800 stations, from which larger projections for the entire radio medium are made.

Media Records, Inc., gathers linage data by product classification and by name of advertisers for ads placed in 237 daily and Sunday newspapers located in 81 cities. Projections from these data lead to estimates of newspaper advertising expenditures in the top 125 markets. Competitive brand data for approximately three-fourths of all newspaper usage by national advertisers are made available to subscribers.

ACB (Advertising Checking Bureau) is another source of competitive data on newspaper usage by national advertisers. The organization secures and measures every daily newspaper and Sunday paper and several hundred United States weeklies. Reports are tailor-made by client, or by product category. ACB is heavily involved in providing proof of performance to advertisers employing the cooperative advertising technique.

The A. C. Nielsen Retail Index furnishes measurable media expenditure data for major competitors in its bimonthly report to client subscribers.

These services do not provide all the information about advertising expenditures that a media planner might desire. Trade associations representing the various advertising media make estimates from time to time, and advertising media representatives offer guesses of competitors' advertising budgets. Little is known, however, about who spends what in such media as direct mail, business publications, or transit advertising.

Information about Media Audiences

The goal of media planning is finding media audiences that possess characteristics similar to the target-market groups that the advertiser wishes to reach. Total audience figures are important to the advertiser, but more information than mere numbers is needed. When one is attempting to match markets and media, there are three types of variables available for defining target markets: demographics, socio-psychographic composition, and product usage.[9]

Every large advertising medium conducts studies which delineate its audience by demographic—and often sociopsychological—characteristics, and it is recognized that the presence of such characteristics may be vital to the purchase or nonpurchase of certain products. Furthermore, the coincidence of product use, such as by the heavy user, and exposure to a specific medium may be important when media decisions are to be made; therefore, many advertising media generate data on the subject. Moreover, media associations in the fields of newspaper, magazine, radio, television, outdoor, and transportation advertising make similar studies. Admittedly these studies stress the value of the media type rather than individual publications, broadcast stations, or other media firms. Both sources of media information spew forth unbelievably large quantities of material which must be evaluated by media planners for possible bias, as stressed in Chapter 16.

To overcome this possible shortcoming, a number of syndicated audience-measurement services have come into existence. This movement has been facilitated by the development of the computer with its ability to process and sort vast quantities of data rapidly. Because these business firms are independent of the various media, their findings possess greater credibility. The A. C. Nielsen Company and the American Research Bureau, for instance, furnish subscribers with data about people who watch television programs. Other research organizations gather radio listenership data.

Most of these services specialize in one form of advertising medium, although several have experimented with multimedia audience measurement. Obviously, the single-medium service is useful only after a decision to include a particular type of medium in the advertising program has been made. In recent years media planners have been putting increased reliance on the services of W. R. Simmons & Associates and Target Group Index (TGI). These competitive firms not only offer demographic breakdowns of audiences, but quantify brand purchasing decisions for many products. This permits a look at media in actual product purchasing or intent-to-purchase patterns;

[9] Barban et al., op. cit., p. 29.

592

PLANNING
AND
MANAGING
THE ADVERTISING
CAMPAIGN

consequently, more is known about the buying habits of media audiences. Studies from Simmons define and describe audiences for 69 magazines, 5 newspaper supplements, 2 national newspapers, and all network television programs. The data are given in terms of audience demographic characteristics and usage or ownership of more than 500 products and services. What TGI data show is volume of usage (heavy, medium, light) and brand loyalty patterns, as well as who influences the purchase. Data can be obtained on loyal users and brand switchers. The service provides an analysis of 120 magazines in the packaged-goods and durable-product areas. TGI also indexes some two dozen psychographic variables against different product usage segments, which is a step beyond what Simmons does.

The methodology used in audience measurement is under careful scrutiny at all times. In the early 1970s quite a flap occurred when the data furnished by Simmons and TGI varied considerably, although the same media were under evaluation. The Advertising Research Foundation (ARF), a nonprofit group established to foster independent research in advertising, acts as an agency for the surveillance of studies made by other groups, thereby enhancing their trustworthiness. ARF also is endeavoring to resolve conflicts between competing data-gathering agencies so that advertising decisions can be made upon sound information. It should be clearly understood that the syndicated research reports do not define markets for the advertiser. The planner still must isolate market segments appropriate to the firm's product and other strengths. The services should be sources of inputs to media selection decisions, not a means of deciding to whom products should be marketed.[10]

The Media-Market Matching Process

With relevant data about the media in hand, the media planner attempts to isolate those media vehicles whose audiences most closely match the target market for the marketing and advertising campaign. Sometimes the process is as simple as finding which media vehicles are exposed to heavy users of the product, and product usage data are the key factors in the decision. More often, knowledge of consumer demographics is necessary, either because product usage information is lacking or because the buying process is more complicated with demographics affecting other elements in the marketing equation. Furthermore, there is often more than one target market to be taken into consideration, and attention may also be given to secondary as well as primary markets for the brand.

[10] Ibid., p. 44.

THE MEDIA PLAN[11]

The media plan is an integral part of the total marketing and advertising plan; therefore, when media objectives are being set down, the needs of the total program must be anticipated. Eight key areas need to be covered in a comprehensive media plan:

1 Creative (including copy and promotional) requirements
2 Competitive pressures
3 Communications principles and/or science
4 Dollar allocation: geographical, seasonal, prospective
5 Budget size
6 Reach and frequency
6 Testing
8 Corporate policy (including personal relationships)[12]

Effective communication and persuasion are the ultimate goal of the media plan, and advertisements are the prime vehicles for this communication and persuasion. The media planner must see that the message appears in the right media environment and at the right time to enhance that effectiveness. Certain messages call for mass audiences, others for more selective groups; media selection accomplishes these objectives. Similarly, some messages need considerable repetition to do the jobs assigned to them; thus frequency becomes a crucial media planning consideration.

The importance of competitive pressures in media planning has already been discussed. What is being sought is a "share of mind" for the advertised product from the target-market group. What other advertisers are doing affects the chances of winning the struggle.

Media planners need to go beyond the potential exposure of the message, which comes from media circulation, and seek to ascertain whether actual communication takes place when a specific medium is employed. Chapter 11 contains a discussion of the communication process. Unfortunately, little is known about what media characteristics enhance communication of the advertising message; the area is in a state of development.

Dollar allocation deals with spending advertising dollars where the business is and takes into account such factors as geographic, seasonal, and prospect differences. Largely a matter of media strategy, the topic is explored in the next section.

[11] Drawn in part from Paul M. Roth, *How to Plan Media*, Time & Space Labs Incorporated, Chicago 1968.
[12] Ibid.

594

PLANNING
AND
MANAGING
THE ADVERTISING
CAMPAIGN

Chapter 17 analyzes the budget-size question, and reach and frequency considerations were examined earlier in this chapter.

As in the case of advertising message development, where creative research is needed on a continuous basis, the media plan should be put up for review regularly. Media testing is that portion of the media plan that evaluates controlled projects to discover empirical criteria or to evaluate media objectives and strategy. The field of media research is a complex and highly specialized subset of the larger field of marketing and advertising research; it has been aided considerably by the development of the computer and by various mathematical models.

Media planners must recognize that their recommendations should be compatible with broader policy considerations laid down by the advertising firm. Furthermore, reasonable willingness to compromise is essential for long-term success in the media planning role.

MEDIA STRATEGY

All this fact gathering, evaluating, weighing, and thinking lead to the adoption of a media plan employing a variation of one of three basic strategies, or approaches, to the use of advertising media. We call these strategies (1) the national plan, (2) the key-market plan, and (3) the skim plan. Other names are given to these plans by some advertising people, but the underlying principles are used by all advertisers.

The National Plan

Some advertisers have achieved nationwide distribution of their products and can advertise nationally. Here we mean nationally in the sense that people living in every corner of the nation are in the target market for the advertiser. The goal is to reach customers wherever they are located. Frequently, media choices for such advertisers will be those which are capable of reaching large numbers of consumers at low costs per impression. The approach is oriented toward quantity of impressions. Thus, the advertiser will probably concentrate the advertising in "mass" national magazines or on network television, although combinations of other media including newspapers, radio, and outdoor advertising may be chosen. The national plan is usually employed after one of the other approaches has been used successfully for a period of time to expand distribution to national levels.

The Key-Market Plan

Many advertisers do not go after the national market. Their strategy is to seek a substantial segment of it. The segment which the advertiser wants to reach may be selected on the basis of consumer characteristics or on the basis of geographical units. A market plan based on division of the market into geographical segments is called the key-market, or zone, approach.

The advertiser who employs the key-market plan decides for one reason or another to concentrate advertising impact upon certain selected marketing areas—a city, county, state, or region. Advertising efforts are not dissipated throughout the entire nation. If distribution is only in certain areas, advertising is in those areas. Creating buyer interest in products which are not readily available is pointless.

The funds available for advertising provide another limiting factor in media planning. The company may have national distribution; yet it may be economically unfeasible to advertise in all markets, or a significant portion of its distribution may be concentrated in a few key markets. For example, four metropolitan areas—New York, Los Angeles, Chicago, and Philadelphia—account for more than one-fifth of all food sales in the United States. In such instances, areas must be chosen where advertising is to be concentrated.

Key markets, however, may be chosen for a variety of other reasons. For example, one region may be the center of a peculiar competitive situation which the advertiser wishes to meet through advertising. Because of their isolation and population composition, other areas may be chosen to be test areas for the introduction of new products, different packages, or experimental advertising approaches. These areas will not receive the same advertising treatment as other regions, even though the advertiser is a national advertiser in the sense previously discussed. National media are rarely used by the advertiser who adopts the key-market approach to company advertising. Instead, local media—newspapers, radio and television stations, and outdoor advertising—are chosen. The national plan, of course, is often the end result of a series of key-market campaigns.

The Skim Plan

An alternative way of approaching segmented markets is to aim at specific consumer groups, regardless of their geographical location. Market segmentation is usually based upon such factors as income, educational level, occupation, social status, and similar qualitative considerations. The advertiser's goal is to concentrate advertising upon those persons who are most likely to buy the product because they are in demographic or psychographic subgroups where possession or desired possession of the product is likely. Once a segment has been tapped and its sales potential wrung out, a second group is chosen and the process is repeated. Often it is hoped that interest in the product will trickle down the social ladder to the point where the product will be accepted by the mass market. In other cases there is no hope that a product will be universally accepted, and the advertiser is

CANNED BARTLETT PEAR IO SECOND TV SPOTS

PROMOTE YOUR STORE BY NAME WITH QUICK, TEMPTING, HOW-TO-SERVE IDEAS IN COLORFUL TV SPOTS IN RETURN FOR AD FEATURES AND HIGH PROFIT DISPLAYS!

PEAR HELENE

Like desserts? Try pear Helene.

Vanilla ice cream, canned pear half and chocolate sauce.

Buy canned pears at (Store Name)

PEARS & CHICKEN

Mmmm...Fried chicken. Festive and delicious when you add canned pear halves...

filled with cranberry sauce or jelly.

Buy canned pears at (Store Name)

PEAR SALAD

Simple, traditional nutritious. Canned pear halves and cottage cheese...

topped with your favorite salad dressing.

Buy canned pears at (Store Name)

PEAR SHORTCAKE

Make Pear Shortcake your next dessert.

Canned pear slices on pound cake, topped with butterscotch sauce.

Buy Canned Pears at (Store Name)

FIGURE 18.4

These two inner pages from a brochure designed for the grocery trade show (1) photoboards of TV commercials for the product and (2) the schedule for airing the commercials. The advertiser is clearly using the key-market strategy, concentrating the campaign in 27 markets.

SATURATION TV SCHEDULE
RETAIL TIE-IN TAGS COMBINE ADVERTISING
AND DISPLAY FOR EXTRA SALES

TELEVISION		NEWSPAPER
MARKET	**WEEKS OF**	**WEEKS OF**
ATLANTA	Nov. 5, 12 & 26	Nov. 5, 12 & 26
BALTIMORE	Nov. 5, 12 & 26	Nov. 5, 12 & 26
BOSTON	Nov. 5, 12 & 26	Nov. 5, 12 & 26
CHICAGO	Nov. 5, 12, 26 & Dec. 3	Nov. 5, 12, 26 & Dec. 3
CINCINNATI	Nov. 5, 12 & 26	Nov. 5, 12 & 26
CLEVELAND	Nov. 5, 12 & 26	Nov. 5, 12 & 26
DALLAS-FT. WORTH	Nov. 5, 12 & 26	Nov. 5, 12 & 26
DENVER	Nov. 5, 12 & 26	Nov. 5, 12 & 26
DETROIT	Nov. 5, 12 & 26	Nov. 5, 12 & 26
HARTFORD-NEW HAVEN	Nov. 5, 12 & 26	Nov. 5, 12 & 26
JACKSONVILLE	Nov. 12, 26 & Dec. 3	Nov. 12, 26 & Dec. 3
KANSAS CITY	Nov. 5, 12 & 26	Nov. 5, 12 & 26
LOS ANGELES	Oct. 29, Nov. 5, 12, 26, Dec. 3 & 10	Oct. 29, Nov. 5, 12, 26, Dec. 3 & 10
MIAMI	Nov. 12, 26 & Dec. 3	Nov. 12, 26 & Dec. 3
MILWAUKEE	Nov. 5, 12 & 26	Nov. 5, 12 & 26
MINNEAPOLIS-ST. PAUL	Nov. 5, 12 & 26	Nov. 5, 12 & 26
NEW YORK	Nov. 5, 12, 26 & Dec. 3	Nov. 5, 12, 26 & Dec. 3
PHILADELPHIA	Nov. 5, 12 & 26	Nov. 5, 12 & 26
PHOENIX	Nov. 12 & 26	Nov. 12 & 26
PITTSBURGH	Nov. 5, 12 & 26	Nov. 5, 12 & 26
PORTLAND	Nov. 5, 12 & 26	Nov. 5, 12 & 26
SACRAMENTO-STOCKTON	Nov. 5, 12 & 26	Nov. 5, 12 & 26
SAN FRANCISCO	Nov. 5, 12. 26 & Dec. 3	Nov. 5, 12, 26 & Dec. 3
SEATTLE	Nov. 5, 12 & 26	Nov. 5, 12 & 26
ST. LOUIS	Nov. 5, 12 & 26	Nov. 5, 12 & 26
WASHINGTON, D. C.	Nov. 5, 12 & 26	Nov. 5, 12 & 26
YORK-LANCASTER	Nov. 12 & 26	Nov. 12 & 26

598

PLANNING
AND
MANAGING
THE ADVERTISING
CAMPAIGN

satisfied to reach a limited market, as in the case of high-priced luxury goods such as Rolls Royces or Cadillacs.

Specialty goods frequently lend themselves to the skim approach. The media chosen are those which tap specialized audiences. Thus, the advertiser of sporting goods may employ special-interest publications, such as *Outdoor Life* or *Surfer* magazine, instead of general magazines. Instead of network radio, advertising messages may be over a number of selected FM stations.

Advertisers do not limit themselves to only one of these basic media strategies in actual practice. They are often used in combination with one another. For example, many large food advertisers use the national approach to give "umbrella" coverage throughout the nation and reinforce this with local media in the most important metropolitan market areas. Regardless of the strategy adopted, the goal is always the same. Advertising media are chosen and used in a manner which will yield the greatest return for the advertiser's dollar.

Once the analysis is completed, the essential media decisions made, and the media plan drawn up, steps must be taken to implement the plan—to execute it through actual placement of advertisements according to the plan.

MEDIA BUYING: IMPLEMENTATION OF THE MEDIA PLAN

Once it has been decided what the media plan is to be, the next step is to carry out the plan. This activity is called *media buying* and involves some routine and detailed procedures and also several scientific and complex processes. The implementation stage is concerned with the actual placement of advertisements according to the media plan.

Scheduling Advertising

In factory management, scheduling is defined as "the determination of when each item of preparation and execution must be performed."[13] Thus, a timetable is prepared and performance is checked against the schedule as a means of control. The term "scheduling" has two meanings in advertising circles. One use of the term is analogous to the factory situation. Procedures are established within the agency setup to make sure that creative work is done on time. The responsibility for seeing that work flows smoothly through the agency is placed with the traffic department. At the heart of this kind of scheduling is the agency work order.

The traffic department issues work orders, or job memos, in order

[13] H. B. Maynard, *Industrial Engineering Handbook*, McGraw-Hill Book Company, New York, 1956.

March 25, 1976

№ 1924

McCANN-ERICKSON, INC.

615 PEACHTREE STREET, N.E., ATLANTA, GEORGIA 30308

Publisher of __Atlanta Journal Constitution__

Address __72 Marietta Street, N.W.__

__Atlanta, Georgia 30301__

Bottler Code No. _____

Product _____

Please insert advertising of __Brown-Freeman Company__ _____

in your publication as specified below and apply the space on our contract, if applicable

Total Space __1000 lines__   Rate $ __.82/line__   Agency Commission __15%__   Cash Disc. __2%__

Other _____

DATES OF INSERTION	SIZE	AD NO.	REMARKS
1976 (M/E)			
April 5	5 x 200 lines	6-BFC-105	"What's It All About"
Material to come from Reilly Graphics, NYC.			

Please avoid placing alcoholic beverages or competitive advertisement on the same page or facing page with this copy.

FIGURE 18.5
By means of this space order, the agency commits the advertiser to a 1,000-line advertisement.

to keep creative work flowing smoothly through the various departments in the agency. The process starts from the closing dates set up by the various advertising media and works backward. Every medium

600

PLANNING
AND
MANAGING
THE ADVERTISING
CAMPAIGN

TABLE 18.1

NORMAL SCHEDULE FOR THE PREPARATION OF A FOUR-COLOR PRINT ADVERTISEMENT

1 Agency account executive initiates copy request (5 working days)
2 Copy completed and layout checked (4 days)
3 Account group approves copy and layout (1 day)
4 Account executive sets up date with client (1 day)
5 Copy and layout submitted to client for approval, rejection, or revision—the first time the advertising manager sees the ad (2 days)
6 Approved copy is set in type and artwork prepared (15 or more days)
7 Art and type are physically put together in "mechanical layout" (2 days)
8 Mechanical layout is approved by account group (1 day)
9 Mechanical layout and finished art submitted to advertising manager for review and approval—the second time the advertising manager sees the ad (1 day)
10 Mechanical layout and art go into the production department or group, which supervises the making of plates by the engraver and the securing of proofs (25 days)
11 Proofs go to the advertising manager for final approval. If corrections are required at this point, there will doubtless be extra costs. This is the last time the advertising manager sees the ad before it is published (2 days)
12 Account executive returns approved proof to agency traffic department (1 day)
13 Agency traffic coordinator then forwards proofs and orders engraver to send plates to publication printer (1 day)
14 Agency traffic or forwarding department sends insertion order with a proof to the publication (same day)

SOURCE: Alfred R. Oxenfeldt and Carroll Swan, *Management of the Advertising Function*, Wadsworth Publishing Company, Inc., Belmont, Calif., 1964, pp. 64–65.

sets a deadline; copy must reach the medium by the specified date, or the advertisement will not be run as scheduled.

Table 18.1 illustrates the step-by-step procedure followed in a normal schedule for preparing a four-color print advertisement. More than two months are involved, and of course, further delays are often possible, thus requiring even more time.

In its second meaning, the term "scheduling" is used to describe an activity closely related to the physical placement of advertisements with media. When all the thinking about which advertising media should be used is finally done, the mechanics of the media job remain. We shall not go into the routine procedures involved in placing advertisements, but we shall explain the use of a tool designed to facilitate the process—the *media schedule*. Although the forms of media schedules may vary greatly, every schedule contains four basic elements: (1) a list of media where the advertisement is to appear; (2) dates of insertion, airing, or posting; (3) space, time, or other units to be used; and (4) the cost. Circulation figures are also sometimes given. A typical schedule is shown in Figure 18.6. Careful study of such schedules, either individually or in comparison with those used by other advertisers, tells a great deal about the campaign strategy being employed. Here the advertiser's thinking about such concepts as reach continuity, frequency, and dominance is dramatically shown.

Scheduling Patterns The advertising effort needs to be allocated, as we have already mentioned, in terms of target-market and geographical patterns. This process is called *media weighting* and is really a *matter of relative emphasis.*[14] Another dimension of the weighting activity is the timing of advertising. One pattern to be adopted, of course, is continuous advertising, wherein ads appear regularly throughout the time period covered on the media schedule. An alternative is to employ a policy of "flighting" or "pulsing" the advertising. These patterns involve heavy media usage for a while, followed by complete abstinence. In addition to budget constraints, which may dictate no advertising for periods of time, such factors as seasonal sales rates, product life cycle, repurchase patterns, and competitive advertising patterns may influence the choice of scheduling pattern.[15]

Patterns for publication advertising. In publication advertising, four basic patterns are available. The *even* schedule calls for the placement of advertisements of equal size at regularly established intervals. Thus, a schedule may include 100-inch advertisements in the local newspaper every Friday morning or a series of full-page advertisements in *Playboy* magazine every month. Advertisers whose products are in demand throughout the time period, or whose campaigns are essentially institutional, may find the even schedule satisfactory.

The *alternating* or *staggered* schedule is a variation of the even strategy. Advertisements continue to appear at regular intervals, but their size alternates in a set manner. For example, a newspaper schedule may include 840-line advertisements on Wednesdays and full pages on Sundays. This schedule is often used as a budget stretcher. By reducing the size of some advertisements, the advertiser is able to keep the message before the potential customer, yet spend less money.

The staggered schedule may be used, of course, over a longer period of time than a week or a month. It may be used to take advantage of intermittent peaks in the demand pattern for such seasonal products as greeting cards. The bulk of the advertising of greeting-card firms, for instance, is scheduled to appear shortly before Christmas, Valentine's Day, and Mother's Day.

The other two scheduling patterns are direct opposites of each other. One schedule calls for starting the advertising campaign with relatively small advertisements. Each succeeding advertisement is somewhat larger than its predecessor until finally a large ad climaxes the campaign. This schedule is frequently used to introduce new models of automobiles and other new products. Initial advertisements are often "teasers," aimed at stimulating consumer interest in the

[14] Barban et al., op. cit., p. 66.
[15] Ibid., p. 68.

602

PLANNING
AND
MANAGING
THE ADVERTISING
CAMPAIGN

MELDRUM AND FEWSMITH, INC.

Advertising

1220 HURON ROAD · CLEVELAND 15, OHIO
TELEPHONE: 241-2141

PRINT MEDIA ESTIMATE

CLIENT REPUBLIC STEEL CORPORATION   **DATE** January 20, 1976
Division: Flat Rolled Division
Product: 1976 Advertising - Hot Rolled Sheet & Plate,   **Est. No.** 3 Revised
Maxi-Form Family

Product Program No. 1-A

Publication	Description and Unit Rate		Total Cost
AUTOMOTIVE ENGINEERING (M)　　12x　41,633	6 - 2 Facing Pages, 4 Color, Bleed (Inside Front Cover & Page 1)	$4,085.	$24,510.
AUTOMOTIVE INDUSTRIES (Semi-M) 11%　45,088	5 - 2 Facing Pages, 4 Color, Bleed	4,423.30	22,116.50
DESIGN NEWS (Semi-M) 12x　122,173	4 - 2 Facing Pages, 4 Color, Bleed	6,080.	24,320.
INDUSTRY WEEK (Metal- working Edition) (W)　　17%　109,075	4 - 2 Facing Pages, 4 Color, Bleed	5,999.24	23,996.96
IRON AGE (W)　　18%　106,832	4 - 2 Facing Pages, 4 Color, Bleed	5,280.80	21,123.20
MATERIALS ENGINEERING (M)　　12x　60,533	3 - 2 Facing Pages, 4 Color, Bleed	4,170.	12,510.
METAL PROGRESS (M)　　24x　47,799	3 - 2 Facing Pages, 4 Color, Bleed	3,945.	11,835.
PRODUCTION (Jan. 1976 Issue) (M)　　10%　79,893	1 - 2 Facing Pages, 4 Color, Bleed	4,986.	4,986.
PURCHASING MAGAZINE (Semi-M) 12x　71,128	3 - 2 Facing Pages, 4 Color, Bleed	5,140.	15,420.
PURCHASING WORLD (M)　　12x　68,144	3 - 2 Facing Pages, 4 Color, Bleed	5,250.	15,750.
WARD'S AUTO WORLD (M)　　6x　48,760	4 - 2 Facing Pages, 4 Color, Bleed	4,320.	17,280.
		TOTAL SPACE PREPARATION	$193,847.66 66,152.34
	HOT ROLLED SHEET & PLATE, MAXI-FORM FAMILY TOTAL		$260,000.

Approved_____

FIGURE 18.6

The various print media to be used by one division of a large steel producer in its advertising program are listed in this form.

forthcoming announcement by arousing curiosity. The opposite schedule starts with a large advertisement, which is followed by successively smaller ads. These patterns are called *step-up* and *step-down* schedules, respectively. The choice is a matter of strategy; the advertiser decides whether an initial smash or a gradual building of interest is desired.

Patterns in Broadcast and Other Media.   Broadcast availabilities and the practice of selling network time for stated periods, such as 13 weeks, make it somewhat difficult to schedule step-up and step-down campaigns. Spot broadcasting, of course, can be employed if time availabilities can be secured. Broadcast campaigns involving many stations in scattered markets require intricate scheduling problems for the media buyer, although computerization has helped make the job considerably easier than it was for many years. Spot broadcasting can increase the advertiser's impact through the use of saturation schedules in chosen markets. For outdoor advertising, the 30-day selling period places a limitation on scheduling flexibility for advertisers wishing to use the medium.

The Media Schedule

The media schedule provides a work sheet against which the person charged with the responsibility of actually placing advertisements can check operations. The schedule is a handy device to show what the advertising program of the company contains. Moreover, it is an instrument of control over advertising expenditures. By totaling scheduled expenditures, one can determine whether the media budget is

FIGURE 18.7

The information contained in Figure 18.6 is also on this "plot sheet." It contains a schedule of the issues of each publication to be used during the year.

Client: REPUBLIC STEEL CORPORATION Period: 1976
Division: Flat Rolled Division Date: February 3, 1976

M&F ADVERTISING

MEDIA	JAN	FEB	MAR	APR	MAY	JUN	JUL	AUG	SEP	OCT	NOV	DEC
Product Program #1-A												
Automotive Engineering		X 2P4CB		X 2P4CB		X 2P4CB		X 2P4CB		X 2P4CB		X 2P4CB
Automotive Industries	15 S-6997-A 2P4CB	15 S9329 DPS:4CB	1 X 2P4CB			1 X 2P4CB					1 2P4CB	
Design News		9 2P4CB S-9329			24 2P4CB		19 2P4CB			11 2P4CB		
Industry Week (Metalworking Ed.)		16 X 2P4CB S-9329			24 X 2P4CB			16 X 2P4CB		18 X 2P4CB		
Iron Age			15 X 2P4CB S-9329			7 X 2P4CB			6 X 2P4CB	4 X 2P4CB		
Materials Engineering		X 2P4CB		DPS:4CB	DPS:4CB							
Metal Progress		S-6997-A 2P4CB		DPS:4CB		DPS:4CB						
Purchasing			9 DPS:4CB S-9329			22 DPS:4CB			7 X 2P4CB			

604

PLANNING
AND
MANAGING
THE ADVERTISING
CAMPAIGN

being exceeded. Finally, the schedule serves as a checklist against which media billing and proof of publication, airing, or posting can be compared.

Buying of Advertising Time and Space

With the media schedule firmly established, the final step in media plan implementation—the actual purchase of advertising—arrives. Three groups participate in buying media: (1) the advertising agency, (2) advertisers, and (3) media buying services. Every advertising agency employs specialists skilled in the buying of broadcast time and publication space. Familiarity with media charges, discount structures, special buying opportunities, and other factors influencing the cost of advertising is the stock-in-trade for these individuals. They are performing one of the three principal functions that the full-service agency renders to its clients—the planning, creation, and *placement* of advertising messages. When the job is well done, advertising efficiency in enhanced.

Retail advertisers traditionally deal directly with the media, buying time and space for advertisements created by store personnel. When advertising is placed by such advertisers, they are not usually given a commission by the media as national advertisers are. The house agency established by some national advertisers may also deal directly with media, with the commission received acting as a reduction in the cost of the advertising.

In the 1960s several independent firms, known as *outside media buying services*, offered to take over the time-buying function for advertisers heavily committed to the broadcast media. At the time the product manager was gaining in popularity, and many organizations started to perform many marketing services in-house. This led to a lessened reliance on the advertising agency.

Media costs, especially for spot television, rose dramatically at the time, accompanied by a general softening of the general economy. The independent buying service sought out special "buys" which deviated from established advertising rates. The buying services buy for cash on the open market, with their profit coming from the differential between the price they pay to media and what they can charge an advertiser. Often the price to the advertiser was appreciably lower than the advertising agency had obtained from the stations, and so use of the buying services could save the advertiser money. Some advertising agencies reacted by strengthening their own buying operations, while others welcomed relief from the burden of buying time. The media buying services have shown that broadcast time costs are negotiable, and they led to improvement on the overall efficiency of time buying, regardless of who does the job.

THE COMPUTER AND MEDIA DECISIONS

Both media planning and media buying are facilitated by the use of the computer. There has been a vast explosion of information about markets and media in recent years; former reliance upon intuition when media were being chosen has become increasingly risky in the economy of the 1970s. When a large number of calculations are to be made, such as in the case of reach and frequency computations, the computer can perform these operations quickly and efficiently, manipulating raw data into useful information. The computer, by processing sales information that shows where or when demand or distribution is the greatest, can aid in the allocation of the advertising budget to regions or to seasons of the year. Advertising can be directed to more dynamic markets or to certain seasons. Similarly, when such factors as market conditions, competitive advertising effort, and media considerations are analyzed prior to the selection of media, vast quantities of data are involved. This point is highlighted by the following quotation:

> As an example of the potential complexity of the media decision . . . in the simplest circumstances, a media buyer selecting 3 media from a group of 6 has 20 potential different choices. The same media buyer selecting 10 media from a group of 100, has 17,310,000,000,000 different alternatives available to him. If he could analyze 1 alternative per second, 24 hours a day, 7 days a week, he could cover all of his choices [in] one-half million years![16]

We should bear in mind that the output of the computer is only as good as its input. Furthermore, the computer is not a substitute for thinking; it makes rapid computations which save laborious, if not humanly impossible, amounts of arithmetic calculations. Proper programming of data for the computer calls for a highly skilled talent.

Computer Models

Extensive experimentation has taken place with the aim of adapting the computer to complex media jobs. There are at least three significant ways the computer has entered the media field: (1) automated cost-estimating systems, (2) simulation models for determining both reach and frequency of schedules, and (3) decision models for determining optimum schedule recommendations. Cost estimating is a highly technical function of the media department and therefore outside of our concern in this book. On the other hand, the decision

---

[16] Joseph St. Georges, "How Practical Is the Media Model," *Journal of Marketing*, pp. 31–32, July 1963.

606

PLANNING
AND
MANAGING
THE ADVERTISING
CAMPAIGN

model can help materially in planning advertising programs. Moreover, models should be useful in explaining how advertising works and why.

Computers can be applied to the problems of media selection in two ways: through linear programming or simulation. These techniques rely upon the ability of the computer to store information, as well as to make rapid computations. In linear programming, the computer functions as a repository of facts, such as media rates, audience size, and profile characteristics. Then the media requirements for a given advertising campaign, including the profile of the target market, the size of the budget, and estimates of the value of advertising exposures in one vehicle contrasted with others, are fed to the computer. Calculations are made, and the computer describes what specific media and quantities (units) will give the maximum exposure for advertising expenditure.

Simulation involves the same general principle. Different kinds of information, however, are stored in the computer at the beginning. Descriptions of hypothetical buyers, including demographic characteristics and media and product usage data, go into the computer's memory box. Then a tentative media plan is fed into the computer, which provides an estimate of how well that particular plan will deliver advertising exposures to consumers.

Both linear programming and simulation rely on innumerable estimates and assumptions. How reliable the "recommendations" of the computer are depends upon the judgment exercised when inputs are being placed into the computer. Linear programming and simulation, however, provide the media planner with comparisons when choices between alternative media plans or media mixes are to be made. Furthermore, the use of the computer provides this additional advantage:

> One of the characteristics of the computer that make it unique among technical achievements is that it has forced men to think about what they are doing with clarity and precision. A man cannot instruct the computer to perform usefully until he has arduously thought through what he's up to in the first place, and where he wants to go from there. . . . Wherever the machine is used, it is improving enormously the quantity and quality of human cogitation; and it is rapidly becoming a kind of Universal Disciplinarian.[17]

Another positive feature of the computer is that it eliminates "reverse rationale;" media choices must be based on data collection and analysis rather than on data uncovered to support decisions already made subjectively.[18]

[17] Gilbert Burck, "The Boundless Age of the Computer," *Fortune*, March 1964, p. 101.
[18] Barban et al., op. cit., p. 84.

Despite the advantages of the computer, its present level of sophistication makes advertising problem solving an uncertain task. Critics contend that presently used data are still not accurate enough to warrant basing a major decision upon a computer recommendation. Another alleged shortcoming is that the availability of the computer has made media buying too mechanical and mathematical, aimed at maximizing discounts and forgetting the power to be found in the imaginative use of media.[19]

Viewed from another angle, successes in linear programming and simulation are not likely to be publicized by their developers. The competitive nature of the advertising activity precludes sharing reasons for success with competitors.

The computer and the discipline it requires undoubtedly will lead to better media decisions in the advertising world of the future. Judgment, art, even intuition, will not become obsolete, however, and the human factor will remain as the key to decision making. But the human being involved, however, must be better trained if he or she is to succeed in the task.

SUMMARY

Media strategy, which calls for creativity similar to that demanded by copy strategy, involves two major processes: media planning and media buying. Media planning requires the analysis of three major factors: market conditions, competitive efforts, and media considerations. There are several sources of information about each of these factors, and the media decision maker must learn to use many kinds of data imaginatively when devising a media plan. The result of this analysis and thinking is the media schedule, which gives detailed information on when and where advertising messages are to appear. Media planning leads to the adoption of one of three strategies: the national plan, the key-market plan, or the skim plan.

Implementation of the media plan takes place through the media buying process. This step is more mechanical than the planning phase and is concerned with such matters as the scheduling and timing of advertising. Scheduling patterns can be even over time, or they can employ the flighting technique.

The actual buying of advertising time or space is usually performed by the advertising agency on behalf of the client. Recently some advertisers are performing the time buying themselves (in-house), and others employ independent media buying services. The goal in all cases is to achieve maximum advertising exposure for dollars spent.

The computer has simplified the complex job of analyzing the quantities of data that need to be examined when media decisions are made. Both linear

[19] Henry Schachte, "They Did It with Media Magic—Can Today's Ways Match Them?" *Advertising Age*, Nov. 24, 1975, p. 35.

608

PLANNING
AND
MANAGING
THE ADVERTISING
CAMPAIGN

programming and simulation models have been developed to help with media selection decisions. Their use is still in the developmental stage.

QUESTIONS FOR DISCUSSION

1 Why is a sound media strategy important to advertising success? Explain.
2 What is involved in media planning? Media selection?
3 What kinds of information are needed before good media planning can be performed? Elaborate with examples.
4 How does the advertising efforts of competitors affect media decisions of the advertiser?
5 Clearly explain how the media concepts of reach, frequency, continuity, and dominance interact within the media decision process.
6 What information sources would you use when seeking data on marketing conditions? On competitive advertising efforts? On media characteristics?
7 Exactly what is involved in the media-market matching process?
8 What are the three main forms of media strategies that are available to the media planner? Describe each briefly.
9 Describe the major scheduling patterns available to the media buyer.
10 How can the computer help in media planning? In media buying? Explain.

FOR FURTHER REFERENCE

Aaker, David A., and John G. Myers: *Advertising Management*, Prentice-Hall, Inc., Englewood Cliffs, N.J., 1975.

Barban, Arnold M., Donald W. Jugenheimer, and Lee F. Young: *Advertising Media*, Sourcebook and Workbook, Grid, Inc., Columbus, Ohio, 1975.

Barban, Arnold M., Stephen M. Cristol, and Frank J. Kopec: *Essentials of Media Planning*, Crain Books, Chicago, 1975.

Barton, Roger: *Media in Advertising*, McGraw-Hill Book Company, New York, 1964.

Heighton, Elizabeth J., and Don R. Cunningham: *Advertising on the Broadcast Media*, Wadsworth Publishing Company Inc., Belmont, Calif., 1976.

Roth, Paul M.: *How to Plan Media*, Time & Space Labs Incorporated, Chicago, 1968.

Sissors, Jack Z.: *Advertising Media Planning*, Crain Books, Chicago, 1975.

CHAPTER 19

CHAPTER 19
COORDINATION OF ADVERTISING WITH OTHER PROMOTIONAL AND MARKETING METHODS

611
COORDINATION
OF ADVERTISING
WITH OTHER
PROMOTIONAL
AND MARKETING
METHODS

Management involves the performance of a number of duties, and one of the principal duties of a manager is coordination of diverse activities. In any context, coordination means the regulation and combination of things into harmonious action. In the context of business, a leading management expert has offered this classic explanation of what coordination involves:

> Coordination . . . the work of assuring that production, sales, finance, personnel, as well as the lesser functional activities, are integrated and interrelated, in terms of both appropriate structures and attitudes, in order to achieve most smoothly the desired end result.[1]

Coordination in business is quite similar to coordination in athletics. We say an athlete must be well coordinated to become a star. The parts of the athlete's body must be capable of working together instantly upon command. For example, the batter's eye sees the oncoming ball, his brain sends signals to needed muscles, and he hits a single. Or the running back sees a hole in the line and breaks through for a first down.

There is another form of coordination in athletics which we often call teamwork. Not only must the individual movements of every person on the team be well coordinated, but these individual movements must be welded together in coordinated joint action aimed at winning the game. Thus, the pitcher counts on the fielders to catch a fly, and the running back relies on the blockers to open a hole in the opposing line. Every player must know the team's plays, strategies, and signals; otherwise all are not moving toward the goal and may even get into one another's way. A winning team consists of individually coordinated members working together as a coordinated unit. In this chapter we discuss the interaction of advertising with a number of other activities that are vitally important to marketing success and to achievement of business management's ultimate goal of long-range profit maximization, combined with consumer welfare.

COORDINATION IN ADVERTISING

Two kinds of coordination exist in advertising. One is analogous to the coordination of the individual athlete and may be called *internal coordination*. As the muscles of the athlete must work together, so must the elements of the advertising program fit together. The advertising

---

[1] Ordway Tead, *The Art of Administration*, McGraw-Hill Book Company, New York, 1951, p. 102.

A 25¢ cup of coffee can save you $37.

A cup of coffee or a soft drink will cost you 25¢. But it'll save you a lot.

Starting April 14, 1975, subject to CAB approval, National Airlines new No Frills Fare will save you 35% off the regular day-coach fare. Instead of paying $98 one way from New York/Newark to Miami/Ft. Lauderdale, you'll pay just $61 including tax plus a nominal security surcharge. That's a savings of $37 off the present daycoach fare.

The fare will apply only to our wide-cabin jets from New York/Newark to Miami/Ft. Lauderdale, on certain days of the week.

On Board

We won't serve you any meals on the flight. No Frills means just that. There'll be No Frills seats on our wide-cabin jets—about 120 on each of our DC-10s and about 200 on each 747. If you like, we'll sell you a cup of coffee or a soft drink for a quarter. When you consider how much you're saving in airfare, that 25¢ cup of coffee is quite a bargain.

Before You Fly

Here's how National's No Frills Fare works. You can make reservations right now. Just purchase your tickets at least 7 days before departure. You fly only on Monday, Tuesday, Wednesday and Thursday. Since the number of seats is limited, you should act as soon as you can. It's first come, first served. You can stay for as long as you like, too. And children 2-11 with an adult fly for about 1/3 off the No Frills Fare.

These fares are good from April 14 through June 30, 1975. And again from September 3 through December 16, 1975. The fares will not be in effect November 25 through December 1, 1975. Should you have to cancel your flight, 10% of the fare or $10 (whichever is higher) is non-refundable.

The Frill Is Gone

We think our No Frills Fare is the best travel news in years. Especially now, when you can really use some good news. We're getting back to basics, and giving you the most value for your money.

Of course, we'll still have our fabulous First Class service. And regular coach service with good food and two free cocktails for all adults. And we'll still have our other special low fare too. Our 7-21 day Midweek Excursion Fare to Florida cities (subject to CAB approval).

The Choice Is Yours.

Frills or No Frills, now the choice is yours. We think it's time you had that choice. For more information or reservations, call your travel agent or National Airlines. In New York call 212-697-9000. In Newark call 201-624-1300. In other areas ask operator for our toll free number.

Miami, Ft. Lauderdale. Only $61.

One way No Frills Fare, effective April 14, subject to CAB approval.

National's ☀ No Frills Fare. Call your travel agent.

National honors American Express, BankAmericard, Carte Blanche, Diners Club, Master Charge/Interbank, UATP, our own card and cash.

message must be appropriate to the medium employed, media choices must reflect budgetary restrictions, and advertisements must be created far enough in advance to meet media deadlines. When many media are used, there is strong need for an integration of all creative efforts so that the total campaign is saying the same thing to prospects at every stage of the promotional effort. No advertising program can succeed if its elements are not coordinated for the right action at the right time.

The other type of advertising coordination is *external*. Just as the pitcher is only part of a baseball team, advertising is only part of a marketing team. Advertising is one element contributing to the overall sales success of the firm. Marketing success is usually dependent upon a desirable product, right distribution channels, correct pricing, personal selling, and advertising; and advertising plays different positions on different marketing teams.

Sometimes the primary burden for selling products is placed in the hands of advertising; advertising is the back who carries the ball. At other times, advertising opens the holes that make room for the personal salesperson to make the touchdown. Regardless of its function in any specific marketing system, advertising must know the plays; its activities must be coordinated with all marketing activities. Moreover, advertising is so closely related to certain other business activities, such as sales promotion and public relations, that coordination with them is essential. External coordination involves more than the meshing of advertising with other elements of the marketing system or with other company functions. Coordination of company efforts with those of outside organizations, especially intermediaries, can be particularly important.

ADVERTISING AND PERSONAL SELLING

Few products are sold by advertising alone. Most marketing organizations employ personal selling in varying amounts. Because both have the same general objective—the making of sales—it is logical that advertising and personal selling require a high degree of coordination. The interrelationship differs, however, for consumer goods and for industrial products.

Securing and maintaining proper levels of product distribution is one of the most important selling tasks for the manufacturer of consumer items. Wholesalers and retailers need to be persuaded to stock and promote the advertiser's product, or consumer advertising is largely wasted. If consumers are unable to locate the products after advertising has stimulated their interest, the advertising expenditure accomplished nothing. Most manufacturers of consumer products therefore maintain sales forces to call upon wholesalers and retailers.

613
COORDINATION
OF ADVERTISING
WITH OTHER
PROMOTIONAL
AND MARKETING
METHODS

FIGURE 19.1
When a special price is offered to the public, its availability needs to be promoted through advertising. From mid-April through June 30 the "no frills" promotion (*opposite page*) generated $4 million in extra revenues from 74,000 passengers who wouldn't have otherwise flown. This called for close coordination of the various parts of the firm's marketing effort.

614

PLANNING
AND
MANAGING
THE ADVERTISING
CAMPAIGN

Trade advertising can be used to assist the salesperson in the field by persuading intermediaries of the advantages to be derived from stocking the manufacturer's products. A favorable climate has already been established before the sales representative calls. The salesperson may even wish to start off the sales conversation with a reference to the advertising, such as "Did you see our advertisement in the latest issue of *Progressive Grocer*?" The ice has been broken by advertising, assuming that it is creatively effective and properly placed in the right media.

Many salespeople unfortunately carry on their selling activities completely independent of the company's trade advertising. It is imperative that the salesperson know what sales themes are being featured in the firm's trade advertising and be encouraged to incorporate these themes in their sales presentations.

Consumer advertising for the product may also assist the field salesperson by providing a talking point when meeting with intermediaries. When the company does extensive consumer advertising, that very fact may be used as another reason why intermediaries should stock and promote the brand. Intermediaries can be shown how advertising stimulation aimed at consumers should speed stock turnover in warehouses and retail outlets. This kind of promotion of consumer advertising to the trade is often called *merchandising the advertising* and is discussed later in this chapter.

Manufacturers of industrial products also maintain sales forces. The primary task of these industrial salespersons is to sell products directly to industrial users. Industrial advertising campaigns may often have as their objective the familiarization of the manufacturer's name with potential buyers. More likely the goal is to obtain leads for the sales force. When an inquiry comes into the home office in response to an industrial advertisement, the inquiry should be passed along to the sales department promptly. Furthermore, the salesperson should follow up the lead before competitors do. When the salesperson knows which advertisement evoked the prospect's interest, the correct buying motive can then be used in the sales presentation. More than space advertising is available to industrial salespersons. One survey indicated that advertising handouts (specialties), product literature, direct-mail advertising, and product publicity were of more value in making industrial sales.[2] It is obvious, therefore, that an integrated and coordinated promotional program is needed in industrial-product areas as well as for consumer goods.

Whether salespersons actually have knowledge of company advertising programs depends largely upon the internal organization of the firm. When advertising and selling are departments under the same marketing executive, chances for communication are greatly

[2] John M. Trytten, Ads Are More than Just a Way to Introduce Your Salesman, *Sales Management*, June 26, 1972, p. 36.

enhanced. Regardless of common leadership, however, interdepartmental communication does not come automatically. Definite steps must be taken if the sales force is to be briefed on the advertising program. The advertising department should take the initiative in this situation. Time to explain the advertising program at every major sales meeting should be aggressively sought. Furthermore, sales supervisors should be asked to check whether salespeople know the details of the program and are using the information in their selling.

The advertising manager, in other words, must be a salesperson who convinces sales management executives that their subordinates should know and use the company's advertising program. The advertising manager should stand ready to convince the sales force of the importance of advertising to the success of the company and to the personal success of the salesperson. Moreover, the advertising manager can receive real help in developing the advertising program from feedback coming via the sales force. For example, regional sales managers are called upon by many firms to help in such activities as media selection, determination of advertising budgets, and choice of advertising themes. Participation in the planning of advertising programs, of course, makes sales-force personnel more favorably disposed toward coordination of advertising and selling activities. If the jobs outlined in this section are conscientiously performed, satisfactory coordination between advertising and personal selling will exist at the manufacturing firm level. The first essential of external advertising coordination will have been achieved.

ADVERTISING AND DISTRIBUTION CHANNELS

Consumer products typically are purchased in retail stores. Ultimate consumers buy most products in one of two ways: (1) through personal selling in the retail outlet or (2) through self-service. Advertising plays an important role regardless of which method of sale is operating; therefore advertising should be coordinated with retail selling and self-service distribution. Products are purchased, or not purchased, at least in part because of consumer familiarity with the brands offered for sale in the retail store. But dealers must also give aggressive support to the product if maximum sales are to be achieved.

There are three major techniques for speeding up the rate of sales of selected brands in retail stores. First, retail salespersons may be tutored in product characteristics and selling points and urged to push particular brands. Sometimes an additional incentive is given to the salesperson in the form of "prize money" or "push money" (pm's) or "spiffs." These incentives are bonuses for the sale of specified items and may be paid by the retailer or the manufacturer. Second, the retailer may display chosen brands advantageously and may select certain point-of-purchase materials for use in the store. Third, the

615
COORDINATION
OF ADVERTISING
WITH OTHER
PROMOTIONAL
AND MARKETING
METHODS

616

PLANNING
AND
MANAGING
THE ADVERTISING
CAMPAIGN

dealer may promote sales by advertising the product over the name of the store.

Advertising can do little directly to stimulate the use of the first technique. If retail salespersons are to be trained to promote a particular brand, the manufacturer's sales representative must convince the retailer of the value of the idea. The retailer or a representative of the manufacturer will then do the actual training. Sales manuals, training films, and other aids may be prepared to facilitate such sales training. These materials are not advertising in the true sense, but they should be related to current advertising themes. In other words, retail salespeople should know as much as possible about the advertising program for reasons similar to those discussed for the manufacturer's representative. Of course, trade advertising can assist in selling the dealer on the advantages of this type of sales training program.

Preferential shelf space for the manufacturer's products and use of point-of-purchase materials are largely ideas which must be sold to the retailer. Once again trade advertising can do part of the sales job, but personal salesmanship usually bears the major burden. The principal hurdle is the intense competition for shelf space and the use of point-of-purchase materials.

Nearly every manufacturer of consumer products is bidding for the favor of the retailer. This important goal is sometimes purchased through dealer allowances. The retailer may be paid an advertising allowance—usually a discount on price—in exchange for agreeing to display merchandise or POP advertising in a prescribed manner. Advertising allowances are controlled by the provisions of the Robinson-Patman Act, which states that such allowances must be made on a proportionately equal basis to all competing buyers, or the practice will be ruled discriminatory, thus illegal.

The third technique—getting dealers to advertise the manufacturer's brand over their own name—also involves personal selling. One procedure, cooperative advertising, has been so thoroughly developed and generally used by national advertisers that the following section is devoted exclusively to a discussion of this method of securing dealer support.

Two other points should be mentioned, however, before we pass on to a discussion of cooperative advertising. First, there is a need for coordination between advertising and retail selling. Products should be on dealers' shelves prior to the appearance of an advertising campaign featuring the products. This warning is especially important when new products are introduced, when established products are featured in a special promotion, or when the product is one of seasonal use. Not only are sales lost when merchandise is absent from dealers' shelves, but ill feeling toward the brand and the manufacturer may be created. Thus, the sales force must contact retailers far enough in advance to permit delivery of the products to be advertised. Moreover, production must be geared to possible expansion in demand patterns caused by the advertising program. Usually advertising cannot be completely efficient if distribution of the product does not precede the appearance of the advertisement. If distribution is achieved too far in advance, however, retailers may logically conclude that the product is unsalable. *Timing is vital.*

Second, there is a need for coordination in retail advertising. Retail advertisements feature an ever-changing variety of products, and the retail salesperson has difficulty keeping track of items. At the same

617

COORDINATION
OF ADVERTISING
WITH OTHER
PROMOTIONAL
AND MARKETING
METHODS

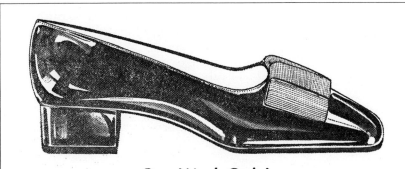

One Week Only!
Our Classic
Julianelli Bow Pump
Now 44.00
Regularly 54.00

How could we improve Mabel Julianelli's elegant, low heel bow pump?
By making it a very special price, this week only. The Classic,
now 44.00. Regularly 54.00. Choose from black, **navy, brown** or
taupe patent; black, navy or brown suede.
All with matching grosgrain bow.
Designer Shoe Salon, Second Floor
Call EL 5-6800, Ext. 268

Add 1.35 outside delivery area and sales tax where **applicable.**
Fifth Avenue at 56th Street, New York.

FIGURE 19.2
Advertisements
featuring special
offers, when limit-
ed in time or
quantity available,
should clearly
inform potential
customers of the
restriction in the
offer.

618

PLANNING
AND
MANAGING
THE ADVERTISING
CAMPAIGN

time, retail advertising is primarily direct action; therefore consumers enter the store intending to buy the advertised product. It is extremely frustrating to receive a blank look from the salesperson when we ask for an item featured in the morning's newspaper. It is equally annoying to learn that the item has been sold out. For these reasons, the retail advertising manager must make sure of two things. First, no item should be advertised unless sufficient quantities are on hand to meet reasonable demand for the merchandise. Short supplies or a limited variety of sizes or models should be clearly stated in the advertisement if the fact is known at the time the advertisement is run. Second, steps should be taken to make certain that salespeople know what merchandise is featured in store advertising. Inasmuch as items are suggested by department heads, the educative responsibility should rest with them. The advertising manager, however, can help by supplying advance proofs of the store's advertisements. These proofs should be posted where employees will examine them before coming on the sales floor. Often a portion of the daily departmental sales meeting is devoted to a discussion of the items featured in current advertising. Professional shoppers, employed by the store, can be used to check salespeople's familiarity with store advertising, and rewards can be given to those who are up to date.

COOPERATIVE ADVERTISING

The term "cooperative advertising" is used in two entirely different ways by advertising executives. It is used to describe joint sponsorship by competitors of an advertising program designed to stimulate consumer demand for the generic products of the industry. For example, the dairies of the nation have banded together to sponsor consumer advertising designed to convince the public of the health and beauty benefits derived from regular consumption of fresh milk and milk products. While this primary-demand campaign is waged in various advertising media, individual dairies continue to compete vigorously with selective-demand advertising programs aimed at convincing consumers of the superiority of their own brands. Thus, competitors are advertising as a group to create a larger-sized pie of demand to be divided among themselves. This type of advertising is sometimes called horizontal cooperative advertising.

Our interest, however, is in the other form of cooperative advertising, variously called vertical cooperative advertising, dealer cooperative advertising, or manufacturer's cooperative advertising. Although each term describes the technique accurately in part, we prefer the third because the initiative for the establishment of such programs comes from the producer rather than the intermediary.

The cooperative arrangement is not difficult to understand, but its implementation is accompanied by many problems. A manufacturer and a retailer who sells the manufacturer's brands enter into an

FIGURE 19.3
This magazine ad is an example of horizontal cooperative advertising.

agreement by which the manufacturer promises to refund a portion of the retailer's advertising costs for those advertisements featuring the manufacturer's products. Quite frequently, the two parties agree to split the advertising costs on a 50–50 basis.

In order to illustrate the procedure, let us assume the following

Clothes for men who dress for women.

WOMAN: When I meet a man, I notice his clothes.

Every woman does.

That's why I'm telling you about Curlee.

Curlee makes men's clothes

I not only notice, I like.

You wear Curlee Clothes

They don't wear you.

I could spend a lot of time with a man who dresses that way.

SUPER: Curlee. For men who dress for women STORE NAME

FIGURE 19.4
This television commercial is part of a vertical cooperative advertising program.

hypothetical situation. The ABC Department Store, located in Hometown, U.S.A., places a full-page advertisement in the Sunday edition of the *Hometown Herald*. The advertisement features a product made by the XYZ Manufacturing Corporation. A manufacturer's cooperative advertising agreement exists between ABC and XYZ; the refund is established at 50 percent. The newspaper bills ABC for $850, its regular page rate for retail advertisers. The bill, along with a tear sheet as proof of actual publication, is sent by ABC to XYZ. The manufacturer sends a check or credit memo for $425 ($850 × 50 percent) to the department store. The two parties have thus advertised under their cooperative advertising agreement. This principle may also apply when a manufacturer's product is featured in multiple-item advertisements, such as those run by supermarkets. The food store is reimbursed on a proportional basis for the space devoted to the manufacturer's brand.

The arrangement gives retailers twice as much advertising for their advertising dollars. At first glance, it seems that the manufacturer receives the same advantage. Because of the differential between rates charged by some media to national and retail advertisers, however, the manufacturer's advantage may be considerably greater. Often the rate differential paid by the national advertiser is as much as 50 percent, depending on the quantity of advertising placed in the particular medium by the retailer. When the differential is at the 50 percent level, the manufacturer actually receives four times as much advertising space than if the messages were placed as national advertising.

If all cases were as simple as the ABC-XYZ illustration, nearly every manufacturer would engage in cooperative advertising. Although it is estimated that more than $3 billion is now spent for cooperative advertising, another estimated $1 billion is not used by retailers. Thus, there must be disadvantages or problems in the arrangement, both from the manufacturer's point of view and from the retailer's.

Cooperative advertising brings many additional costs to the manufacturer. An important one is in the preparation of the advertisement itself. It is customary for the manufacturer to provide the retailer with the materials for reproduction of the advertising messages used in the cooperative program. This practice gives the retailer more professional and more effective advertising messages than can usually be generated by the store or the advertising medium. Moreover, the basic advertising theme is carried to the retail level by these advertisements, which present the product in local media in the way desired. Because the advertisements appear exactly the same throughout the nation, except for differing retailer signatures, the advantages of repetition are gained. Nevertheless, preparation of the advertisements and the reproduction materials are appreciable costs for the manufacturer.

Considerable paperwork is caused by a cooperative advertising program. Tear sheets of print ads must be checked to see that advertisements are run according to instructions. Checking on the broadcast half of advertising is even more complicated. Logs main-

622
PLANNING
AND
MANAGING
THE ADVERTISING
CAMPAIGN

FIGURE 19.5
When the product cannot be found in local stores, the consumer is urged to order directly from the manufacturer.

tained by broadcast stations can be examined, and special-service groups do provide monitoring for a fee. The usual practice, however, tends to center on the use of signed affidavits wherein an executive of the broadcast station certifies that the commercial was, in fact, aired. Getting better proof is expensive and time-consuming.

Media bills must be audited and paid. Abuses can occur, such as the practice of "double billing". A bill for advertising space or time used is prepared by the local advertising medium for a higher amount of money than the retailer actually pays the medium. The manufacturer then ends up paying more than contemplated under the terms of the agreement.

Wasted circulation is another potential cost in cooperative advertising. Retailers may choose media which are not good vehicles for advertising the manufacturer's product. However, that shortcoming can be controlled by the terms of the agreement. Furthermore, presently about 75 percent of all cooperative advertising is run in newspapers, with direct mail serving as second in importance. The broadcast media, particularly television, are, however, aggressively seeking a higher rate of participation.

Retailers fail to engage in cooperative advertising arrangements with manufacturers because of inertia, because of a feeling that it is of little benefit to their operation's profitability, or because of the considerable amount of detailed paperwork involved. Despite the disadvantages, retailers can benefit from cooperative advertising. The following section describes how manufacturers can incorporate cooperative advertising into their promotional mix with good results.

When to Use Cooperative Advertising

Manufacturer's cooperative advertising is often employed when products are sold through exclusive or selective distribution methods. These distribution patterns call for the sale of the manufacturer's brand in

623
COORDINATION
OF ADVERTISING
WITH OTHER
PROMOTIONAL
AND MARKETING
METHODS

FIGURE 19.6
Manufacturers often offer to send literature and dealers' names to prospects. Consulting the yellow pages in the telephone directory may also be suggested.

624

PLANNING
AND
MANAGING
THE ADVERTISING
CAMPAIGN

one—or a few—retail outlets in a marketing area. It is important, therefore, for the consumer to know where the product can be purchased. National advertising may stimulate initial interest in the brand, but identification of the local retail outlet is essential if such interest is to be translated into buying action. For this reason telephone directory advertising is high on the approved media lists of most manufacturers engaging in cooperative advertising. Clothing, tires, gasoline, paint, cosmetics, most department-store items, and appliances constitute a partial list of products featured in cooperative advertisements.

Cooperative advertising rarely can be used successfully to introduce a new product or to help move a small-volume item. In such cases, the retailer wants to know whether the product can be sold at all. The retailer believes the manufacturer has the responsibility of building demand. After the product has been established at satisfactory levels of volume, cooperative advertising is probably more advantageous for both the manufacturer and the retailer.

Convenience-type products, such as food, soap, and drugs, are also given cooperative advertising support. The reason, more than likely, is to give the retailer a price discount. In other words, cooperative advertising is not used as an inducement for the retailer to advertise the brand. Instead advertising allowances and cooperative advertising are used as a means of obtaining distribution for products. Such inducements may be given in a discriminatory fashion despite the Robinson-Patman Act provision that advertising allowances must be made proportionately available to all competing buyers.

MERCHANDISING THE ADVERTISING

"Merchandising" is a term that has many different meanings in the language of marketing. For our purposes here, "merchandising" is a synonym for "selling," and "merchandising the advertising" means "selling the advertising program." The manufacturer using this technique desires to arouse enthusiasm and support for the advertising program where so many dollars are invested. According to its advocates, merchandising the advertising, when used effectively, can double the value of the firm's investment in advertising.

The two most important groups to be influenced are the manufacturer's own sales force and intermediaries, particularly the retailers handling the brands. The manufacturer wants both groups to feel that the advertising program is a positive force, designed to make their respective tasks easier and to increase their sales volume. The salespeople are told how the consumer advertising will make it easier to convince retailers of the advisability of stocking the manufacturer's product. They are also briefed on how the trade advertising program provides another inducement for retailers to buy and promote the brand. The manufacturer's sales force generally receives this type of motivation from advertising department personnel, supplemented by agency and sales executives and direct-mail promotion.

Retailers must be convinced that the manufacturer's consumer advertising program will provide a ground swell of demand for the product, thereby facilitating a rapid stock turnover. Retailers will then decide to stock the brand and, more important, to promote the product so that each retailer can get a fair share of the sales springing from the interest created by the manufacturer's advertising. So persuaded, the retailer may promote the product in the various ways already discussed—preferential shelf position, display of merchandise, use of point-of-purchase materials, advertising the manufacturer's brand over the retailer's name, and dealer tie-in campaigns.

Retailers are reached primarily through salespeople employed by the manufacturer, broker, or wholesaler and through trade advertising, including magazines, direct mail, and advertising portfolios. Some advertising media employ merchandising personnel who contact retailers on behalf of advertisers using the particular newspaper, magazine, or broadcasting network or station. These merchandising persons urge retailers to support the advertised product in their own advertising and sales promotional efforts.

In his autobiography, *How to Make $100,000,000 in a Hurry*, Jeno Paulucci attests to the value of merchandising the advertising in the success of the Chun King Corp. When his company was in its infancy, a four-color, full-page ad was run in *Life* to launch a new 3-pound package. With the ad scheduled to run in February, Chun King sales representatives started to show millions of preprints to the trade as early as the previous June. The advertisement cost $30,000, a staggering drain on company resources at the time, but it lent prestige to the company and its product and aided in securing wide distribution in retail stores.[3]

Placing the responsibility for the program of merchandising company advertising is a difficult task. Surely the advertising department must bear a heavy share of the burden, for its personnel are in the best position to know the details of the advertising program. Moreover, advertising people should have the most enthusiasm for the company's advertising program since they develop it. On the other hand, the sales department is largely the instrument for transmitting such information to both retailers and the sales force. When a separate sales promotion department is maintained within the organizational structure of the firm, this department often carries out the assignment.

The philosophy behind the technique of merchandising the advertising is well expressed in this short quotation: "Many people are so

[3] *Advertising Age*, June 9, 1969, p. 78.

626

PLANNING
AND
MANAGING
THE ADVERTISING
CAMPAIGN

K-D Tools presents the biggest hand-tool promotion in history.

And every part of it is designed to send you customers.

1. The largest hand-tool advertisement ever kicks it off. The 68-page insert you see here will also appear in April issues of MOTOR SERVICE and SERVICE STATION MANAGEMENT. Result? The ad—and the insert—will be read by professional mechanics in 311,000 service stations and repair shops! Over one million of your best customers will see and read about the 791 K-D hand tools it describes!

Tools designed to solve their special automotive service problems. Best-selling K-D tools to make tough jobs easy…on disc brakes, air conditioning units, ignition systems, electrical systems, engines. You name it and K-D makes it. Start planning now for big K-D tool sales.

2. The big K-D Sweepstakes. Every customer has to come to you to see if he's a winner. One of your customers may win a trip for two to fabulous Acapulco. Or any one of the 175 other prizes of up to $200 worth of K-D tools in our great new K-D Tools Sweepstakes.

And here's your pay-off. Look for heavy customer traffic as soon as April issues reach mechanics in your area. They'll be coming to you to see if the numbers in their K-D inserts match one of the numbers listed on *your* K-D tool display. And to buy the tools they need from the special K-D insert. You can't lose!

busy getting out the next ad that they haven't time to do a good job in 'putting over' the ad they just got out." All in all, merchandising the advertising is a concept that warrants more cultivation.

ADVERTISING AND PRODUCT MANAGEMENT

The advertising program should be coordinated with product innovation, packaging, pricing, and other components making up the total

627

COORDINATION
OF ADVERTISING
WITH OTHER
PROMOTIONAL
AND MARKETING
METHODS

product. For instance, the advertising department should be aware of the development of new products. Research and development people should brief advertising executives on activities far enough in advance for creative personnel to have time to develop good sales themes to be used in product promotion. Moreover, since lags exist in the process, time must be allowed for the mechanical production and media placement of advertisements. The product development department cannot suddenly announce a new discovery and expect the advertising department to develop an outstanding campaign designed to

628
PLANNING
AND
MANAGING
THE ADVERTISING
CAMPAIGN

introduce the product to the market. For one thing, many forms of advertising media must be contracted for months in advance. This area of coordination, however, is often overlooked even in well-managed firms. The desire for secrecy furnishes a partial explanation. The commercial researcher wishes to keep news of activities away from competitive organizations. The greater the number of people in on a secret, the greater the chance of an information leak. Employment mobility of sales and advertising executives, particularly agency personnel, intensifies this problem. When people move, secrets may go with them.

Coordination between the production and advertising departments may be viewed from another perspective: advertising executives should inform production officials of changes which advertising is expected to stimulate in the marketplace. If it is important to have merchandise on retailers' shelves at the time an advertising campaign is launched, adequate time must be allowed to produce the items and get them into distribution pipelines. Production schedules must be adjusted to fit anticipated demand for products, and advertising can be an important factor in changing patterns. For example, ice cream is no longer consumed in the summer months only; advertising has helped to convince the public that ice cream is good to eat all year around.

The price of the product must be realistic and competitive. The advertising department or agency often decides whether price will be stressed as a buying appeal in company advertising. Thus, advertising executives are often in a position to know a great deal about pricing conditions. Their opinions should be weighed along with those of other marketing executives and those of production and accounting officials. Price changes anticipated in the future must be made known to advertising executives far enough in advance to permit inclusion of the changes in advertising copy if price is to be featured.

ADVERTISING AND SALES PROMOTION

Our discussion to this point has dealt with the need for coordination of advertising with three elements of the marketing mix: the product, its price, and distribution channels. Advertising's relationship to personal selling was also examined. We now look at how advertising relates to the other promotional tools, namely, sales promotion and public relations.

The Nature of Sales Promotion

The activity known in marketing circles as sales promotion is an elusive one to define. One writer does so in these words:

Sales promotion, as the conjunction of the two words implies, lies halfway between the two functions of face-to-face selling and the promotion of a product or service through media advertising; it could perhaps be described as the adhesive which bonds the two together. Its main application is in marketing situations where there are intermediaries between the producer and the consumer—agents, distributors, wholesalers, retailers—situations more typical of consumer than industrial marketing.[4]

629
COORDINATION
OF ADVERTISING
WITH OTHER
PROMOTIONAL
AND MARKETING
METHODS

Sales promotion occupies a sort of middle-ground position. Without being either personal selling or advertising, it possesses characteristics of both as well as of publicity. Sales promotion is supplementary to personal selling and advertising; it acts as a coordinative force between the two activities, helping to make each activity more effective. And although sales promotion itself may be carried on continuously, specific sales promotional activities are noncontinuous in operation. Frey distinguishes sales promotion from advertising on the basis of media used by each activity. He observes that advertising messages appear in media owned and controlled primarily by persons other than the advertiser, while "sales promotion . . . 'educates' and arouses the enthusiasm of salesmen, middlemen, consumers, and perhaps others through a variety of materials, tools, and devices *that the company itself controls.*"[5] In other words the basic tools of sales promotion are internally created and distributed, whereas advertising relies upon outside media to disseminate messages created by persons external to the company's personnel. There is, of course, a gray area where the media of advertising and the media of sales promotion touch. A very succinct definition of sales promotion is: "a short term incentive to the trade or consumer to induce purchase of the product."[6]

Rather surprisingly, the importance of sales promotion has only recently received the attention of marketers. There are few, if any, college-level courses on the subject, and the number of textbooks dealing with the activity are few in number. Yet approximately the same amount of money is spent on sales promotion as for advertising. One estimate placed the total sales promotion expenditures in 1973 at $23.5 billion.[7] Specialized sales promotion agencies have been established and appear to be prospering.[8] In recent years the most popular workshops sponsored by the Association of National Advertisers

---

[4] Colin McIver, *Marketing for Managers*, Longmans Group, Ltd., London, 1972, p. 139.
[5] Albert W. Frey, *The Role of Sales Promotion*, Tuck School, Dartmouth University, Hanover, N.H., 1957, p. 4.
[6] *The Tools of Promotion*, Association of National Advertisers, Inc., New York, 1975, p. 1.
[7] Russell D. Bowman, "Merchandising and Promotion Grow Big in Marketing World; Investments Boom," *Advertising Age*, Dec. 30, 1974, p. 21.
[8] Louis J. Haugh, "48 Sales Promotion Agencies," *Advertising Age*, May 26, 1975, p. 40.

630
PLANNING
AND
MANAGING
THE ADVERTISING
CAMPAIGN

involved the complexities of managing the sales promotional activities of advertising firms. Projections place the annual growth of advertising at 5.5 percent, while sales promotion's growth rate is at 9.2 percent.[9] Thus, the topic warrants a rather thorough examination.

Sales promotion is basically a motivating activity. Its efforts are aimed principally at three different groups: company salespeople, intermediaries, and consumers. Our explanation of how advertising is merchandised to salespeople and distributors illustrates one phase of the typical sales promotional program carried on by many manufacturers. The motivation of these two groups so crucial to company success in marketing products should be stimulated, of course, in areas other than the company's advertising program. For instance, company products are promoted through demonstrations, exhibits, training films, sales manuals, catalogs, and a number of other ways. The general principles involved in merchandising advertising apply, nevertheless, to every other sales promotional device directed at company salespersons and intermediaries.

Consumer-directed Sales Promotion

The various kinds of consumer-directed sales promotion are familiar to all of us in our roles as consumers. Our daily newspaper apprises us of special deals being offered on products through cents-off coupons and so forth. Furthermore, magazine ads tell us of premiums we can receive if we buy the featured product, or we learn of prizes to be won in contests sponsored by manufacturers. This section of the chapter examines this important area of sales promotion. These sales promotion activities furnish advertising with an important and interesting adjunct. Consumer-oriented sales promotion and advertising must be closely coordinated if total sales performance is to be improved through their combined efforts. The devices used in reaching consumers are sometimes called either *quick-action stimuli* or *forcing methods*.

National advertising is primarily indirect-action in its appeal. Behind most national advertisements is the goal of implanting favorable attitudes in the minds of consumers so that the advertised brand will be considered when purchases are made. Sellers often wish to supplement indirect approaches with something more positive. Sales promotion devices are designed to move buyers to immediate action.

Luick and Ziegler classify consumer-product sales promotion devices in two groups, according to the manufacturer's objective: (1) to induce consumers to try a new product or (2) to increase the purchase of established products.[10] For example, a sales promotion device may

[9] Bowman, op, cit., p. 21.
[10] John F. Luick and William Lee Ziegler, *Sales Promotion and Modern Merchandising*, McGraw-Hill Book Company, New York, 1968, pp. 37, 65.

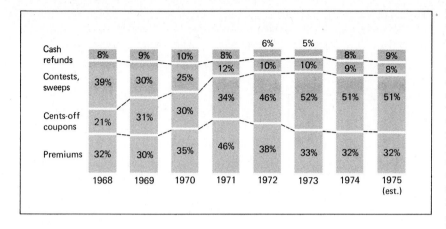

FIGURE 19.8
The changing popularity of consumer promotions is shown in this bar graph, which spans an eight-year period. Included are the major advertised promotions by type as they appeared in magazines and newspaper supplements. [*Reprinted from* Advertising Age *by special permission.*]

persuade the skeptical homemaker to try a new breakfast cereal, whereas mere claims of product superiority would not accomplish the same thing. In this instance, the stimulus is more than likely applied upon the child in the family, who persuades the parent to purchase the brand in order to be able to exchange its boxtop for a desired premium. In a different situation, the homemaker may choose one brand of flour over another, even though there is no outstanding difference among the popular brands, because the manufacturer is currently sponsoring a contest and the first prize is a two-week vacation in Europe for two.

The sales promotion method in either case is relatively short-lived, as all sales promotional activities by definition are. The offerer of the special inducement to consumer action is interested in more than immediate sales, however. If the forcing method is employed to induce sampling of a new product, the underlying hope is that the consumer will like the product and include it on future shopping lists. The goal in the case of an established product is to reinforce a buying pattern favoring the promoted brand. The philosophy supporting this strategy is the belief that consumers are creatures of habit who tend to buy the same brand time after time unless a strong reason for changing brands is presented to them. Sales promotion devices, therefore, have become almost standard in some highly competitive fields, such as cereals, soaps, toiletries, and several other consumer-product categories. It is not uncommon for consumers to switch brand preferences for such products because of quick-buying stimuli placed before them.

The Relationship Between Advertising and Consumer-directed Sales Promotion

Before looking at the most common methods of forcing consumer action, we should establish their relationship to advertising. At the

632

PLANNING
AND
MANAGING
THE ADVERTISING
CAMPAIGN

FIGURE 19.9
This ad, directed at young women, appeared in *Cosmopolitan*, *Glamour*, *Mademoiselle*, *People*, and *Seventeen*. Note the offer of a booklet explaining how to grow avocado trees, a secondary use for the advertised product.

outset it should be realized that the success of any promotional device is dependent upon consumer awareness of its existence. Advertising is the primary method of informing the public of the details of specific sales promotional efforts; therefore, many people think that advertising and forcing methods are the same thing. Others think that they are substitutes for each other. Neither point of view is correct. As a matter of fact, the decision to use forcing methods almost always brings about an increased need for advertising. The stimulation behind the special promotion is usually additional advertising. The reason is simple; the typical advertisement announcing the manufacturer's current sales promotion device has very little to say about the product itself; therefore regular indirect-action advertising is continued or the reputation of the product in the eyes of the consuming public will gradually decline. The primary objective of advertisements featuring quick-action stimuli is to make some sort of special offer, whereas the objective of most regular advertising is to sell the product through a dramatization of its consumer benefits. These objectives are not the same, and their achievement calls for different strategies and copy approaches.

633

COORDINATION
OF ADVERTISING
WITH OTHER
PROMOTIONAL
AND MARKETING
METHODS

Advertising featuring sales promotion devices may strengthen the overall reputation of a brand because increased mention of the product name in mass media generally increases consumer familiarity with the product. On the other hand, this condition precludes the use of some devices—or the use of any sales promotion devices at all—for some prestige products. The aura of quality surrounding a product can be dissipated if the product is sold by means of a something-for-nothing appeal. Quick-action stimuli must be appropriate to the product whose purchase is being encouraged. Too frequent use of such promotions may also tend to cheapen a product in the public mind and result in sales increases that are artificial and followed by lower than normal repeat sales. The typical home medicine cabinet is full of products which were purchased primarily because of some sort of special offer; yet the purchaser has not continued to buy the product.

Sales Promotion Planning and Strategy

Careful planning is as much needed for sales promotion programs that are being formulated as for advertising programs. Objectives should be set and strategies for their attainment developed. The manufacturer seeking to lead consumers into buying action has a bewildering array of promotion devices to consider. This decision is complicated by the patterns of fad and fashion that are common in sales promotion. For instance, contests requiring participants to write jingles or statements "in 25 words or less" were extremely popular at one time. This approach is seldom seen today. On the other hand, coupon offers and rebates were in vogue during the 1974–1975 recession. The choice

634

PLANNING
AND
MANAGING
THE ADVERTISING
CAMPAIGN

should be in tune with consumer preferences of the moment. To illustrate this problem of choice the following chart of promotional devices in actual use by national marketers during the fall of 1975 is provided:[11]

Premiums		52.3%
Self-liquidators[12]	17.8%	
Free offers	14.0%	
Recipe books	20.5%	
Cents-off coupons		31.8%
Refund offers		4.7%
Prize offers		11.2%
Sweepstakes	9.3%	
Contests, skill	1.9%	

The promotion must be different enough to attract consumer attention, yet be in tune with current promotional trends. The primary goal in promotion is to find a fresh approach which is not too unusual; to put a fresh twist on a time-tested method. Only a few of the thousands of different promotions launched annually are overwhelmingly successful. Many fail completely.

MAJOR CONSUMER-DIRECTED SALES PROMOTION ALTERNATIVES

The basic nature, advantages and disadvantages, and possible uses of the major alternatives available to the sales promotion decision maker are now given. When new products are being introduced, three major kinds of sales promotion may be used: (1) consumer sampling, (2) couponing, and (3) money-refund offers. On the other hand, when the objective is to increase the use of established products, the major alternatives are (1) price-off promotions, (2) premiums, and (3) consumer contests and sweepstakes.[13] The core group of sales promotion devices consists of four kinds of promotion: deals, coupons, premiums, and contests; each type is now examined.

Deals

There are basically two different kinds of special offer: the money refund for products in the introductory stage and the price-off promo-

[11] *The Promotional Marketing News Bulletin*, a D. L. Blair publication, August/September 1975.
[12] A self-liquidator is a premium for which the consumer pays a certain amount of money, usually the actual cost of the item to the firm offering the premium.
[13] Luick and Ziegler, loc. cit.

tion for established products. The term "deal" is commonly used to describe these promotional devices which are promotions essentially price-oriented in appeal. Outright price reduction is avoided, as the price is reduced for a limited time and that fact is made clear to the consumer. When the promotion is over, the consumer should be willing to pay the regular price for the item. The deal promotion can be implemented in two different ways, through (1) special prices and sales and (2) combination offers.

635

COORDINATION
OF ADVERTISING
WITH OTHER
PROMOTIONAL
AND MARKETING
METHODS

Special Price Offers The special price is sometimes used to introduce a new product, but there is a built-in danger in this approach. Consumers may come to think of the special price as the regular charge for the item. Raising the price later then becomes difficult. This hazard is reduced by the money-refund offer. The customer is required to furnish proof of purchase to the manufacturer in order to receive the price reduction; for instance, the package label must be mailed in to the company, which then sends the stipulated amount of money to the buyer. The short-run nature of the offer must be stressed, and the consumer must be furnished a reasonable explanation why the price is temporarily reduced.

Special offers by manufacturers are frequently expressed in terms of "cents-off" specials. Such cents-off promotions have been popular in supermarkets in recent years and reached maximum use during the recession of the mid-1970s. The level of price reduction is highly important in the success of a particular promotion of this type. If brand share is to be influenced at all, the reduction should be at least in the 11 to 12 percent range. Moreover, the advantage is only for a short time. Of course, the stimulation of immediate sales is an important motivating factor, but the establishment of habit patterns involving the featured brand is still in the strategic background. Most of that task, however, must remain in the hands of advertising and quality of the product itself. The deal merely gets the consumer to try the product one time.

The special price is not used only for low-priced items, as many durable consumer products are offered in this manner. A classic example was the "rebate" offers made by automobile makers in 1975. Faced with huge inventories of unsold new cars, and a new model year approaching, the manufacturers offered rebates ranging from $200 to $400 if consumers would buy a car. Chrysler, who started the rebate trend, dubbed its $10 million advertising and rebate promotion a "Car Clearance Carnival." The promotion is an example of the special offer which had believability.

Too frequent use of the special price, or the special sales event, may create skepticism in the minds of consumers. Special prices and sales are used in industrial as well as consumer selling. Furthermore, "trade deals" are extensively employed to get intermediaries to stock

636

PLANNING
AND
MANAGING
THE ADVERTISING
CAMPAIGN

Good Sense.   **Good Taste.**

FIGURE 19.10
This coupon offer is distributed in a magazine advertisement. The consumer clips the coupon and receives 10 cents off at the store when the product is purchased.

You're going to love Kellogg's Product 19. The sensible side of you gets 100% of the U.S. Recommended Daily Allowance for ten vitamins and iron. And the other side of you gets that good, crunchy Kellogg's taste. Kellogg's® Product 19® cereal. For the two of you.

The Common Sense Cereal.

particular brands. This technique is a reduced price given to the retailer instead of the ultimate consumer. The retailer then has the option to pass along the savings to the customer or to retain it as additional profit.

Combination Offers   A combination offer brings two or more products together at a price less than consumers would have to pay if the items were purchased separately. For example, toothpaste manufacturers may combine their brand of dentifrice with a toothbrush, and razor makers offer a razor along with blades and shaving foam. The purchaser pays slightly more for the combination than for the host item alone, if the deal promotion is well designed. These two examples illustrate an important principle of creating good combination offers; the items in a combination offer should be interrelated in consumer use. The combination offer may be used to introduce new products, and the unknown item is then tied to a well-established product. The consumer who is planning to buy the old product is persuaded to pay a little bit more—or maybe no more—to get an additional new product. "What have I got to lose?" is the prevailing attitude, and the consumer is "forced" into trying the new product.

Combination offers are also useful in switching brand loyalties in highly competitive fields. Obviously the retailer's support is necessary to the success of a consumer deal; otherwise consumers will not be able to find the featured products.

637
COORDINATION
OF ADVERTISING
WITH OTHER
PROMOTIONAL
AND MARKETING
METHODS

Coupon Offers

The coupon is an extension or variation of the consumer deal strategy, serving to implement cents-off deals. Each coupon offers a price reduction on a specific item in the manufacturer's product line. When these coupons are presented at the grocery store at the time of purchase of the featured item, the amount specified on the face of the coupon is deducted from the regular price.

The couponing technique has been experiencing a great deal of popularity in recent years. In 1970, 16.4 billion coupons were distributed to consumers by manufacturers, but in 1975 the number had more than doubled to 35.7 billion[14] with nearly 60 percent of all households using coupons as part of their regular buying behavior.

The advantage of coupons over special prices is that the product is never marked at a price lower than the established one. Psychologically the coupon carries the ideas of urgency and temporariness better than special prices. The coupon offer is more frequently used to stimulate the sales of established products than to help introduce new products. Coupons have also been described as "tie-breakers in an era of parity products."[15] The coupon sometimes is the only advantage when discriminating between products.

One important management problem is choosing what method of distribution to use in getting the coupons to potential users. Five methods available are (1) by direct mail, (2) by door-to-door placement,

[14] *The Nielsen Researcher*, no. 1, 1976, p. 3.
[15] *Advertising Age*, Aug. 12, 1974, p. 36.

638

PLANNING
AND
MANAGING
THE ADVERTISING
CAMPAIGN

(3) through newspaper advertisements, (4) through magazine and newspaper supplement advertisements, and (5) in or on package locations. Currently popular is the so-called in-ad coupon technique used by most major packaged-goods manufacturers. Through a cooperative agreement with food and drug retailers, the manufacturer's product is featured through a coupon offer in the retailer's advertisement.

Another success story has been the "freestanding insert," which has been described for the uninitiated as "that part of the Sunday paper that falls either on the floor or on your lap when you open the paper."[16] This method of delivery results in high redemption rates, and like the in-ad technique, appears in a medium that the retail trade regards highly, the newspaper, and thus has high acceptance by retailers. Each of the methods has its own advantages and limitations; therefore the manufacturer using coupons needs to become knowledgeable in the various distribution alternatives.

Retailer cooperation is essential if coupon redemption is done in the store. One of the controversial points in the manufacturer-retailer relationship arises over this process. Retailers claim that redeeming coupons slows up the sales transaction procedure without providing a compensating advantage. Manufacturers answer that such offers speed the rate of stock turnover; retailers counter than coupon offers merely cause consumers to switch brands without any increase in total sales in the product category. Retailers do receive a nominal payment of 5 cents each for redeeming and handling coupons for the manufacturer. The manufacturer often makes arrangements with coupon redemption specialists such as A. C. Nielsen to handle the flow of coupons from retailers. These services may be more expensive, but they do relieve the advertiser of many headaches.

A troublesome abuse is misredemption. Some retailers give the customer credit for the amount of the coupon's face value even though the product was not in fact purchased. The threat of criminal prosecution for fraud is one way of controlling this abuse. Once the Universal Product Code becomes an operating fact in retail-store operations, it will be easy to accommodate proper redemption. The coupon will carry the same marking as the product being offered at "cents-off," and the computer will automatically make the proper deduction from the register total.

Premiums

Premiums, the basis of an industry amounting to $4.5 billion annually, are often confused with advertising specialties. In most cases both advertising specialties and premiums are low in monetary value. The

---

[16] David L. Ryan, "Couponing," in *The Tools of Promotion*, op. cit., p. 1.

639
COORDINATION
OF ADVERTISING
WITH OTHER
PROMOTIONAL
AND MARKETING
METHODS

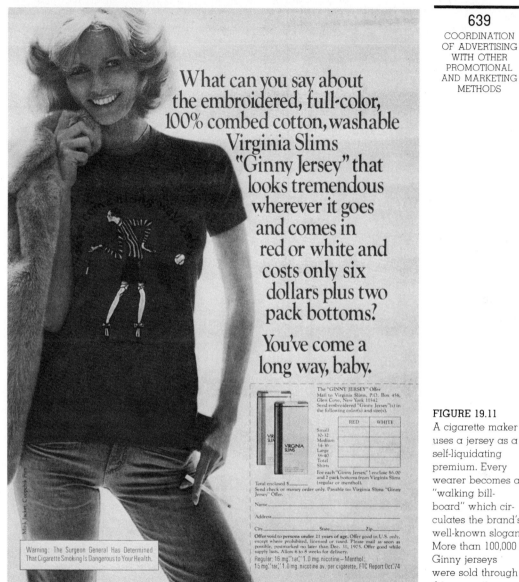

FIGURE 19.11
A cigarette maker uses a jersey as a self-liquidating premium. Every wearer becomes a "walking billboard" which circulates the brand's well-known slogan. More than 100,000 Ginny jerseys were sold through this promotion.

specialty item, however, is an advertising medium in itself with the name of the giver imprinted on the item. Premiums, on the other hand, do not carry such marks of giver identification. The fundamental distinction between these two sales promotional devices is that the advertising specialty is given in anticipation of future business, while the premium is tied to current sales. If there is no sale, no premium is given.

640

PLANNING
AND
MANAGING
THE ADVERTISING
CAMPAIGN

The premium is offered to the consumer as a reason for buying a particular product. If he or she buys the item, the premium comes as a gift. Thus, cereal manufacturers give toys in exchange for box tops, and soap manufacturers give household aids for soap wrappers. Cosmetic manufacturers offer a sample package or a related gift item, such as a scarf or handbag, when a purchase of a certain amount, say $5, is made. The premium and the product sponsoring it are not usually interrelated in use, as in the case of the combination offer. The premium is chosen for its uniqueness or desirability to the person who might want the item but does not wish to spend money for its purchase. Premium offers are based on the assumption that most people have the "something-for-nothing" motivation in their personality makeup.

Often a more attractive premium can be featured through the use of the self-liquidating technique. The consumer sends not only proof of purchase but a specified amount of money. The amount often approximates the cost of the premium to the manufacturer who buys in large quantities, and the offer liquidates itself as consumer money comes in. The buyer does not suffer, for the cost is usually less than the cost for the item in local stores. The manufacturer still must pay for the promotion and handling of the offer. The average value of self-liquidators has been increasing in recent times, and some of the featured items are relatively expensive. For instance, in 1973 Kool Cigarettes redeemed over 20,000 sailboats at $88.00 plus 10 empty packages as proof of purchase.[17]

Distribution of the premiums poses a managerial challenge. Common methods of distribution include mailings, retailers, placement in the package, and attachments to the package. When the request comes to the manufacturer through the mails, a system for premium fulfillment must be established to ensure that consumers obtain the premium within a reasonable time after sending in for it; otherwise dissatisfaction with the company results. Special fulfillment houses provide this kind of service for many manufacturers.

The promotional possibilities inherent in premium offers are dramatized by the self-liquidating offers made by Texaco, Inc., in the 1960s. For many years a toy fire engine was featured at $3.98. More than 1 million units were distributed annually, and estimates placed the number of new customers generated by the offer at 150,000 per year. How a premium offer may outperform a price reduction is shown in this statement Herman W. Lay, chairman of the board, Pepsico, Inc., made when he was president of the Frito-Lay Company, manufacturers of potato chips and other snack foods:

> You can't give a customer a price reduction of less than 10¢ to 15¢ and have it mean anything. But we have been highly successful in forcing

[17] Robert L. Uebele, "Premiums," in ibid., p. 9.

sales of our Corn Fritos and Potato Chips by using premiums that cost six tenths of a cent on the average. We're using recipe booklets, flower packets, plastic roses and orchids, and miniature plastic dinosaurs, particularly in our Twin-Paks. We're violently opposed to off-price promotions, but these premiums do an outstanding job for us.[18]

641
COORDINATION
OF ADVERTISING
WITH OTHER
PROMOTIONAL
AND MARKETING
METHODS

In 1974 Coca-Cola USA distributed 8,400,000 old-fashioned Coke glasses to consumers sending in bottle cap liners, and in 1975 a similar offer was made with distribution made in retail stores.

Premiums are also used to stimulate industrial and trade buying, although the practice causes problems when the gift is viewed as a form of commercial bribery, or "payola." In the field of sales management gift incentives are a very popular form of motivation, but the given item actually is not a premium in the sense that we are using the term.

Trading Stamps

Trading stamps are a mechanism for obtaining customer loyalty for retailers rather than quick-action stimuli designed to motivate rapid sales for the manufacturer's brand. The trading stamp is proof that the holder spent a small amount of money, usually 10 cents, at a store sponsoring a particular stamp plan. The stamps, which are collected by 37 million American households, are accumulated until a sufficient quantity is available to exchange for merchandise of considerable monetary value.

Although the primary purpose of trading stamp plans is to win store loyalty for the sponsoring retailer, many retailers violate the basic principles underlying this form of sales promotion. Trading stamps must be promoted aggressively; the retailer cannot distribute stamps grudgingly to customers. Every customer should be encouraged to save the retailer's featured stamp if customer loyalty is to be built by use of the device.

The energy crisis of the 1970s brought hard times to the trading stamp industry. Between May 1973 and mid-February 1974 Sperry and Hutchinson Company, whose Green Stamps dominate the field, lost 90 percent of its business with service stations.[19] Many food retailers stopped using the promotional device as consumers became extremely price-conscious, and "discount pricing" was substituted for trading stamps. As with all promotional tools, trading stamps experience periods of popularity and then seem to go into an eclipse only to return again when circumstances warrant a different strategy. If gasoline retailing once again becomes more competitive, stamps will likely

---

[18] *Sales Management*, Aug. 7, 1964, p. 67.
[19] *Annual Report, 1974*, The Sperry and Hutchinson Company, p. 7.

642

PLANNING
AND
MANAGING
THE ADVERTISING
CAMPAIGN

return to the pump islands. In the meantime selected retailers might well benefit from retaining the trading stamp as a means of reaching those consumers who remain loyal to the means of getting merchandise without a direct outlay of cash.

Contests

There are two kinds of contests: those of skill and those of chance.

Contests of Skill   When skill is involved in the contest, the participating consumer is asked to do something which is judged, and prizes are awarded for superior performances. Devising a new brand name, writing an essay, composing a limerick, and thinking up a slogan about the sponsor's product are examples of the kind of creative effort required.

Another approach is to require the consumer to use the manufacturer's product in its normal way and have the end product judged. The Pillsbury Bake-Off Contest is a classic example of this kind of skill

FIGURE 19.12
The Pillsbury Flour Bake-Off is probably the most successful skill-type contest available to consumers.

contest. The Pillsbury promotion commenced in 1949, when after a six-months promotional program the 100 winners from 250,000 women who had submitted favorite recipes were flown to New York City where they cooked their recipes in the ballroom of the Waldorf-Astoria Hotel. Each succeeding year the Bake-Off has continued to garner large numbers of entries, who must purchase flour to experiment with their concoctions. Furthermore, the contest is advertised heavily and, more importantly, receives large amounts of free publicity in the family sections of the nation's newspapers. In spite of this success story, skill contests are comparatively rare. When being developed, care must be exercised to make certain that typical consumers can perceive themselves as possible winners. Highly complicated rules convey the feeling that the average consumer has little chance of winning, and so a "Why enter?" attitude develops. It is also common knowledge that "professional" contest entrants do win many of the prizes in contests of skill.

Sweepstakes   When the chance, or sweepstakes, approach is employed, the consumer's name is pooled with the names of all entrants. The winner is selected at random; therefore all entrants have an equal chance of winning. Obviously, the number of people likely to enter is much higher than in the case of contests of skill. One sweepstakes contest operated by Lever Brothers pulled over 10.5 million entries, and in 1968 more than 6.8 million consumers won prizes in sweepstakes contests. The recession year of 1975 saw sweepstakes contests still in use. For instance, Pepsi-Cola offered 65,000 prizes ranging from $1 to $50 worth of groceries, and Eveready batteries offered "a trip to the Super Bowl and a $10,000 trip to the supermarket (of your choice)."[20] The prizes had a practical flavor to them. The sweepstakes event offers broad merchandising opportunities for the product, and it gets a high level of consumer involvement. The device is ideal for the mass marketer who wishes to reach women ages twenty-five to forty-five with one to three children since three-quarters of all participants in sweepstakes contests are from this demographic group.[21]

Each entry in the typical contest requires the purchase of one unit of the sponsor's product, and a contest in which every entrant has an equal chance to win carries considerable attraction when the top prizes are expensive. One problem in the contest of chance is that it must be designed to be legal. Lotteries are often outlawed as a form of gambling. Illegal lotteries involve the payment of money—"consideration" in legal jargon—by participants. As a general rule, the purchase of merchandise is not ruled to be sufficient consideration to classify the contest as a lottery. Currently, contestants are offered an

643
COORDINATION
OF ADVERTISING
WITH OTHER
PROMOTIONAL
AND MARKETING
METHODS

[20] *Advertising Age*, Jan. 5, 1976, p. 34.
[21] *The Promotional Marketing News Bulletin*, a D. L. Blair publication, July/August 1974.

644

PLANNING
AND
MANAGING
THE ADVERTISING
CAMPAIGN

opportunity to do something different than purchase the product—to draw a facsimile of the label or print the product name, for instance—and still qualify as an entrant.

The sweepstakes contest, particularly the so-called game variety, went through difficult times in the late 1960s, and the promotional device went out of favor. Guidelines were established by the FTC

645
COORDINATION
OF ADVERTISING
WITH OTHER
PROMOTIONAL
AND MARKETING
METHODS

Free Food for Life!

Win Dial's "Free Food for Life" Sweepstakes.

111 cash prizes that could pay your food bills for a week— for a year—even for life!

Imagine having enough money to pay all your food bills for life! That's the **Grand Prize** in Dial's "Free Food for Life" Sweepstakes . . . $200 food money sent to you every month—for life! **10 Second Prize** winners will receive $50 food money every week for an entire year. **100 Third Prizes** of $50 food money will also be given away. 111 prizes in all!

Thanks to the Dial family of fine products—Dial Soap, Dial Anti-Perspirant and Dial Shampoo— you could be one of the 111 "Free Food for Life" winners. All prizes will be awarded. Just follow these easy rules:

1. On an entry form or on any piece of paper, print your name, address, and zip code. Mail your entry to DIAL'S "FREE FOOD FOR LIFE" Sweepstakes, P.O. Box 9120, Kankakee, Illinois 60901.
2. Each entry must be accompanied by two complete wrappers from any size Dial Soap or write the code number from the bottom of any size Dial Anti-Perspirant, Dial Deodorant can or any size Dial Shampoo or the word "DIAL" printed on a plain piece of paper. Residents of the State of Washington should disregard rule #2.
3. All entrants must be at least 18 years of age or older to be eligible to win.
4. Submit as many entries as you wish, but mail each entry separately. Entries must be received on or before July 5, 1974. Your chances of winning depend on the number of times you enter and the total number of entries received.
5. One GRAND PRIZE winner will receive a life annuity issued by the Prudential Insurance Company of America guaranteeing such GRAND PRIZE winner $200 per month for the rest of his/her life. The initial payment shall begin the 15th of the month following determination of the winner. GRAND PRIZE winner may elect an alternate prize of $20,000 cash. Ten SECOND PRIZE winners will each receive the equivalent of $50 per week for one year which shall be paid in one payment of $2,600 the 15th of the month following determination of winners. 100 THIRD PRIZE winners will each receive a $50 check.
6. All prizes will be awarded. Winners will be determined by random drawing by an independent judging agency whose decisions are final. Winners will be notified by mail by August 15, 1974. Only one prize per family. Prizes are non-transferable.
7. Winners will be liable for any federal, state or local taxes.
8. Contest open to all U.S.A. residents including Florida and Puerto Rico, except employees and their immediate families of the Greyhound Corporation, Armour-Dial, Inc. and their subsidiaries and affiliated companies, their advertising agencies, the independent judging agency, and Promotional Service Center. Winners may be required to furnish proof of eligibility. Offer void in Missouri, Alaska and Idaho and where prohibited by law.
9. NO PURCHASE REQUIRED.

Mail to: **Dial's "Free Food for Life" Sweepstakes.**
P.O. Box 9120
Kankakee, Illinois 60901

Name_____

Address_____

City_____

State_____Zip Code_____

FIGURE 19.13
This two-page sweepstakes promotion ran at the height of the consumer's concern over inflation and high food prices in 1974. [*Armour-Deal Inc.*]

which overcame the major criticism of the contests as they were being conducted. In many instances not all the prizes were distributed, as the appropriate numbers were not picked; now all prizes must be awarded. In the mid-1960s more than 1,000 sweepstakes were conducted annually. With the legal problems clarified, it appears that sweepstakes are in the midst of a revival.

646

PLANNING
AND
MANAGING
THE ADVERTISING
CAMPAIGN

The sponsor of a contest must decide whether to emphasize a few fabulous prizes or a large number. Some contests include both approaches, and in some everyone is a winner. Every contest should be designed to capture the imagination of the audience. Topical themes, such as baseball, football, or politics, in their respective seasons, may be used to accomplish this goal. Deciding what category of prize—money, travel, or merchandise—has highest current appeal is an intriguing and perplexing question.

Appropriateness of the contest and of its prizes to the product is an important consideration. For some products the contest approach may cheapen the brand image. Generally speaking, contests are used in the promotion of frequently purchased merchandise, because the contest offer must coincide with demand for the generic product if many consumers are going to be moved to action by the forcing method.

As with other promotional methods, the success of a contest depends to a large degree upon how well consumers are informed of its existence. Advertising can do a great deal to engender public interest in a consumer contest. A plus factor in favor of the contest is that this form of promotional effort often contains suitable material for publicity campaigns, and thereby increases the sponsor's return from the contest.

Product Sampling

"A good product promotes itself" is a recognized marketing axiom, and distributing a small taste of the product to potential customers is an important way of promoting a product. Many sellers feel that sampling is the best way to promote their products. Although sampling does not require the aggressive promotion that other devices need, sampling programs should be coordinated with advertising programs for maximum effectiveness. If both sampling and advertising are in the promotional mix, consumers should receive samples shortly after exposure to advertising messages about the product's benefits. The combination is somewhat like the one-two punch in boxing. Sampling, however, is costly; to the expense of the give-away item itself must be added those incurred in getting the sample to the consumer.

The physical distribution of the sample is an important operational problem when this technique is employed. When sampling is defined as including "any method possible to get an actual product into the consumer's hands," the following methods are alternatives:[22]

1 Mail

2 House-to-house delivery

[22] Roy Harris, "Sampling," in *The Tools of Promotion*, op. cit., p. 1.

3   Point-of-purchase areas in stores

4   Newspaper or magazine offer

5   Offer included in another product

6   Refund offer

7   Cents-off coupon

647

COORDINATION
OF ADVERTISING
WITH OTHER
PROMOTIONAL
AND MARKETING
METHODS

Another perplexing decision concerns the size of the sample. Should it be trial size or actual size? Enough of the product must be provided to let the consumer give it a satisfactory use; yet the supply should not be so large that the consumer will be kept out of the market for a long period of time.

Where the size given away is the size most consumers normally purchase, retailers often object to the sampling program because they lose sales while the sample is being used. For instance, a major coffee roaster decided to send 1-pound cans of the firm's brand to 1 million homes in a certain geographical section of the United States. As far as retail stores in the area were concerned, coffee sales declined 1 million pounds. Of course, consumers who were given samples may have shifted their brand preference, but the total demand for coffee was not increased. Retailers naturally prefer promotional methods which bring sales volume to their outlets, as consumer deals do.

Mass sampling involves its own peculiar form of promotional waste. It is estimated that 20 percent of all products given away as samples are wasted. Some recipients are not interested in the product, such as the nonsmoker who gets a sample packet of cigarettes. Or the receiver may already be a user of the item. Specialized firms are available to help with the planning and execution of sampling programs and claim their efforts reduce these hazards. The program's effectiveness is measured in terms of how many recipients bought the product again, for building sales is the purpose of sampling, as it is for all forms of sales promotion.

ADVERTISING AND PUBLIC RELATIONS

One coordinative area remains to be analyzed, that of advertising and public relations. We are not speaking here of the need to coordinate product advertising and public relations, or corporate, advertising although it is obvious that this task is an integral part of the internal coordination to be done within every advertising program. At this juncture we are interested in external coordination between advertising, regardless of kind, and the business management function known as public relations.

Public relations, like sales promotion, means different things to different people. One useful definition reads as follows:

Money can't buy this kind of advertising:

Esquire
THE MAGAZINE FOR MEN AUGUST 1975

VW's new Rabbit is significant because it is a complete departure for Volkswagen, and also because it is the specific type of car that Detroit will be building in the 1980's.

The statistics speak for themselves: accommodation for four, a seventy-horsepower engine, fuel consumption of thirty-eight mpg and a weight of under two thousand pounds.

What they came up with was

Volkswagen is evidently confident in its new model, because it is covered by the VW Owner's Security Blanket, which is as good as you can get.

Personally, I think that VW's Rabbit is one very good idea ahead of its time.

Popular Mechanics
APRIL 1975

The most important new import for 1975 is the VW Rabbit. The 1800-pound Rabbit is a mechanical masterpiece. It gets up to 60 mph in about 12 seconds—giving it the edge on some V8 subcompacts. Its hatchback design provides 24.7 cubic feet of luggage capacity with the rear seat folded. VW got the greatest possible amount of usable interior space into the smallest possible outer shell—and an exterior with some style.

"a car that doesn't have an ounce of fat, one which provides excellent operating economy, as well as performance and value."

VW's note: The 1976 EPA estimates for the standard shift model are 39 mpg on the highway, 25 mpg in the city. Your actual mileage may vary, depending on the type of driving you do, your driving habits, your car's condition and optional equipment.

Popular Science
JUNE 1975

A totally new kind of small car. Volkswagen's Rabbit, may make things difficult for U.S. small-car makers in the coming months.

Its speed through the maneuvering courses matched or exceeded the best times of the other

test cars, and the feeling of control is ever present, even at high speed and in extreme turning tests.

Economy means light weight, small engines. VW has it now. The others have a way to go.

ROAD & TRACK
MAY 1975

The winner, and not by a hare (sorry, couldn't resist). This car does it all: it's small, light, roomy and fast, with nimble and responsive steering, ride and handling. A modern and sophisticated car with a handsome Giugiaro-designed hatchback body, the Rabbit offers one of the most space-saving mechanical layouts we've seen

yet: front-wheel drive, transverse engine and a unique, independent rear suspension featuring an integral anti-roll bar and using so little space it's remarkable.

Seats are firm in the German manner and you sit high, viewing the world through an expansive greenhouse.

The Rabbit has a solid feel and an ultramodern look to it. Best of all it is almost sinfully enjoyable to drive.

ROAD TEST
JULY 1975

The Volkswagen Rabbit should be recognized as a true worldcar. it would be as at home commuting in Los Angeles, on a ski trip in the Alps, or chasing kangaroos across Australia. It is the finest example to date of a totally integrated passenger car, useful anywhere in the world and is qualified as no other imported car of 1975 for the Road Test Engineering Award.

CAR and DRIVER
APRIL 1975

Whole populations of drivers will live for years with this car, strongly impressed by its generally nimble disposition and its sensitive feel of the road through the steering wheel and

brake pedal. It slips through city traffic like a bicycle and thrives on the parking-space it remains most cars pass by. You can stuff enough groceries for a football team through the

rear hatch while the back seat folds and pivots forward out of the way. The only thing you'll need a trailer for is objects too heavy to boost across the high lift-over.

FIGURE 19.14
Here an advertiser makes an unusual use of favorable publicity about the product.

Public relations is that specific operating philosophy by which management sets up policies designed to serve both in the company's and the public's interest. It is, further, the *basis* of communication techniques which management employs to achieve good relations with the public.[23]

649
COORDINATION
OF ADVERTISING
WITH OTHER
PROMOTIONAL
AND MARKETING
METHODS

This definition clearly establishes public relations as a component of the promotional mix, along with advertising, personal selling, and sales promotion. A look at the primary function of each activity will help explain their interrelationship. Although advertising is widely used for such public interest objectives as traffic safety and community fund raising, within a marketing system advertising is basically concerned—in one way or another—with the distribution of products. So are personal selling and sales promotion. On the other hand, public relations is concerned with ideas which may or may not include products. The relationship is sometimes explained by comparing the common marketing goal which seeks to increase the seller's "share of the market" with the public relations goal of obtaining a larger "share of the mind" of the public.

We distinguished between advertising and publicity in the first chapter of this book. Publicity is information placed in media because of its newsworthiness. The company benefiting therefrom does not pay for its appearance, nor is the company usually identified as the source. Advertising, on the other hand, appears in the same media, but the sponsor is identified and pays for the privilege of telling the story in one's own words. Not only do publicity and advertising appear in the same media, but each has the same long-range objective—to promote the company and its products. The need for coordination is, therefore, clear-cut. Publicity releases about company products, for instance, must contain product claims which are compatible with similar claims made in company advertising, and vice versa. Any inconsistencies will be obvious to the discerning prospect or customer.

By the same token, advertising messages should be consistent with the company image sought by the public relations program in its entirety. The company cannot wear two different hats when appearing in public; every advertisement should make a contribution to the public relations goals of the company.

SUMMARY

Coordination of activities is an essential business function. The goal is to achieve maximum efficiency in business operations. Advertising activities are no exception; they must be coordinated both internally and externally if maximum returns are to be derived from the use of advertising. Internal

[23] Charles S. Steinberg, *The Mass Communicators: Public Relations, Public Opinion, and Mass Media*, Harper & Row, Publishers, Incorporated, New York, 1948, p. 198.

650

PLANNING
AND
MANAGING
THE ADVERTISING
CAMPAIGN

coordination of advertising involves meshing the various parts of the advertising program together into a smoothly functioning system. Timing and scheduling are at the heart of this kind of coordination.

External coordination of advertising is accomplished at two levels. It must be coordinated with other elements that compose the balance of the promotional mix, and it must be coordinated with the product and distribution subsystems to produce an efficient, integrated marketing system. Advertising is an effective selling tool for the manufacturer's sales force and for the distributive organization. Selling time can be reduced if customers have been made aware of the product and its benefits through advertising. This is true whether the customers are consumers, industrial buyers, or intermediaries. Furthermore, consumer advertising can persuade retailers to stock and display the manufacturer's products, and it is important for the manufacturer to get active promotional support from intermediaries. Cooperative advertising programs have been developed to encourage such dealer support. The advertising programs of many manufacturers are aggressively sold to their own salesforce and to intermediaries through a process called merchandising the advertising. The objective is to see that the advertising program is understood and used as a sales tool by both groups.

Advertising must be coordinated with sales promotion, public relations, and publicity, as well as with personal selling. It is particularly important to see that the use of such quick-action promotional devices as premiums, deals, coupons, and contests is properly related to the advertising which is necessary to inform both intermediaries and customers of the special offer.

Public relations, in a broad sense, involves any activity which may affect the attitudes of a number of different "publics" about the company. These publics include not only customers for the company's products, but also employees, suppliers, stockholders, legislators, and residents of the communities where the company has production or distribution facilities. Publicity is the activity most closely associated with public relations. Inasmuch as the underlying purpose of publicity and advertising is the same—to inform the public of the company and its products—the information that both present should jibe. Of course, advertising should be coordinated with the overall public relations program for the same reason.

QUESTIONS FOR DISCUSSION

1 How does a field salesperson working for a manufacturer of a consumer product use consumer-directed advertising from the company to make the sales job easier? Would the salesperson representing an industrial-goods manufacturer use advertising in the same way?

2 Explain the role of advertising in the distribution of goods purchased through the self-service principle.

3 Does advertising play a part in the promotion of goods in which retail selling is the key factor in the consumer's decision? How?

4 Distinguish clearly between the two forms of cooperative advertising, and explain when each form is used.

5 How and to whom is advertising "merchandised?" Explain.

6 What are the key differences between the respective roles of advertising and sales promotion? Does the use of one preclude the employment of the other? Explain.

7 Psychologically, why did the automobile industry decide to offer rebates in 1975 instead of just reducing the price? How would you classify this type of promotion?

8 Why do the various forms of consumer-directed sales promotion come into popularity and then fade from the scene for awhile? What forms seem to be most popular today?

9 Why is product sampling viewed as the "best" kind of promotion? What are the problems in implementing such a program?

10 When is an emphasis on public relations preferable to one based on advertising? Are the two promotional techniques mutually exclusive in day-to-day use? Explain.

FOR FURTHER REFERENCE

Canfield, Bertrand R., and H. Frazier Moore: *Public Relations: Principles Cases, and Problems*, 6th ed., Richard D. Irwin, Inc., Homewood, Ill., 1973.

Crimmins, Edward C.: *A Management Guide to Cooperative Advertising*, Association of National Advertisers, Inc., New York, 1970.

Cutlip, Scott M., and Allen H. Center: *Effective Public Relations*, 4th ed., Prentice-Hall, Inc., Englewood Cliffs, N.J., 1971.

Engel, James F., Hugh G. Wales, and Martin R. Warshaw: *Promotional Strategy*, 3d ed., Richard D. Irwin, Inc., Homewood, Ill. 1975.

Fox, Harold W.: *The Economics of Trading Stamps*, Public Affairs Press, Washington, 1968.

Hurwood, David L., and Earl L. Bailey: *Advertising, Sales Promotion and Public Relations—Organizational Alternatives*, The National Industrial Conference Board, Inc., New York, 1968.

Levy, Sidney J.: *Promotional Behavior*, Scott, Foresman and Company, Glenview, Ill., 1971.

Luick, John F., and William Lee Ziegler: *Sales Promotion and Modern Merchandising*, McGraw-Hill Book Company, New York, 1968.

Marquis, Harold H.: *The Changing Corporate Image*, American Management Association, Inc., New York, 1970.

Mertes, John E.: *Corporate Communications: The Promotional View*, Bureau for Business and Economic Research, University of Oklahoma, Norman, 1972.

Steinberg, Charles S., *The Creation of Consent: Public Relations in Practice*, Hastings House, New York, 1975.

Riso, Ovid (ed.): *Sales Promotion Handbook*, 6th ed., The Dartnell Corporation, Chicago, 1973.

Wolfe, Harry D., and Dik W. Twedt: *Essentials of the Promotional Mix*, Appleton Century Crofts, New York, 1970.

CHAPTER 20
THE LEGAL FRAMEWORK OF ADVERTISING

Unethical behavior can be a problem in the field of advertising as well as in any business or profession. There are dishonest men and women in all walks of life. Abuses in advertising, however, can have unfortunate effects on consumers, ranging from misspent money on an item that did not live up to its expectations to hazardous accidents resulting from the misrepresentation of faulty goods. To protect consumers against misleading or fraudulent advertising, three institutions police advertising: (1) governmental agencies acting to enforce laws against offenders, (2) industry associations that impose self-regulation upon their members, and (3) advertisers themselves, through enlightened self-interest and a sense of social responsibility.

When advertising is viewed as a communication process, rather than as a marketing technique, this third form of protection is paramount. Not only is advertising self-publicizing, but unlike a personal sales appeal or a telephone solicitation, the content of the message is a matter of public record. Consumers and competitors alike are in a better position, therefore, to expose dishonest advertising. As most advertisers thrive on repeat business for survival, truthful advertising, which leads to consumer satisfaction, is good strategy; whereas false or misleading ads soon bring customer dissatisfaction and indignation, and garnering loyal customers is difficult, if not impossible.

A report of the Sub-Council on Advertising and Promotion of the National Business Council for Consumer Affairs, issued in 1972, supports this philosophy. Five recommendations were made to chief executives of corporations to help them implement a desire that the advertising and promotion practices of their corporations reflect the beliefs and principles of the corporation as articulated by its top management:[1]

1 The chief executive officer of the corporation should be involved in the development of the statements of advertising policy and procedures.

2 The statements should be reduced to writing.

3 The statements should be disseminated to all individuals involved in the organization's advertising and promotion functions.

4 The statements should be made available to interested individuals outside of the organization.

5 The statements should be subject to continuing review and revision.

Although this approach may appear idealistic, the company which strives to follow it will likely find itself with fewer legal entangle-

---

[1] Robert J. Keith, Chairman, *Corporate Policies and Procedures on Advertising & Promotion*, Report of the Sub-Council on Advertising & National Business Council for Consumer Affairs, Washington, 1972, pp. 11–13.

654

PLANNING
AND
MANAGING
THE ADVERTISING
CAMPAIGN

ments such as are discussed later in this chapter. As in many other professions, moreover, advertising possesses an organization to promote self-regulation and to establish professional standards for the industry.

LEGAL RESTRICTIONS ON ADVERTISING

Legal restrictions are one of the uncontrollable variables facing every advertiser as well as most businesspeople. The consumer movement of the 1960s and 1970s has led to the passage of laws affecting the content of advertising. This is not, however, a new phenomenon; the federal government became interested in the control of certain advertising practices as early as 1914 when the Federal Trade Commission Act was enacted.

Making the advertising student an expert on advertising law is not our goal. Rather, this commentary should emphasize the need to consult a well-qualified lawyer when questions arise. The impact of regulations upon the advertising industry should be better appreciated if more than the specific nature of the restrictions is known; the thinking and events leading to their passage shed additional light and bring greater understanding. Thus, the content of several important laws and their background are presented in this chapter.[2]

Late in the nineteenth century there was a decided shift in public attitude toward business. The policy of laissez faire, based on the idea that the public benefits to the greatest extent in an environment which lets the forces of free competition operate untrammeled, gave way to one which permitted certain business activities to be controlled by governmental bodies. The number of business activities subject to governmental regulation has increased with the passage of years. More laws have been enacted, and judicial interpretations have extended the areas of governmental control of business activity.

The new regulations touch nearly every facet of business operations. Our concern is primarily with the segment of the body of law known in legal circles as trade regulation. This field encompasses those laws and judicial rulings which control the buying and selling process. Such business practices as pricing, selling below cost, quantity discounting, terms of sale, trademarking, labeling, and advertising are included. Our aim at this point is to show briefly how advertising is currently affected by various laws and why these laws were passed.

[2] The most useful source of additional information on laws affecting advertising is Marshall C. Howard, *Legal Aspects of Marketing*, McGraw-Hill Book Company, New York, 1964, especially chap. 5, "Advertising and Labeling," pp. 105–130.

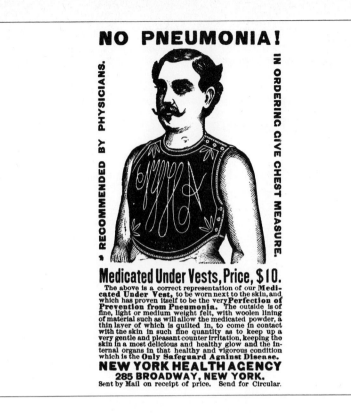

FIGURE 20.1
The lack of truth-
fulness in old-time
ads was common.

Regulation of False and Deceptive Advertising

False claims about products, when made in advertisements, destroy public faith in all advertising. So do statements, although not technically false, which mislead buyers. Thus, the area of false and misleading advertising is highly important to any discussion of advertising regulation, and it is important to be familiar with the legislation which has been enacted to control this abuse of the privilege of advertising one's wares to the public. Two legislative bodies regulate advertising: the federal government and the state governments.

Federal Trade Commission Act The Sherman Act was passed by Congress in 1890 and amended by the Clayton Act in 1914. These two acts were designed to cover more effectively such business behavior as price discrimination, exclusive dealing and tie-ins, acquisition of stock, and interlocking directorates. It was felt that those practices led to monopoly and should be attacked at their roots. Another act passed in 1914, the Federal Trade Commission Act, provided for additional control of business activity.[3]

[3] Public Law 203, approved Sept. 26, 1914, 2nd Sess., 63rd, U.S. Stat. L., vol. 38, pp. 717–724.

656

PLANNING
AND
MANAGING
THE ADVERTISING
CAMPAIGN

FIGURE 20.2
Modern-day advertising can also be untruthful. The Federal Trade Commission found this firm's advertising and personal selling methods to be deceptive and unfair competition. [*FTC Docket 8690.*]

The Federal Trade Commission Act created the Federal Trade Commission and defined its powers and duties. In time the FTC was to become the "policeman of advertising." Its power evolved from the provisions contained in Section 5 of the act:

> Be it enacted . . . that unfair methods of competition in commerce are hereby declared unlawful.

> The Commission is hereby empowered and directed to prevent persons, partnerships, or corporations, except banks and common carriers subject to the Acts to regulate commerce, from using unfair methods of competition in commerce.

This section continues with a detailed description of the cease-and-desist-order procedure to be followed by the FTC and the recourse to judicial action available to the commission and to the defendants in a particular case.

Uncertainty about whether false advertising could be treated as an unfair method of competition existed for many years. This point was apparently settled by a Supreme Court decision in 1922.[4] The power of the commission over the content of advertisements, however, was still considered to be somewhat weak. Strengthening legislation was passed later.

Wheeler-Lea Act Congress passed the Wheeler-Lea Act in 1938, substantially amending the Federal Trade Commission Act.[5] Among other things, the important Section 5 was rewritten to read:

> (a) Unfair methods of competition in commerce, and unfair or deceptive acts or practices in commerce, are hereby declared to be unlawful.

The addition of the phrase "unfair or deceptive acts or practices" reflected considerable change in thinking about the role of government in the regulation of business between the years 1914 and 1938. In 1914 it was felt that if competition were maintained, the public interest would be protected. With the change made in 1938 it was no longer necessary for the FTC to show that competition had been injured in a case under scrutiny. If the act was unfair or deceptive, a prima facie action was established against the defendant.

Several new sections were added to the Federal Trade Commission Act by passage of the Wheeler-Lea Act. Section 12 provided:

> (a) It shall be unlawful for any person, partnership, or corporation to disseminate, or cause to be disseminated, any false advertisement—
>
> (1) By United States Mails, or in commerce by any means, for the purpose of inducing, or which is likely to induce, directly or indirectly, the purchase of food, drugs, devices, or cosmetics; or
>
> (2) By any means, for the purpose of inducing, or which is likely to induce, directly or indirectly, the purchase in commerce of food, drugs, devices, or cosmetics.
>
> (b) The dissemination or the causing to be disseminated of any false advertisement within the provisions of subsection (a) of this section shall be an unfair or deceptive act or practice in commerce within the meaning of Section 5.

Thus, Congress placed a specific responsibility upon the shoulders of the Federal Trade Commission to guard against the false advertising

---

[4] *F.T.C. v. Winsted Hosiery Co.*, 258 U.S. 483, 42 S. Ct. 384, 66 L. Ed. 729 (1922).
[5] Public Law 447, approved Mar. 21, 1938, 3d Sess., 75th Cong., U.S. Stat. L., vol. 52.

658

PLANNING
AND
MANAGING
THE ADVERTISING
CAMPAIGN

FIGURE 20.3
The cartoonist
pokes fun at the
truth-in-advertising
issue. [*Reprinted
from* Advertising
Age *by permis-
sion.*]

"Has this truth in advertising hurt your business any?"

of specified product categories. While the Food and Drug Administration (FDA) retained control over the contents and labeling of products in these categories, the FTC became active in controlling advertising of them. As a matter of fact, the work of the commission in the advertising-regulation area has tended to be concentrated on the advertising of the food, drug, and cosmetic products specifically mentioned in the 1938 amendment.

Important procedural changes were also contained in the Wheeler-Lea Act. Moreover, Section 15 defined false advertising in these words:

> The term "false advertisement" means an advertisement, other than labeling, which is misleading in a material respect; and in determining whether any advertisement is misleading, there shall be taken into account (among other things) not only representations made or suggested by statement, word, design, device, sound, or any combination thereof, but also the extent to which the advertisement fails to reveal facts material in the light of such representations or material with respect to consequences which may result from the use of the commodity to which the advertisement relates under the conditions prescribed in said advertisement, or under such conditions as are customary or usual.

Magnuson-Moss Warranty–Federal Trade Commission Improvement Act This act, passed by Congress early in 1975, contains two parts, or "titles."[6] The first deals with consumer product warranties and reflects consumer pressure for clearer warranties. Its provisions are, of course, vitally important to any marketer whose total product package includes a warranty. Our interest, however, is in the second part of the act, which bears the heading "Title II—Federal Trade Commission Improvements."

Section 201 broadened the jurisdiction of the FTC by providing that Section 5 of the Federal Trade Commission Act be amended by striking out "in commerce" and substituting the phrase "in or affecting commerce." Furthermore, the administrative body's rule-making authority was extended by the insertion of a new section:

> **Sect. 18. (a) (1)** The Commission may prescribe—(A) interpretive rules and general statements of policy with respect to unfair or deceptive acts or practices in or affecting commerce. . . . and (B) rules which define with specificity acts or practices which are unfair or deceptive acts or practices in or affecting commerce. . . . Rules under this subparagraph may include requirements prescribed for the purpose of preventing such acts or practices.

The act continues with detailed provisions dealing with hearing procedures, rules of evidence, judicial review, and so forth.

One implication of the legislation is that the jurisdiction of the FTC is now broadened by law where it had been done in the past primarily by judicial interpretation. At the time of this writing, the full impact of these "improvements" is difficult to predict. The FTC did send out copies of selected decisions to 88 companies, placing these firms on notice that if they engaged in any of the specified practices they would be considered to be doing something false and misleading. It appears that the commission position is that offenders can be brought before a federal district court under the provisions of the act instead of issuing a formal complaint as had been the procedure in the past. The enforcement strategy being employed is apparently based on the assumption that firms can be fined $10,000 per offense if they knowingly act in a way prohibited by a decision in an earlier litigated case, even if that case involved a different company. Advertisers and students of trade regulations law are concerned that due process may be denied should the earlier procedure, which called for a full hearing by the commission before an advertising or selling practice were to be judged false or misleading, be abandoned. It is quite certain that the Magnuson-Moss Act will be tested in the courts over the next several years and its true consequences clarified.

---

[6] Public Law 93–637, 93d Cong., S. 356 (Jan. 4, 1975).

660

PLANNING
AND
MANAGING
THE ADVERTISING
CAMPAIGN

Printers' Ink Model Statute   Control of false advertising by the federal government alone would leave a great deal of advertising unregulated, for interstate commerce must be shown before federal agencies, such as the Federal Trade Commission, have jurisdiction. Prosecution, if any, must be based in many cases upon violation of state laws. Such laws do exist today, and most of them are based upon the Printers' Ink Model Statute which was drawn up in 1911 by the editors of a leading advertising journal of that period. Subsequently some 27 states and the District of Columbia adopted the model statute, and 17 additional states have enacted variations of it. Its provisions, including revisions made in 1945, are as follows:

> Any person, firm, corporation or association or agent or employee thereof, who, with intent to sell, purchase or in any wise dispose of, or to contract with reference to merchandise, real estate, service, employment, or anything offered by such person, firm, corporation or association, or agent or employee thereof, directly or indirectly, to the public for sale, purchase, distribution, or the hire of personal services, or with intent to increase the consumption of or to contract with reference to any merchandise, real estate, securities, service, or employment, or to induce the public in any manner to enter into any obligation relating thereto, or to acquire title thereto, or an interest therein, or to make any loan, makes, publishes, disseminates, circulates, or places before the public, or causes, directly or indirectly, to be made, published, disseminated, circulated, or placed before the public, in this state, in a newspaper, magazine or other publication, or in the form of a book, notice, circular, pamphlet, letter, handbill, poster, bill, sign, placard, card, label, or over any radio or television station or other medium of wireless communication, or in any other way similar or dissimilar to the foregoing, an advertisement, announcement, or statement of any sort regarding merchandise, securities, service, employment, or anything so offered for use, purchase or sale, or the indirect, terms or conditions upon which such loan will be made to the public, which advertisement contains any assertion, representation or statement of fact which is untrue deceptive, or misleading, shall be guilty of a misdemeanor.[7]

Laws patterned after these specifications provide the basic mechanism for the control of misleading advertising at state or municipal levels. Use of the word "intent" in the model law has made enforcement of these state laws quite difficult. Proponents of stricter consumer protection legislation, however, point out that some states have no laws affecting advertising; and that only 19 states have satisfactory laws controlling deceptive selling practices. Moreover, vigilant enforcement of such laws, if they are on the statute books, depends directly on the

[7] Copyright 1959 by Printers' Ink Publishing Corporation. Used by permission.

extent of public interest. In many communities this has not been great enough to make effective use of existing legal machinery.

Regulation of the Use of Advertising Allowances

Clayton Act   The Clayton Act[8] was passed by Congress in 1914. Its goal was to strengthen the Sherman Act in a number of ways; the most significant for our purpose was control of the practice of price discrimination among buyers. Price discrimination was felt to be an important means of bringing about the establishment of monopolies. Thus Section 2 of the Clayton Act provided that "it shall be unlawful . . . to discriminate in price between different purchasers . . . where the effect of such discrimination may be to substantially lessen competition or to tend to create a monopoly." Provisions were made for price variation when the sale involved products of different quality, grade, or quantity; and a differential in price was permitted when the costs of selling or transportation varied among competing buyers.

Many ways were found to circumvent the Clayton Act. The advertising allowance was one device. Some intermediaries were given an allowance for promotion of the manufacturer's products. While many buyers may have actually expended these funds for this purpose, some took the allowance as a form of price discrimination. During the 1930s there was considerable feeling in our country against the chain store as a business institution. People felt chains, because of their bigness, were driving small independent merchants out of business. Recourse was made to Congress, and the Robinson-Patman Act was passed in 1936.[9]

Robinson-Patman Act   Essentially designed to put teeth into the price-discrimination provisions of the Clayton Act, the Robinson-Patman Act strengthened the wording of Section 2 of the parent act. These two subsections vital to the advertising field were added:

> **2(d)**   It shall be unlawful for any person engaged in commerce to pay or contract for payment of anything of value to or for the benefit of a customer of such person in the course of such commerce as compensation or in consideration for any services or facilities furnished by or through such customer in connection with the processing, handling, sale, or offering for sale of any products or commodities manufactured, sold, or offered for sale by such person, unless such payment or consideration is available on proportionally equal terms to all other customers competing in the distribution of such products or commodities.

[8] Public Law 212, approved Oct. 15, 1914, 2d Sess., 63d Cong., U.S. Stat. L., vol. 38, pp. 730–740.
[9] Public Law 692, approved June 19, 1936, 2d Sess., 74th Cong., U.S. Stat. L., vol. 49, p. 1526.

662

PLANNING
AND
MANAGING
THE ADVERTISING
CAMPAIGN

2(e) It shall be unlawful for any person to discriminate in favor of one purchaser against another purchaser or purchasers of a commodity bought for resale, with or without processing, by contracting to the furnishing of any services or facilities connected with the processing, handling, sale, or offering for sale of such commodity so purchased upon terms not accorded to all purchasers on proportionally equal terms.

These two sections mean that the manufacturer must treat all the intermediaries equally when giving advertising allowances. The manufacturer can elect to grant such allowances; but once granted, every competing reseller must be afforded the privilege on "proportionate terms." In a 1968 case it was held that Section 2(d) requires a supplier to make available on proportionally equal terms promotional allowances to retailers who buy from wholesalers and who compete with a favored direct-buying retailer.[10] These provisions of the Robinson-Patman Act have had considerable influence on the use of such devices as manufacturers' cooperative advertising programs. Some of the buying advantage of large buyers has been taken away by the act. It is also quite possible that some sellers have avoided the use of advertising allowances because of the legal uncertainties involved in their use.

Legal Protection of Trademarks

The use of trademarks is closely tied in with the advertising process. An advertisement usually contains a reproduction of the featured product's trademark, for the trademark is one means of assuring buyers that they are getting the specific product they want. Their desire for the product may well have been stimulated by exposure to advertisements. While all the intricacies of trademark law cannot be explained in a few short paragraphs, it is hoped that this treatment may provide an understanding of the rudiments of legislation designed to protect trademarks.

Lanham Act For nearly a century the only protection of trademarks in the United States was to be found in the common law. In 1881 and in 1905 Congress passed laws setting forth more specifically the rights of persons who possess certain trademarks. In 1946 Congress again examined this area and decided that new legislation was needed. The Trademark Law of 1946, commonly known as the Lanham Act, was enacted.[11]

Basically, the Lanham Act set up registration procedures to be followed by persons and business firms wishing to protect their rights

---

[10] *F.T.C. v. Fred Meyer, Inc.*, 390 U. S. 341 (1968).
[11] Public Law 489, approved July 5, 1946, by the 79th Cong., 60 Stat. 427.

to certain trademarks. Two registers, known as the Principal Register and the Supplemental Register, were established. If a trademark qualified for placement on one of the registers, its owner was entitled to certain rights, and legal recourse was provided in case these rights were violated by other parties.

Trademarks registrable on the Principal Register are listed in Section 2:

No trademark by which the goods of the applicant may be distinguished from the goods of others shall be refused registration on the principal register on account of its nature unless it—

(a) consists of or comprises immoral, deceptive, or scandalous matter; or matter which may disparage or falsely suggest a connection with persons, living or dead, institutions, beliefs, or national symbols, or bring them into contempt, or disrepute;

(b) consists of or comprises the flag or coat of arms or other insignia of the United States, or of any State or municipality, or of any foreign nation, or any simulation thereof;

(c) consists of or comprises a name, portrait, or signature identifying a particular living person except by his written consent, or the name, signature, or portrait of a deceased President of the United States during the life of his widow, if any, except by the written consent of the widow;

(d) consists of or comprises a mark which so resembles a mark registered in the Patent Office or a mark or trade name previously used in the United States by another and not abandoned, as to be likely, when applied to the goods of the applicant, to cause confusion, or mistake or to deceive purchasers.

Marks registrable on the Supplemental Register are set forth in Section 23:

All marks capable of distinguishing applicant's goods or services and not registrable on the principal register provided in this chapter, except those declared to be unregistrable under subsections (a), (b), (c), and (d) of Section 1052 of this title, which have been in lawful use in commerce by the proprietor thereof, upon or in connection with any goods or services for the year preceding the filing of the application, may be registered on the supplemental register upon the payment of the prescribed fee and compliance with the provisions of section 1051 of this title so far as they are applicable.

Other sections permit the registration of service, collective, and certification marks in the same manner as trademarks. Section 45 defines these terms in the following way:

664

PLANNING
AND
MANAGING
THE ADVERTISING
CAMPAIGN

Trade-mark. The term "trade-mark" includes any word, name, symbol, or device or any combination thereof adopted and used by a manufacturer or merchant to identify his goods and distinguish them from those manufactured or sold by others.

Service mark. The term "service mark" means a mark used in the sale or advertising of services to identify the services of one person and distinguish them from the services of others and includes without limitation the marks, names, symbols, titles, designations, slogans, character names, and distinctive features of radio or other advertising used in commerce.

Certification mark. The term "certification mark" means a mark used upon or in connection with the products or services of one or more persons other than the owner of the mark to certify regional or other origin, material, mode of manufacture, quality, accuracy or other characteristics of such goods or services or that the work or labor on the goods or services was performed by members of a union or other organization.

Collective mark. The term "collective mark" means a trademark or service mark used by the members of a cooperative, an association or other collective group or organization and includes marks used to indicate membership in a union, an association or other organization.

The marks used by laundries, dry cleaners, restaurants, hotels, and other service establishments are examples of service marks. Certification marks are used by Underwriters' Laboratories, *Parent's Magazine*, American Dental Association, and other organizations which rate, recommend, or approve products. The "Sunkist" mark used by the Sunkist Growers, Inc., is an example of a collective mark.

Two main advantages accrue from registration on the Principal Register. First, such registration gives "constructive notice" of the registrant's claim of ownership. Other parties cannot start using the mark after the date of registration, even if done in good faith or without knowledge of the registrant's use of the mark. Second, after five years on the Principal Register a mark may become incontestable, and the registrant then has exclusive right to its use even though another party may have used the mark prior to its registration by the registrant.

Detailed statements of remedies for infringements are contained in other sections of the act, which contains a total of 50 sections.

Legislation Respecting the Content and Dissemination of Advertising Messages

Advertising copy is governed by the laws of defamation, libel, and slander. No untrue statements may be made about other persons, nor may they be held up to contempt. Moreover, the use of an individual's name, picture, or statement without his or her consent is an invasion of the right of privacy and grounds for action for damages. As a result, careful procedure to obtain legal releases from persons pictured or mentioned in an advertisement is standard practice in the field. But if the advertisement exposes the person to ridicule or contempt, or is otherwise defamatory, the publisher, the advertiser, and the agency are all liable, even though standard releases have been obtained.

Various regulatory bodies are also interested in the content of advertisements. Fraudulent advertising, as well as obscene materials, is denied the use of the mails by the U.S. Postal Service. This agency is also concerned, along with various state governments, with the control of lotteries. The lottery laws of the different states vary greatly in content and interpretation. Basically, a lottery is present if a prize, some form of consideration, and chance are present. Advertisements promoting lotteries may be ruled illegal. The Securities and Exchange Commission controls misrepresentation in the offering of securities to the public. The Federal Communications Commission works closely with the Federal Trade Commission to control false or misleading advertising which reaches the public through radio or television.

Congress enacted in 1965 legislation prohibiting the placement of billboards and other signs within 660 feet of the Interstate Highway System and the Primary Road System. The Public Health Cigarette Smoking Act was passed by Congress in 1970.[12] Probably the most far-reaching legislation affecting advertising, the law restricts the advertising of cigarettes. All advertising for the product category was banned from the broadcast media, effective January 2, 1971, and after July 1, 1971, the FTC was given authority to require cigarette advertising in print media to contain health warnings similar to those that were required to be placed on packages containing cigarettes.

THE INTERPRETATION AND ENFORCEMENT OF LAWS AFFECTING ADVERTISING

Laws do not solve problems unless they are enforced. Enforcement can come about through the decisions of courts of law and through rulings by appropriate administrative bodies.

Some Interesting and Important Cases

All of the many cases that have served as landmarks in the development of the law of advertising cannot be discussed in this chapter. We would, however, like to mention briefly several important cases so that readers may better understand the complexity of advertising legislation and its interpretation. Some of these cases involved court decisions, others rulings by the Federal Trade Commission.

[12] Public Law 91–222, passed on Apr. 1, 1970; House Res. 6543.

666
PLANNING
AND
MANAGING
THE ADVERTISING
CAMPAIGN

The Regimen Case   The Drug Research Corp., through its advertising agency, Kastor, Hilton, Chesley, Clifford & Atherton, Inc., started to advertise Regimen tablets in 1957. These pills were promoted as being capable of bringing about large losses in body weight in humans without the reduction of food intake. In 1965 a federal court jury found the advertiser—and its agency—guilty of defrauding the public through false advertising. Involved in the fraud were faked laboratory reports and the use of television models who participated in drastic dieting instead of using Regimen as claimed. The Kastor, Hilton agency maintained that it acted as an agent carrying out the orders of its principal, and thus was not liable. The court, however, for the first time, placed a legal obligation upon an advertising agency, alongside its moral obligation to make certain that claims in the advertising created for clients be true.

The "Mock-up" Cases   As television came to be the dominant advertising medium for many product categories, the need for firm ground rules concerning the use of demonstrations "on the tube" became apparent. Television demonstrations were attacked in the early 1960s on two points: (1) nonexistence of a claimed superiority and (2) failure of the demonstration to prove what it purported to prove. The first instance is plainly a case of false advertising. A new legal concept was involved in the second case.

The so-called White Jacket cases actually came before the 1960s. Actors wearing medical clothing were used to present medical and dental products; these commercials were ruled misleading because the viewer might believe the medical doctors and dentists were in fact urging use of the advertised product. Commercials purporting to show the ability of one brand of aluminum foil to preserve food better than competitive brands, an auto wax's resistance to heat and cold, a cigarette filter's ability to absorb tar and nicotine, the moisture content of oleomargarine, and the comparative safety of a razor came under FTC scrutiny and were ordered ceased.

In these earlier cases the advertisers involved consented to stop the demonstrations; thus the courts were not brought into the fray. It wasn't until the "Rapid Shave" case reached the courts that a legal ruling on television commercials became available. The commercial in question presented the "moisturizing" qualities of the advertised shaving cream by apparently removing the same from sandpaper with one stroke of a safety razor immediately following application of the cream. Sandpaper was not used, however, in the demonstration; instead a simulated "mock-up" of sand on Plexiglas was employed. The advertiser claimed that the substitution was made because of the technical limitation inherent in the television medium. While the use of mock-ups in television was not ruled illegal per se, the case established that tests performed on television must be as purported. In other words, the undisclosed use and substitution of mock-ups or props in demonstrations showing "proof" of product claims is an illegal misrepresentation. This case finally reached the Supreme Court in 1965, when the FTC position was upheld.

The Campbell Soup Company Case In 1970 FTC action against the Campbell's Soup Company was resolved by a consent order prohibiting the company from using false advertising to sell soup or any other food product.[13] Campbell had placed marbles at the bottom of a bowl of soup which was used in television commercials. The marbles raised the solid ingredients to the top, thereby giving the illusion of more vegetables in the soup than were actually present. The Campbell case dramatizes the "damned if you do, damned if you don't" dilemma which sometimes faces advertisers. Without the marbles the soup picture understates the case—showing no vegetables. With marbles it shows the vegetables but implies so many vegetables that they rise above the broth surface. Since vegetables settle to the bottom, there is no way you can show the vegetables without some kind of contrived situation.

The case had been originally pressed by a consumer group, SOUP (Students Opposed to Unfair Practices), and its leaders objected strenuously to the consent order. They advocated affirmative disclosure by Campbell in future advertising; these disclosures would be designed to overcome and dissipate any residual deception of the public resulting from past misrepresentations. This line of reasoning was rejected by the majority of the commissioners, but it did set in motion the concept of corrective advertising to be discussed shortly.

The Clorox Case In 1957 Procter & Gamble acquired the assets of the Clorox Chemical Company. The Federal Trade Commission, late in 1963, ordered P & G to divest itself of its Clorox holdings under the provisions of Section 7 of the Clayton Antitrust Act, contending that the acquisition "may be substantially to lessen competition, or to tend to create a monopoly" in the household liquid bleach industry.

Our interest in the case springs from the reasoning behind the FTC ruling. "Of particular significance was the Commission's characterization of Proctor [sic] & Gamble's strength as advertising might which could be wielded to monopolize the bleach market and to prevent any other company from becoming an effective competitor."[14] P & G, because of its size, gets maximum volume discounts in television advertising; after the merger Clorox was able to get 33$\frac{1}{3}$ percent more advertising exposure for its advertising expenditures. After several trials, the Supreme Court agreed with the Federal Trade Commission's

[13] FTC Dkt. C–1741, CCH 19,261 (May 1970).
[14] *Journal of Marketing*, vol. 28, no. 2, p. 82., April 1964.

668

PLANNING
AND
MANAGING
THE ADVERTISING
CAMPAIGN

position, and in 1967 (10 years after its acquisition of Clorox) Procter & Gamble was ordered to divest itself of control of the bleach manufacturer.[15]

The Borden Case The Borden Company manufactures evaporated milk which it sells both under its own label and to resellers who sell the milk under their private labels. In 1958 the FTC issued a complaint against the company, claiming discrimination in price among different purchasers, a violation of the Robinson-Patman Act. Borden admitted that there was no chemical difference between the Borden brand and the privately branded milk. However, it was contended that the products were not of "like grade and quality" because of consumer acceptance of the Borden brand. The FTC disagreed and issued a cease-and-desist order against Borden, who appealed to the circuit court. When this court agreed with Borden's position, the FTC appealed to the Supreme Court, which remanded to the circuit court. Once again the court held that there was no substantial evidence that Borden had engaged in illegal price discrimination.[16]

One commentary on the case shows its importance for advertising:

> This case is in the nature of a landmark decision as it recognizes the fact that value has been created for a product by promotion. Though there is no change in the grade or quality, there may be an economic value attached to a brand name product over its private brand counterpart.[17]

The ITT Continental Baking Company Case The FTC alleged in 1971 that the advertising for Wonder bread, Hostess snacks, and Profile bread was false, and cease-and-desist orders were issued. In the case of Profile the baking company, which advertised that the bread was lower in calories than competitive brands, agreed to an order which required that at least 25 percent of each advertisement for the next year consist of a clear disclosure that the FTC had alleged false advertising of the product—that it had no unusual capability for people seeking weight reduction. Profile ads in 1972 did contain such disclosures, admitting that the slices were thinner than those of competing brands, and for that reason alone were lower in calories.

The company resisted similar orders for Wonder bread and Hostess snacks. The FTC claimed that the advertising for Wonder bread exploited children's aspirations for rapid and healthy growth by showing the product as an extraordinary food whereas it was no

---

[15] *Federal Trade Commission v. Procter & Gamble Co.*, 87 S. Ct. 1224 (1967).

[16] *The Borden Company v. F.T.C.*, 381 F. 2d 175 (5th Cir., 1967).

[17] Morris L. Mayer, Joseph B. Mason, and Einar A. Orbeck, "The Borden Case: A Legal Basis for Private Brand Price Discrimination," *MSU Business Topics*, Winter 1970, p. 61.

different from competitive breads. Furthermore, it was claimed that the advertising for both the bread and snack items tended to exploit parents' concern for children's healthy growth and the nutritional effects of children's snacks.

An administrative law judge dismissed the proceedings against both products in late 1972. Appeal to the commission led to the dismissal of charges alleging false advertising of Hostess snack cakes. A cease-and-desist order requiring the company to stop advertising Wonder bread as more nutritious than other foods was issued in 1973.[18] At the many hearings over these matters exhaustive consumer surveys and expert witness testimony were employed by both sides of the case, which served as an important breakthrough for the use of behavioral science concepts in adjudication of legal matters. In the end, the FTC decided not to use the corrective advertising remedy, and the future of several other important regulatory concepts introduced during the case was left dangling.

The Dry Ban Case   This case was the most discussed of all FTC action in 1975 and probably was the most significant for national advertisers in the past several years. An administrative law judge found that Bristol Myers, the manufacturer of Dry Ban deodorant, and its advertising agency, Ogilvy & Mather, used false demonstrations in television commercials promoting the product. The alleged false representation was that the product was a dry spray, not wet when applied to the body, left no residue, and was superior to competing products for these reasons. When reviewed by the commissioners, they perceived the ads represented the product's dryness only as compared to a leading competitive spray; there was no claim in the commercial that Dry Ban was absolutely dry.[19] In other words, it was held that relative rather than absolute claims were made in the commercial. Inasmuch as the FTC case was based upon the theory of absolute claim, its position failed for lack of proof.

In its dismissal statement, the FTC noted the circumstances under which such charges would be ruled to be not in the public interest. The presence of the following factors is the key:

> Those persons affected do not constitute a particularly vulnerable group; there are no health or safety considerations that might legitimately demand further expenditure of public funds; there was no significant economic harm to a consumer who purchased the product (Dry Ban) and found it 'less dry' than anticipated; the advertising in question was terminated over four years earlier; there was no indication on the record

---

[18] FTC Dkt. 8860, CCH 20,464 (October 1973).
[19] FTC Dkt. 8897, CCC 20,900 (April 1975).

670

PLANNING
AND
MANAGING
THE ADVERTISING
CAMPAIGN

that competition was adversely affected by whatever deception might be proved; nor was the case dealing with intentional wrongdoers.[20]

These criteria, thus, provide guidelines of reason when the FTC is contemplating action against an advertiser. When the potential harm to the consumer's physical or economic well-being is trivial, action is not warranted. Resources for prosecution of cases are limited and should be reserved, according to this line of reasoning, for more serious offenses. However, the key commissioners holding these views have already left the Federal Trade Commission. We can predict that the FTC will always pursue some blatantly false ads, even though they may be trivial in health, safety, or economic dimensions.

Some Recent Policies of the FTC

The mandate given to the Federal Trade Commission is a broad one: to ensure fairness within the economic environment of the nation. One area of regulatory concern is over industry structure and competition; the second focuses on direct marketing practices involving consumers. This activity is sometimes labeled "consumer protection." Since 1970 this facet of FTC work has received increased emphasis. In trying to discharge its obligation, the commission has tried several new approaches which affect advertising, or at least may affect it in the future. Advertising students and practitioners need to understand the general nature of these policies and their implication. Several are discussed in alphabetical order.

Advertising Substantiation   Since 1971 the Federal Trade Commission has maintained a program for the substantiation of advertising claims. If the Federal Trade Commission requests it, an advertiser must supply the commission with documentation in support of claims made in its advertising, such as claims of product safety performance, efficacy, quality, or comparative price. In addition to submitting documentation advertisers must also show that they relied on the documentation when preparing the advertising in question. The rationale for this program is that the possibility that the advertiser will be required to provide the documentation to the FTC will act as a deterrent to unfounded claims. Additionally, the advertising substantiation program has raised the question of what kind of documentation will constitute reasonable substantiation for various types of claims. The response to this question in any particular circumstance is determined by a variety of factors, including such issues as the potential effect of the advertising and the product on consumer health, safety, or economic well-being; the state of the art with regard to testing of the

---

[20] Quoted from *Journal of Marketing*, p. 92, January 1976.

particular product; and the extent to which consumers would be likely to rely on the advertising claim in question.[21]

In addition to the requirement for the support of advertising claims, the FTC is concerned over uniqueness claims. The uniqueness of a product attribute cannot be implied unless it, too, can be supported. As Wilkes and Wilcox point out, this portion of commission policy:

> . . . differs sharply from the "unique selling point" (U.S.P.) approach to developing advertising copy first advocated in the 1940s by Ted Bates and Company. This concept challenges an advertiser to make a proposition to consumers that competition cannot or does not make, one that is unique to the brand or *is not already being made*. Under the substantiation program, however, nonsupported claims as well as preemptive claims that imply uniqueness when none exists are likely to be challenged by the commission.[22]

However, the implied-uniqueness approach has not been successful for the FTC so far.

Affirmative and Full Disclosure of Information Based upon the premise that consumers should have sufficient information to make valid comparisons between purchasing alternatives, laws have been passed and regulatory body rulings promulgated to require that specific kinds of information be provided to them. The FDA, for instance, set up a program in 1975 requiring that the labels on packages of processed food list the nutritional value of the contents. The Federal Trade Commission was also considering at the time requiring that nutritional information appear in all food advertising. This potential rule is being resisted, largely because it is felt that the impact of advertisements such as 30-second television commercials would be lost if they became a mere recitation of nutritional facts about the featured product.

Affirmative disclosure is a concept which would require that advertisers tell not only the positive story about their products, but also the salient negative side. Thus, in addition to any full disclosure of information about the product that might be required, advertisers would have to tell about product deficiencies and limitations. The makers of Geritol, for instance, have been required to disclose in their ads that the "great majority of people who experience symptoms of tiredness do not experience them because of vitamin deficiency." And in a more specific instance, a consent order for Forever Young, a chemical designed for use in the removal of wrinkles and skin

---

[21] Pfizer, Inc., 3 Trade Reg. Rep. ¶ 20,056 (FTC., July 11, 1972).
[22] Robert E. Wilkes and James B. Wilcox, "Recent FTC Actions: Implications for the Advertising Strategist," *Journal of Marketing*, p. 57, January 1974.

672

PLANNING
AND
MANAGING
THE ADVERTISING
CAMPAIGN

blemishes, prescribes that at least 15 percent of all advertising for the product must disclose the dangers inherent in the use of the product.

Bait-and-Switch Advertising   This variation of consumer deception is not new; however, the FTC has recently shown increased interest in the sharp practice. As is humorously shown in the accompanying cartoon (Figure 20.4), the retailer advertises an enticingly low price for a consumer item; when the consumer goes to the store, he or she hears that (1) the item is not in stock, or (2) it is inferior in quality. The salesperson then proceeds in an attempt to switch the prospect's interest to another (higher-priced) model.

One of the nation's largest retailers brought consumers to its outlets with an advertisement featuring an attractive sewing machine at $58. According to an FTC complaint issued in 1974, salespeople disparaged the item with statements including: "(1) the advertised sewing machines are noisy, and are not guaranteed for as long a period of time as the firm's more expensive models; (2) certain of them will not sew straight stitch, zig zag stitch, or in reverse; (3) none of the advertised sewing machines is available for sale and, if ordered, there will be long delays in delivery."[23] It was further alleged that rates of compensation of salespersons was greater when higher-priced models were sold.

Comparison Advertising   Sometimes called comparative advertising, *Comparison advertising* is defined as advertising that:

1   Compares two or more specifically named or recognizably presented brands of the same generic product or service class, and

2   Makes such a comparison in terms of one or more specific product or service attributes.[24]

Examples include the classic Plymouth advertising of the 1930s, when the relatively unknown brand of automobile asked consumers to "Look at All Three," and the Avis campaign of the 1960s, wherein a comparison was made to Hertz—because Avis was number two in the rent-a-car business, the claim that its employees "tried harder" was given as a reason for doing business with the firm.[25] In the 1970s Datril,

---

[23] *In re Sears, Roebuck & Co.*, CCH 20,652 (July 1974); BNA ATRR no. 672 (July 16, 1974), A–20. Quoted material from *Journal of Marketing*, p. 101, January 1975.

[24] William L. Wilkie and Paul W. Farris, "Comparison Advertising: Problems and Potential," *Journal of Marketing*, p. 7, October 1975.

[25] Ibid. Also see Terence A. Shimp, "Comparison Advertising in National Television Commercials: A Content Analysis with Specific Emphasis Devoted to the Issue of Incomplete Comparative Assertions," in Edward M. Mazze (ed.), *1975 Combined Proceedings*, American Marketing Association, Chicago, 1975, pp. 504–508.

FIGURE 20.4
Bait-and-switch advertising is humorously depicted in this newspaper cartoon. [*King Features Syndicate, Inc.*]

an over-the-counter headache relief medicine, made direct comparisons with Tylenol, which was dominant in the product category at the time; here the message was that the competitive product was just as effective, yet was being sold at much lower prices.

In this instance the practice of comparison advertising is encouraged by consumer groups and by the FTC under the theory that such messages provide consumers with additional information upon which to make purchasing decisions. From an implementation viewpoint, there is a critical question whether a given message constitutes disparagement of the competitor and the product. Still unresolved is whether comparison advertising is effective in persuading consumers to the advertiser's point of view. If the cognitive dissonance theory of explaining consumer behavior is being followed, a case can be made that such comparisons hurt the advertiser. This thought is expressed in the following quotation:

What the comparative spot does is tell the user of the compared-to brand

674

PLANNING
AND
MANAGING
THE ADVERTISING
CAMPAIGN

Remarkable achievement. $23,976

Mercedes 450 SLC Sports Coupe

Remarkable achievement. $4,189*

Ford Granada Sports Coupe

*Manufacturer's suggested retail price excluding title, taxes, destination charges.

Pictured at top is perhaps the world's finest sports coupe, and a remarkable achievement in automotive engineering.

From its fully independent suspension system to the design of its interior, the Mercedes 450 SLC is a possession of pride for those who can easily afford its formidable price tag. Those who cannot, please read on.

The second car pictured above is a dramatically styled edition of one of the best-selling cars in America:

New Ford Granada Sports Coupe

You may notice that the Granada Sports Coupe is virtually the same size as the Mercedes 450 SLC. (See specifications) But no car can be categorized "sports coupe" on its dimensions alone.

For road performance at the sporting level this Granada is equipped with a heavy duty suspension, heavy duty shock absorbers, heavy duty rear springs and steel-belted radials. Inside it features reclining bucket seats, leather wrapped steering wheel and floor shift. Wiper/washer

SELECTED SPECIFICATIONS	MERCEDES 450 SLC	GRANADA SPORTS COUPE
WHEELBASE (IN.)	111.0	109.9
LENGTH	196.4	197.7
WIDTH	70.5	71.2
HEIGHT	52.4	53.3
BODY CONST.	UNIT	UNIT
ENG. DISPLACEMENT (CU. IN.)	275.8	200 (OPT. 250, 302, 351)
COMP. RATIO	8.0:1	8.3:1 (200 CID)
BORE X STROKE (IN.)	3.62 X 3.35	3.68 X 3.126
†GEAR RATIO: 1ST	2.31:1	2.46:1
2ND	1.46:1	1.46:1
3RD	1.00:1	1.00:1

†These are automatic transmission gear ratios.

controls are positioned for instant reach on turn signal lever, European-style.

And to further enhance the performance of your car, the Granada Sports Coupe offers a great range of special equipment to order from. Including a powerful 351 CID V-8 engine and SelectShift transmission. Even 4-wheel disc brakes are available (Granada is one of the few American cars to offer them).

A sporting choice

If money is really no object, you should certainly consider the Mercedes 450 SLC. It is a remarkable achievement in automotive engineering. Under any circumstances, consider the new Granada Sports Coupe. Starting at $4,189* it is a remarkable achievement by almost any standard.

See your local Ford Dealer

FORD GRANADA

FORD DIVISION

FIGURE 20.5

The comparative advertising technique is well illustrated by this car advertisement.

that he/she is in fact using the wrong product—that a wrong decision has been made. Rather than improve the position of the brand being advertised, the comparison spot focusing on cognitive dissonance might be alienating the consumer.[26]

[26] Thomas E. Barry and Roger L. Tremblay, "Comparative Advertising: Perspectives and Issues," *Journal of Advertising*, vol. 4, no. 4, p. 17, 1975.

There is need for a great deal more research into the effectiveness of this advertising strategy. If the practice continues to grow in popularity—which appears likely—regulatory bodies, such as the FTC, may be called upon to serve as referees. If this comes to pass, the question of correct testing procedures to be employed when assessing advertising claims will surface. The Committee on Improving Advertising of the American Association of Advertising Agencies (4As) developed a Policy Statement and Guidelines for Comparative Advertising which was adopted in early 1974. Similar policy statements in 1966 and 1969 tended to "discourage" comparative advertising. In the mid-1970s it was accepted by the 4As as a reality. The three television networks were accepting commercials employing the technique, and some major advertisers used it. Thus, it was decided that self-regulation by the advertising industry was desirable.

Corrective Advertising   This is advertising run by a commercial sponsor to correct *misimpressions* resulting from that sponsor's earlier ads. This concept sits high in the priorities of the Federal Trade Commission, having first employed the technique in the Profile bread case discussed earlier. The rationale for corrective ads is that they are designed to:

1 Dispel the "residual effects" of such deceptive advertising
2 Restore competition to the stage that prevailed before the unfair practice
3 Deprive firms from falsely obtained gains to which advertising may have contributed[27]

A potentially monumental case over corrective advertising came in late 1975 when the FTC ordered Warner-Lambert to engage in corrective advertising for its mouthwash, Listerine. The commission felt that a misleading impression was created by advertising for the brand in that Listerine prevents colds or lessens their severity. The FTC stated that the "deception" could not be dispelled until Warner-Lambert spent a total of $10,200,000 for advertising containing the statement: "Contrary to prior advertising, Listerine will not prevent colds or sore throats or lessen their severity." The company promised to test the commission's ruling in the courts; this would bring about a judicial ruling on the corrective advertising remedy and whether or not the commission can order a company to spend its own money in this manner. All previous cases were handled without court action through the consent decree procedure.

[27] Stanley E. Cohen, "Enforcer Pitofsky Explains FTC's New Get Tough Policy," *Advertising Age*, Jan. 18, 1971, pp. 1, 14. Also see Dorothy Cohen, "Remedies for Consumer Protection: Prevention, Restitution, or Punishment," *Journal of Marketing*, p. 27, October 1975.

676

PLANNING
AND
MANAGING
THE ADVERTISING
CAMPAIGN

One important question is expressed by Keith Hunt in these words: "Given that an ad is judged deceptive, how do we decide whether a deceptive residual exists?[28] He goes on to prescribe extensive research and concludes that the burden of proving or disproving the presence of a deceptive residual should be placed on the advertiser, given that deception has been proved.

Counter Advertising   Messages given access to the broadcast media in order to present views opposite to those of commercials being aired are called *counter advertising*. This concept, as espoused by the Federal Trade Commission, is not much more than a gleam in its eye rather than a practical reality. The Federal Communications Commission had earlier broadened the fairness doctrine so that broadcasters, who use the public airwaves, must present contrasting viewpoints on controversial matters of significant public interest. Thus, before cigarette advertising was banned from broadcast media, antismoking commercials were aired over radio and television starting in 1967. Early in 1972 the FTC attached to this line of reasoning and advocated that public interest firms should be granted the right of access to the public airwaves by the FCC for the purpose of disseminating answers to messages involving controversial issues. Anyone wishing to pay for air time would be permitted to use the broadcast media to counter product claims and advertising themes of controversial nature; furthermore, if the group cannot afford to buy the time, it should be granted on a gratis basis. The refusal of the FCC to support the concept and require stations to permit counter advertising has lessened its impact. Networks don't have to accept counter advertising, and they don't do so.

FIGURE 20.6
The beginning of the Declaration of Independence is set up in the form of an advertising space order (*opposite page*). The message is changed as believed necessary if current rules and regulations facing copywriters had been in effect. In other words, if the Declaration had been "legaled" today, it would read in the manner shown. [*Edward A. McCabe, Scali, McCabe, Sloves Advertising.*]

Implications and Conclusions

What implications and conclusions can be drawn from this brief discussion of cases and policies involving the interpretation and enforcement of laws affecting advertising? For one thing, it should be clear that the legal restrictions on advertising are becoming more numerous and complex, and consumers are becoming more critical. No decision about advertising strategy can be safely made without weighing its legal consequences. Advertising men and women are frequently heard to say in their day-to-day deliberations, "Let's legal it." Translated, this expression means to check out the matter with an attorney.

Many of these legal restrictions have tended to hamstring the creative side of the advertising business.[29] In an effort to avoid legal

[28] H. Keith Hunt, "Corrective Advertising—Who Proves the Deceptive Residual?," paper presented before the American Academy of Advertising, Knoxville, Tenn., April 1974.
[29] The titles to two talks given before the Western Region Convention of the American Association of Advertising Agencies in 1975 reflect this concern: "Regulation—Creative Friend or Foe?" by Neal W. O'Connor and "How to Write Advertising and Stay Out of Jail" by Harold Riney.

Jefferson, Hancock & Wythe, Inc.
INDEPENDENCE HALL, PHILA., PENNSYLVANIA

Client_____ House   Date_____ 7/4/76

Job No._____ 1   Space_____ --

Medium_____ Parchment   Publ. Date___ ASAP

OK only if everybody showed up

Copy

A DECLARATION
By the Representatives of the United States of America
In General Congress (Assembled.)

When in the Course of human Events, it becomes necessary for one People to dissolve the Political Bands which have connected them with another, and to assume among the Powers of the
Earth, the separate and equal Station to which the (Laws of Nature)
(and of Nature's God entitle them) a decent Respect to the Opinions
of Mankind requires that they should declare the causes which im-
pel them to the Separation.

must prove existence of such laws. No copies on file!

We hold these (Truths to be self-evident) that (all Men are)
(created equal) that they are endowed by their Creator with certain
unalienable Rights, that (among) these are Life, (Liberty) and the Pursuit of Happiness--That to secure these Rights, Governments are
instituted among Men, deriving their just Powers from the Consent
of the Governed, that whenever any Form of Government becomes
destructive of these Ends, it is the Right of the People to alter or
to abolish it, and to institute new Government, laying its Foundation on such Principles, and organizing its Powers in such Form,
as to them shall seem most likely to effect their Safety and Happiness. Prudence, indeed, will dictate that Governments long established should not be changed for light and transient Causes; and
accordingly (all) Experience hath shewn, that Mankind are more disposed to suffer, while Evils are sufferable, than to right themselves
by abolishing the Forms to which they are accustomed. But when
a (long Train of Abuses and Usurpations) pursuing invariably the
same Object, evinces a Design to reduce them under absolute
Despotism, it is their Right, it is their Duty, to throw off such
Government, and to provide new Guards for their future Security.
Such has been the (patient) Sufferance of these Colonies; and such is
now the Necessity which constrains them to alter their former
Systems of Government. The History of the present (King of Great)
(Britain) is a History of repeated Injuries and Usurpations, all having
in direct Object the Establishment of an absolute Tyranny over these
States. To prove this, let (Facts) be submitted to a candid World.

No! must be substantiated

This is an implied guarantee. Copy must state that we don't guarantee it.

Are we prepared to disclose others?

Can't say 'all'. Qualify.

Someone may challenge this!!

Can't substantiate

Need a signed release.

Since when are your opinions facts?

He has refused his Assent to Laws, the most wholesome and
necessary for the public Good.

Disparaging! Do we have adequate research to back up?   Continued....

678

PLANNING
AND
MANAGING
THE ADVERTISING
CAMPAIGN

pitfalls, messages are often written with extreme caution, for truth always puts some limits on everything, including creativity. Resulting ads tend to be bland compared to ads where creative license with truth is freely taken. How one advertising man believes the Declaration of Independence would have to be written today, if it were to avoid being labeled as deceptive, is shown in Figure 20.6.

At several places we have highlighted the need for additional research. Present laws and policies of regulatory bodies are based upon assumptions respecting the effects of advertising messages on consumers; these assumptions may or may not be valid. It would appear that behavioral science concepts and research methodology are of potential value as the theories underlying advertising regulation are being tested. Substantial research is being done by the advertising industry and academic people to discover the correctness of these assumptions.

There is no doubt that deceptive advertising does exist. What is deceptive is sometimes hard to define, and how to redress its effects on consumers and prevent its reoccurrence are truly troublesome matters. The FTC is a political body whose membership changes with the passage of time and administrations; these changes bring shifts in emphases and philosophy. There is some evidence that the commission is moving from its former role perception as the preventer of false, misleading, or deceptive advertising to one of establishing standards based on its concept of what is good for the consumer. The advertising practitioner and the student of advertising must, therefore, continuously study its actions, and those of other regulatory bodies, closely. The activities of legislative bodies similarly need to be regularly monitored in order to see that new laws affecting advertising are passed only after advertising's point of view has had a hearing. Good laws and good regulation are to be welcomed by professionals in the advertising business. The reverse—bad laws and poor regulation—should be resisted.

The Role of FTC Rules and Guides

The Federal Trade Commission has the duty of obtaining compliance with the statutes it administers. To facilitate this process the FTC informs and guides business people about the requirements of such statutes. Sellers and advertisers are aided by two kinds of documents frequently issued by the commission: *Industry Guides* and *Trade Regulation Rules*.

Industry Guides are designed to clarify legal approaches to such single-industry concerns as cigarette advertising, tire advertising, and shoe labeling. Other guides discuss practices which cut across industry lines—deceptive pricing and bait advertising are examples. These guides are essentially statements on how the FTC would interpret the law should an actual case arise. They alert the industries involved, and they can also help to educate consumers and protect them from being victimized by improper sales practices.

Trade Regulation Rules (TRR) present the conclusions of the commission about the legality of certain business practices. A given rule may apply nationwide, or it may be limited to certain markets or geographic areas. The rules have the full force and effect of law; violation of a TRR is considered tantamount to violation of the FTC Act. Industry cooperation is sought when the guides and rules are being written; they are designed to remove uncertainty in situations where matters are not perfectly clear. The advertising of pet food, claims of broadcast audience ratings, the granting of advertising allowances, premium offers to children, and the use of endorsements in advertising have all received this kind of an FTC consideration.

SELF-REGULATION OF ADVERTISING

The advertising profession has long been committed to the idea of self-regulation of the industry. As indicated earlier, the impetus for state laws against deceptive advertising came from an advertising trade publication, *Printers' Ink*, in 1911. More recent developments are now discussed.

Better Business Bureaus

The Better Business Bureau (BBB) idea was first developed by the Advertising Club of Cleveland, Ohio. Today, over 240 of these bureaus operate at both local and national levels to fight illegal advertising and to raise the standards of advertising practice. Advertisers, advertising agencies, and advertising media work together to stamp out deceptive advertising through the BBB approach. Each bureau acts as a watch-dog within its community. When fraudulent advertising is alleged and called to the attention of bureau personnel, an investigation is made. If the advertising appears to be deceptive, the advertiser is contacted and an attempt is made to persuade him or her to cease the practice. The bureau has no legal power, although it may work with local law enforcement officials to help prosecute violators of laws against fraudulent advertising and other sharp practices. Moreover, the bureau maintains a file of consumer complaints about operators in the community. Consumers, in turn, may call the bureau which will report the number and nature of complaints on file with them. There is, of course, no claim that the complaints are justified; however, normally a high level of them on file should be fair warning to the inquirer.

The effectiveness of BBBs varies greatly from city to city. This is due, in part, to the quality of leadership operating local units. Another

680

PLANNING
AND
MANAGING
THE ADVERTISING
CAMPAIGN

factor is the amount of financial and other support provided the bureaus. Each bureau depends solely on the voluntary contributions of advertisers, media, and agencies; this support can vary greatly. There are no tax revenues involved.

The focus of interest of the BBBs is upon people operating within the local area, retailers and service establishments primarily. A great deal of BBB caseload centers on the "one-shot" huckster with his or her scheme to fleece the unwary public. This situation contributes to a frequently held attitude that such agencies are not overly successful in achieving their worthwhile objectives; the ending of one unsavory practice seems only to be followed by another equally undesirable one. Without its BBB, however, the local scene would quite likely be far more hazardous for consumers in many communities.

National Advertising Review Board

For many years the National Association of Better Business Bureaus expended some effort on the self-regulation of national advertising, while the local bureaus concentrated on local and retail advertising. A reorganization took place in the early 1970s when the Council of Better Business Bureaus (CBBB) was established; the new group became much more involved in national advertising regulation. The CBBB set up a policy-making group known as the National Advertising Review Council, which consists of eight members drawn from the chairmen and presidents of the four leading professional associations serving the field of advertising—American Association of Advertising Agencies, Association of National Advertisers, American Advertising Federation, and the CBBB.

The National Advertising Review Board (NARB) was then established. The board has 50 members: 40 are advertising professionals and 10 are public members. The NARB acts as the supreme court of the self-regulation system of advertising and is broken up into "panels" of five members, or "judges."

Another part of the self-regulation mechanism is the National Advertising Division (NAD) of the CBBB, which is also staffed by advertising professionals. Complaints about national advertising go first to the NAD. This body investigates and often settles complaints at the staff level through suggestions made to the offending advertiser.

When the advertiser will not agree to cease or modify the advertising found to be misleading by the NAD, the matter is referred to a NARB panel for adjudication. The panel can agree with the decision by the NAD or can find the complaint without merit and rule for the advertiser. How the review system operates is shown by the flowchart presented in Figure 20.7. In its first 40 months, NARB called together a panel for a total of 23 times. Twelve of these cases were decided in favor of the advertiser, with the remainder decided against the advertiser. Over the same span of time the NAD received 787

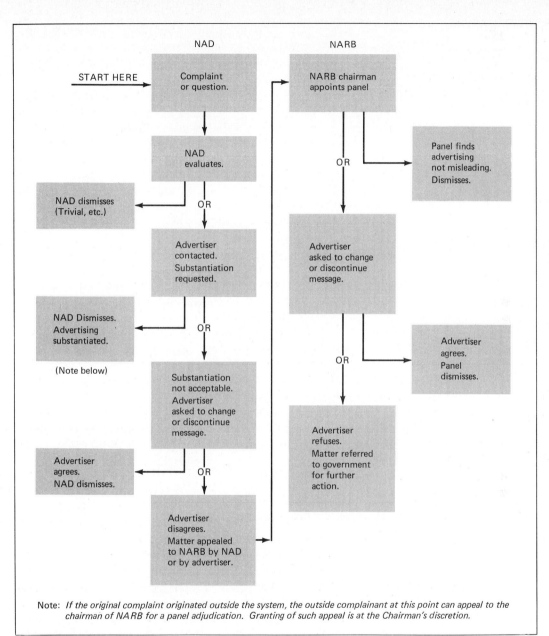

FIGURE 20.7
This flowchart traces the steps followed when a complaint is lodged against an advertisement for handling through the self-regulatory procedures established by the advertising industry. [*The National Advertising Review Board: 1971–1975, p. 12, published by NARB, 1975.*]

complaints. The source of these complaints consists of the following: consumers, 17 percent; consumer groups, 21 percent; competitors, 8 percent; local BBBs, 25 percent; NAD monitoring, 25 percent; and other,

682

PLANNING
AND
MANAGING
THE ADVERTISING
CAMPAIGN

4 percent. It is believed that the scarcity of cases coming to the NARB is due to the effective settlement of claims at the NAD level. Of course, the availability of this self-regulation mechanism is not widely known to the public.

The evolution of the NAD-NARB system has established two fundamental principles for self-regulatory bodies: (1) public exposure of all regulatory decisions, (2) willingness to explore problem areas before problems become critical. The groups issue monthly reports which tend to dissipate suspicion and help to set practical norms for the advertising industry. For example, in April 1975 the NAD reported that seven advertisers, including General Mills and Calgon Corporation, agreed to modify or discontinue questioned ad claims, while another seven adequately substantiated claims. The stance is corrective in nature rather than defensive.[30]

The value of the activity is shown by a statement from Thomas Rosch, director of the FTC's Bureau of Consumer Protection, that the "NARB helps relieve us (FTC) of much of the burden in the regulatory area."[31] Advertisers escape the adverse publicity which often springs from FTC action against them, and issues are settled much more expeditiously. Review boards have now been established in many communities with the goal of solving similar disagreements about possibly misleading advertising at the local level through this quasi-arbitration approach.

Another product of the joint effort for self-policing was the development of a code for consumer advertising, as shown in Table 20.1. The statement provides a useful guideline when self-regulation of advertising abuses is undertaken. Surely every advertiser should refer to the code when evaluating advertising messages about to be released to the media for dissemination.

Self-Regulation by Advertising Media

All advertising media reserve the right to reject any advertising submitted if it is considered objectionable to their readers, listeners, or viewers, even if it is not misleading. *Sunset* magazine, for instance, has banned any advertising for products containing dangerous insecticides since 1969. When the decision was made, the magazine carried more advertising for insecticides than any other nonfarm magazine.

In the area of broadcast advertising, the National Association of Broadcasters (NAB) through the operation of its Code Authority has established extensive sets of guidelines for advertisers wishing to use radio and television in their media mixes. Of particular interest has been advertising directed primarily to children. Self-regulation has zeroed in on such specific areas of child-oriented efforts as host selling,

---

[30] Drawn from *The Gallagher Report*, July 22, 1974, p. 1.
[31] *Advertising Age*, June 6, 1975, p. 66.

TABLE 20.1

THE ADVERTISING CODE OF AMERICAN BUSINESS

I *Truth.* Advertising shall tell the truth, and shall reveal significant facts, the concealment of which would mislead the public.

II *Responsibility.* Advertising agencies and advertisers shall be willing to provide substantiation of claims made.

III *Taste and decency.* Advertising shall be free of statements, illustrations or implications which are offensive to good taste or public decency.

IV *Disparagement.* Advertising shall offer merchandise or service on its merits, and refrain from attacking competitors unfairly or disparaging their products, services or methods of doing business.

V *Bait advertising.* Advertising shall offer only merchandise or services which are readily available for purchase at the advertised price.

VI *Guarantees and warranties.* Advertising of guarantees and warranties shall be explicit. Advertising of any guarantee or warranty shall clearly and conspicuously disclose its nature and extent, the manner in which the guarantor or warrantor will perform and the identity of the guarantor or warrantor.

VII *Price claims.* Advertising shall avoid price or savings claims which are false or misleading, or which do not offer provable bargains or savings.

VIII *Unprovable claims.* Advertising shall avoid the use of exaggerated or unprovable claims.

IX *Testimonials.* Advertising containing testimonials shall be limited to those of competent witnesses who are reflecting a real and honest choice.

Explanatory note: This code was part of a program of industry self-regulation pertaining to national consumer advertising announced jointly on September 28, 1971, by the American Advertising Federation, the American Association of Advertising Agencies, the Association of National Advertisers, and the Council of Better Business Bureaus, Inc.

toy advertising, and premium offers. In fact, a statement titled "Children's Television Advertising Guidelines" runs approximately the length of three pages in this textbook. Furthermore, the guidelines have caused the creative approaches used by many advertisers to be changed materially. In some instances it was decided to exclude children from designated target audiences for advertising messages.

The advertising of alcoholic beverages is either prohibited or carefully controlled by the Radio Code and the Television Code. Moreover, how personal products, such as sanitary napkins and tampons, are advertised is prescribed. The objective, of course, is to forestall governmental regulation of advertising over the airwaves.

Advertising by Members of the Professions

Codes of ethics for such professional groups as medical doctors and lawyers have long prohibited advertising by members. A formal announcement that an office location has been changed, a new partner added, or a practice established was the only advertising allowed. In the case of dentistry, dentists in some states can advertise

Which relative will be executor of your estate?

Americans, you are amazing. No people protects its individual liberties like you do.

You go crazy every time the government tries to run your lives for you. To make your decisions.

You protest. You demonstrate. You march.

But when the government makes the biggest decision of all for you, you don't raise a whimper.

Mostly because you're not around to.

That decision is called "What happens to my property after I die?" And the government makes it every day. Because millions of Americans can't be bothered. And their familes suffer for it.

You need a will. And you need legal help. We're Littleford and Weekley, Attorneys. And we'd like you to come in and talk to us. It won't cost you a penny.

Then, if you still don't want to make out a will—OK. You're under no obligation.

Except the one to your family.

Littleford and Weekley, Attorneys: Your partners in law.

without losing their licenses. In some states advertising by professionals is prohibited by statute.

In the mid-1970s the prohibition against such advertising was under pressure. The Justice Department took action to end the self-imposed advertising ban by physicians, lawyers, architects, engineers, and opticians. Furthermore, the FTC issued a complaint against the American Medical Association charging illegal restraint of trade because of the prohibition of advertising. A long litigation over the question is anticipated; thus at the time this is being written, predicting the outcome is difficult. However, an advertising agency, Foote, Cone & Belding, prepared prototype ads for adaptation by members of the American Bar Association when the time is appropriate. In February 1976 the ABA voted a relaxation of its ban on advertising by lawyers. Its canon of ethics was changed to permit lawyers to advertise fees, credit arrangements, office hours, specialties, and background information in telephone directories (yellow pages) and legal directories.

State laws or state pharmacy board rules forbidding prescription drug advertising were also under attack in the mid-1970s. This event provided an interesting situation, as consumer groups, which normally are critical of advertising, were found to be advocating its use. The rationale offered was that the price of prescription drugs would be lower if advertising were permitted. A similar case was made for the advertising of eyeglasses.

Conclusion on Self-Regulation

The self-regulation of any industry practice faces hard sledding. For one thing, there is an ever-present skepticism concerning such efforts which the outside observer may view as self-serving, even collusive, and designed to circumvent the law. There is a serious limitation, furthermore, in the enforcement arena. The policing body usually has no real power to force compliance with its rulings; instead reliance is placed upon persuasion and pressure from the other members of the industry group and the implicit threat that the matter will go to the FTC if not satisfactorily settled at the self-regulation level. Thus, compliance is difficult to accomplish if significant numbers of industry members decide not to participate in the self-regulatory effort; all broadcast stations, for instance, do not subscribe to the Radio and Television Codes. Enlightened self-interest, however, should encourage advertisers to support such efforts with vigor and enthusiasm. If governmental regulation and control are forestalled thereby, the advertising business will benefit. Quite likely the interest of consumers will also be protected at a lower net cost and probably more readily than through the legal processes discussed earlier.

FIGURE 20.8
On the opposite page is an advertising agency's idea of how lawyers might advertise if permitted to do so. [*Foote, Cone & Belding.*]

686

PLANNING
AND
MANAGING
THE ADVERTISING
CAMPAIGN

SUMMARY

Deceptive advertising and other forms of unethical behavior do occur in the field of advertising. Protection is available in three forms: law, industry self-regulation, and enlightened self-interest on the part of advertisers. Many legal restrictions have been placed upon advertisers in order to control the unethical behavior of those who fail to invoke the self-interest philosophy. False and deceptive advertising is one of the concerns of the Federal Trade Commission. When businesses are found to be dealing deceptively with consumers, the FTC issues cease-and-desist orders and accepts consent decrees from violators. The use of advertising allowances is regulated by the FTC. What is said in advertising messages and where they may appear are also subject to legal control in several ways.

Interpreting and enforcing laws affecting advertising is a complex task. Over time an extensive body of law has developed which is based on a series of landmark cases. The rules of law set down in these cases provide guidelines to persons who create advertising messages, sometimes, it is believed, to the detriment to creativity. The FTC, moreover, in its efforts to protect consumers adopts policies which affect how advertising can be carried out in the United States. Policies of current interest and possible concern are advertising substantiation, affirmative disclosure, bait-and-switch advertising, comparison advertising, corrective advertising, and counter advertising.

Self-regulation by the advertising industry itself may help to forestall additional regulation of promotional activities.

QUESTIONS FOR DISCUSSION

1 Why is an attitude of enlightened self-interest so vitally important to the development of a sound advertising program. Explain.

2 Briefly describe the provisions of the Federal Trade Commission Act as it affects advertising. How was the power of the FTC over advertising affected by the Wheeler-Lea Act? The Magnuson-Moss Act?

3 What does the Robinson-Patman Act have to do with advertising? The Lanham Act? The Printers' Ink Model Statute?

4 What was the key issue in the so-called mock-up and Campbell Soup cases? What is your personal opinion about this matter?

5 Why was the Dry Ban case considered to be so important to the future of advertising? Explain.

6 Briefly define each of the following FTC policies: (a) advertising substantiation, (b) affirmative disclosure, (c) comparison advertising, (d) corrective advertising, and (e) counter advertising.

7 Have you ever been a target for what appeared to be a bait-and-switch scheme? Describe how it operated and your reactions to it.

8 In your college library locate a recent FTC Industry Guide and a Trade

Regulation Rule that affect advertising. Summarize each and bring them to class; be ready to discuss and debate the suitability of the guide and the rule provided.

9 From the pages of a recent issue of *Advertising Age*, or other periodical, locate a recent decision by the NARB. Bring a summary of the ruling to class for discussion; if possible, bring a copy of the advertisement involved.

10 Can self-regulation lessen the need for the control of advertising by governmental agencies? Explain.

FOR FURTHER REFERENCE

Brozen, Yale (ed.): *Advertising and Society*, New York University Press, New York, 1974.

Divita, S. F.: *Advertising and the Public Interest*, American Marketing Association, Chicago, 1974.

Howard, John A., and James Hulbert: *Advertising and the Public Interest*, Crain Communications, Inc., Chicago, 1973.

Howard, Marshall C.: *Legal Aspects of Marketing*, McGraw-Hill Book Company, New York, 1964.

Kintner, Earl W.: *A Primer on the Law of Deceptive Practices*, The Macmillan Company, New York, 1971.

Preston, Ivan L.: *The Great American Blow-up: Puffery in Advertising and Selling*, The University of Wisconsin Press, Madison, 1975.

Stridsberg, Albert B.: *Effective Advertising Self-Regulation: A Survey of Current World Practice and Analysis of International Patterns*, International Advertising Association, New York, 1974.

Wright, John S., and John E. Mertes: *Advertising's Role in Society*, West Publishing Company, St. Paul, Minn., 1974.

SIX

THE FUTURE OF ADVERTISING

The last section of this textbook is a look into the future. Admittedly, prediction is a hazardous process; nevertheless, everyone is curious about what the future holds for the individual and for the society of which he or she is a part. Some of what we say may not come to pass; yet an understanding of the forces at work should add meaning to events as they transpire.

We attempt to divine where advertising is headed over the next decade. In doing so, we first look at its future in the United States, then throughout the rest of the world. Finally, the future of advertising as a career for college graduates is analyzed.

CHAPTER 21
WHERE ADVERTISING IS HEADED

Advertising, like other disciplines that function in modern society, must adapt to changes in life-styles, and advertising people must know about the forces—political, economic, and social—that create these changes. If any word characterizes the pace of the years following World War II, it is "change." Almost overused to the point of becoming a cliche, "change" is the best term to sum up our present lives. Two best-sellers of the early 1970s—*Future Shock* by Alvin Toffler and *Greening of America* by Charles Reich—described the impact of rapid change on society and provided useful guidebooks to marketing and advertising planners.

Among the forces that created our present life-style is the political unrest of the late 1960s and early 1970s, which contained the Vietnam War, followed by corresponding campus unrest and national political scandal. Prior to these events, there was an enormous social upheaval in the civil rights movements of the 1960s, which many people feel caused the women's movement and aroused the consciousness of other minorities besides blacks. The 1960s brought high levels of economic growth, and new levels of affluence were reached by many members of society. Economic conditions in the 1970s, however, were not as kind, and the United States along with the entire developed world experienced sharp inflation accompanied by the unemployment of many workers—several million in the United States alone. Forecasting from these conditions, we can anticipate equal or greater demographic, economic, social, political, and technological changes in the late 1970s. For any facet of advertising to function in this kind of world, adaptability to change is an essential requirement. Because of the shortage of some vital resources, which changes market conditions, advertising will once again have to adapt, as it will to the changing nature of affluence in our country.

This chapter examines those changes which may affect the future of advertising. In assessing where advertising is heading, we must remember that it is essentially a subsystem of marketing which in turn is a subsystem of business. The economy and society which business serves must be dissected, and advertising placed in its proper perspective in the total environment. Advertising is a dynamic activity which has shown great ability to change in response to shifts in environmental forces. Its future success is dependent upon how well advertising continues to adapt and serve.

THE FUTURE OF ADVERTISING IN THE UNITED STATES

Our discussion of advertising's future in the United States is divided into three parts; advertising is considered (1) as an economic force, (2) as a social institution, and (3) as a communicative art. Of course, some of the ideas discussed carry over in application to the international scene, which is the topic of a later portion of this chapter.

The Economic Role of Advertising in the Future

Advertising became an integral part of the economic system when the Industrial Revolution brought about mass production of goods. As manufacturers became concentrated in special localities where power, labor, or raw materials were readily available, consumers and producers were separated geographically. Furthermore, specialization of labor spread into the distribution phase of business, and intermediaries took over the marketing of products. Consumers could no longer ask the person who made the product about its qualities. A communication system between the producer and the intermediaries also became necessary. Advertising came to fill these communications gaps. It is obvious that the economic future of advertising is dependent upon the continuation and intensification of the separation between the production and consumption functions in our society. All signs point in that direction. Moreover, many other changes are occurring which favor the growth of advertising.

Mass Consumption

Markets consist of (1) people, with (2) money and (3) willingness to spend. A new economic order that has developed in the United States, in Europe, and even in parts of Asia, such as Japan, is called the *mass consumption society*. Three important features characterize this society: (1) affluence of the population, (2) consumer power over the growth of the economy, and (3) increasing importance of consumer psychology. In this economic environment "not a few individuals, nor a thin upper class, but the majority of families now have discretionary purchasing power and constantly replace and enlarge their stock of consumer goods."[1] The editors of *Fortune* point out that "the United States was the first nation in which economic growth transformed the mass consumer market from a low-income to a middle-income market,"and go on to predict that "the United States is entering the era of the mass high-income market."[2] We first look at people and their roles in an expanding economy.

Population Trends Following 1945 the United States population grew at an annual rate of 1.7 percent for 15 years. This was the famous

---

[1] George Katona, *The Mass Consumption Society*, McGraw-Hill Book Company, New York, 1964.
[2] Editors of *Fortune, Markets of the Seventies*, The Viking Press, Inc., New York, 1969, p. 100.

post-World War II "baby boom." Demand for many products and services came almost automatically with the increase in population.

By the late 1960s the growth rate had declined to 1 percent, but an upturn was predicted for the late 1970s when the children born following 1945 would be entering the family-building stage of their life cycle. However, changing attitudes concerning early marriage and the desirable number of children in the "ideal family," along with the advent of the oral contraceptive, may make this expectation erroneous. The preliminary figure for the fertility rate (births per 1,000 females aged 15 to 44) for 1974 was 68.5, a considerable drop from the 1970 rate of 87.5, and there was much talk of a zero population growth (ZPG). It seemed clear, then, that opportunities for sales would not expand indefinitely solely because of greater numbers of people in our nation. However, death rates also are declining. This trend plus immigration gains will result in population growth, but a lower rate than in the past. The population of the United States is expected to expand to about 224 million by 1980, from 204.9 million in 1970, an average annual rate of growth of about 0.9 percent.

More significant to marketing and advertising is the changing composition of our population. A dramatic increase in the number of people in the key buying years will occur over the coming decade. Past experience has shown that people in the 25-to-39-year range are the prime market for most consumer goods and services. In early 1976 approximately 43 million people were in this age group, about 20 percent of the country's total population. The number will stand at 51 million by 1980 and 58 million in 1985. The last figure will represent one-fourth of all Americans. As families are formed, consumer durables are purchased to furnish new homes; children are born, even if at lower rate per family. The market potential created by this changed composition of the population is staggering to contemplate. Advertising should aid in informing and persuading consumers about alternative products and services available to satisfy their needs. Of course, whether this potential will result in actual sales depends, for one thing, upon whether consumers will have sufficient money to purchase them.

Family Income Trends An interruption in the long-term trend of ever-increasing family incomes in the United States was brought about by the serious recession of 1974–1975. Because advertising is an institution of affluence, a vital question is whether our nation will return to a state of general affluence. It is our position that a return is likely, and the following discussion is based upon this assumption.

Increases in *disposable income* (money left over after payment of taxes) and in *discretionary income* (money left over after the purchase of necessities) are important factors in the demand for products and services. As the experiences of undeveloped countries reveal, population alone does not create sufficient demand to bring about national

FIGURE 21.1
This ad attempts to tap supernumerary income available in many American households. It is also an interesting use of an American art form (similar to that of Norman Rockwell) by a foreign manufacturer.

prosperity. The Conference Board, an independent business research organization, has coined the term "disposable supernumerary income" to describe the after-tax money available for luxury spending (somewhat similar to discretionary income).[3] In the 20 years preceding 1975, supernumerary income, measured in 1974 dollars, rose from

[3] Fabian Linden, "The Arithmetic of Affluence," *Consumer Markets*, September 1975. Data in this paragraph are from this source.

about $15 billion to over $80 billion. This means there was an annual growth rate of about 10 percent, twice the growth of total disposable income in the period. By 1980 Linden predicts that spendable supernumerary income will exceed $150 billion and account for 17 percent of total family disposable income. Expressed another way—in terms of family income—over 12 million, or 22 percent, of all United States families had incomes of $20,000 or more (in 1974 dollars), whereas only 6 million, or 12 percent, were at that level of affluence in 1965.

*what advertising is (different definitions)

Projections for 1980 predict the number will then stand at near 21 million families. At least $1 out of every $6 of consumer spending power will be spent by 1980 for goods and services that may be classified as beyond the necessities of living. Obviously, advertising should play a significant role for businesses attempting to tap this potential.

Thus, we see that the United States market is increasing in numbers, albeit at a slower rate than in the past; furthermore, disposable supernumerary income is growing at a rapid rate. This leaves the third factor—willingness to buy—as an opportunity area for advertising. Once the majority of the people of a country move above the subsistence level, advertising's ability to present product benefits to masses of people becomes essential in the marketing system. Advertising serves as a means of stimulating people out of buying ruts established when family incomes were lower. Advertising persuades people to buy things they can now afford. This function has social implications because the country's economic health is based largely upon high levels of personal consumption; otherwise unemployment results. Advertising provides an essential communication system for business firms wishing to participate in the larger markets resulting from more people with more money. Advertising would undoubtedly continue if these trends were reversed, but its rate of use would be slowed down materially.

Other Socioeconomic Trends   Several additional trends on the American scene bode well for the future of advertising, and at the same time pose challenges to it. Citizens of the United States, regardless of their socioeconomic and ethnic grouping, have experienced more formal *education* than in previous generations. Adults with at least a high school diploma numbered 60 million in 1970; the number will approach 84 million by 1980. By that date, more than 35 million Americans will have had some college training, more than one-half with bachelor's degrees. More education generally means greater earning capacity. Furthermore, it means different tastes for products and changing levels of aspiration. Advertising assists people who are seeking to learn the value systems of their new station in life. Advertisements are consulted for appropriate ways to manifest new lifestyles. More education, at the same time, has made these people more sophisticated, and advertising appeals need to be geared to their new levels of accomplishments. When consumers have greater education and higher income levels, markets tend to be more fragmented than was the case of the old-style mass middle-class environment. A specific example is the nonwhite population, which consisted of 24.1 million blacks and 3.2 million other nonwhites in 1975.[4] This group is charac-

[4] *The Gibson Report* as quoted in *Business Week*, Feb. 23, 1976, p. 96.

terized as "the 9th largest consumer market in the world." Spending by nonwhites in 1976 was placed at $73 billion, and the segment will have an aggregate income of $120 billion by 1980. With greater market segmentation, whatever the basis, different advertising approaches should be employed if the seller is to tap the full market potential.

Mobility is another influential force on the American scene. In the first five years of the 1970s, nearly one-half of the population changed their place of residence; for persons in their late twenties, eight out of ten moved. The movement of population continues to be into metropolitan areas, with the central city suffering losses to suburbia and exurbia. People now have access to more retail stores and to a more sophisticated merchandising environment. The changes bring about a need for a different kind of advertising. When in a new environment, the consumer looks for new retail sources and therefore is open to new and useful information. Advertisements provide clues about whether a particular store is the place where the person wants to shop. New patterns of product preference are created through the relocation process. When one moves up the socioeconomic ladder, one tends to adapt to the tastes of the new neighborhood. Once again, advertising provides clues to acceptable consumption behavior.

Working women are a powerful factor in the expansion of the markets of the future. Approximately 39 percent of all women aged 16 years or older were working in 1965. By 1970 the figure approached 43 percent, climbed to 46 percent in 1975, and is projected to reach 48.5 percent by 1980. The income level of many women workers is increasing as well. This change was brought about by new attitudes concerning the role of women in our society and by legislation which opened up employment opportunities to them. Family income obviously increases when two wage earners contribute to it, especially as the pay differential between men and women narrows. The two-worker family unit moves into the supernumerary income class faster than the one-worker family. Moreover, the woman's traditional role as the household purchasing agent is altered. More responsibility for family shopping is discharged by the male and by the children, thus requiring different advertising strategies to reach these buyers. When the woman still performs the shopping function, it is done in a much different manner—less leisurely, more businesslike, and with less comparison of product offerings in several stores. Advertising is relied upon more heavily as a source of information about products and prices in order to save shopping time. Product reputation, created in part by advertising, is more important to the busy shopper. The increase in the numbers of women workers has also increased the market for prepackaged, prepared foods and other items with timesaving features built into them. Advertising has the job of explaining these products and their availability to working women.

Longer vacations and *earlier retirements* are definite trends in the

FIGURE 21.2
Information about new products is disseminated through advertising. In recent years the slow cooker has been widely adopted by American households. The original brand, CROCK-POT, is featured in this holiday-season magazine ad which carries the photograph of the product spokesman in its television commercials.

The Original SLOW ELECTRIC STONEWARE COOKER.

CROCK·POT

"...worth its wait in flavor"

"We've had our Crock-Pot two years," Joe says. "It's no rookie when it comes to good things to eat."

Rival's Crock-Pot started the exciting swing to tender flavorful Slow Cooking. Stopped the stirring and sticking, slowed the timing, zipped up the good taste.

Try the Crock-Pot for stews, soups, baked beans, seafood, vegetables, bread and cakes. Or an unforgettable pot roast — from an economy cut of beef. Put in the ingredients in the morning. Set it on Low and forget it. Don't peek. Don't stir. Above all, don't worry. Let Crock-Pot simmer for 8, 10 or 12 hours. You'll agree with Joe, "it's worth its wait in flavor!"

Cooks all day while the cook's away. On no more current than a 75-watt light bulb (about 3¢). And you get a wonderful 84-page Cookbook with over 150 recipes.

The perfect gift. Don't settle for second best. Insist on the Crock-Pot, the ORIGINAL, the one that STARTED Slow Cooking.

Crock-Pot sizes for all; 2, 3, 3½, 5 qts. in pretty kitchen colors.

RIVAL· RIVAL MANUFACTURING COMPANY
Kansas City, Mo. 64129 • In Canada: Montreal

United States. These trends have created what is known as the *leisure market*. Do-it-yourself urges are stimulated in part by more free time and are accentuated by the scarcity and expensiveness of skilled artisans, such as painters, carpenters, and gardeners. Advertising acts as a stimulus to this trend by showing how the various tasks can be performed. Active sports, world travel, and various creative hobbies including oil painting and woodworking are also part of the leisure market that advertising is called upon to reach. Many other forces could be added to this discussion; combined, they spell out an increased need for more advertising in the United States. As the same conditions obtain in other nations, increased demand for the services of advertising should result.

Changes on the Business Scene

Demographic and other socioeconomic changes in the consumer market are not the only forces affecting the future of advertising.

New Products and Advertising   In addition to increased supernumerary income, a continued flow of new products contributes to an increasing need for advertising. Certainly the innovator of a mass-market item should employ mass communications to tell potential users about its existence. Although there was a slacking off of research and development (R&D) investment during the mid-1970s, our nation nevertheless spent $32 billion on R&D in 1975. This figure amounted to 2.3 percent of the gross national product (GNP), whereas we were spending at a 3.0 percent rate in the 1964–1967 period. The decline represents, in our opinion, a pause in direction reflecting an end to the space program and other major research projects. Once we decide to do something about the energy problem, such as developing a system of solar heating, the former levels of R&D spending will probably be again reached. Our point is that the successful launching of new consumer products is heavily dependent upon larger-than-average expenditures for advertising. As long as companies look for growth through new products, there will be a need for advertising designed to inform consumers of the product's availability in the marketplace.

Mergers and Conglomerates   The trend toward the consolidation of business into the hands of fewer producers, as well as the increased diversification in the products marketed by producers, is another example of changes on the business scene which act to perpetuate advertising as a significant economic force in our society. Larger firms and varied product lines frequently lead to impersonal attitudes toward, and lack of producer identification by, customers. However, advertising can provide a means whereby large-scale producers can communicate with customers and establish rapport with them. Without advertising such manufacturers are often left at the mercy of intermediaries insofar as consumer contact is concerned. Related to this situation is the problem of the conglomerate form of business. Blending together a number of businesses, often not related as to product line, into a larger entity creates a serious identification problem. "Just whom are we dealing with?" is the buyer's question. Advertising can explain.

In his book, *Madison Avenue, USA*, Martin Mayer suggests that advertising appropriations grow as a company prospers. Professor Harry G. Johnson phrases Mayer's point in this manner:

> Advertising is a form of insurance for the corporation against the risks of managerial mortality.

Another reason for the continuance of advertising expenditures at high levels is given by Johnson in these words:

> The rise of Madison Avenue to date has been associated on the one hand with technical progress both in communication and in the techniques employed by communications media, which made possible the elaborate centrally planned and executed advertising campaign, and on the other hand with the rising relative cost of labor, which has given a progressive cost advantage to "absentee salesmanship" by means of advertising aimed at the buyer. . . .[5]

Marion Harper once said "that for many companies the public's knowledge of these companies and brands is their biggest asset."[6] Public acceptance of a company comes from many sources, including advertising.

The Gross National Product and Advertising   One common way to evaluate the importance of advertising in a nation's economy is to relate advertising expenditures to the gross national product. Advertising has not fared well on this score. Prior to 1940 the level of investment in advertising averaged close to 3 percent of the GNP. During World War II with its shortages of consumer goods, the ratio fell to slightly over 1 percent. The figure now stands at an even 2 percent. Products, in other words, are apparently being sold in the United States today with relatively less advertising support than in the 1930s. Rising costs of advertising may be one factor, as well as greater efficiency of advertising. Furthermore, the character of the GNP has changed and now has a substantial governmental segment and a very high service industry quotient, neither of which are as advertisable as the traditional components of GNP.

It is fair to state, however, that advertising now represents a declining part of the consumer sector of the economy and that advertising-to-sales ratios are diminishing for national manufacturing

---

[5] Harry G. Johnson, "The Consumer and Madison Avenue," in Perry Bliss (ed.), *Marketing and the Behavioral Sciences*, Allyn and Bacon, Inc., Boston, 1963, p. 124. Originally published in *Current Economic Comment*, August 1960.
[6] Quoted from "Obstacles, Opportunities, Optimism, and Obligations," a talk by John Crichton, 4As Central Region Annual Meeting, Nov. 7, 1974.

companies, especially in the packaged-goods field.[7] Bogart believes that "this may reflect the fact that we are approaching the limits of consumers' capacity to absorb additional advertising communication" and that "it may mean a shift in the balance of advertising and other forms of sales promotion."[8]

Before looking at some other countervailing forces which are operating to decrease the role of advertising, we would like to raise a pertinent question: "Are businesspeople advertising enough?" Probably not, if we agree with the following remarks made by Peter Drucker about advertising's parent, marketing:

> Wherever conditions do not resemble . . . extreme scarcity . . . new technology needs, above all, effective marketing. It needs an understanding of the market and its dynamics. Indeed this is necessary to direct the technological efforts. . . . It takes innovative marketing to create the new perception for the customer so that he can use the new to expand his horizon, to raise his expectations and aspirations, and to derive new satisfactions.
>
> Economic advance is not greater satisfaction of old needs and wants. It is new choice. It is the widening of the horizon of expectations and aspirations. This is largely a function of marketing which, therefore, is needed to make the technological change economically productive, that is, result in the satisfaction of human needs and wants.[9]

And, of course, advertising is an important element in the marketing mix for most firms.

Economic Forces Decreasing Demand for Advertising

There are several forces acting as a drag on consumer spending, which in turn will tend to decrease the need for advertising. For one thing, bigger tax bites from all governmental levels are to be anticipated for many years ahead. Larger portions of family income will go for such essentials as transportation and fuel costs unless the energy shortage is relieved by a technological breakthrough. At least in the short run consumers are presently less optimistic about their ability to "continue to improve their economic condition—and this surely affects buying habits. . . ."[10] However, as long as incomes keep pace with the rate of inflation, and unemployment declines, the consumer pessimism should dissipate.

[7] Personal communication, Leo Bogart, Executive Vice-President and General Manager, Newspaper Advertising Bureau, Inc., dated Feb. 11, 1976.
[8] Ibid.
[9] Peter Drucker, *The Age of Discontinuity*, Harper & Row, Publishers, Incorporated, New York, 1969, p. 54.
[10] Herbert Zeltner, "New Kinds of Consumer Buying Data Seen Ahead," *Advertising Age*, Nov. 10, 1975, p. 70.

With services obtaining larger portions of consumer dollars, there will be less relative need for advertising unless the advertising of services is increased. More effective use of advertising, as in the case of Anheuser-Busch reaching heavy beer drinkers, means that at least for some advertisers there will be fewer dollars spent for it. As various media, such as television, become saturated with advertising messages—the so-called clutter factor—some sellers may well decide to seek other alternatives in their efforts to persuade consumers to buy their products. If done with some frequency, the total of advertising would be reduced.

Consumerism, which has been described as "a social movement seeking to augment the rights and power of buyers in relation to sellers,"[11] became a major social issue in the late 1960s under the leadership of Ralph Nader. The movement is critical of advertising on many scores, and its activity has led to greater governmental control of advertising and possibly may have brought about some decline in its use. There have been many efforts to tax advertising in a manner similar to the sales tax on goods. Some people advocate limiting the amount of money that may be spent to advertise certain classifications of goods such as drugs and foods. Similarly, the sellers of goods and services employing the use of scarce commodities such as electric utilities would be denied the right to advertise, or at least to declare such expenditures as a tax deduction. Since its surfacing in the 1960s, the consumer movement has apparently established itself as a permanent force. Its primary thrust is not aimed at the elimination of advertising per se. Instead consumerists desire that the content of the advertising message be informational rather than persuasive. In their demands however, these individuals sometimes show a lack of understanding of how the marketplace operates, the fundamentals of consumer behavior, and the rudiments of creating advertisements. The advertising industry should endeavor to build communication bridges with consumer leaders and adapt to their needs when feasible.

Conclusions

Balancing these positive and negative forces on the demand for advertising in the future is a challenging task. Dollar figures, of course, show advertising growing at a tremendous rate. In 1940 advertising expenditures in the United States were $2 billion; thirty-five years later the figure was nearly $30 billion, a fifteenfold increase. Much of the increase was, undoubtedly, due to inflation. It seems likely that the past rate of growth is likely to continue. At any rate, advertising should continue to be an important business tool in future years.

[11] Philip Kotler, "What Consumerism Means for Marketers," *Harvard Business Review*, May–June 1972, p. 49.

THE FUTURE OF ADVERTISING AS
A SOCIAL INSTITUTION

Advertising does exert considerable influence upon social behavior patterns in our society. It is an institution of social control, as well as one of economic force. Attacks upon advertising have been around for many years. Recently, however, the tempo of these attacks seems to have increased. Furthermore, these attacks have been more and more concerned with its social functioning. A wide assortment of philosophers, theologians, social scientists, historians, and other social commentators have shown interest in the social role of advertising; their opinions have received wide circulation.

The attacks upon advertising are basically of two types. First, advertising is accused of being dishonest—of being fraudulent or misleading. Second, advertising is accused of being a corrupting influence upon our society. Advertising not only is often in bad taste, runs the argument, but also causes people to develop unhealthy attitudes and to set undesirable personal goals. Advertising, in other words, debases the public mind and spirit.

These charges are strong ones and are often couched in powerful language by extremely vocal critics who are gifted in their articulative abilities. If the charges are true, the future of advertising is in serious jeopardy, for the continuance of advertising—although serving economic and business purposes—cannot be permitted if the public welfare is injured in the process.

Truth in Advertising

Chapter 20 explores this topic rather thoroughly; therefore our discussion at this point is brief. Obviously, there is such a thing as dishonesty in advertising, as may be found in all walks of life. Enforcement of existing laws and better education of consumers remain the best protections against false and fraudulent advertising.

A more difficult area appears when we move to misleading advertising. One of the accepted tenets of the common law is that the seller has the right to "puff" his or her wares. What this means is that the law recognizes—and believes that the buyer does too—that when someone has something to sell, he or she tries to put the item in the best possible light. A certain amount of excess enthusiasm about the product should be expected and taken for granted. Ivan L. Preston, a teacher of advertising at the University of Wisconsin, wrote a 368-page book published in 1975 which traces the history of puffery in advertising and selling in the United States.[12] He concludes and advocates that this legal defense should be taken away from sellers.

---

[12] Ivan L. Preston, *The Great American Blow-up: Puffery in Advertising and Selling*, The University of Wisconsin Press, Madison, 1975.

Drawing the line, however, between acceptable overstatement and false or fraudulent statements is not always easy; opinions differ on the point. Thus, a symposium of clergymen sponsored by the Toronto School of Theology, when charged to investigate "truth in advertising," concluded their deliberations with this recommendation: ". . . that TRUTH be the sole basic moral criterion in advertising in North America."[13] This conclusion was explained by these words:

> Although emotion-tinged exasperated concern might promote an initial recommendation of other criteria, further consideration will reveal that *only the truth-criterion can be enforced* without courting the dangers of arbitrariness, excessive Puritanism, paternalism and even serious abridgment of human liberties.

Most advertising in modern-day America is truthful. When untruthful advertising is found, it should be eliminated and the perpetrators aggressively prosecuted. We anticipate that legislation and judicial interpretation in future years, as well as self-regulation by the advertising industry and enlightened business practice by advertisers, will lessen the relevancy of this criticism of advertising. Continued efforts to limit advertisers to the use of only the coldest factual information in their advertisements are to be anticipated. However, in an affluent society, psychological satisfactions have become more important for most consumers than material ones; furthermore, it is well to remember that a feature or an "image" of a product that is meaningless to one person may be quite meaningful to someone belonging to a different sex, age bracket, ethnic group, or social group. Deciding such issues on behalf of consumers is fraught with the possibilities enumerated by the ministers quoted above. We would be well advised to concentrate, as they recommend, on the truth criterion.

Advertising as a Corrupter

Some critics of advertising claim that most advertising is in bad taste. Advertising illustrations are said to represent low levels of aesthetic appreciation. Moreover, some advertisements deal with offensive or delicate subjects, such as body odor, bad breath, indigestion, and intimate wearing apparel. Furthermore, these critics claim advertising dollars are used to sponsor mass media featuring inane or vulgar subject matter. Many television programs, for instance, carry crime, violence, or sex as their principal themes, nor are the print media

[13] *Truth in Advertising*, Fitzhenry & Whiteside, Ltd., Harper & Row, Publishers, Inc., Toronto, 1972, pp. 5–6, as reprinted in John S. Wright and John E. Mertes (eds.), *Advertising's Role in Society*, West Publishing Company, St. Paul, Minnesota, 1974, pp. 299–300.

innocent of such offenses. The essence of these criticisms is that advertising is turning us into a bunch of cultural morons.

Once again, we must look critically at the charges. Advertising has a responsibility if it has the degree of influence in our society which is claimed for it. Some advertisements are offensive. Generally speaking, media—acting individually or as an industry—attempt to screen out such advertisements. But taste is a subjective matter. The ads in *Playboy* are not meant for the audience of the *Nation's Business* nor that of the *Ladies Home Journal*.

Keeping these violations of standards in mind, one gets the feeling, nevertheless, that the critics are attempting to foist their own standards upon the general public. As Leo Rosten says:

> Most intellectuals do not understand the inherent nature of the mass media. . . . They project their own tastes, yearnings, and values upon the masses—who do not, unfortunately, share them.[14]

Who should determine what an individual's preference in art and entertainment should be? Advertisers strive to reach potential customers in the most efficient way. Choosing media already popular with potential customers is one way of doing so.

This matter soon becomes a chicken-and-egg situation, with the critics of the cultural level of advertising advocating that advertisers should lead the public in the development of higher levels of cultural taste. Some advertisers, as a matter of fact, have done a great deal along these lines. Modern art, for instance, has reached its present heights of acceptance with the assistance of advertisers who were courageous enough to use new art forms in their advertisements. Similarly, good music has been fostered by those advertisers who use "good music" radio stations as their medium of advertising. Advertisers underwrite many other kinds of cultural and educational programs. The documentary which explores current social and economic problems is an example. Public affairs broadcasts of political conventions, state occasions, and historical events are in the same vein. Much of public broadcasting is underwritten by grants from corporations which get the most modest of credits for doing so. Some authorities contend that advertising should not lead but rather should reflect social and cultural trends.

As far as advertising connected with bodily processes is concerned, it has promoted high levels of personal cleanliness and hygiene among our people. For example, the importance of brushing

[14] Leo Rosten, "The Intellectual and the Mass Media," *Daedalus*, Spring 1960. Reprinted by permission of *Daedalus* and D. Van Nostrand Company, Inc., publishers of *Jacob's Culture for the Millions* (1961). See also John S. Wright and Daniel S. Warner (eds.), *Speaking of Advertising*, McGraw-Hill Book Company, New York, 1963, p. 175.

FIGURE 21.3

This print advertisement for ice cream is an example of the beautiful artwork often seen in advertising today. The ad appeared in color. Because of the wide exposure of such advertising, the level of art appreciation among the population should gradually be raised.

teeth regularly was learned from advertising messages as well as from the family dentist. Furthermore, personal standards of what is proper vary a great deal. What appears to be jarring to the sensitive person may result in long-range benefit to the entire group, including the sensitive one. It seems that the best interests of the advertiser and the media provide adequate controlling forces in the difficult-to-define area of taste.

Another group of advertising critics feel that advertising encourages the development of unsatisfactory standards of personal behavior. Advertising, they argue, persuades people to want things they do not need or should not have. It gets people to place false value on things—in other words, to be materialistic. Moreover, advertising is accused of fostering wastefulness and self-indulgence. This point of view implies that the critic is the best judge of how people should lead their lives. In a free-choice economy, however, the individual has the right to spend his or her time and money as he or she chooses as long as fellow humans are not hurt by the activity. Perhaps greater consumer efficiency might be achieved if the production and distribution of goods were centrally controlled, although the results achieved in totalitarian societies indicate otherwise. A certain amount of waste is probably the price we pay for freedom of choice, whether in the marketplace or in government, religion, or education. Moreover, the upward movement of consumer preferences for products is part and parcel of a pattern of rising standards of living. When advertising creates a desire for additional goods and services, individuals may be expected to exert themselves and produce more to obtain them. Thus, the gross national product increases.

Conclusions

The sheer volume of advertising criticism on the social side of the ledger seems to confirm the claim that advertising exerts a considerable influence in our society. The question is not whether advertising is or is not a social institution, but rather how its influence should be directed. Although most criticisms leveled at advertising are exaggerations derived from isolated instances and not from general practices, its critics perform a worthwhile service for advertising. The pokes and jibes tend to keep advertising people alert to a latent danger; they are reminded of the responsibility which accompanies advertising's influence.

The influence of advertising seems likely to increase rather than decline. Advertising was the principal supporter of mass media during their years of development and is well entrenched within their operational frameworks today. Advertising, moreover, is accepted and expected by most Americans. In the main, they do not resent its presence; instead they look to it as one guide in their personal behavior. Advertising is being employed in many new areas, as is indicated in the following section. Its sphere of influence is increasing. By and large, the accusations that advertising is dishonest and a corrupting influence are outweighed by its overall honesty and its influence for the general good. Nevertheless, vigilance is needed if advertising's present status of influence is to be enhanced, or even preserved.

THE FUTURE OF ADVERTISING AS COMMUNICATION

Once it has been established that advertising has a future both as an economic force and as a social institution, more discussion of the subject is probably unnecessary. There are, however, two additional areas where current developments are both important and interesting. One area involves the increased emphasis being placed upon advertising as a communicative art; the other deals with the emergence of international advertising.

Advertising Application to Nonbusiness Problems: Social Advertising

This textbook is oriented toward the use of advertising to help in the distribution of goods and services. The facts of business warrant this orientation, for most advertising effort and expenditures are made for business purposes. However, there is a growing use of marketing and advertising for nonbusiness purposes.[15] Such developments increase the volume of advertising; it is estimated that 10 percent of all advertising now emanates from nonprofit organizations. Moreover, they tend to raise its stature in the public eye. Advertising takes on some of the prestige of the activity it promotes. At least such use of advertising leads to it being looked at from a different point of view. If an advertising critic's favorite cause, say, the Sierra Club, successfully employs advertising to promote membership or sales of its books, it is natural that he or she look at advertising differently.

Kotler calls these efforts *social advertising*, which he divides into five subgroups: political advertising, social cause advertising, philanthropic organization advertising, government organization advertising, and private nonprofit organization advertising.[16]

Political Advertising Political candidates once relied upon speeches before live audiences as their main vote-getting method. Candidates traveled throughout their voting areas and spoke to as many voters as possible in groups and singly. This approach is like personal selling in

[15] See Philip Kotler, *Marketing for Nonprofit Organizations*, Prentice-Hall, Inc., Englewood Cliffs, N.J., 1975.
[16] Ibid., pp. 202–203.

the marketing mix for products. Development of mass media and increased population led candidates to seek ways of placing their stories before the voting public in nonpersonal form, and advertisements were inserted in newspapers and on outdoor signs. Radio allowed voters to hear the candidate's voice, and President Franklin D. Roosevelt became a master of the radio medium in his political campaigning.

Television now permits candidates to address large numbers of people at one time and allows millions of voters to see as well as hear candidates. Dwight Eisenhower's successful campaign for the Presidency in 1952 was aided by short commercials which caused the opposition to state that "the presidency is being sold like a bar of soap." Many political experts believe John F. Kennedy won the presidency in 1960 because of his ability to project youthfulness and vigor over television. Being photogenic on television has become a decided plus for any aspirant for political office.

Presidential candidates in 1972 spent $80 million for advertising, and candidates for other offices spent another $320 million. More and more political campaign strategy relies on television; the medium allows the candidate to reach more people, more often, at less cost per impression than platform appearances can yield. Greater interest in political affairs has probably resulted from the easy way in which voters can now learn about the candidates.

Social Cause Advertising Many public interest causes employ advertising when trying to get messages before the general public. Thus, we see the Planned Parenthood League, NOW, and similar groups among those employing advertising for social purposes.

Social cause advertising has been greatly facilitated by the work of the Advertising Council, which was started during World War II as a means of securing public support for such causes as the purchase of war bonds, donation of blood, and the enlistment of women into the armed services. Advertising agencies and advertising departments volunteer the skills of their employees to develop advertising programs for those causes selected for promotion under the aegis of the Advertising Council. The finished ads are then published or broadcast by media either as a free public service or in return for the payment of media charges by the sponsoring advertiser. Social causes received $529,152,292 of advertising in 1975 through the operation of the Advertising Council.

Philanthropic Organization Advertising Social cause advertising is primarily propagandistic in intent, whereas philanthropic advertising focuses on fund raising for worthwhile causes.[17] Mass appeals are

---

[17] Ibid.

It happened to us once.
It can happen again.
And again.

FIGURE 21.4
"Advocacy advertising" is adopted when a company feels the media are not providing the public with all sides of a controversial issue. In effect, the ads are "paid editorials."

made to enlist the support of the people for the United Fund campaign in many cities, as well as to obtain financial assistance for the Red Cross, Christmas Seals, Easter Seals, and so forth. Philanthropic organizations often spend a considerable portion of the monies raised for the very advertising designed to raise funds. Direct mail is often the medium used in these efforts.

Government Organization Advertising Many state governments and some municipalities employ advertising to attract tourists and new industries to their areas. Similarly, units of local government, such as park commissions and police departments, dispatch advertising messages concerning recreational opportunities, local events, and safety tips to residents of the community. Since abolition of the military draft, the armed services of the United States government have become major advertisers, spending in excess of $100 million annually, in their efforts to sign up volunteers.

Private Nonprofit Organization Advertising Colleges and universities, particularly those which are privately financed, use advertising to interest students in the possibilities of enrolling at their particular institutions. Kotler reminds us that "museums, symphonies, hospitals, and religious organizations all have strong communication responsibilities and are involved in preparing annual reports, direct mailings, classified ads, broadcast messages, and other forms of advertising."[18]

Conclusions These various forms of social advertising are not alone in the public interest arena. Many corporations carry on institutional or corporate advertising campaigns. A considerable portion of these campaigns is devoted to public service themes. In the mid-1970s the energy crisis spawned many advertisements addressed to this problem's solution. Furthermore, some corporations engage in "advocacy" advertising, wherein the corporation expresses its opinions on matters of controversy when it is felt that the established media are not presenting both sides of the issue. In effect, the ads are paid editorials which appear in the media in the form of advertisements.

Greater use of advertising for nonbusiness purposes is anticipated in future years. Charities nearly always have difficulty raising needed funds; personal solicitation is both costly and time-consuming, and if volunteers are used, often relatively ineffective. Any device which materially reduces such costs is to be welcomed. Political candidates will look more and more to the communications techniques of advertising to accomplish their communication goals. Governmental agencies seek to communicate their goals to the public in order to be more effective and to reduce taxpayers' resistance to requests for more money. Religious organizations are turning to advertising as a way of promoting their causes. Such activities increase not only the pervasiveness of advertising but also its recognition as an important institution in modern society. In a world characterized by a "knowledge explosion" and a "communication revolution," the advertising profession has a challenging opportunity to employ its innovative skills to facilitate dissemination of new thoughts, as well as information about new products.

[18] Ibid., p. 203.

Increased Emphasis on Scientific Methods

The days of the self-made advertising man or woman appear to be at an end. No longer can a flair for words guarantee success. Quantifiable methods are being developed at an accelerating rate in advertising. As a result, careers in advertising should be more rewarding, in both the material and creative senses, for persons knowledgeable in the use of the new methods. What are some of the developments on this front?

First of all, sincere efforts are being made to more precisely define key principles of mass communication. In recent years, this search has been conducted on an industry wide basis, especially through the efforts of the Advertising Research Foundation. As a nonprofit organization supported by advertisers, agencies, media, and universities, the ARF has been a strong force in improving methods of advertising research and in distributing this knowledge widely. It has conducted studies of printed media readership and broadcast audience measurements, established basic criteria for evaluating research reports, consulted on the design of projects for individual sponsors to meet accepted standards, and provided confidential appraisals of published research. In addition, especially since it began the publication of the *Journal of Advertising Research* in 1960, the foundation has materially stimulated the development of techniques and the refinement of methodology, and has disseminated the results of such experiments to all its members.

Use of the behavioral sciences in the practice of advertising is now a reality. Psychology, sociology, anthropology, and related fields are being tapped to help fathom the minds of consumers to determine their wants and needs more accurately. We are on the road to better understanding of that complex subject, consumer behavior.

The role of the computer, with its linear programming and simulation potentialities, is destined to become increasingly important to advertising decision making. The solution of advertising problems is becoming more analytical, and rule-of-thumb and formula advertising are giving way to advertising approaches which are both more scientific and more imaginative.

Another trend, the feeling that creativity is something that can be learned, aims at the creation of more productive advertising. Alex Osborn pioneered this concept and maintained that everyone possesses creative ability to a degree. Its lack results from failure to use and develop a capacity that is originally almost universal. He made a strong case for the idea that creativity not only can be developed or learned, but can also be taught. Osborn's book, *Applied Imagination*, presents guiding principles around which this theory is developed.[19]

The greater dissemination of scientific research about advertising

[19] Alex F. Osborn, *Applied Imagination*, rev. ed., Charles Scribner's Sons, New York, 1963.

and the increased recognition of the importance of scientific methods in the application of advertising to marketing and social problems promise new opportunities for a variety of skills in the advertising field. At the same time, the need for people with highly developed creative and communicative abilities is as great—or greater—than ever before. Leo Burnett puts it this way:

> If people could tell you in advance what they want, there would never have been a wheel, a lever, much less an automobile, an electric refrigerator or a TV set. There would never have been a Barnum and Bailey circus, a *South Pacific* or a modern magazine. Somebody with the urge, the inspiration and the drive had to think it up and push it through. That goes for new advertising ideas, too. Somebody has to think them up and push them through. And somebody has to have imagination and guts enough to buy them.[20]

THE FUTURE OF ADVERTISING IN WORLD TRADE

The interdependence between the nations of the world is now generally recognized as a fact of life. Although foreign trade still accounts for less than 10 percent of our gross national product, it is fair to state that American economic abundance is tied to the world economy and its general good health. This point is dramatized when we learn that 20 percent of all corporate earnings for United States firms currently come from overseas sales. For selected firms, the contribution to earnings from foreign operations can be much higher; for example, Coca-Cola's overseas share of total profits stands at 55 percent; Gillette's at 51 percent; IBM, 54 percent; Sperry Rand, 50 percent; Revlon, 38 percent—the list could be extended indefinitely.[21] The United Nations estimated in 1973 that there existed approximately 7,300 multinational firms in the world; these companies are so designated because they have substantial investments, sales, and profits from outside their domestic operations. These MNC (multinational companies) in most cases employ international advertising agencies to assist in the promotion of their products throughout the world. Most international advertising is a part of the United States advertising industry. In 1975 the estimated total expenditures for world advertising was set at $55 billion, of which $30 billion was done in the United States; the total worldwide advertising expenditure is predicted to be $85 billion by 1980.[22] In sum, international advertising is already important on the world business scene and appears destined to grow in magnitude and significance.

[20] Leo Burnett, *Communication of an Advertising Man*, privately printed, Chicago, 1961, pp. 78–79.
[21] *Business Week*, Jan. 12, 1974, p. 53.
[22] Robert J. Coen, Vice-President, McCann-Erickson, as quoted in *Advertising Age*, Nov. 10, 1975, p. 6.

THANK YOU Please come again.

We mean what we say.
We do sincerely hope to see you again.
In fact again and again.
Both at our first store in Causeway Bay,
and the soon-to-be-opened
McDonald's at Repulse Bay.
McDonald's gives you the tastiest hamburgers
in the world, the crispiest french fries,
the thickest shakes and the hottest apple pies.
And it's all part of that great one minute
meal we're famous for.
Because no matter how busy we may be,
McDonald's will always have time to serve you.
And serve you fast! After all, that's what
has made McDonald's your favourite
eating place.

From tomorrow, a McDonaldland book cover
will be given away FREE with each
Big Mac purchased. And tomorrow afternoon,
Ronald McDonald, everyone's
favourite clown, will be at our store
to personally thank you for coming down
to McDonald's, and to hand out special
gifts to all our little friends.

McDonald's, the All-American Taste.

4, Paterson Street, Causeway Bay, Hong Kong, (near Daimaru)
Open daily from 8 a.m. to midnight

FIGURE 21.5
A familiar product
is presented to
English-language
residents of Hong
Kong.

The International Advertising Agency

Facing intensified competition for international markets as other nations increased their productive capacities and improved their marketing techniques, United States producers expanded their overseas advertising efforts. One study revealed that 72 percent of American

笑容不祗代表
我們的謝意.....

在麥當勞，你會發現我們每一位職員
臉上都很自然的流露着笑容，
它不祗代表我們的謝意，同時也代表着
我們愉快的心情。

正因為我們都以服務閣下為樂，
所以忙得也特別起勁。無論你要什麼…
美味的漢堡飽、甘香鬆脆的薯條，
濃香的美國奶昔或最新鮮的蘋果批，
我們只需要一分鐘便可以準備妥當。

為再表謝意，凡購買麥當勞巨無霸，
我們將送贈麥當勞萬能彩畫，
可用作課本封面、書枱墊紙及海報等
三種用途，印製精美，色彩鮮艷。
同時麥當勞叔叔特備禮物於明天下午
在麥當勞送給小朋友。
請即到銅鑼灣百德新街「麥當勞」，
便知詳細。

麥當勞　純美國口味

McDonald's麥當勞　　營業時間：每日上午八時至晚上十二時　香港銅鑼灣百德新街四號（近大丸）

FIGURE 21.6
The same basic message directed to Chinese-language residents of the city.

companies selling products in foreign markets employ advertising in their marketing mixes.[23] Major United States agencies went interna-

[23] Billy I. Ross, "A Study of the Advertising Practices and Procedures of U.S. Firms Selling Products Overseas," brochure published by the Department of Marketing, Texas Tech University, undated.

tional in their operations in order to defend domestic business by serving their American clients' international needs and also to develop new profit potential for themselves. Thus, in 1975 we see J. Walter Thompson, the largest United States agency with total billings of $900.0 millions of which $467.3 came from outside the country.[24] [Dentsu, a Japanese agency, billed more ($1.004 billion in 1975) than J. Walter Thompson, but approximately 90 percent of its total was in domestic Japanese billings.] Another American agency, McCann-Erickson, billed $544.3 million outside the United States in 1975, which made it the biggest agency insofar as international advertising goes.

The agencies which went international at an early date, such as J. Walter Thompson and McCann-Erickson, established branch offices in many of the principal cities of the world; the choices depended upon client marketing patterns. Later entrants into the international field purchased existing agencies, as with the Leo Burnett acquisition of the London Press Exchange. A third alternative is the partnership route whereby the American agency enters into a joint ownership arrangement with a strong foreign agency and provides it with a highly developed system of multinational coordination and uniformity of standards for planning and development of marketing strategy and creative execution. This approach has been adopted by Grey Advertising Inc., which has partners in Argentina, Australia, Austria, Belgium, Canada, France, Germany, Holland, Italy, Japan, South Africa, Spain, Sweden, United Kingdom, and Venezuela. This arrangement is advantageous when nationalistic attitudes bring about restrictions concerning foreign ownership of business firms within a nation.

International Advertising Decisions

Deciding whether to use an American agency or a foreign one is the first step to be taken by the United States seller who wishes to advertise in another land. Because of the dominance of the world's agency structure by the American-related organizations, that decision is usually made in favor of those international agencies headquartered in the United States.

Closely related to the agency choice is another critical problem area for the international advertising decision maker: creating the advertising message itself. One approach is to merely take copy used in domestic advertising and translate it into the language of the country where the advertisement is to appear. Such important considerations as local taboos, customs, or prejudices are likely to be overlooked.[25] International creative strategy should, however, strive for

---

[24] *Advertising Age*, Feb. 23, 1976, p. 1.

[25] See David Ricks, Marilyn Y. C. Fu, and Jeffrey S. Arpan, *International Business Blunders*, Grid, Inc., Columbus, Ohio, 1974, especially chap. 2, for some hilarious examples.

a degree of uniformity where the product and buying patterns will permit. Emphasis should be placed upon common denominators, not on differences. The correct philosophy, one held by Coca-Cola, is for the advertising to possess "one sound, one sight, one sell."

The international advertising executive must, therefore, know a great deal about the people of the country where the advertising is to run. Cultural differences are still very important, even as our world tends to become one due to the prevalence of mass communications throughout the continents. Knowledge of foreign media is also needed. In many countries, television stations are not permitted to air commercial messages, or their use is greatly restricted in a way that limits their effectivness. Theater advertising is a primary medium in some countries, and radio is highly important where illiteracy limits the circulation of printed media.

Advertising in Other Countries

Earlier we discussed the increasing use of advertising methods in communist, planned economies, such as found in Russia and in Eastern Europe. Of late, there has been a great surge of interest in advertising in the countries of the Middle East where economic development is accelerating rapidly due to the increased flow of cash brought about the pricing strategies of the oil cartel (OPEC). Thus, an Arabic business magazine published in Bierut, *Alam Attijarat* (World of Business), which has a controlled circulation of 14,000, showed a 75 percent increase in advertising in the first half of 1974 over 1973.[23] Figure 21.7 is an advertisement for an American-made product as it appeared in the publication.

Western European countries are employing advertising techniques which were developed primarily in the United States. And Japanese advertising, as shown in Figure 21.8, is quite imitative of the United States advertising. Application of American techniques has crossed both political and geographical boundaries to become truly worldwide.

Advertising by Foreign Firms and Countries

A number of foreign firms have made significant penetrations into the American market assisted by aggressive advertising campaigns. One of the all-time great success stories is that of Volkswagen, the German car manufacturer that fulfilled the desire of a segment of American motorists wishing an economical compact automobile not available from Detroit car makers. The advertising created to promote the "Bug," as done by Doyle Dane Bernbach, won many plaudits for its creativity

[26] *The New York Times*, July 18, 1974.

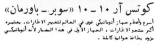

FIGURE 21.7
An American-
made industrial
product is adver-
tised in the
Arabic-language
edition of *Automo-
bile International*.
Tire changers are
featured.

and also sold millions of Volkswagen cars. Japanese autos, Datsun and Toyota, were equally successful later on, again aided by advertising designed by American agencies. Similarly, Japanese motorcycles were outstanding marketing successes. Nations of the world have advertised themselves as desirable tourist attractions, thereby tapping some of America's supernumerary income. Efforts by the United States to stimulate return visits have met with minimal success, although it is now becoming a common event to see a Japanese tour group taking in the sights in major American cities. Advertising is an institution which has helped the peoples of the world feel a closer kinship.

THE FUTURE OF ADVERTISING AS A CAREER

The importance of advertising and its promising future as a means of communication have just been presented. The prestige of advertising is growing throughout most of the world, along with the level of advertising expenditures. Its role in nonbusiness endeavors is also expanding. Added together, these positive forces make a case for advertising holding career opportunities for many young people today. Those who are not satisfied with the daily humdrum will find advertising filled with variety and challenge, as well as monetary rewards.

The critical question for the student, once he or she recognizes that the field of advertising possesses many vocational opportunities, is whether advertising will offer a viable career. To assess the possibilities the person needs to know the following: (1) How many jobs are there in advertising? (2) Who hires advertising personnel? (3) What are the different kinds of jobs available? (4) What talents are needed to qualify for these jobs? (5) How does one go about getting an advertising job? We provide some answers to these questions in this chapter, and additional insights can be obtained from the references suggested and from talking with men and women actively engaged in advertising.

Size of the Advertising Business

Media, agencies, supplier groups, and advertisers, the four basic components of the advertising business, provide the jobs to be found in advertising. Because no specialized census of advertising employment is made in the United States, it is difficult to ascertain the comparative number of positions in each category. The 1972 Census of Business revealed that 9,599 establishments with 104,826 employees were engaged in advertising service businesses. The advertising agency

コットンフィールドの風。

晴れた日は

野にでて

キャベツでもつくり、

雨の日は

レイ・ブラッドベリの短編でも

ゆっくり読みかえしてみる。

晴耕雨読の

ラングラージーンズ。

ラングラージーンズは、アメリカ南部の、あのふりそそぐ
陽光と澄みきった大気が育てたU.S.コットンを使用。
ラングラージーンズは、アメリカのベストブランドです。
(株)ラングラー・ジャパン本社
東京都品川区上大崎2-12-2 TEL444-3171

FIGURE 21.8

An American product is sold in Japan through advertising. (Note the American models.) The Wrangler brand was propelled from an unknown status to the number one selling USA brand in less than three years. The copy on the left-hand side reads as follows:

THE WIND FROM THE COTTONFIELDS
Clear days are when I go out
to the field,
to tend by cabbage crop.
But on a rainy day,
I stay home
And leaf through Ray Bradbury's short shorts.
But rain or shine,
Always in my Wrangler Jeans.

Wrangler Jeans are made from U.S. cotton grown by abundant sunshine and the crystal air of America's Deep South.
Wrangler Jeans, the best U.S. brand.

Bye. Bye. Grossingers.

Hello Grossingers. You should only live and be well.

As far as going to the country goes, you're about the biggest and the best your country has to offer.

But if anybody who goes to Grossingers would like once in a while a little something different, have we got a country for you!

Holland. It isn't the biggest country in Europe. But every square inch of us is like one giant resort.

We Dutch are so tuned in to welcoming people, we'll really make you feel at home.

Not just in our large cities like Amsterdam, Rotterdam and The Hague. With their museums, night clubs and excitements.

But in the countryside as well. A countryside made familiar by artists for centuries.

You'll find that every village and hamlet in Holland has facilities designed to take good care of people. Family people. With kids, grandkids, and in-laws and uncles and aunts.

In fact, you'll find a whole nation of Dutch uncles just waiting to entertain yours.

In times like these it's also good to remind you that Holland is a country that really likes Americans. (We liked America so much we bought Manhattan. Remember?)

And we'll never forget what you Americans did for us during World War II. (Who could forget that?)

So for a change come to Holland. To our dikes and windmills and tulips and seasides and countrysides and citysides.

And so it shouldn't be a total loss, remember. When you go back to Grossingers, you'll have a lot to talk about.

Holland.
Don't visit us. Live with us.

For complete details on a Dutch vacation, see your travel agent or write for our free booklet: "Getting into Dutch." It will tell you about some of the most unusual tours you'll find anywhere in Europe. Or anywhere. Write: The Netherlands National Tourist Office, 576 Fifth Avenue, New York, New York 10036.

HOLLAND

FIGURE 21.9
Foreign travel is encouraged by ads such as this one sponsored by Holland. Appearing in the *New York Times Magazine* and *The New Yorker*, the ad is aimed at an upper-middle-class market, consumers that are affluent and urban and in the 30 to 50 age bracket. Primary prospects are women who have previously taken at least two trips through Europe.

portion stood at 6,719 agencies with 73,378 employees. There are no specific data on the number of people in advertising-related positions working for advertisers such as manufacturers and retailers. Similarly, a breakout of the number of media employees who perform in advertising jobs is lacking. Of course, not everyone working in advertising does so in a specialized, nonclerical capacity; these businesses need routine employees such as typists and mail-room clerks. However, these jobs often provide break-in opportunities for persons wishing to enter the advertising field. A conservative estimate is that more than 100,000 men and women are employed in professional or other positions requiring specialized advertising skills. Somewhere in the

neighborhood of 7,500 to 10,000 new positions should thus develop annually due to death, retirement, and people leaving the advertising business, as well as the need to handle new businesses that are opening up.

Certainly the opportunities for jobs with an advertiser or advertising medium are much greater than with an advertising agency, as these organizations have greater needs for personnel. Less premium, moreover, is usually placed on experience and specialized skills by these employers. The newcomer to advertising may, therefore, have a better chance for initial employment with them. Surely the job seeker should know something about the nature of the various jobs in advertising and the qualifications needed to fill them.

Advertising Jobs and the Talents Needed to Fill Them

Peter Allport, president of the Association of National Advertisers, Inc., believes that the advertising business needs 10 different kinds of professionals:

1 The Writer
2 The Artist
3 The Dramatist or Theatrical Producer
4 The Salesman
5 The Marketer, The Decision Maker
6 The Psychologist
7 The Statistician
8 The Media Analyst
9 The Financial Manager
10 The People Manager, The Project Manager, and The Entrepreneur[27]

From these titles alone, one can readily see the diversity of jobs to be found in advertising. Furthermore, in a general way, the talents needed are implicit in these job titles. However, some amplification may be in order.

A common tendency is to equate employment in advertising with the possession of certain creative talents. Frequently advertising people are thought of as being skilled in the use of words or other symbols. In other words, advertising, to these people, consists in copywriting, art, layout, or broadcast production. These jobs are certainly at the core of advertising; such forms of creativity are basic to the advertising field, and many persons who like to write or draw find outlets for their creative talents in advertising. But other talents, as well as other forms of creativity, are vitally needed in advertising.

Probably most people in advertising work in selling. Media organizations must sell space and time if their business enterprises are to succeed. Special-service groups must also sell what they have to offer. In a different sense, the advertising agency must sell its services; first of all, in getting the account, and later on in keeping the client

[27] Peter W. Allport, "Professionalism in Advertising," *Journal of Advertising*, vol. 3, no. 4, p. 19, 1974.

FIGURE 21.10
Job opportunities to
be found in adver-
tising are varied.
This account group
at Bozell & Jacobs,
Inc., Dallas, is per-
sonally trying out
the client's cosmet-
ic product.

happy with the performance of the agency. There is a pressing need
for selling talent in advertising, as James Webb Young emphasizes in
his concise book, *How to Become an Advertising Man*.[28]

All advertising organizations are businesses; as such, they must
do more than sell to survive; they must be managed. People must be
hired and fired; work assignments must be made; payrolls met; and
many other managerial tasks performed. Advertising, therefore, has a
need for people with managerial talents. Most advertising executives
reach managerial positions by moving up the ladder from other
positions. Thus, the creative person may eventually perform business
administration tasks instead of writing copy.

Another talent sought by advertising organizations is analytical
ability, a talent that is vital in the creation of advertisements. People
working in advertising research and media selection must be able to
wrestle with problems, tackling them in a logical manner. Computer
technology has further strengthened the emphasis on analytical ability. And, of course, whoever has the responsibility for the advertising
budget must be able to analyze figures and come up with meaningful

[28] James Webb Young, *How to Become an Advertising Man*, Advertising Publications,
Inc., Chicago, 1963, pp. 9–11.

ROLLING STONE

Meet Don Welsh, our new Advertising Director (and a puzzle to his mother).

Don Welsh comes to Rolling Stone via Ohio, Columbia University, law, and five highly successful years of selling at Fortune.

Don's latest move has puzzled a few people. His mother, for one.

She can't quite figure why Don would want to leave the hallowed halls of Time, Inc., forsake The Establishment and all the Good Things that go with it, for a magazine that…"Well, among my friends here in Youngstown, I don't know *anyone* who reads it."

Don's reason, Mother, is that he knows where he wants to go, and it's up. And he knows how he wants to get there, and it's fast. Last year, Rolling Stone went up in advertising revenue farther and faster than any other national magazine except one. And in 1975 (when just about everybody else is down) the climb continues (30% ahead in pages this quarter).

That's *part* of the reason Rolling Stone is a red-hot magazine. Here's the rest of it. It just *could be* that our more than 2,500,000 readers are onto something significant. Maybe this whole new kind

of exciting, totally honest, totally involved, frankly biased, fearless, gutsy, prize-winning journalism of Hunter Thompson, Joe Eszterhas, Tom Wolfe, Michael Rogers, Tim Crouse, Ben Fong Torres, Annie Leibovitz is the way of the future.

If it is, then maybe *you* should take a closer, longer look.

Why not give Don Welsh a call. **(212/486-9560)** Let him tell you everything you ought to know about Rolling Stone and where it's going. You'll like his enthusiasm, his professional approach. Time, Inc.-trained, and you know what *that* means.

ROLLING STONE, 78 EAST 56TH STREET, NEW YORK 10022. (212/486-9560) WASHINGTON/CHICAGO/SAN FRANCISCO/LOS ANGELES/LONDON

FIGURE 21.11
This advertisement, which appeared in advertising trade publications, dramatizes the career opportunities that are available in media sales.

answers. As a matter of fact, these four talents—creative, selling, managerial, and analytical—are useful to advertising personnel regardless of job assignment. It is primarily a matter of emphasis. No person, however, is likely to be endowed with all four talents, at least not equally. Thus, each person must analyze his or her own strengths and weaknesses to learn where the greatest opportunity for success lies. At the same time, each person should strive to develop abilities in all four areas, especially if executive status in advertising is sought.

Career Planning

A common question is "How do I prepare myself for a career in advertising?" An understanding of human behavior, of the art of mass communications, and of the principles of marketing is fundamental in any area of advertising. Creativity can be developed; it is no longer thought of as a God-given gift. Writing and rewriting provide the opportunity for the development of copywriting skills. The ability to state ideas clearly and concisely is to be cultivated, for advertising has no place for pedantic or verbose writing. Advertising artists need formal training in the techniques and methods of commercial design, and an appreciation of graphic as well as verbal communication is helpful in any creative advertising position.

Analytical ability is developed through the study of mathematics, statistics, logic, computer programming, and the natural and social sciences. The manager needs to know something about accountancy and office management and be able to use good human relations practices. Advertising relies heavily on people to get its work done. One adage in advertising is that all the assets of an agency go down the elevator at 5 P.M. Since people are sometimes temperamental, the manager must be able to keep them productive. Selling talents are developed largely through practice, although an understanding of buyer behavior and communications principles is important.

The Role of College   Most of these talents can be developed through formal education. A pertinent question, therefore, is whether college is needed for a career in advertising. There are successful advertising people who do not possess college degrees, especially in the creative areas, but today the noncollege person will have difficulty getting started in the field. Most employers require a college degree as one of their minimum standards of employment. In a survey of 1,800 advertising managers and advertising agency executives, it was reported that slightly over 80 percent believed that "a college education is helpful because it gives a general intellectual background, maturity and improves the ability to think."[29] These same individuals were asked to rank several college courses as to their importance to their present work; the findings are reported in Table 21.1.

The question thus becomes one of what kind of college education should be sought; there are different viewpoints on this subject. Three avenues are open: a major in liberal arts, in business administration, or in communications or journalism. Those advocating the liberal arts feel that a young person liberally educated can learn the techniques of advertising on the job and will perform better in the long run because of the breadth of his or her formal training.

---

[29] William A. Cather, "What It Takes to Become an Adman—as Admen See It," *Advertising Age*, Dec. 23, 1974, p. 17.

FIGURE 21.12
An advertising professor explains the fine points of typography to a student in an advertising production class. [*Department of Advertising, The University of Tennessee.*]

Other employers prefer the beginner who is already prepared in the fundamentals of advertising. Both business schools and journalism or communications schools offer programs designed to prepare young people for advertising careers. In business schools, the emphasis is more on selling, merchandising, and marketing research: on how advertising is used in the marketing program. In journalism-communications schools, the emphasis is more on the planning and creation of advertising. A major in one area and a minor in the other is recognized by most employers as an excellent educational background for a career in advertising.

TABLE 21.1
IMPORTANCE OF SELECTED COLLEGE COURSES TO WORK IN ADVERTISING
(Ranked on a scale of 1 to 10)

COURSES	AGENCY EXECS	AD MANAGERS
Writing	7.8	7.9
Psychology	6.8	6.6
Marketing	6.7	7.9
Literature	6.4	5.9
Sociology	5.6	5.1
Advertising	5.5	6.8
Economics	5.5	6.4

SOURCE: *Advertising Age*, Dec. 23, 1974, p. 17.

Self-Development Formal education is only one facet of vocational preparation. Many other activities in our lives contribute to personal development. For a prospective career in advertising, various work experiences can provide worthwhile insights. Selling—from door to door and in certain kinds of retail establishments where customers need and expect sales assistance—is extremely helpful. Good marketing and advertising are customer-oriented; therefore, time spent serving buyers furthers a person's understanding of what motivates them to buying action. Any activity which brings us close to people in their everyday living furnishes a storehouse of such information.

Success in advertising depends in part on the ability to observe; you should try to develop your powers of observation, regardless of the activity of the moment. Imagination is also a highly desirable quality for the advertising person to possess; you should seek to perceive interesting interrelationships in the world around you. Remember that prospective employers try to decide whether applicants have the potentialities for success in a field where precise job specifications are difficult to set down. Whatever you can do to broaden your perspective will help to develop a person who is attractive to such employers. Moreover, this kind of orientation should be employed by the individual working in advertising throughout his or her career.

Breaking into Advertising

To get a job in advertising you must at least offer a potential that an employer can use profitably. Educational background and work experience are the two areas most closely scrutinized by the employer, who is naturally also interested in personality and personal appearance because your first communication to others is delivered nonverbally by your appearance and demeanor. If you have worked hard to develop your creative, analytical, managerial, and selling talents, you must still sell yourself to the employer. This job consists largely in presenting your qualifications in an appealing way. Advertising employers often put a great deal of stock in this phase of the employment process,

FIGURE 21.13
The importance of demographic data is explained to an advertising class. [*Department of Advertising, The University of Tennessee.*]

reasoning that since the employee is being hired to help sell products, he or she should show some imagination in presenting the case for employment. When the number of applicants is high, the choice is frequently made on the basis of this sort of intangible. But in any situation the job applicant should prepare a neat, concise résumé of his or her background and experience, such as the one shown in Figure 21.14, and present it to each potential employer.

Employment in advertising differs from employment in many other fields. Generally speaking, the industry operated until recently under the philosophy of letting prospective employees seek out the job. In other words, advertising agencies, for example, rarely conducted talent searches on college campuses. Some leaders in the field feel that such a policy is a mistake; therefore, as the number of qualified people diminishes, we see major advertising agencies following the lead of their clients by conducting on-campus recruiting programs. While some organizations have formal training programs, on-the-job training is common practice. Beginning salaries, as in many professions, are often below the level of vocations requiring less education and background; but ultimate financial opportunities in advertising are almost unlimited. Success in the field can come fast, as seniority is rarely the basis for advancement.

Even if you recognize that beginning pay may be lower than in many other fields and you are ready to accept this as a condition of employment, you may not be able to step right into the job you desire. For instance, your goal might be that of working for a leading advertising agency, but you might be unable to secure a job with an

MARTHA SUSAN PIERCE
7029 Downing Drive
Knoxville, Tennessee 37919

Telephone: (615) 588-2855

EDUCATION

1976   UNIVERSITY OF TENNESSEE, KNOXVILLE, TENNESSEE
            B.S. Communications. Concentration in Advertising

1975   Bickel Foundation Scholarship - for demonstrated professional
            promise

PROFESSIONAL
EXPERIENCE 1975 - 1976, University of Tennessee Daily Beacon, Knoxville,
            Advertising Manager

            1975, University of Tennessee Daily Beacon, Assistant
            Advertising Manager

            1974, University of Tennessee Daily Beacon, Advertising Sales

            1974, Knoxville Bureau of Recreation, Playground leader

            1973, Miller's Department Store, Knoxville, Tennessee,
            Departmental Sales

            1970, Knoxville Bureau of Recreation, Camp Counselor

HONORS AND
AFFILIATIONS Member, Alpha Lambda Delta, freshman honorary for women
              Student Senator, Student Government Association
              Alpha Omicron Pi social sorority, Scholarship Chairperson and
              Judicial Board Chairperson
              Member, ADS, national advertising fraternity
              Member, Chancellor's Honor Banquet Committee
              Member, West Hills Presbyterian Church, Knoxville

PERSONAL   Age 21...Single...5'4", 120 lbs., excellent health...will relocate

REFERENCES Professor Richard Joel, Head, Department of Advertising,
            University of Tennessee, Knoxville, Tennessee 37916

            Dean Donald G. Hileman, College of Communications, University of
            Tennessee, Knoxville

            Mr. Les Hyder, Director of Student Publications, University of
            Tennessee, Knoxville

FIGURE 21.14

A concise personal résumé is an essential ingredient in a young person's promotional
program when seeking to break into advertising.

YOUR RESUME MAY LEAD TO A GREAT NEW JOB

Media Supervisor. Planner/Buyers.	MW/SE/NE	$15-20,000
Packaged Goods Account Executives	MW	$26,32,000
All-Media Agency Art Directors	MW/NE	$18-24,000
Creative Supervisor/Writer	MW	$18,24,000
Sr. Marketing/Direct Response	MA	$35-40,000
Market Planning/Research Managers	MW	$18-25,000

Our employers require 2 to 10 years experience directly in these job areas; stable records; good references. Also other agency and corporate work in account/advertising/product management, market research, PR. All fees, interviewing paid. Fully confidential yet we actively promote you. Send your resume/base salary in confidence, today!

Dick Wilkinson

CADILLAC ASSOCIATES, INC.
32 W. Randolph St., Chicago, IL 60601
(312) 346-9400

FIGURE 21.15 Advertising trade publications contain many employment advertisements such as this one by an executive search firm.

agency. Seeking other employment in advertising—where you will learn more about advertising—is the recommended course of action. The advertising field seldom penalizes a person who moves from one job to another, as long as the job progression is upward. Advertising is characterized by employee mobility. While advertising jobs are often considered tension-filled, tension and excitement go hand in hand. If one has the temperament for it, there are few jobs as rewarding—financially and in self-satisfaction.

SUMMARY

Advertising will undoubtedly grow in volume and importance. Conditions on the economic scene in the United States and throughout the world call for the increased use of advertising to achieve economic, social, and political goals. Concentration of production in the hands of fewer and larger manufacturers and greater population mobility are trends which separate the producers even further from buyers which thus necessitates greater needs for advertising.

People who possess more supernumerary income also expand the need for advertising. The development of new products requires that potential users be informed of their existence and to their benefits of consumers. As more women enter the work force, traditional shopping patterns will break down and advertising should receive more attention by busy consumers. Similarly, other markets are created by changes in the quality of life of all minority groups.

There will be an even greater emphasis on truthfulness in advertising, as the forces of consumerism and higher levels of education combine to press for

FIGURE 21.16
A concept developed by an American college student was the basis for this car advertisement. The Japanese car manufacturer sponsored a copy-thinking contest for advertising students in the United States. This ad was one of seven winners in the contest and ran in *America* magazine.

this desirable state. The use of advertising for nonbusiness purposes is already increasing in relative importance. Social advertising in its many forms will assist many causes and at the same time enhance the status of advertising as an institution in our society.

Advertising increases in importance when economies of various countries around the world become more economically developed. Currently, such developed nations as Japan and West Germany employ American-style advertising.

Advertising careers, while hard for individuals to launch initially, appear to be growing in numbers and opportunity. Proper preparation through formal education and work experience will help the person wishing to break into the advertising business. Success in this kind of career depends on imagination and the ability to work hard, a willingness to start at the bottom, and the drive to continue to study the many complex facets of the advertising field.

QUESTIONS FOR DISCUSSION

1 What are five socioeconomic changes you foresee over the next five years that will have significant impact on the demand for more advertising in the United States? Can you name any changes which may lead to a lessening of such demand?

2 If zero population growth is reached in the United States, what impact will this development have on advertising's future as a business? How about changes in the age composition of our population?

3 What is supernumerary income? Explain how its presence affects advertising.

4 Working women, family marketing, longer vacations, and earlier retirements are all considered to be trends important to advertising's future. Explain how each fits into the advertising scheme of things.

5 How can R&D affect advertising? Conversely, how can advertising affect R&D?

6 What is "social advertising"? Enumerate and explain its five subtypes. Bring an example of each subtype to class.

7 Does advertising affect the national "taste"? In a positive or negative way? Explain.

8 Bring examples of ads to class which illustrate how a foreign manufacturer is using American advertising techniques to successfully secure sales for the firm's product in the United States market.

9 What problems are encountered when an American firm desires to advertise in a foreign country? How are these obstacles overcome?

10 Assume that you wish to enter the advertising business upon completion of college. Write a marketing plan outlining how you will prepare yourself to be an attractive prospect for such a job, including your present strengths and areas which you feel can be improved between now and then.

FOR FURTHER REFERENCE

Boland, Charles Michael: *Careers and Opportunities in Advertising*, E. P. Dutton & Co., Inc., New York, 1964.

Buell, Victor P.: *Changing Practices in Advertising Decision-Making and Control*, Association of National Advertisers, Inc., New York, 1973.

Fayerweather, John: *International Marketing*, Prentice-Hall, Inc., Englewood Cliffs, N.J., 1970.

Greer, Thomas V.: *Marketing in the Soviet Union*, Frederick A. Praeger, Inc., New York, 1973.

Kahn, E. J., Jr.: *The American People*, Weyleright and Talley, New York, 1974.

Kotler, Philip: *Marketing for Nonprofit Organizations*, Prentice-Hall, Inc., Englewood Cliffs, N.J., 1975.

Miracle, Gordon E., and Gerald S. Albaum: *International Marketing Management*, Richard D. Irwin, Inc., Homewood, Ill., 1970.

Preston, Ivan L., *The Great American Blow-up: Puffery in Advertising and Selling*, The University of Wisconsin Press, Madison, 1975.

Ricks, David, Marily Y. C. Fu, and Jeffrey S. Arpan, *International Business Blunders*, Grid, Inc., Columbus, Ohio, 1974.

Terpstra, Vern, *International Marketing*, The Dryden Press, Inc., Hinsdale, Ill., 1972.

Thorelli, H. B. (ed.): *International Marketing Strategy*, Penguin Books, Inc., Baltimore, 1973.

Weiss, E. B.: *Marketing to the New Society*, Crain Communications, Inc., Chicago, 1973.

Wright, John S., and John E. Mertes: *Advertising's Role in Society*, West Publishing Company, St. Paul, Minn., 1974.

Young, James Webb: *How to Become an Advertising Man*, Advertising Publications, Inc., Chicago, 1963.

GLOSSARY

AAA American Academy of Advertising. A professional organization of college teachers of advertising and practitioners interested in furthering advertising education.

AAAA (4A's) American Association of Advertising Agencies. An organization of leading United States advertising agencies.

AAF American Advertising Federation. An association of advertising clubs, advertisers, agencies, media, and allied companies, with the objective of making advertising more effective for business and more useful to the public.

ABC Audit Bureau of Circulations. An organization sponsored by publishers, agencies, and advertisers to validate the circulation statements of magazines and newspapers.

ABP American Business Press. An organization of technical, professional, industrial, and other business publications formed by merger of the Associated Business Publications and National Business Publications groups.

AFTRA American Federation of Television and Radio Artists. A guild of broadcast announcers and performers.

AM Amplitude modulation. The standard radio broadcasting method, with tone modulation governed by variations in the height of waves rather than by their frequency.

AMA American Marketing Association. A professional organization of marketing teachers, marketing research practitioners, and marketing executives.

ANA Association of National Advertisers. A national organization of advertisers, with larger manufacturers constituting the majority of the members.

ANPA American Newspaper Publishers Association. An organization of publishers of daily newspapers in the United States and Canada.

APA Agricultural Publishers Association. An association of farm magazine and farm newspaper publishers.

ARB American Research Bureau. A broadcast program rating service for television only; it uses both the viewer diary method and an electronic recording and tabulating system known as *Arbitron*.

ARF Advertising Research Foundation. A nonprofit organization of advertisers, agencies, and media, with colleges and universities as academic members, to promote greater effectiveness in advertising and marketing through impartial, objective research.

ASCAP American Society of Composers, Authors, and Publishers. An organization that administers the licensing of and collection of fees from networks and stations for music and other program material.

Account An advertiser. Used to refer to the client of an advertising agency or to a firm placing advertising direct with media.

Account executive The member of an advertising agency who supervises the planning and preparation of advertising for one or more clients, and who is responsible for the primary liaison between agency and advertiser. Sometimes called *account supervisor* or *contact man*.

Adjacencies Programs immediately preceding or following a specific commercial time period or program.

Advertising As defined by the AMA, any paid form of nonpersonal presentation and promotion of ideas, goods, and services by an identified sponsor to a group.

Advertising From the communications viewpoint, controlled, identifiable information and persuasion by means of mass communications media.

Advertising Council A nonprofit organization of advertisers, agencies, and media formed to plan, create, and distribute public service advertising programs. Founded as the War Advertising Council in 1941.

Advertising registers Directories of national advertisers or advertising agencies, published annually in separate editions.

Advertising specialties A form of direct advertising. Products bearing the name and address or slogan of a business firm are given away free by the advertiser to present or prospective customers. Sometimes called *remembrance advertising*.

Advertising substantiation Advertisers must be able to supply the FTC with documentation in support of claims made in their advertising; they must also be able to show that they relied on the documentation when preparing the advertising.

Affiliate A broadcast station belonging to or carrying the programs of a specific network.

Affirmative disclosure A procedure which would require advertisers to tell not only the positive story about their products, but also the negative side.

Agate line A unit of measurement for advertising space, one column wide and one-fourteenth inch deep.

Agent One who represents or handles business contacts for artists, actors, musicians, or writers. Also an owner or partner in an advertising agency.

Aided recall A research technique used to measure the impression made by an advertisement or other communication, and in which the interviewer shows the respondent an advertisement, program log, or other aid to memory.

Airbrush A commercial art method of painting by use of a fine spray to produce tonal gradations and to retouch photographs.

Air check A recording of a broadcast program or commercial made to evaluate production and delivery techniques.

Alternate sponsorship Two advertisers sharing the same program, with one dominant one week, the other the following week. Also, two advertisers sharing the same time period, each using his own program.

Animatic film A film of storyboards with a sound track attached. Used to pretest television commercials.

Animation Movement added to static objects. Usually applied to cartoon drawings filmed for television, or to POP material or outdoor advertisements with moving parts.

Arbitron An instantaneous system for obtaining television program ratings by means of electronic devices placed in homes and wired to a central tabulating headquarters. See *ARB*.

Area sampling A probability sampling technique which divides the total geographical area under study into a number of smaller areas and then uses random selection to determine the specific areas or specific respondents to be interviewed.

Audience The total number of people who *may* receive an advertising message delivered by a medium or combination of media.

Audience composition The proportion of various types of people, classified by characteristics demographic or psychographic reached by an advertising medium or message.

Audience flow The gain or loss in audience during a broadcast program, or from one program channel to another.

Audimeter An electromechanical device used by A. C. Nielsen Company to record station tuning of TV receivers by a sample of viewers.

Audio Sound or pertaining to sound. In television, the transmission or reception of sound as opposed to the picture portion, or video.

Audiotape Tape used for radio broadcasting to record sound only, in contrast to videotape, which records both sound and visual portions of telecasts.

Availability Broadcast time offered to an advertiser for sponsorship.

BBB Better Business Bureau. Local organizations supported by business firms to discourage false or misleading advertising.

BCU In television, big close-up. See *ECU*.

b.f. Abbreviation for boldface type.

BMI Broadcast Music Incorporated. A music copyright organization formed by stations and networks to perform functions similar to ASCAP.

B of A Bureau of Advertising, American Newspaper Publishers Association. Promotes the use of daily newspapers as advertising media.

BPA Business Publications Audit of Circulations. An auditing organization for business publications primarily concerned with controlled circulation.

BPAA Business and Professional Advertisers Association A professional organization of marketing and advertising executives in the business products field. Formerly the Association of Industrial Advertisers.

Back to back Adjacent time periods, programs, or commercials.

Bait advertising Advertising exceptional prices or terms for a product in order to attract prospects to a store, where they find it difficult or impossible to buy the product as advertised.

Basic network The minimum number of broadcast stations an advertiser can use in a specific network. Now obsolete in radio, as advertisers may select almost any combination of stations desired.

Basic station A television station included in the list of network affiliates which advertisers must buy if they use the network.

Billboard The opening routine of a broadcast program, including identification, credits to performers, producers, and the like. Also, a poster panel in outdoor advertising.

Billing The total amount of money charged to clients by an advertising agency, including media bills, production costs, and service charges.

Bleed Printing to the very edge of the page, leaving no margin.

Block In broadcasting, either a group of consecutive time periods or the same time period from day to day. In printing, a metal or wood base on which the plate is mounted to make it type high.

Body copy Main copy block or blocks of an advertisement, as distinguished from headline, subheads, coupon copy, etc.

Body type Type used for body copy in an advertisement, in contrast to display type used for headlines and subheads.

Boldface Type that is heavier in strokes than other designs of the same type family, or heavier than text type with which it is used.

Boutique A form of limited-service advertising agency, usually performing only the creative function for a fee.

Box-top offer An offer of a premium based on the return of the box top from a package or other proof of purchase.

Broadside A giant folder, often sent as a self-mailer, used especially in direct-mail advertising to the trade.

Brochure An elaborate or impressive booklet.

Broker A manufacturer's sales representative who receives commissions on sales made to wholesalers or retailers in a specified territory.

Budget attrition The process whereby the advertising budget gets used up for nonadvertising activities.

Bulk discount A discount for quantity purchases.

Bulk mailing Third-class mail delivered to the post office in bundles, sorted by states and cities.

Bulk sales Large quantities of a publication bought for redistribution.

Business advertising A collective word to describe all forms of advertising designed to sell goods and services for purposes other than personal satisfaction.

CATV Community Antenna Television System. A system for extending the coverage of TV stations through the use of coaxial cable connections to subscribers in weak viewing areas.

CU Close-up. A camera shot to show a single object or part of it at close range.

Camera chain Equipment for live television pickup includes a TV camera, monitor, and in-studio control equipment.

Caps In typography, capital, or uppercase, letters in contrast to small, or lowercase, letters.

Caption Explanatory text accompanying an illustration. Also, the heading of a chapter, page, or section.

Center spread A single sheet of paper that forms the two facing pages in the center of a publication and permits printing across the fold, or gutter.

Chain break A pause in network broadcasting to permit local station identification. Also, a commercial broadcast during this pause.

Channel The frequency in the

broadcast spectrum assigned to a station for its transmissions.

Character An individual letter, figure, or other unit of type.

Checking copy Copy of a publication delivered to an agency or advertiser to verify insertion of an advertisement as ordered.

Chroma In color, the dimension of strength or intensity. Two other dimensions are required in color measurement: *hue*, the quality that distinguishes one color from another, and *value*, or depth, the degree of lightness or darkness.

Circular An inexpensive form of direct advertising consisting of small sheets of paper printed on one or both sides for delivery by mail or by hand, and frequently distributed as inserts with letters, statements, or catalogs. Also called *leaflets*.

Circulation The number of copies of a publication distributed. Used loosely to refer to the number of homes regularly tuned to a broadcast station.

City zone The portion of a newspaper's coverage area that includes the corporate city plus adjacent areas which have the characteristics of the city.

Classified advertising Advertising arranged according to the product or service advertised, and usually restricted in size and format. *Display classified* permits illustrations and greater variety in size and format. See *display advertisement*.

Clear channel station A radio station with interference-free broadcasting rights on a particular frequency and broadcasting power up to 50,000 watts.

Clear time In broadcasting, either the reservation of time periods for an advertiser with a station or a check on the availability of time periods by a network with its affiliated stations.

Client An agency or media term referring to an advertiser with whom business is done.

Closing date The final date on which advertising must be delivered to a medium if it is to appear in a specific issue or time slot.

Coaxial cable A special type of cable used to transmit telephone, telegraph, and television impulses.

Coincidental survey A method of checking viewers or listeners of a broadcast program while it is on the air. Usually conducted by telephone.

Collateral In advertising, used in reference to noncommissionable media used in a campaign.

Color separation In full-color advertisements, either a black-and-white negative of one primary color in the full-color original or the process of breaking down full-color copy into its primary-color components.

Column inch A unit of publication space one column wide and one inch deep.

Combination rate A special rate for advertising in two or more publications under the same ownership.

Company magazine A publication issued regularly by a business firm for its employees, dealers, prospects, or other groups. A house organ.

Comparative advertising See *comparison advertising*.

Comparison advertising Advertising which contrasts two or more specifically named brands of the same generic product class and makes such a comparison in terms of one or more specific product attributes. Also called *comparative advertising*.

Composition Setting type and assembling it with engravings.

Comprehensive A layout prepared

to resemble the finished advertisement as closely as possible.

Consumer behavior The study of those activities dealing with the buying of products and the reasons for such action.

Consumer jury A method of pretesting products or advertisements by exposing them to potential purchasers or users.

Contest A form of sales promotion whereby consumers of the featured product may win prizes either through skill or by chance. Designed to stimulate quick buying action.

Continuity Script for radio, television, or film production; or the script for the spoken words which give a continuous flow to a station's programming.

Continuity in advertising Repetition of the same basic theme, layout, or commercial format. Continuity in media refers to the regularity with which messages appear in advertising media.

Continuous tone A screened photographic image which contains gradient tones from black to white.

Controlled circulation The circulation of business publications delivered free, or largely free, to individuals selected by job category or other relevant criteria. To meet BPA standards, the publication must be issued quarterly or oftener and must contain no less than 25 percent editorial material. See *qualified circulation*.

Cooperative advertising Most commonly used to refer to advertising paid for jointly by a national advertiser and his wholesalers or retailers; sometimes called a *dealer's, manufacturer's, or vertical* cooperative. Also applied to advertising sponsored by several national advertisers or several local advertis-

ers, and classed as a *horizontal* cooperative.

Copy Broadly, all elements, both verbal and visual, which will be included in the finished advertisement. In a narrow sense, the verbal elements only, or the material to be set by a compositor.

Copy chief Head of a copy group in an agency or advertising department.

Copy fitting Counting the number of characters or words in a piece of copy in order to determine how much space it will require if set in a specified type face and size. The same procedure is used to determine the amount of copy needed to fill a fixed amount of space. Also called *copy casting*.

Copy plan The *copy-thinking* phase in the creation of advertisements. Also sometimes referred to as *copy policy, copy outline,* or *copy platform*.

Copyright Legal protection granted an artist or author against the reprinting, use, or sale of an original work without express consent.

Copy testing Measuring the effectiveness of an advertising campaign, an advertisement, or elements of an advertisement.

Corporate advertising Advertising that stresses the resources, skill, or character of the advertising firm rather than promoting a product or a brand. See *institutional advertising*.

Corrective advertising Advertising run by a sponsor to correct misimpressions resulting from earlier advertising. Done at the request or order of the FTC.

Cosponsoring Two or more advertisers sharing proportionately the cost of a single broadcast program.

Cost per inquiry The cost of producing one inquiry about the product from an advertisement or an advertising campaign.

Cost per thousand The cost to the advertiser for the delivery of a message to 1,000 readers, viewers, etc. May be applied to a variety of bases, such as *cost per thousand homes*, cost per thousand *circulation*, or cost per thousand prospects.

Counter advertising Advertisements aired on broadcast media to present views opposite of those being expressed in other commercials. Based upon the Fairness Doctrine as promulgated by the FCC.

Counter card Point-of-purchase material with an easel on the back, to be placed on the counter or near the product.

Coupon A form of sales promotion whereby consumers can exchange the coupon for a reduction in price or refund when purchasing the featured product.

Coverage The percentage of households or individuals who are exposed to a specific advertising medium in a given area.

Coverage map A map showing the geographical area reached by transmission from a broadcast station. Usually divided into primary and secondary coverage areas for both day and night.

Creative research Research applied to the development and evaluation of the creative product—advertisements and commercials.

Crop To remove portions of an illustration by trimming the edges, either to eliminate undesirable content or to change illustration proportions.

Cumulative audience The total number of persons or homes reached by a number of successive issues of a publication or successive broadcasts. In broadcasting, sometimes referred to as *cumulative reach.*

Cut A trade term for a printed illustration, or for the engravings used to reproduce it. Also, to delete portions of copy or program material to fit space or time period. In broadcasting, an abrupt stop in a program or an instant switch from one television picture to another without fading.

Cut-in The insertion of a local announcement into a network commercial.

DMMA Direct Mail Marketing Association. An organization of producers and users of direct advertising materials.

Deadline The hour or day after which advertising will not be accepted for appearance in a specific edition of a publication or specific broadcast time period. See *closing date*.

Dealer imprint A dealer's name and address, or other identification, placed on material produced by a national advertiser.

Delayed broadcast A repeat broadcast of a program by tape or film. Frequently used to compensate for time differences between station locations in network operations.

Demarketing A state in which demand exceeds the level at which the marketer feels able or motivated to supply it.

Demographics The statistical description of a market or other population group based upon such facts as age, sex, marital status, education, etc. See *psychographics*.

Depth interview A research method based on the use of open-end questions and stimulation of the respondent to talk freely and at length about the subject.

Direct advertising Printed advertising delivered to prospects by mail, salespeople, dealers, or canvassers, in contrast to advertising delivered by publications or by broadcast or position media.

Direct-mail advertising Direct advertising delivered to prospects through the mails.

Direct marketing The consummation of a sale of a product by mail, without aid of intermediaries or personal, face-to-face selling. Similar to mail-order advertising.

Director In broadcasting, the person responsible for on-the-air production of a program. See *producer*.

Directory advertising Advertising in printed directories, such as telephone, industrial, and city directories.

Display advertisement In publications, advertisements using attention-attracting elements, such as illustrations, typographical variety, white space, or color, in contrast to classified advertising.

Display type Type used for headline or other emphasized elements; also, any type larger than 14-point.

Dissolve In television or film production, the technique of bringing one scene into full focus as a previous one fades or is wiped out.

Double-page spread An advertisement appearing on two facing pages.

Drive time The peak period for radio listenership, when people are driving to and from work.

Drop shipment Merchandise that is shipped direct from manufacturer to retailer, but invoiced to a wholesaler, who in turn bills the retailer.

Dubbing In broadcasting, adding pictures or sound after the original recording has been made. Also, making duplicate recordings of original material.

Dummy In direct advertising, a model indicating the size, shape, and layout of the finished printed product. In periodicals, a facsimile of the proposed issue.

Duplication Two or more advertising media reaching the same individual or household.

ECU Extreme close-up. In television, a very close camera shot to show maximum detail. See *BCU*.

EDP Electronic data processing. The storing, retrieving, and analyzing of masses of data by use of computers and other electronic equipment.

ET Electrical transcription. A recording of a radio program for later broadcasts.

Earned rate The rate an advertiser pays for space or time actually used within a specific time period.

Editorial matter The news, educational, or entertainment portion of a publication or broadcast, as distinguished from the advertising.

Electric spectacular An outdoor advertisement using electric lights to form words and designs, and usually animated.

Electrotype A duplicate of an engraving or type form made electrolytically.

Em The square of any type size; derived from the letter M, which is as wide as it is high. Unless specified otherwise, the *pica-em*, or 12-point em, is equal to $\frac{1}{6}$ inch.

Embossing Relief printing, using two dies to raise the printed surface above the rest of the sheet.

Engraving An original printing plate. Also, a method of reproducing a design for printing by cutting or etching metal plates.

Envelope stuffer Direct-mail advertising inserted in mailings of statements or other correspondence.

FCC Federal Communications Commission. The government agency that licenses broadcast stations and regulates broadcasting.

FDA Food and Drug Administration. The government agency responsible for enforcement of the Food, Drug and Cosmetic Act, which forbids interstate commerce in such products if misbranded or adulterated. Also regulates advertising of these product categories.

FM Frequency modulation. A method of modulating tone in broadcasting by frequency of waves rather than their amplitude. More limited in coverage area than AM, but less affected by static. See *AM.*

FTC Federal Trade Commission. A government agency concerned with the regulation of interstate commerce, including interstate advertising.

Face The style or design of type. Also, the printing surface of a type character or engraving.

Fact sheet An outline of key product facts supplied to copywriters, or to broadcast announcers who use it as a basis for ad-libbed rather than prepared commercials.

Fair trade Laws which restrain retailers from selling products at prices less than those established by agreement between manufacturer and retailer. More properly called *resale price maintenance.*

Family of type One design of type in a complete range of sizes and variations, as Caslon Bold, Caslon Bold Condensed, Caslon Bold Italic, Caslon New, Caslon Old Style, etc.

Feed To transmit a broadcast from one station or location to another.

Feedback The response or reaction to a communication which tells the sender how his or her message is being interpreted.

Field intensity In broadcasting, the measurement of station signal strength at different locations. Field intensity contour maps indicate station coverage patterns. See *coverage map.*

Fifteen and two The standard discounts to advertising agencies allowed by most media. Fifteen percent of the gross bill is the commission retained by the agency; two percent of the net bill is a cash discount normally passed on to the advertiser.

50 showing In outdoor advertising, a standard poster showing consisting of approximately half the number of panels included in a 100 showing. See *100 showing.*

Film clip A short section of film footage.

Flat bed A letterpress printing press with a flat base on which the page forms are locked.

Flat rate A uniform rate for advertising space or time, with no discounts for volume or frequency.

Flight saturation Maximum concentration of spot commercials in a short time period.

Flush Printed matter set even with other material or with the edge of the page.

Focus-group interview A form of qualitative research involving a joint depth interview with several respondents selected because of their similarities.

Font A complete assortment of type characters in one face and size, including numbers, punctuation marks, etc.

Format The size, shape, style, and appearance of a publication, printed page, or advertisement. In broadcasting, the organization of each element in a program.

Four-color process A printing process that reproduces a full range of colors by overprinting red, yellow, blue, and black.

Frequency The number of times an advertising message is delivered within a set period of time. Also, the number of impulses per second sent out by a broadcast transmitter.

Frequency discount A reduction in advertising rates based on the number of insertions or commercials used in a given period.

Frequency modulation See *FM*.

Fringe time Time periods in which normal broadcast audiences are unavailable.

Full color See *four-color process*.

Full disclosure Manufacturers of specified products must disclose specific kinds of information about them; for example, processed food makers list the nutritional value of their products on labels and in advertisements.

Full position A special preferred position for newspaper advertisements, either next to and following reading matter or at the top of the column next to reading matter.

Full showing In transit advertising, a message on each bus or other unit of the system. Also used loosely to refer to a 100 showing of outdoor advertising.

GRP See *gross rating point*.

Gallup-Robinson A research organization, best known for impact studies of TV and magazine advertisements.

General advertising National or nonlocal advertising in newspapers.

Generic name A name used to describe a product category rather than a specific brand.

Gimmick Any clever idea or device.

Giveaway A broadcast program offering prizes to studio contestants, or to listeners or viewers. Also, a premium available without charge.

Government organization advertising A form of social advertising sponsored by government agencies to get the public to join the armed services, travel in a certain area, and so forth.

Grade A coverage The primary coverage area of a television station.

Grade B coverage The secondary coverage area of a television station.

Gravure A printing process which transfers image to paper with ink retained in depressions in the plate. See *intaglio*.

Gross rating point (GRP) A measurement of the saturation for a given media effort. One gross rating point equals one percent of the TV homes in a given market. Computed by multiplying the rating figure by the frequency number. Used in buying television coverage.

Group discount In broadcasting, a special discount for the use of a group of stations simultaneously.

Gutter The two inside margins of facing pages in a newspaper or magazine.

Half showing In transit advertising, a card in every other vehicle of the system. Loosely used for a 50 showing of outdoor advertising.

Halftone An engraving made by photographing through a screen which breaks up the subject into small dots of varying size, reproducing continuous shades or tones.

Handbill A small form of direct advertising distributed by hand.

Hand composition Hand-set type, in contrast to type set by machine.

Hand lettering Lettering drawn by hand, in contrast to that set in type.

Hand tooling Processing an engraving by hand to improve its reproduction qualities.

Head-on position An outdoor advertising location directly facing traffic, as distinguished from either an angled or a parallel position.

Heaviside layer A region of ionized air beginning about 65 miles above the earth's surface. At night it reflects AM broadcast signals back to earth, but does not affect FM transmissions.

Hidden Offer A special offer buried in the body copy of a print advertisement as a test of readership.

Hi-Fi Color In newspaper advertising, preprinted color ads which feed into the press like wallpaper so that the paper may be cut at any point without damaging the effect of the ad.

Hitchhike In broadcasting, a commercial at the end of a program, but within the sponsor's time, which features one of the sponsor's products not advertised in the other commercials.

Hold An instruction to a typographer to keep type set up for future use. Also called *hold order*.

Holding power In broadcasting, the degree to which a program retains its audience for the duration of the program.

Holdover audience In broadcasting, the audience that is retained from a previous program over the same network or station.

Horizontal publication A business publication edited for readers employed in similar job categories in different industries, such as *Product Engineering, Purchasing*, and *Journal of Accountancy*.

House agency An advertising agency controlled by a single advertiser.

House organ A publication issued regularly by a business firm for its employees, dealers, prospects, or other groups. See *company magazine*.

Hue In color, the dimension that distinguishes one color from another, as red from yellow.

ID Identification announcement. A broadcast term for a brief commercial between programs and preceding the station identification announcement.

IOA Institute of Outdoor Advertising. An educational and promotional organization of the outdoor advertising field.

Impact The degree to which an advertisement, an advertising campaign, or a medium affects the audience receiving it.

Imprint The printing of additional copy on previously printed material. See *dealer imprint*.

Impulse purchase Unpremediated purchase of consumer goods.

Industrial advertising Advertising goods or services to businesses for use in the production or distribution of other goods and services.

Inherited audience The portion of a broadcast audience that remains tuned to a succeeding program.

In-house agency An advertiser firm that performs agency functions for itself instead of engaging an advertising agency. See *house agency*.

Inquiry test A method of testing advertisements or media by comparing the number of inquiries received from readers, listeners, or viewers.

Insert A special page printed by the advertiser and forwarded to a publisher who binds it in the publication. Also, an advertising tabloid placed inside a newspaper.

Insertion order Written authorization for a publication to print an advertisement of a specified size in a particular issue at a stated rate.

Institutional advertising Advertising created primarily to build long-range goodwill or prestige for the advertiser, rather than stimulating immediate product purchase. See *public relations* and *corporate advertising*.

Intaglio The process of printing from a depressed surface. See *gravure*.

Island display A store display centered in an aisle or other open space.

Island position A newspaper advertisement position entirely surrounded by editorial matter or page margin; rarely available.

Jingle A musical commercial.

Job ticket A card or envelope with complete instructions that accompanies a printing job through all departments and provides records on the progress of the work.

Junior unit A unit of space that permits an advertiser to use the same plates for large- and small-page magazines. Plates prepared for full-page space in the smaller magazine appear in the larger one with editorial material on two or more sides.

Justify type To arrange type so that letters are properly spaced and lines are of even length. Machine-set type is justified automatically.

Keying an advertisement Putting a code number or letter in a coupon or in the advertiser's address so that the particular advertisement or medium producing an inquiry can be identified. See *inquiry test*.

Keynote idea The underlying theme for an advertising campaign.

Key plate In color-process printing, the plate with maximum detail to which other plates must be registered.

Key station The station or stations at which the principal programs of a broadcast network originate.

Lanham Act The Federal statute governing registration of trademarks and the other identifying symbols on products sold in interstate commerce.

Layout The arrangement of creative elements on a printed page: headlines, copy blocks, illustrations, logotypes, and other items which serve as a blueprint for the finished ad.

Leading Pronounced *ledding*. The insertion of metal strips, or leads, between lines of type to provide greater space and improve readability and appearance.

Letterpress printing A method of printing in which the ink is carried on a raised, or relief, surface.

Letter spacing Spacing between type characters to extend them over a wider type measure.

Licensee In broadcasting, the owner of a station.

Life-style A distinctive mode of living, focusing on how people go about their daily routines.

Lightface A type design that has thin, light lines, in contrast to *boldface*.

Linage Any amount of advertising space measured in agate lines.

Line A unit for measuring the depth of advertising space. See *agate line*.

Line charges In broadcasting, the cost for microwave relay, coaxial cable, or telephone lines to transmit a network or remote program to a radio or TV station. See *remote*.

Line cut (plate) An engraving made without a screen; reproduces only solid lines or areas, without intermediate shades or tones. See *halftone*.

Line drawing A brush or pen drawing consisting of solid lines or masses without continuous tonal gradations.

Line-of-sight signal In broadcasting, the FM signal, which cannot be received at any significant distance from the point where it becomes tangent to the earth's surface.

Linotype A trademarked machine that sets and casts type one line at a time. The *Intertype* machine performs the same functions.

Lip sync In television, the synchronization of an actor's lip movements with separately recorded spoken lines.

List broker A commission agent who rents direct-mail lists to advertisers.

Listener diary In broadcasting, a method of research in which respondents maintain a continuing record of listening or viewing.

List price The manufacturer's or wholesaler's recommended retail price.

Lithography The process of printing from a flat surface on which the ink for the image is retained by a greasy or albuminous deposit; planographic printing.

Live program Simultaneous performance and broadcasting, in contrast to broadcasting from magnetic tape or film.

Local advertising Advertising that is placed by a local entrepreneur, in contrast to national or general advertising.

Local channel station A radio station with restricted power, limiting its coverage area to a radius of approximately 50 miles.

Log In broadcasting, an hourly chronological record of all programs and commercials aired by a station.

Logotype The signature or standard name plate of an advertiser.

Loss leader A product offered at cost or below to attract store traffic.

Lowercase Small letters, in contrast to capital letters.

MAB Magazine Advertising Bureau. A bureau within the MPA to promote the sale of advertising space in consumer magazines. See *MPA*.

MPA Magazine Publishers Association. An organization of consumer magazine publishers.

Machine composition Type set mechanically, or machine-set in contrast to hand-set.

Magnuson-Moss Warranty–Federal Trade Commission Improvement Act An amendment to the FTC Act, passed in 1975, broadening the scope of the FTC.

Mail-order advertising Advertising designed to produce orders direct from prospects by mail; any type of medium may be used to deliver the advertising message.

Make good Repeating an advertisement without charge, or refunding space or time charges, as compensation for an advertisement omitted or containing a significant error.

Markdown The amount of reduction below original price, in either a percentage or dollars and cents.

Market People who have the ability and inclination to buy, or prospects for a product or service. Also, a geographical area which includes a significant number of prospects.

Marketing A total system of interacting business activities designed to plan, price, promote, and distribute want-satisfying products and services to present and potential customers.

Marketing concept A unifying approach marshaling and directing the total resources of the business firm toward the determination and satisfaction of customer and consumer wants and needs in a way planned to enhance the firm's overall profit performance.

Marketing mix The blending of product, price, distribution channels, personal selling, and advertising into a suitable marketing program for the firm.

Market profile Facts about the prospects, or an analysis by age, sex, income, possessions, etc., of people who constitute the market for a product or service. See *demographics*, and *psychographics*.

Market segmentation Dividing the market for a product into homogeneous subsections in order that each segment may be treated in the most appropriate manner.

Market share One firm's share of the industry's total sales volume.

Markup The increase, in either dollars and cents or a percentage, between cost and selling price.

Mass communication The delivery of large numbers of identical messages simultaneously by communication organizations, or media, in contrast to personal or individual communication.

Mat service A commercial organization supplying advertisers, publications, and printers with ready-made mats and illustrations through a subscription service.

Matrix A mold of impregnated paper pulp, plastic, or other substance taken from type or plates. Molten lead cast in this mold produces a duplicate printing plate called a *stereotype*. Also, called a *mat*.

Maximil rate A newspaper's milline rate based on its highest rate.

Media characteristics The various dimensions by which advertising media may be compared, including selectivity, coverage, flexibility, cost, editorial environment, production quality, permanence, trade acceptability, and merchandising cooperation.

Media director An agency executive responsible for the selection and scheduling of advertising media.

Media planning The process of designing a course of action that shows how advertising time and space will be used to contribute to the achievement of marketing objectives.

Media Records, Inc. An organization that publishes records of the space used by different advertisers in newspapers that subscribe to the service.

Media representative An individual or firm which sells advertising space or time for a number of noncompeting publications or broadcast stations. Often called *reps.*

Medium Any vehicle used to convey an advertising message, such as television, magazines, or direct mail. Also, the methods and tools used by an artist, such as pen and ink, crayon, or photography.

Merchandising Any activity to stimulate trade interest in moving the product or service to the prospect.

Merchandising the advertising The promotion of a consumer advertising program to members of the advertiser's sales force and to the trade.

Microwave relay A method of relaying television signals by use of ultrahigh frequency relay stations at high topographic locations or in mobile equipment.

Middle break In broadcasting, a station identification or commercial at the halfway point in a program.

Milline rate A theoretical unit for comparison of newspaper advertising rates in relation to circulation; the cost of one agate line for one million circulation.

Millivolts per meter (MV/M) A measurement of broadcast signal strength, used in determining the coverage of a station.

Minimil A newspaper's milline rate based upon its lowest rate.

Mixing In broadcasting, mixing different audio effects, as music and voice, or leveling of volume from scene to scene.

Mock-up A facsimile of products or packages used in television.

Monitor To listen to or view a broadcast program. Also, a television receiver in the control room or studio used by production personnel or performers to follow the action of a program.

Motivation research (MR) Research which attempts to relate behavior to underlying desires, emotions, and intentions, in contrast to research which merely enumerates behavior or describes a situation; it relies heavily on the use of techniques adapted from psychology and other social sciences.

Moving shot In television, following the action with a camera.

Multiplexing In broadcasting, the use of special equipment to transmit more than one program service from the same station, such as an FM station "storecasting" music and commercials to supermarkets and broadcasting regular programs to home listeners.

NAB National Association of Broadcasters. An organization of radio and television stations and networks.

NAD National Advertising Division of the Council of Better Business Bureaus. The entry gate for complaints registered against national advertisers as part of the advertising industry's self-regulation procedure. The complaint moves up to NARB if not resolved at this level.

NARB National Advertising Review Board. The final arbiter of complaints registered against national advertisers as part of the advertising industry's self-regulatory machinery. Uses moral suasion to get undesirable practices stopped.

NOAB National Outdoor Advertising Bureau. A cooperative organization for placement and inspection of outdoor advertising, owned and used by advertising agencies.

NRMA National Retail Merchants Association. Department, chain, and specialty stores retailing apparel, shoes, dry goods, etc. For-

merly National Retail Dry Goods Association.

NSAD National Society of Art Directors. A professional organization of art directors for agencies, media, advertisers, and advertising suppliers.

National advertising The advertising of a manufacturer or wholesaler, in contrast to the advertising of a retailer or local advertiser. Also, any advertising in media with nationwide circulation.

National brand A brand distributed widely through many different outlets, in contrast to a *private brand* or *private label* owned by a distributor or retailer.

Net audience An unduplicated number of homes, or of readers, viewers, or listeners, reached over a period of time, or by a combination of different media.

Net profit Profit after payment of all costs of operation. *Net before taxes* is profit after payment of all operating costs except taxes.

Net rate A medium's published rate less agency commission. See *gross rate.*

Network In broadcasting, a group of stations affiliated by contract and usually interconnected for simultaneous broadcast of the same programs.

Network affiliate One of the stations in a broadcasting network.

Network cooperative program A network broadcast available for local sponsorship, with local commercials inserted on cue.

Network option time Time on affiliated stations for which the network has first priority, but the availability of which is dependent on acceptance of the network program by the local station. Also called *network time. See station option time.*

Next to reading matter (NR) An advertisement position immediately adjacent to reading matter or editorial content.

Nielsen Drug (Food) Index Reports on the market movement of products, by type and brand, through panels of drugstores and food stores.

Nielsen rating In broadcasting, the percentage of TV homes in a given area tuned to a given television program, as reported by the A. C. Nielsen Company.

OAAA Outdoor Advertising Association of America. An association of plant owners operating standardized outdoor advertising facilities.

O and O station A broadcast station owned and operated by a network.

Off camera In television, action or sound outside camera range and not visible to the audience.

Off mike In broadcasting, voice or sound away from microphone. Opposite of *on mike.*

Offset A lithographic printing process in which the image is first transferred to a rubber roller, or blanket, which in turn makes the impression on the paper.

On camera In television, action or sound within camera range and visible to the audience.

100 showing A standard showing of outdoor posters. The number of poster panels in a 100 showing varies with the size of the market, but is considered sufficient to expose the message to practically every mobile person in the market during a 30-day period.

One-time rate The rate paid by an advertiser who does not use enough space or time to earn volume discounts. The same as *transient rate.*

Open rate An advertising rate subject to discounts for volume or frequency.

Operations research An interdisciplinary approach to marketing and advertising research using physical or mathematical models which are subjected to possible courses of action.

Outdoor advertising Signs placed alongside highways and streets which meet the standards established by the OAAA. Includes posters and painted bulletins.

Outline halftone A halftone with the background removed. Also called a *silhouette halftone.*

Out-of-home advertising A collective term to describe advertising media that depend upon people or traffic passing the location of the medium. Includes outdoor advertising, nonstandardized signs, and transit advertising. Sometimes called *traffic* or *position media.*

Overrun The number of pieces of printed material in excess of the specified quantity. An advertiser usually accepts up to 10 percent overrun at pro rata cost.

PIB Publishers Information Bureau. An organization which furnishes periodic reports on the expenditures of national advertisers in magazines and network television.

POP Point-of-purchase, or point-of-sale, advertising; any displays or advertising material used in or around a retail store.

POPAI Point-of-Purchase Advertising Institute. An organization of advertisers, agencies, and producers of point-of-purchase advertising material.

Package insert Advertising material packed with a product, usually to advertise a different product.

Package program In broadcasting, a complete program, including all elements except commercials, sold as a unit; may be either live or transcribed, or on film or tape.

Packaging Institute An organization of manufacturers and users of packing materials, machinery, and services.

Page proof A proof of type and illustrations in page form as they will finally appear, usually pulled after *galley proofs* have been corrected.

Painted bulletin An outdoor advertisement that is painted on a panel, in contrast to one of printed paper pasted on.

Pan or **panning** In television, to move the camera up and down or from left to right, in contrast to moving it to or from the subject.

Panel A group of respondents used repeatedly to supply data in marketing or advertising research. Also, the portion of an outdoor board on which printed paper is pasted.

Paper See *poster*.

Participation program A regularly scheduled network or station program on which advertisers may place spot announcements without any responsibility for program content.

Pass-along reader A person who reads a publication not purchased by him or by a member of his household.

Paste-up A layout in which illustration and type material are combined on one sheet for reproduction as a single engraving.

Pay TV A plan which allows TV viewers to receive special programs after payment of a specific fee.

Penetration The ability of an advertising medium to reach a certain percentage of homes or prospects in a given geographical area. See *coverage*.

Philanthropic organization advertising A form of social advertising

designed to raise funds for worthwhile causes.

Photocomposition A photographic method of setting type, rapidly gaining favor in newspaper and other printing production. Cold type.

Photoengraving A relief printing plate made by a photochemical process. Also, prints made from such a plate, or the process itself.

Photostat A rapid and inexpensive process for copying text or illustrations. Also, the copies so made, often called *stats*.

Pica A unit of measurement for type or other printed material; six picas equal one inch.

Piggyback Two broadcast commercials aired one after the other featuring two different products of the advertiser.

Pilot program In broadcasting, a representative program from a series, produced either for the purpose of pretesting audience reaction or as a sample for prospective sponsors.

Planographic printing Lithography, whether direct or offset.

Plate A term loosely applied to any material used to make a printed impression by letterpress, gravure, or lithography.

Plated stock Paper with a hard, smooth surface and a high gloss, the result of pressing between polished sheets of metal.

Playback In broadcasting, playing a transcription immediately after recording, to check performance or production. Also, the machine used for this purpose.

Point A unit of vertical type measurement equal to $1/72$ inch.

Point-of-purchase advertising See *POP*.

Political advertising A form of social advertising used to support the candidacy of individuals in election campaigns.

Portfolio test A method of pretesting advertisements by interspersing them among editorial matter in a book similar to a photo album.

Positioning See *product positioning*.

Poster An advertising message printed on large sheets of paper and pasted on boards or panels.

Poster panel A standard structure on which posters are pasted.

Poster plant The local organization that builds and maintains standard outdoor advertising facilities.

Predate issue An edition of a publication that is released before the date it actually bears.

Preemption In broadcasting, the appropriation of time from regularly scheduled programs to permit broadcast of special programs of higher priority, such as a presidential speech.

Preferred position Any advertisement position in publications for which the advertiser must pay a premium when specifically ordered.

Premium An offer of merchandise, either free or at nominal cost, as an immediate inducement to purchase a product.

Preprint A reproduction of an advertisement prior to publication.

Press proof A proof made on the regular printing press before or during the actual press run.

Press run The printing of a specific job. Also, the number of copies printed.

Primary colors In printing, red, yellow, and blue.

Primary coverage The area in which the reception of a radio station is consistently good to excellent. Corresponds to *grade A coverage* in television.

Primary demand In economics, the demand for a type of product without regard to a specific brand.

Printers' Ink Model Statute A model legislative act against fraudulent or misleading advertising, first sponsored by *Printers' Ink* in 1911.

Private-label goods Goods produced for exclusive labeling by distributors, retailers, or other intermediaries.

Private nonprofit organization advertising A form of social advertising sponsored by nonprofit organizations with goods and services for sale: symphony tickets, college tuition, church attendance, and the like.

Probability sampling A method of sampling in which each unit of the universe has a known or equal chance of selection. See *quota sampling*.

Process plates Printing plates to reproduce the message in two, three, or four colors.

Process printing Printing in which one color is printed over another with transparent inks to produce different hues.

Producer In broadcasting, the person responsible for program production. The producer is primarily concerned with overall administration rather than on-the-air production. See *director*.

Product positioning A marketing strategy which takes into consideration how consumers perceive a product relative to competitive offerings.

Product reputation advertising Advertising which highlights product features as reason for purchase of the product.

Production department In an advertising agency or advertising department, those persons responsible for the conversion of copy and artwork into printed advertising material. In broadcasting, those responsible for the production and presentation of a program.

Professional advertising Advertising aimed at such professional persons as doctors, dentists, and architects for the purpose of getting them to recommend the featured product to clients.

Program rating The percentage of a sample of radio or TV homes tuned to a specific program at a particular time.

Progressive proofs A set of engraver's proofs used in color process printing, showing each color plate separately and in combination.

Projective techniques Motivational research methods, including thematic apperception tests, used to discover why individuals behave as they do.

Psychographics The statistical description of a market or other population group based upon psychological criteria such as interests, innovativeness, life-style, sophistication, etc. See *demographics*.

Publicity A story or message about a product or a company prepared as editorial rather than advertising material and published or broadcast without cost.

Publisher's representative An independent organization or individual that sells advertising space for a publication or group of them.

Publisher's statement The statement of circulation issued by a publisher.

Puffery A legal concept which recognizes that when someone has something to sell, he or she tries to put the item in the best possible light. Such puffery is to be expected and is not actionable under the common law.

Pulse The Pulse, Inc. A research organization that reports the percentage of homes tuned to a given television or radio program. Also engages in newspaper audience and market research studies.

Qualified circulation A term now preferred by BPA to *controlled circulation*.

Qualitative research A variety of indirect methods of research attempting to answer the "why" question in marketing and advertising.

Quarter showing In transit advertising, a message in every fourth unit of the system. Loosely used for a 25 showing in outdoor.

Quota A specific sales goal, in terms of units or dollars, which is established in advance.

Quota sampling A method of sampling in which interviewers look for specific numbers of respondents with known characteristics. Each unit in the universe does not have a known or equal chance of selection. Also called *judgment sampling*. See *probability sampling*.

RAB Radio Advertising Bureau. An organization of representatives, stations, and networks to promote radio as an advertising medium.

ROP Run-of-paper. A term that indicates the position of an advertisement will be at the publisher's discretion. See *preferred position*.

Random sampling A form of probability sampling in which each unit of the universe has an equal chance of selection. See *quota sampling*.

Rate card A card or folder issued by an advertising medium listing rates for space or time and providing mechanical requirements and other data usually required by advertisers.

Rate holder The minimum size advertisement that must appear in a medium during a specified period if the advertiser is to earn a frequency discount rate.

Rating In broadcasting, the same as *program rating.*

Reach The numbers of different homes, people, or prospects reached by one or a group of commercials or advertisements.

In broadcasting, a synonym for *cumulative net audience.*

Readership The percentage of audience who recall a specific advertisement or editorial item in a given issue of a publication.

Rebroadcast A broadcast program repeated at a different time, usually to reach people in a different time zone.

Recall test A method for testing advertising in which respondents are provided with clues and then asked to recall particular ads and the various elements of those ads.

Recognition The acceptance by a medium or media association of an advertising agency as one entitled to receive standard agency commissions.

Recognition test A method for testing advertising copy in which respondents are shown an ad and asked whether they saw it, read the copy, noted the illustration, etc.

Relay stations See *microwave relay.*

Release A signed statement by a person quoted or photographed which authorizes use of the statement or photograph for advertising purposes. Also, authorization to a medium for the insertion of an advertisement.

Relief printing Printing from a raised surface; letterpress, in contrast to gravure, planographic, or silk-screen printing.

Remembrance advertising Another name for advertising specialties.

Remote A broadcast originating outside the regular station or network studios, such as a football game or a convention. Also called *remote pickup.*

Rep Representative. See *publisher's representative and media representative.*

Reprint A copy of an advertisement printed after its appearance in a publication.

Repro proof Reproduction proof. A clean, sharp proof of type used for reproduction by photoengraving or offset or gravure printing.

Resizing The production of an advertisement in various sizes for different units of space.

Respondent The individual interviewed or subjected to test in marketing and advertising research.

Retail advertising Advertising designed to attract people to the retail outlet to purchase merchandise in stock.

Retail trading zone The area lying outside the city zone, the residents of which patronize city retailers to an important degree. See *city zone.*

Retouching Correcting or improving photographs or other artwork prior to the production of printing plates.

Robinson-Patman Act Federal legislation restricting price or promotional discrimination between customers in interstate commerce.

Roman type A race of type distinguished by variation in the weight of strokes and the inclusion of serifs. Also, all type faces that are not italic.

Rotation Repeating a series of advertisements in the order in which they first appeared.

Rotogravure High-speed gravure printing on rotary presses.

Rough A preliminary sketch submitted for approval before the finished illustration or layout is completed.

Run-of-paper See *ROP.*

SAG Screen Actors Guild. An organization of film talent which negotiates collective bargaining agreements with motion-picture and television producers.

S.C. The typographical abbreviation for small capital letters.

SRDS Standard Rate & Data Service, Inc. An organization which publishes current information on advertising rates, mechanical requirements, closing dates, and similar data on publication, broadcast, and transit media. Accepted as the standard source of advertising media information.

Saddle stitching The binding of a publication or booklet by means of wire staples through the center fold. This method of binding permits the pages to lie flat when opened. See *side stitching.*

Sales promotion Any sales activity that supplements or coordinates personal selling and advertising, but which cannot be strictly classified as either.

Sampling In research, selecting a representative portion of the universe. Also, the distribution of miniature or full-size trial packages of a product to introduce it or promote use.

Sans serif A type face that has no cross strokes, or *serifs*, at the top or bottom of the characters.

Satellite station A television station that carries little or no local programming, but tends to restrict its broadcasting to duplicating programs of a parent station.

Saturation campaign The intense use of broadcast media in a market, such as 20 TV or 100 radio commercials a week over a single station; usually purchased at special low rates.

Schedule A listing of proposed advertisements, by specific media, with dates of appearance, amount of space or time, etc.

Scratchboard A special drawing board coated with India ink, on which the artist scratches a design in white with a stylus.

Screening A method of printing based on the stencil principle; ink is squeezed through a screen that has the design to be printed imposed upon it.

Script A face of type that resembles handwriting. Also, in broadcasting, the written material used to produce a program or commercial.

Secondary coverage The area in which the reception of a radio station is generally fair, but subject to variation. Corresponds to *grade B coverage* in television.

Selective demand In economics, the demand for a particular brand of product. See *primary demand.*

Self-mailer A direct-mail piece that can be mailed without a wrapper or envelope.

Semantic differential A method of measuring the meaning of words or concepts which employs bipolar scales separated by an odd number of equal intervals.

Serifs The short cross strokes at the top and bottom of the characters in certain designs of type, especially those of the Roman race.

Sets in use A term used to designate the percentage or number of television or radio homes in a given area with sets turned on at a specific time.

Set solid Lines of type set without leading.

Share of audience In broadcasting, the percentage of homes with sets in use tuned to a particular program or station.

Share of market The ratio of an advertiser's sales to total industry sales on either an actual or a potential basis.

Short rate The higher rate an advertiser must pay if he or she fails to use the amount of space or time specified in the contract.

Shoulder of type The portions of a unit of type which extend above and below the type character, and which do not print.

Side stitching In binding a magazine or booklet, a method of stitching through the edges of the folded pages from front to back. The pages will not lie flat when opened. See *saddle stitching.*

Signature The advertiser's name in an advertisement. Also, a single sheet of paper which, when folded, will form four, or multiples of four, pages. In broadcasting, a sound effect or music that identifies a program or commercial.

Signs In outdoor advertising, non-standardized posters and painted bulletins which do not meet the specifications of OAAA. See *outdoor advertising.*

Silhouette halftone See *outline halftone.*

Silk screen A method of printing based on the stencil principle. Ink is squeezed through a cloth screen that has the design to be printed imposed upon it in reverse.

Simmons (W. R.) and Associates A syndicated service providing advertisers and agencies with information on the characteristics of selected media audiences.

Simulcast A program broadcast simultaneously over rradio and television, or over AM and FM radio.

Social advertising Advertising for nonbusiness reasons by nonprofit organizations.

Social cause advertising A form of social advertising used to get public interest causes before the public; primarily propagandistic in intent.

Sound on film (SOF) In broadcasting, film footage with a sound track, usually recorded simultaneously.

Space buyer An advertising agency employee who helps plan printed advertising campaigns, and who selects and buys space in publication, outdoor, and transit media. See *time buyer.*

Specialties See *advertising specialties.*

Spectacolor A more sophisticated version of *Hi-Fi Color* in which pre-printed ads are fed into the press, but the point at which the paper is cut is critical to the sense of the ad.

Spectacular A large outdoor electric sign, usually animated. Also, in broadcasting, an elaborate special program irregularly scheduled, usually an hour or more in length.

Speculative presentation A demonstration by an agency to a prospective client showing how it would handle the account if awarded the business. A "pitch."

Split run Two or more advertisements of the same size in the same position in different copies of the same issue of a publication. Used to test different versions of an advertisement, or to feature different products in the regional editions of a national magazine.

Sponsor A radio or television advertiser. In a strict sense, one who pays for program time as distinguished from an advertiser who pays only for announcement or commercial time.

Spot announcement A short commercial, one minute or less in length, inserted between radio or television programs, or included in participating programs.

Spot broadcasting An approach to national broadcast advertising, by which the advertiser selects specific markets and specific stations. The opposite of network broadcasting.

Spread Two facing pages in a publication.

Starch A research organization, best known for readership studies of magazine advertisements.

Station break The identification or call letters of a radio or television station, or the allowable time between two programs for this identification. Also referred to as *station identification.*

Station option time The time over which a network affiliate station has first sales priority, in contrast to network option time. Also called *station time.*

Station representative An individual or organization selling spot broadcasting time on a specific station or group of them. See *publisher's representative.*

Stereophonic broadcasting The broadcasting of two signals for reception on two separate sets in stereophonic sound. The two signals may be transmitted by a single station using multiplexing, or by two different stations—two FM, one AM and one FM, or a TV station plus either an AM or FM station.

Stereotype A duplicate printing plate cast from a matrix of impregnated paper pulp or plastic.

Still In television, a photograph or similar material inserted into a program or commercial.

Stop motion A photographic technique for animating inanimate objects.

Storecasting Broadcasting at the point-of-purchase, usually offering music and news as well as commercials.

Storyboard A series of sketches, with accompanying copy, providing in parallel sequence the video and audio portions of a TV program or commercial. A "layout" for television.

Super or **superimposition** In television, the imposition of the image from one camera over the image from another; usually refers to a name, trademark, or slogan.

Supplement A special feature section, often in magazine format, distributed with a newspaper.

Sustaining program An unsponsored broadcast program on a commercial station.

Syndication The practice of taking a series of successful network television programs and rerunning them on local stations in hours not covered by network programming. Programming, in addition to former network programs, can be specially created for syndication.

Systems approach An orderly discipline for dealing with complex problems under uncertainty.

TAA Transit Advertising Association. An organization of firms selling transit advertising.

TAB Traffic Audit Bureau. An organization that furnishes uniform, impartial data on outdoor advertising circulation.

TGI Target Group Index. A syndicated service providing advertisers and agencies with information on the characteristics of selected media audiences.

TvB Television Bureau of Advertising. An organization of networks, stations, and representatives to improve and promote the use of TV as an advertising medium.

Tabloid A newspaper usually about one-half the standard size.

Tabloid insert Advertising sections prepared by retailers and other sellers for inclusion in newspapers. Usually presented in a tabloid format.

Tag In broadcasting, an addition to a commercial, such as a voice-over message following a transcribed message, or an announcement or musical bit that serves as a finale.

Talent In broadcasting, actors, musicians, announcers, or other performers.

Tape In broadcasting, either audiotape or videotape used to record programs or commercials.

Target market A group of the population which is believed to hold the greatest sales potential for the product. The advertiser tries to isolate media which reach the target market and designs messages which communicate with its members.

the advertising budget. Objectives are set; then the amount of advertising needed to achieve the objectives is determined and the amount of money necessary to do so becomes the budget.

Tear sheet A page containing an advertisement, clipped from a publication and sent to the advertiser for checking purposes.

Teaser Any advertisement designed to stimulate curiosity by withholding identification of the advertiser or product, but promising more information in future messages.

Theme The central idea of an advertisement, campaign, or program. Also, in broadcasting, the musical identification of a program or commercial.

Thirty sheet A 30-sheet outdoor poster. Uses the same poster panel as the 24-sheet, but provides a copy area 11 inches higher and 25 inches wider.

Three sheet A vertically proportioned outdoor poster, pasted on a panel approximately $8^{1}/_{2}$ feet high and 5 feet wide. The panels are usually located near retail outlets or public transportation stations

and are designed to reach pedestrian rather than vehicular traffic.

Thumbnail A rough layout in miniature.

Till forbid (TF) Instructions to a medium to continue running an advertisement as scheduled until further notice.

Time buyer An advertising agency employee who helps plan campaigns in broadcast media, and who selects and purchases radio and television time. See *space buyer*.

Time clearance The process of making a specific program period available on particular stations, as when certain affiliated stations have been ordered as part of a network.

Trade advertising Advertising directed at wholesalers or retailers.

Trade character An animate being or animated object designed to identify and personify a product or an advertiser.

Trademark A word or symbol attached to merchandise or its package to identify the maker or origin. See *trade name*.

Trade name The name under which a firm does business, or by which the firm or its products or services are usually identified. Also called *brand name*. See *trademark*.

Traffic department In an advertising agency, the department that schedules the work of other departments and is responsible for its completion according to schedule. In broadcasting, the department responsible for the scheduling of all programs and announcements to be aired.

Transient rate The flat or one-time rate for advertising, without quantity or frequency discounts.

Transit advertising A form of out-of-home media; depends upon consumer usage of commercial transportation facilities—buses, airlines, and subway and commuter trains—and upon pedestrians viewing the advertising from the streets. Also called *transportation advertising.*

Translator station A television station that rebroadcasts programs from another station on another channel, but has no local studio and is not permitted to originate programs or commercials locally.

Transportation advertising See *transit advertising.*

Traveling display An exhibit of point-of-purchase material which is the property of the advertiser and is moved from one dealer or one location to another. Also, transit advertising on the outside of vehicles.

Trendex Trendex, Inc. A research organization engaged in consumer and industrial market research, including audience studies for various media.

Triple spotting Broadcasting three commercials in succession, without intervening news or entertainment.

Twenty-four sheet A 24-sheet outdoor poster, 104 inches by 234 inches. Originally it required 24 separate sheets of paper, but now it may be produced with 10. See *thirty sheet.*

Type family A group of type faces of the same basic design, but with variations in width of characters, boldness or lightness of strokes, and the like. For example, Bodoni, Bodoni Bold, Bodoni Bold Italic, Bodoni Book, etc.

Type page The total area of a page minus the margins, or the space that can be occupied by printed matter.

Typo An error in typography made by the compositor. Also loosely applied to errors in typed copy.

UHF Ultrahigh frequency, or television channels 14 through 84.

Unaided recall A research technique in which respondents must answer questions without any aids to memory. See *aided recall.*

Uppercase Capital letters.

Use payment In broadcasting, fees paid talent for use of commercials in which they appear; established by SAG or AFTRA codes.

VHF Very high frequency, or television channels 2 through 13.

VTR Videotape recording. See *videotape.*

Value The quality of a color by which it is seen as light or dark. See *hue* and *chroma.*

Vertical publication A business publication edited for persons in a particular industry or profession, regardless of specific job categories, in contrast to a *horizontal* publication.

Video Loosely used as a synonym for television; more accurately, the visual portion of a television broadcast.

Videotape An electronic unit that simultaneously records both audio and video on the same tape, and permits immediate playback and rapid editing.

Visualization The process of picturing in the mind how an ad will look before it is produced. Also used to denote a rough layout or storyboard.

Voice-over (VO) In television, narration with the narrator not visible on the screen.

Wait order An order to a medium to hold an advertisement for release at a date to be specified later. A hold order.

Wash drawing A drawing similar to watercolor, executed with brush in varying shades of gray and black; reproduced by halftone engraving.

Waste circulation Advertising in a geographical area where the advertiser has no distribution for the advertised product. Also, that portion of the circulation of a medium which cannot be considered to reach logical prospects for a product because they are unable to use it or unable to pay for it.

Weight of type The relative blackness of a particular type face.

Wheeler-Lea Act An amendment enacted in 1938 to the Federal Trade Commission Act, designed to protect the consumer against unfair trade practices in interstate commerce, and especially against false or misleading advertising of food, drugs, and cosmetics.

Widow A single word or short line of type at the end of a paragraph, particularly at the top of a column or page.

Wipe In television, a rapid transition shot replacing one image on the screen with another.

Zoom In television, a rapid change of focus which makes the image grow larger (zoom in) or smaller (zoom out). Done with a special lens or rapid dollying.

INDEX